Vocabulary Change

A Study of Variation in Regional Words in Eight of the Southern States

by Gordon R. Wood

Southern Illinois University Press
Carbondale and Edwardsville
Feffer & Simons, Inc.
London and Amsterdam

Printed in the United States of America
ISBN 0-8093-0433-3
Library of Congress Catalog Card Number 76-86183

To Sara

who helped
at all stages
of its writing

Contents

List of Figures

List of Maps

Preface

To a casual observer his language may seem as firm and unchanging as the earth under foot, an impression that must surely be altered if he looks attentively at either. And so the present essay is a look at a language, American English, as it both continued and changed between the eighteenth century and the twentieth Actually it is not a look at the whole language but only at a small part of it, the regional vocabularies found in eight of the Southern states.

As the title suggests, I have used the word "change" frequently and, I must confess, without being always explicit about what the before and middle stages are that characterize linguistic shifts. What we all need is a true chronology of the westward spread of American English; I have even hinted in the text about the research procedure to follow in gathering evidence for that chronology. But I am also sure that we agree to a general idea of shift in vocabulary from that of "all Indian—no English" to a condition of "mostly English." It is this latter end of things, the product of changes, that perforce I have written about.

The essay is based on a list of words collected from persons born, reared, and living in Alabama, Arkansas, Florida, Georgia, Louisiana, Mississippi, Oklahoma, and Tennessee. My original intent, fulfilled here, was to prepare a word geography of the region. But as I worked with the evidence I became increasingly aware of the complex mingling of regional vocabularies which had occurred. When I began to notice that two or three dialects of American English had been brought together so that they could interact with each other, I knew that I had found something new about the history of American English. What follows, then, is an extended redefinition of the changing Southern dialect as the term "dialect" is used to label a major division of our native language.

This book analyzes the responses of a thousand or so persons to a printed vocabulary questionnaire. Chapter 1 introduces the patterns of settlement, urbanization, and commerce which help me to account for the presence and importance of regional words in some communities and not in others. Chapter 2 discusses technical problems arising from the use of questionnaires to gather information about regional English and from the use of computers to classify and count the responses. Chapter 3 discusses gross word counts which range from zero (complete denial of use) to over one thousand affirmative responses and examines them as clues to linguistic change. Chapter 4 considers the geography of selected regional words and the zones of dialectal gradation. Chapter 5 offers a new static model of the Southern dialect and its major subdialects. Chapter 6 examines word by word the relative importance of synonyms as they are reported in each state of the eight under study; the order of presentation reflects social changes from pioneer, agricultural vocabularies to urban words introduced into American English in the nineteenth century or later. And Chapter 7 does what ending chapters do: It summarizes and projects.

Computer processes play a large part in what is said. Unpublished printouts lie behind the detailed maps and some of the tables; it is hoped that they will be made available later in the form of computer tapes. Printouts published here as a part of this text provide evidence not only for conclusions now reached but also for extensions of the present work. If someone wishes to draw additional maps, then column C of Table I is the starting point. If someone else wishes to test theories of meaning, the workings of communication theory, the role of transformational or structural grammars in word formation, or the process of simulation as applied to language change, the tables provide raw data in abundance.

The book began to be written in 1957 when I proposed to members of the American Dialect Society that we send out printed questionnaires as a first step in extending the Linguistic Atlas surveys to unexplored areas in the South. With the assurance of computer technicians to buoy me, I believed that mimeographed questionnaires could be sent out and returned quickly and that they then could be sorted and tabulated by computer within less than a year's time. Thanks to the help of many persons, the first came true. And thanks to all sorts of things, including the intricacies of computer analysis, the sorting and tabulation took longer; the interpretation took longest of all.

My first computer sortings were tables, county by county and age group by age group, of the responses of every informant to every entry in the questionnaire. The resulting pages are too bulky to print here; they are best consulted on computer tape and I have suggested that the tape record be made available to scholars who wish to study individual words by county and by age group. At the moment there is general agreement that this is a good idea, but we prefer to wait until the computer industry has made it easier to send a record prepared on one kind of machine to another kind of machine (even made by the same company) with a reasonable expectation that the second machine can read the tape prepared for the first.

From these early printouts I deduced in 1961 that the vocabulary of the Southern dialect was distributed in far different ways from those I had expected to find. The definition of *Southern* offered here is the interpretation that seems best, all things considered. A later attempt at mapping by computer is planned, but the sole criteria to be used will be lexical if the attempt is made.

Early support for the preparation and distribution of questionnaires came from research funds of the University of Chattanooga augmented by a grant from the Modern Language Association of America. Colleagues at other colleges and universities found ways to support distribution within the legitimate areas of interest of their institutions. They and their 1957–58 academic homes are Lalia P. Boone, University of Florida; John O. Eidson and Calvin S. Brown, University of Georgia; E. H. Criswell, University of Tulsa; John Murphy, Central State College (Oklahoma); Rudolph Fiehler, Louisiana Polytechnic Institute; Luke M. Grande, Christian Brothers College (Tennessee); Elizabeth H. Jackson, Maryville College; Mary C. Parler, University of Arkansas; I. Willis Russell, University of Alabama. To these I must add the name of the late Miss Betty Blocker, Alumni Secretary of the University of Chattanooga, who gave me the names of a host of intermediaries. Without these and the academic intermediaries, the record would have been skimpy. As it was, they produced some three thousand informants whose responses to the questionnaire let me choose the one thousand best informants whose answers are the data for this study.

A grant from the American Philosophical Society made possible the first full-scale analysis of all data from all selected informants. The more recent computations, those printed in this book, were supported by funds from the Office of Research and Projects, Southern Illinois University, Edwardsville, Illinois. Additional support from the Edwardsville campus is acknowledged: For summer research funds and for released time to write this book, the Humanities Division and the English Faculty. For programming of the calculations printed here: Mr. Gerald H. Beine, then of the Data Processing Center. From the Carbondale campus came mapping service from the Cartographic Laboratory; the maps were drawn under the supervision of Messrs. Tso-Hwa Lee and Lawrence Dusek. And for printing the book, the guidance and help of the Southern Illinois University Press is appreciated.

Permission to use map data from copyrighted sources has been granted. In order to avoid engulfing some maps here with a list of contributors, the sources are specified now in detail: Hans Kurath, *A Word Geography of the Eastern United States,* University of Michigan

Press, Ann Arbor, 1949, Figures 3, 4, 5a, 27, 28, 29, 30, 32, 33, 34, 71; E. Bagby Atwood, *The Regional Vocabulary of Texas,* University of Texas Press, Austin, 1962, Maps 69, 119–25; Harold B. Allen, *Publication of the American Dialect Society,* XXX, Map 1; Albert H. Marckwardt, *Publication of the American Dialect Society,* XXVII, Maps 2, 4, 5; Gordon R. Wood, *Publication of the American Dialect Society,* XXXV, Maps 3, 4; University of Alabama Press, University, 1957, 1961 respectively; Charles O. Paullin, *Atlas of the Historical Geography of the United States,* Carnegie Institute of Washington, Washington, D.C., and the American Geographical Society of New York, N.Y., 1932, Plates 60, 76 B, C, D, E, F, G, 142 A.

GORDON R. WOOD

Collinsville, Illinois
1969

Vocabulary Change

1

The Setting for Uniformity or Variation

The vocabulary of a living language reflects a multitude of adjustments between personal idiosyncrasy and community order. When that linguistic community stretches across an entire continent, as American English does, the elements of order may obscure an ever present variety in usage.

It is, indeed, not too difficult to think that the apparent uniformity of American English arose during the eighteenth and nineteenth centuries, a product of formal education no less. As one scholar put it, "Noah Webster gave the United States its amazing uniformity of language."[1] That Webster hoped to accomplish this is common knowledge. In his 1798 *Dissertations on the English Language* he argued that the thirteen states should act for the benefit of the whole republic.

> We have therefore the fairest opportunity of establishing a national language, and of giving it uniformity and perspicuity, in North America, that ever presented itself to mankind. Now is the time to begin the plan. The minds of the Americans are aroused by the events of a revolution.[2]

From his special vantage point in Hartford, Connecticut, two things appeared certain: Local usages would "corrupt the national language", and furthermore,

> Nothing but the establishment of schools and some uniformity in the use of books, can annihilate differences in speaking and preserve the purity of the American tongue.[3]

Not everyone agreed with him, for there was in his day an inclination to admire practical skill and local self-sufficiency. In words attributed to Patrick Henry as he addressed some of his backwoods constituents in Virginia, "*Naiteral* parts *is* better than all the *larnin* upon *yearth*."[4]

Even if people had agreed on Webster's goal, national conditions during the first century of the republic worked against uniformities in education. Consider for instance the difference in academic training of two contemporary presidents born on the Kentucky frontier, Abraham Lincoln and Jefferson Davis. Lincoln's schooling was catch as catch can; Davis's, on the other hand, included study at Transylvania University, an early college west of the Appalachians, and then at West Point. Obviously, something in addition to formal education provided them with an American English suited to their great tasks of leadership.

By mid-nineteenth century or later many factors favored diversity in American English. Movement from place to place was limited to the distance one could walk or ride in a day—a maximum perhaps of twenty-five miles. Forests, mountains, rivers, prairies, and deserts were formidable barriers to communication. Nor do these conditions seem to have appreciably changed with the arrival of steamboats on the inland rivers. Indeed, one can observe that truly national communication did not begin to emerge until after railroads were built and telegraph lines strung.

If conditions in the nineteenth century favored regional variations in American English which had developed during the colonial period, how does one account for its apparent uniformity in the twentieth century? This is a basic question to which the present discussion is addressed. That is, given a body of regional English words on the Atlantic seaboard, what can one discover about their present occurrence in a part of the nation settled during the nineteenth century? And having found the words, what can one conclude about the relative changes in uniformity in current local use?

The vocabulary itself has been gathered in a region called the Interior South in this discussion[5] and made up of these eight states: Tennessee, Georgia, Florida, Alabama, Mississippi, Louisiana, Arkansas, and Oklahoma. An area of over four hundred thousand square miles, its northern mountains give way to piedmont and then to coastal plains. The Mississippi cuts the mountain mass and, on its way to the Gulf of Mexico, receives the southeastern flow of rivers from Oklahoma, Arkansas, and Louisiana. From eastern uplands its rivers flow into the Atlantic Ocean, the Ohio River, or the Gulf.

In terms of human movement overland from the eastern seaboard into the interior in the eighteenth or early nineteenth centuries, three main directions are possible. One is along the coastal plain which curves around the southern part of the mountain and hill mass; a second is in the Cumberland-Shenandoah corridor which lies west of the Blue Ridge and extends southwest to the headwaters of the Tennessee River; and a third is down the valley of the Ohio and its tributaries along the western edge of the Appalachians (Figure 1).

The uplands of what are now Tennessee and Kentucky started to fill with English-speaking pioneers before the Revolutionary War began even though that part of the wilderness had been formally reserved for the Indian tribes in the Proclamation of 1763. Land hunger augmented by wealth or poverty, by political and personal disputes, and by the absence of suitable farm land in the colonies led pioneer families westward. Once a decision to enter the wilderness had been made, pioneer hunter-farmers were attracted to the new lands by their own views of a good soil and the suitable climate. That is, these pioneers settled mountain valleys resembling colonial lands already in cultivation. Their experience and that of others told them that bottom land could be cleared for crops, that water would be sufficient for a family and its domestic animals, that frosts in October and November and the return of spring in late February would permit planting corn, wheat, and other familiar crops in season. Furthermore, in times of emergency, the farmer-hunter could sustain himself, his family, and their animals from familiar trees, plants, and animals of the wilderness itself.

Because we will be concerned later with the importation of regional words from the original colonies and their successor states into the Interior South, let us notice the migration of a representative of the first hunter-farmer families. A Quaker, Daniel Boone, and his family left the Quaker settlements of Pennsylvania in 1753 and moved southwest with the frontier into the Cumberland and Shenandoah valleys. By 1759 a deed placed him as a "planter" in the Yadkin Valley of North Carolina. From there in association with a North Carolina land speculator, William Henderson, Boone explored the Tennessee and Kentucky wilderness. By 1775 Boone, his family, and other pioneer families (some of whom had crossed the Blue Ridge from eastern Virginia or from North Carolina) had established a permanent settlement at Boonesborough, Kentucky.[6] Close behind them other pioneer settlers from Pennsylvania or further north would soon work their way down the Ohio, the second route into the Interior South.

Two points need to be noted. First, the earliest advance into this region is from Pennsylvania; the language of its colonial settlers is, in some particulars, not that of coastal Virginia and the Carolinas. Second, Boonesborough is a village if not a city in the wilderness; it is a forerunner of other towns and villages which provide urbanizing influences of some sort on the frontier. Thus, if urbanizing brings linguistic uniformities, these settlements are indications of its presence on the western frontier while it is still a wilderness.

Although the mountain valleys were being settled in the pre-Revolutionary period, English-speaking inhabitants of eastern Georgia and adjacent parts of the Carolinas did not skirt the mountain barrier and push west into the Gulf Coastal Plain even though that direction of advance looks easy on the maps (Figures 1, 2). If one seeks to explain the relative slowness of this westward advance, he must weigh these restraints at least: Hostile Indian tribes had to be defeated and forced to give up the land. Besides, there may have been no real pressures of population in eastern South Carolina and Georgia for persons to find new land. Fur-

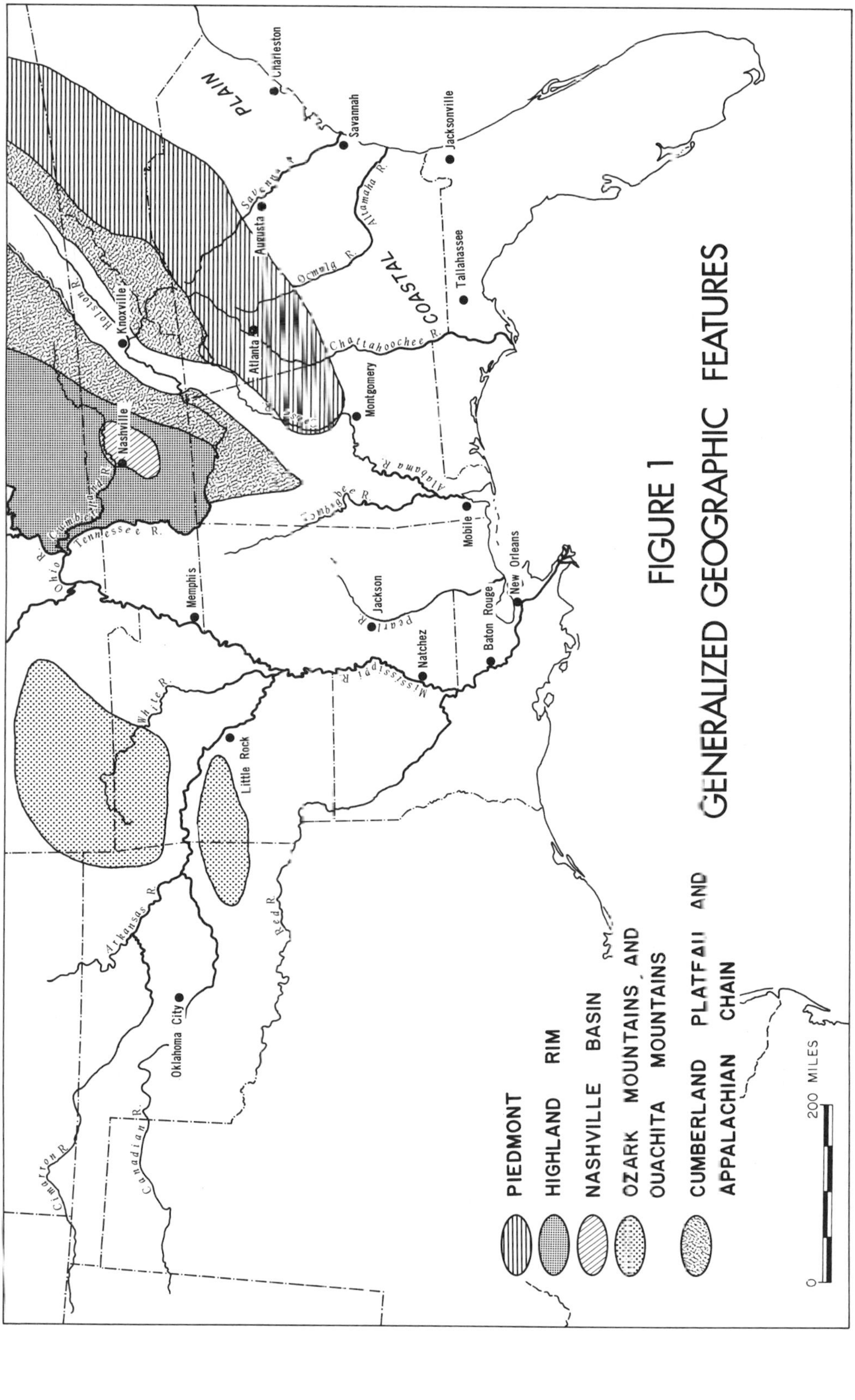
PIEDMONT
HIGHLAND RIM
NASHVILLE BASIN
OZARK MOUNTAINS AND OUACHITA MOUNTAINS
CUMBERLAND PLATEAU AND APPALACHIAN CHAIN
0
200 MILES
COASTAL
PLAIN
Charleston
Savannah
Jacksonville
Augusta
Tallahassee
Atlanta
Montgomery
Knoxville
Nashville
Memphis
Mobile
Jackson
New Orleans
Baton Rouge
Natchez
Little Rock
Oklahoma City
Altamaha R.
Chattahoochee R.
Alabama R.
Tennessee R.
Holston R.
Ohio R.
Pearl R.
Mississippi R.
White R.
Arkansas R.
Red R.
Canadian R.
Cimarron R.

FIGURE 1
GENERALIZED GEOGRAPHIC FEATURES

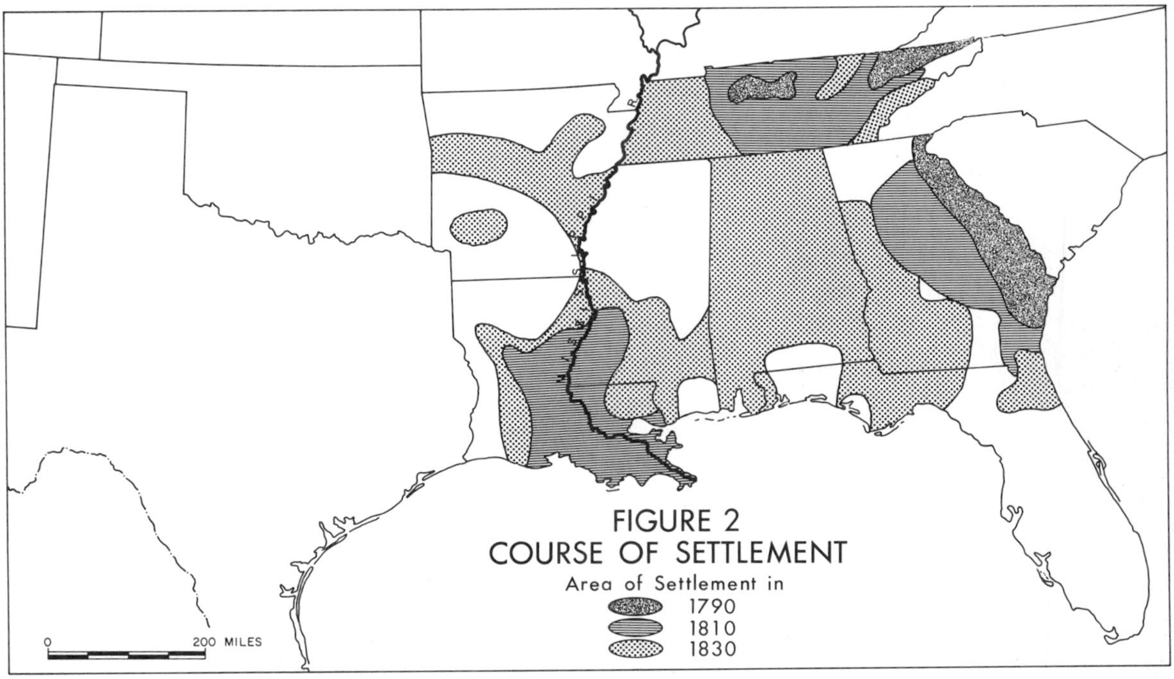
0 200 MILES

FIGURE 2
COURSE OF SETTLEMENT
Area of Settlement in
1790
1810
1830

ther there were variable combinations of natural barriers—southward flowing rivers to be crossed with great difficulty, and the presence of piney woods, a sign of soil unsuited to the familiar crops. And then there was the climate. As Goldsmith viewed it in *The Deserted Village,* in Georgia blazing suns "shed intolerable day" where "oft in whirls the mad tornado flies."

A commercial change made this hostile region worth the effort to convert it to agriculture and in fact caused the rapid settlement of lands particularly suited to the needs of a new cash crop, short staple cotton. A quarter of a century after the founding of Boonesborough, the invention of the cotton gin and the perfection of machines to spin cotton thread made the growing of short staple cotton profitable. This plant requires two hundred frost-free days and twenty annual inches of rain, ten of which must be in the fall months. These natural demands thus place the cotton economy in an area south of those which are suitable for older, more familiar crops (Figure 3).

After 1800 the cotton economy attracted to the Interior South a wide range of persons: Northerners and their slaves, one-time pioneer hunter-farmers and their families, and Southern planters and their slaves.[7] National lore does not provide a name for a representative of the Southern planter group. Lacking such but needing a stock figure comparable to Daniel Boone for the hunter-farmers, let us use the description given by a Virginian, a Dr. Ruffin, of his fellow Virginians.

> When their agriculture fails them at home, rather than let mines, and coal beds, and water-falls, and timber-forests, and the finest tide-rivers and harbors in America, allure them to manufactures and commerce, they will take their negroes and emigrate a thousand miles.[8]

For our purposes assume that this migration took with it those habits of American English which in colonial times had developed east of the Blue Ridge in Virginia and in corresponding parts of the Carolinas and Georgia. Let me insist that this sharp division of linguistic influences into two major streams separated by the Blue Ridge is for illustrative conveniences; later its proper flow will be considered in detail.

At the moment it is sufficient to notice that census evidence before 1860 points to a very considerable number of free Southerners who settled all parts of the Interior South. Virginia and North Carolina were the main colonizers

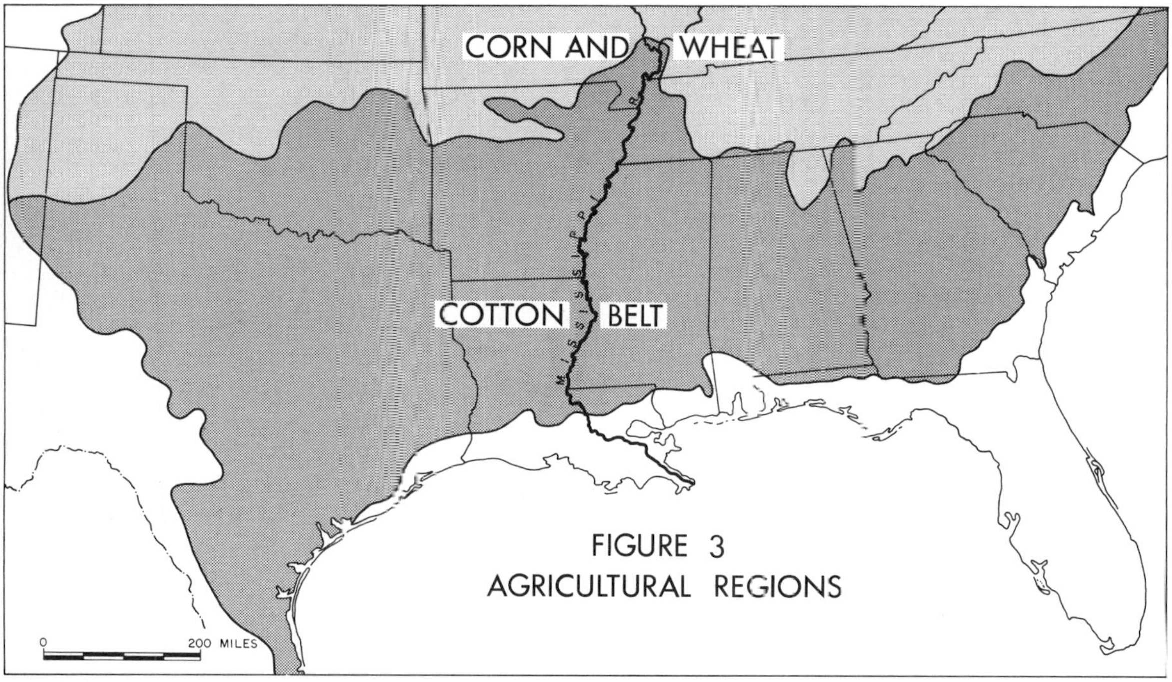
CORN AND WHEAT
COTTON BELT
MISSISSIPPI R.
0 200 MILES

FIGURE 3
AGRICULTURAL REGIONS

of Tennessee, while South Carolina and Georgia furnished the greater number of migrants to Alabama. Mississippi in turn drew its population from Alabama, South Carolina, Georgia, North Carolina, and Tennessee. Arkansas, first settled by native Tennesseeans, received an influx of immigrants who came down river from Illinois. Louisiana, in addition to replenishing itself from its own French stock, attracted migrants from Alabama, Georgia, and New York.[9] Northern Florida was settled mainly by Georgians. And Oklahoma, reserved for the greater part of the nineteenth century as Indian Territory, was settled by land rushes beginning in 1889; part of its pattern of American English is a westward extension of influences originating in the Carolinas and Georgia, but obviously its social history presents very special problems to interpreters.

In the first half of the nineteenth century, communities and individual farms or plantations were isolated from each other by the difficulties of travel. This isolation began to be broken in the second quarter of the century when one could count over sixty steamboats on the western waters. At approximately the same time, railroads and the telegraph were introduced, the forerunners of all of those more recent influences which accompany a national interchange of people, commodities, and information.[10] The speakers whose responses are examined in this study are, then, the intellectual and actual children of those who settled the region and of those who at the end of the nineteenth and the beginning of the twentieth centuries joined them in daily use of American English.

2

Procedures and Assumptions

Some questions about the nature of twentieth-century American English can be answered by means of an inventory of selected details. If, as in the present instance, a basic interest is to discover variables in local vocabulary and then relate them to other segments of a language, a tested procedure is to take a language census. As stated, the undertaking appears simple enough. In practice, though, the actualities of selecting the right investigative tool, of choosing the persons to respond, and of tabulating and interpreting the records are a source of problems for the scholar.

Among other things, the linguistic census itself rests on the hypothesis that a chosen vocabulary will provide us with a representative sample of the whole language and some of its subdivisions. A related hypothesis is that single individuals found to use parts of the special vocabulary represent the usage habits of the entire town or county in which those individuals grew up. From the responses which the census taker obtains, one can then deduce that change has or has not taken place, that the regional vocabulary has or has not come into the area from some other region, and so on.

The selected instrument for the present study was a printed questionnaire. When that selection was made, two forms of a similar collecting instrument were at hand and were not chosen. The first and newer of the two at that time, a pictorial interview technique, required an interviewer to show an informant a series of numbered pictures and capture his responses by means of a tape recorder. The second, highly regarded then and quite familiar to linguistic interviewers in the United States, was that developed for the Linguistic Atlas of the United States and Canada; it required the services of a trained field worker who asks his informant an ordered set of questions and transcribes the answers on worksheets, a procedure which recently has been augmented by the use of a tape recorder.[1]

Practical considerations at the time led to the use of printed questionnaires as the only possible means of conducting a census with the consequent rejection of any method of spoken interview. This choice carried with it, moreover, a number of advantages, one of which is that the text of the questionnaire is based on evidence in the Linguistic Atlas files. Thus it could be related to Hans Kurath's then newly published *A Word Geography of the Eastern United States*.[2] As other Atlas studies were published, the present work could be linked with them (Figure 4).

The questionnaire has three parts: A cover page with directions which guide informants in marking words,[3] the text proper, and a biographical final page. Of these, the ten pages of text raise linguistic issues. The design itself is straightforward: An *item* number precedes each set of words; it is followed by a definition, and then by an alphabetical list of synonyms. Item 114, for instance, has three details:

> 114. INSECT THAT GLOWS AT NIGHT: fire bug, firefly, glow worm, June bug, lightning bug.

Three issues are immediately apparent: a parallel between the language of the definition and that of some word choices might influence actual selections. Or the printed sequence of synonyms might favor one word over those next to it. Or an informant's special familiarity with a word might lead to his marking it no matter what definition has been given. Let us examine these.

The text of the questionnaire as it is printed later in this study does indeed show that words in particular definitions also occur in the synonym lists that follow them. The word *rollers* in Item 14, for instance, is echoed in *roller shades*. One test of the hypothesis that a word in this or any definition has led to the choice

FIGURE 4
ADJACENT REGIONAL STUDIES

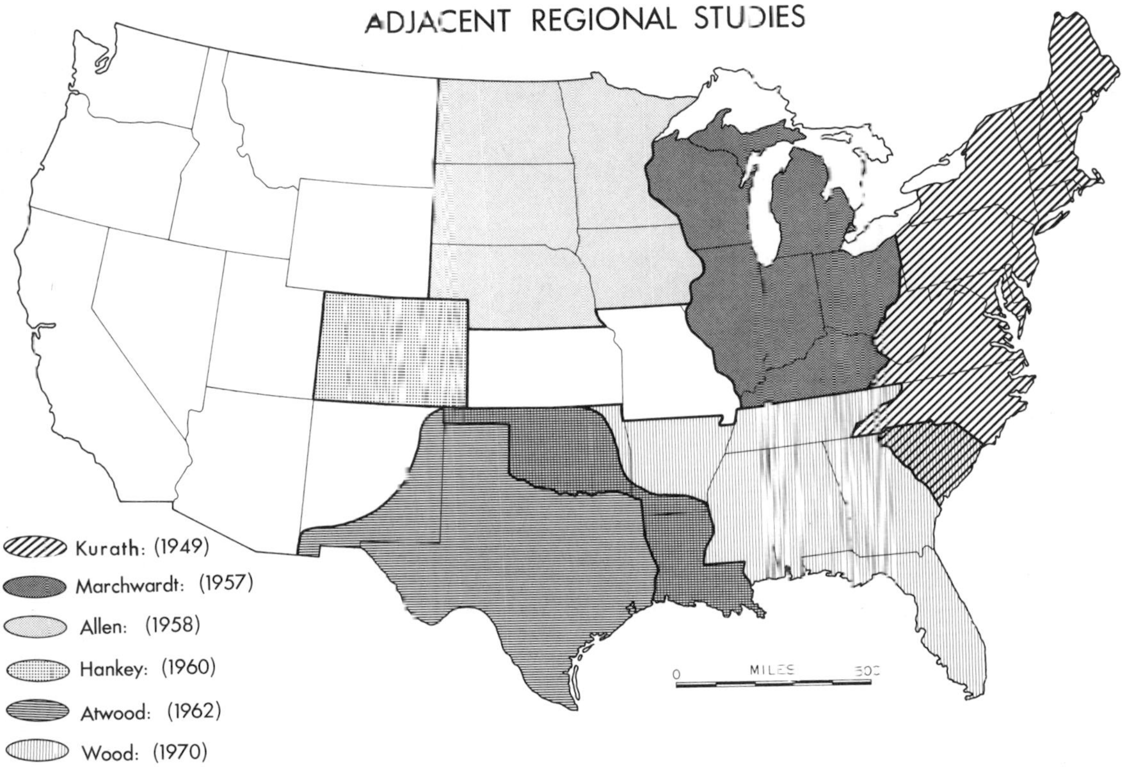
Kurath: (1949)
Marchwardt: (1957)
Allen: (1958)
Hankey: (1960)
Atwood: (1962)
Wood: (1970)
0
MILES

of a synonym is that its influence will be equally strong everywhere. A second is that the same pattern of equal occurrences will appear in each item which has an echoic element in its definition and word list. Thus, in tabulations which show percentages of response anyone would expect to find this evidence shown in equal degrees of word choice in the north and south or east and west subdivisions of every state, and from state to state in the Interior South. That balanced pattern is not evident in the tabulated responses under *roller shades*. Readers may easily apply these same tests to all of Table I.[4]

Similarly a hypothesis that word order has exerted an undue influence on word choice can be tested in the same table. There any word at the top of each list is the one immediately adjacent to the definition as printed in the questionnaire; left to right sequence in the questionnaire text is found in a corresponding top to bottom order in that same table. If the left word in the questionnaire is the one ordinarily selected, then that selection will be shown by the state-by-state percentages which are greater for every top word than for any word below it. Similarly if any other word position in the questionnaire—for example the rightmost one—is unduly influential, that undue influence will be apparent in all items tabulated. Again, there is insufficient evidence to support this hypothesis.

Different issues arise in connection with meaning. Instructions in the questionnaire tell informants to encircle those words that they actually use, to leave unmarked those that they do not, and to write beside an entry any other familiar synonyms that should have been included. These instructions and the format of the items themselves raise questions of "understanding" that have characterized twentieth-century discussions of the meaning of meaning.

A researcher must assume that informants do indeed use each marked word in the sense defined; to do anything else is to engage in mind reading at a great distance. At the same time he recognizes at least three possible sources of semantic confusion as embodied in the doctrine of private linguistic worlds, in that of restrictive definition, and in that of historical nimbus.

The doctrine of private linguistic worlds is that each person's experience with words and events is unique; thus, the same word cannot mean the same thing to any two people.[5] To put it another way, let us assume that two or more people do have an idea in common but each has different English symbols for it. Within that doctrine is it not appropriate to assume that for one person the idea is brought forth by means of the token *roller shades,* for another by *ship,* for a third by *sealing wax?* Only one of them could select *roller shades* in the list of synonyms provided in the questionnaire; the others would omit it and perhaps volunteer one of the other words because of their private linguistic experiences. Questionnaire responses do not support the concept of privateness.

The doctrine of a restrictive effect of definition is that a word is meaningless until a definition is given to it. Once the definition is given, then users must hold to that sense alone. Familiar examples, of course, are definitions of *point, line,* and *plane* in geometry and of *sentence, morpheme,* and *phoneme* in language study. It is the position articulated by Humpty Dumpty when he said that a word "means just what I choose it to mean, neither more nor less." From that doctrine it follows that every word in each synonym list whether familiar or not will mean exactly what the accompanying definition states that it must mean. If informants could be expected to observe this convention, they would be obliged to mark all synonyms.

Finally, the doctrine of historical nimbus derives from our knowledge of ranges of meanings associated with words. One collegiate dictionary, for instance, traces the meanings of *snack* and *lunch* respectively to early concepts such as "to snap" and a blending of "noon," "drink," and "pour."[6] And it records *corn* in a British sense of "wheat" and an American sense of "maize." Thus an informant's response may be a reflection of any of the possible senses of a word and not necessarily that one given in the questionnaire.

A researcher cannot easily demonstrate the weakness of this doctrine. But in order to use a questionnaire as his source of information he must assume that the presence of that nimbus is not influential in this specific setting; otherwise his and the informants' discussion of word choices is pointless. Second, he may recognize the possibility that his informants know more meanings of a word than a definition presents, and he will identify those meanings as recorded in pertinent historical and dialectal reference works.[7] But his sole guides to word selection are in the stated definition. It serves in conjunction with the synonymous words listed to limit the sense in which the informant understands these words. At the same time it does not impose on anyone a need to accept as synonymous a word which he knows only in a different sense or not at all.

It is on grounds of common sense that a researcher accepts a count of the same marked word in several questionnaires as being a count also of "the same meaning."

Having recognized a set of limiting characteristics of the research tool and having decided to use it, his next concern is with the distribution of a sufficient number of questionnaires so that he will get back an appropriate sample of the language of a proper number of persons in a proper number of places. The sampling technique used in this study has roughly the same aims as that devised for the Linguistic Atlas. If other sampling techniques seem better for this kind of inquiry into human conduct, their proponents can demonstrate that excellence by comparing their findings with those reported here. Meanwhile the present record is assumed to illustrate an adequate sample.

The initial plan of distribution and collection tried to take into account most mishaps which might occur. If one wishes to have a sufficient number of useful documents from all parts of a region, he should assume that some informants will not return their questionnaires and that other informants will later be found unsuitable. In actual performance, this meant that roughly three thousand questionnaires were mailed in order to obtain a slightly over one thousand best records for this study.

The questionnaires were sent to all counties and parishes within the region, an indirect way of reaching those localities of historical and social importance which an interviewer for the Linguistic Atlas would select by specific research. Informants within those counties or parishes had already been identified by intermediaries who presumably knew the locale. When the completed questionnaires were returned, a representative linguistic community was developed from the biographical part of the questionnaire. (Map 3 and Appendix A).

The selected members of this community are white, native-born, lifetime residents of their respective home counties. They are descendants of earlier settlers of the Inter or South and adjacent states. Roughly half are males. The oldest members, past seventy, ended their schooling with the second reader; the youngest, eighteen to twenty years in age, were enrolled in college at the time. Their occupations—*student, farmer, housewife, county judge,* and *forest ranger*, for example—include nearly every type of employment, a spectrum so wide that simpler classifications for an attempted link between employment and vocabulary proved impracticable.[8]

Having chosen the best available evidence, the researcher's next task is to sort the evidence and interpret it, a task made more exhaustive by means of digital computers.

A printed questionnaire is better suited to computer analysis than is a collection of worksheets gathered for the Linguistic Atlas, though the latter can be analyzed by computer after some editing. But uniformities of printed questionnaires permit a direct coding of all responses since each possible response occurs in a numbered item and in the same position in its own list. Further each accepted questionnaire is given its unique classificational number which identifies it by state, county, and place. This number is followed by a coded record of the informant's age, sex, race, and education. These codes, the item number of the synonym entry, and the codes of the individual synonyms as chosen or omitted are then punched on cards to be sorted by computer and tabulated.[9]

Among early hypotheses tested by means of these tabulations is the one that men and women differ in their choices of certain synonyms. The results were negative. And so, except for this comment, no further discussion of this hypothesis occurs in the present study. Silence is an explicit statement that the questionnaire elicited no positive evidence that sex differences are reflected in word choice.[10]

The next hypothesis to be tested is that chronological change in vocabulary can be discovered in the difference in word choice among age groups. To this end the entire collection of responses was sorted into three age groups, those from persons between eighteen and thirty, those between forty and sixty, and those between seventy and ninety. A county by county word list of every word choice for each age group was printed and provides evidence for discussions of obsolescence and for the word maps. This computer printout itself is far too bulky and awkward to print here.[11]

After these county tabulations had been made and the maps prepared, the next steps were to compile and print a gross count for each word, a body of computations which convert these gross figures to percentages for each according to its presence in any or all of the eight states, and a list of volunteered words according to the states from which they had come. These are reproduced in the text.

In sum, computer tabulations lie behind three kinds of synchronic models—the maps, the percentile and numerical listings, and the list of volunteered words. Each can be compared with the other since all derive from the same raw evidence collected in the same way. But readers may properly ask whether this group of models can be compared with other models which are based on Atlas field interviews and derive from evidence gathered over longer and different periods of time.

A comparison of synchronic with diachronic models is justified in this instance since informants for both are contemporaries who share the twentieth-century developments of American English common to their respective communities. The language models themselves may reflect a different moment of collection as well as a different gap between collecting and publication, but this does not introduce so great an element of difference in linguistic time as to provide a measurable disparity in the available vocabularies. And since my concern with vocabulary uniformity or change is directed only to the evidence from the Interior South, I can see no clouding of that analysis by noting that words in the Interior South are also recorded in earlier vocabulary studies of surrounding states.[12]

The propriety of comparing evidence collected by different techniques is a more troublesome issue. One can argue that regardless of the printed spelling, a word found by spoken interview is at the level of speech while a word spelled in the same way but found by means of a printed questionnaire is at the level of print. Some researchers hesitate to cross from level to level in order to find similarities in vocabulary. My view is that we have somehow confused ourselves by giving undue attention to the ways in which evidence is gathered. One can easily elicit *faucet* from some persons by showing a picture, by asking a well-phrased question, or by inviting choices from a printed list of synonyms. The result when it occurs at the level of a conventionally spelled word will not be a string of separated letters *f* + *a* + *u* and so on, or a string of phonemic-phonetic symbols beginning with /f/; instead it will be *faucet*. As such and at the level of vocabulary, each instance of *faucet* can be compared with every other occurrence of it. Of course, a matter of interpretation does arise when two variant conventional spellings such as *spicket, spigot* occur.[13] Here the procedure has been to treat them as a single word, to note the presence of the two forms and comment on that fact, and to indicate that field interviews are needed if one wishes to establish local limits for either pronunciation at a given moment.

As for relative differences between a spontaneous spoken record and the evidence of contemplative choice encouraged by a printed questionnaire, this too is hardly a barrier to comparisons. When spontaneous and contemplative choices agree, one can not avoid a conclusion that the two are parts of the same linguistic processes in American English. Each independent choice of the same word is evidence of its presence in the Interior South and of its relationships to regional English vocabulary collected elsewhere in the United States. As for the influence of contemplation, one should notice that all who read and answer the questionnaire are given a uniform opportunity to consider all of the choices. As a result, we obtain both a record of instances in which a word is reported as being in use to some degree as well as those synonyms chosen seldom or not at all.

In those circumstances a researcher can say that as a tool the printed questionnaire gives him a record of vocabulary which can properly be compared with other regional vocabularies. In addition it gives him a scaled report of preference which extends from unanimous choice to unanimous rejection.

3

Gradations in Uniformity

Change is an aspect of language reflected in part by gradation just as gradation is a part of linguistic uniformity.[1] When changes in the language are in part a response to the presence of competing dialect vocabularies, the investigator must search for the actual presence of the two or more dialects before he can examine their interaction if any.

Gross counts of the local vocabulary provide a good starting point. For the Interior South these counts provide first answers to questions like these: How much of the regional word choice can be traced to the migration of Boone and his neighbors and their successors? How much to the planters and slaves from Virginia and other South Atlantic states? And, in response to later urban intrusions, how much to commerce and technology? But counted word choices should not be read as a claim that they are a measure of precise linguistic causes and effects. Even if such an unlikely attempt were to be made, the missing local history of English words in the Interior South would doom it to failure.[2] What is proposed here is a report of the gross numbers of choices of words first found on the seaboard and now reported from the interior. But before we examine the proposed links, let us consider the reasons for caution in proposing single explanations as illustrated by the geography of the name of an insect, a food, and some commercial artifacts.

It is self-evident truth that migrants from the Atlantic states to the interior brought with them words that had become a part of American English almost at the moment of first colonization. *Mosquito hawk* seems an indisputable instance of movement of words along the coast in the South Atlantic states and then westward into our region (Map 44). Consider two pieces of evidence. Among other interesting creatures of the New World as labeled and displayed in John Lawson's 1709 *A New Voyage to Carolina* is a dragon fly with the name "muskeetoe hawk." The current presence of that word on the coast is attested to in Kurath's *Word Geography;* its distribution in Georgia and other states of the Interior South seems readily explained by postulating a westward dissemination as the planter class established cotton plantations in the Gulf plain. This explanation is clouded by the discovery that *mosquito hawk* is known in the upper Midwest.[3] Since it reached there by some strange passage overland, it could also have reached parts of the Interior South by routes equally mysterious.

Present records show that *tow sack* is a North Carolina word. It doubtless accompanied those North Carolinians who settled the uplands of Tennessee, and went with them or their descendants into other parts of the Interior South as the frontier was pushed back (Map 42).[4] Since *dog irons* and *fire dogs,* or *goobers* and *pinders* have similar distinctive patterns of occurrence, one can assume that they too reflect early lines of migration from Virginia, the Carolinas, and Georgia (Maps 33, 48). But *goobers* and *pinders* are recorded fairly late in American English though they may have entered it much earlier. Because they are African words, they may reflect part of the path of forced slave migration from an older South to the newer cotton plantations; if so, the words could have entered general usage fairly late. If not, then they must have done so toward the beginning of the nineteenth century. Either possibility leaves unanswered such questions as these: When did diffusion into general English as distinguished from slave English begin? And when, by whom, and for how long were *pinders* and *goobers* a part of actively transmitted westward moving vocabularies?

A second set of problems is linked to responses to urban influences. The direction in which trade moves becomes a possible way of exporting regional words from one locality to a more distant one. *Gunny sack,* for example, is a local word in Ohio and adjacent states. In the early days of the republic, Pittsburgh and Wheeling had become "centers of trade dominating the upper Ohio Valley."[5] It seems likely that the presence of *gunny sack* further south is a token of that trade and of the growth of Ohio and other midwestern states as suppliers of food shipped downriver (Map 62). Of course, its presence in the Interior South can also be explained as a sign of the migration of persons from the *gunny sack* area or by a combination of the two. On the other hand, the dissemination of *guano sack* in Georgia seems to point to distribution from the Savannah River and especially to commercial influences from Savannah and Augusta (Map 61). The importation of guano from Peru began early in the nineteenth century, a time when the Savannah Valley could be said to have a stable population which was supplied from the two cities named.[6] In part, the presence of *guano sack* is a possible indication of the area influenced by the urbanizing presence of Savannah and Augusta, rather than of any significant shift of population.

The words *coal oil* and *kerosene* are of particular interest since they show how brief a period is required for the spread of regional words and for one of them to decline in our esteem. These two industrial names appeared in the 1850's. In 1853 application was made for American patents on the process of making *kerosene,* a trade name coined from Greek; a contemporary law suit established the right to use *coal oil* as a name of the same product. Kerosene was manufactured in New York state while competing coal oil works produced the same illuminating oil in West Virginia and Ohio.[7] Trade routes apparently explain the presence of *kerosene* as a local word in the North and parts of the Old South; certainly West Virginia and Ohio distribution downstream accounts for much of the use of *coal oil* in the Interior South (Maps 13, 72). After 1860 *kerosene* shifted from a regional to a national word for the product, but one can only marvel at social processes which led more recent users to decide that *coal oil* is inelegant. As informants put it, "We called it coal oil but we knew it really should be kerosene."

The city extended its influence subtly through education even though a person had ended his formal schooling with the second reader. Print—magazines, catalogs, newspapers, books—intruded upon local vocabularies as the wilderness was being tamed. That is, a local word from Philadelphia, or New York, or Boston replaced an equally useful synonym somewhere else. *Mantel,* for example, became a catalog word.[8] So, as soon as Oklahoma was settled, rural free delivery of catalogs may have contributed more to its acceptance and to the corresponding absence of *fireboard* than did difficulties of travel westward through the Arkansas Ozarks where the latter is still known (Map 34).

The advent of formal, public education introduced a variety of urbanizing terms. Consider those related closely to the school itself. When schools were opened, people who had had no occasions to speak of it before began to discuss *playing hookey.* Similarly, school board members and teachers who knew the informal homemade devices began to discuss from catalogs the kinds of *seesaw* the school could buy. As for textbooks, Odonata and Annelida appeared in elementary science texts with the labels *dragon fly* and *earthworm,* a surprise doubtless to those adults who had always known them as *mosquito hawks* and *red worms.* When the influence is strong enough, the original local name gives way to a book word; otherwise, the latter is reserved for class use and the former for daily conversation.

With these variables in mind, one can understand that the implied history of regional vocabulary is more complex than the visible history that is offered here. Simplifications must guide us as we now interpret the evidence in three records. The first are the printed gross counts of word occurrences and the printed list of volunteered words as found in Tables II and III. The second, four kinds of percentile statements are given in Table I. And the third, not printed in this book, are the computer listings of the county by county sum of individual responses classified by age groups.

The report of the numbers of persons who chose each word in the questionnaire is in Table II. A quick glance at it shows a gradation from no response to over one thousand choices. Its significance as a record is that at the negative end we have a clear indication that over one thousand persons do not use one set of words. From that negative affirmation, the pattern of choice gradually shifts until all or nearly all persons in the Interior South may be said to know and use the upper segment of this vocabulary.

To begin with negative evidence, no persons chose the local words *eaceworm, cubbie, lattermath, creeper, chance, goose drownder, tempest, overden, Dutch cap, hay doodles, loppered milk, cook jack,* and *freight.* A single choice characterizes the next twenty-five, making for all practical purposes a list of thirty-nine unknown or unreported usages. As one moves toward the other end of this scale, he discovers that half of the informants or more report using one hundred questionnaire words. The choices of one thousand or more persons are *rock, shuck, tongue, seesaw, corn bread, crawls, rail fence, pallet, lightning bug,* and *haystack.*

The list of volunteered words hints at similar gradations in choice. With caution one can deduce that in frequency *baker bread, fiddle worm,* and *seasoning meat* should fall somewhere in the middle frequency of responses and that *chifferobe, plunder house, shiplap, fat splinters,* and some thirty other words would occur regularly in responses throughout the entire region. To hazard a guess, they would be reported by over half of the informants.[9]

A different view of the ranges of choice is furnished by Table I where all responses are expressed as percentages within the framework of a total state response.[10] Let us consider the measures of relative frequency and relative importance as shown in columns A and B of that table: The first gives the state total as a percentage of occurrences east or west of the Mississippi as is appropriate for that state. The second gives the state total as a percentage of the maximum of possible responses in that state. While these could be charted separately here they are combined to form the axes of scattergrams which display relative frequency and relative importance at the same time.

The first list of regional words is a representative sample of that part of the local vocabulary which presumably originated in Pennsylvania or in states still further north. A simple dissemination southward into the interior is assumed.[11]

	Item no.
pitch pine	12
blinds	14
clapboards	15
eaves troughs	16
spouting	16
spouts	16
overhead	18
haycocks	20
stoop	25
stone wall	30
worm fence	31
pail	32
skillet	34
poke	37
burlap sack	38
fills	42
thills	42
whiffletree	43
armload	46
coal hod	51
coal oil	53
lamp oil	53
comforter	55
hap	55
bawl	67
sook (ie)	71
lead horse	79
near horse	79
little piece	80
bread	83
johnny cake	84
fried cake	85
flannel cakes	86
flitch	87
side meat	87
ponhaws	90
lobbered milk	93
thick milk	93
Dutch cheese	94
smearcase	94
piece meal	95
pit	97
cling	98
freestone peach	99
green beans	103
husk	107
grinnie	110

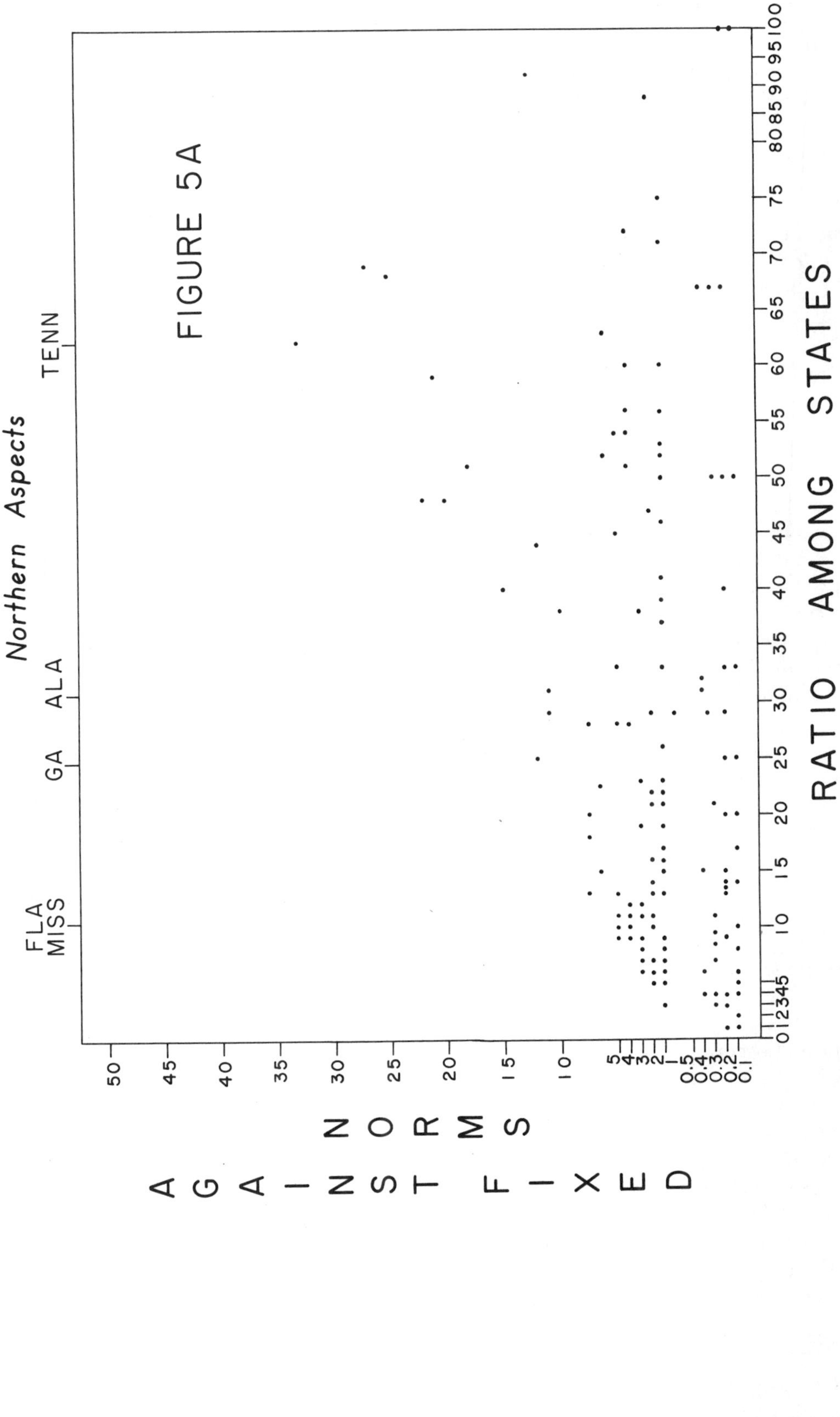
Northern Aspects
FLA
MISS
GA
ALA
TENN
RATIO AMONG STATES
AGAINST FIXED NORMS

FIGURE 5A

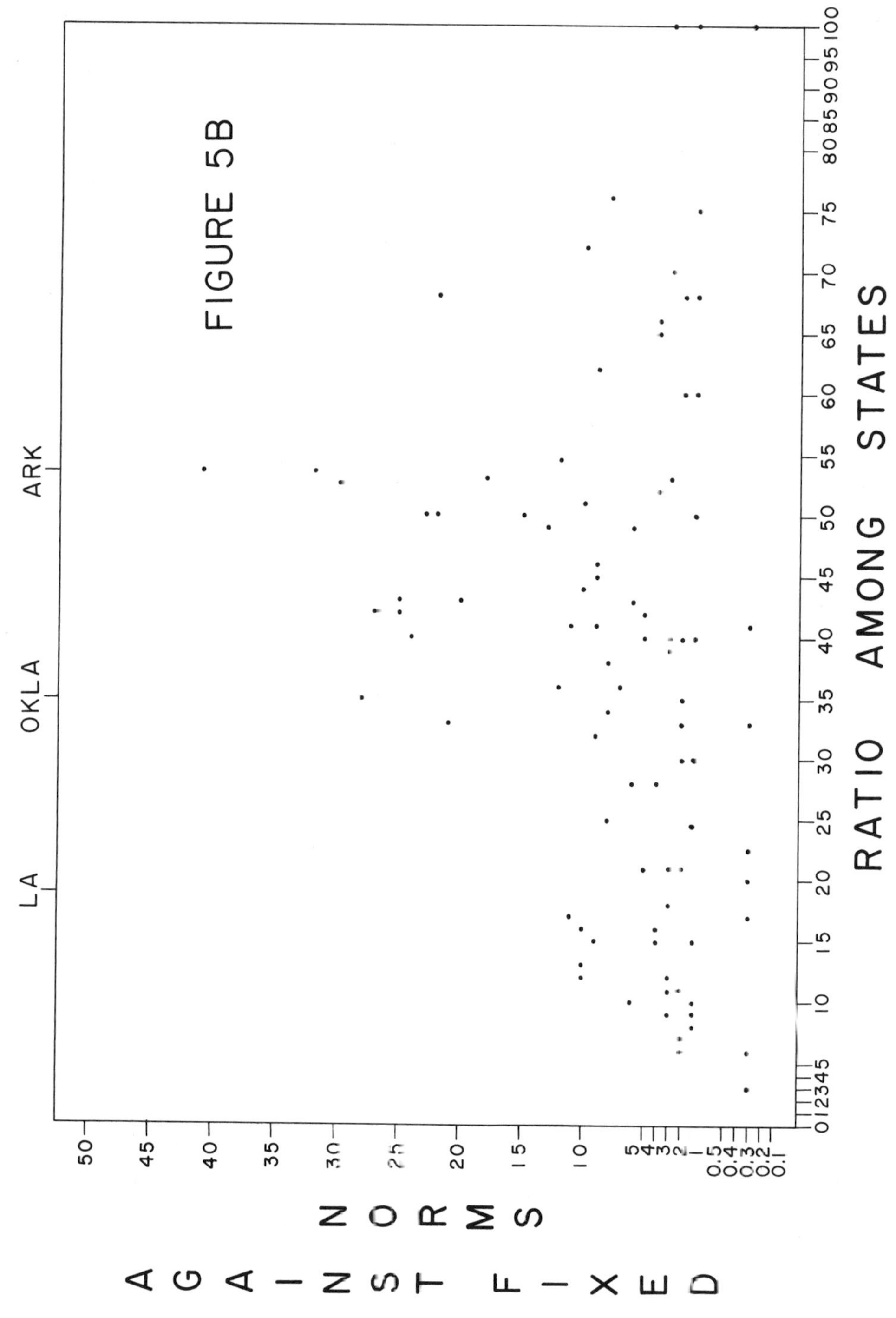
FIGURE 5B
LA
OKLA
ARK
RATIO AMONG STATES
AGAINST FIXED NORMS

	ITEM NO.
darning needle	115
snake feeder	115
sugar bush	119
baby buggy	125
sick on his stomach	136
horning	139

The resulting scattergram (Figures 5A and B) shows a range of gradations that go from nearly zero to somewhat above one-third and then, according to importance, diminish at the right of the plotted data.[12] However, this figure does not indicate the relative contributions of each state to the whole display, a matter which will be clarified now. In each instance let us mark the lowest percentage point for the individual states and, selecting a high point of preference and a separate high point of state occurrence, join the three to form a triangle which includes the bulk of other points recorded for that specific state.[13] The triangles for Florida, Georgia, and Tennessee are shown in Figure 6.

The Alabama and Mississippi responses are displayed separately because of a need for additional clarity and emphasis. Since each of these states has a smaller number of counties and thus of informants, the statistical record forces their contributed data to be plotted to the left where it tends to be lost if displayed with the record of other states. But when displayed separately, some data points fall outside the triangular frame which has served for analysis elsewhere. Be that as it may, the frame drawn for Alabama and Mississippi does enclose a significant number of plotted points. In terms of relative contributions to the total sectional response, Mississippi reaches seventeen percent and Alabama thirty-three. On the scale of relative importance of words within the state, the peak is at five percent of the possible maximum (Figure 7).

West of the Mississippi the maximum range

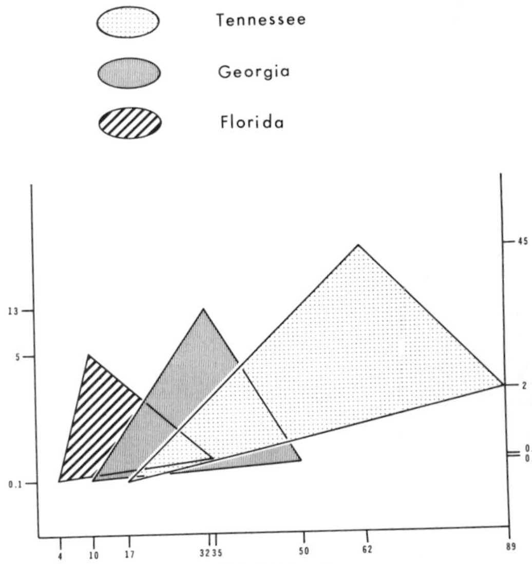
Tennessee
Georgia
Florida
13
5
0.1
45
2
0.3
0.2
4
10
17
32
35
50
62
89

FIGURE 6

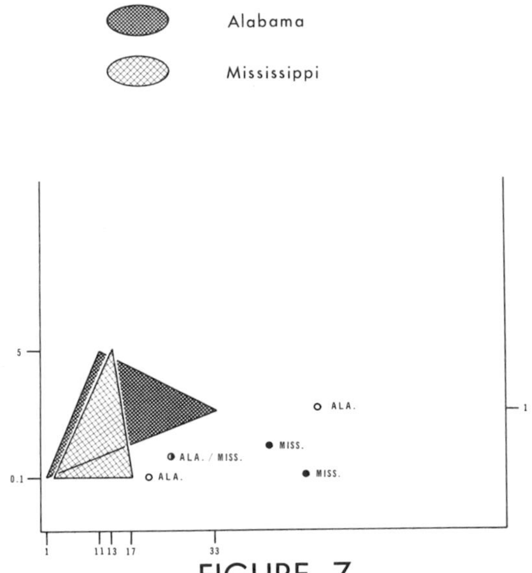
Alabama
Mississippi
5
0.1
1
ALA.
MISS.
ALA. / MISS.
MISS.
ALA.
MISS.
1
11
13
17
33

FIGURE 7

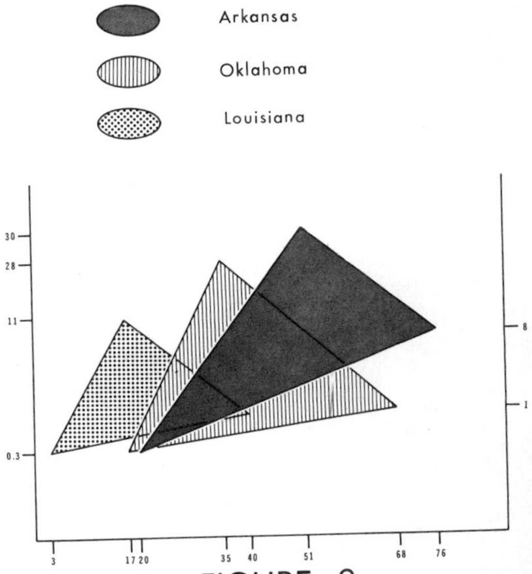
Arkansas
Oklahoma
Louisiana
30
28
11
0.3
8
1
3
17
20
35
40
51
68
76

FIGURE 8

of this vocabulary is from one-third to three-fourths on the scale of total importance. In terms of the separate states in the sectional total, the greatest distribution is from one-tenth to slightly less than one-half (Figure 8).

The second list contains regional words reported from Maryland southward, and Pennsylvania words which have no northern extensions and which may or may not be found in the South Atlantic states.

	ITEM NO.
quarter till	4
fireboard	10
dog irons	11
fire dogs	11
fatwood	12
lightwood	12
weatherboards	15
weatherboarding	15
hay shocks	20
clothes press	22
paling fence	29
rock fence	30
bucket	32
spicket	35
spigot	35
croker sack	38
crocus sack	38
French harp	40
mouth harp	40
singletree	43
toting	44
turn	46
sawbuck	47
seesaw	48
ridy horse	49
whet rock	52
comfort	55
nicker	68
whicker	68
pully bone	69
co-wench	71
come up	74
light bread	83
corn pone	84
ash cake	84
batter bread	84
fat cake	85
middling(s)	87
middlin meat	87
clabber	93
clabber milk	93
clabber cheese	94
snack	95
press peach	98
soft peach	98
snap beans	103
salad	104
goobers	105
pinders	105
shuck	107
roasting ears	108
polecat	111
earthworm	113
red worm	113
mosquito hawk	115
snake doctor	115
sugar tree	118
granny	127
granny woman	127
jackleg preacher	129
Christmas gift	143
pack	147

The shape of the second pair of scattergrams (Figures 9A and B) resembles the first. State records, however, differ in several particulars. The pattern for Florida, Georgia, and Tennessee rises higher in indications of preference and extends further to the right. If one uses Georgia as an example, the indications of relative importance of the words has increased by fifteen units over that in the first list; its indication of state preference has increased by twenty-five. For the same reasons that applied earlier, the Alabama and Mississippi details are less expansive (Figures 10 and 11).

West of the Mississippi, a notable increase is approximately twenty units upward and thirty to the right for Louisiana. In Arkansas and Oklahoma the differences are modest. (Figure 12.)

These models of word choice show that regional vocabularies whether from Pennsylvania and further north or from the coastal and piedmont sections of the South Atlantic states have mingled complexly in the Interior South. For each of the purported source vocabularies, moreover, the range of use extends from slight to highly significant whether one measures this range as an element physically present in a section of geographic space or as an expression

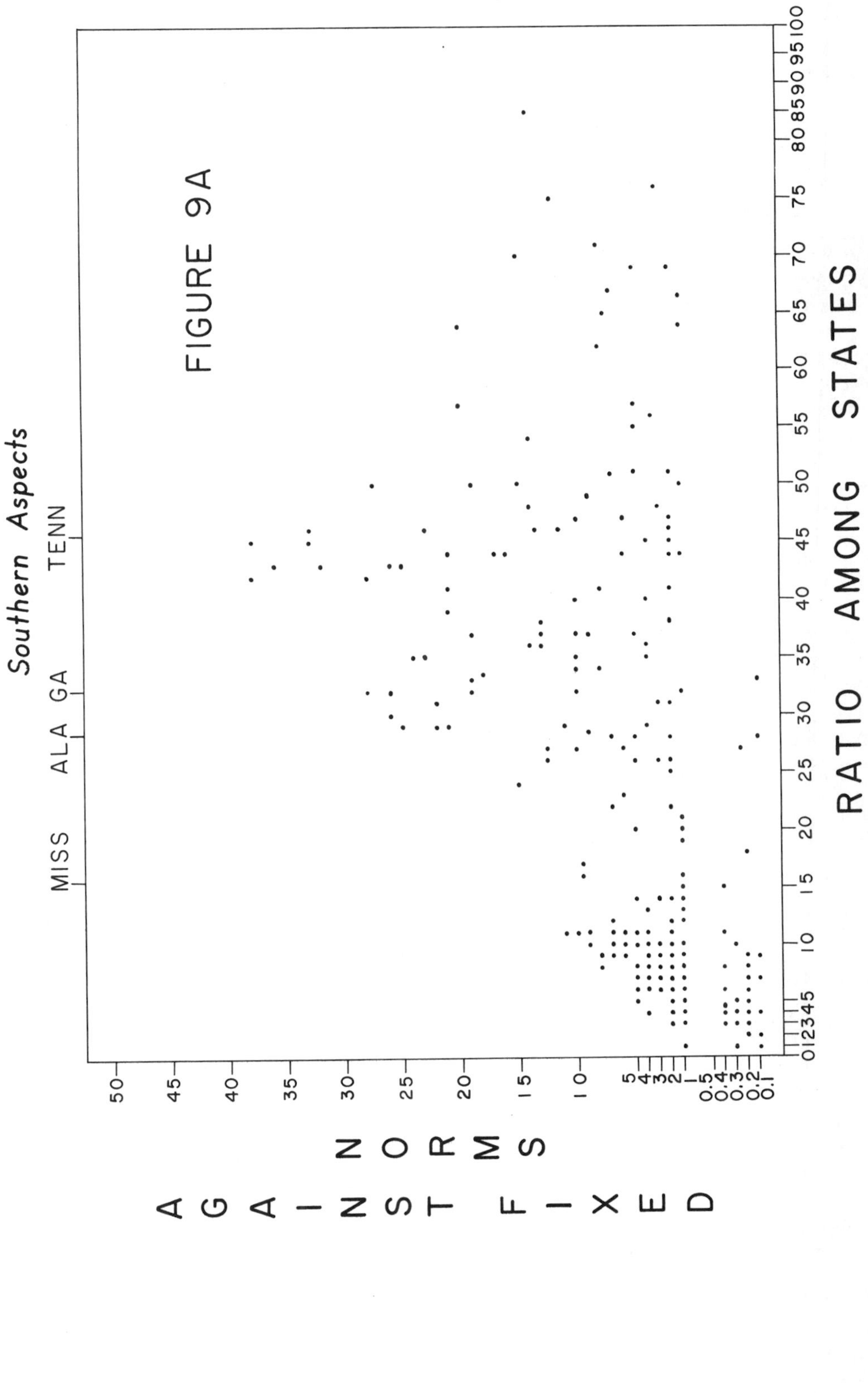
Southern Aspects
MISS
ALA
GA
TENN
RATIO AMONG STATES
AGAINST FIXED NORMS

FIGURE 9A

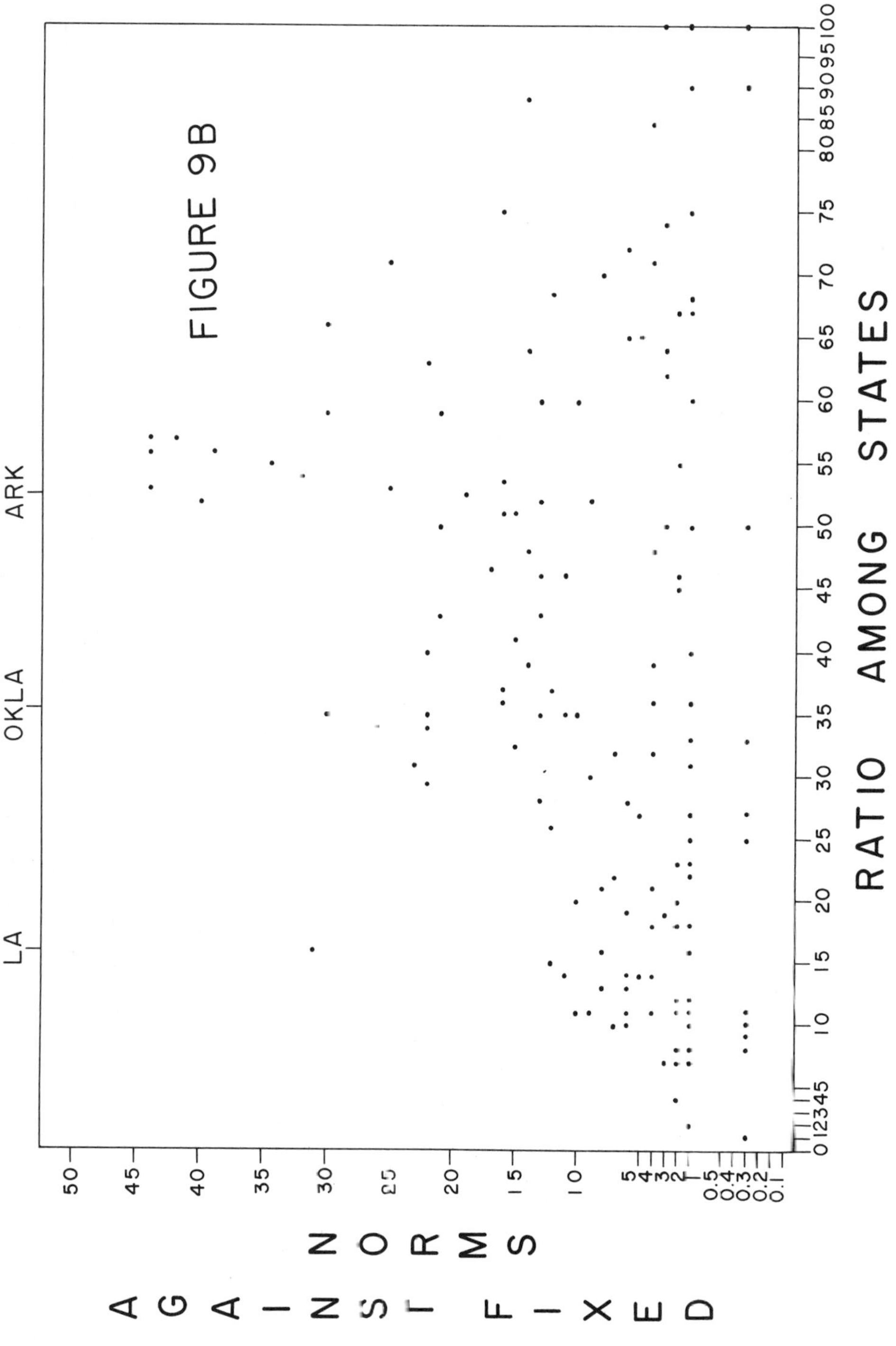
FIGURE 9B
LA
OKLA
ARK
RATIO AMONG STATES
NORMS AGAINST FIXED
0 1 2 3 4 5 10 15 20 25 30 35 40 45 50 55 60 65 70 75 80 85 90 95 100
50 45 40 35 30 25 20 15 10 5 4 3 2 1 0.5 0.4 0.3 0.2 0.1

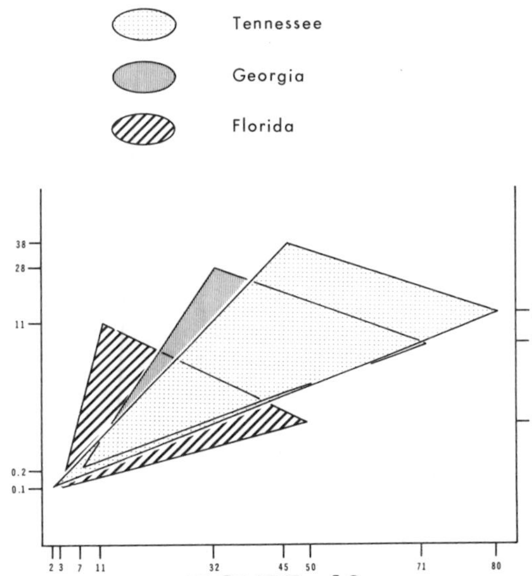
Tennessee
Georgia
Florida
38
28
11
0.2
0.1
14
8
1
2 3 7 11 32 45 50 71 80

FIGURE 10

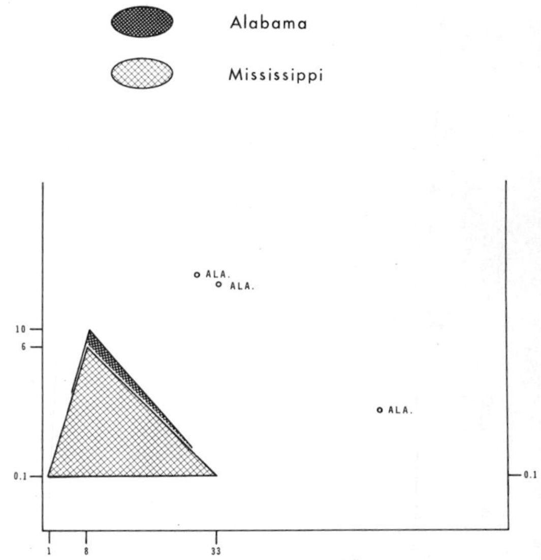
Alabama
Mississippi
ALA.
ALA.
ALA.
10
6
0.1
0.1
1 8 33

FIGURE 11

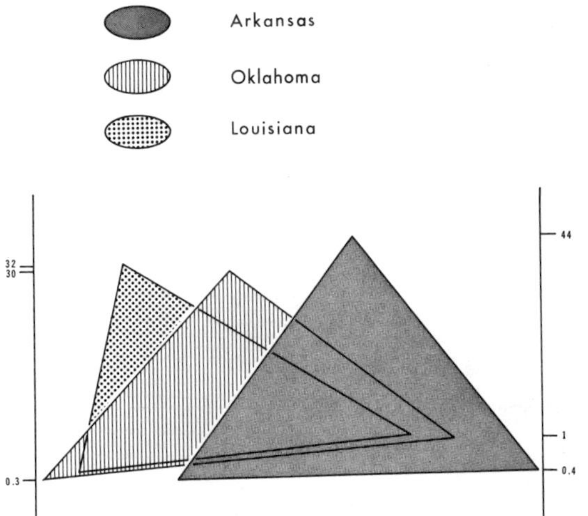
Arkansas
Oklahoma
Louisiana
32
30
0.3
44
1
0.4
1 8 16 25 35 57 68 75 88

FIGURE 12

of relative preference in choice. Whatever the measure of gradation, it occurs in similar patterns on both sides of the Mississippi. Briefly, if a mingling of regional vocabularies is a potential source of change in word usage, then such a potential is amply displayed in these models.

Preference has been given as one factor in the measured display of word frequencies. Let us examine variables which contribute to preference as they appear in the county by county tabulations.

Again it is perfectly obvious that indications of preference are hard to count. If *armoire* is "old fashioned" according to one informant and *pinders* is "used by hired hands" according to another, how is the researcher to measure the relative value of these words as an expression of the language of hired hands or of old-fashioned informants elsewhere? Or how much attention must he give to the impact of reference books and other formal guides? If one had been influenced by dictionaries published at the beginning of this century, he might have avoided *tote* because it was labeled "dialectal"; within the past few years, however, he, his wife, and their contemporaries have bought, used, and talked about *tote bags* apparently without any linguistic qualms. Is the recorded preference for *tote* a sign here of an upward change in the acceptability of disapproved regional words? Again, given a comment about preferences on the Atlantic, how does one measure its impact on the vocabulary of the interior with such a guide as this? "*Sitting room* is now rather a rural expression. *Living room* is fully established in the cities and among the younger generation in the country."[14] Quantifying is difficult.

The procedure used here is suggested by Atwood's Texas study and is indebted to it for words chosen to show decreasing or increasing preference according to age groups—choices according to obsolescence and expansion. His operational definition of "obsolescence," for instance, is that the percentages of occurrence are highest among the oldest informants and decrease progressively.[15] At first glance it would seem that percentages of choice could be compared between the Texas analysis and the present tabulations. But when one examines the actual record for each age group within the eight separate states of the Interior South, he finds statistical awkwardnesses that make such an attempt unrewarding. Consider, for instance, the percentile design needed to show relative preferences for a word that is known-unknown-increasing-decreasing all at the same time from age group to age group and place to place. East of the Mississippi *turn*, meaning "an armful" will serve. These are the numbers of persons who marked it in each age group.

	70–90	40–60	18–30
Tennessee	4	3	0
Georgia	26	40	9
Florida	19	15	3
Alabama	2	0	2
Mississippi	0	0	0

Assuming that we agree on a way to derive the percentages (within the states separately? within the two main subsections of the Interior South? within the entire area under study?), we would still be at something of a loss when we sought to compare these with their counterparts in Atwood.

Rather let the Texas analysis provide a word list and a set of labels for their linguistic status there. From the present evidence an answer can then be given to questions about their relative obsolescence or expansion in the Interior South. The selected words, sorted according to increasing numerical occurrence as listed in Table II and sorted again according to their presence in the computer tabulations of age groups, are given in ascending order in the next few pages. Words in the left-hand column are the choice of older Texans; those at the right are shown to be expanding there. As for the numbers in parentheses, they represent a specific age group in the computer printouts: (1) persons from the Interior South eighteen to thirty years old, (4) persons forty to sixty years old, and (7) those seventy years old and older. If no number is given, its absence means that the word is reported in all age groups with about the same frequency.

In this first list all words are "obsolescent" in the Texas record and should be viewed as "obsolescent" here since nearly all occur fewer than one hundred times. But notice that *garret* is reported by the youngest and the middle-aged but not the oldest; under those circumstances it could be interpreted as an expanding word which in time would replace the widespread *attic*.[16]

Instance	Age Group	Synonym	Total Occurrence
whiffletree	(7)	....	
garrett	(1, 4)	attic	689
griddle cakes		....	
crocus sack	(7)	....	
coverlid	(4, 7)	....	
lunch	(4, 7)	snack	947
parlor		....	
poke		....	
hayseed	(7)	....	
corn dodger	(4, 7)	....	
clearseed peach	(4, 7)	....	

Foods, a piece of equipment now antique, and two words that are phonological variants of more widely used words—*crocus sack, coverlid*—these are entries for which no synonym is listed above. *Croker sack* occurs over six hundred times; it is not discussed later in this chapter; *pancakes* and *bedspread* are.

In the next group, *firefly* is listed in Atwood among expressions gradually increasing.[17] It is included here because its total occurrence is 128, not a strong candidate to replace *lightning bug* at over one thousand. This group in ascending order begins with one hundred and ends with 399.

Instance	Age Group	Synonym	Total Occurrence
granny		....	
turn		....	
....		firefly	128
bad man		....	
counterpane		bedspread	889
flapjacks		pancakes	667
riled		....	
plum peach		....	
middlins		....	
tote		....	
paling fence		picket fence	772
batter cakes		hot cakes	280
French harp		harmonica	367
shavs		....	
court		....	
shivaree		....	

Foods again are prominent in the list. *Flapjacks, batter cakes,* and *hot cakes* may in time give way to *pancakes* since the latter word is now the usual field label on packages, in published recipes, and in other commercial settings. Commercial influences surely favor *bedspread* and *picket fence* over *counterpane* and *paling fence*; the degree differs since one can observe that bedspreads are apt to be advertised more widely and more often than are picket fences. Advertising does not, however, seem to have given *harmonica* any appreciable gain over *French harp*.

As for social customs, *shivaree* has been replaced by the practice of marking the car of newly wedded persons, but no name was volunteered for the latter. And *court* has given way to *date*, a word which has risen to national respectability since the beginning of this century. No count of the latter is given here since it is among the volunteered words.

The final group begins with words occurring four hundred times or more and can most readily be displayed in units of one hundred.

	Age Group	Synonym	Total Occurrence
400 Occurrences			
lead horse		....	
snap beans		green beans	503
nicker		....	
roasting ears	(4, 7)	....	
600 Occurrences			
poison oak		poison ivy	671
pole cat		skunk	740
....		cottage cheese	685
clabber		....	
booger man	(4, 7)	....	
slop bucket		....	
700 Occurrences			
double tree		....	
souse			
light bread		white bread	91
800 Occurrences			
pully bone		wishbone	426
butter beans		lima beans	439

The supposedly obsolescent words occurring in

over four hundred responses do not appear to be actively so in the Interior South except perhaps for *booger man* and *roasting ears* for which almost no reports come from the youngest informants.

Some innovating words are well established at approximately the same frequency as those words which they are to replace *White bread,* on the other hand, occurs less than a hundred times and does not seem to be in a favorable position to replace *light bread* soon. It may, however, have unsuspected forces supporting it just as community preferences may have brought about the expansion of *quarter of* an hour and especially *ten forty five.* The first occurs roughly one hundred forty times and the second two hundred forty; both seem to be on their way to wider acceptance. This is particularly apparent in the expression *ten forty five,* accepted in all age groups but the oldest in Louisiana; technological precision must be at work.

From these numerical models of regional English, one can draw certain conclusions with regard to choice. For the entire Interior South the range extends from complete denial to complete acceptance. That is, roughly one thousand persons indicated that they did not use one set of words but did use another; between those extremes their preferences gradually shifted. For the two major sections, that is the geographic and political units east and west of the Mississippi, the smaller body of regional words shows similar gradations from low to high preference. An interesting aspect of this latter model is that it shows similar patterns of preference regardless of the eighteenth- and early nineteenth-century regional origins of the vocabularies used. As for the relative obsolescence or innovation characteristic of particular words, the evidence seems to be that a few are roughly as obsoloscent in the Interior South as they are in Texas. The rest are somewhat more stable, particularly those that more than half of the informants marked. Words in this range must be interpreted as regionally standard and acceptable.

4

The Geography of Some Words

Geographic models let us see how far a vocabulary has spread and where it is to be found among native speakers. For in drawing these models, a word geographer along with most other geographers has to decide on the features that are worth considering and the ways to map them. From Table I, for instance, one could devise a system of shading for percentages and apply that system to the gross divisions of each state. Or, as in the instance of *pail,* meaning "a large, open, wooden vessel" he could show its presence and the presence of competing terms like *bucket* with a graph (Item 32, Map 4).[1] The present maps, however, are derived from plotting the county by county responses, first separately and then in increasingly elaborate combinations.

The county map is an absolute. If a word occurs there it is shown as a dot or a circle; if not, the map is blank. That means that a single dot shows at least one occurrence in the county or parish but does not show how many more informants responded. Imagine that one county has a single response from a young man and that an adjacent county has eighteen responses, two of which are actually at the county seat and the remainder at other points from ten to thirty miles distant; its informants consist of one very old person, thirteen middle-aged persons, and the rest college freshmen. Regardless of simplicity or complexity of these facts each county record will be shown as a single dot or circle of the same size.[2]

The course of presentation in this chapter and the general ordering of maps in the word geography itself reflect historical matters that have already been mentioned. The first maps have as points of presumed origin those movements of American English which began in the North and Middle Atlantic states; the second, those in the South Atlantic states; and the third, a relationship that has been hinted at before, the ties between Louisiana and more northerly sites along the Mississippi River and its tributaries.[3] To put it in terms of dialect areas, it is a progression that moves from considering "Northern," "North Midland," and "Midland" dialect characteristics to "South Midland," "Southern" and "Louisianian" ones.[4] Its circular course is generalized in the composite map of *stone wall, tow sack,* and *bayou* (Map 5).

For the "Northern," "North Midland," and "Midland" elements each map shows unique vocabulary diffusions in the Interior South. *Stone wall* occurs fairly uniformly in the northern tier of these states; its southernmost occurrences extend into Florida and the Gulf states. *Burlap sack* appears in the same general areas but seems to have a somewhat wider distribution everywhere, perhaps partly because of commerce and partly because of an absence of enough stones in certain localities to justify talking about a wall of them. *Coal hod* and *eaves troughs* have a more limited area, less than that of one sense of *clothes press.* As for *coal oil* and one of its synonyms, *lamp oil,* the shape of the mapped occurrences must surely be that produced by commercial distribution. In sum, these and the maps of *teeter board, blinds, comforter,* and perhaps *curtains*[5] show unique patterns of spread which some words followed as they were first brought into the Interior South from the Middle Atlantic states and later from adjacent states in the Midwest (Maps 6–13). For the sake of simplicity one may view this dissemination as going from north to south.

The next elements are "Southern" and "South Midland." In part, their spread into the interior parallels that of the group which we have just examined. One difference is that their presumed origin is in the South Atlantic states and their most likely dissemination is either by way of the great valley system leading from the

Shenandoah to the Tennessee or south of the Appalachian barrier into the Gulf plain, or both (Figure 1). *Tow sack* illustrates the first; *fire dogs* and *dog irons* illustrate the second and third. From these maps one should notice the unique distributions westward, from northwest Georgia toward central Louisiana, southward into Florida or the Gulf states, and, selectively for those words disseminated from southern Georgia, a spread into the cotton growing region (Figure 3).

Starting with Virginia origins and working southward along the Atlantic, these illustrate unique patterns of westward dissemination. None appears to depend for its presence on an urbanizing influence or commercial distribution. They are *paling fence, rock fence; snake doctor* and *snake feeder; red worm; wheel horse* and *line horse, nicker* and *whicker; granny* in the sense of "a midwife"; *jackleg preacher; salad* and especially its phonological variant *sallet;* four names of a fruit: *plum peach, press peach, freestone peach,* and *soft peach; clabber cheese;* three names for bacon: *fat back, middlins,* and *middling meat; pully bone,* breadstuffs: *ash cake, batter cakes, batter bread, corn pone,* and one sense of *fritters; dog irons* and *fire dogs;* and *pack* meaning "to carry" (Maps 14–35, 42).

The last major group is linked with the social history of the cotton belt (Figure 3). It is "Southern" and "Louisianian" in origin and for convenience may be associated with the planter class.[6] This is not to say that the cotton aristocrats chose to use the Africanisms *pinder* or *goober* when less distinguished persons used *peanuts.* Rather it is to say that after the three words became available in American English, circumstances would make two of them the language of hired hands; each, then, was diffused at a different pace.

From the eastern part of the region, *croker sack, crocus sack,* and *mouth harp* are loosely associated with commerce, though their spread does not seem to reflect a flow of products from any particular urban center. *Mutton corn, spider* as the name of a skillet, *fatwood,* and *cowench* are mainly found in Florida and Georgia. *Lightwood, turn of wood, lowing, mosquito hawk, piazza, snap beans,* and the verb *tote* all extend further north in Georgia and have unique distributions westward. The "Louisianian" presence is shown by *bayou;* its outward spread, however, presents a puzzle. If one assumes that the Indian name had already entered French by the eighteenth century and that French-speaking persons had already named the localities now called bayous, how was the word introduced into local English? If it entered English in the nineteenth century and then was spread, why did it replace *slough* or other existing English words? At any rate, we may want to think that it is an early nineteenth-century addition to English at all of the points mapped. *Armoire* and *gallery* depend on a later presence of wealth and of a desire to live in the style of important New Orleans families for instance; language reflects the diffusion of style. *Gallery* as a term in domestic architecture and *armoire* as a name for furniture now smack of the antique. They serve, however, to remind us that from present evidence some hints can be gained about the regional spread of language influences from New Orleans and other river cities to counties and parishes which surround them[7] (Maps 36–51).

We have come to the end of a circular path of observations. And considering them, it is appropriate to look at Map 5 again and ask ourselves whether any overall patterns can be developed from the succession of unique maps which show current locations of words whose diffusions cross each other in three directions at least. One answer lies in the construction of a different sort of geographic model, combining the unique maps into a composite display of those regions where information from all maps is regularly found, with shading for those regions where uniqueness is prominent. The gradations shown on these will be from "all" to "some" and, if appropriate, to "none," a changing from dialectal abundance to absence.

The first composite made of word maps associated with *stone wall* may surprise some readers. If one were to judge solely by its evidence, he would conclude that the dialect features prominent in the Interior South are "Northern" and "North Midland" (Map 76). The area of greatest prevalence of these dialectal features is shown by the presence of *coal hod* and five other words; the next gradation has only those four words—*burlap sack, clothes press, comfort,* and *stone wall*; the blank areas have no responses.

The next composite is of maps of "Southern" and "South Midland" words from the South Atlantic states. In this model (Map 77) portions of Georgia and of Oklahoma have been excluded because they will be considered separately. The result of combining fourteen representative maps is to establish that this vocabulary occurs chiefly in upland Tennessee, Georgia, Alabama, Mississippi, and Arkansas. From these locations fingers extend southward into the Gulf plain and westward into Oklahoma. Outer areas are defined first by the relative absence of *pack, dog irons, fireboard,* and *snake feeder,* and second by the total absence of all words used.[8]

The third composite is of "Southern" words reported in Georgia, Florida, and the southeastern corner of Tennessee (Map 78). This restriction serves to focus attention on Georgia which has a special role in later analyses of dialect boundaries.[9] Here one notices for the first time a north and south spread of a regional vocabulary represented by ten words. A central area is marked by their presence in mid-Georgia; the marginal areas in the Georgia mountains, along eastern and western rivers, and in southwestern Florida, are determined by the absence first of *co-wench,* then of others such as *spider, turn of wood,* and *mosquito hawk*;[10] no zero element is shown.

The region west of the Mississippi has been described in part already, but since it is a difficult region to analyze in terms of vocabulary patterns, it is well to draw a second composite, placing an arbitrary right boundary at the Mississippi River. Within Louisiana, Arkansas, and Oklahoma, the zero area is that part of southwest Louisiana which is French speaking. In the rest of this western region one finds *earthworm, mosquito hawk, plum peach, sallet,* and *dog irons* to some degree, but no similarly wide distribution of words like *fireboard* and *jackleg preacher.* The central area, then, is defined by the presence of seventeen words; the peripheral areas by absences of one or more members of clusters of those words.[11] This "Midland" region includes the Arkansas and Louisiana uplands, its fingers extend out into the Mississippi Valley (an indication of migration from the hill country to the cotton lands?), and along the Red River Valley and thence northward into central Oklahoma (Map 79). The "Midland" vocabulary obviously mingles with "Southern."

Given these occurrences, can we discover anything else within the area by repeating the same techniques in some fashion? Yes. Of several procedures that suggest themselves, that of establishing a density map is worth considering. That is, the researcher examines county records and keeps track of specific counties from which the greatest number of different instances of regional vocabulary are reported; the useful evidence is selected by occurrence without reference to possible origin. To be specific, in Arkansas *tin panning, mosquito hawk,* and *tied quilt* are significant in the formation of one part of a density map there while *dog irons, fairing off,* and *tow sack* provide evidence for a concurrent density map in another portion of the same state. That individual sections of these density patterns derive from distinct basic records is shown by variations in shading on Map 84.[12]

What is gained by using this device? First, we have established specific centers of vocabulary concentration as such and have placed them within a larger setting of similar regional words. It is a mapped analog to the numerical gradations of occurrence made earlier by counting the times each word is reported. Second, we have gained an additional clue to possible relationships between events, geography, people, and language change. Consider that restricted area in northwest Arkansas where one density pattern is greatest. The site of the University of Arkansas is within this area, a clue to the relative ease of access from eastern parts of the state and of the cultural diversity in this locality. To the south are mountains and a river barrier, to the west mountains and until the end of the nineteenth century the full reservation of Oklahoma for tribes of American Indians. In sum, it is as though here is a kind of dam to the south and west behind which is impounded a linguistic lake.

Trade and movement along rivers may account for the more extensive density patterns described in Arkansas and Oklahoma. If so, a counterpart seems to be in two valley systems east of the Mississippi. There one pattern extends along the valley of the Tombigbee, a possible reflection of inland traffic between Memphis, Tennessee, and its environs, and Mobile, Alabama. A second originates more generally in the eastern curve of the big bend of the Tennessee River and extends southward along several river systems in Georgia. Whether or not this explanation of the patterns is accepted, one must agree that density patterns show that vocabulary stability and change are variables which shift from one section of the Interior South to another.

Change as gradation in word choice has been shown in three degrees of abstraction. The most abstract model is the density map which identifies centers of particular usages or dialect characteristics. At the next lower level of abstraction is the map of a dialect area which distinguishes the main dialect localities from their peripheries. At the lowest level are the unique maps of words which show two states—present or absent. Each level is a notation on the dynamics and the possibility of choice.

5

The *Southern* Dialect Area Redefined

Dynamic models of regional word distribution have the merit of suggesting that change is at work in regional American English. At the same time, in the form that they have been drawn for the Interior South they have some possible limitations. Boundaries, for instance, seem to fade forever. Intermingled parts are not clearly separated from each other. And their general appearance is such as to make very difficult any comparisons with the familiar maps of the American English dialects.

These limitations can be overcome by drawing a traditional map with appropriate isoglosses, a map which extends the Atlantic speech boundaries (Map 1) into the interior.[1] But readers must remember that what is included in a "Midland" area or a "Southern" area west of the Appalachians is ordinarily a more varied local vocabulary than is reported in the region bearing the same name in the Atlantic states. In brief, a western speech area as named requires a redefinition of the distinctive elements which identify that dialect.

A first step in such a redefinition is to discover whether the "Southern" vocabulary fills the entire Interior South regardless of infusions of "Northern" and "Midland" words. The test vocabulary is *barn lot, corn shucks, light bread,* and *pallet;* to these one may cautiously add two words linked to urbanizing influences, *kerosene* and *snack,* if one assumes a simple diffusion from "Southern" areas in the east. Their exclusion would not materially change the appearance of a composite map (Map 80) derived from the unique maps of the other words. "Southern" as defined at this point by these words occurs everywhere in the Interior South but in the French-speaking parishes of Louisiana.

A further possibility is that the "Southern" dialect extends west beyond the panhandle counties in Oklahoma. In fact, Atwood's discussion of the Texas vocabulary includes the remark that "the Southern vocabulary finally comes to an end somewhere on the slopes of the southern Rockies."[2] But how does one reconcile that statement with another conclusion based also on vocabulary evidence? "Southern comes to an end along the Chattahoochee River"[3] in Georgia. The distance between these two western boundaries for "Southern" is well over a thousand miles.

Part of the difficulty arises from the choice of test words which are to be used in characterizing the "Southern" dialect and from terminological confusions relating to that label and its sublabels in operational definitions given in Kurath's *Word Geography.*[4] A second part of the difficulty, indeed a different class of difficulties, relates to the act of extending Atlantic isoglosses westward. If we examine the second difficulty first, we can at the same time begin to establish subordinate dialect areas of *Southern* as that term will be redefined here.

Isogloss boundaries from the seaboard will have to be linked to their continuations in the interior. The linking is not easy if we assume that the seaboard lines are true isoglosses, single lines separating one linguistic feature from another. In the Interior South few such lines can be drawn as the reader may have already suspected from discussion in the preceding chapters. (*Gallery* and *piazza* are in fact the only synonyms which can be separated by an isogloss.) As for the line itself, it must represent a composite of responses. Let us recall that in mapping individual responses, a single dot stands for the word marked by one informant or by a half dozen. A boundary line made by joining the separate county dots that mark the edge of some reported word is, then, a generalization of variable numbers of responses and ages of informants. Thus on theoretical grounds

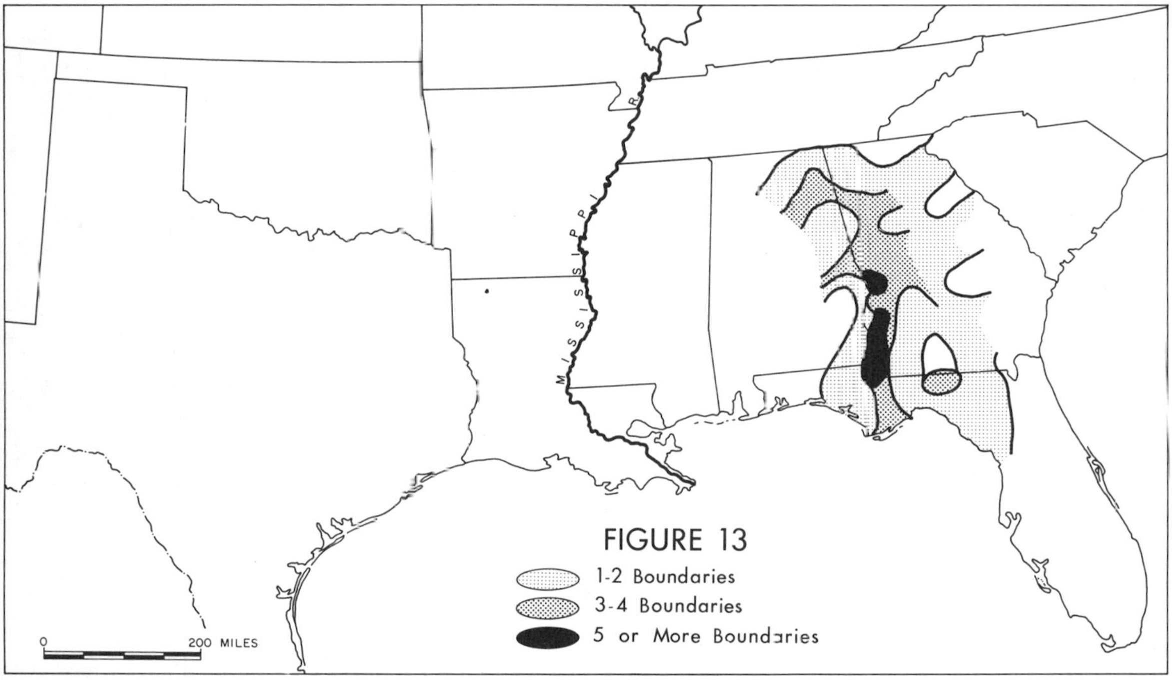
MISSISSIPPI R.
1-2 Boundaries
3-4 Boundaries
5 or More Boundaries
0 200 MILES

FIGURE 13

one could argue against drawing the line with a uniform width and perhaps even against joining it to the lines mapped for the Atlantic states. Practical advantages, however, seem to outweigh theoretical objections so long as we are aware of what the objections are. Eastern boundaries, for example, call for western extensions.

After the isogloss boundaries of individual words have been brought together on one map, it is clear that some boundaries converge while others occur in parallel patterns rather like the grain in a wooden board.[5] In the first instance, the presence and location of the boundary is indicated by converging lines; in the second, the actuality of a single line and its placing are more nearly intuitive.

A single example of the first type occurs in the Interior South. In western Georgia and eastern Alabama a dozen or so boundary isoglosses converge. Unique boundaries of *fire dogs, salad, lightwood, co-wench, spider, turn* (of wood), *whicker, fireboard, batter cakes, press peach, clabbered milk,* and *rock fence* come together to form a composite zone of composites shaped vaguely like a tree. The trunk is fairly compact in southwest Georgia; further north its branches diverge east and west (Figure 13).

Some central boundary within this figure is to be drawn in such a way that it will be an extension of an Atlantic boundary. This boundary as defined by the words mapped here must reflect the presence of "Southern" and "Midland" or "South Midland" characteristics. That is, it must obviously be an extension of the line which in Kurath follows the crest of the Blue Ridge to divide the "Southern" dialect from "Midland" (Map 1); it must lie along some prominent geographic feature after the Kurath example; and it must originate at the terminus of the "Midland-Southern" boundary in the hills of South Carolina. One geographic feature that falls within the composite linear map is the course of the Chattahoochee River, originating in the Georgia mountains and curving southwest and then south to form the political and physical boundary between Georgia and Alabama (Figure 1). The forces of settlement history, of river travel, and so on have seemed to combine to form this linguistic boundary. But notice that when drawn, its direction confines "Southern" to an area east of the Blue Ridge-Chattahoochee line. The new definition of

Southern will propose a different interpretation of that boundary.

As this boundary bends southward, some of its "Midland" elements branch away and begin to parallel the unique isoglosses of *pack, red worm, snake doctor,* and *tow sack.* Their westward extensions suggest that a boundary of "South Midland" will follow their course. These isoglosses, however, do not converge. Rather they belong to the second type; they generally parallel each other at varying distances. The linguistic boundary must therefore be drawn mainly in terms of a major geographic feature lying within the area where the isoglosses are found. Since these are words reported in the hill country, a convenient line would separate the upland culture from the cotton culture of the plains and piedmont. Such a line east of the Mississippi would begin along the upper Chattahoochee, would follow the high ground south and west of the Tennessee River and then would turn back along the Cumberland. West of the Mississippi, a similar boundary would enclose the Ozark and Ouachita mountain ranges. "Southern" and "South Midland" thus delimited in the Interior South would leave "Midland" as the most readily available title for language elements outside those boundaries (Maps 82, 83).

Agreed that "Southern" and "South Midland" words can be discerned readily within the areas so delimited; and granted further that according to the evidence of vocabulary, these "Southern" and "South Midland" vocabularies change gradually as one moves westward. Yet "Midland" in the Interior South contains far too many extraneous features of vocabulary to allow us to say that it is essentially the same as that "Midland" in Pennsylvania, Ohio, Illinois, and so on. In the midst of "Midland" in the Mississippi Valley and in parts of Oklahoma are "Northern," "Southern," "General Southern" (Atwood's label) and "Louisianian" words as we have already seen. It is time to elaborate the redefinition of *Southern* and the labeling of its subareas.

Southern is defined by the presence of regional words such as *light bread.* As a dialect of American English it occurs in the South Atlantic states and extends westward to the Rockies.[6] Based on outside evidence, its northern boundary, i.e. the boundary between it and "Midland," should be shifted from the Blue Ridge at least to the Ohio until that river reaches the Mississippi; then the boundary should go north of the Missouri Ozarks and return to the northern political boundary of Oklahoma for its westward continuation[7] (Map 83).

Within the *Southern* dialect are subdialect areas which have special vocabularies within their boundaries:[8] *Coastal Southern* has its western boundary along the Blue Ridge-Chattahoochee line as shown, replacing "Southern" as the area label. *MidSouthern* (a term modelled on "South Midland") is found generally in the uplands of the South; in the interior it has been infiltrated by words from "Northern" and "Midland" dialects. *Gulf Southern* is that mixed vocabulary found in the Mississippi Valley and the adjacent Gulf plain; it contains words from the several Atlantic dialects as well as Louisiana words. *Plains Southern* applies to that transitional vocabulary which appears in Oklahoma and in parts of Texas and presumably diminishes further westward (Map 82).

Southern, as defined, has these characteristics of vocabulary which are of interest to anyone examining the nature of word change there. Some of its words such as *earthworm* have moved from local to national usage; others like *dragon fly* have imposed an urban element on the regional synonyms. Synonyms in turn—*mosquito hawk, snake doctor, darning needle, red worm*—fall within certain boundaries drawn for the subdialect areas and serve when mapped individually to define the geographic extent of those subdialects. As for the social standing of the regional words, a count of users must enter into one's evaluation along with less easily measured information. So few people use *spider* as a synonym for *skillet* or *frying pan* that it can hardly be viewed as a competitor for either except in extremely limited settings. But *light bread* and *pallet,* reported by a thousand persons and thus standing for the usages of additional thousands, do have in the Interior South a standing equal to that of *bread* and *sleeping bag*. In a national context either synonym should be found acceptable, but one must leave these decisions about regional and national usage labels to the descriptive vagaries of dictionary makers.[9]

The remapping of *Southern* and its subdivisions has provided us with a generalized guide to the areas of the Interior South in which particular developments of local vocabulary have occurred. As such it is a convenient abstract indication of past events. But it may also be viewed as a generalized predictive model for gradations in future changes within this regional vocabulary. The prediction is of this sort: Along the boundary lines are the greatest instabilities; there one regional vocabulary is most apt to be replaced by its neighbor. Next are the enclosed subregions which will in turn be influenced by vocabulary diffusions across boundaries. At the other end of the scale of changes are the *Southern* words found in the entire Interior South; their rate of change will be very slow. Time will tell whether predictive interpretations of this static model of the *Southern* dialect are in accord with linguistic actuality.

6

The Choice of Synonyms

The *Southern* dialect which has been described up to this point has been presented according to the presence of a few words everywhere and of larger numbers of other words here and there in the Interior South. But the total list of test words for any aspect of *Southern* is smaller than the number of words given in the questionnaire itself. If one can account for some aspects of local vocabulary as evidence of the influence of migration, commerce, and urbanization on regional word change, one must also recognize that choices among synonyms has had its influence within that same region. To that end the present chapter is directed as it considers, word by word, the varying degrees of preference shown for each group of synonyms. Its thesis is that vocabulary change is implicit if not explicit in the degrees of preference calculated from individual choices among synonyms.

The design of the questionnaire is that of instructions and word lists. For the latter, the patterns stand as prophecy if not as a stated hypothesis: "Each word listed as a synonym will occur with equal frequency in use no matter where in the United States this questionnaire is answered." What kind of performance does this imply? The questionnaire presents one hundred and forty-seven numbered items, each with its own group of synonyms—one hundred and forty-seven unique linguistic universes whose synonymous members occur just once in a list. If actuality imitated this model, all persons would mark every word in item 10, in item 43, and item 99 with complete uniformity. But this sort of performance is not really expected. In fact, the questionnaire directs the answerer to encircle the word or words which he ordinarily uses and to leave unmarked all other synonyms given beside it. One calculated model of these responses is found in column D of Table I; that model lies behind the general discussions that follow.

In this chapter the order of presentation derives from the historical change from rural to urban interests that took place in the nineteenth and early twentieth centuries. In so far as it has been possible to do so, the writer has put concepts relating to the natural world at the beginning of the analysis and those relating to the city at the end.[1] This sequence, however, is not that of the questionnaire itself, but the necessary connections are made within the text. If for instance the reader has turned to the subdivision STORMS, the heading *Items 6, 7* refers him to the questionnaire printout as it appears in Table I; there the items are arranged in the ascending numerical order of the questionnaire itself.

Comments within the discussion of individual words serve as a summary of relationships displayed in Table I, with each Item being considered as its own unique, complete model of vocabulary preference in the Interior South. From the evidence in column D, one can be sure that *back log* is reported everywhere while its synonyms *back chunk* and *back stick* are chosen according to one pattern of preference east of the Mississippi and a different one west of it. (In Table I all Louisiana responses are west of the Mississippi.) The assumed ranges of change are for *back log* a high degree of stability; for *back chunk* and *back stick* a possible decrease in and eventual loss from regional use. For the measured differences in every instance, readers will turn to Table I.

The Natural Setting

Appropriate vocabularies for the weather, for gross features of the natural landscape, for North American plant and animal life, and for imprecise measures of time and distance were well established in American English before the westward migrations began, at least so one would imagine. Among the words presented under this general heading, *bayou* appears to be the sole word in this class to enter American English west of the Appalachians.

Climate and Weather

STORMS

Items 6, 7 Map 53

Fifteen words in the questionnaire relate to rain storms. Six of these refer to rains accompanied by thunder and lightning; the remaining nine to short, heavy rains. For the first sort approximately half of the responding informants chose *thunder storm* in preference to *electrical storm,* the latter having been chosen by less than one-third. The general word *storm* and the more specific *thunder shower* are known at a level of choice which in column D sinks at times to four and eight percent. *Tempest* is not chosen at all, though one can imagine informants using that word in the proverbial *a tempest in a tea pot.*

A violent and brief rain is called a *downpour* first and a *cloudburst* second everywhere but in Oklahoma; there the order is reversed. The degree of difference in choice is so slight that either could serve for the other except in Louisiana and Florida. The words *flaw* and *squall* are rare, though one does find *squall* in coastal counties. As for other synonyms, less formal in tone, *lightwood knot floater, toad strangler,* and *trash mover* occur now and then east of the Mississippi; only *toad strangler* is reported west of the Mississippi. While *gully washer* has about the same frequency of use that is given for *cloudburst, goose drownder* does not occur at all.

A rain accompanied by thunder and lightning is apparently well enough named in the text of the questionnaire. The other, a short and heavy rain, is not. Informants volunteered *(bull) frog strangler, cloud break, deluge, flood, trash toter,* and *washout,* terms which range from the jocular to the semitechnical *flood* and *washout.*[2]

IMPROVING WEATHER

Item 5 Map 54

When informants take notice of the passing of a storm or of cloudy weather, they regularly say that it is *clearing up* in all states but Georgia; there the preference is for *fairing off,* an expression not reported from Oklahoma. *Clearing off* and *fairing up* occur often; *breaking away,* on the other hand, is not reported in Mississippi; in the other states its choice is slight.[3]

ICE

Item 9

Although the southern tip of Florida may not often be excessively cold, a large part of the Interior South does experience freezing weather. When a thin covering of ice forms on ponds, the common term is *skim;* its next nearest competitor is *shale ice.* Scattered instances of *anchor ice, mush ice, shale,* and *scum* are recorded.

Among the volunteered words *skif ice* or *skif of ice* is widespread east of the Mississippi.[4]

Landscape

LOW DRY GROUND

Item 57

It was stated earlier that the first settlers sought out fertile land along the course of rivers and creeks, land that was renewed by the silt from spring floods and then became sufficiently dry to be arable. *Bottom land* is the usual term everywhere except in Arkansas where a second synonym, *bottoms,* is preferred; either will serve for this sense throughout the region. The third term, *intervale,* is unreported.

Of the volunteered words, *flat* occurs widely. *Delta,* a formal and technical term, needs further exploration in the Mississippi Valley.[5]

MOIST AREA

Item 58 Maps 5, 50

The questionnaire sought names of three kinds of low land. One is "swampy ground with a small stream running through it." The second "a slight depression, sometimes with a little stream," and the third "a low grassland." Obviously the physical characteristics of each of these will differ from place to place; the Florida Everglades may be called a swamp, yet that wilderness exceeds the concept of *marsh* or *swamp* in the experience of many informants.

For swampy ground, the preferred term is *swamp,* with a somewhat greater preference shown east of the Mississippi. Next is *marsh* or *slough. Swale, seep,* and *draw* are not often reported in this sense, nor is *bog. Bayou,* an eighteenth-century innovation from American Indian languages by way of Louisiana French, is reported in this sense from Tennessee, and particularly from Mississippi, Louisiana, and Arkansas.

For a slight depression, the preferred word east of the Mississippi is *seep* followed by *draw,* except in Alabama where these preferences are reversed. West of the Mississippi *draw* is preferred in Arkansas and is almost the only choice in Oklahoma. Louisiana choices are between *draw* and *coulee,* the latter being Canadian French in origin. A few scattered instances of *swale* occur.

The main word for low grassland is *meadow* everywhere except in Florida where *prairie,* a second preference in other states, is first. *Coulee, swale, intervale,* and *dago* rarely are reported. *Bayou* in this additional sense is a second preference in Mississippi.[6]

GROUPS OF TREES

Item 120

An isolated group of trees growing in open country is ordinarily called a *grove* everywhere except in Florida where it is a *clump,* the second term in other states. The two are close enough in frequency of choice to be interchangeable; perhaps preferences are determined by the formality of statement if *grove* has literary overtones for its user. *Bluff* in this sense is more frequent east of the Mississippi than west of it.

The volunteered words *shinnery* and *thicket* need additional local investigation. *Shinnery* has been reported extensively from Texas; it has been volunteered from many states in the Interior South. *Thicket* in this sense is found in parts of the Midwest.[7]

SUGAR MAPLES

Item 118

One tree with sweet sap is almost always called a *sugar maple.* Its synonym in all states except Florida and Louisiana is *sugar tree.* In Florida the second synonym is *rock maple,* a word not reported west of the Mississippi. The second choice in Louisiana is *hard maple* which is also known in all other states but Alabama and Oklahoma.[8]

A STAND OF MAPLES

Item 119

The questionnaire listed twelve synonyms for the name of a place where sap is gathered. As the volunteered word *cane patch* suggests, weather conditions in the South do not lead to a sugaring such as is common in Vermont maple groves; commercial production in the South is from cane. Even so, there are preferences for the names given to groves of maple trees which are distributed generally in the region. In Tennessee the first four in descending order of preference are *sugar tree grove, maple grove, sugar maple grove,* and *sugar grove.* In Georgia it is *sugar maple grove, maple grove, maple orchard,* and *sugar tree grove.* The first choice in Alabama, Mississippi, Louisiana, Arkansas, and Oklahoma is *maple grove* and the second *sugar maple grove;* in Florida, on the other hand, the choices are *maple orchard* and *maple grove.* Scattered instances are given of *sap orchard, sugar bush, sugar lot, sugar orchard,* and *sugar place* east and west of the Mississippi; *sugar lot* is reported only in Tennessee and Alabama. *Sugar camp,* found everywhere but in Florida, has its greatest frequency of choice in Louisiana.[9]

IRRITANT PLANT

Item 121

A vine or bush with three lobed leaves and irritant sap is called either *poison ivy* or *poison oak;* only in Oklahoma and Florida are there sufficient differences in percentage to show that one is preferred. Some informants wrote to say that *poison ivy* is a vine and *poison oak* a bush; others gave the same information but reversed the names. *Poison vine* is clearly a third choice in Tennessee; elsewhere it competes equally with *poison ivory,* a folk etymology. The volunteered *poison sumac* needs investigation for its meaning and occurrences.[10]

POISONOUS FUNGUS

Item 109

The poisonous fungus distinguished by a cap and a stem is ordinarily called a *toadstool;* its synonym, *frogstool,* is seldom reported or not at all. The volunteered *mushroom* needs further investigation to determine whether the words are truly synonymous or are restricted to distinguishing the edible variety from its poisonous likeness. *Devil's snuffbox,* also volunteered, is applied in the writer's experience to a different fungus.[11]

Wild Creatures

AN ODORIFEROUS ANIMAL

Item 111

Early settlers called the small, furry, bushy-tailed, striped animal by the English name *polecat* (the name of a different animal in Europe) or by a word out of the American Indian languages, Anglicized as *skunk*. Both terms are common in the Interior South, with *skunk* being preferred slightly in Tennessee, Alabama, and Mississippi, and markedly in Louisiana, Arkansas, and Oklahoma.[12]

A SQUIRREL-LIKE ANIMAL

Item 110

A small animal that runs on the ground and looks somewhat like a squirrel is called a *ground squirrel* in more than fifty percent of the responses. *Chipmunk,* from American Indian languages, is the only synonym except for a few scattered instances of *grinnie* in Tennessee and north Georgia.[13]

AN AMPHIBIAN

Item 112

The hopping, dry-land amphibian is known first as a *toad frog* and second as a *toad;* in Oklahoma only is *hop toad* in one fourth of the choices. *Dry-land frog, grey frog, wart frog,* and *warty toad* seldom occur. Volunteered words such as *bullfrog* seem to apply to the true amphibian.[14]

A GLOWING INSECT

Item 114

An insect that glows at night has five different names in the questionnaire. From these, three-fourths or more of the choices are *lightning bug.* Of the rest *firefly* is next. In Mississippi *fire bug* is third as is *glow worm* in Tennessee; the latter accounts for a fraction of the choices in Georgia, Florida, Arkansas, and Oklahoma. Instances of *June bug* are reported.[15]

A LARGE INSECT

Item 115 Maps 16, 44, 77, 78, 79

Large, four winged insects seen flying over bodies of water have the general book name *dragon fly* and at least six local names. *Dragon fly* is the word of first preference only in Alabama and Oklahoma; it is second or third in the other states. Two words, *snake doctor* and *snake feeder,* are the first choice in Tennessee; elsewhere *snake feeder* is not reported or is chosen in one-tenth of the instances or less. *Snake doctor* is the first choice in Georgia, Mississippi, and Arkansas. *Mosquito hawk* is the first choice in Florida and Louisiana and ties with *dragon fly* for first choice in Arkansas. *Ear sewer* has a slight distribution east of the Mississippi; *darning needle, devil's darning needle,* and *sewing needle* are known in scattered instances. Of the volunteered words, the Louisiana *cigalle* needs investigation as an instance of local French.[16]

WEBS

Item 117

Webs that spiders weave indoors and out sometimes have the same name and sometimes different ones. *Cobweb* is the first preference everywhere but in Georgia for the indoors variety; *spider web* is preferred for the outside web everywhere. *Cobweb* and *spider's web* are generally the second choice for the outside web except in Louisiana where only *cobweb* is second. *Spider's web* is used for the web inside with some frequency; only scattered instances of *dust web* and *web* are reported in this sense. *Web* is used for the outside form in from two to five percent of the choices; *dew web* and *spider nest* occur infrequently.

CRUSTACEANS
Item 116

The freshwater shellfish that has claws and swims backward is a *crawfish* in the choices of over half of the informants except in Oklahoma where it is that of less than one-third. *Crayfish* is the second choice in Alabama, Mississippi, and Louisiana, and ties for second with *crabs* in Georgia; the latter word is also second in Florida—raising the question whether coastal informants have confused the salt water with the fresh water crustacean. *Crawdad(dies)* is the second choice in Tennessee and Arkansas, the first choice in Oklahoma, and is reasonably well reported from the other states except for Georgia; there the frequency of choice is a fraction of a percent. The volunteered words are phonological variants of *crawdad*.[17]

WORM USED FOR BAIT
Item 113 Maps 17, 77, 79

For the smaller worm used as bait in fishing, twelve synonyms are given. *Red worm* is preferred in Tennessee and Arkansas; *earthworm* in Georgia (just one point more than *fish bait*), Alabama, Mississippi, Florida, Louisiana, and Oklahoma. *Red worm* is the second preference in Georgia, Alabama, Mississippi (just five points more than *fishing worm*), Louisiana (tied with *fish bait, fishing worm*), but not in Oklahoma where *fishworm* is second (three points more than *red worm*). No response is reported for *eace worm,* and only scattered responses for *angledog, bait worm, eel worm, mudworm,* and *rainworm.*

For a large worm used in fishing, four synonyms are given. *Night crawler* is the first choice in Tennessee, Mississippi, Louisiana, Arkansas, and Oklahoma; *Georgia wiggler* or *wiggler* is the first choice in Georgia, Alabama, and Florida; it is the second choice in the other states, along with *dew worm* in Tennessee and Oklahoma. Of the volunteered words, *grub worm* and *swagers* or *swayers* are from the greatest number of states.[18]

Ideas of Quantity

The industrial and scientific revolutions brought with them a need for greater precision in measuring time, distance, and weight. Very little of this influence is reflected in the questionnaire or in the volunteered responses that arose from answering it. Rather, these are familiar usages from earlier periods.

Measures

GENERAL UNITS OF TIME
Items 1, 2, 3

The latter part of daylight hours before supper is either *afternoon* or *evening*; informants in Tennessee, Georgia, and Florida expressed a slight preference for *afternoon. Twilight* was volunteered, but in my experience it is not a word that would ordinarily be substituted in the sentence *They will meet him this afternoon/evening.*

The break of day is either *sunrise* or *sunup.* Tennessee, Alabama, Florida, and Arkansas informants prefer the first; those in other states prefer *sunup.* And the close of day is either *sundown* or *sunset.* Tennessee preference is equally divided; Louisiana preference is for *sunset*; other informants choose *sundown.* The volunteered words are variants of *dusk-dark.*[19]

RESTRICTED UNITS OF TIME
Items 4, 70 Map 73

In all states except Oklahoma the time when animals are attended to is first *feeding time* and second *time to feed.* In Oklahoma the choices are *chore time* and *feeding time. Chore time* is almost a second choice in Arkansas; it is third of the three choices in Louisiana where *feed time* is unreported; *feed time* is third in the other states except Oklahoma which uses *time to feed.*

The questionnaire sought to determine a choice not only of prepositions in statements of "fifteen minutes before the hour" but also of a different system of expressing that concept. *Quarter till eleven* is the first preference everywhere except in Florida and Oklahoma where it is second. *Quarter of* and *quarter to* are second or third preferences in all states but Arkansas where *of* is second and *before* and *to* third. The precise sounding *ten forty five* is reported in more than one-fifth of the choices except in Mississippi where it sinks markedly. If *ten forty five* is an urban innovation, its spread merits further inquiry.[20]

DISTANCE

Item 80

East of the Mississippi, except in Florida, the preferred expression for a short, unspecified distance is *a little piece* or *a little way(s)*. In Florida *a little ways* is more prevalent than *a little piece,* a usage found west of the Mississippi in Arkansas and Oklahoma. *A piece* is generally distributed throughout the region; *a ways,* however, is reported only from Tennessee, Alabama, Georgia, Arkansas, and Oklahoma.[21]

BULK

Item 46 Maps 39, 78

The questionnaire phrased the definition in this item as "the amount of wood' that one can carry; perhaps a rephrasing in terms of sacks of groceries would have been more productive. The first and second choices are between *armful* and *armload* everywhere except in Georgia; there the second choice is *turn,* an important third choice in Florida. *Load* is reported generally, *chance* not at all.[22]

The Human Condition

Family relationships and human passions did not change in the course of founding the nation. But local occupations, attitudes, and social customs did alter in some new ways, and entertainment began to respond to national sale of manufactured instruments.

Kinship

PARENTS

Items 122, 123

Within a family the male parent is mainly called *daddy,* or somewhat less often *dad* and *papa.* Although the choices of *father* range from four to twelve percent, one should keep in mind Atwood's comment on Texas usage (*Regional Vocabulary of Texas,* p. 66): "It is somewhat doubtful that *Father* is often used in real family situations." *Pa, paw,* and *pop* occur with about the same frequency as *father* does; *pappy* is not reported from Alabama or Mississippi.

The usual words for the female parent are, in descending order, *mama, mother, ma,* and *mom. Maw, mommer, mommy,* and *mammy* are reported less often and in some states not at all. Local investigation may show that the formality of the occasion governs choice.[23]

RELATIVES

Item 124

The questionnaire asked the names of close and distant relations. For the first, the members of the immediate family, *my family* and *my folks* are first and second choices. The third, *my parents,* provides a special problem because its semantic range is narrower than that of the other synonyms. In the larger sense of "immediate family" *my people* and *my relatives* occur generally; *my relations* are unreported in Alabama, Mississippi, Louisiana, and Arkansas.

For the second sense, "others related by blood," the preferred words are *my kinfolks* and *my relatives,* followed by *my family, my kin,* and *my relations. My people* and *my relation* are less widely reported.[24]

A LIKENESS

Item 126

When a person wishes to say that a child looks more like one of its parents than the other, his probable first word choice is *looks like.* The next choice could be any one of these three: *favors, resembles,* or *takes after.* The least likely choice is *features,* a word not reported in Mississippi, Louisiana, and Oklahoma.[25]

Outsiders

MIDWIFE

Item 127 Map 20

A woman who helps at childbirth is regularly known by the book word *midwife.* Three other names in general though lesser use are *godmother, granny,* and *granny woman.* Instances of *granny doctor* are reported everywhere except in Alabama and Oklahoma.[26]

UNTRAINED PREACHER

Item 129 Maps 21, 79

A part-time preacher whose professional training may lie only in what he has read from the Bible goes under several names; nine are given in the questionnaire, and about the same number were volunteered. *Brother-so-and-so* is preferred in all states except Tennessee and Georgia where *jackleg preacher* is the first choice and *local preacher* is second, competing in Tennessee with *Brother-so-and-so* (one substitutes a person's name for *so-and-so*). *Parson* and *the reverend* are also widely reported. *Bible banger, chair backer,* and *yard ax* are barely mentioned, while *domine* is unreported everywhere.[27]

A RUSTIC

Item 130

If a simple, rural life appeals to city people, their admiration for it does not extend to persons who live at some distance from the cities. The questionnaire offers nineteen names, of which only *sharecropper* has a neutral sense in part; all the rest are adverse. Informants provided at least ten additional words, of which only *pioneer* and *farmer* have a neutral sense. The first choice in Tennessee, Georgia, Alabama, Mississippi, Louisiana, Arkansas, and Oklahoma is *hillbilly*; in Florida it is *cracker,* one of the second choices in Georgia, but not reported west of the Mississippi. Other second preferences are *clodhopper, country man,* and *hick. Red neck,* which was adequately used in the presidential campaign of 1968, is reported in less than one-tenth of the instances. As for other words, *hoosier* provides a special problem in that it occurs alone in small percentages and yet is a frequently volunteered word in combinations such as *backwoods hoosier. Backwoodsman, country jake, hayseed, share cropper,* and *yokel* are known throughout the region. *Country gentleman, mossback, stump farmer, swamp angel,* and *yahoo* are reported on both sides of the Mississippi but not from every state. *Cracker,* as has already been noted, and a few instances of *jackpine savage* occur east of the Mississippi. *Mountain boomer, pumpkin husker,* and *rail splitter* are not reported.[28]

A HOBGOBLIN

Item 142

Some parents threaten a child with a supernatural creature who will get him if he does not mind. The common word is *booger man* and its phonological equivalent *boogey man.* The next most frequent are *bad man, old scratch,* and *rawhead and bloody bones.* Scattered instances occur of *black man, old Harry,* and *old Nick. Plat eye* is rare.[29]

Social Life

AFFECTION

Item 137

When a young man and woman show an attachment for each other, he is said to *go with her* in roughly half of the choices; the next most frequent choice is *court.* Next are *spark with* and *talk to. Keep company with* and *sit up to* are not reported in Louisiana and *walk out with* is not reported in Alabama and Florida. So familiar a word as *woo* is unreported in Mississippi, and is chosen in no more than a twentieth of the instances elsewhere. *Date,* among the volunteered words, needs study for its currency and usage levels.[30]

REJECTION

Item 138

When a woman tires of her suitor and rejects him she is said to *turn him down* except in Louisiana; there she will *give him the cold shoulder,* the second choice in Tennessee and one of two second choices in Georgia. An alternate second choice in Georgia and second choice in six other states is *jilt him. Give him the air* is also widely used. *Give him the bounce* or *the mitten, kick him,* and *throw him over* are reported but not from every state. The list of volunteered words is quite long, suggesting that mankind is more impressed by rejection than by courtship. Some phrases such as *give him the shaft* and *give him a dear John* reflect a recent impact of military speech on civilians.[31]

A CELEBRATION

Item 139 Map 52

The local custom of greeting newly wedded persons with a noisy mock celebration is known east of the Mississippi first as a *serenade* and second as a *shivaree* (from French *charivari*); west of the Mississippi this preference is reversed. The next choice is *tin panning*, followed by scattered instances of *horning* and *belling*. *Belling bee, bull banding, calathump, horning bee,* and *skimmelton* are reported east of the Mississippi. The volunteered *reception* is a jocular use of a term regularly employed in connection with dignified activities.[32]

TRUANCY

Item 140 Map 74

Children resist the urbanizing influences of school by absenting themselves from classes. The main term for this action is to *play hookey*. In Tennessee and Georgia the next term is to *lay out*; in the other states it is either to *skip class* or to *skip school*. The only other usage known generally is to *slip off from school*. *Lie out* may simply be an elegant variation of *lay out*; if so its scattered distribution is an indication of the results from classroom drill in the differences between *lie* and *lay*. *Bag school, bolt,* and *run out of school* are reported occasionally east of the Mississippi. *Cook jack* is unknown. On a more formal level, to *play truant* is reported everywhere except in Louisiana. As for volunteered words, *cut class(es)* is the usage most widely suggested.[33]

Recreation

PLAYGROUND EQUIPMENT

Items 48, 49 Map 11

School and park playgrounds have merry-go-rounds and seesaws, play equipment that at one time could be improvised at home and more recently, as a result of twentieth-century commerce, can be purchased for use in one's yard. Of the playground equipment specifically listed in the questionnaire, *seesaw* was chosen in over three-fourths of all possibilities. East of the Mississippi and including Louisiana, the second is *ridy horse*; in Arkansas and Oklahoma second preference is *teeter* and *teeter board*. *Hicky horse, cock horse,* and *dandle* have a slight distribution east of the Mississippi and little or none west of it.

For the second device, the homemade merry-go-round, *whirlygig* and *ridy horse* alternate as first and second choices. A phonological variant *whirlyjig* is chosen in from six to twenty-four percent of the preferences east of the Mississippi, and in thirteen percent in Oklahoma; it is unreported in Louisiana and Arkansas. *Flying Dutchman* and *flying jenny* are reported with absolute identity in each of the eight states, a coincidence which arouses suspicions about the computer program at this point. The rest of the calculations, however, have the expected variety; *flying mare*, for instance, is shown as unrecorded for Mississippi, Florida, and Louisiana.[34]

MARBLES

Item 50 Map 75

The language of playing marbles is apt to be learned more by word of mouth than from books. If the game requires its players to shoot from a line drawn on the ground, the prevalent name of that line is *taw* except in Oklahoma where *taw line* is the more frequent. Other well-distributed usages are *lag line, lagging line,* and *starting line*. Among the frequently volunteered words is *head taw* (or *tow*), perhaps from a misreading of synonyms in the questionnaire.[35]

MUSICAL INSTRUMENTS

Item 40 Maps 40, 70, 71, 77

Two manufactured musical instruments, dissimilar in appearance, have names in common. The names of the small instrument (played by blowing against its metallic reeds) are distributed strangely. The first and second preferences alternate between *French harp* and *harmonica* everywhere but in Florida where the pair is *harmonica* and *harp*. The range of preference for *jew's harp* and its phonological equivalent, *juice harp*, is as widely variable as is that for *mouth harp* and *mouth organ*. *Breath harp* is barely present in Tennessee and Oklahoma.

The second one, a harp with a kind of tine which is plucked while one blows against it, is known first as a *jew's harp* and second as a *juice harp*. *Mouth harp* occurs in all states and has a range that does not exceed one-tenth of the responses. Again *French harp* is not reported in Florida; in other states its range is like that of *mouth harp*. Instances of *breath harp* in this sense are reported from Tennessee, Alabama, Georgia, and Oklahoma.[36]

TO COAST OR HIT FACE DOWN
Items 144, 145

When someone who is diving hits the water face down or (during brief periods of snow in the South) coasts lying down flat, this action is expressed by *belly* plus another word. For the condition of swimming it is *belly buster* in three-fourths of the choices or more. *Belly bust* is next, followed by *belly flop* and *belly flopper,* the last of these being unreported in Alabama.

For the act of coasting while lying down flat, nineteen synonyms are given. To this number some informants added *belly slide* and *gut ripper*. The common choices are *belly buster, belly bust, belly booster,* and *belly bumper,* the first three of which occur in all eight states.[37]

GREETING
Item 143

The usual Christmas greeting is *Merry Christmas*. Less general but still reported is *Christmas gift*. A few of the choices in Tennessee and Georgia are *Christmas box*. *Christmas gift,* as natives of the region will point out, is a part of a Christmas morning game and thus has a different function from that of exchanging the greeting *Merry Christmas*.[38]

Condition of Health and Emotions
ILLNESS
Items 134, 135, 136

The usual expression for becoming ill is to *get sick*. The next most common are to *be taken sick* or to *take sick,* the latter being chosen somewhat more frequently west of the Mississippi.

When the illness is a cold, one is said to *catch, catch a, get a, take,* or *take a cold*. The preferred usage everywhere except in Georgia and Arkansas is *catch a cold*; in those two states it is *take cold*. The expression chosen least often is *get a cold*.

When illness brings nausea with it, the first informative word *sick* is followed by a choice of *at, in, on, to,* or *of* and then *his stomach*. The choice of *at* is clearly the regional preference. The second and lesser choice in Tennessee and Arkansas is *in*; in Georgia, Alabama, Mississippi, and Florida it is *on*; except for a few instances in Arkansas this usage is not reported west of the Mississippi. In Louisiana, the second is *of,* followed by *to*. The *of* usage is not reported in Mississippi and Oklahoma.[39]

FATIGUE
Item 133

The questionnaire offered fifteen expressions for the state of exhaustion; informants volunteered seven additional ones. Of these latter, the most widespread is *pooped (out)*. Roughly one quarter of the choices are *worn out*. Less than that but near or above one-tenth are *all in, fagged out,* and *give out*. Next in general distribution are *bushed, petered out, played out, tuckered,* and *tuckered out*. Least widely distributed are *beat out* (not reported in Florida), *done out* (not reported in Mississippi, Florida, Louisiana, and Oklahoma), *perished* (not reported in Mississippi, Florida, Louisiana), *killed* (one percent or less in Georgia and Arkansas), and *used up* (not reported in Alabama and Arkansas).[40]

ANGER
Item 132

When a person shows anger, he is generally said to become awfully *mad*. The use of *awfully* in the questionnaire may have encouraged more than half the informants to choose *mad* and to exclude *angered* from the volunteered words despite school instruction against the first and for the second. *Riled* is a second choice everywhere except in Mississippi where *hot* is preferred slightly more often; *roiled* is present in a few instances in each state east of the Mississippi and in Oklahoma. *Hot* and *ugly* are reported everywhere though seldom in more than one-tenth of the choices. *Ashy, het up, owly,* and *wrathy* have a limited occurrence. *Hot* may occur frequently in the volunteered expression *hot under the collar*.[41]

OBSTINATE
Item 131

One word, *owly,* was given both for this concept and that of anger. In each instance its reported use is slight. Of the nine other words *stubborn* and *bullheaded* are the first and second preferences, followed by *contrary, headstrong,* and *ornery,* and then by *pig headed,* and *set.* Scattered instances of *sot* occur in Tennessee, Georgia, Alabama, Florida, and Oklahoma; its choice, however, may be influenced by the informant's attitude toward *sot* as an old-fashioned or unrefined word. *Otsny* (pig Latin for *snotty?*) is almost unknown. A frequently volunteered word is *worked up,* an instance of the addition of *up* to convey this specific thought.[42]

ACTIVITIES
Items 24, 44, 146, 147 Maps 35, 47, 77

A baby moving across the floor ordinarily *crawls,* though in a few instances outside of Louisiana he *creeps.*

When someone picks up and transports a heavy object such as a suitcase, he *carries* it in half of the responses. Or he *lugs* or *totes* it, the latter being the second preference in Alabama, Louisiana, Arkansas, and Oklahoma. *Tote* occurs in over one-fifth of the preferences in Louisiana and with a similar or greater degree of preference in the states east of the Mississippi. *Hike* and *pack* also occur, but *freight* is unreported.

Transporting wood in a wagon is called *hauling* in nearly all of the choices. *Carting, drawing, teaming,* and *toting* occur in a few instances; of these, *carting* and *toting* are the most widespread, and *teaming* is almost unknown.

In doing housework, a woman ordinarily uses the words *clean up* or, less frequently, *straighten up.* Occasionally the choice is *tidy up* or *do up;* seldom is it *redd up* or *ridd up.*[43]

Rural Life

The stage of rural life which is investigated in this vocabulary is chronologically somewhere between the pioneer clearing of fields and current mechanized farming. The crops are those which can be grown locally in most of the Interior South as well as in the rest of the nation; the domestic animals are those that thrive in the temperate zone; and the foods are those which can be prepared at home without the intervention of a national system of food processing. Those things that are found only in the semitropics—oranges and grapefruits, for instance—are not considered. At the same time, one must recall that foods began to be distributed commercially during the lifetime of the oldest informants.

Agriculture

THE GARDEN
Item 96

Domestic crops cultivated on a limited scale for domestic use are grown in a *garden* or a *vegetable garden.* The term preferred less often than those two is *garden patch. Family garden* is reported in one-tenth of the choices in Georgia, less often in all of the other states but Louisiana which does not report it at all. *Kitchen garden* is unreported in Louisiana and Arkansas; elsewhere it is a minor preference.[44]

BEANS
Items 102, 103, 106 Maps 46, 79

In more than half of the instances the preferred name of large, flat, yellowish beans particularly when they are out of the pod is *butter beans.* Next is *lima beans.* Just barely known in the region are *sewee beans* and *sivvy beans.* Enough persons volunteered the remark that *butter beans* are larger and yellower than *lima beans* to justify further local inquiry. The commercial use of *lima beans* on canned and frozen food containers is an influence.

String beans, snap beans, and *green beans* are the chief terms, with *snap beans* and *string beans* alternating in preference everywhere but in Tennessee and Oklahoma; there *green beans* is the more frequent choice over *string beans.* In Arkansas the percentages are so close that one could assume that choices are a matter of free variation. The more inclusive word *beans,* the shortened form *snaps,* and the variant *sallet beans* occur in seven states or fewer. Commercial labels on cans and packages of frozen foods are *green beans* or, less frequently, one of the volunteered words, *shelly beans*. The distribution of the latter is worth field investigation.

When a housewife removes beans from their pods, she regularly is said to *shell* them; preferences for this expression go beyond eighty percent. Next is to *hull* them. Scattered instances of to *pod* or to *shuck* are reported.[45]

COVERS

Items 100, 107 Map 55

The words *cap, husk, shell,* and *shuck* are applied to several distinct coverings. *Shuck* is almost the only choice when users refer to the green, leafy cover of an ear of corn. *Husk* is chosen less than one-fifth of the time except in Oklahoma where it almost reaches one-third. *Cap* has a small distribution in Tennessee, Mississippi, and Oklahoma.

Hull is the preferred name for the green outer cover of a walnut. This is followed by *shell* or *husk,* neither of which exceeds one-third of the preferences. *Shuck* is reported from everywhere but Louisiana.

The hard inner cover of a walnut is a *shell* in over one-third of the choices. In descending order are *hull, husk,* and *shuck,* the last being unreported from Louisiana.[46]

INDIAN CORN

Item 108 Maps 36, 78

The word *corn* has already served to illustrate a shift in meaning of an English word when it reached North America. With reference to "maize," informants chose *corn on the cob* at least half of the time when they referred to the variety of corn eaten at the table as distinguished from field corn. Their next preference is *roasting ears* and *sweet corn. Garden corn, green corn, mutton corn,* and *sugar corn* are seldom reported.[47]

PEANUTS

Item 105 Maps 48, 78

The common word is *peanut*. Two Africanisms, *pinders* and *goobers,* are known; *goobers* is reported more often than its synonym except in Florida. *Ground peas* and *ground nuts* do not occur west of the Mississippi. One informant noted that *goobers* occurs in the speech of "hired hands." *Peanuts,* the commercial term, should eventually replace the others.[48]

EDIBLE TOPS

Item 104 Maps 22, 79

The edible tops of some plants go generally by the name *greens*. The other choice is *salad* and, less often, its phonological variant *sallet*. Volunteered words show that informants identify the kind of greens by linking the name of the plant to it as in *beet greens*.[49]

EARLY ONIONS

Item 101

The usual name of edible onions that appear in the spring is *green onions* everywhere but in Georgia; there *spring onions* has a somewhat greater preference. *Shallots* and *spring onions* are second and third preferences in seven states; Florida divides its preferences among *scallions, multipliers,* and *young onions;* Louisiana reports *shallots* one-third of the time, perhaps with local French as a contributing factor in its increased use. Some informants state that *shallots* differ from the other onions named. In any event, *live forevers, potato onions, rare ripes* are rarely reported; *shell oats,* presumably a folk etymology, is reported from all states but Oklahoma.[50]

PEACHES

Items 98, 99 Maps 23, 24, 78

The names of two kinds of peach derive in part from the difficulty or ease of separating its meat from the seed. The first, the one with meat that sticks to the seed, is a *cling,* a *cling peach,* or a *clingstone* in a complex set of choices. East of the Mississippi a second preference is *plum peach* in Tennessee, Alabama, and Mississippi; this word is unreported in Florida and Louisiana, but is close to second preference in Arkansas. *Press peach* is the second choice in Georgia and close to that position in Mississippi, Florida, and Louisiana.

Thirteen words are given in the questionnaire as names of a peach with meat that separates easily from the seed. Of these *clear seed* is most frequently reported in Georgia, Alabama, and Mississippi. In Florida it shares frequency of occurrence with *freestone,* the other word most frequently chosen in Tennessee, Florida, Arkansas, and Oklahoma. Louisiana shares its preference for *freestone* with *freestone peach.* Second preferences are *freestone peach* (Tennessee, Arkansas, and Oklahoma), *freestone,* (Alabama and Mississippi), *clearseed peach,* (Georgia and Alabama) and *clear seed* (Louisiana). *Soft peach,* reported in seven states, has its greatest preference in Tennessee. *Cleavestone* and *openstone* appear east of the Mississippi only; *free peach, open peach, open seed, open seed peach,* and *openstone peach,* occur occassionally on either side of that river.[51]

PROPAGATIVE PART

Item 97

The usual choice for the propagative part of a cherry or peach is a *seed.* In secondary statements of preference, these distinctions appear. Everywhere but in Georgia *stone* is the name of the peach seed; there it is *kernel.* The word for cherry seed is *pit,* a word of Dutch origin. The synonyms, *heart* and *kernel,* are least prevalent in either sense.[52]

PILES OF STALKS

Items 19, 20, 21, 82

In the course of harvesting, stalks of wheat, hay, and oats are gathered into bundles or piles. Since wheat and oats are not major crops everywhere in the Interior South, the distribution of terms may reflect other piles such as those of corn stalks. With that possibility in mind, one notices that the first and second names for wheat that has been gathered and bound are *bundle* and *sheaf.* As for hay, the small piles in the field are *hay shocks* or *shocks* everywhere but in Florida and Louisiana where the first preference is for *hay piles* and the second for *hay shocks.* The other synonyms, *hand stacks, heaps, ricks, haycocks, hay tumbles, mows,* and *tumbles,* are given here in roughly diminishing occurrence. A large pile of hay outside is ordinarily a *haystack. Hay rick, rick, barrack,* and *hay cap* occur in one-twentieth or less of the choices. *Dutch cap* is not reported. And, finally, a pile of bundles of wheat is usually called a *shock. Shook* and *stock* occur in less than one-tenth of the choices.[53]

Foods

As has been noted in the discussion of names of beans, the growth of commercial processing and distribution of meat, milk products, and bread has had an influence on the local names of these foods. Although it is still possible to witness the home preparation of pork and other products at hog killing time, most informants doubtless buy commercially dried, salted, and fresh meats, loaves of bread, sacks or boxes of flour and meal, and cheese and milk from a store. Central distribution from processors to these stores has grown with increased rail, truck, and air transportation and with the introduction of refrigeration.[54] Local choice is complexly related to national labels.

DRIED BEEF

Item 89

Dried thin strips of beef are commonly called *dried beef;* the commercial *chipped beef* accounts for the choices of one-fifth or more of the informants. *Jerked beef* or *jerky* is reported at eight percent or less on both sides of the Mississippi. If *jerky* is a popular alteration of the Spanish *charqui,* ultimately from the Quechua Indian language according to *The Random House Dictionary of the English Language* (1967), the problems of its dissemination in the United States and of its absence in the reported Texas *pilón* need investigation.[55]

MEAT FROM HOGS

Items 87, 88, 91 Maps 26, 27, 66, 67

Blocks of meat cut from the sides of a hog and salted are ordinarily called *salt meat* in Tennessee, Georgia, and Alabama; it and *side pork* have about equal preference in Mississippi; in the other states *side pork* is preferred. *Middlin(g)s* and *bacon* range in choice from one-tenth to nearly one-third everywhere but in Oklahoma where *bacon* is the more frequent. It is likely that a semantic shift is in process because of the commercial label *bacon* which is placed on packages of the thin strips, often sugar cured for breakfast use. To return to the salted product, *side pork, sow belly,* and *fatback* are less frequently used. Among volunteered words, *streak-o-lean* and *salt bacon* may serve to identify linguistic subareas.

Meat from the hog's head and jowls can be pressed into a loaf, called *souse* according to one-third of the choices. Varying in preference are *head cheese, hog's head cheese,* and *pressed meat.* Among the volunteered words *head meat* comes from the largest number of states.

The tough covering of bacon is either *rind* or *skin,* the former being first preference in all states but Georgia. A volunteered word, *meat skins,* has commercial distribution as part of a label on appetizers—*fried meat skins.*[56]

MILK AND CHEESE

Items 93, 94 Maps 25, 77, 79

Before the days of commercial processing, sweet milk would sour, turn thick and remain edible. The resulting substance is called *clabber* or a variant of that name—*clabber milk* or *clabbered milk.* A half dozen other synonyms occur in small distributions with the exception of *loppered milk* which is not reported at all. The volunteered *buttermilk* suggests that clabber is no longer a familiar food or that the definition in the questionnaire is misleading.

A kind of cheese once made at home is sometimes known as *clabber cheese.* The commercial term *cottage cheese,* however, is the first choice of almost half of the informants. A frequent choice of *home made cheese* may reflect an influence of the questionnaire itself. *Curds* is an important synonym in Florida only. *Smearcase,* adapted from German, is reported in Tennessee, Mississippi, Florida, Arkansas, and Oklahoma; it is perhaps a reflection of migrations from the Pennsylvania German area reinforced by German arrivals from Europe in the nineteenth century.[57]

BREAD

Items 83, 84 Maps 29, 30, 31, 63, 64, 65, 77, 81

Homemade bread (or its commercial equivalent) made of wheat flour and baked in loaves is generally called *light bread. Loaf bread* is next in Georgia and Alabama; in Tennessee it shares equally with *bread,* the second preference in the other five states. *White bread* is next, particularly in Florida, Louisiana, Arkansas, and Oklahoma. The other three items have scattered distributions.

Breads made from corn meal have a wide range in shape and consistency. None of these in itself is nationally distributed by a commercial bakery, but the meal and the mixes in which corn meal is a significant part are commercially packaged. Accompanying recipes use some of the regional words.

The bread in its firmer states is called *corn bread.* Next most frequent, and of a different shape, is *hoe cake,* followed by *corn pone* and *pone bread,* and then by *corn dodger,* unreported in Louisiana. *Johnny cake* has scattered occurrences on both sides of the Mississippi. A special kind of corn bread baked in the ashes is known in descending order of preferences as *ash cake, ash pone,* and *ash bread.*

The soft, mushy forms of this bread are first *spoon bread* and second *batter bread. Awendaw bread* may have a wider actual use than the questionnaire discovered simply because informants did not recognize their pronunciation [əwendə] in that spelling. Of the volunteered words, *kush kush* needs study as another instance of the introduction of Africanisms into American English.[58]

MEAT-AND-MEAL LOAF

Item 90

Scrapple is a general name for a loaf made of corn meal, meat scraps, and meat juice. *Cripple,* reported everywhere but in Louisiana, has its greatest preference in Alabama and Mississippi. *Ponhaws* and a phonological variant *ponhoss* occur irregularly in the region; its reasonably frequent occurrence in Louisiana may indicate German influences there. It should be noted that *chittling bread,* among the volunteered words already discussed, may belong to this class of foods rather than to the ones above with which it has been grouped.[59]

DOUGHNUTS AND PANCAKES

Items 85, 86 Maps 30, 32

Doughnuts are made with baking powder or with yeast. The general term for either confection is *doughnut* everywhere but in Georgia where a slight preference is given to *raised doughnut* for the one made with yeast. For the one made with baking powder other names—*fat cake, fried cake, raised doughnut* and the Dutch *crull* or *cruller*—appear occasionally; the only large second choice is that of *cake doughnut* in Arkansas and Oklahoma. For the yeast doughnut the second choice in Georgia is *doughnut;* in Tennessee, Alabama, and Mississippi it is Dutch *cookie.* West of the Mississippi and in Florida the second choice is *raised doughnut,* a choice that is third in Tennessee. *Bread doughnut* occurs in less than one-fifth of the choices in the region; *crull, cruller, fat cake, fried cake,* and *nut cake* are scattered in a somewhat greater frequency east of the Mississippi than west of it. Among volunteered words, *tea cake* is interesting because it shows that one semantic range of these words extends beyond the concept of a confection with a hole in the center, and because it appears in Atwood's analysis of the Texas vocabulary.

Pancakes is chosen in from one-third to half of the state responses. The second preference east of the Mississippi is *batter cakes,* and west of it *hot cakes. Flapjacks* is reported in approximately ten percent of the responses in the region; *griddle cakes* is lowest in general choice. *Flannel cakes, flitters, fritters, slap jacks,* and *wheat cakes* are far more limited in occurrence. Commercial packaging and labeling, cook books, and the like have doubtless influenced the choice of *pancakes* and, to a lesser extent, the choices of *batter cakes, hot cakes,* and *flapjacks.*[60]

MISCELLANEOUS

Items 69, 92, 95 Maps 28, 79

A sweet liquid served with pudding is customarily called *sauce,* a word reinforced by commercial labels such as "plum pudding with hard sauce." *Dressing gravy* is the second preference in Georgia, Alabama, Mississippi, Florida, and Louisiana; *dip* is second preference in Tennessee, Arkansas, and Oklahoma.

A bone shaped like a Y and found in chicken breasts is a *pully bone* in at least half of the choices, and *wishbone* in one-fourth of them. *Lucky bone* and *breakbone* are reported in scattered instances.

Food eaten between meals is commonly a *snack,* a word reinforced by such commercial uses as *snack bar.* The next preference, chosen in no more than one-fifth of the instances, is a *bite* which shares this position with a *piece* only in Oklahoma. The choice of *lunch* ranges below one-tenth of the choices; one assumes that *lunch* as a name of the noon meal has an influence both on choice and sense here, but supporting evidence needs to be gathered from direct interviews. *Nick nacks,* volunteered from Tennessee, is known as far west as Texas.[61]

Domestic Animals

DOGS

Item 65

A dog of mixed and uncertain breed is ordinarily a *cur* or a *mongrel,* the latter term having preference in Alabama, Louisiana, and Oklahoma. Next are *cur dog* and *no count,* then *common dog, fiste, scrub,* and *heinz.* The least widely reported are *fice* and *sooner.* Returning to *heinz* for a moment, notice that it and the volunteered *duke's mixture,* appear to reflect an influence of commercial developments after the middle of the nineteenth century: Heinz 57 varieties of canned foods, and Duke's Mixture for tobacco.[62]

HORSES

Items 68, 74, 75, 79 Maps 18, 19, 77, 79, 81

Although horses on farms and in cities have been largely replaced by motorized equipment, informants still know a vocabulary to use in connection with them. For the horse on the left side of a team the general word is *lead horse.* In some states *leader* is the second preference; in others it is *wheel horse. Line horse, near horse, nigh horse,* and *saddle horse* are next. Scattered reports of *near-side horse* occur in Tennessee, Florida, Arkansas, and Oklahoma.

Responses to the questionnaire suggest that some informants were confused by the question or by actuality itself. Indicating this confusion are the volunteered words *gee horse* and *haw horse,* since "gee" calls for a turn in one direction and "haw" in the opposite.

When a person wishes to call horses in from the pasture, he whistles or calls them by name. If he wishes to use a customary word, he calls *kope,* or *co-jack; come* and *come up* occasionally serve in some states, but not in all of them. If he wishes to urge them on when driving or riding, he may make a clucking sound. It is more likely that he will say *get up* or one of its phonological variants.

As for the gentle sound that a horse makes, it is a *nicker* in Tennessee, Georgia, Alabama, and Arkansas, and a *whinny* in Mississippi, Florida, Louisiana, and Oklahoma. *Whicker* is frequently reported in Georgia and Florida. Known but less often reported are *laugh, whinker,* and *whinner.*[63]

COWS

Items 66, 67, 71, 72, 73 Maps 38, 43, 78

Similar calls serve to bring cows and calves in from the pasture as in *bossie, come bossie, soo,* and *sook.* The usual term is *sook cow* or *sook calf(ie)* except in Florida where *co-bossie* is preferred. *Co-wench* occurs less often as a call for cows than does *bossie* or *here bossie.* There is no equivalent distribution of calls for calves.

The usual command given to make cows stand still at milking time is *saw* or in Florida *so;* the second preference is *sah,* or in Florida and in Oklahoma *so-bossie,* distributions which may simply reflect the difficulties of presenting these sounds in print for intelligent general choice. *Here, histe,* and *so-wench* are reported from a few of the states.

The gentle sound that a cow makes at feeding time is *moo* or, for less than one-third of the choices, *low.* Less often the variants *loo* and *mew, bawl, beller* or *bellow,* and *hum* occur. The loud sound, on the other hand, which a cow makes when a calf is taken away is *bawl* in Tennessee, Alabama, Mississippi, Arkansas, and Oklahoma, *low* in Georgia and Florida, and *moo* in Louisiana. The same words plus *beller* and *bellow* occur as second and third preferences. *Cry, loo,* and *mew* are seldom reported. As for the sounds a calf makes when being weaned, *bawl* is preferred in Tennessee, Alabama, Mississippi, Louisiana, Arkansas, and Oklahoma. *Blate* is in Georgia and Florida; its importance is increased if one combines with it the phonological variants *blat* and *bleat.*[64]

SHEEP

Item 77

The call to get sheep in from the pasture is *coo-sheep* or *sheepie, co-sheep* (except for Florida and Oklahoma) or *sheep; come nannie* is reasonably frequent in Georgia, Arkansas, and Oklahoma, as is *co-nin(nie)* in Oklahoma and *nan(nie)* in Louisiana. The other words have a scattered response mainly east of the Mississippi.

PIGS

Item 76

Customary calls for pigs at feeding time are *piggy, piggy,* or in Mississippi and Oklahoma, *soo-pig;* aside from these, *soo-wee* and *hoo-ee,* are the only ones reported from all states.[65]

CHICKENS

Item 78

The main calls for chickens at feeding time are *chick, chick* and *chickie, chickie. Biddie* is the only other choice made in all of the states; its range does not exceed one-tenth of the choices.[66]

Nature Methodized

The questionnaire reflects in these entries the American scene of the 1890's before extensive use of barbed wire or other wire fences had developed. Yards and farm fields have been fenced to some degree. If stone is available, farm fences are of stone; otherwise they are of wood. Cattle have been restricted to fenced lots at least part of the time, and barns and other buildings are built from sawed lumber rather than from rough logs.

Enclosures

WALLS AND FENCES

Items 29, 30, 31, 64 Maps 5, 6, 14, 15, 76, 77

Walls made by piling stones on each other are *rock walls* in Tennessee and Georgia, *stone walls* in Alabama, Mississippi, Florida, and Louisiana, and both in Arkansas and Oklahoma. The second choice in Louisiana, Arkansas, and Oklahoma is *rock fence*. In passing it should be noted that if a boy picks up something to throw, he throws a *rock* almost always, and a *stone* less than one-fifth of the time. In a few rare instances he will throw a *donnick* or *dornick*.

It is reported, in sometimes as often as one hundred percent of the responses, that the only important name of one kind of wooden fence is *rail fence*. In Oklahoma alone is any other important choice: *worm fence* is reported there in roughly one-tenth of the instances. A more carefully fashioned fence, one that is placed around homes rather than as a boundary for fields, is a *picket fence;* the second choice, *paling fence* and *palings* in Georgia, is unreported in Louisiana.[67]

FENCED LOTS

Items 26, 27, 28 Map 56

Fenced yards or lots for certain animals are called *barn yards* and *barn lots,* or with specific reference to a particular animal, *cow pens, cow lots. Feed lot* is also in general use though not quite so often as are the others. *Cow brake, cow pound, cuppin,* and *farm lot* are chosen more often east of the Mississippi than west of it. The volunteered *cow woods* reflects the continuity of a pioneer custom of letting cattle roam at large in wooded areas; local inquiry needs to establish whether the term is now the semantic equivalent of *cow lot* and *barn yard.*

Pigs are kept in lots which sometimes have a special shelter as well. Prevailing names for the lot and its shelter, if any, are *hog pen* and *pig pen* everywhere but in Georgia; there *hog lot* is the second term, a degree of preference close to that shown in Tennessee, Alabama, Mississippi, Arkansas, and Oklahoma. *Hog house, hog boist, hog crawl, pig sty,* and *sty* are reported also.[68]

STORAGE PLACES

Items 17, 18

Outbuildings and some of their parts provide storage places for equipment and fodder. The upper part of a barn is one such. This part is ordinarily a *barn loft, hay loft,* or *loft. Barn chamber, hay mow, mow, overhead,* and *scaffold* are reported less often; *overden* is not reported anywhere. In passing, note *scaffle* [skæfəl] which may have a wider distribution than is shown by the responses to the spelling *scaffold.*

A storage building attached to a house is mainly a *storeroom.* The next choices are *lean-to shed, tool shed,* and *wood shed,* followed by *tool house* and *wood house.* If the building is freestanding, it is known as a *smokehouse,* a *store room,* or simply a *shed. Tool house, tool shed, wood house,* and *wood shed* also apply to these separate buildings. The range of volunteered words is impressively long and shows a complex of changing influences. *Cotton house, pump house,* and *wash house* for example, reflect earlier domestic requirements which have doubtless vanished; the building may now be used as a garage or for some other purpose. *Utility room,* on the other hand, is a recent national usage disseminated through home magazines, builders, and the like.[69]

Urbanization

During the latter part of the nineteenth century and all of the twentieth, urban influences entered rural life through print and other means of national dissemination. Ease of travel brought city and country closer together in a new kind of physical unity. And the city itself expanded, absorbing homes and property that at one time were at a considerable distance from its center. At the same time aspects of the old continued beside the new. In domestic architecture, for instance, the local design of one house might reflect a regional evolution of the log cabin while a house adjacent to it would show the influence of current fashions found in a book.[70]

The House

EXTERIOR

Items 15, 16, 25 Maps 45, 51, 69

Overlapping, milled boards used to form the outer walls of frame houses are *weatherboarding* or *weatherboards* in Tennessee, Georgia, Alabama, and Mississippi, but are *siding* in Florida, Louisiana, and Oklahoma, and both in Arkansas. The other term presented in the questionnaire, *clapboards,* is reported in one-tenth of the instances in Tennessee, Alabama, Mississippi, Florida, and Arkansas. *Boxing* and *shiplap* are widely volunteered.

In naming devices at the edge of the roof to carry off rain, the questionnaire listed *eaves* along with *gutters.* Local interviews will be needed to discover whether the words refer to the same thing; in any event, no informant stated that the two words had different meanings. The first preference is *gutters,* the trade name. *Eaves* is the second preference. Of the words that clearly refer to the conduit and not to the edge of the roof, *rain troughs* occurs everywhere, with the greatest preference recorded in Oklahoma. *Water gutter* has a similar region-wide distribution with the greatest preference in Arkansas. *Eaves troughs* occurs everywhere but in Mississippi; *eaves spouts, spouting,* and *spouts* have scattered occurrences and may be influenced by the commercial *down spouts. Water spouts* and *water trough* are widely volunteered.

The questionnaire sought the names of small uncovered porches and large covered ones. For the smaller, *porch* and *stoop* (Dutch in origin) alternate everywhere but in Louisiana; there the choice is first *porch* and second *steps. Platform* is reported from one-twentieth of the responses in Tennessee, Georgia, Alabama, Florida, and Arkansas, as is *portico* in Tennessee, Georgia, Alabama, Florida, and Arkansas, and *step* or *steps* in all states. *Veranda* occurs in less than one-fifth of the choices east of the Mississippi and in Arkansas. For a large porch with a roof, the main choice of half of the informants or more is simply *porch. Gallery* is a frequent second choice in Mississippi and Louisiana, perhaps reinforced by French influences in Louisiana. At least one-twentieth of the choices in each state are *veranda.* The other terms *piazza, portico,* and *stoop* are reported in scattered instances east and west of the Mississippi. Among the volunteered words, *patio* is a sign of a newer fashion in domestic architecture publicized by itself or in conjunction with a Spanish look in furnishings. Local meanings may show that the word is used to signify both a covered porch and an open terrace, or only the latter.[71]

INTERIOR

Items 8, 10 Maps 34, 57, 77, 79

Visitors are entertained in the *living room,* or according to the other and lesser choices, in the *front room,* the *parlor,* or the *sitting room.* Taste in the choice of terms is influenced to some extent by home magazines and similar arbiters of elegance; witness the introduction of *family room* for a more casual part of the home as contrasted to the room meant by the words given above. *Best room* and *big house* occur infrequently. On the other hand, the volunteered words *fireplace room* and *Florida room* have a reasonably wide distribution.

Big house is often used to refer to a mansion or other imposing home as a means of distinguishing it from other dwellings nearby; in the special sense used in the questionnaire its name may reflect a pioneer practice of building a one-room log cabin and then, as time permitted, linking additional one-room cabins to it.

The fireplace in a living room has a shelf above it, ordinarily called a *mantel* or *mantelpiece,* a name reinforced by commercial usage. In decreasing order of preference, the other synonyms are *mantel board, fireboard, mantel shelf, shelf,* and *clock shelf.* This *fireboard* must not be confused with the one which is placed in front of the fireplace either to close the opening or to shield persons sitting in front of an open fire.[72]

INTERIOR STORAGE PLACES

Items 22, 23 Maps 8, 49, 76

Domestic architecture did not at first provide separate small rooms for the storage of clothes. A person used chests and other pieces of furniture for this purpose. The piece of furniture in which clothes can be hung is ordinarily called a *wardrobe*. Its synonyms, *clothes press* and *press*, occur in Tennessee, Georgia, Alabama, Florida, and Oklahoma. The French *armor* and *armoire* occur in more than one-fifth of the choices in Louisiana; occurrences in Georgia, Mississippi, and Arkansas, however, do not reach one-tenth. Volunteered words such as *chiffonier* indicate commercial influences.

When a storage room is a part of the floor plan, it is ordinarily called a *closet* or a *clothes closet* if that is its function. *Wardrobe*, with the greatest preference in Tennessee, is reported with this meaning in all states but Mississippi. *Press* and *clothes press* have scattered occurrences.

An unfinished room at the top of a house is ordinarily an *attic*. Lesser preferences are *loft* (also used to refer to the upper part of a barn), *garrett*, and scattered instances of *cock loft* and *sky parlor*.[73]

FARM AND HOUSEHOLD GOODS AND EQUIPMENT

Many implements and possessions considered in this section were once made at home or in a nearby establishment such as a smithy. With the extension of commerce into all parts of the nation, the local product was replaced when worn out by its commercial equivalent as described in a catalog or sold in a store. An original name, as in *harrow*, may continue in use while the thing itself is improved, whatever "improved" may mean to a manufacturer and his salesman.

BEDS AND BEDCLOTHING

Items 54, 55, 56 Maps 10, 58, 59, 60, 76

When there are more overnight guests than beds, a host and hostess may improvise beds on the floor. The only name of major importance for these beds is *pallet*. The word *bunk* is also reported but is a serious competitor only in Louisiana where one-fifth of the preferences are given to it. In furniture catalogs *bunk* is the name for a particular style of manufactured bed; local interviews will be needed to discover the degree of intermingling of the two senses. *Lodge* and *shakedown* are reported only in Tennessee and Oklahoma.

Two kinds of bed covering are listed. The first is a fancy daytime cover ordinarily removed before the bed is used. The preferred name is *bedspread* followed by the phonological variants of a synonym, *counterpane, counterpin*. The least frequently chosen are *coverlet*, reported from all states, and its phonological variant *coverlid*, unreported from Florida, Louisiana, and Oklahoma. *Bedspread, counterpane*, and *coverlet* occur in catalogs and help to set semantic limits for these words.

The second covering is one for warmth; it is filled with cotton held together by tying rather than quilting. The first preference is *comfort* followed by *comforter*, a word chosen in one-third or less of the instances. *Tied quilt* is third. *Comfortable* and *hap*, unknown west of the Mississippi, are reported in scattered instances east of it.[74]

WINDOW COVERING

Item 14 Maps 12, 79

One device for regulating the amount of light that enters through a window is a piece of stiff cloth attached to a roller. When this product was introduced commercially, at least six words became associated with it. Of these, *shades* and *window shades* are ordinarily preferred. *Blinds* and *window blinds* (except for the absence of the latter from Mississippi choices) are reported, particularly in Arkansas and Oklahoma. *Roller shades* and *curtains* are last in order of preference. The latter word raises the problem of the degree to which the sense of "cloth hanging from rods" has shifted to "window covering on rollers." The volunteered word *Venetian blinds* illustrates a commercial influence in terms of product and name, and shows that in some instances a volunteered word names a device which differs markedly from that described in the questionnaire.[75]

SUPPORTS

Items 11, 47 Maps 33, 77, 78, 79

Devices for supporting logs in a fireplace are *dog irons*, the first choice in Tennessee, second choice in Louisiana, Arkansas, and a shared second choice in Oklahoma; *andirons*, the second choice in Tennessee and first choice in the other states; *fire dogs,* the second choice in Georgia, Alabama, and Florida; and *log irons,* the other part of the shared second choice in Oklahoma. *Log irons, dogs, fire irons,* and *hand irons* have small and scattered distributions.

Carpenters and others support wood on two kinds of frames when sawing it. If the wood to be sawed is firewood, the supports of the frame are shaped like an X. This device is ordinarily called a *saw horse* with second preference being given to *rack* everywhere but in Louisiana where *rack* and *horse* share second. *Sawbuck* is preferred over *horse* in some states. *Buck, jack, saw jack, trestle,* and *wood buck* occur in scattered distributions.

If the piece of wood is a board, the appropriate equipment has the form of an A. It too is a *saw horse* or *horse*. The other scattered terms —*jack, rack, sawbuck, saw jack,* and *trestle*—do not exceed one-tenth of the choices made in any state; ordinarily they are well below the figure.[76]

VESSELS

Items 32, 33, 51 Maps 4, 9, 76, 81

A large open vessel for water or milk was once wood; it has been replaced by commercial products made of metal or plastics. The questionnaire sought the names of both the wooden and metal vessels. The preferred word for either is *bucket;* the synonym *pail,* however, is represented by responses that range from seven to thirty percent. The volunteered *piggen,* a locally made wooden container with one long stave serving as a handle, may provide a useful test for regional obsolescence.

A container used to carry food to hogs is nearly always called a *slop bucket*. Scattered instances of *slop pail, swill bucket,* and *swill pail* are reported. Atwood (*Regional Vocabulary of Texas,* p. 46) notes that the container for waste food in the city is a *garbage can*. To this some persons could add newer words for disposing of food scraps by a device that grinds them and sends them into the sewage lines. As with other new products, one trade name may become a generic word for all such devices.

When a person brings coal from the coal pile into the house, he uses a *coal bucket* or a *coal scuttle*. *Coal bucket* is the first preference in Tennessee, Florida, Louisiana, Arkansas, and Oklahoma, and the second preference in Georgia, Alabama, and Mississippi. The first and second preferences for *coal scuttle* reverse the pattern. *Coal hod* and *coal pail* are reported in scattered instances.[77]

KITCHEN EQUIPMENT

Items 34, 35 Maps 36, 78

A large iron utensil used for boiling meat and potatoes is either a *pot* or *kettle,* the former having a preference that ranges from half to nearly all of the responses.

Another iron utensil, the one used for frying, is a *frying pan* or a *skillet*. The latter is preferred in Tennessee, Mississippi, Louisiana, Arkansas, and Oklahoma; *frying pan* is preferred in the other states. *Spider,* at or above one-tenth of the choices in Georgia and Florida, is unreported in Mississippi, Louisiana, and Oklahoma. *Fryer* and *fry pan* have a scattered distribution; *creeper* is not reported at all. *Fryer* and *skillet* in various combinations are current names in commerce as is *fry pan*.[78]

STOPPERS

Item 39

A device made of cork used in closing bottles is a *stopper* or a *cork* in the first preferences everywhere but in Georgia; there it is *cork stopper,* a second or third preference in other states. When made of glass the same sort of device is a *glass cork* in Tennessee, Georgia, Alabama, Mississippi, and Arkansas in first preferences; in Florida, Louisiana, and Oklahoma it is a *cork stopper*. The word *stopple* is used for both cork and glass stoppers, though the marked preference is for the sense of *glass stopper*.[79]

A VALVE

Item 36

A device attached to barrels and used to control the flow of liquid from them is a *faucet* or a *spigot* (and its phonological variant *spicket*), or somewhat less often a *tap*. With the introduction of home plumbing, *faucet* is the preferred word for the hand valve over a sink; *spicket, spigot* is the second preference in this sense in Tennessee, Georgia, and Florida; *hydrant* is the second preference everywhere but in Mississippi where it and *spicket* are equal. *Tap* is reported from all states except Florida. When this same sort of device controls the flow of water from a pipe in the yard or garden, it is first a *hydrant* everywhere but in Florida and Louisiana. In Florida the preference is for *spicket;* in Louisiana *faucet* and *hydrant* share first preference. *Faucet* is the second preference, and *spigot, spicket* the third in the states east of the Mississippi; the latter pair is scarcely reported west of it. Scattered instances of *tap* occur. Commercial terminology may favor *faucet* for the indoor device.[80]

ANIMAL DRAWN EQUIPMENT

Items 41, 42, 43, 45

An implement with teeth used to break clods after plowing is a *harrow;* its synonym *drag* is chosen in no more than twenty-three percent of the instances. The volunteered *disc* indicates that an innovation in agricultural implements has helped shape local vocabulary.

With regard to horse-drawn vehicles, that part between which a single horse stands is called *shafts* or its phonological variant *shavs.* The other terms, *fills* or *thills,* are almost never reported. The bar to which a single horse is hitched in drawing a wagon is a *singletree* or *swingletree.* A few instances of *swiveltree, whiffletree,* and *shippletree* are given. The shaft between two horses hitched to a farm wagon is a *tongue.* In Mississippi that is the only word; in the other states *pole* is reported. *Neap, neb,* and *spear* occur in a few instances. The bar for two horses is a *doubletree* or, less often, a *double singletree;* its phonological variant *double swingletree* is reported in all states. *Double evener,* and *spreader* are present in a few states.[81]

SACKS

Items 37, 38 Maps 5, 7, 41, 42, 61, 62, 76, 77, 79, 81

A manufactured paper container for carrying groceries is called first a *bag* everywhere but in Arkansas and Oklahoma; there it is a *sack.* The second preference is *sack* except again in Arkansas and Oklahoma where it is a *bag. Poke* is reported everywhere but in Louisiana; its greatest preference reported in Tennessee and Arkansas does not exceed fifteen percent. Schooling may contribute to its disappearance by condemning it as inelegant except in "To buy a pig in a poke." The Pennsylvania German *toot* occurs in a few instances east of the Mississippi.

A large loosely woven cloth bag goes under half-a-dozen names. First preference in Tennessee, Alabama, and Arkansas is *tow sack;* in Georgia, Mississippi, Florida, Louisiana it is a *croker sack;* in Oklahoma it is *gunny sack.* Second preferences are *burlap bag, croker sack, gunny sack,* and *tow sack. Burlap sack* is reported in all states. The other names are restricted in distribution. *Coffee sack* occurs east of the Mississippi as does *crocus sack* in all but one instance. *Gunny bag,* on the other hand, has a greater frequency west of the Mississippi. *Guano sack* has its chief occurrences in Georgia, Florida, and Alabama. And *jute bag, jute sack,* and *seagrass sack* appear in scattered instances.[82]

A VEHICLE FOR A BABY

Item 125

One pushes a young baby in a *baby buggy* or a *baby carriage,* both in commercial use. *Baby cab* drew a small number of responses, and *baby coach* none. The volunteered words are trade names for a different sort of vehicle for a baby.[83]

A SHARPENER

Item 52

A flat piece of rock used to sharpen knives is a *whet rock* everywhere but in Oklahoma where it is *whet stone,* the second preference in the other states. *Whet, whet seed,* and *whetter* are occasionally chosen. The volunteered *grind stone* refers to a larger rock, disc shaped and mounted on an axle; at one time powered by hand, it is now a common motor-driven accessory on work benches.[84]

COMBUSTIBLES

Items 12, 13, 53 Maps 13, 37, 72, 78, 79

Some influences of nineteenth and twentieth-century developments in kinds of domestic fuel are not reflected in the questionnaire. Rather the emphasis is on wood as used in stoves and open fireplaces. Pieces of wood used to start a fire are called *kindling* in at least half of the indications of preference. In Georgia, Alabama, Mississippi, and Florida *lightwood* is an important synonym; *pine* shares second place with it in Alabama and Mississippi; in all of the other states but Florida *pine* is the second choice. *Fat pine, fatwood,* and *pitch pine* are reported in scattered examples.

A large log placed at the back of a fireplace is a *backlog* in more than half of the preferences. *Back stick,* the second choice, ranges near one-third. Tennessee, Georgia, Alabama, Mississippi, and Arkansas have the larger percentages. *Back chunk* is reported everywhere but in Arkansas. Of the volunteered words, *liteard* and *lightered wood* suggest that some informants did not recognize that the spelling *lightwood* in the questionnaire stood for a pronunciation reflected in their spellings. *Back log* is nationally used in a metaphorical sense as in "a backlog of orders."

An exception must be made for means of illumination. After the middle of the nineteenth century, the introduction of a manufactured oil for lamps led to the dissemination of the names *carbon oil, coal oil, kerosene,* and *lamp oil. Coal oil* and *kerosene* are the chief regional words everywhere but in Georgia; there *lamp oil* is preferred somewhat more often than *coal oil. Carbon oil* is reported everywhere but in Georgia and Louisiana.[85]

Construction

FOR FIRE ENGINES

Item 141

Fire engines are kept in a *fire station* or, in Tennessee, a *fire hall.* The second preference in Georgia and Alabama is *fire hall* (a word unreported in Arkansas and Oklahoma), *fire station* in Tennessee, and *fire house* in the other states.[86]

FOR TRANSPORTATION

Items 59, 60, 61

The twentieth-century building of roads in the cities and towns and extending those roads into the countryside introduced specific references for a number of words. The principal name for roads with a bituminous surface is *blacktop,* an expected response to its appearance. For roads paved with concrete, three preferences occur: *concrete road* is the first choice in Tennessee and Florida; *paved road* is first in Georgia, Alabama, Mississippi. Louisiana, and Arkansas; and *pavement* is first in Oklahoma. The second choice in Tennessee for the roads with a bituminous surface is *oiled road* with *pavement, hard surface road,* and *macadam road* close to it. The second choice in Georgia, Alabama, and Mississippi is *pavement;* in the other states it is *hard surface road. Macadam road* is everywhere but in Louisiana; a few instances of *tarvia* or *tarvia road* are known, mainly in Alabama.

The second choice for the road paved with concrete is *paved road* in Tennessee, Florida, and Oklahoma; *concrete road* in Georgia, Alabama, and Mississippi; and *pavement* in Louisiana and Arkansas. The preference for *pavement* goes beyond one-tenth of choices in all of the states. *Cement road* is next; *hard road* and *hard surface road* have scattered occurrences; in Arkansas, however, *hard road* is an important term, exceeding the reported preferences for *pavement. Slab* has its chief preferences in Arkansas and Oklahoma; *pike* and *pave* are seldom reported. When wet, roads are either *slick* or *slippery,* though highway signs tend to say "slippery when wet."

In examining the tables of percentages, readers will notice that one definition has words which may have contributed to choices of *concrete road* and *paved road* and thus is a matter for verification in the course of field interviews.[87]

FOR ESTHETICS OR DRAINAGE

Items 62, 63

In towns and cities when sidewalks are constructed a grass strip is sometimes left between the sidewalk and street. It is regularly called a *sidewalk plot* in Tennessee, Georgia, and Mississippi; this choice is shared with *parkway* in Alabama and with *boulevard* in Louisiana. *Parkway* is the first choice in Arkansas, and *parking* is first in Oklahoma. The choice of *boulevard* occurs everywhere in a second or lesser preference as does *boulevard strip,* and *parking strip. Tree lawn* is reported everywhere but in Mississippi; *parking* is unreported in Alabama, Mississippi, Florida, and Louisiana; *parkway* is unreported in Louisiana; and *berm* in this sense is barely known in any state; it is wholly unreported in Mississippi, Louisiana, and Oklahoma.

The effects of road grading are often more visible outside the city than within it. A ditch provided in the course of such grading is simply a *ditch* everywhere but in Oklahoma where the first preference is for *bar ditch.* The second preference in Tennessee, Georgia, and Alabama is *gutter;* in Mississippi, Louisiana, and Arkansas it is *bar pit;* and in Oklahoma it is *ditch. Grader ditch,* the second preference in Florida, is chosen in about the same degree in Georgia, Arkansas, and Oklahoma. Scattered instances of *barrow pit, borrow pit,* and *borrow ditch* occur.[88]

The record shows that two synonyms are seldom chosen with equal frequency in the Interior South. As a characteristic of the *Southern* dialect, and presumably of all of American English, it is clear that one of a set of synonyms is preferred within a state, or in one of the two major geographic subdivisions east and west of the Mississippi, or in the entire Interior South. Less frequently named synonyms are more restricted in their actual presence in the interior states, but the patterns of major and minor distributions do not consistently match from state to state. Thus if vocabulary change consists of replacing a major word by its minor synonym, the available word or words may vary widely from Georgia to Oklahoma and from Tennessee to Florida.

7

The Accomplished Facts of Change

In the use of a language, community order and personal idiosyncrasy have somehow combined to bring American English to its present stages of development. To imagine what has occurred in greater or lesser degree in the entire nation, one need consider no more than the details which have been provided in this study of the *Southern* vocabulary. In the South as elsewhere the "purity of the American tongue" has been maintained by less formal means than those proposed by Noah Webster.

In the Interior South, the *Southern* dialect shows directly for itself and metaphorically for the other dialects the impact of diverse influences. Here one finds a record of the mingling of dialect vocabularies, indications of changes in material surroundings, and an increasing presence of city influences which came first as new books and later as new roads. Within the Interior South are words of such general acceptability that they could readily be placed beside *earthworm* and *kerosene* as words that are national; two of these are *light bread* and *pallet*. On the other hand, here as elsewhere are words so locally confined that they seem likely to disappear within a generation or so—*big house* and *mutton corn,* for instance. But in an age of instant communications one need not be surprised when the most unlikely regionalism becomes nationally known: the scorned *tote* is now in the language of the cultivated in the form *tote bag*. Linguistic prophesy, however, is not the function of this essay.

The vocabulary examined was transmitted by word of mouth before urbanizing influences began the propagation of standard vocabularies. Today this same process of transmission surely must account for the informants' first encounter with most of these words. *Lag line* or *taw line* move from generation to generation during the course of playing marbles and are stored in the remote parts of memory when marbles give way to some other game. Even the book word *earthworm* may be heard long before it is met on a printed page. In some instances word distribution seems to provide an explicit marker for migration and trade, as in the maps of *tow sack* and *coal oil;* in other instances—the development of the cotton plantations, for example—the links between words and social change are hinted at as in the maps of *mosquito hawk, pinders,* and *guano sack*.

When several synonyms emerge from this mixture of spoken and printed instruction, the users in a region tend to select one as the chief symbol and reserve the others for special uses. At least such an inference is possible from the tables of relative frequency given here. But what guides this preference (in those general instances when some idea of elegance is not associated with the synonym) has not emerged from the tabulations or from comments that informants wrote.

The vocabulary of the *Southern* dialect has been used in conjunction with other evidence to define that dialect according to its twentieth-century geographic limits. Extending from the South Atlantic states to the slopes of the Rockies, its northern boundary follows the course of the Ohio to the confluence of that river and the Mississippi, then passing north of the Missouri Ozarks it extends west along the northern boundary of Oklahoma. Within the Interior South four main vocabulary areas have been defined and delimited according to the presence and absence of selected words; at varying degrees within the political boundaries of each state an intricate balance of preferences among synonyms is apparent. And within the same area the total vocabulary ranges in generality of use from "very small" to "complete." These conclusions and the remarks on gradation which occur in several chapters derive from an examination of a closed system, that system of vocabulary preferences explicitly chosen in the entries in the questionnaire. That the *Southern* dialect of American English is not a closed system at all is clear from the list of volunteered words which has been frequently mentioned here; the unclosed part invites further study.

The form of future investigations of regional American English will doubtless enlarge the boundaries of this closed system by including greater quantities of information and by examining larger segments of continuous discourse; at least, this is the potential of one sort of computational linguistics. Until that occurs the present study provides a detailed, computer based model of the occurrence of regional words in the eight state area called the Interior South. As such it furnishes a guide to recent changes that have occurred in the *Southern* dialect of American English.

Appendices

Tables

Maps

Appendix A

Ancestral Origins of Informants

This table shows by state the origins of the informant's parents and grandparents as that data was given in the biographical part of the questionnaire.

The place of birth of the parent(s) is given in the left column; that of the grandparent(s) is underlined in the right column.

	TO															
	ALA.		ARK.		FLA.		GA.		LA.		MISS.		OKLA.		TENN.	
FROM																
Alabama	132	135	7	26	7	17	14	25	3	7	11	20	8	11	12	25
Arkansas			121	97		2			3	1		1	10	15		
Florida					103	82	6	8						1		
Georgia	13	29	8	26	33	88	440	585		4	1	5	1	6	13	25
Louisiana	1	3	7	8					47	52	2	7		4	1	1
Mississippi	3	7	17	23				1	3	9	72	97	2	9	5	8
Oklahoma			1	2							1		48	20		1
Tennessee	4	5	13	65	3	3	17	42		1	3	10	5	18	330	844
Kentucky	1	4	6	11	2	2						5	3	10	15	35
Missouri			3	11				1	1	1		2	14	27	4	4
North Carolina	2	18	3	26	6	14	6	41			2				20	65
South Carolina	3	15	4	6	8	19	12	49	2	1	1	3		3	1	11
Texas	2	2	[illegible]	6		1			2	4	1	4	20	25	1	1
Virginia		17	2	19	4	8	3	13		2	1	5	2	15	4	49
Illinois		2	3	7	3	1					1		6	11	1	4
Indiana	1	1		1		2						1	1	4	3	4
Iowa				1									2	9	4	4
Kansas													12	6		
Maine						1							1	1	1	1
Maryland			1	3											1	1
Massachusetts				1		1				1						
Michigan		2	3	7	3	1					1		6	11	1	4
Minnesota													1	2		
Nebraska		1											5	2		
New Jersey				1												
New York		1	2	2	3	1	3					2			1	7
North Dakota					1											
Ohio	2	5	6	7		1							3	7	7	15
Pennsylvania	1	4			1										1	7
Rhode Island						1										
West Virginia															1	4
Wisconsin				1		1					1	1				
Canada				1	1	1		3		3		1			1	2
England		7		2	1	6		4		1				5		6
Ireland		3	1	5	4			8		1	1	2		5	8	26
Scotland	5	5			1	3		8						3		5
Austria				3									2	2		
Bohemia														1	1	2
Czechoslovakia														1	1	2
Denmark					1											
France		1	1	8		1		4						1	3	3
Germany	2	8	1	8	1	8		3	2	8		2	2	8	4	14
Holland		1		1				3		1						4
Italy									1						2	
Luxembourg										1						

Appendix B

Questionnaire Format

The questionnaire contained a page of instructions, an extensive text reported completely in Table I, and a biographical page.

The page of instructions began with a general explanation and then gave these directions to the informant:

1. Please put a circle around the word in each group which you ordinarily use.
2. IF you ordinarily use more than one word in a group, put a circle around each of the words you use.
3. DON'T put a circle around any word you don't actually use, even though you may be familiar with it.
4. IF the word you ordinarily use is not listed in the group, please write it in the space below the item.
5. IF you never use any word in the group because you never need to refer to the thing described, don't mark the word.
6. THE MATERIAL IN CAPITALS IS EXPLANATORY ONLY

   EXAMPLE: TOWN OFFICER: selectman, trustee, (supervisor,) reeve, councilman.

The biographical page contained these entries with appropriate space for completion:

Sex   Race   Age   Highest Grade Reached in School

State   County   Town (or equivalent)

How long have you lived here (years)?

Birthplace: Town   State

Other towns, states or countries you have lived in (approximate dates)

Have you traveled much outside your native state (yes or no)?
If so, where?

Relatives' birthplace (state or country):

Father   Grandfather

Grandmother

Mother   Grandfather

Grandmother

Do you speak any non-English language (yes or no)? If so, which?

Occupation:

Appendix C

Data Processing Notes

If the supporting computer tapes are made available, details will be furnished about the way that data is stored on them. The present notes are a general description of the steps from questionnaire to the printed results which appear in this study.

The selected questionnaires were punched on data cards which were divided into two fields, a biographical one and a textual one. The first field contained twelve columns for coded information: columns 1–6, a numerical code for state, county or parish, and place; 7–8, a numerical code for each informant within the county; 9–12, numerical codes for sex, race, age and level of education. Columns 13–80 contained the coded text and the necessary sequence numbers.

The first computer printout from these cards was a listing by state (coded) and county (spelled out) of the number of responses each age group gave in its item by item choice of questionnaire words. The second was a compilation and consolidation of this body of responses into a record of responses in groups of ten adjacent counties, a record that is still too bulky and awkward to print.

From those two records and a new set of cards containing volunteered words, the computations and lists printed here were prepared. Table I is a set of computations from the preceding block of computations for ten county units. Table II is the grand total of occurrences of each word, including negative responses arranged in increasing order of total occurrence. Table III is an alphabetizing of the volunteered words. And the index of words, though not a photocopy of a computer printout, was prepared in draft form by computer.

Appendix D

List of Participating Counties

This list shows all of the counties from which information was obtained. The counties are arranged in alphabetical order by state.

Alabama

Baldwin
Blount
Bullock
Butler
Calhoun
Cherokee
Chilton
Choctaw
Clarke
Clay
Cleburne
Coffee
Colbert
Cullman
Dallas
De Kalb
Etowah
Fayette
Franklin
Geneva
Hale
Henry
Houston
Jackson
Jefferson
Lamar
Lee
Limestone
Marion
Marshall
Mobile
Monroe
Montgomery
Morgan
Pickens
Randolph
St. Clair
Sumter
Tuscaloosa
Walker
Washington
Winston

Arkansas

Arkansas
Ashley
Benton
Boone
Bradley
Carroll
Chicot
Clark
Cleveland
Crawford
Crittenden
Cross
Dallas
Desha
Drew
Faulkner
Franklin
Fulton
Garland
Grant
Greene
Hempstead
Howard
Independence
Izard
Jackson
Jefferson
Lee
Logan
Lonoke
Madison
Miller
Mississippi
Monroe
Nevada
Newton
Ouachita
Perry
Phillips
Pike
Polk
Pope
Prairie
Pulaski

Arkansas—continued

St. Francis
Saline
Scott
Sebastian
Sevier
Sharp
Stone
Union
Washington
White
Yell

Florida

Alachua
Baker
Bay
Bradford
Calhoun
Citrus
Collier
Columbia
Dade
De Soto
Duval
Escambia
Flagler
Franklin
Gadsden
Gilchrist
Glades
Hamilton
Hardee
Hernando
Hillsborough
Holmes
Jackson
Jefferson
Lake
Lee
Leon
Levy
Liberty
Madison
Manatee
Marion
Martin
Monroe
Nassau
Okeechobee
Orange
Osceola
Palm Beach
Pinellas
Putnam
St. Lucie
Sarasota
Seminole
Suwannee
Taylor
Union
Washington

Georgia

Appling
Arkinson
Baker
Banks
Barrow
Bartow
Ben Hill
Berrien
Bibb
Bleckley
Brantley
Brooks
Bulloch
Burke
Butts
Calhoun
Camden
Chandler
Carroll
Catoosa
Charlton
Chatham
Chattooga
Cherokee
Clarke
Clay
Clayton
Clinch
Cobb
Coffee
Colquit
Columbia
Cook
Coweta
Crawford
Crisp
Dade
Decatur
De Kalb
Dodge
Douglas
Early
Echols
Fannin
Fayette
Floyd
Forsyth
Franklin
Fulton
Gilmer
Glascock
Gordon
Grady
Greene
Gwinnett
Habersham
Hall
Hancock
Haralson
Harris

Georgia—continued

Hart
Heard
Henry
Houston
Irwin
Jackson
Jasper
Jeff Davis
Jefferson
Johnson
Jones
Lamar
Lanier
Laurens
Lincoln
Lowndes
Lumpkin
McDuffie
Macon
Madison
Meriwether
Miller
Mitchell
Monroe
Murray
Muscogee
Newton
Oconee
Oglethorpe
Paulding
Peach
Pickens
Pierce
Pike
Polk
Pulaski
Putnam
Quitman
Rabun
Randolph
Richmond
Rockdale
Schley
Seminole
Spalding
Stewart
Talbot
Tattnall
Taylor
Telfaire
Terrell
Thomas
Tift
Towns
Troup
Turner
Twiggs
Union
Upson
Walker
Walton
Warren
Wayne
Wheeler
White
Wilkes
Wilkinson
Worth

Louisiana

Assumption
Avoyelles
Bienville
Caddo
Claiborne
East Baton Rouge
Evangeline
Iberia
Iberville
Lafayette
Lafourche
Lincoln
Madison
Natchitoches
Orleans
Rapides
Red River
St. Martin
Tangipahoa
Terrebonne
Webster
West Carroll
West Feliciana
Winn

Mississippi

Adams
Calhoun
Carroll
Chicasaw
Clarke
Coahoma
Copiah
Grenada
Hinds
Jackson
Jasper
Jones
Kemper
Lafayette
Lamar
Lauderdale
Leake
Lee
Leflore
Lowndes
Marion
Marshall
Monroe
Oktibbeha
Perry
Pike
Scott
Simpson
Tallahatchie
Tippah

Mississippi—continued

Tishomingo
Union
Yalobusha
Yazoo

Oklahoma

Alfalfa
Bryan
Caddo
Carter
Choctaw
Cleveland
Coal
Comanche
Creek
Custer
Ellis
Garvin
Grady
Hughes
Jackson
Johnston
Kay
Kingfisher
Latimer
Le Flore
McClain
McCurtain
Muskogee
Noble
Oklahoma
Okmulgee
Osage
Pawnee
Pittsburg
Pontotoc
Pottawatomie
Pushmataha
Rogers
Seminole
Sequoyah
Texas
Washita
Woods

Tennessee

Anderson
Bedford
Benton
Bledsoe
Blount
Bradley
Cannon
Carroll
Cheatham
Chester
Claiborne
Cocke
Coffee
Cumberland
Davidson
Decatur
De Kalb
Dickson
Dyer
Fayette
Fentress
Franklin
Gibson
Giles
Grainger
Greene
Grundy
Hamilton
Hancock
Hardeman
Hardin
Hawkins
Henry
Hickman
Humphreys
Jackson
Jefferson
Johnson
Knox
Lake
Lauderdale
Lawrence
Lewis
Lincoln
Madison
Marion
Marshall
Maury
McMinn
McNairy
Meigs
Monroe
Montgomery
Moore
Morgan
Obion
Overton
Perry
Polk
Putnam
Rhea
Roane
Robertson
Rutherford
Scott
Sevier
Shelby
Smith
Stewart
Sullivan
Sumner
Tipton
Unicoi
Union
Van Buren
Warren
Washington
Wayne
Weakley
White
Williamson
Wilson

Table I

Occurrence of Local Words

This table contains the questionnaire text and the percentages of individual response to each entry under a given Item.

The heading consists of an Item number from the questionnaire, the informational setting or definition supplied for that entry, and a Work Sheet number. This last element provides for interested scholars the number assigned to the Linguistic Atlas work sheets in publications such as *A Compilation of the Work Sheets of The Linguistic Atlas of the United States and Canada and Associated Projects,* compiled by Raven I. McDavid, Jr. and Virginia McDavid, mimeo. (Michigan, 1951). Successive entries in Table I are arranged in ascending order by Item number.

The left-hand column contains the words that the informant was given in the questionnaire; the top word is the leftmost in the questionnaire list, the bottom word is the rightmost in the string of synonyms. Percentile responses are given state by state under columns A, B, C, D, and are shown by state total opposite the abbreviation ST, and by subdivisional total within the state opposite the directional abbreviations EW for Tennessee and NS for the other states. For subdivisions see Map 2.

These are the computations for the respective columns:

A. The state total as a percent of the sectional total. Tennessee's total, for instance, as a percent of the state totals east of the Mississippi (Tennessee, Georgia, Alabama, Mississippi, Florida); or Louisiana's total as a percent of the state totals west of the Mississippi (Louisiana, Arkansas, Oklahoma).

B. The state total as a percent of the maximum number of possible choices of a given word within that state. The maximum is different for each state and remains constant in each computation for the entire list of synonyms in the questionnaire.

C. The separate locational totals as a percent of the total for that state by itself; each state total is set at one hundred percent.

D. The individual synonym total in a state as a percent of the synonym totals in that state for that Item. That is, for each new Item there are eight separate statewide counts for all synonyms listed under that Item; the individual synonym count is expressed as a percent of the total within each separate state as that state record is computed.

ITEM (1)
WORK SHEET (2)

UNITS OF TIME
THE LATTER PART OF THE DAYLIGHT HOURS BEFORE SUPPER

		TENNESSEE A	TENNESSEE B		GEORGIA A	GEORGIA B	ALABAMA A	ALABAMA B	MISSISSIPPI A	MISSISSIPPI B	FLORIDA A	FLORIDA B	LOUISIANA A	LOUISIANA B	ARKANSAS A	ARKANSAS B	OKLAHOMA A	OKLAHOMA B
AFTERNOON	W	17	5	N	15	5	7	2	3	1	7	2	4	1	25	8	25	8
	E	30	9	S	12	4	3	1	1	.2	5	1	4	1	20	6	23	7
	ST	47	14		27	8	10	3	4	1	12	4	7	2	45	14	48	14
EVENING	W	14	4	N	12	3	8	2	5	1	7	2	11	4	20	7	15	5
	E	30	9	S	13	4	4	1	4	1	3	1	10	4	21	8	25	9
	ST	44	13		25	7	12	4	9	2	9	3	21	8	40	15	39	14

		TENNESSEE C	TENNESSEE D		GEORGIA C	GEORGIA D	ALABAMA C	ALABAMA D	MISSISSIPPI C	MISSISSIPPI D	FLORIDA C	FLORIDA D	LOUISIANA C	LOUISIANA D	ARKANSAS C	ARKANSAS D	OKLAHOMA C	OKLAHOMA D
AFTERNOON	W	36	19	N	56	30	69	32	83	28	60	34	50	11	55	27	53	26
	E	64	34	S	44	23	31	14	17	6	40	23	50	11	45	22	48	24
	ST		53			53		46		33		57		22		48		50
EVENING	W	32	15	N	47	22	68	37	58	39	69	30	52	41	49	25	38	19
	E	68	32	S	53	25	32	17	42	28	31	13	48	37	51	27	63	31
	ST		47			47		54		67		43		78		52		50

ITEM (2)
WORK SHEET (3)

UNITS OF TIME
THE SUN APPEARS AT

		TENNESSEE A	TENNESSEE B		GEORGIA A	GEORGIA B	ALABAMA A	ALABAMA B	MISSISSIPPI A	MISSISSIPPI B	FLORIDA A	FLORIDA B	LOUISIANA A	LOUISIANA B	ARKANSAS A	ARKANSAS B	OKLAHOMA A	OKLAHOMA B
SUNRISE	W	18	5	N	11	3	8	2	4	1	9	3	4	1	24	9	23	8
	E	34	11	S	6	2	4	1	2	1	4	1	11	4	21	8	19	7
	ST	52	16		17	5	11	4	6	2	13	4	15	5	44	16	41	15
SUNUP	W	14	4	N	16	5	6	2	5	1	7	2	11	4	23	9	18	7
	E	22	7	S	20	6	2	1	2	1	5	2	5	2	16	6	27	10
	ST	36	11		36	11	8	2	7	2	12	4	16	6	39	15	45	17

		TENNESSEE C	TENNESSEE D		GEORGIA C	GEORGIA D	ALABAMA C	ALABAMA D	MISSISSIPPI C	MISSISSIPPI D	FLORIDA C	FLORIDA D	LOUISIANA C	LOUISIANA D	ARKANSAS C	ARKANSAS D	OKLAHOMA C	OKLAHOMA D
SUNRISE	W	34	20	N	66	22	68	40	67	31	72	38	27	13	53	28	55	26
	E	66	39	S	34	11	32	19	33	15	28	15	73	34	47	24	45	21
	ST		60			33		59		46		53		47		52		47
SUNUP	W	38	15	N	46	31	75	31	67	36	56	26	71	38	59	28	40	21
	E	62	25	S	54	37	25	10	33	18	44	21	29	16	41	20	60	32
	ST		40			67		41		54		47		53		48		53

TABLE I

ITEM (3)
WORK SHEET (3)

UNITS OF TIME
THE SUN DISAPPEARS AT

		TENNESSEE A	TENNESSEE B		GEORGIA A	GEORGIA B	ALABAMA A	ALABAMA B	MISSISSIPPI A	MISSISSIPPI B	FLORIDA A	FLORIDA B	LOUISIANA A	LOUISIANA B	ARKANSAS A	ARKANSAS B	OKLAHOMA A	OKLAHOMA B
SUNDOWN	W	15	5	N	16	6	6	2	5	2	8	3	8	4	27	12	20	9
	E	23	8	S	19	7	3	1	2	1	4	1	4	2	17	8	23	10
	ST	38	14		34	12	9	3	7	2	12	4	12	5	45	19	43	19
SUNSET	W	17	4	N	9	2	9	2	4	1	7	2	7	2	17	5	19	6
	E	39	9	S	4	1	3	1	3	1	4	1	13	4	20	6	23	7
	ST	56	13		13	3	12	3	7	2	12	3	20	6	37	11	42	13

		TENNESSEE C	TENNESSEE D		GEORGIA C	GEORGIA D	ALABAMA C	ALABAMA D	MISSISSIPPI C	MISSISSIPPI D	FLORIDA C	FLORIDA D	LOUISIANA C	LOUISIANA D	ARKANSAS C	ARKANSAS D	OKLAHOMA C	OKLAHOMA D
SUNDOWN	W	39	19	N	46	36	69	37	70	41	67	41	67	31	61	39	46	28
	E	61	31	S	54	43	31	17	30	18	33	20	33	16	39	25	54	32
	ST		50			79		54		59		61		47		64		60
SUNSET	W	31	15	N	68	14	74	34	63	26	63	25	35	19	45	16	46	18
	E	69	34	S	32	7	26	12	38	15	37	14	65	34	55	20	54	22
	ST		50			21		46		41		39		53		36		40

UNITS OF TIME
A TIME OF DAY

ITEM (4)
WORK SHEET (4)

		TENNESSEE A	TENNESSEE B		GEORGIA A	GEORGIA B	ALABAMA A	ALABAMA B	MISSISSIPPI A	MISSISSIPPI B	FLORIDA A	FLORIDA B	LOUISIANA A	LOUISIANA B	ARKANSAS A	ARKANSAS B	OKLAHOMA A	OKLAHOMA B
QUARTER BEFORE ELEVEN	W	21	.3	N	14	.2	7	.1	7	.1	7	.1	**	**	50	1	**	**
	E	29	.4	S	14	.2	**	**	**	**	**	**	**	**	33	1	17	.3
	ST	50	1		29	.4	7	.1	7	.1	7	.1	**	**	83	2	17	.3
QUARTER OF ELEVEN	W	13	1	N	11	1	5	1	5	1	12	1	9	1	22	3	22	3
	E	27	3	S	12	1	3	.3	1	.1	11	1	13	1	22	3	13	1
	ST	40	5		23	3	8	1	6	1	23	3	22	3	44	5	34	4
QUARTER TILL ELEVEN	W	14	4	N	12	4	7	2	5	1	6	2	8	3	25	8	18	6
	E	32	9	S	15	4	3	1	4	1	2	1	7	2	22	7	21	7
	ST	46	13		28	8	10	3	8	2	8	2	14	5	47	16	30	13
QUARTER TO ELEVEN	W	24	2	N	11	1	8	1	7	1	9	1	9	1	14	1	5	.3
	E	19	2	S	8	1	6	1	2	.2	7	1	27	2	9	1	36	3
	ST	43	4		19	2	14	1	9	1	16	2	36	3	23	2	41	3
TEN FORTY FIVE	W	16	3	N	17	3	8	1	1	.1	10	2	9	3	23	7	21	6
	E	32	5	S	11	2	3	.4	1	.1	2	.3	2	1	20	6	26	8
	ST	48	8		28	5	11	2	1	.2	12	2	11	3	43	13	46	14

		TENNESSEE C	TENNESSEE D		GEORGIA C	GEORGIA D	ALABAMA C	ALABAMA D	MISSISSIPPI C	MISSISSIPPI D	FLORIDA C	FLORIDA D	LOUISIANA C	LOUISIANA D	ARKANSAS C	ARKANSAS D	OKLAHOMA C	OKLAHOMA D
QUARTER BEFORE ELEVEN	W	43	1	N	50	1	100	1	100	2	100	1	**	**	60	3	**	**
	E	57	1	S	50	1	**	**	**	**	**	**	**	**	40	2	100	1
	ST		2			2		1		2		1		**		5		1
QUARTER OF ELEVEN	W	32	5	N	48	7	67	9	86	14	52	15	43	8	50	7	64	7
	E	68	10	S	52	8	33	4	14	2	48	14	57	11	50	7	36	4
	ST		15			15		13		16		29		19		14		12
QUARTER TILL ELEVEN	W	30	13	N	45	21	71	29	58	33	75	21	54	19	53	23	46	17
	E	70	30	S	55	25	29	12	42	23	25	7	46	16	47	20	54	20
	ST		43			46		41		56		28		35		42		37
QUARTER TO ELEVEN	W	56	8	N	58	6	57	12	78	16	56	11	25	5	60	3	11	1
	E	44	6	S	42	5	43	9	22	5	44	8	75	16	40	2	89	9
	ST		14			11		20		21		19		22		5		10
TEN FORTY FIVE	W	33	8	N	61	16	76	19	50	2	84	19	78	19	54	19	45	18
	E	67	17	S	39	10	24	6	50	2	16	4	22	5	46	16	55	22
	ST		25			26		25		5		22		24		34		40

TABLE I

WEATHER
AFTER A STORM THE WEATHER IS

ITEM (5)
WORK SHEET (5)

		TENNESSEE A	TENNESSEE B		GEORGIA A	GEORGIA B	ALABAMA A	ALABAMA B	MISSISSIPPI A	MISSISSIPPI B	FLORIDA A	FLORIDA B	LOUISIANA A	LOUISIANA B	ARKANSAS A	ARKANSAS B	OKLAHOMA A	OKLAHOMA B
CLEARING OFF	W	26	4	N	14	2	7	1	4	1	2	.3	4	1	24	6	29	8
	E	39	6	S	6	1	1	.2	1	.1	1	.1	**	**	19	5	24	6
	ST	64	10		20	3	8	1	5	1	3	.4	4	1	43	11	53	14
CLEARING UP	W	15	5	N	10	3	8	3	5	1	11	3	8	3	22	9	17	7
	E	31	9	S	9	3	4	1	1	.4	6	2	10	4	16	7	26	11
	ST	46	14		19	6	13	4	6	2	16	5	18	8	39	16	43	18
FAIRING OFF	W	5	1	N	20	2	4	1	6	1	10	1	26	2	21	1	**	**
	E	4	1	S	35	4	4	.4	9	1	3	.3	21	1	32	2	**	**
	ST	10	1		55	7	8	1	15	2	12	1	47	3	53	4	**	**
FAIRING UP	W	16	1	N	4	.2	6	.3	4	.2	6	.3	22	1	44	1	11	.3
	E	45	2	S	12	1	**	**	**	**	6	.3	**	**	11	.3	11	.3
	ST	61	3		16	1	6	.3	4	.2	12	1	22	1	56	2	22	1
BREAKING AWAY	W	8	.1	N	33	.4	8	.1	**	**	**	**	15	1	31	1	8	.3
	E	33	.4	S	8	.1	**	**	**	**	8	.1	**	**	8	.3	38	2
	ST	42	1		42	1	8	.1	**	**	8	.1	15	1	38	2	46	2

		TENNESSEE C	TENNESSEE D		GEORGIA C	GEORGIA D	ALABAMA C	ALABAMA D	MISSISSIPPI C	MISSISSIPPI D	FLORIDA C	FLORIDA D	LOUISIANA C	LOUISIANA D	ARKANSAS C	ARKANSAS D	OKLAHOMA C	OKLAHOMA D
CLEARING OFF	W	40	13	N	69	12	83	16	86	14	75	4	100	8	55	18	55	22
	E	60	20	S	31	6	17	3	14	2	25	1	**	**	45	15	45	18
	ST		34			18		19		16		5		8		32		40
CLEARING UP	W	33	16	N	51	18	66	40	78	32	65	43	43	24	58	27	40	21
	E	67	33	S	49	17	34	21	22	9	35	23	57	32	42	20	60	31
	ST		50			35		60		41		66		57		47		52
FAIRING OFF	W	55	2	N	37	14	56	8	41	16	79	15	56	14	40	4	**	**
	E	45	2	S	63	25	44	6	59	23	21	4	44	11	60	6	**	**
	ST		4			39		14		39		19		24		10		**
FAIRING UP	W	27	3	N	25	1	100	5	100	5	50	4	100	5	80	4	50	1
	E	73	8	S	75	4	**	**	**	**	50	4	**	**	20	1	50	1
	ST		11			5		5		5		8		5		5		2
BREAKING AWAY	W	20	.3	N	80	2	100	2	**	**	**	**	100	5	80	4	17	1
	E	80	1	S	20	1	**	**	**	**	100	1	**	**	20	1	83	5
	ST		2			3		2		**		1		5		5		6

ITEM (6)
WORK SHEET (6)

WEATHER
VERY HEAVY RAIN THAT DOES NOT LAST LONG

		TENNESSEE A	TENNESSEE B		GEORGIA A	GEORGIA B	ALABAMA A	ALABAMA B	MISSISSIPPI A	MISSISSIPPI B	FLORIDA A	FLORIDA B	LOUISIANA A	LOUISIANA B	ARKANSAS A	ARKANSAS B	OKLAHOMA A	OKLAHOMA B
GOOSE DROWNDER					(NO RESPONSE)													
					(NO RESPONSE)													
					(NO RESPONSE)													
GULLY WASHER	W	21	4	N	9	2	3	1	6	1	3	1	9	2	29	7	24	6
	E	37	7	S	13	2	2	.3	3	1	2	.3	**	**	15	4	24	6
	ST	58	10		23	4	5	1	9	2	5	1	9	2	44	11	47	12
TRASH MOVER	W	**	**	N	65	2	4	.1	8	.2	**	**	100	1	**	**	**	**
	E	12	.3	S	8	.2	4	.1	**	**	**	**	**	**	**	**	**	**
	ST	12	.3		73	2	8	.2	8	.2	**	**	100	1	**	**	**	**
TOAD STRANGLER	W	3	.1	N	7	.2	7	.2	**	**	28	1	20	1	20	1	20	1
	E	21	1	S	14	.4	**	**	**	**	21	1	**	**	33	2	7	.3
	ST	24	1		21	1	7	.2	**	**	48	1	20	1	53	3	27	1
LIGHTWOOD KNOT FLOATER	W	**	**	N	**	**	**	**	**	**	21	.3	**	**	**	**	**	**
	E	7	.1	S	71	1	**	**	**	**	**	**	**	**	**	**	**	**
	ST	7	.1		71	1	**	**	**	**	21	.3	**	**	**	**	**	**
SQUALL	W	**	**	N	**	**	**	**	**	**	11	.1	**	**	**	**	**	**
	E	**	**	S	11	.1	33	.3	11	.1	33	.3	100	.3	**	**	**	**
	ST	**	**		11	.1	33	.3	11	.1	44	.4	100	.3	**	**	**	**
FLAW	W	100	.1	N	**	**	**	**	**	**	**	**	**	**	**	**	**	**
					(NO RESPONSE)													
	ST	100	.1		**	**	**	**	**	**	**	**	**	**	**	**	**	**
DOWNPOUR	W	16	4	N	12	3	9	2	5	1	10	3	9	3	24	9	13	5
	E	29	8	S	9	2	3	1	2	1	5	1	12	4	16	6	27	10
	ST	45	12		21	6	12	3	7	2	15	4	21	8	40	14	40	14
CLOUDBURST	W	18	4	N	11	2	9	2	3	1	7	2	3	1	19	6	23	8
	E	29	7	S	14	3	4	1	3	1	2	.4	4	1	21	7	29	9
	ST	47	11		25	6	12	3	6	1	9	2	8	3	40	13	52	17

(CONTINUED) VERY HEAVY RAIN THAT DOES NOT LAST LONG

ITEM (6)		TENNESSEE C	TENNESSEE D		GEORGIA C	GEORGIA D	ALABAMA C	ALABAMA D	MISSISSIPPI C	MISSISSIPPI D	FLORIDA C	FLORIDA D	LOUISIANA C	LOUISIANA D	ARKANSAS C	ARKANSAS D	OKLAHOMA C	OKLAHOMA D
GOOSE DROWNDER					(NO RESPONSE)													
					(NO RESPONSE)													
	ST		**			**		**		**		**		**		**		**
GULLY WASHER	W	37	11	N	41	9	67	8	63	20	63	6	100	15	67	18	50	13
	E	63	19	S	59	13	33	4	38	12	38	3	**	**	33	9	50	13
	ST		30			21		12		31		9		15		26		26
TRASH MOVER	W	**	**	N	89	9	50	1	100	4	**	**	100	7	**	**	**	**
	E	100	1	S	11	1	50	1	**	**	**	**	**	**	**	**	**	**
	ST		1			10		3		4		**		7		**		**
TOAD STRANGLER	W	14	.2	N	33	1	100	3	**	**	57	9	100	7	38	3	75	2
	E	86	2	S	67	2	**	**	**	**	43	7	**	**	63	4	25	1
	ST		2			3		3		**		16		7		7		3
LIGHTWOOD KNOT FLOATER	W	**	**	N	**	**	**	**	**	**	100	3	**	**	**	**	**	**
	E	100	.2	S	100	5	**	**	**	**	**	**	**	**	**	**	**	**
	ST		.2			5		**		**		3		**		**		**
SQUALL	W	**	**	N	**	**	**	**	**	**	25	1	**	**	**	**	**	**
	E	**	**	S	100	1	100	4	100	2	75	3	100	2	**	**	**	**
	ST		**			1		4		2		5		2		**		**
FLAW	W	100	.2	N	**	**	**	**	**	**	**	**	**	**	**	**	**	**
					(NO RESPONSE)													
	ST		.2			**		**		**		**		**		**		**
DOWNPOUR	W	36	13	N	56	17	72	31	72	25	64	29	43	22	60	21	33	11
	E	64	22	S	44	13	28	12	28	10	36	16	57	29	40	14	68	22
	ST		35			30		43		35		45		51		35		33
CLOUDBURST	W	39	12	N	44	13	70	25	50	14	79	17	43	7	47	15	45	17
	E	61	19	S	56	16	30	11	50	14	21	5	57	10	53	17	55	21
	ST		31			29		36		27		22		17		32		38

RAIN WITH THUNDER AND LIGHTNING

ITEM (7)
WORK SHEET (6)

TEMPEST		TENNESSEE A	TENNESSEE B		GEORGIA A	GEORGIA B	ALABAMA A	ALABAMA B	MISSISSIPPI A	MISSISSIPPI B	FLORIDA A	FLORIDA B	LOUISIANA A	LOUISIANA B	ARKANSAS A	ARKANSAS B	OKLAHOMA A	OKLAHOMA B
					(NO RESPONSE) (NO RESPONSE) (NO RESPONSE)													
THUNDER SHOWER	W	14	1	N	12	1	5	1	7	1	6	1	4	.3	28	3	16	1
	E	24	2	S	23	2	1	.1	3	.3	3	.3	12	1	20	2	20	2
	ST	38	4		35	3	6	1	11	1	10	1	16	1	48	4	36	3
THUNDER STORM	W	17	6	N	14	5	6	2	5	2	7	3	10	5	21	10	21	10
	E	30	11	S	11	4	3	1	2	1	3	1	6	3	17	8	25	12
	ST	47	18		25	9	9	4	8	3	10	4	16	8	38	18	46	21
ELECTRIC(AL) STORM	W	10	1	N	13	2	12	2	2	.3	12	2	2	.3	33	6	18	3
	E	25	4	S	15	2	3	.4	2	.3	6	1	6	1	22	4	18	3
	ST	36	5		27	4	15	2	4	1	18	2	8	1	55	10	37	6
ELECTRIC(AL) SHOWER	W	11	.1	N	**	**	**	**	**	**	11	.1	50	.3	**	**	**	**
	E	11	.1	S	56	1	**	**	**	**	11	.1	**	**	**	**	50	.3
	ST	22	.2		56	1	**	**	**	**	22	.2	50	.3	**	**	50	.3
STORM	W	14	1	N	4	.3	11	1	1	.1	4	.3	6	1	19	2	16	2
	E	48	4	S	6	.4	6	.4	3	.2	3	.2	9	1	22	3	28	3
	ST	62	5		10	1	17	1	4	.3	7	1	16	2	41	5	44	5

TEMPEST		TENNESSEE C	TENNESSEE D		GEORGIA C	GEORGIA D	ALABAMA C	ALABAMA D	MISSISSIPPI C	MISSISSIPPI D	FLORIDA C	FLORIDA D	LOUISIANA C	LOUISIANA D	ARKANSAS C	ARKANSAS D	OKLAHOMA C	OKLAHOMA D
					(NO RESPONSE) (NO RESPONSE)													
	ST		**			**		**		**		**		**		**		**
THUNDER SHOWER	W	36	4	N	33	6	83	7	70	15	67	8	25	3	58	7	44	4
	F	64	0	S	67	13	17	1	30	6	33	4	75	9	42	5	56	5
	ST		12			19		8		21		12		11		12		9
THUNDER STORM	W	36	21	N	55	29	65	31	71	43	68	33	62	37	55	27	46	27
	E	64	36	S	45	24	35	17	29	17	32	15	38	23	45	22	54	32
	ST		57			53		47		60		49		60		49		58
ELECTRIC(AL) STORM	W	29	5	N	46	10	80	22	50	6	67	21	25	3	59	16	50	9
	E	71	11	S	54	11	20	6	50	6	33	10	75	9	41	11	50	9
	ST		16			21		28		13		31		11		27		18
ELECTRIC(AL) SHOWER	W	50	.3	N	**	**	**	**	**	**	50	1	100	3	**	**	**	**
	E	50	.3	S	100	3	**	**	**	**	50	1	**	**	**	**	100	1
	ST		1			3		**		**		3		3		**		1
STORM	W	23	3	N	43	2	67	11	33	2	60	4	40	6	46	6	36	5
	E	77	11	S	57	2	33	6	67	4	40	3	60	9	54	7	64	9
	ST		15			4		17		6		6		14		13		14

TABLE I

THE HOME
WHERE GUESTS ARE ENTERTAINED

ITEM (8)
WORK SHEET (7)

		TENNESSEE A	TENNESSEE B		GEORGIA A	GEORGIA B	ALABAMA A	ALABAMA B	MISSISSIPPI A	MISSISSIPPI B	FLORIDA A	FLORIDA B	LOUISIANA A	LOUISIANA B	ARKANSAS A	ARKANSAS B	OKLAHOMA A	OKLAHOMA B
BEST ROOM	W	**	**	N	**	**	**	**	**	**	**	**	**	**	100	.3	**	**
	E	100	.2	S	**	**	**	**	**	**	**	**	**	**	**	**	**	**
	ST	100	.2		**	**	**	**	**	**	**	**	**	**	100	.3	**	**
BIG HOUSE	W	40	.2	N	**	**	**	**	**	**	20	.1	**	**	**	**	**	**
	E	40	.2	S	**	**	**	**	**	**	**	**	100	.3	**	**	**	**
	ST	80	.4		**	**	**	**	**	**	20	.1	100	.3	**	**	**	**
FRONT ROOM	W	12	1	N	18	1	3	.2	5	.4	9	1	4	1	25	5	26	5
	E	32	2	S	9	1	**	**	5	.4	5	.4	6	1	17	3	23	4
	ST	45	3		27	2	3	.2	11	1	15	1	9	2	42	8	49	9
LIVING ROOM	W	16	8	N	13	7	8	4	4	2	8	4	8	5	22	13	19	11
	E	29	15	S	13	7	3	1	2	1	4	2	7	4	20	12	23	14
	ST	45	23		27	14	11	6	6	3	11	6	15	9	42	25	42	25
PARLOR	W	32	1	N	18	1	5	.2	7	.3	7	.3	36	1	18	1	**	**
	E	5	.2	S	5	.2	7	.3	7	.3	9	.4	18	1	9	.3	18	1
	ST	36	2		23	1	11	1	14	1	16	1	55	2	27	1	18	1
SITTING ROOM	W	8	.1	N	33	.4	8	.1	**	**	8	.1	17	.3	33	1	17	.3
	E	25	.3	S	8	.1	**	**	**	**	8	.1	**	**	17	.3	17	.3
	ST	33	.4		42	1	8	.1	**	**	17	.2	17	.3	50	1	33	1

		TENNESSEE C	TENNESSEE D		GEORGIA C	GEORGIA D	ALABAMA C	ALABAMA D	MISSISSIPPI C	MISSISSIPPI D	FLORIDA C	FLORIDA D	LOUISIANA C	LOUISIANA D	ARKANSAS C	ARKANSAS D	OKLAHOMA C	OKLAHOMA D
BEST ROOM	W	**	**	N	**	**	**	**	**	**	**	**	**	**	100	1	**	**
	E	100	1	S	**	**	**	**	**	**	**	**	**	**	**	**	**	**
	ST		1			**		**		**		**		**		1		**
BIG HOUSE	W	50	1	N	**	**	**	**	**	**	100	1	**	**	**	**	**	**
	E	50	1	S	**	**	**	**	**	**	**	**	100	3	**	**	**	**
	ST		1			**		**		**		1		3		**		**
FRONT ROOM	W	27	3	N	65	8	100	3	50	9	64	9	40	5	59	13	54	14
	E	73	8	S	35	4	**	**	50	9	36	5	60	8	41	9	46	12
	ST		12			12		3		17		14		13		22		26
LIVING ROOM	W	35	28	N	50	40	74	65	69	48	67	49	52	34	52	37	45	31
	E	65	51	S	50	40	26	23	31	22	33	24	48	32	48	34	55	38
	ST		79			80		87		70		73		66		70		70
PARLOR	W	88	5	N	80	5	40	3	50	7	43	4	67	11	67	2	**	**
	E	13	1	S	20	1	60	5	50	7	57	5	33	5	33	1	100	2
	ST		6			6		8		13		9		16		3		2
SITTING ROOM	W	25	.3	N	80	2	100	2	**	**	50	1	100	3	67	2	50	1
	[illegible]						**	**	**	**	50	1	**	**	33	1	50	1

FIRST THIN LAYER OF ICE ON LAKE OR POND

ITEM (9)
WORK SHEET (7)

		TENNESSEE A	TENNESSEE B		GEORGIA A	GEORGIA B	ALABAMA A	ALABAMA B	MISSISSIPPI A	MISSISSIPPI B	FLORIDA A	FLORIDA B	LOUISIANA A	LOUISIANA B	ARKANSAS A	ARKANSAS B	OKLAHOMA A	OKLAHOMA B
ANCHOR ICE	W	**	**	N	**	**	**	**	100	.1	**	**	**	**	33	.3	33	.3
	E	**	**	S	**	**	**	**	**	**	**	**	**	**	33	.3	**	**
	ST	**	**		**	**	**	**	100	.1	**	**	**	**	67	1	33	.3
MUSH ICE	W	11	1	N	5	.2	**	**	2	.1	5	.2	**	**	44	3	13	1
	E	73	3	S	5	.2	**	**	**	**	**	**	**	**	31	2	13	1
	ST	84	4		9	.4	**	**	2	.1	5	.2	**	**	75	4	25	1
SHALE ICE	W	10	.1	N	10	.1	10	.1	30	.3	10	.1	25	.3	25	.3	25	.3
	E	30	.3	S	**	**	**	**	**	**	**	**	25	.3	**	**	**	**
	ST	40	.4		10	.1	10	.1	30	.3	10	.1	50	1	25	.3	25	.3
SHALE					(NO RESPONSE)													
	E	67	.2	S	**	**	**	**	**	**	[illegible]	.1	**	**	**	**	100	1
	ST	67	[illegible]		**	**	**	**	**	**	33	.1	**	**	**	**	100	1
SKIM	W	23	5	N	20	5	7	2	6	1	4	1	**	**	22	4	22	4
	E	23	5	S	16	4	**	**	1	.2	.4	.1	2	.3	24	4	30	5
	ST	46	11		36	8	7	2	7	2	4	1	2	.3	46	8	52	9
SCUM	W	14	.1	N	29	.2	14	.1	14	.1	**	**	**	**	67	2	11	.3
	E	**	**	S	14	.1	**	**	14	.1	**	**	**	**	11	.3	11	.3
	ST	14	.1		43	.3	14	.1	29	.2	**	**	**	**	78	3	22	1

		TENNESSEE C	TENNESSEE D		GEORGIA C	GEORGIA D	ALABAMA C	ALABAMA D	MISSISSIPPI C	MISSISSIPPI D	FLORIDA C	FLORIDA D	LOUISIANA C	LOUISIANA D	ARKANSAS C	ARKANSAS D	OKLAHOMA C	OKLAHOMA D
ANCHOR ICE	W	**	**	N	**	**	**	**	100	5	**	**	**	**	50	2	100	3
	E	**	**	S	**	**	**	**	**	**	**	**	**	**	50	2	**	**
	ST		**			**		**		5		**		**		4		3
MUSH ICE	W	14	3	N	50	2	**	**	100	5	100	14	**	**	58	16	50	6
	E	86	22	S	50	2	**	**	**	**	**	**	**	**	42	11	50	6
	ST		25			4		**		5		14		**		27		11
SHALE ICE	W	25	1	N	100	1	100	6	100	14	100	7	50	33	100	2	100	3
	E	75	2	S	**	**	**	**	**	**	**	**	50	33	**	**	**	**
	ST		3			1		6		14		7		67		2		3
SHALE					(NO RESPONSE)													
	E	100	1	S	**	**	**	**	**	**	100	7	**	**	**	**	100	6
	ST		1			**		**		**		7		**		**		6
SKIM	W	50	35	N	55	50	100	88	87	59	90	64	**	**	48	24	42	31
	E	50	35	S	45	41	**	**	13	9	10	7	100	33	52	27	58	42
	ST		70			91		88		68		71		33		51		72
SCUM	W	100	1	N	67	2	100	6	50	5	**	**	**	**	86	13	50	3
	E	**	**	S	33	1	**	**	50	5	**	**	**	**	14	2	50	3
	ST		1			3		6		9		**		**		16		6

TABLE I

THE HOME
SHELF OVER FIREPLACE

ITEM (10)
WORK SHEET (8)

		TENNESSEE			GEORGIA		ALABAMA		MISSISSIPPI		FLORIDA		LOUISIANA		ARKANSAS		OKLAHOMA	
		A	B		A	B	A	B	A	B	A	B	A	B	A	B	A	B
FIREBOARD	W	11	.4	N	11	.4	8	.3	**	**	3	.1	**	**	70	3	**	**
	E	65	2	S	3	.1	**	**	**	**	**	**	**	**	20	1	10	.3
	ST	76	3		14	1	8	.3	**	**	3	.1	**	**	90	3	10	.3
MANTEL	W	19	7	N	7	3	10	4	6	2	6	2	5	3	21	12	22	12
	E	39	14	S	3	1	3	1	2	1	4	2	5	3	22	12	26	14
	ST	59	21		10	4	13	5	8	3	10	4	9	5	42	23	48	27
MANTEL BOARD	W	8	.2	N	25	1	13	.3	4	.1	4	.1	14	1	43	2	**	**
	E	17	.4	S	17	.4	**	**	8	.2	4	.1	**	**	21	1	21	1
	ST	25	1		42	1	13	.3	13	.3	8	.2	14	1	64	3	21	1
MANTELPIECE	W	9	2	N	24	5	1	.3	4	1	13	3	18	3	13	2	8	1
	E	9	2	S	27	6	4	1	3	1	4	1	32	4	13	2	16	2
	ST	19	4		51	11	6	1	7	2	17	4	50	7	26	4	24	3
MANTEL SHELF	W	10	.2	N	**	**	**	**	**	**	20	.4	25	.3	25	.3	25	.3
	E	10	.2	S	45	1	**	**	**	**	15	.3	**	**	**	**	25	.3
	ST	20	.4		45	1	**	**	**	**	35	1	25	.3	25	.3	50	1
SHELF	W	**	**	N	**	**	**	**	**	**	**	**	**	**	**	**	100	.3
					(NO RESPONSE)													
	ST	**	**		**	**	**	**	**	**	**	**	**	**	**	**	100	.3
CLOCK SHELF					(NO RESPONSE)													
	E	**	**	S	**	**	100	.1	**	**	**	**	**	**	**	**	**	**
	ST	**	**		**	**	100	.1	**	**	**	**	**	**	**	**	**	**

ITEM (10) (CONTINUED) SHELF OVER FIREPLACE

ITEM (10)		TENNESSEE C	TENNESSEE D		GEORGIA C	GEORGIA D	ALABAMA C	ALABAMA D	MISSISSIPPI C	MISSISSIPPI D	FLORIDA C	FLORIDA D	LOUISIANA C	LOUISIANA D	ARKANSAS C	ARKANSAS D	OKLAHOMA C	OKLAHOMA D
FIREBOARD	W	14	1	N	80	2	100	5	**	**	100	1	**	**	78	7	**	**
	E	86	8	S	20	1	**	**	**	**	**	**	**	**	22	2	100	1
	ST		10			3		5		**		1		**		10		1
MANTEL	W	33	24	N	72	15	76	54	75	45	58	26	50	19	49	34	46	38
	E	67	49	S	28	6	24	17	25	15	42	18	50	19	51	35	54	44
	ST		73			21		71		60		44		39		69		82
MANTEL BOARD	W	33	1	N	60	4	100	5	33	2	50	1	100	6	67	6	**	**
	E	67	1	S	40	2	**	**	67	4	50	1	**	**	33	3	100	3
	ST		2			6		5		6		2		6		10		3
MANTELPIECE	W	50	7	N	47	31	25	5	56	19	75	33	37	19	50	5	33	3
	E	50	7	S	53	34	75	14	44	15	25	11	63	33	50	5	67	7
	ST		14			65		18		34		44		53		11		10
MANTEL SHELF	W	50	1	N	**	**	**	**	**	**	57	5	100	3	100	1	50	1
	E	50	1	S	100	5	**	**	**	**	43	4	**	**	**	**	50	1
	ST		1			5		**		**		9		3		1		2
SHELF	W	**	**	N	**	**	**	**	**	**	**	**	**	**	**	**	100	1
					(NO RESPONSE)													
	ST		**			**		**		**		**		**		**		1
CLOCK SHELF					(NO RESPONSE)													
	E	**	**	S	**	**	100	2	**	**	**	**	**	**	**	**	**	**
	ST		**			**		2		**		**		**		**		**

HOUSEHOLD EQUIPMENT
SUPPORTS FOR LOGS IN FIREPLACE

ITEM (11)
WORK SHEET (8)

		TENNESSEE			GEORGIA		ALABAMA		MISSISSIPPI		FLORIDA		LOUISIANA		ARKANSAS		OKLAHOMA	
		A	B		A	B	A	B	A	B	A	B	A	B	A	B	A	B
ANDIRONS	W	17	5	N	16	5	9	3	6	2	9	3	5	2	25	9	25	9
	E	19	6	S	14	4	4	1	2	1	5	2	6	2	23	8	18	6
	ST	36	11		29	9	12	4	8	3	14	4	11	4	47	17	42	16
DOGS	W	18	.2	N	18	.2	9	.1	**	**	9	.1	**	**	100	1	**	**
	E	45	1	S	**	**	**	**	**	**	**	**	**	**	**	**	**	**
	ST	64	1		18	.2	9	.1	**	**	9	.1	**	**	100	1	**	**
DOG IRONS	W	20	3	N	7	1	4	1	6	1	2	.3	17	3	40	7	2	.3
	E	55	9	S	4	1	**	**	1	.2	1	.1	2	.3	19	3	19	3
	ST	75	12		11	2	4	1	8	1	3	.4	19	3	60	10	21	4
FIRE DOGS	W	2	.2	N	23	2	4	.4	**	**	20	2	25	1	25	1	13	.3
	E	3	.3	S	33	3	5	1	4	.4	5	1	**	**	25	1	13	.3
	ST	5	1		55	5	10	1	4	.4	25	2	25	1	50	1	25	1
FIRE IRONS	W	**	**	N	8	.2	13	.3	4	.1	**	**	9	.3	9	.3	18	1
	E	54	1	S	13	.3	4	.1	4	.1	**	**	9	.3	27	1	27	1
	ST	54	1		21	1	17	.4	8	.2	**	**	18	1	36	1	45	2
HAND IRONS					(NO RESPONSE)													
	E	**	**	S	**	**	**	**	**	**	100	.2	**	**	**	**	**	**
	ST	**	**		**	**	**	**	**	**	100	.2	**	**	**	**	**	**
LOG IRONS	W	22	.4	N	22	.4	11	.2	6	.1	**	**	**	**	**	**	18	1
	E	33	1	S	**	**	**	**	**	**	6	.1	**	**	9	.3	73	3
	ST	56	1		22	.4	11	.2	6	.1	6	.1	**	**	9	.3	91	4

ITEM (11) (CONTINUED) SUPPORTS FOR LOGS IN FIREPLACE

ITEM		TENNESSEE C	TENNESSEE D		GEORGIA C	GEORGIA D	ALABAMA C	ALABAMA D	MISSISSIPPI C	MISSISSIPPI D	FLORIDA C	FLORIDA D	LOUISIANA C	LOUISIANA D	ARKANSAS C	ARKANSAS D	OKLAHOMA C	OKLAHOMA D
ANDIRONS	W	48	20	N	53	28	70	44	72	41	64	37	45	21	52	29	58	36
	E	52	22	S	47	25	30	19	28	16	36	21	55	25	48	26	42	26
	ST		42			53		63		57		58		46		55		61
DOGS	W	29	1	N	100	1	100	2	**	**	100	1	**	**	100	2	**	**
	E	71	2	S	**	**	**	**	**	**	**	**	**	**	**	**	**	**
	ST		3			1		2		**		1		**		2		**
DOG IRONS	W	26	12	N	65	7	100	10	83	23	75	4	89	33	68	22	10	1
	E	74	33	S	35	4	**	**	17	5	25	1	11	4	32	10	90	13
	ST		45			10		10		27		5		38		32		14
FIRE DOGS	W	40	1	N	41	13	44	7	**	**	78	25	100	8	50	2	50	1
	E	60	1	S	59	18	56	8	100	9	22	7	**	**	50	[illegible]	50	1
	ST		2			30		15		9		32		8		5		3
FIRE IRONS	W	**	**	N	40	1	75	5	50	2	**	**	50	4	25	1	40	3
	E	100	5	S	60	2	25	2	50	2	**	**	50	4	75	3	60	4
	ST		5			3		7		5		**		8		5		7
HAND IRONS (NO RESPONSE)	E	**	**	S	**	**	**	**	**	**	100	3	**	**	**	**	**	**
	ST		**			**		**		**		3		**		**		**
LOG IRONS	W	40	2	N	100	2	100	3	100	2	**	**	**	**	**	**	20	3
	E	60	2	S	**	**	**	**	**	**	100	1	**	**	100	1	80	11
	ST		4			2		3		2		1		**		1		14

TABLE I

FUEL
WOOD USED TO START A FIRE

ITEM (12)
WORK SHEET (8)

		TENNESSEE A	TENNESSEE B		GEORGIA A	GEORGIA B	ALABAMA A	ALABAMA B	MISSISSIPPI A	MISSISSIPPI B	FLORIDA A	FLORIDA B	LOUISIANA A	LOUISIANA B	ARKANSAS A	ARKANSAS B	OKLAHOMA A	OKLAHOMA B
FAT PINE	W	10	.1	N	10	.1	10	.1	**	**	20	.2	**	**	**	**	**	**
	E	**	**	S	10	.1	**	**	20	.2	20	.2	**	**	100	1	**	**
	ST	10	.1		20	.2	10	.1	20	.2	40	.4	**	**	100	1	**	**
FATWOOD	W	**	**	N	**	**	**	**	**	**	43	1	**	**	**	**	**	**
	E	**	**	S	50	1	**	**	**	**	7	.1	**	**	**	**	**	**
	ST	**	**		50	1	**	**	**	**	50	1	**	**	**	**	**	**
KINDLING WOOD	W	20	9	N	12	5	7	3	6	2	6	2	7	4	23	15	19	12
	E	34	15	S	7	3	3	1	2	1	4	2	8	5	19	12	23	14
	ST	54	24		19	8	10	4	8	3	10	4	15	9	43	27	42	27
LIGHTWOOD	W	**	**	N	28	3	1	.1	1	.1	15	2	100	1	**	**	**	**
	E	1	.1	S	39	4	6	1	2	.2	7	1	**	**	**	**	**	**
	ST	1	.1		67	7	7	1	3	.3	22	2	100	1	**	**	**	**
PINE	W	3	.1	N	13	.4	22	1	6	.2	**	**	27	1	27	1	**	**
	E	50	2	S	3	.1	**	**	3	.1	**	**	**	**	27	1	18	1
	ST	53	2		16	1	22	1	9	.3	**	**	27	1	55	2	18	1
PITCH PINE	W	100	.1	N	**	**	**	**	**	**	**	**	**	**	**	**	**	**
	E	**	**	S	**	**	**	**	**	**	**	**	**	**	100	1	**	**
	ST	100	.1		**	**	**	**	**	**	**	**	**	**	100	1	**	**

		TENNESSEE C	TENNESSEE D		GEORGIA C	GEORGIA D	ALABAMA C	ALABAMA D	MISSISSIPPI C	MISSISSIPPI D	FLORIDA C	FLORIDA D	LOUISIANA C	LOUISIANA D	ARKANSAS C	ARKANSAS D	OKLAHOMA C	OKLAHOMA D
FAT PINE	W	100	.3	N	50	1	100	2	**	**	50	3	**	**	**	**	**	**
	E	**	**	S	50	1	**	**	100	5	50	3	**	**	100	2	**	**
	ST		.3			1		2		5		5		**		2		**
FATWOOD	W	**	**	N	**	**	**	**	**	**	86	8	**	**	**	**	**	**
	E	**	**	S	100	4	**	**	**	**	14	1	**	**	**	**	**	**
	ST		**			4		**		**		9		**		**		**
KINDLING WOOD	W	37	34	N	61	30	74	54	73	59	57	32	46	39	55	48	46	45
	E	63	58	S	39	19	26	19	27	22	43	24	54	45	45	40	54	53
	ST		92			49		74		80		55		84		88		97
LIGHTWOOD	W	**	**	N	41	17	14	2	33	2	70	21	100	6	**	**	**	**
	E	100	.3	S	59	25	86	11	67	5	30	9	**	**	**	**	**	**
	ST		.3			42		12		7		30		6		**		**
PINE	W	6	.3	N	80	2	100	12	67	5	**	**	100	10	50	4	**	**
	E	94	6	S	20	1	**	**	33	2	**	**	**	**	50	4	100	3
	ST		7			3		12		7		**		10		7		3
PITCH PINE	W	100	.3	N	**	**	**	**	**	**	**	**	**	**	**	**	**	**
	[illegible]	[illegible]	[illegible]	S	**	**	**	**	**	**	**	**	**	**	100	2	**	**
	[illegible]		[illegible]			[illegible]		[illegible]		[illegible]		[illegible]		[illegible]		[illegible]		**

ITEM (13)
WORK SHEET (8)

FUEL
LARGE LOG AT BACK OF FIRE

		TENNESSEE A	TENNESSEE B		GEORGIA A	GEORGIA B	ALABAMA A	ALABAMA B	MISSISSIPPI A	MISSISSIPPI B	FLORIDA A	FLORIDA B	LOUISIANA A	LOUISIANA B	ARKANSAS A	ARKANSAS B	OKLAHOMA A	OKLAHOMA B
BACK CHUNK	W	15	.2	N	23	.3	8	.1	8	.1	8	.1	**	**	**	**	25	.3
	E	15	.2	S	23	.3	**	**	**	**	**	**	25	.3	**	**	50	1
	ST	31	.4		46	1	8	.1	8	.1	8	.1	25	.3	**	**	75	1
BACKLOG	W	21	13	N	14	8	6	4	5	3	10	6	8	5	31	19	14	9
	E	23	14	S	13	8	2	1	2	1	5	3	5	3	26	17	16	10
	ST	44	27		27	16	8	5	7	4	15	9	13	8	57	36	30	19
BACK STICK	W	16	4	N	29	7	8	2	3	1	1	.2	6	1	52	6	**	**
	E	39	9	S	3	1	**	**	2	.4	**	**	**	**	35	4	6	1
	ST	54	12		32	7	8	2	5	1	1	.2	6	1	87	10	6	1

		TENNESSEE C	TENNESSEE D		GEORGIA C	GEORGIA D	ALABAMA C	ALABAMA D	MISSISSIPPI C	MISSISSIPPI D	FLORIDA C	FLORIDA D	LOUISIANA C	LOUISIANA D	ARKANSAS C	ARKANSAS D	OKLAHOMA C	OKLAHOMA D
BACK CHUNK	W	50	1	N	50	1	100	2	100	2	100	1	**	**	**	**	33	2
	E	50	1	S	50	1	**	**	**	**	**	**	100	4	**	**	67	3
	ST		1			3		2		2		1		4		**		5
BACKLOG	W	48	33	N	53	35	79	56	68	52	66	64	61	54	54	43	47	43
	E	52	35	S	47	32	21	15	33	25	34	33	39	35	46	36	53	48
	ST		67			67		71		77		97		88		79		91
BACK STICK	W	29	9	N	92	28	100	27	64	13	100	2	100	8	59	13	**	**
	E	71	22	S	8	3	**	**	36	8	**	**	**	**	41	9	100	3
	ST		32			30		27		21		2		8		21		3

HOUSEHOLD EQUIPMENT
WINDOW COVERING ON ROLLERS

ITEM (14)
WORK SHEET (9)

		TENNESSEE A	TENNESSEE B		GEORGIA A	GEORGIA B	ALABAMA A	ALABAMA B	MISSISSIPPI A	MISSISSIPPI B	FLORIDA A	FLORIDA B	LOUISIANA A	LOUISIANA B	ARKANSAS A	ARKANSAS B	OKLAHOMA A	OKLAHOMA B
BLINDS	W	25	2	N	15	1	11	1	6	.4	4	.3	5	1	27	4	27	4
	E	28	2	S	6	.4	1	.1	1	.1	1	.1	3	.3	16	2	22	3
	ST	54	4		21	2	13	1	7	1	6	.4	8	1	43	6	49	6
CURTAINS	W	28	1	N	11	1	9	.4	7	.3	11	1	**	**	18	1	18	1
	E	20	1	S	7	.3	2	.1	2	.1	4	.2	9	.3	**	**	55	2
	ST	48	2		17	1	11	1	9	.4	15	1	9	.3	18	1	73	3
ROLLER SHADES	W	19	.4	N	10	.2	5	.1	**	**	5	.1	20	.3	20	.3	20	.3
	E	24	1	S	14	.3	5	.1	10	.2	10	.2	**	**	20	.3	20	.3
	ST	43	1		24	1	10	.2	10	.2	14	.3	20	.3	40	1	40	1
SHADES	W	18	6	N	16	5	10	3	4	1	7	2	5	1	16	4	18	4
	E	26	9	S	11	4	3	1	2	1	4	1	8	2	26	6	27	6
	ST	44	15		27	9	13	4	7	2	10	4	13	3	42	9	45	10
WINDOW BLINDS	W	28	1	N	13	1	10	.4	**	**	10	.4	4	.3	56	5	20	2
	E	18	1	S	15	1	3	.1	**	**	3	.1	**	**	4	.3	16	1
	ST	46	2		28	1	13	1	**	**	13	1	4	.3	60	5	36	3
WINDOW SHADES	W	21	11	N	21	11	5	2	4	2	8	4	8	4	29	15	12	6
	E	23	12	S	11	6	2	1	3	2	4	2	8	4	23	12	21	11
	ST	43	23		32	17	7	4	6	3	12	6	16	9	51	27	32	17

		TENNESSEE C	TENNESSEE D		GEORGIA C	GEORGIA D	ALABAMA C	ALABAMA D	MISSISSIPPI C	MISSISSIPPI D	FLORIDA C	FLORIDA D	LOUISIANA C	LOUISIANA D	ARKANSAS C	ARKANSAS D	OKLAHOMA C	OKLAHOMA D
BLINDS	W	47	4	N	73	4	89	8	80	6	75	3	67	5	63	7	56	9
	E	53	4	S	27	1	11	1	20	2	25	1	33	3	38	4	44	7
	ST		8			5		9		8		3		8		12		16
CURTAINS	W	59	3	N	63	2	80	4	75	5	71	4	**	**	100	1	25	2
	E	41	2	S	38	1	20	1	25	2	29	2	100	3	**	**	75	5
	ST		5			3		5		6		6		3		1		7
ROLLER SHADES	W	44	1	N	40	1	50	1	**	**	33	1	100	3	50	1	50	1
	E	56	1	S	60	1	50	1	100	3	67	2	**	**	50	1	50	1
	ST		2			2		2		3		3		3		1		2
SHADES	W	41	13	N	58	18	79	34	64	21	66	20	38	8	38	7	39	10
	E	59	19	S	42	13	21	9	36	12	34	10	63	13	62	12	61	15
	ST		32			31		43		33		30		21		19		25
WINDOW BLINDS	W	61	2	N	45	2	80	4	**	**	80	3	100	3	93	10	56	4
	E	39	2	S	55	2	20	1	**	**	20	1	**	**	7	1	44	4
	ST		4			4		5		**		4		3		11		8
WINDOW SHADES	W	47	23	N	65	36	68	24	55	27	66	35	50	32	56	31	36	15
	E	53	26	S	35	19	32	11	45	23	34	18	50	32	44	24	64	27
	ST		[illegible]			[illegible]		[illegible]		[illegible]		[illegible]		[illegible]		55		42

ITEM (15)
WORK SHEET (11)

THE HOME
OVERLAPPING HORIZONTAL BOARDS ON OUTSIDE OF HOUSE

		TENNESSEE A	TENNESSEE B		GEORGIA A	GEORGIA B	ALABAMA A	ALABAMA B	MISSISSIPPI A	MISSISSIPPI B	FLORIDA A	FLORIDA B	LOUISIANA A	LOUISIANA B	ARKANSAS A	ARKANSAS B	OKLAHOMA A	OKLAHOMA B
CLAPBOARDS	W	36	3	N	10	1	3	.3	10	1	9	1	**	**	34	4	7	1
	E	13	1	S	5	1	5	1	3	.3	4	.4	3	.3	41	4	14	1
	ST	49	5		15	1	9	1	13	1	13	1	3	.3	76	8	21	2
SIDING	W	14	2	N	10	2	5	1	3	.4	16	3	10	4	23	9	24	10
	E	22	4	S	11	2	3	1	3	1	13	2	4	2	17	7	23	9
	ST	36	6		22	4	8	1	6	1	29	5	14	6	39	16	47	19
WEATHERBOARDS	W	22	5	N	17	4	9	2	5	1	6	1	6	1	29	5	4	1
	E	25	5	S	10	2	2	1	2	1	2	.4	21	4	23	4	17	3
	ST	47	10		27	6	11	2	7	2	8	2	27	5	52	9	21	4
WEATHERBOARDING	W	19	9	N	23	11	6	3	3	1	5	2	4	1	48	10	5	1
	E	27	13	S	13	6	1	.4	2	1	1	1	3	1	27	6	13	3
	ST	46	23		36	18	7	4	5	2	6	3	7	1	75	16	18	4

		TENNESSEE C	TENNESSEE D		GEORGIA C	GEORGIA D	ALABAMA C	ALABAMA D	MISSISSIPPI C	MISSISSIPPI D	FLORIDA C	FLORIDA D	LOUISIANA C	LOUISIANA D	ARKANSAS C	ARKANSAS D	OKLAHOMA C	OKLAHOMA D
CLAPBOARDS	W	73	8	N	64	3	38	4	75	16	67	8	**	**	45	7	33	2
	E	27	3	S	36	2	63	6	25	5	33	4	100	3	55	9	67	5
	ST		11			5		10		21		12		3		16		7
SIDING	W	39	5	N	47	6	62	10	44	7	56	24	69	32	58	19	52	35
	E	61	8	S	53	7	38	6	56	9	44	19	31	15	42	14	48	32
	ST		13			12		16		16		43		47		33		67
WEATHERBOARDS	W	47	11	N	61	13	79	24	67	17	75	12	23	9	56	10	20	2
	E	53	13	S	39	8	21	6	33	9	25	4	77	29	44	8	80	10
	ST		24			21		30		26		15		38		10		12
WEATHERBOARDING	W	41	21	N	65	40	89	39	64	24	77	23	50	6	64	21	27	4
	E	59	31	S	35	22	11	5	36	14	23	7	50	6	36	12	73	10
	ST		52			62		44		38		30		12		33		14

TABLE I

THE HOME
DEVICES AT EDGES OF ROOF TO CARRY OFF RAIN

ITEM (16)
WORK SHEET (11)

		TENNESSEE			GEORGIA		ALABAMA		MISSISSIPPI		FLORIDA		LOUISIANA		ARKANSAS		OKLAHOMA	
		A	B		A	B	A	B	A	B	A	B	A	B	A	B	A	B
EAVES	W	15	3	N	21	4	7	1	4	1	12	2	13	3	18	4	24	5
	E	11	2	S	20	4	4	1	4	1	3	1	4	1	24	5	18	4
	ST	25	5		41	8	11	2	8	2	15	3	16	3	42	8	42	8
EAVES SPOUTS	W	29	.2	N	43	.3	**	**	**	**	**	**	**	**	25	.3	**	**
	E	29	.2	S	**	**	**	**	**	**	**	**	**	**	50	1	25	.3
	ST	57	.4		43	.3	**	**	**	**	**	**	**	**	75	1	25	.3
EAVES TROUGHS	W	4	.1	N	22	1	**	**	**	**	11	.3	9	1	43	4	17	1
	E	37	1	S	11	.3	4	.1	**	**	11	.3	**	**	9	1	22	2
	ST	41	1		33	1	4	.1	**	**	22	1	9	1	52	4	39	3
GUTTERS	W	20	14	N	17	11	7	5	4	3	6	4	7	4	26	15	15	9
	E	28	19	S	9	6	2	2	2	2	4	3	11	6	25	14	16	9
	ST	49	33		25	17	9	6	7	4	10	7	18	10	52	30	31	18
RAIN TROUGHS	W	24	1	N	17	1	14	.4	**	**	7	.2	6	.3	47	3	12	1
	E	21	1	S	3	.1	7	.2	7	.2	**	**	**	**	**	**	35	2
	ST	45	1		21	1	21	1	7	.2	7	.2	6	.3	47	3	47	3
SPOUTING	W	50	.1	N	**	**	**	**	**	**	**	**	**	**	**	**	**	**
	E	50	.1	S	**	**	**	**	**	**	**	**	**	**	**	**	**	**
	ST	100	.2		**	**	**	**	**	**	**	**	**	**	**	**	**	**
SPOUTS	W	14	.1	N	**	**	14	.1	14	.1	**	**	**	**	33	1	**	**
	E	14	.1	S	14	.1	**	**	29	.2	**	**	17	.3	33	1	17	.3
	ST	29	.2		14	.1	14	.1	43	.3	**	**	17	.3	67	1	17	.3
WATER GUTTER	W	23	1	N	12	1	8	.4	2	.1	8	.4	6	.3	31	2	6	.3
	E	17	1	S	29	2	**	**	2	.1	**	**	6	.3	38	2	13	1
	ST	40	2		40	2	8	.4	4	.2	8	.4	13	1	69	4	19	1

ITEM (16) (CONTINUED) DEVICES AT EDGES OF ROOF TO CARRY OFF RAIN

		TENNESSEE C	TENNESSEE D		GEORGIA C	GEORGIA D	ALABAMA C	ALABAMA D	MISSISSIPPI C	MISSISSIPPI D	FLORIDA C	FLORIDA D	LOUISIANA C	LOUISIANA D	ARKANSAS C	ARKANSAS D	OKLAHOMA C	OKLAHOMA D
EAVES	W	57	6	N	51	14	65	14	53	12	79	21	78	16	43	7	57	14
	E	43	5	S	49	13	35	8	47	11	21	6	22	5	57	9	43	11
	ST		11			27		22		23		26		21		16		24
EAVES SPOUTS	W	50	.4	N	100	1	**	**	**	**	**	**	**	**	33	1	**	**
	E	50	.4	S	**	**	**	**	**	**	**	**	**	**	67	1	100	1
	ST		1			1		**		**		**		**		2		1
EAVES TROUGHS	W	9	.2	N	67	2	**	**	**	**	50	3	100	5	83	7	44	4
	E	91	2	S	33	1	100	1	**	**	50	3	**	**	17	1	56	5
	ST		3			3		1		**		6		5		8		10
GUTTERS	W	42	32	N	66	39	75	49	63	42	62	39	39	26	51	29	49	26
	E	58	44	S	34	20	25	16	37	25	38	24	61	40	49	28	51	27
	ST		76			59		66		66		62		65		57		52
RAIN TROUGHS	W	54	2	N	83	2	67	4	**	**	100	2	100	2	100	6	25	2
	E	46	1	S	17	.3	33	2	100	3	**	**	**	**	**	**	75	6
	ST		3			2		6		3		2		2		6		9
SPOUTING	W	50	.2	N	**	**	**	**	**	**	**	**	**	**	**	**	**	**
	E	50	.2	S	**	**	**	**	**	**	**	**	**	**	**	**	**	**
	ST		.4			**		**		**		**		**		**		**
SPOUTS	W	50	.2	N	**	**	100	1	33	2	**	**	**	**	50	1	**	**
	E	50	.2	S	100	.3	**	**	67	3	**	**	100	2	50	1	100	1
	ST		.4			.3		1		5		**		2		3		1
WATER GUTTER	W	57	3	N	29	2	100	4	50	2	100	4	50	2	45	3	33	1
	E	43	2	S	71	5	**	**	50	2	**	**	50	2	55	4	67	2
	ST		5			7		4		3		4		5		8		3

TABLE I

OTHER BUILDINGS
A SEPARATE BUILDING FOR KEEPING VARIOUS THINGS

ITEM (17)
WORK SHEET (10)

		TENNESSEE A	TENNESSEE B		GEORGIA A	GEORGIA B	ALABAMA A	ALABAMA B	MISSISSIPPI A	MISSISSIPPI B	FLORIDA A	FLORIDA B	LOUISIANA A	LOUISIANA B	ARKANSAS A	ARKANSAS B	OKLAHOMA A	OKLAHOMA B
SHED	W	26	5	N	13	2	5	1	7	1	8	2	5	1	21	4	16	3
	E	19	4	S	10	2	3	1	4	1	4	1	21	4	16	3	21	4
	ST	45	9		23	4	8	2	10	2	13	2	26	5	37	8	37	8
SMOKEHOUSE	W	16	6	N	23	8	7	2	3	1	6	2	6	1	46	11	14	3
	E	28	10	S	13	5	2	1	2	1	1	.3	**	**	20	5	14	3
	ST	44	16		36	13	9	3	5	2	7	2	6	1	66	16	28	6
STOREROOM(A)	W	23	5	N	17	3	7	1	2	.4	14	3	8	3	24	7	10	3
	E	16	3	S	13	3	3	1	3	1	4	1	4	1	31	9	24	7
	ST	38	8		30	6	10	2	5	1	18	4	12	4	55	17	33	10
TOOL HOUSE(A)	W	15	2	N	22	3	9	1	8	1	10	1	17	1	17	1	22	2
	E	17	2	S	10	1	5	1	3	.3	3	.3	4	.3	22	2	17	1
	ST	31	4		32	4	14	2	10	1	12	1	22	2	39	3	39	3
TOOL SHED(A)	W	21	3	N	19	3	5	1	3	.4	3	.4	7	1	28	4	19	3
	E	28	4	S	11	2	1	.2	4	1	5	1	14	2	21	3	12	2
	ST	49	7		30	4	7	1	7	1	8	1	21	3	49	8	30	5
WOOD HOUSE(A)	W	30	2	N	28	2	4	.3	2	.2	6	1	**	**	33	.3	**	**
	E	21	2	S	6	1	1	.1	1	.1	**	**	**	**	67	1	**	**
	ST	51	4		35	3	5	.4	4	.3	6	1	**	**	100	1	**	**
WOOD SHED(A)	W	15	2	N	22	3	4	1	5	1	5	1	9	1	27	2	9	1
	E	36	5	S	6	1	1	.1	4	1	3	.4	9	1	27	2	18	1
	ST	51	7		28	4	5	1	8	1	8	1	18	1	55	4	27	2

ITEM (17) (CONTINUED) A SEPARATE BUILDING FOR KEEPING VARIOUS THINGS

ITEM (17)		TENNESSEE C	TENNESSEE D		GEORGIA C	GEORGIA D	ALABAMA C	ALABAMA D	MISSISSIPPI C	MISSISSIPPI D	FLORIDA C	FLORIDA D	LOUISIANA C	LOUISIANA D	ARKANSAS C	ARKANSAS D	OKLAHOMA C	OKLAHOMA D
SHED	W	58	9	N	56	6	67	10	63	15	65	12	20	6	57	8	43	9
	E	42	7	S	44	5	33	5	37	9	35	7	80	26	43	6	57	13
	ST		16			12		15		23		19		32		14		22
SMOKEHOUSE	W	36	10	N	63	21	80	24	56	11	87	16	100	9	70	19	50	9
	E	64	18	S	37	12	20	6	44	9	13	2	**	**	30	8	50	9
	ST		29			34		30		20		19		9		28		19
STOREROOM(A)	W	59	9	N	56	9	68	13	40	5	78	23	70	15	43	13	29	8
	E	41	6	S	44	7	32	6	60	7	22	7	30	6	57	17	71	21
	ST		14			16		19		12		29		21		30		29
TOOL HOUSE(A)	W	47	3	N	68	7	63	10	75	11	79	9	80	9	44	3	56	5
	E	53	4	S	32	3	38	6	25	4	21	2	20	2	56	3	44	4
	ST		7			10		16		15		11		11		6		9
TOOL SHED(A)	W	42	5	N	63	7	78	7	44	5	36	3	33	6	57	8	62	8
	E	58	7	S	38	4	22	2	56	6	64	6	67	13	43	6	38	5
	ST		13			11		9		11		9		19		14		14
WOOD HOUSE(A)	W	59	5	N	82	6	75	3	67	2	100	4	**	**	33	1	**	**
	E	41	3	S	18	1	25	1	33	1	**	**	**	**	67	1	**	**
	ST		8			8		4		4		4		**		2		**
WOOD SHED(A)	W	29	4	N	78	8	86	6	58	9	64	6	50	4	50	4	33	2
	E	71	10	S	23	2	14	1	42	6	36	3	50	4	50	4	67	4
	ST		14			11		7		15		9		9		8		6

OTHER BUILDINGS
SUCH A BUILDING BUILT ONTO A HOUSE

ITEM (17)
WORK SHEET (10)

		TENNESSEE A	TENNESSEE B		GEORGIA A	GEORGIA B	ALABAMA A	ALABAMA B	MISSISSIPPI A	MISSISSIPPI B	FLORIDA A	FLORIDA B	LOUISIANA A	LOUISIANA B	ARKANSAS A	ARKANSAS B	OKLAHOMA A	OKLAHOMA B
LEAN-TO SHED	W	27	4	N	12	2	6	1	2	.3	10	1	3	1	33	7	18	4
	E	30	4	S	5	1	1	.1	2	.2	6	1	3	1	22	5	20	4
	ST	57	7		17	2	6	1	4	1	16	2	7	1	55	12	38	8
STOREROOM(B)	W	20	8	N	16	7	9	4	5	2	6	2	7	3	26	11	16	7
	E	21	8	S	14	5	3	1	3	1	2	1	9	4	24	10	18	8
	ST	41	16		30	12	12	5	8	3	9	3	16	7	50	21	34	14
TOOL HOUSE(B)	W	19	1	N	17	1	11	.4	6	.2	8	.3	**	**	20	.3	20	.3
	E	25	1	S	8	.3	3	.1	**	**	3	.1	**	**	40	1	20	.3
	ST	44	2		25	1	14	1	6	.2	11	.4	**	**	60	1	40	1
TOOL SHED(B)	W	15	1	N	23	1	2	.1	3	.2	8	1	7	.3	14	1	7	.3
	E	33	2	S	11	1	**	**	2	.1	3	.2	14	1	36	2	21	1
	ST	48	3		34	2	2	.1	5	.3	11	1	21	1	50	3	29	1
WOOD HOUSE(B)	W	32	1	N	18	.4	**	**	5	.1	5	.1	**	**	**	**	**	**
	E	14	.3	S	18	.4	**	**	5	.1	5	.1	**	**	**	**	**	**
	ST	45	1		36	1	**	**	9	.2	9	.2	**	**	**	**	**	**
WOOD SHED(B)	W	18	2	N	27	3	6	1	1	.1	4	.4	7	.3	47	3	**	**
	E	24	3	S	15	2	1	.1	4	.4	2	.2	**	**	33	2	13	1
	ST	42	5		42	5	7	1	4	1	5	1	7	.3	80	4	13	1

		TENNESSEE C	TENNESSEE D		GEORGIA C	GEORGIA D	ALABAMA C	ALABAMA D	MISSISSIPPI C	MISSISSIPPI D	FLORIDA C	FLORIDA D	LOUISIANA C	LOUISIANA D	ARKANSAS C	ARKANSAS D	OKLAHOMA C	OKLAHOMA D
LEAN-TO SHED	W	47	10	N	71	7	88	10	60	6	65	18	50	7	61	18	48	15
	E	53	12	S	29	3	13	1	40	4	35	10	50	7	39	11	52	17
	ST		22			10		12		10		28		15		29		32
STOREROOM(B)	W	48	23	N	55	29	77	52	68	44	73	33	42	30	53	27	48	27
	E	52	25	S	45	24	23	16	32	21	27	13	58	41	47	25	53	30
	ST		47			52		68		65		46		70		52		56
TOOL HOUSE(B)	W	44	2	N	67	3	80	6	100	4	75	4	**	**	33	1	50	1
	E	56	3	S	33	1	20	1	**	**	25	1	**	**	67	2	50	1
	ST		5			4		7		4		6		**		3		3
TOOL SHED(B)	W	31	3	N	67	6	100	1	67	4	71	7	33	4	29	2	25	1
	E	69	6	S	33	3	**	**	33	2	29	3	67	7	71	4	75	4
	ST		9			10		1		6		10		11		6		6
WOOD HOUSE(B)	W	70	2	N	50	2	**	**	50	2	50	1	**	**	**	**	**	**
	E	30	1	S	50	2	**	**	50	2	50	1	**	**	**	**	**	**
	ST		3			4		**		4		3		**		**		**
WOOD SHED(B)	W	43	6	N	64	14	88	10	20	2	67	6	100	4	58	6	**	**
	E	57	8	S	36	8	13	1	80	8	33	3	**	**	42	4	100	3
	ST		[illegible]			21		12		10		8		4		11		3

OTHER BUILDINGS
UPPER PART OF BARN, USED FOR STORING HAY

ITEM (18)
WORK SHEET (14)

		TENNESSEE A	TENNESSEE B		GEORGIA A	GEORGIA B	ALABAMA A	ALABAMA B	MISSISSIPPI A	MISSISSIPPI B	FLORIDA A	FLORIDA B	LOUISIANA A	LOUISIANA B	ARKANSAS A	ARKANSAS B	OKLAHOMA A	OKLAHOMA B
BARN CHAMBER					(NO RESPONSE)													
	E	20	.1	S	80	.4	**	**	**	**	**	**	**	**	**	**	100	.3
	ST	20	.1		80	.4	**	**	**	**	**	**	**	**	**	**	100	.3
BARN LOFT	W	16	6	N	26	10	6	2	3	1	1	.4	3	1	43	10	12	3
	E	40	15	S	4	2	1	1	1	.4	1	.4	**	**	21	5	21	5
	ST	56	21		30	11	8	3	4	2	2	1	3	1	64	16	33	8
HAY LOFT	W	24	9	N	14	6	6	3	4	2	11	4	5	3	29	17	17	10
	E	16	7	S	14	5	3	1	4	2	3	1	8	4	22	12	19	11
	ST	40	16		28	11	10	4	8	3	14	6	13	7	61	29	36	21
HAY MOW	W	25	.2	N	25	.2	**	**	**	**	**	**	13	.3	25	1	63	2
	E	[illegible]	.1	S	13	.1	13	.1	**	**	13	.1	**	**	**	**	**	**
	ST	38	.3		30	.3	13	.1	**	**	13	.1	13	.3	25	1	63	2
LOFT	W	19	5	N	16	4	8	2	4	1	8	2	17	4	16	3	14	3
	E	20	5	S	16	4	2	.4	2	1	5	1	12	3	22	5	19	4
	ST	39	10		32	8	10	3	6	1	13	3	29	6	38	8	33	7
MOW	W	**	**	N	17	.1	**	**	17	.1	17	.1	**	**	**	**	**	**
	E	33	.2	S	17	.1	**	**	**	**	**	**	**	**	**	**	**	**
	ST	33	.2		33	.2	**	**	17	.1	17	.1	**	**	**	**	**	**
OVERHEAD	W	20	.1	N	20	.1	20	.1	**	**	**	**	**	**	**	**	**	**
	E	20	.1	S	20	.1	**	**	**	**	**	**	**	**	**	**	100	.3
	ST	40	.2		40	.2	20	.1	**	**	**	**	**	**	**	**	100	.3
OVERDEN					(NO RESPONSE)													
					(NO RESPONSE)													
					(NO RESPONSE)													
SCAFFOLD	W	50	.1	N	**	**	**	**	**	**	**	**	**	**	**	**	**	**
	E	**	**	S	50	.1	**	**	**	**	**	**	**	**	**	**	**	**
	ST	50	.1		50	.1	**	**	**	**	**	**	**	**	**	**	**	**

TABLE I

(CONTINUED) UPPER PART OF BARN, USED FOR STORING HAY

ITEM (18)		TENNESSEE C	TENNESSEE D		GEORGIA C	GEORGIA D	ALABAMA C	ALABAMA D	MISSISSIPPI C	MISSISSIPPI D	FLORIDA C	FLORIDA D	LOUISIANA C	LOUISIANA D	ARKANSAS C	ARKANSAS D	OKLAHOMA C	OKLAHOMA D
BARN CHAMBER					(NO RESPONSE)		**	**	**	**	**	**	**	**	**	**	100	1
	E	100	.2	S	100	1		**		**		**		**		**		1
	ST		.2			1												
BARN LOFT	W	28	12	N	86	30	82	25	73	18	50	4	100	5	67	20	36	8
	E	72	31	S	14	5	18	5	27	7	50	4	**	**	33	10	64	13
	ST		43			35		30		25		8		5		29		21
HAY LOFT	W	59	20	N	50	18	66	27	52	26	78	44	40	20	58	31	47	26
	E	41	14	S	50	17	34	14	48	25	22	13	60	30	43	23	53	29
	ST		33			35		41		51		56		50		54		54
HAY MOW	W	67	.4	N	67	1	**	**	**	**	**	**	100	3	100	1	100	5
	E	33	.2	S	33	.3	100	1	**	**	100	1	**	**	**	**	**	**
	ST		1			1		1		**		1		3		1		5
LOFT	W	48	10	N	49	13	84	23	64	15	59	20	59	25	41	6	42	8
	E	52	11	S	51	13	16	4	36	8	41	14	41	18	59	9	58	10
	ST		21			26		27		23		33		43		15		18
MOW	W	**	**	N	50	.3	**	**	100	2	100	1	**	**	**	**	**	**
	E	100	.4	S	50	.3	**	**	**	**	**	**	**	**	**	**	**	**
	ST		.4			1		**		2		1		**		**		**
OVERHEAD	W	50	.2	N	50	.3	100	1	**	**	**	**	**	**	**	**	**	**
	E	50	.2	S	50	.3	**	**	**	**	**	**	**	**	**	**	100	1
	ST		.4			1		1		**		**		**		**		1
OVERDEN					(NO RESPONSE)													
					(NO RESPONSE)													
	ST		**			**		**		**		**		**		**		**
SCAFFOLD	W	100	.2	N	**	**	**	**	**	**	**	**	**	**	**	**	**	**
	E	**	**	S	100	.3	**	**	**	**	**	**	**	**	**	**	**	**
	ST		.2			.3		**		**		**		**		**		**

ITEM (19)
WORK SHEET (14)

CROPS
LARGE PILE OF HAY OUTSIDE

		TENNESSEE A	TENNESSEE B		GEORGIA A	GEORGIA B	ALABAMA A	ALABAMA B	MISSISSIPPI A	MISSISSIPPI B	FLORIDA A	FLORIDA B	LOUISIANA A	LOUISIANA B	ARKANSAS A	ARKANSAS B	OKLAHOMA A	OKLAHOMA B
BARRACK	W	33	.1	N	**	**	33	.1	**	**	**	**	**	**	**	**	**	**
	E	33	.1	S	**	**	**	**	**	**	**	**	**	**	**	**	100	.3
	ST	67	.2		**	**	33	.1	**	**	**	**	**	**	**	**	100	.3
DUTCH CAP					(NO RESPONSE)													
					(NO RESPONSE)													
					(NO RESPONSE)													
HAY CAP	W	**	**	N	25	.1	**	**	**	**	**	**	**	**	**	**	**	**
	E	25	.1	S	25	.1	**	**	**	**	25	.1	**	**	**	**	**	**
	ST	25	.1		50	.2	**	**	**	**	25	.1	**	**	**	**	**	**
HAY RICK	W	23	1	N	10	.3	13	.4	3	.1	**	**	**	**	80	1	**	**
	E	43	1	S	7	.2	**	**	**	**	**	**	**	**	20	.3	**	**
	ST	67	2		17	1	13	.4	3	.1	**	**	**	**	100	2	**	**
HAYSTACK	W	18	16	N	20	17	7	6	4	4	7	6	6	5	28	24	15	13
	E	25	22	S	12	10	2	2	2	2	3	3	8	6	23	19	19	16
	ST	43	38		31	28	9	8	6	6	11	9	14	12	51	43	35	29
RICK(A)	W	39	1	N	6	.1	6	.1	6	.1	6	.1	**	**	80	1	**	**
	E	28	1	S	11	.2	**	**	**	**	**	**	**	**	**	**	20	.3
	ST	67	1		17	.3	6	.1	6	.1	6	.1	**	**	80	1	20	.3

		TENNESSEE C	TENNESSEE D		GEORGIA C	GEORGIA D	ALABAMA C	ALABAMA D	MISSISSIPPI C	MISSISSIPPI D	FLORIDA C	FLORIDA D	LOUISIANA C	LOUISIANA D	ARKANSAS C	ARKANSAS D	OKLAHOMA C	OKLAHOMA D
BARRACK	W	50	.2	N	**	**	100	1	**	**	**	**	**	**	**	**	**	**
	E	50	.2	S	**	**	**	**	**	**	**	**	**	**	**	**	100	1
	ST		.4			**		1		**		**		**		**		1
DUTCH CAP					(NO RESPONSE)													
					(NO RESPONSE)													
	ST		**			**		**		**		**		**		**		**
HAY CAP	W	**	**	N	50	.3	**	**	**	**	**	**	**	**	**	**	**	**
	E	100	.2	S	50	.3	**	**	**	**	100	1	**	**	**	**	**	**
	ST		.2			1		**		**		1		**		**		**
HAY RICK	W	35	2	N	60	1	100	5	100	2	**	**	**	**	80	3	**	**
	E	65	3	S	40	1	**	**	**	**	**	**	**	**	20	1	**	**
	ST		5			2		5		2		**		**		4		**
HAYSTACK	W	43	39	N	63	61	74	68	64	61	67	66	45	45	55	51	44	43
	E	57	52	S	37	36	26	24	36	35	33	32	55	55	45	42	56	54
	ST		91			96		93		96		98		100		93		98
RICK(A)	W	58	2	N	33	.3	100	1	100	2	100	1	**	**	100	3	**	**
	E	42	1	S	67	1	**	**	**	**	**	**	**	**	**	**	100	1
	ST		3			1		1		2		1		**		3		1

TABLE I

CROPS SMALL PILE OF HAY IN THE FIELDS

ITEM (20)
WORK SHEET (14)

		TENNESSEE A	TENNESSEE B		GEORGIA A	GEORGIA B	ALABAMA A	ALABAMA B	MISSISSIPPI A	MISSISSIPPI B	FLORIDA A	FLORIDA B	LOUISIANA A	LOUISIANA B	ARKANSAS A	ARKANSAS B	OKLAHOMA A	OKLAHOMA B
COCKS	W	35	1	N	45	1	5	.1	**	**	**	**	**	**	100	1	**	**
	E	10	.2	S	5	.1	**	**	**	**	**	**	**	**	**	**	**	**
	ST	45	1		50	1	5	.1	**	**	**	**	**	**	100	1	**	**
DOODLES	W	100	.1	N	**	**	**	**	**	**	**	**	**	**	**	**	**	**
					(NO RESPONSE)													
	ST	100	.1		**	**	**	**	**	**	**	**	**	**	**	**	**	**
HAND STACKS	W	8	.3	N	31	1	8	.3	6	.2	14	1	25	.3	50	1	**	**
	E	6	.2	S	22	1	3	.1	**	**	3	.1	**	**	**	**	25	.3
	ST	14	1		53	2	11	.4	6	.2	17	1	25	.3	50	1	25	.3
HAYCOCKS	W	26	1	N	26	1	5	.1	**	**	5	.1	40	1	40	1	20	.3
	E	26	1	S	11	.2	**	**	**	**	**	**	**	**	**	**	**	**
	ST	53	1		37	1	5	.1	**	**	5	.1	40	1	40	1	20	.3
HAY DOODLES					(NO RESPONSE)													
					(NO RESPONSE)													
					(NO RESPONSE)													
HAY SHOCKS	W	17	4	N	19	5	6	2	4	1	4	1	7	1	41	9	14	3
	E	37	10	S	8	2	1	.2	2	.4	2	1	2	.3	24	5	14	3
	ST	54	14		27	7	7	2	6	1	6	2	8	2	64	14	27	6
HAY TUMBLES	W	**	**	N	**	**	33	.1	**	**	**	**	**	**	100	.3	**	**
	E	33	.1	S	33	.1	**	**	**	**	**	**	**	**	**	**	**	**
	ST	33	.1		33	.1	33	.1	**	**	**	**	**	**	100	.3	**	**
HEAPS	W	8	.3	N	42	2	3	.1	6	.2	14	1	14	.3	14	.3	**	**
	E	11	.4	S	8	.3	**	**	3	.1	6	.2	14	.3	43	1	14	.3
	ST	19	1		50	2	3	.1	8	.3	19	1	29	1	57	1	14	.3
MOWS	W	13	.1	N	38	.3	38	.3	**	**	**	**	**	**	33	.3	33	.3
	E	**	**	S	**	**	**	**	13	.1	**	**	33	.3	**	**	**	**
	ST	13	.1		38	.3	38	.3	13	.1	**	**	33	.3	33	.3	33	.3
PILES	W	17	3	N	23	4	7	1	4	1	12	2	7	1	21	3	10	1
	E	8	1	S	22	4	3	1	2	.4	4	1	12	2	24	4	26	4
	ST	24	5		45	8	9	2	6	1	15	3	19	3	45	7	36	5
RICKS(B)	W	32	1	N	14	.4	7	.2	7	.2	4	.1	10	.3	30	1	30	1
	E	32	1	S	4	.1	**	**	**	**	**	**	**	**	10	.3	20	1
	ST	64	2		18	1	7	.2	7	.2	4	.1	10	.3	40	1	50	2
SHOCKS(A)	W	27	7	N	16	4	7	2	3	1	2	.4	2	1	36	11	21	6
	E	33	9	S	7	2	2	1	2	1	1	.3	1	.3	21	6	18	5
	ST	60	15		23	6	9	2	5	1	3	1	4	1	57	17	39	12
TUMBLES	W	25	.1	N	**	**	**	**	**	**	**	**	**	**	100	.3	**	**
	E	50	.2	S	25	.1	**	**	**	**	**	**	**	**	**	**	**	**
	ST	75	.3		25	.1	**	**	**	**	**	**	**	**	100	.3	**	**

(CONTINUED) SMALL PILE OF HAY IN THE FIELDS

ITEM (20)		TENNESSEE C	TENNESSEE D		GEORGIA C	GEORGIA D	ALABAMA C	ALABAMA D	MISSISSIPPI C	MISSISSIPPI D	FLORIDA C	FLORIDA D	LOUISIANA C	LOUISIANA D	ARKANSAS C	ARKANSAS D	OKLAHOMA C	OKLAHOMA D
COCKS	W	78	2	N	90	3	100	1	**	**	**	**	**	**	100	2	**	**
	E	22	1	S	10	.3	**	**	**	**	**	**	**	**	**	**	**	**
	ST		2			4		1		**		**		**		2		**
DOODLES	W	100	.2	N	**	**	**	**	**	**	**	**	**	**	**	**	**	**
					(NO RESPONSE)													
	ST		.2			**		**		**		**		**		**		**
HAND STACKS	W	60	1	N	58	4	75	4	100	4	83	8	100	4	100	2	**	**
	E	40	1	S	42	3	25	1	**	**	17	2	**	**	**	**	100	1
	ST		1			7		6		4		9		4		2		1
HAYCOCKS	W	50	1	N	71	2	100	1	**	**	100	2	100	9	100	2	100	1
	E	50	1	S	29	1	**	**	**	**	**	**	**	**	**	**	**	**
	ST		3			3		1		**		2		9		2		1
HAY DOODLES					(NO RESPONSE)													
					(NO RESPONSE)													
	ST		**			**		**		**		**		**		**		**
HAY SHOCKS	W	32	11	N	72	18	89	23	71	22	63	15	80	17	63	20	50	11
	E	68	24	S	28	7	11	3	29	9	38	9	20	4	37	11	50	11
	ST		35			25		26		30		24		22		31		22
HAY TUMBLES	W	**	**	N	**	**	100	1	**	**	**	**	**	**	100	1	**	**
	E	100	.2	S	100	.3	**	**	**	**	**	**	**	**	**	**	**	**
	ST		.2			.3		1		**		**		**		1		**
HEAPS	W	43	1	N	83	6	100	1	67	4	71	8	50	4	25	1	**	**
	E	57	1	S	17	1	**	**	33	2	29	3	50	4	75	2	100	1
	ST		2			7		1		7		11		9		3		1
MOWS	W	100	.2	N	100	1	100	4	**	**	**	**	**	**	100	1	100	1
	E	**	**	S	**	**	**	**	100	2	**	**	100	4	**	**	**	**
	ST		.2			1		4		2		**		4		1		1
PILES	W	68	8	N	51	15	71	17	64	15	75	32	38	13	47	7	27	5
	E	32	4	S	49	15	29	7	36	9	25	11	63	22	53	8	73	15
	ST		11			30		24		24		42		35		16		21
RICKS(B)	W	50	2	N	80	1	100	3	100	4	100	2	100	4	75	2	60	4
	E	50	2	S	20	.3	**	**	**	**	**	**	**	**	25	1	40	3
	ST		5			2		3		4		2		4		3		7
SHOCKS(A)	W	44	17	N	71	15	77	24	62	17	57	6	67	9	63	25	55	25
	E	56	22	S	29	6	23	7	38	11	43	5	33	4	38	15	45	21
	ST		39			21		31		28		11		13		39		45
TUMBLES	W	33	.2	N	**	**	**	**	**	**	**	**	**	**	100	1	**	**
	E	67	1	S	100	.3	**	**	**	**	**	**	**	**	**	**	**	**
	ST		1			.3		**		**		**		**		1		**

TABLE I

ITEM (21)
WORK SHEET (14)

CROPS
PILE OF BUNDLES OF WHEAT OR OATS

		TENNESSEE			GEORGIA		ALABAMA		MISSISSIPPI		FLORIDA		LOUISIANA		ARKANSAS		OKLAHOMA	
		A	B		A	B	A	B	A	B	A	B	A	B	A	B	A	B
SHOCK(B)	W	18	13	N	23	16	6	4	4	3	5	4	7	5	32	22	19	13
	E	27	19	S	13	9	1	1	2	1	1	1	2	1	21	14	19	13
	ST	45	32		36	25	8	5	5	4	7	5	9	6	53	36	38	26
STOOK	W	55	1	N	18	.2	**	**	**	**	9	.1	**	**	**	**	100	.3
	E	9	.1	S	**	**	**	**	**	**	9	.1	**	**	**	**	**	**
	ST	64	1		18	.2	**	**	**	**	18	.2	**	**	**	**	100	.3
SHOOK	W	29	.4	N	7	.1	7	.1	14	.2	14	.2	**	**	**	**	**	**
	E	7	.1	S	7	.1	**	**	7	.1	7	.1	100	.3	**	**	**	**
	ST	36	1		14	.2	7	.1	21	.3	21	.3	100	.3	**	**	**	**

		TENNESSEE			GEORGIA		ALABAMA		MISSISSIPPI		FLORIDA		LOUISIANA		ARKANSAS		OKLAHOMA	
		C	D		C	D	C	D	C	D	C	D	C	D	C	D	C	D
SHOCK(B)	W	40	39	N	64	63	81	80	69	64	79	71	76	72	60	60	51	50
	E	60	58	S	36	35	19	19	31	28	21	19	24	22	40	40	49	49
	ST		96			98		98		92		90		94		100		99
STOOK	W	86	2	N	100	1	**	**	**	**	50	2	**	**	**	**	100	1
	E	14	.3	S	**	**	**	**	**	**	50	2	**	**	**	**	**	**
	ST		2			1		**		**		4		**		**		1
SHOOK	W	80	1	N	50	.4	100	2	67	5	67	4	**	**	**	**	**	**
	E	20	.3	S	50	.4	**	**	33	3	33	2	100	6	**	**	**	**
	ST		2			1		2		8		6		6		**		**

ITEM (22)
WORK SHEET (9)

THE HOME
SMALL ROOM FOR HANGING CLOTHES

		TENNESSEE			GEORGIA		ALABAMA		MISSISSIPPI		FLORIDA		LOUISIANA		ARKANSAS		OKLAHOMA	
		A	B		A	B	A	B	A	B	A	B	A	B	A	B	A	B
CLOSET	W	16	7	N	14	6	8	4	5	2	6	3	10	5	19	9	18	9
	E	29	13	S	12	5	3	1	3	1	4	2	11	5	16	8	25	12
	ST	45	20		26	12	11	5	8	4	10	4	22	10	36	17	43	21
CLOTHES CLOSET	W	16	3	N	17	3	4	1	4	1	12	2	5	1	28	9	23	7
	E	22	4	S	14	2	4	1	1	.2	5	1	3	1	16	5	25	8
	ST	38	7		31	5	8	1	5	1	17	3	8	3	44	14	48	15
CLOTHES PRESS(A)					(NO RESPONSE)													
	E	**	**	S	**	**	100	.1	**	**	**	**	**	**	**	**	**	**
	ST	**	**		**	**	100	.1	**	**	**	**	**	**	**	**	**	**
PRESS(A)	W	**	**	N	33	.1	**	**	**	**	33	.1	**	**	**	**	**	**
	E	**	**	S	**	**	**	**	33	.1	**	**	**	**	**	**	**	**
	ST	**	**		33	.1	**	**	33	.1	33	.1	**	**	**	**	**	**
WARDROBE(A)	W	9	.4	N	7	.3	2	.1	**	**	7	.3	14	.3	43	1	**	**
	E	72	3	S	2	.1	2	.1	**	**	**	**	**	**	29	1	14	.3
	ST	80	4		9	.4	4	.2	**	**	7	.3	14	.3	71	2	14	.3

		TENNESSEE			GEORGIA		ALABAMA		MISSISSIPPI		FLORIDA		LOUISIANA		ARKANSAS		OKLAHOMA	
		C	D		C	D	C	D	C	D	C	D	C	D	C	D	C	D
CLOSET	W	36	24	N	55	36	73	54	65	50	60	33	48	38	54	28	42	24
	E	64	42	S	45	30	27	20	35	27	40	23	52	41	46	24	58	33
	ST		66			66		74		77		56		78		52		57
CLOTHES CLOSET	W	41	9	N	54	16	50	11	78	16	69	27	57	11	64	27	48	20
	E	59	13	S	46	14	50	11	22	5	31	12	43	8	36	15	52	22
	ST		21			31		22		20		39		19		42		42
CLOTHES PRESS(A)					(NO RESPONSE)													
	E	**	**	S	**	**	100	2	**	**	**	**	**	**	**	**	**	**
	ST		**			**		2		**		**		**		**		**
PRESS(A)	W	**	**	N	100	1	**	**	**	**	100	1	**	**	**	**	**	**
	E	**	**	S	**	**	**	**	100	2	**	**	**	**	**	**	**	**
	ST		**			1		**		2		1		**		**		**
WARDROBE(A)	W	11	1	N	75	2	50	2	**	**	100	4	100	3	60	3	**	**
	E	89	11	S	25	1	50	2	**	**	**	**	**	**	40	2	100	1
	ST		13			2		3		**		4		3		5		1

HOUSEHOLD EQUIPMENT
A MOVABLE PLACE FOR HANGING CLOTHES

ITEM (22)
WORK SHEET (9)

		TENNESSEE			GEORGIA		ALABAMA		MISSISSIPPI		FLORIDA		LOUISIANA		ARKANSAS		OKLAHOMA	
		A	B		A	B	A	B	A	B	A	B	A	B	A	B	A	B
CLOTHES PRESS(B)	W	**	**	N	18	.2	**	**	**	**	18	.2	**	**	**	**	**	**
	E	36	.4	S	18	.2	**	**	**	**	9	.1	**	**	**	**	100	1
	ST	36	.4		36	.4	**	**	**	**	27	.3	**	**	**	**	100	1
PRESS(B)	W	11	.1	N	11	.1	**	**	**	**	**	**	**	**	**	**	100	.3
	E	56	1	S	11	.1	11	.1	**	**	**	**	**	**	**	**	**	**
	ST	67	1		22	.2	11	.1	**	**	**	**	**	**	**	**	100	.3
WARDROBE(B)	W	16	8	N	15	8	8	4	5	3	7	4	7	3	30	15	20	10
	E	26	13	S	14	7	2	1	2	1	4	2	3	1	20	10	20	10
	ST	42	21		29	15	10	5	7	3	12	6	9	5	50	25	40	20
ARMOIRE	W	40	.2	N	20	.1	**	**	**	**	**	**	14	.3	14	.3	**	**
	E	20	.1	S	**	**	**	**	20	.1	**	**	57	1	14	.3	**	**
	ST	60	.3		20	.1	**	**	20	.1	**	**	71	2	29	1	**	**
ARMOR					(NO RESPONSE)													
	E	**	**	S	50	.1	**	**	50	.1	**	**	100	2	**	**	**	**
	ST	**	**		50	.1	**	**	50	.1	**	**	100	2	**	**	**	**

		TENNESSEE			GEORGIA		ALABAMA		MISSISSIPPI		FLORIDA		LOUISIANA		ARKANSAS		OKLAHOMA	
		C	D		C	D	C	D	C	D	C	D	C	D	C	D	C	D
CLOTHES PRESS(B)	W	**	**	N	50	1	**	**	**	**	67	3	**	**	**	**	**	**
	E	100	2	S	50	1	**	**	**	**	33	2	**	**	**	**	100	3
	ST		2			3		**		**		5		**		**		3
PRESS(B)	W	17	.4	N	50	1	**	**	**	**	**	**	**	**	**	**	100	2
	E	83	2	S	50	1	100	2	**	**	**	**	**	**	**	**	**	**
	ST		3			1		2		**		**		**		**		2
WARDROBE(B)	W	39	36	N	52	49	80	78	76	71	64	61	69	39	59	58	51	48
	E	61	58	S	48	46	20	20	24	23	36	34	31	17	41	39	49	47
	ST		94			95		98		94		95		57		97		95
ARMOIRE	W	67	1	N	100	1	**	**	**	**	**	**	20	4	50	1	**	**
	E	33	.4	S	**	**	**	**	100	3	**	**	80	17	50	1	**	**
	ST		1			1		**		3		**		22		3		**
ARMOR					(NO RESPONSE)													
	E	**	**	S	100	1	**	**	100	3	**	**	100	22	**	**	**	**
	ST		**			1		**		3		**		22		**		**

THE HOME
UNFINISHED ROOM AT THE TOP OF THE HOUSE

ITEM (23)
WORK SHEET (9)

		TENNESSEE			GEORGIA		ALABAMA		MISSISSIPPI		FLORIDA		LOUISIANA		ARKANSAS		OKLAHOMA	
		A	B		A	B	A	B	A	B	A	B	A	B	A	B	A	B
ATTIC	W	16	8	N	14	8	7	4	5	3	8	4	8	5	21	14	20	13
	E	28	15	S	12	6	3	1	2	1	5	2	7	4	20	13	23	15
	ST	44	23		26	14	10	5	7	4	13	7	15	10	41	26	44	28
COCK LOFT	W	100	.1	N	**	**	**	**	**	**	**	**	**	**	**	**	**	**
					(NO RESPONSE)													
	ST	100	.1		**	**	**	**	**	**	**	**	**	**	**	**	**	**
GARRET	W	23	.3	N	15	.2	15	.2	**	**	**	**	40	1	**	**	40	1
	E	38	1	S	**	**	**	**	**	**	8	.1	**	**	**	**	20	.3
	ST	62	1		15	.2	15	.2	**	**	8	.1	40	1	**	**	60	1
LOFT(B)	W	12	1	N	15	1	5	.4	4	.1	7	1	8	1	40	4	8	1
	E	30	3	S	15	1	7	1	2	.2	2	.2	12	1	20	2	12	1
	ST	42	4		31	3	12	1	6	1	10	1	20	2	60	5	20	2
SKY PARLOR	W	**	**	N	50	.2	**	**	**	**	25	.1	**	**	**	**	**	**
	E	**	**	S	25	.1	**	**	**	**	**	**	**	**	**	**	**	**
	ST	**	**		75	.3	**	**	**	**	25	.1	**	**	**	**	**	**

		TENNESSEE			GEORGIA		ALABAMA		MISSISSIPPI		FLORIDA		LOUISIANA		ARKANSAS		OKLAHOMA	
		C	D		C	D	C	D	C	D	C	D	C	D	C	D	C	D
ATTIC	W	36	30	N	54	44	73	59	70	62	63	55	56	44	52	43	47	42
	E	64	54	S	46	37	27	21	30	26	37	32	44	35	48	40	53	48
	ST		84			81		80		88		87		79		83		91
COCK LOFT	W	100	.3	N	**	**	**	**	**	**	**	**	**	**	**	**	**	**
					(NO RESPONSE)													
	ST		.3			**		**		**		**		**		**		**
GARRET	W	38	1	N	100	1	100	3	**	**	**	**	100	6	**	**	67	2
	E	63	2	S	**	**	**	**	**	**	100	1	**	**	**	**	33	1
	ST		3			1		3		**		1		6		**		4
LOFT(B)	W	29	4	N	50	8	40	7	60	7	75	8	40	6	67	11	40	2
	E	71	9	S	50	8	60	10	40	5	25	3	60	9	33	6	60	4
	ST		13			16		16		12		11		15		17		6
SKY PARLOR	W	**	**	N	67	1	**	**	**	**	100	1	**	**	**	**	**	**
	E	**	**	S	33	1	**	**	**	**	**	**	**	**	**	**	**	**
	ST		**			2		**		**		1		**		**		**

ACTIVITIES
TO DO THE HOUSEWORK

ITEM (24)
WORK SHEET (10)

		TENNESSEE A	TENNESSEE B		GEORGIA A	GEORGIA B	ALABAMA A	ALABAMA B	MISSISSIPPI A	MISSISSIPPI B	FLORIDA A	FLORIDA B	LOUISIANA A	LOUISIANA B	ARKANSAS A	ARKANSAS B	OKLAHOMA A	OKLAHOMA B
CLEAN UP	W	16	9	N	14	7	7	4	5	2	8	4	9	5	22	13	19	12
	E	28	15	S	13	7	3	2	2	1	4	2	9	5	19	12	23	14
	ST	44	23		27	14	10	5	7	4	12	7	17	11	40	25	42	26
DO UP	W	14	.1	N	**	**	**	**	**	**	**	**	**	**	**	**	33	.3
	E	29	.2	S	29	.2	**	**	14	.1	14	.1	33	.3	**	**	33	.3
	ST	43	.3		29	.2	**	**	14	.1	14	.1	33	.3	**	**	67	1
REDD UP	W	20	.1	N	**	**	**	**	**	**	**	**	**	**	**	**	100	.3
	E	60	.3	S	**	**	20	.1	**	**	**	**	**	**	**	**	**	**
	ST	80	.4		**	**	20	.1	**	**	**	**	**	**	**	**	100	.3
RIDD UP	W	**	**	N	**	**	**	**	**	**	**	**	**	**	100	.3	**	**
					(NO RESPONSE)													
	ST	**	**		**	**	**	**	**	**	**	**	**	**	100	.3	**	**
STRAIGHTEN UP	W	14	2	N	16	2	6	1	4	1	6	1	4	1	25	5	21	4
	E	33	5	S	11	2	4	1	3	.4	4	1	8	1	11	2	32	6
	ST	46	7		27	4	9	1	7	1	10	1	11	2	36	7	53	10
TIDY UP	W	14	.3	N	23	1	9	.2	**	**	14	.3	10	.3	20	1	20	1
	E	9	.2	S	18	.4	5	.1	**	**	9	.2	**	**	20	1	30	1
	ST	23	1		41	1	14	.3	**	**	23	1	10	.3	40	1	50	2

		TENNESSEE C	TENNESSEE D		GEORGIA C	GEORGIA D	ALABAMA C	ALABAMA D	MISSISSIPPI C	MISSISSIPPI D	FLORIDA C	FLORIDA D	LOUISIANA C	LOUISIANA D	ARKANSAS C	ARKANSAS D	OKLAHOMA C	OKLAHOMA D
CLEAN UP	W	37	28	N	53	39	71	54	71	53	65	49	50	39	54	40	45	30
	E	63	47	S	47	35	29	22	29	22	35	27	50	39	46	34	55	37
	ST		74			74		75		76		76		79		74		67
DO UP	W	33	.3	N	**	**	**	**	**	**	**	**	**	**	**	**	50	1
	E	67	1	S	100	1	**	**	100	2	100	1	100	3	**	**	50	1
	ST		1			1		**		2		1		3		**		2
REDD UP	W	25	.3	N	**	**	**	**	**	**	**	**	**	**	**	**	100	1
	E	75	1	S	**	**	100	1	**	**	**	**	**	**	**	**	**	**
	ST		1			**		1		**		**		**		**		1
RIDD UP	W	**	**	N	**	**	**	**	**	**	**	**	**	**	100	1	**	**
					(NO RESPONSE)													
	ST		**			**		**		**		**		**		1		**
STRAIGHTEN UP	W	29	6	N	58	12	62	12	60	13	64	11	33	5	68	14	39	10
	E	71	15	S	42	9	38	7	40	9	36	6	67	11	32	6	61	16
	ST		22			21		19		22		17		16		20		26
TIDY UP	W	60	1	N	56	3	67	3	**	**	60	4	100	3	50	2	40	2
	E	40	1	S	44	2	33	1	**	**	40	2	**	**	50	2	60	3
	ST		2			5		4		**		6		3		4		5

THE HOME
A LARGE PORCH WITH ROOF

ITEM (25)
WORK SHEET (10)

		TENNESSEE A	TENNESSEE B		GEORGIA A	GEORGIA B	ALABAMA A	ALABAMA B	MISSISSIPPI A	MISSISSIPPI B	FLORIDA A	FLORIDA B	LOUISIANA A	LOUISIANA B	ARKANSAS A	ARKANSAS B	OKLAHOMA A	OKLAHOMA B
GALLERY	W	32	1	N	**	**	5	.1	11	.2	**	**	32	3	5	.3	**	**
	E	**	**	S	**	**	16	.3	37	1	**	**	41	3	5	.3	18	1
	ST	32	1		**	**	21	.4	47	1	**	**	73	6	9	1	18	1
PIAZZA	W	25	1	N	25	1	5	.1	**	**	10	.2	**	**	**	**	**	**
	E	5	.1	S	15	.3	**	**	**	**	15	.3	100	.3	**	**	**	**
	ST	30	1		40	1	5	.1	**	**	25	1	100	.3	**	**	**	**
PORCH(A)	W	15	8	N	14	7	6	3	4	2	8	4	7	4	26	15	19	11
	E	31	17	S	14	7	3	2	2	1	4	2	5	3	18	10	25	14
	ST	46	25		27	15	9	5	6	3	12	7	12	7	44	25	44	25
PORTICO(A)	W	**	**	N	**	**	40	.2	40	.2	**	**	[illegible]	1	14	.3	29	1
	E	20	.1	S	**	**	**	**	**	**	**	**	**	**	14	.3	14	.3
	ST	20	.1		**	**	40	.2	40	.2	**	**	29	1	29	1	43	1
STOOP(A)	W	**	**	N	**	**	**	**	17	.1	33	.2	**	**	100	.3	**	**
	E	17	.1	S	33	.2	**	**	**	**	**	**	**	**	**	**	**	**
	ST	17	.1		33	.2	**	**	17	.1	33	.2	**	**	100	.3	**	**
VERANDA(A)	W	18	1	N	30	1	16	1	7	.3	5	.2	4	.3	24	2	24	2
	E	9	.4	S	7	.3	**	**	**	**	9	.4	4	.3	32	3	12	1
	ST	27	1		36	2	16	1	7	.3	14	1	8	1	56	5	36	3

		TENNESSEE C	TENNESSEE D		GEORGIA C	GEORGIA D	ALABAMA C	ALABAMA D	MISSISSIPPI C	MISSISSIPPI D	FLORIDA C	FLORIDA D	LOUISIANA C	LOUISIANA D	ARKANSAS C	ARKANSAS D	OKLAHOMA C	OKLAHOMA D
GALLERY	W	100	2	N	**	**	25	2	22	5	**	**	44	18	50	1	**	**
	E	**	**	S	**	**	75	5	78	16	**	**	56	22	50	1	100	5
	ST		2			**		[illegible]		20		**		40		2		5
PIAZZA	W	83	2	N	63	3	100	2	**	**	40	3	**	**	**	**	**	**
	E	17	.3	S	38	2	**	**	**	**	60	4	100	3	**	**	**	**
	ST		2			5		2		**		6		3		**		**
PORCH(A)	W	33	29	N	50	43	69	53	69	45	66	55	58	28	59	46	43	35
	E	67	61	S	50	42	31	24	31	20	34	28	42	20	41	33	57	47
	ST		90			85		77		66		83		48		79		81
PORTICO(A)	W	**	**	N	**	**	100	3	100	5	**	**	100	5	50	1	67	2
	E	100	.3	S	**	**	**	**	**	**	**	**	**	**	50	1	33	1
	ST		.3			**		3		5		**		5		2		3
STOOP(A)	W	**	**	N	**	**	**	**	100	2	100	3	**	**	100	1	**	**
	E	100	.3	S	100	1	**	**	**	**	**	**	**	**	**	**	**	**
	ST		.3			1		**		2		3		**		1		**
VERANDA(A)	W	67	3	N	81	8	100	11	100	7	33	3	50	3	43	7	67	7
	E	33	2	S	19	2	**	**	**	**	67	5	50	3	57	9	33	3
	ST		5			9		11		7		8		5		16		10

THE HOME
A SMALL PORCH, OFTEN WITH NO ROOF

ITEM (25)
WORK SHEET (10)

		TENNESSEE			GEORGIA		ALABAMA		MISSISSIPPI		FLORIDA		LOUISIANA		ARKANSAS		OKLAHOMA	
		A	B		A	B	A	B	A	B	A	B	A	B	A	B	A	B
PLATFORM	W	20	1	N	7	.3	**	**	**	**	9	.4	**	**	73	3	**	**
	E	43	2	S	9	.4	2	.1	5	.2	5	.2	**	**	27	1	**	**
	ST	64	3		16	1	2	.1	5	.2	14	1	**	**	100	4	**	**
PORCH(B)	W	16	3	N	12	2	9	2	9	2	5	1	11	4	21	7	17	6
	E	28	5	S	10	2	4	1	3	1	4	1	8	3	15	5	28	10
	ST	44	8		22	4	13	2	12	2	9	2	19	6	36	12	45	16
PORTICO(B)	W	18	1	N	20	1	15	1	**	**	10	.4	9	.3	36	1	9	.3
	E	25	1	S	10	.4	**	**	**	**	3	.1	**	**	36	1	9	.3
	ST	43	2		30	1	15	1	**	**	13	1	9	.3	73	3	18	1
STEP	W	**	**	N	**	**	11	.2	11	.2	6	.1	5	.3	20	1	50	4
	E	39	1	S	22	.4	6	.1	**	**	6	.1	5	.3	15	1	5	.3
	ST	39	1		22	.4	17	.3	11	.2	11	.2	10	1	35	3	55	4
STEPS	W	19	1	N	17	1	3	.1	8	.3	6	.2	8	1	16	1	20	2
	E	31	1	S	11	.4	**	**	**	**	6	.2	12	1	12	1	32	3
	ST	50	2		28	1	3	.1	8	.3	11	.4	20	2	28	3	52	5
STOOP(B)	W	14	4	N	23	6	6	2	3	1	12	3	3	.3	30	4	15	2
	E	22	6	S	14	4	2	1	1	.3	3	1	3	.3	35	5	15	2
	ST	36	10		37	10	8	2	4	1	15	4	5	1	65	9	30	4
VERANDA(B)	W	27	2	N	15	1	12	1	3	.2	5	.3	**	**	100	2	**	**
	E	19	1	S	12	1	3	.2	2	.1	2	.1	**	**	**	**	**	**
	ST	46	3		27	2	15	1	5	.3	7	.4	**	**	100	2	**	**

ITEM (25)

(CONTINUED) A SMALL PORCH, OFTEN WITH NO ROOF

		TENNESSEE C	TENNESSEE D		GEORGIA C	GEORGIA D	ALABAMA C	ALABAMA D	MISSISSIPPI C	MISSISSIPPI D	FLORIDA C	FLORIDA D	LOUISIANA C	LOUISIANA D	ARKANSAS C	ARKANSAS D	OKLAHOMA C	OKLAHOMA D
PLATFORM	W	32	3	N	43	2	**	**	**	**	67	5	**	**	73	8	**	**
	E	68	7	S	57	2	100	2	100	5	33	3	**	**	27	3	**	**
	ST		10			4		2		5		8		**		11		**
PORCH(B)	W	35	11	N	54	12	71	26	77	40	59	13	56	36	59	20	37	20
	E	65	19	S	46	10	29	11	23	12	41	9	44	29	41	14	63	33
	ST		30			22		37		52		22		64		35		53
PORTICO(B)	W	41	3	N	67	4	100	9	**	**	80	5	100	4	50	4	50	1
	E	59	4	S	33	2	**	**	**	**	20	1	**	**	50	4	50	1
	ST		6			6		9		**		6		4		8		2
STEP	W	**	**	N	**	**	67	3	100	5	50	1	50	4	57	4	91	12
	E	100	3	S	100	2	33	2	**	**	50	1	50	4	43	3	9	1
	ST		3			2		5		5		3		7		7		14
STEPS	W	39	3	N	60	3	100	2	100	7	50	3	40	7	57	4	38	6
	E	61	4	S	40	2	**	**	**	**	50	3	60	11	43	3	62	10
	ST		7			5		2		7		5		18		7		16
STOOP(B)	W	38	13	N	61	32	76	25	70	17	78	40	50	4	46	12	50	7
	E	62	22	S	39	20	24	8	30	7	23	12	50	4	54	14	50	7
	ST		35			52		32		24		51		7		27		15
VERANDA(B)	W	59	6	N	56	5	78	11	67	5	75	4	**	**	100	5	**	**
	E	41	4	S	44	4	22	3	33	2	25	1	**	**	**	**	**	**
	ST		10			9		14		7		5		**		5		**

THE HOUSE AND ITS ENVIRONS
PLACE WHERE COWS ARE ENCLOSED

ITEM (26)
WORK SHEET (15)

		TENNESSEE A	TENNESSEE B		GEORGIA A	GEORGIA B	ALABAMA A	ALABAMA B	MISSISSIPPI A	MISSISSIPPI B	FLORIDA A	FLORIDA B	LOUISIANA A	LOUISIANA B	ARKANSAS A	ARKANSAS B	OKLAHOMA A	OKLAHOMA B
COW BRAKE	W	20	.1	N	20	.1	20	.1	**	**	**	**	**	**	**	**	**	**
	E	**	**	S	20	.1	20	.1	**	**	**	**	**	**	**	**	**	**
	ST	20	.1		40	.2	40	.2	**	**	**	**	**	**	**	**	**	**
COW LOT(A)	W	23	10	N	20	9	6	3	4	2	4	2	3	1	36	20	16	9
	E	29	13	S	9	4	2	1	1	1	1	1	3	1	17	9	25	14
	ST	52	24		30	14	8	4	5	2	5	2	5	3	53	29	42	23
COW PEN	W	11	5	N	18	7	9	4	4	2	13	5	12	4	21	7	11	4
	E	13	5	S	19	8	4	2	4	2	6	2	8	3	32	11	15	5
	ST	24	10		37	15	13	5	8	3	19	8	21	7	53	18	27	9
COW POUND	W	33	.1	N	33	.1	**	**	**	**	33	.1	**	**	**	**	**	**
					(NO RESPONSE)													
	ST	33	.1		33	.1	**	**	**	**	33	.1	**	**	**	**	**	**
COW YARD	W	39	1	N	6	.1	6	.1	**	**	**	**	**	**	33	1	17	.3
	E	44	1	S	6	.1	**	**	**	**	**	**	17	.3	33	1	**	**
	ST	83	2		11	.2	6	.1	**	**	**	**	17	.3	67	1	17	.3
CUPPIN	W	25	.1	N	**	**	**	**	**	**	**	**	**	**	**	**	**	**
	E	25	.1	S	25	.1	**	**	25	.1	**	**	100	.3	**	**	**	**
	ST	50	.2		25	.1	**	**	25	.1	**	**	100	.3	**	**	**	**

		TENNESSEE C	TENNESSEE D		GEORGIA C	GEORGIA D	ALABAMA C	ALABAMA D	MISSISSIPPI C	MISSISSIPPI D	FLORIDA C	FLORIDA D	LOUISIANA C	LOUISIANA D	ARKANSAS C	ARKANSAS D	OKLAHOMA C	OKLAHOMA D
COW BRAKE	W	100	.2	N	50	.3	50	1	**	**	**	**	**	**	**	**	**	**
	E	**	**	S	50	.3	50	1	**	**	**	**	**	**	**	**	**	**
	ST		.2			1		2		**		**		**		**		**
COW LOT(A)	W	44	29	N	69	32	77	31	74	30	74	17	50	13	68	40	39	27
	E	56	38	S	31	14	23	9	26	11	26	6	50	13	32	19	61	43
	ST		67			46		40		40		23		27		60		70
COW PEN	W	47	13	N	49	25	70	40	52	30	69	52	60	40	39	15	42	12
	E	53	15	S	51	26	30	17	48	28	31	24	40	27	61	23	58	16
	ST		28			52		57		58		76		67		38		29
COW POUND	W	100	.2	N	100	.3	**	**	**	**	100	1	**	**	**	**	**	**
					(NO RESPONSE)													
	ST		.2			.3		**		**		1		**		**		**
COW YARD	W	47	2	N	50	.3	100	1	**	**	**	**	**	**	50	1	100	1
	E	53	2	S	50	.3	**	**	**	**	**	**	100	3	50	1	**	**
	ST		4			1		1		**		**		3		3		1
CUPPIN	W	50	.2	N	**	**	**	**	**	**	**	**	**	**	**	**	**	**
	E	50	.2	S	100	.3	**	**	100	2	**	**	100	3	**	**	**	**
	ST		[illegible]			[illegible]		**		2		**		3		**		**

ITEM (27)
WORK SHEET (15)

OTHER BUILDINGS
SHELTER AND YARD FOR HOGS

		TENNESSEE A	TENNESSEE B		GEORGIA A	GEORGIA B	ALABAMA A	ALABAMA B	MISSISSIPPI A	MISSISSIPPI B	FLORIDA A	FLORIDA B	LOUISIANA A	LOUISIANA B	ARKANSAS A	ARKANSAS B	OKLAHOMA A	OKLAHOMA B
HOG HOUSE	W	27	1	N	24	1	2	.1	6	.3	**	**	5	.3	53	4	5	.3
	E	27	1	S	10	1	**	**	4	.2	**	**	5	.3	11	1	21	1
	ST	55	3		33	2	2	.1	10	1	**	**	11	1	63	4	26	2
HOG LOT	W	22	5	N	21	5	8	2	2	.4	3	1	8	1	35	5	19	3
	E	32	8	S	11	3	.4	.1	1	.3	.4	.1	**	**	22	3	16	2
	ST	54	13		32	8	8	2	3	1	3	1	8	1	57	8	35	5
HOG BOIST					(NO RESPONSE)													
	E	**	**	S	100	.1	**	**	**	**	**	**	**	**	**	**	**	**
	ST	**	**		100	.1	**	**	**	**	**	**	**	**	**	**	**	**
HOG CRAWL	W	**	**	N	33	.1	**	**	**	**	**	**	**	**	**	**	**	**
	E	33	.1	S	**	**	**	**	**	**	33	.1	**	**	**	**	100	.3
	ST	33	.1		33	.1	**	**	**	**	33	.1	**	**	**	**	100	.3
HOG PEN	W	17	9	N	18	9	7	4	3	2	9	5	6	3	31	15	12	6
	E	23	12	S	14	8	2	1	3	2	4	2	7	3	25	12	19	9
	ST	40	21		32	17	9	5	6	3	13	7	13	6	56	27	31	15
PIG PEN	W	21	7	N	15	5	7	2	6	2	7	2	9	4	19	8	17	7
	E	28	9	S	6	2	4	1	3	1	4	1	7	3	24	10	25	10
	ST	48	15		21	7	11	3	9	3	11	4	16	7	42	18	42	18
PIG STY	W	25	1	N	8	.2	**	**	**	**	21	1	14	.3	**	**	29	1
	E	25	1	S	**	**	8	.2	4	.1	8	.2	43	1	**	**	14	.3
	ST	50	1		8	.2	8	.2	4	.1	29	1	57	1	**	**	43	1
STY	W	24	.4	N	18	.3	6	.1	**	**	6	.1	**	**	33	.3	33	.3
	E	24	.4	S	6	.1	12	.2	6	.1	**	**	**	**	**	**	33	.3
	ST	47	1		24	.4	18	.3	6	.1	6	.1	**	**	33	.3	67	1

(CONTINUED) SHELTER AND YARD FOR HOGS

ITEM (27)		TENNESSEE C	TENNESSEE D		GEORGIA C	GEORGIA D	ALABAMA C	ALABAMA D	MISSISSIPPI C	MISSISSIPPI D	FLORIDA C	FLORIDA D	LOUISIANA C	LOUISIANA D	ARKANSAS C	ARKANSAS D	OKLAHOMA C	OKLAHOMA D
HOG HOUSE	W	50	3	N	71	4	100	1	60	4	**	**	50	2	83	6	20	1
	E	50	3	S	29	2	**	**	40	3	**	**	50	2	17	1	80	4
	ST		5			5		1		7		**		4		8		4
HOG LOT	W	41	10	N	65	15	95	18	57	5	88	6	100	7	62	8	54	6
	E	59	14	S	35	8	5	1	43	4	13	1	**	**	38	5	46	5
	ST		24			23		19		10		7		7		13		11
HOG BOIST					(NO RESPONSE)													
	E	**	**	S	100	.3	**	**	**	**	**	**	**	**	**	**	**	**
	ST		**			.3		**		**		**		**		**		**
HOG CRAWL	W	**	**	N	100	.3	**	**	**	**	**	**	**	**	**	**	**	**
	E	100	.1	S	**	**	**	**	**	**	100	1	**	**	**	**	100	1
	ST		.1			.3		**		**		1		**		**		1
HOG PEN	W	42	16	N	55	28	80	35	53	23	68	39	47	18	55	26	39	14
	E	58	23	S	45	22	20	9	47	21	32	18	53	20	45	21	61	22
	ST		39			50		44		44		58		38		47		36
PIG PEN	W	43	12	N	70	14	67	21	67	25	65	18	58	24	44	14	41	18
	E	57	16	S	30	6	33	10	33	12	35	10	42	18	56	18	59	25
	ST		28			19		31		37		28		42		32		43
PIG STY	W	50	1	N	100	1	**	**	**	**	71	4	25	2	**	**	67	2
	E	50	1	S	**	**	100	2	100	1	29	2	75	7	**	**	33	1
	ST		2			1		2		1		6		9		**		3
STY	W	50	1	N	75	1	33	1	**	**	100	1	**	**	100	1	50	1
	E	50	1	S	25	.3	67	2	100	1	**	**	**	**	**	**	50	1
	ST		2			1		3		1		1		**		1		2

THE HOUSE AND ITS ENVIRONS
YARD ADJOINING THE BARN

ITEM (28)
WORK SHEET (15)

		TENNESSEE A	TENNESSEE B		GEORGIA A	GEORGIA B	ALABAMA A	ALABAMA B	MISSISSIPPI A	MISSISSIPPI B	FLORIDA A	FLORIDA B	LOUISIANA A	LOUISIANA B	ARKANSAS A	ARKANSAS B	OKLAHOMA A	OKLAHOMA B
BARN LOT	W	25	8	N	13	4	5	2	4	1	3	1	6	1	44	12	14	4
	E	37	12	S	9	3	.3	.1	1	.3	3	1	3	1	19	5	14	4
	ST	62	20		22	7	6	2	5	2	6	2	8	2	64	17	28	7
BARN YARD	W	16	8	N	20	10	8	4	4	2	9	5	7	4	21	12	17	9
	E	22	11	S	10	5	3	2	3	2	4	2	7	4	24	13	23	12
	ST	38	20		31	16	11	6	7	4	13	7	15	8	46	25	40	21
COW LOT(B)	W	8	1	N	22	2	5	.4	8	1	12	1	9	1	27	2	18	1
	E	7	1	S	34	3	3	.2	1	.1	**	**	**	**	23	2	23	2
	ST	15	1		55	4	8	1	9	1	12	1	9	1	50	4	41	3
FARM LOT	W	33	.3	N	33	.3	**	**	**	**	**	**	**	**	**	**	**	**
	E	11	.1	S	11	.1	**	**	**	**	11	.1	**	**	**	**	100	.3
	ST	44	.4		44	.4	**	**	**	**	11	.1	**	**	**	**	100	.3
FEED LOT	W	24	1	N	11	.4	5	.2	5	.2	8	.3	10	1	25	2	20	1
	E	16	1	S	19	1	8	.3	3	.1	**	**	5	.3	20	1	20	1
	ST	41	2		30	1	14	1	8	.3	8	.3	15	1	45	3	40	3

		TENNESSEE C	TENNESSEE D		GEORGIA C	GEORGIA D	ALABAMA C	ALABAMA D	MISSISSIPPI C	MISSISSIPPI D	FLORIDA C	FLORIDA D	LOUISIANA C	LOUISIANA D	ARKANSAS C	ARKANSAS D	OKLAHOMA C	OKLAHOMA D
BARN LOT	W	40	19	N	60	14	94	20	81	22	50	9	67	12	70	24	50	10
	E	60	28	S	40	10	6	1	19	5	50	9	33	6	30	10	50	10
	ST		46			24		21		27		18		18		34		21
BARN YARD	W	43	20	N	66	37	69	45	56	32	69	47	50	33	47	24	42	26
	E	57	27	S	34	19	31	20	44	25	31	21	50	33	53	27	58	35
	ST		46			55		65		57		68		67		51		61
COW LOT(B)	W	55	1	N	39	6	67	5	86	10	100	9	100	6	55	4	44	4
	E	45	1	S	61	9	33	2	14	2	**	**	**	**	45	4	56	5
	ST		3			15		7		12		9		6		8		9
FARM LOT	W	75	1	N	75	1	**	**	**	**	**	**	**	**	**	**	**	**
	E	25	.2	S	25	.3	**	**	**	**	100	1	**	**	**	**	100	1
	ST		1			1		**		**		1		**		**		1
FEED LOT	W	60	2	N	36	1	40	2	67	3	100	3	67	6	56	4	50	4
	E	40	1	S	64	3	60	4	33	2	**	**	33	3	44	3	50	4
	ST		4			4		6		5		3		9		7		8

THE HOUSE AND ITS ENVIRONS
A KIND OF WOODEN FENCE

ITEM (29)
WORK SHEET (16)

		TENNESSEE			GEORGIA		ALABAMA		MISSISSIPPI		FLORIDA		LOUISIANA		ARKANSAS		OKLAHOMA	
		A	B		A	B	A	B	A	B	A	B	A	B	A	B	A	B
PALE FENCE	W	20	.4	N	45	1	5	.1	**	**	**	**	**	**	40	1	**	**
	E	10	.2	S	10	.2	**	**	5	.1	5	.1	**	**	40	1	20	.3
	ST	30	1		55	1	5	.1	5	.1	5	.1	**	**	80	1	20	.3
PALING FENCE	W	36	9	N	13	3	6	1	6	1	5	1	**	**	60	9	**	**
	E	21	5	S	11	3	1	.2	1	.3	1	.2	**	**	28	4	12	2
	ST	57	14		23	6	7	2	7	2	6	1	**	**	88	14	12	2
PICKET FENCE	W	13	8	N	18	11	7	4	3	2	8	5	7	5	23	16	17	12
	E	27	16	S	11	7	3	2	3	2	4	3	10	7	24	17	21	14
	ST	40	24		30	18	11	6	6	4	13	8	16	12	46	32	37	26
PALINGS	W	12	1	N	19	1	4	.3	6	.4	10	1	**	**	38	2	8	.3
	E	25	2	S	21	1	1	.1	**	**	1	.1	**	**	38	2	15	1
	ST	37	3		40	3	6	.4	6	.4	12	1	**	**	77	4	23	1
SLAT FENCE	W	23	1	N	35	1	**	**	**	**	4	.1	**	**	75	1	**	**
	E	15	.4	S	19	1	**	**	**	**	4	.1	**	**	25	.3	**	**
	ST	38	1		54	1	**	**	**	**	8	.2	**	**	100	1	**	**
PALE GARDEN	W	29	.2	N	43	.3	**	**	**	**	**	**	**	**	100	1	**	**
	E	14	.1	S	14	.1	**	**	**	**	**	**	**	**	**	**	**	**
	ST	43	.3		57	.4	**	**	**	**	**	**	**	**	100	1	**	**

		TENNESSEE			GEORGIA		ALABAMA		MISSISSIPPI		FLORIDA		LOUISIANA		ARKANSAS		OKLAHOMA	
		C	D		C	D	C	D	C	D	C	D	C	D	C	D	C	D
PALE FENCE	W	67	1	N	82	3	100	1	**	**	**	**	**	**	50	1	**	**
	E	33	.4	S	18	1	**	**	100	2	100	1	**	**	50	1	100	1
	ST		1			4		1		2		1		**		3		1
PALING FENCE	W	63	21	N	55	11	88	17	82	24	85	11	**	**	68	18	**	**
	E	37	12	S	45	9	13	2	18	5	15	2	**	**	32	8	100	6
	ST		33			19		19		29		13		**		26		6
PICKET FENCE	W	33	18	N	62	37	69	52	51	32	66	49	41	41	49	30	45	40
	E	67	38	S	38	23	31	23	49	31	34	26	59	59	51	31	55	49
	ST		57			61		75		63		75		100		61		89
PALINGS	W	32	2	N	48	5	75	4	100	7	88	7	**	**	50	3	33	1
	E	68	4	S	52	5	25	1	**	**	13	1	**	**	50	3	67	2
	ST		6			10		5		7		8		**		7		4
SLAT FENCE	W	60	1	N	64	3	**	**	**	**	50	1	**	**	75	2	**	**
	E	40	1	S	36	2	**	**	**	**	50	1	**	**	25	1	**	**
	ST		2			5		**		**		2		**		3		**
PALE GARDEN	W	67	.4	N	75	1	**	**	**	**	**	**	**	**	100	1	**	**
	E	33	.2	S	25	.3	**	**	**	**	**	**	**	**	**	**	**	**
	ST		1			1		**		**		**		**		1		**

THE HOUSE AND ITS ENVIRONS
A WALL MADE OF ROCKS OR STONES

ITEM (30)
WORK SHEET (16)

		TENNESSEE			GEORGIA		ALABAMA		MISSISSIPPI		FLORIDA		LOUISIANA		ARKANSAS		OKLAHOMA	
		A	B		A	B	A	B	A	B	A	B	A	B	A	B	A	B
STONE WALL	W	19	7	N	17	6	8	3	6	2	6	2	6	3	24	10	14	6
	E	21	8	S	12	4	4	1	3	1	4	1	12	5	27	11	18	7
	ST	40	15		29	11	11	4	9	3	10	4	18	7	50	21	32	13
STONE FENCE	W	23	1	N	9	1	6	.3	8	.4	8	.4	18	1	27	1	18	1
	E	15	1	S	15	1	2	.1	4	.2	11	1	18	1	9	.3	9	.3
	ST	38	2		25	1	8	.4	11	1	19	1	36	1	36	1	27	1
ROCK WALL	W	11	4	N	26	10	8	3	2	1	5	2	4	1	39	14	15	5
	E	33	13	S	10	4	1	1	1	1	3	1	**	**	20	7	22	8
	ST	44	17		36	14	9	4	3	1	8	3	4	1	59	21	37	13
ROCK FENCE	W	40	6	N	7	1	3	1	2	.3	7	1	10	1	31	5	14	2
	E	29	4	S	10	2	**	**	1	.2	**	**	2	.3	24	4	19	3
	ST	69	11		17	3	3	1	3	1	7	1	12	2	55	8	33	5

		TENNESSEE			GEORGIA		ALABAMA		MISSISSIPPI		FLORIDA		LOUISIANA		ARKANSAS		OKLAHOMA	
		C	D		C	D	C	D	C	D	C	D	C	D	C	D	C	D
STONE WALL	W	48	16	N	59	22	68	33	69	40	62	26	35	21	47	19	44	18
	E	52	17	S	41	15	32	15	31	18	38	16	65	39	53	21	56	22
	ST		33			37		48		58		43		61		40		40
STONE FENCE	W	60	3	N	38	2	75	4	67	7	40	5	50	6	75	2	67	2
	E	40	2	S	62	3	25	1	33	4	60	7	50	6	25	1	33	1
	ST		5			5		5		11		11		12		3		3
ROCK WALL	W	25	10	N	73	36	86	35	58	13	67	23	100	12	66	27	41	17
	E	75	29	S	27	13	14	6	42	9	33	11	**	**	34	14	59	24
	ST		38			49		41		22		34		12		41		41
ROCK FENCE	W	58	14	N	42	4	100	6	60	5	100	11	80	12	57	9	43	7
	E	42	10	S	58	5	**	**	40	4	**	**	20	3	43	7	57	9
	ST		24			9		6		9		11		15		16		16

THE HOUSE AND ITS ENVIRONS
A FENCE MADE OF WOODEN RAILS

ITEM (31)
WORK SHEET (16)

		TENNESSEE A	TENNESSEE B		GEORGIA A	GEORGIA B	ALABAMA A	ALABAMA B	MISSISSIPPI A	MISSISSIPPI B	FLORIDA A	FLORIDA B	LOUISIANA A	LOUISIANA B	ARKANSAS A	ARKANSAS B	OKLAHOMA A	OKLAHOMA B
RAIL FENCE	W	19	16	N	18	15	7	6	4	4	7	6	6	5	30	25	15	12
	E	26	22	S	12	10	2	2	2	2	3	3	6	5	24	19	19	16
	ST	45	38		29	25	9	8	6	5	11	9	12	10	54	44	34	28
SNAKE FENCE	W	13	.1	N	13	.1	13	.1	**	**	**	**	**	**	33	.3	33	.3
	E	50	.4	S	13	.1	**	**	**	**	**	**	**	**	**	**	33	.3
	ST	63	1		25	.2	13	.1	**	**	**	**	**	**	33	.3	67	1
WORM FENCE	W	14	.1	N	**	**	**	**	**	**	**	**	**	**	**	**	100	3
	E	57	.4	S	29	.2	**	**	**	**	**	**	**	**	**	**	**	**
	ST	71	1		29	.2	**	**	**	**	**	**	**	**	**	**	100	3
ZIGZAG FENCE	W	20	.1	N	**	**	**	**	**	**	20	.1	**	**	100	.3	**	**
	E	20	.1	S	20	.1	20	.1	**	**	**	**	**	**	**	**	**	**
	ST	40	.2		20	.1	20	.1	**	**	20	.1	**	**	100	.3	**	**

		TENNESSEE C	TENNESSEE D		GEORGIA C	GEORGIA D	ALABAMA C	ALABAMA D	MISSISSIPPI C	MISSISSIPPI D	FLORIDA C	FLORIDA D	LOUISIANA C	LOUISIANA D	ARKANSAS C	ARKANSAS D	OKLAHOMA C	OKLAHOMA D
RAIL FENCE	W	42	41	N	60	59	74	73	67	67	70	69	52	52	56	55	44	39
	E	58	56	S	40	39	26	25	33	33	30	30	48	48	44	44	56	50
	ST		97			98		98		100		99		100		98		89
SNAKE FENCE	W	20	.2	N	50	.4	100	1	**	**	**	**	**	**	100	1	50	1
	E	80	1	S	50	.4	**	**	**	**	**	**	**	**	**	**	50	1
	ST		1			1		1		**		**		**		1		2
WORM FENCE	W	20	.2	N	**	**	**	**	**	**	**	**	**	**	**	**	100	9
	E	80	1	S	100	1	**	**	**	**	**	**	**	**	**	**	**	**
	ST		1			1		**		**		**		**		**		9
ZIGZAG FENCE	W	50	.2	N	**	**	**	**	**	**	100	1	**	**	100	1	**	**
	E	50	.2	S	100	.4	100	1	**	**	**	**	**	**	**	**	**	**
	ST		1			.4		1		**		1		**		1		**

ITEM (32)
WORK SHEET (17)

HOUSEHOLD EQUIPMENT
A LARGE OPEN WOODEN VESSEL FOR WATER, MILK, ETC.

		TENNESSEE A	TENNESSEE B		GEORGIA A	GEORGIA B	ALABAMA A	ALABAMA B	MISSISSIPPI A	MISSISSIPPI B	FLORIDA A	FLORIDA B	LOUISIANA A	LOUISIANA B	ARKANSAS A	ARKANSAS B	OKLAHOMA A	OKLAHOMA B
PAIL(A)	W	16	1	N	17	1	4	.3	2	.2	10	1	5	.3	32	3	18	1
	E	27	2	S	11	1	7	1	1	.1	4	.3	5	.3	18	1	23	2
	ST	43	4		28	2	11	1	4	.3	14	1	9	1	50	4	41	3
BUCKET(A)	W	15	8	N	13	7	8	4	5	3	8	4	7	5	22	14	19	12
	E	29	16	S	13	7	4	2	2	1	4	2	8	5	19	12	24	16
	ST	44	24		26	14	11	6	7	4	11	6	16	10	41	27	43	28

		TENNESSEE C	TENNESSEE D		GEORGIA C	GEORGIA D	ALABAMA C	ALABAMA D	MISSISSIPPI C	MISSISSIPPI D	FLORIDA C	FLORIDA D	LOUISIANA C	LOUISIANA D	ARKANSAS C	ARKANSAS D	OKLAHOMA C	OKLAHOMA D
PAIL(A)	W	37	5	N	61	9	33	4	67	5	73	11	50	3	64	8	44	5
	E	63	8	S	39	6	67	9	33	3	27	4	50	3	36	5	56	6
	ST		13			14		13		8		15		7		13		10
BUCKET(A)	W	35	30	N	51	44	68	59	69	64	67	56	46	43	54	47	44	39
	E	65	57	S	49	42	32	28	31	28	33	28	54	50	46	40	56	51
	ST		87			86		87		92		85		93		87		90

ITEM (32)
WORK SHEET (17)

HOUSEHOLD EQUIPMENT
A LARGE OPEN TIN VESSEL FOR WATER, MILK, ETC.

		TENNESSEE A	TENNESSEE B		GEORGIA A	GEORGIA B	ALABAMA A	ALABAMA B	MISSISSIPPI A	MISSISSIPPI B	FLORIDA A	FLORIDA B	LOUISIANA A	LOUISIANA B	ARKANSAS A	ARKANSAS B	OKLAHOMA A	OKLAHOMA B
PAIL(B)	W	18	3	N	15	2	5	1	6	1	6	1	7	1	21	4	19	4
	E	26	4	S	13	2	4	1	1	.1	7	1	7	1	21	4	26	5
	ST	43	6		28	4	9	1	6	1	13	2	14	3	41	9	45	9
BUCKET(B)	W	14	7	N	14	7	7	4	5	2	8	4	7	4	23	12	18	9
	E	30	14	S	13	6	3	2	2	1	3	2	9	5	20	10	22	11
	ST	44	21		27	13	11	5	7	3	11	5	16	8	43	22	40	21

		TENNESSEE C	TENNESSEE D		GEORGIA C	GEORGIA D	ALABAMA C	ALABAMA D	MISSISSIPPI C	MISSISSIPPI D	FLORIDA C	FLORIDA D	LOUISIANA C	LOUISIANA D	ARKANSAS C	ARKANSAS D	OKLAHOMA C	OKLAHOMA D
PAIL(B)	W	41	9	N	54	13	54	11	89	20	47	13	50	13	50	14	42	13
	E	59	14	S	46	11	46	10	11	3	53	14	50	13	50	14	58	18
	ST		23			24		21		23		27		26		28		31
BUCKET(B)	W	33	25	N	53	40	69	55	68	53	71	51	43	32	54	39	46	31
	E	67	52	S	47	36	31	24	32	25	29	21	57	42	46	33	54	37
	ST		77			76		79		78		73		74		72		69

ITEM (33)
WORK SHEET (17)

HOUSEHOLD EQUIPMENT
A VESSEL FOR CARRYING FOOD TO HOGS

		TENNESSEE A	TENNESSEE B		GEORGIA A	GEORGIA B	ALABAMA A	ALABAMA B	MISSISSIPPI A	MISSISSIPPI B	FLORIDA A	FLORIDA B	LOUISIANA A	LOUISIANA B	ARKANSAS A	ARKANSAS B	OKLAHOMA A	OKLAHOMA B
SLOP BUCKET	W	15	8	N	15	8	7	4	5	3	7	4	7	4	25	15	19	11
	E	30	16	S	14	7	3	2	2	1	3	2	7	4	20	12	23	14
	ST	44	24		29	15	10	6	7	4	10	5	14	8	45	27	41	25
SLOP PAIL	W	26	1	N	5	.1	11	.2	5	.1	5	.1	**	**	40	1	**	**
	E	32	1	S	5	.1	**	**	**	**	11	.2	**	**	**	**	60	1
	ST	58	1		11	.2	11	.2	5	.1	16	.3	**	**	40	1	60	1
SWILL BUCKET	W	26	1	N	**	**	**	**	**	**	26	1	**	**	20	.3	**	**
	E	26	1	S	9	.2	**	**	**	**	13	.3	**	**	40	1	40	1
	ST	52	1		9	.2	**	**	**	**	39	1	**	**	60	1	40	1
SWILL PAIL	W	**	**	N	**	**	**	**	**	**	33	.2	**	**	**	**	100	1
	E	17	.1	S	17	.1	**	**	**	**	33	.2	**	**	**	**	**	**
	ST	17	.1		17	.1	**	**	**	**	67	.4	**	**	**	**	100	1

		TENNESSEE C	TENNESSEE D		GEORGIA C	GEORGIA D	ALABAMA C	ALABAMA D	MISSISSIPPI C	MISSISSIPPI D	FLORIDA C	FLORIDA D	LOUISIANA C	LOUISIANA D	ARKANSAS C	ARKANSAS D	OKLAHOMA C	OKLAHOMA D
SLOP BUCKET	W	34	30	N	52	50	72	70	74	71	70	54	52	52	55	51	45	41
	E	66	60	S	48	47	28	27	26	26	30	23	48	48	45	43	55	50
	ST		91			97		96		97		77		100		94		91
SLOP PAIL	W	45	2	N	50	1	100	4	100	3	33	1	**	**	100	3	**	**
	E	55	2	S	50	1	**	**	**	**	67	3	**	**	**	**	100	4
	ST		4			1		4		3		4		**		3		4
SWILL BUCKET	W	50	2	N	**	**	**	**	**	**	67	9	**	**	33	1	**	**
	E	50	2	S	100	1	**	**	**	**	33	4	**	**	67	3	100	3
	ST		5			1		**		**		13		**		4		3
SWILL PAIL	W	**	**	N	**	**	**	**	**	**	50	3	**	**	**	**	100	3
	E	100	.3	S	100	1	**	**	**	**	50	3	**	**	**	**	**	**
	ST		.3			1		**		**		6		**		**		3

HOUSEHOLD EQUIPMENT
A HEAVY IRON UTENSIL FOR FRYING

ITEM (34)
WORK SHEET (17)

		TENNESSEE A	TENNESSEE B		GEORGIA A	GEORGIA B	ALABAMA A	ALABAMA B	MISSISSIPPI A	MISSISSIPPI B	FLORIDA A	FLORIDA B	LOUISIANA A	LOUISIANA B	ARKANSAS A	ARKANSAS B	OKLAHOMA A	OKLAHOMA B
CREEPER					(NO RESPONSE)													
					(NO RESPONSE)													
					(NO RESPONSE)													
FRYER	W	**	**	N	30	.3	**	**	**	**	20	.2	17	.3	67	1	**	**
	E	**	**	S	40	.4	10	.1	**	**	**	**	**	**	17	.3	**	**
	ST	**	**		70	1	10	.1	**	**	20	.2	17	.3	83	2	**	**
FRYING PAN	W	11	3	N	18	5	9	3	3	1	8	2	3	1	21	5	24	6
	E	19	6	S	19	6	5	2	3	1	5	2	13	3	9	2	31	8
	ST	30	9		37	11	14	4	6	2	13	4	16	4	29	7	54	13
FRY PAN	W	29	.2	N	14	.1	**	**	**	**	14	.1	**	**	**	**	25	.3
	E	14	.1	S	14	.1	**	**	**	**	14	.1	**	**	25	.3	50	1
	ST	43	.3		29	.2	**	**	**	**	29	.2	**	**	25	.3	75	1
SKILLET	W	20	8	N	13	5	7	3	6	2	4	2	9	5	23	13	19	11
	E	38	15	S	6	2	2	1	2	1	3	1	7	4	19	11	23	14
	ST	57	22		18	7	9	4	8	3	8	3	15	9	42	25	43	25
SPIDER	W	2	.1	N	7	.3	2	.1	**	**	32	1	**	**	100	.3	**	**
	E	5	.2	S	44	2	**	**	**	**	7	.3	**	**	**	**	**	**
	ST	7	.3		51	2	2	.1	**	**	39	2	**	**	100	.3	**	**

		TENNESSEE C	TENNESSEE D		GEORGIA C	GEORGIA D	ALABAMA C	ALABAMA D	MISSISSIPPI C	MISSISSIPPI D	FLORIDA C	FLORIDA D	LOUISIANA C	LOUISIANA D	ARKANSAS C	ARKANSAS D	OKLAHOMA C	OKLAHOMA D
CREEPER					(NO RESPONSE)													
					(NO RESPONSE)													
	ST		**			**		**		**		**		**		**		**
FRYER	W	**	**	N	43	1	**	**	**	**	100	2	100	3	80	4	**	**
	E	**	**	S	57	2	100	1	**	**	**	**	**	**	20	1	**	**
	ST		**			3		1		**		2		3		5		**
FRYING PAN	W	36	10	N	49	25	63	32	56	21	59	26	18	5	70	15	43	15
	E	64	18	S	51	27	38	19	44	17	41	17	82	24	30	6	57	19
	ST		28			52		52		38		43		30		21		34
FRY PAN	W	67	1	N	50	.4	**	**	**	**	50	1	**	**	**	**	33	1
	E	33	.3	S	50	.4	**	**	**	**	50	1	**	**	100	1	67	2
	ST		1			1		**		**		2		**		1		3
SKILLET	W	34	24	N	70	23	80	36	73	46	59	20	56	38	54	39	45	28
	E	66	46	S	30	10	20	9	27	17	41	14	44	30	46	33	55	35
	ST		70			33		45		63		34		68		72		63
SPIDER	W	33	.3	N	14	1	100	1	**	**	81	15	**	**	100	1	**	**
	E	67	1	S	86	9	**	**	**	**	19	3	**	**	**	**	**	**
	ST		1			10		1		**		19		**		1		**

HOUSEHOLD EQUIPMENT
IRON UTENSIL WITH LARGE OPEN TOP FOR BOILING MEAT, POTATOES, ETC.

ITEM (35)
WORK SHEET (17)

		TENNESSEE			GEORGIA		ALABAMA		MISSISSIPPI		FLORIDA		LOUISIANA		ARKANSAS		OKLAHOMA	
		A	B		A	B	A	B	A	B	A	B	A	B	A	B	A	B
KETTLE	W	21	4	N	6	1	7	1	4	1	2	.4	4	1	28	7	37	9
	E	49	9	S	6	1	1	.2	1	.2	3	1	**	**	9	2	22	5
	ST	70	13		12	2	8	1	6	1	5	1	4	1	37	9	59	14
POT	W	15	6	N	18	7	6	3	6	2	11	4	9	4	22	10	11	5
	E	18	8	S	16	7	4	2	3	1	4	2	13	6	23	10	23	10
	ST	33	14		34	14	10	4	8	3	15	6	22	10	45	20	33	15

		TENNESSEE			GEORGIA		ALABAMA		MISSISSIPPI		FLORIDA		LOUISIANA		ARKANSAS		OKLAHOMA	
		C	D		C	D	C	D	C	D	C	D	C	D	C	D	C	D
KETTLE	W	30	15	N	50	7	86	22	80	19	44	6	100	10	76	24	63	31
	E	70	34	S	50	7	14	4	20	5	56	7	**	**	24	8	38	19
	ST		49			14		26		24		13		10		31		49
POT	W	45	23	N	52	45	63	46	69	52	72	63	41	37	49	34	32	16
	E	55	28	S	48	41	38	28	31	24	28	24	59	53	51	35	68	35
	ST		51			86		74		76		87		90		69		51

HOUSEHOLD EQUIPMENT
OVER A SINK

ITEM (36)
WORK SHEET (18)

		TENNESSEE A	TENNESSEE B		GEORGIA A	GEORGIA B	ALABAMA A	ALABAMA B	MISSISSIPPI A	MISSISSIPPI B	FLORIDA A	FLORIDA B	LOUISIANA A	LOUISIANA B	ARKANSAS A	ARKANSAS B	OKLAHOMA A	OKLAHOMA B
FAUCET(A)	W	17	8	N	14	7	8	4	5	3	7	3	7	5	23	15	19	12
	E	30	14	S	11	5	3	1	2	1	3	2	8	5	19	12	23	14
	ST	47	23		25	12	11	5	7	4	10	5	16	10	42	27	42	27
HYDRANT(A)	W	18	1	N	11	1	11	1	2	.1	2	.1	5	.3	10	1	10	1
	E	24	1	S	7	.3	18	1	7	.3	**	**	5	.3	19	1	52	4
	ST	42	2		18	1	29	1	9	.4	2	.1	10	1	29	2	62	5
SPICKET(A)	W	2	.2	N	16	2	4	.4	4	.4	18	2	**	**	50	.3	50	.3
	E	24	2	S	24	2	**	**	**	**	8	1	**	**	**	**	**	**
	ST	26	3		40	4	4	.4	4	.4	26	3	**	**	50	.3	50	.3
SPIGOT(A)	W	9	.4	N	22	1	9	.4	4	.2	9	.4	**	**	33	.3	33	.3
	E	11	1	S	22	1	7	.3	**	**	9	.4	33	.3	**	**	**	**
	ST	20	1		43	2	15	1	4	.2	17	1	33	.3	33	.3	33	.3
TAP(A)	W	21	.3	N	29	.4	7	.1	7	.1	**	**	**	**	30	1	10	.3
	E	14	.2	S	7	.1	7	.1	7	.1	**	**	10	.3	10	.3	40	1
	ST	36	1		36	1	14	.2	14	.2	**	**	10	.3	40	1	50	2

		TENNESSEE C	TENNESSEE D		GEORGIA C	GEORGIA D	ALABAMA C	ALABAMA D	MISSISSIPPI C	MISSISSIPPI D	FLORIDA C	FLORIDA D	LOUISIANA C	LOUISIANA D	ARKANSAS C	ARKANSAS D	OKLAHOMA C	OKLAHOMA D
FAUCET(A)	W	37	29	N	55	34	72	47	74	54	67	39	46	41	55	47	46	36
	E	63	50	S	45	28	28	18	26	20	33	19	54	47	45	39	54	43
	ST		79			61		66		74		58		88		86		79
HYDRANT(A)	W	42	3	N	63	3	38	7	25	2	100	1	50	3	33	2	15	2
	E	58	4	S	38	2	62	11	75	7	**	**	50	3	67	5	85	12
	ST		7			4		17		9		1		6		7		14
SPICKET(A)	W	8	1	N	41	9	100	5	100	9	68	21	**	**	100	1	100	1
	E	92	8	S	59	12	**	**	**	**	32	10	**	**	**	**	**	**
	ST		9			21		5		9		31		**		1		1
SPIGOT(A)	W	44	1	N	50	5	57	5	100	4	50	5	**	**	100	1	100	1
	E	56	2	S	50	5	43	4	**	**	50	5	100	3	**	**	**	**
	ST		3			11		9		4		10		3		1		1
TAP(A)	W	60	1	N	80	2	50	1	50	2	**	**	**	**	75	3	20	1
	E	40	1	S	20	1	50	1	50	2	**	**	100	3	25	1	80	4
	ST		2			3		3		4		**		3		5		5

HOUSEHOLD EQUIPMENT
ON A BARREL

ITEM (36)
WORK SHEET (18)

		TENNESSEE A	TENNESSEE B		GEORGIA A	GEORGIA B	ALABAMA A	ALABAMA B	MISSISSIPPI A	MISSISSIPPI B	FLORIDA A	FLORIDA B	LOUISIANA A	LOUISIANA B	ARKANSAS A	ARKANSAS B	OKLAHOMA A	OKLAHOMA B
FAUCET(B)	W	18	4	N	17	3	7	1	4	1	9	2	12	3	25	6	11	3
	E	22	4	S	17	3	2	.4	2	.4	3	1	14	3	15	4	23	5
	ST	40	8		34	7	9	2	6	1	12	2	26	6	40	9	34	8
SPICKET(B)	W	8	1	N	13	2	8	1	6	1	7	1	5	.3	32	3	18	1
	E	37	5	S	16	2	3	.3	1	.1	4	1	**	**	18	1	27	2
	ST	44	5		28	4	10	1	7	1	11	1	5	.3	50	4	45	4
SPIGOT(B)	W	18	2	N	18	3	7	1	6	1	9	1	6	1	25	6	28	7
	E	24	3	S	9	1	2	.3	2	.3	5	1	4	1	21	5	16	4
	ST	41	6		27	4	10	1	8	1	14	2	10	3	46	11	44	11
TAP(B)	W	15	2	N	12	1	12	1	7	1	8	1	**	**	13	1	20	2
	E	27	3	S	9	1	5	1	2	.2	5	1	10	1	23	3	33	4
	ST	42	4		20	2	17	2	9	1	13	1	10	1	37	4	53	6

		TENNESSEE C	TENNESSEE D		GEORGIA C	GEORGIA D	ALABAMA C	ALABAMA D	MISSISSIPPI C	MISSISSIPPI D	FLORIDA C	FLORIDA D	LOUISIANA C	LOUISIANA D	ARKANSAS C	ARKANSAS D	OKLAHOMA C	OKLAHOMA D
FAUCET(B)	W	45	15	N	50	21	78	23	67	20	74	25	47	29	62	20	32	9
	E	55	19	S	50	21	22	7	33	10	26	9	53	32	38	13	68	19
	ST		34			42		30		30		34		61		33		28
SPICKET(B)	W	17	4	N	44	9	75	15	88	18	62	12	100	4	64	9	40	5
	E	83	19	S	56	12	25	5	13	3	38	7	**	**	36	5	60	8
	ST		23			22		20		20		19		4		14		13
SPIGOT(B)	W	43	10	N	68	16	77	17	73	20	63	18	57	14	55	22	63	24
	E	57	14	S	32	8	23	5	27	8	37	10	43	11	45	18	37	14
	ST		24			23		22		28		28		25		39		38
TAP(B)	W	35	7	N	57	8	71	20	78	18	62	12	**	**	36	5	38	8
	E	65	12	S	43	6	29	8	22	5	38	7	100	11	64	9	63	13
	ST		19			13		28		23		19		11		14		21

ITEM (36)
WORK SHEET (18)

HOUSEHOLD EQUIPMENT
IN THE YARD OR GARDEN

		TENNESSEE			GEORGIA		ALABAMA		MISSISSIPPI		FLORIDA		LOUISIANA		ARKANSAS		OKLAHOMA	
		A	B		A	B	A	B	A	B	A	B	A	B	A	B	A	B
FAUCET(C)	W	9	2	N	12	2	5	1	5	1	9	2	11	2	7	1	24	4
	E	31	5	S	16	3	4	1	1	.2	6	1	28	5	4	1	26	4
	ST	40	7		28	5	9	2	7	1	15	3	39	6	11	2	50	8
SPICKET(C)	W	4	1	N	14	2	5	1	4	1	14	2	**	**	100	.3	**	**
	E	28	4	S	23	3	1	.1	1	.1	6	1	**	**	**	**	**	**
	ST	32	5		37	5	6	1	5	1	21	3	**	**	100	.3	**	**
SPIGOT(C)	W	4	.2	N	30	2	6	.3	2	.1	11	1	**	**	**	**	**	**
	E	21	1	S	17	1	2	.1	**	**	8	.4	100	.3	**	**	**	**
	ST	25	1		47	3	8	.4	2	.1	19	1	100	.3	**	**	**	**
HYDRANT(B)	W	[illegible]	[illegible]	N	14	4	10	3	5	2	3	1	6	4	25	15	20	12
	E	25	7	S	8	2	4	1	4	1	2	1	5	3	21	12	23	13
	ST	50	14		21	6	14	4	9	3	5	1	11	6	46	27	43	25
TAP(C)	W	67	.2	N	**	**	**	**	**	**	**	**	**	**	**	**	25	.3
	E	33	.1	S	**	**	**	**	**	**	**	**	25	.3	**	**	50	1
	ST	100	.3		**	**	**	**	**	**	**	**	25	.3	**	**	75	1

		TENNESSEE			GEORGIA		ALABAMA		MISSISSIPPI		FLORIDA		LOUISIANA		ARKANSAS		OKLAHOMA	
		C	D		C	D	C	D	C	D	C	D	C	D	C	D	C	D
FAUCET(C)	W	22	6	N	44	11	56	13	82	20	62	20	28	13	60	4	48	11
	E	78	20	S	56	15	44	10	18	4	38	13	72	34	40	2	52	13
	ST		25			26		24		24		33		47		6		24
SPICKET(C)	W	11	2	N	38	11	88	10	86	13	69	25	**	**	100	1	**	**
	E	89	15	S	62	17	13	1	14	2	31	11	**	**	**	**	**	**
	ST		17			28		12		16		37		**		1		**
SPIGOT(C)	W	15	1	N	64	9	75	4	100	2	60	8	**	**	**	**	**	**
	E	85	4	S	36	5	25	1	**	**	40	5	100	3	**	**	**	**
	ST		5			14		6		2		13		3		**		**
HYDRANT(B)	W	51	26	N	64	21	73	43	58	33	57	10	56	26	55	51	47	34
	E	49	25	S	36	11	28	16	42	24	43	8	44	21	45	42	53	39
	ST		52			32		59		58		18		47		93		73
TAP(C)	W	67	1	N	**	**	**	**	**	**	**	**	**	**	**	**	33	1
	E	33	.3	S	**	**	**	**	**	**	**	**	100	3	**	**	67	2
	ST		1			**		**		**		**		3		**		3

HOUSEHOLD EQUIPMENT
PAPER CONTAINER FOR GROCERIES ETC.

ITEM (37)
WORK SHEET (19)

		TENNESSEE A	TENNESSEE B		GEORGIA A	GEORGIA B	ALABAMA A	ALABAMA B	MISSISSIPPI A	MISSISSIPPI B	FLORIDA A	FLORIDA B	LOUISIANA A	LOUISIANA B	ARKANSAS A	ARKANSAS B	OKLAHOMA A	OKLAHOMA B
BAG	W	13	5	N	14	5	7	2	4	2	9	3	7	2	31	10	16	5
	E	32	12	S	12	4	3	1	2	1	5	2	16	5	18	6	13	4
	ST	44	17		25	10	10	4	7	3	14	5	23	7	49	16	28	9
POKE	W	11	1	N	15	1	6	.3	2	.1	2	.1	**	**	64	3	**	**
	E	60	3	S	2	.1	**	**	**	**	2	.1	**	**	21	1	14	1
	ST	72	4		17	1	6	.3	2	.1	4	.2	**	**	86	4	14	1
SACK	W	23	6	N	15	4	8	2	5	1	8	2	9	4	16	8	23	10
	E	19	5	S	14	4	3	1	1	.4	4	1	2	1	19	9	30	14
	ST	42	12		29	8	10	3	6	2	12	3	12	5	35	16	53	25
TOOT	W	25	.1	N	**	**	**	**	25	.1	**	**	**	**	**	**	**	**
	E	25	.1	S	**	**	**	**	**	**	25	.1	**	**	**	**	**	**
	ST	50	.2		**	**	**	**	25	.1	25	.1	**	**	**	**	**	**

		TENNESSEE C	TENNESSEE D		GEORGIA C	GEORGIA D	ALABAMA C	ALABAMA D	MISSISSIPPI C	MISSISSIPPI D	FLORIDA C	FLORIDA D	LOUISIANA C	LOUISIANA D	ARKANSAS C	ARKANSAS D	OKLAHOMA C	OKLAHOMA D
BAG	W	28	15	N	54	28	67	36	64	36	66	38	30	17	63	27	56	15
	E	72	37	S	46	24	33	18	36	20	34	20	70	40	37	16	44	12
	ST		51			51		54		57		58		57		43		26
POKE	W	16	2	N	89	4	100	4	100	2	50	1	**	**	75	9	**	**
	E	84	10	S	11	1	**	**	**	**	50	1	**	**	25	3	100	2
	ST		12			5		4		2		2		**		12		2
SACK	W	54	20	N	53	23	75	31	76	30	67	26	80	34	47	21	43	31
	E	46	16	S	47	20	25	10	24	9	33	13	20	9	53	24	57	41
	ST		36			44		42		39		38		43		45		72
TOOT	W	50	.3	N	**	**	**	**	100	2	**	**	**	**	**	**	**	**
	E	50	.3	S	**	**	**	**	**	**	100	1	**	**	**	**	**	**
	ST		1			**		**		2		1		**		**		**

ITEM (38)
WORK SHEET (19)

HOUSEHOLD EQUIPMENT
LARGE BAG LOOSELY WOVEN

		TENNESSEE			GEORGIA		ALABAMA		MISSISSIPPI		FLORIDA		LOUISIANA		ARKANSAS		OKLAHOMA	
		A	B		A	B	A	B	A	B	A	B	A	B	A	B	A	B
BURLAP BAG	W	18	2	N	12	1	9	1	3	.3	10	1	8	1	50	5	12	1
	E	33	4	S	9	1	3	.4	2	.2	1	.1	**	**	19	2	12	1
	ST	51	6		22	3	12	1	4	1	11	1	8	1	69	6	23	2
BURLAP SACK	W	15	1	N	12	1	6	.4	1	.1	7	1	5	.3	15	1	15	1
	E	45	3	S	7	1	3	.2	**	**	3	.2	25	2	15	1	25	2
	ST	60	4		19	1	9	1	1	.1	10	1	30	2	30	2	40	3
COFFEE SACK	W	**	**	N	25	.1	**	**	**	**	**	**	**	**	**	**	**	**
	E	25	.1	S	25	.1	**	**	25	.1	**	**	**	**	**	**	**	**
	ST	25	.1		50	.2	**	**	25	.1	**	**	**	**	**	**	**	**
CROKER SACK	W	3	1	N	10	3	6	1	9	2	15	3	40	3	**	**	5	.3
	E	2	.4	S	27	5	5	1	4	1	11	2	25	2	25	2	5	.3
	ST	5	1		46	8	11	2	13	2	26	5	65	5	25	2	10	1
CROCUS SACK	W	3	.1	N	25	1	**	**	8	.3	28	1	**	**	50	.3	**	**
	E	**	**	S	22	1	6	.2	3	.1	6	.2	**	**	50	.3	**	**
	ST	3	.1		47	2	6	.2	11	.4	33	1	**	**	100	1	**	**
GUNNY SACK	W	21	1	N	5	.2	3	.1	11	.4	8	.3	7	2	22	6	33	9
	E	34	1	S	**	**	**	**	8	.3	11	.4	7	2	4	1	26	7
	ST	55	2		5	.2	3	.1	18	1	18	1	14	4	26	7	60	16
GUNNY BAG	W	50	.1	N	**	**	**	**	**	**	**	**	**	**	17	1	25	1
	E	**	**	S	**	**	**	**	**	**	50	.1	8	.3	**	**	50	2
	ST	50	.1		**	**	**	**	**	**	50	.1	8	.3	17	1	75	3
GUANO SACK	W	**	**	N	27	1	3	.1	**	**	15	1	**	**	100	.3	**	**
	E	**	**	S	45	2	9	.3	**	**	**	**	**	**	**	**	**	**
	ST	**	**		73	2	12	.4	**	**	15	1	**	**	100	.3	**	**
JUTE BAG	W	50	.1	N	**	**	**	**	**	**	**	**	**	**	**	**	**	**
	E	**	**	S	50	.1	**	**	**	**	**	**	**	**	**	**	**	**
	ST	50	.1		50	.1	**	**	**	**	**	**	**	**	**	**	**	**
JUTE SACK	W	**	**	N	100	.3	**	**	**	**	**	**	**	**	**	**	**	**
					(NO RESPONSE)													
	ST	**	**		100	.3	**	**	**	**	**	**	**	**	**	**	**	**
SEAGRASS SACK	W	33	.2	N	**	**	**	**	**	**	**	**	**	**	**	**	50	1
	E	67	.4	S	**	**	**	**	**	**	**	**	**	**	25	.3	25	.3
	ST	100	1		**	**	**	**	**	**	**	**	**	**	25	.3	75	1
TOW SACK	W	28	7	N	10	2	9	2	5	1	**	**	8	3	31	12	10	4
	E	47	11	S	.4	.1	.4	.1	.4	.1	.4	.1	**	**	28	10	23	9
	ST	75	18		10	2	9	2	5	1	.4	.1	8	3	59	22	33	12

(CONTINUED) LARGE BAG LOOSELY WOVEN

ITEM (38)		TENNESSEE C	TENNESSEE D		GEORGIA C	GEORGIA D	ALABAMA C	ALABAMA D	MISSISSIPPI C	MISSISSIPPI D	FLORIDA C	FLORIDA D	LOUISIANA C	LOUISIANA D	ARKANSAS C	ARKANSAS D	OKLAHOMA C	OKLAHOMA D
BURLAP BAG	W	36	7	N	56	7	71	15	60	6	92	13	100	5	72	11	50	3
	E	64	12	S	44	6	29	6	40	4	8	1	**	**	28	4	50	3
	ST		19			13		21		9		14		5		16		6
BURLAP SACK	W	25	3	N	62	4	67	6	100	2	71	5	17	3	50	3	38	3
	E	75	10	S	38	3	33	3	**	**	29	2	83	13	50	3	63	5
	ST		13			7		9		2		8		15		5		8
COFFEE SACK	W	**	**	N	50	1	**	**	**	**	**	**	**	**	**	**	**	**
	E	100	.3	S	50	1	**	**	100	2	**	**	**	**	**	**	**	**
	ST		.3			1		**		2		**		**		**		**
CROKER SACK	W	56	2	N	40	17	53	15	70	30	57	29	62	20	**	**	50	1
	E	44	1	S	60	25	47	13	30	13	43	22	38	13	100	4	50	1
	ST		3			42		28		43		51		33		4		2
CROCUS SACK	W	100	.3	N	53	5	**	**	75	6	83	11	**	**	50	1	**	**
	E	**	**	S	47	4	100	3	25	2	17	2	**	**	50	1	**	**
	ST		.3			9		3		8		13		**		2		**
GUNNY SACK	W	38	3	N	100	1	100	1	57	8	43	3	50	13	84	14	56	23
	E	62	4	S	**	**	**	**	43	6	57	4	50	13	16	3	44	18
	ST		7			1		1		13		8		25		17		41
GUNNY BAG	W	100	.3	N	**	**	**	**	**	**	**	**	**	**	100	2	33	3
	E	**	**	S	**	**	**	**	**	**	100	1	100	3	**	**	67	6
	ST		.3			**		**		**		1		3		2		9
GUANO SACK	W	**	**	N	38	5	25	1	**	**	100	5	**	**	100	1	**	**
	E	**	**	S	63	8	75	4	**	**	**	**	**	**	**	**	**	**
	ST		**			12		6		**		5		**		1		**
JUTE BAG	W	100	.3	N	**	**	**	**	**	**	**	**	**	**	**	**	**	**
	E	**	**	S	100	1	**	**	**	**	**	**	**	**	**	**	**	**
	ST		.3			1		**		**		**		**		**		**
JUTE SACK	W	**	**	N	100	2	**	**	**	**	**	**	**	**	**	**	**	**
					(NO RESPONSE)													
	ST		**			2		**		**		**		**		**		**
SEAGRASS SACK	W	33	1	N	**	**	**	**	**	**	**	**	**	**	**	**	67	2
	E	67	1	S	**	**	**	**	**	**	**	**	**	**	100	1	33	1
	ST		2			**		**		**		**		**		1		3
TOW SACK	W	38	21	N	96	12	95	30	92	21	**	**	100	20	52	28	29	10
	E	62	35	S	4	1	5	1	8	2	100	1	**	**	48	25	71	23
	ST									[illegible]		[illegible]		20		53		32

ITEM (39)
WORK SHEET (20)

HOUSEHOLD EQUIPMENT
MADE OF CORK

		TENNESSEE A	TENNESSEE B		GEORGIA A	GEORGIA B	ALABAMA A	ALABAMA B	MISSISSIPPI A	MISSISSIPPI B	FLORIDA A	FLORIDA B	LOUISIANA A	LOUISIANA B	ARKANSAS A	ARKANSAS B	OKLAHOMA A	OKLAHOMA B
CORK	W	18	3	N	12	2	8	2	6	1	7	1	7	2	16	5	28	9
	E	26	5	S	5	1	6	1	3	1	8	2	9	3	12	4	29	9
	ST	44	8		17	3	14	3	9	2	15	3	16	5	28	9	57	18
CORK STOPPLE	W	10	.1	N	20	.2	**	**	**	**	20	.2	**	**	**	**	**	**
	E	30	.3	S	20	.2	**	**	**	**	**	**	**	**	**	**	**	**
	ST	40	.4		40	.4	**	**	**	**	20	.2	**	**	**	**	**	**
CORK STOPPER(A)	W	13	3	N	18	4	7	1	3	1	9	2	14	2	34	4	11	1
	E	21	4	S	23	5	4	1	1	.2	1	.1	6	1	26	3	9	1
	ST	34	7		41	8	11	2	4	1	9	2	20	3	60	8	20	3
STOPPER	W	19	5	N	12	3	5	1	5	1	7	2	6	2	33	10	15	5
	E	36	9	S	7	2	1	.2	3	1	6	1	6	2	22	7	18	5
	ST	55	14		19	5	6	2	7	2	13	3	12	4	55	17	33	10
STOPPLE(A)	W	**	**	N	**	**	20	.1	**	**	40	.2	**	**	**	**	**	**
	E	20	.1	S	20	.1	**	**	**	**	**	**	100	.3	**	**	**	**
	ST	20	.1		20	.1	20	.1	**	**	40	.2	100	.3	**	**	**	**

		TENNESSEE C	TENNESSEE D		GEORGIA C	GEORGIA D	ALABAMA C	ALABAMA D	MISSISSIPPI C	MISSISSIPPI D	FLORIDA C	FLORIDA D	LOUISIANA C	LOUISIANA D	ARKANSAS C	ARKANSAS D	OKLAHOMA C	OKLAHOMA D
CORK	W	40	12	N	72	14	58	23	71	28	46	16	43	19	56	15	49	29
	E	60	17	S	28	6	42	17	29	12	54	19	57	25	44	12	51	30
	ST		29			20		41		40		35		44		27		59
CORK STOPPLE	W	25	.3	N	50	1	**	**	**	**	100	2	**	**	**	**	**	**
	E	75	1	S	50	1	**	**	**	**	**	**	**	**	**	**	**	**
	ST		1			2		**		**		2		**		**		**
CORK STOPPER(A)	W	38	9	N	44	21	64	22	75	14	94	21	71	16	57	13	57	5
	E	62	14	S	56	28	36	13	25	5	6	1	29	6	43	10	43	3
	ST		23			49		34		19		22		22		23		8
STOPPER	W	34	16	N	61	17	87	20	61	26	55	21	50	16	60	30	46	15
	E	66	31	S	39	11	13	3	39	16	45	17	50	16	40	20	54	17
	ST		46			28		23		42		38		31		51		33
STOPPLE(A)	W	**	**	N	**	**	100	2	**	**	100	2	**	**	**	**	**	**
	E	100	.3	S	100	1	**	**	**	**	**	**	100	3	**	**	**	**
	ST		.3			1		2		**		2		3		**		**

HOUSEHOLD EQUIPMENT
MADE OF GLASS

ITEM (39)
WORK SHEET (20)

		TENNESSEE			GEORGIA		ALABAMA		MISSISSIPPI		FLORIDA		LOUISIANA		ARKANSAS		OKLAHOMA	
		A	B		A	B	A	B	A	B	A	B	A	B	A	B	A	B
CORK STOPPER(B)	W	21	3	N	9	1	3	.4	4	1	15	2	14	4	17	4	19	5
	E	24	4	S	6	1	1	.2	4	1	13	2	13	3	17	4	20	5
	ST	45	7		14	2	4	1	8	1	28	4	27	7	34	9	39	10
STOPPLE(B)	W	19	1	N	19	1	2	.1	5	.2	7	.3	**	**	20	.3	**	**
	E	30	1	S	14	1	5	.2	**	**	**	**	20	.3	20	.3	40	1
	ST	49	2		33	1	7	.3	5	.2	7	.3	20	.3	40	1	40	1
GLASS CORK	W	15	2	N	13	2	9	1	6	1	6	1	4	1	34	6	18	3
	E	28	5	S	15	2	3	1	3	.4	2	.3	**	**	22	4	22	4
	ST	43	7		28	5	12	2	9	1	8	1	4	1	56	10	40	7

		TENNESSEE			GEORGIA		ALABAMA		MISSISSIPPI		FLORIDA		LOUISIANA		ARKANSAS		OKLAHOMA	
		C	D		C	D	C	D	C	D	C	D	C	D	C	D	C	D
CORK STOPPER(B)	W	46	19	N	60	15	67	14	45	19	54	39	53	45	50	22	48	27
	E	54	23	S	40	10	33	7	55	22	46	33	47	41	50	22	52	29
	ST		42			26		21		41		72		86		44		55
STOPPLE(B)	W	38	5	N	57	10	33	4	100	7	100	6	**	**	50	2	**	**
	E	62	9	S	43	8	67	7	**	**	**	**	100	5	50	2	100	4
	ST		14			18		11		7		6		5		4		4
GLASS CORK	W	34	15	N	45	26	74	50	71	37	75	17	100	9	61	31	45	18
	E	66	29	S	55	31	26	18	29	15	25	6	**	**	39	20	55	22
	ST		44			56		68		52		22		9		52		41

ITEM (40)
WORK SHEET (20)

SOCIAL LIFE
INSTRUMENT TO BE BLOWN ON

		TENNESSEE A	TENNESSEE B		GEORGIA A	GEORGIA B	ALABAMA A	ALABAMA B	MISSISSIPPI A	MISSISSIPPI B	FLORIDA A	FLORIDA B	LOUISIANA A	LOUISIANA B	ARKANSAS A	ARKANSAS B	OKLAHOMA A	OKLAHOMA B
BREATH HARP	W	100	.2	N	**	**	**	**	**	**	**	**	**	**	**	**	**	**
	E	**	**	S	**	**	**	**	**	**	**	**	**	**	**	**	100	.3
	ST	100	.2		**	**	**	**	**	**	**	**	**	**	**	**	100	.3
FRENCH HARP(A)	W	27	6	N	12	3	9	2	6	1	**	**	9	3	29	10	19	7
	E	42	9	S	1	.3	**	**	2	.4	**	**	2	1	19	7	22	8
	ST	69	15		14	3	9	2	8	2	**	**	11	4	48	17	41	15
HARMONICA	W	15	4	N	14	4	7	2	4	1	6	2	8	3	18	7	19	8
	E	32	8	S	11	3	4	1	2	.4	5	1	11	5	20	8	24	10
	ST	47	12		25	7	11	3	6	2	11	3	19	8	38	16	43	18
HARP	W	8	1	N	18	2	6	1	5	1	14	1	**	**	38	1	25	1
	F	8	1	S	31	3	5	1	2	.2	3	.3	**	**	13	.3	25	1
	ST	16	2		49	5	11	1	7	1	17	2	**	**	50	1	50	1
JEWS HARP(A)	W	16	1	N	16	1	9	.4	9	.4	2	.1	9	1	36	3	14	1
	E	27	1	S	9	.4	2	.1	2	.1	9	.4	**	**	32	3	9	1
	ST	42	2		24	1	11	1	11	1	11	1	9	1	68	5	23	2
JUICE HARP(A)	W	20	1	N	4	.2	2	.1	10	1	6	.3	13	.3	13	.3	**	**
	E	36	2	S	10	1	4	.2	4	.2	4	.2	**	**	13	.3	63	2
	ST	56	3		14	1	6	.3	14	1	10	1	13	.3	25	1	63	2
MOUTH HARP(A)	W	3	.1	N	9	.3	3	.1	**	**	31	1	33	.3	**	**	**	**
	E	6	.2	S	17	1	11	.4	6	.2	14	1	33	.3	**	**	33	.3
	ST	9	.3		26	1	14	1	6	.2	46	2	67	1	**	**	33	.3
MOUTH ORGAN	W	7	1	N	25	2	5	.4	1	.1	23	2	**	**	18	1	36	1
	E	8	1	S	17	1	6	1	1	.1	6	1	**	**	**	**	45	2
	ST	16	1		42	4	11	1	2	.2	29	2	**	**	18	1	82	3

(CONTINUED) INSTRUMENT TO BE BLOWN ON

ITEM (40)		TENNESSEE C	TENNESSEE D		GEORGIA C	GEORGIA D	ALABAMA C	ALABAMA D	MISSISSIPPI C	MISSISSIPPI D	FLORIDA C	FLORIDA D	LOUISIANA C	LOUISIANA D	ARKANSAS C	ARKANSAS D	OKLAHOMA C	OKLAHOMA D
BREATH HARP	W	100	1	N	**	**	**	**	**	**	**	**	**	**	**	**	**	**
	E	**	**	S	**	**	**	**	**	**	**	**	**	**	**	**	100	1
	ST		1			**		**		**		**		**		**		1
FRENCH HARP(A)	W	39	16	N	90	13	100	24	76	24	**	**	82	24	60	25	46	17
	E	61	26	S	10	1	**	**	24	7	**	**	18	5	40	17	54	19
	ST		42			14		24		31		**		29		42		36
HARMONICA	W	32	11	N	56	18	67	23	73	20	57·	17	41	24	47	18	45	19
	E	68	23	S	44	14	33	11	27	7	43	13	59	34	53	20	55	23
	ST		34			31		34		27		29		58		38		43
HARP	W	50	2	N	37	9	55	8	71	9	82	15	**	**	75	3	50	2
	E	50	2	S	63	15	45	6	29	4	18	3	**	**	25	1	50	2
	ST		5			24		14		13		18		**		4		3
JEWS HARP(A)	W	37	2	N	64	3	80	5	80	7	20	1	100	5	53	7	60	3
	E	63	3	S	36	2	20	1	20	2	80	4	**	**	47	6	40	2
	ST		5			5		6		9		5		5		13		4
JUICE HARP(A)	W	36	3	N	29	1	33	1	71	9	60	3	100	3	50	1	**	**
	E	64	5	S	71	2	67	3	29	4	40	2	**	**	50	1	100	4
	ST		8			3		4		13		5		3		2		4
MOUTH HARP(A)	W	33	.2	N	33	1	20	1	**	**	69	12	50	3	**	**	**	**
	E	67	1	S	67	3	80	5	100	4	31	5	50	3	**	**	100	1
	ST		1			4		6		4		17		5		**		1
MOUTH ORGAN	W	46	2	N	60	10	44	5	50	2	79	20	**	**	100	2	44	3
	E	54	2	S	40	7	56	6	50	2	21	5	**	**	**	**	56	4
	ST		4			17		11		4		25		**		2		8

ITEM (40)
WORK SHEET (20)

SOCIAL LIFE
HARP HELD BETWEEN THE TEETH AND PICKED

		TENNESSEE			GEORGIA		ALABAMA		MISSISSIPPI		FLORIDA		LOUISIANA		ARKANSAS		OKLAHOMA	
		A	B		A	B	A	B	A	B	A	B	A	B	A	B	A	B
BREATH HARP(B)	W	25	.2	N	13	.1	25	.2	**	**	**	**	**	**	**	**	**	**
	E	**	**	S	25	.2	13	.1	**	**	**	**	**	**	**	**	100	1
	ST	25	.2		38	.3	38	.3	**	**	**	**	**	**	**	**	100	1
FRENCH HARP(B)	W	17	1	N	8	.4	13	1	2	.1	**	**	**	**	17	1	6	.3
	E	48	2	S	10	1	2	.1	**	**	**	**	6	.3	28	2	44	3
	ST	65	3		19	1	15	1	2	.1	**	**	6	.3	44	3	50	3
JEWS HARP(B)	W	19	8	N	22	9	8	3	5	2	8	3	8	3	30	13	16	7
	E	21	8	S	9	4	3	1	2	1	4	2	6	3	25	10	16	7
	ST	40	16		31	12	10	4	7	3	12	5	14	6	54	23	32	14
JUICE HARP(B)	W	19	6	N	19	6	6	2	4	1	8	3	7	2	30	8	13	3
	E	26	8	S	14	4	2	1	2	1	1	.3	6	1	20	5	24	6
	ST	45	14		33	10	7	2	6	2	9	3	13	3	50	13	37	9
MOUTH HARP(B)	W	19	1	N	14	1	11	.4	8	.3	6	.2	**	**	57	1	**	**
	E	19	1	S	11	.4	3	.1	6	.2	3	.1	14	.3	14	.3	14	.3
	ST	39	1		25	1	14	1	14	1	8	.3	14	.3	71	2	14	.3

		TENNESSEE			GEORGIA		ALABAMA		MISSISSIPPI		FLORIDA		LOUISIANA		ARKANSAS		OKLAHOMA	
		C	D		C	D	C	D	C	D	C	D	C	D	C	D	C	D
BREATH HARP(B)	W	100	1	N	33	.4	67	3	**	**	**	**	**	**	**	**	**	**
	E	**	**	S	67	1	33	1	**	**	**	**	**	**	**	**	100	3
	ST		1			1		4		**		**		**		**		3
FRENCH HARP(B)	W	26	2	N	44	2	86	8	100	2	**	**	**	**	38	3	11	1
	E	74	7	S	56	2	14	1	**	**	**	**	100	4	63	4	89	11
	ST		9			4		9		2		**		4		7		12
JEWS HARP(B)	W	48	22	N	71	35	75	38	67	36	65	39	56	33	55	31	50	25
	E	52	24	S	29	14	25	13	33	18	35	21	44	26	45	26	50	25
	ST		46			50		51		54		60		59		57		50
JUICE HARP(B)	W	42	17	N	57	24	74	22	65	22	90	33	56	19	60	19	35	12
	E	58	24	S	43	18	26	8	35	12	10	4	44	15	40	13	65	22
	ST		40			42		29		34		36		33		31		34
MOUTH HARP(B)	W	50	2	N	56	2	80	5	60	6	67	3	**	**	80	4	**	**
	E	50	2	S	44	2	20	1	40	4	33	1	100	4	20	1	100	1
	ST		4			4		6		10		4		4		4		1

FARM EQUIPMENT
SHAFT BETWEEN TWO HORSES HITCHED TO A FARM WAGON

ITEM (41)
WORK SHEET (20)

		TENNESSEE A	TENNESSEE B		GEORGIA A	GEORGIA B	ALABAMA A	ALABAMA B	MISSISSIPPI A	MISSISSIPPI B	FLORIDA A	FLORIDA B	LOUISIANA A	LOUISIANA B	ARKANSAS A	ARKANSAS B	OKLAHOMA A	OKLAHOMA B
NEAP	W	17	.1	N	17	.1	17	.1	**	**	**	**	**	**	**	**	**	**
	E	33	.2	S	17	.1	**	**	**	**	**	**	**	**	**	**	100	1
	ST	50	.3		33	.2	17	.1	**	**	**	**	**	**	**	**	100	1
POLE	W	20	.4	N	25	1	10	.2	**	**	**	**	**	**	44	1	**	**
	E	20	.4	S	15	.3	5	.1	**	**	5	.1	11	.3	11	.3	33	1
	ST	40	1		40	1	15	.3	**	**	5	.1	11	.3	56	2	33	1
TONGUE	W	18	15	N	19	16	7	6	4	4	8	6	7	6	30	23	16	13
	E	24	20	S	12	10	2	2	2	2	3	3	5	4	25	19	17	14
	ST	42	35		31	26	9	8	7	5	11	9	12	10	54	43	34	27
NEB	W	40	.2	N	40	.2	**	**	**	**	**	**	100	.3	**	**	**	**
	E	**	**	S	20	.1	**	**	**	**	**	**	**	**	**	**	**	**
	ST	40	.2		60	.3	**	**	**	**	**	**	100	.3	**	**	**	**
SPEAR	W	25	.1	N	**	**	**	**	**	**	**	**	**	**	33	.3	**	**
	E	50	.2	S	**	**	25	.1	**	**	**	**	**	**	**	**	67	1
	ST	75	.3		**	**	25	.1	**	**	**	**	**	**	33	.3	67	1

		TENNESSEE C	TENNESSEE D		GEORGIA C	GEORGIA D	ALABAMA C	ALABAMA D	MISSISSIPPI C	MISSISSIPPI D	FLORIDA C	FLORIDA D	LOUISIANA C	LOUISIANA D	ARKANSAS C	ARKANSAS D	OKLAHOMA C	OKLAHOMA D
NEAP	W	33	.2	N	50	.3	100	1	**	**	**	**	**	**	**	**	**	**
	E	67	1	S	50	.3	**	**	**	**	**	**	**	**	**	**	100	2
	ST		1			1		1		**		**		**		**		2
POLE	W	50	1	N	63	2	67	3	**	**	**	**	**	**	80	3	**	**
	E	50	1	S	38	1	33	1	**	**	100	1	100	3	20	1	100	4
	ST		2			3		4		**		1		3		4		4
TONGUE	W	43	41	N	61	58	80	75	68	68	69	69	59	55	55	52	49	44
	E	57	55	S	39	37	20	19	32	32	31	30	41	38	45	43	51	47
	ST		96			95		94		100		99		93		95		91
NEB	W	100	1	N	67	1	**	**	**	**	**	**	100	3	**	**	**	**
	E	**	**	S	33	.3	**	**	**	**	**	**	**	**	**	**	**	**
	ST		1			1		**		**		**		3		**		**
SPEAR	W	33	.2	N	**	**	**	**	**	**	**	**	**	**	100	1	**	**
	E	67	1	S	**	**	100	1	**	**	**	**	**	**	**	**	100	2
	ST		1			**		1		**		**		**		1		2

ITEM (42)
WORK SHEET (20)

FARM EQUIPMENT
PART OF A ONE-HORSE VEHICLE

		TENNESSEE A	TENNESSEE B		GEORGIA A	GEORGIA B	ALABAMA A	ALABAMA B	MISSISSIPPI A	MISSISSIPPI B	FLORIDA A	FLORIDA B	LOUISIANA A	LOUISIANA B	ARKANSAS A	ARKANSAS B	OKLAHOMA A	OKLAHOMA B
FILLS	W	**	**	N	**	**	**	**	**	**	**	**	**	**	33	.3	33	.3
	E	**	**	S	**	**	**	**	**	**	**	**	**	**	**	**	33	.3
	ST	**	**		**	**	**	**	**	**	**	**	**	**	33	.3	67	1
SHAFTS	W	23	10	N	19	8	10	4	5	2	6	3	5	2	30	13	15	6
	E	19	8	S	10	4	2	1	2	1	4	2	7	3	29	12	14	6
	ST	42	18		29	13	12	5	7	3	10	4	12	5	59	25	29	12
THILLS	W	43	.3	N	**	**	**	**	**	**	**	**	**	**	100	.3	**	**
	E	29	.2	S	29	.2	**	**	**	**	**	**	**	**	**	**	**	**
	ST	71	1		29	.2	**	**	**	**	**	**	**	**	100	.3	**	**
SHAVS	W	13	4	N	22	7	4	1	3	1	8	2	6	1	49	11	14	3
	E	28	8	S	15	5	1	.4	2	1	3	1	**	**	17	4	13	3
	ST	41	12		37	11	6	2	5	2	11	3	6	1	67	15	27	6

		TENNESSEE C	TENNESSEE D		GEORGIA C	GEORGIA D	ALABAMA C	ALABAMA D	MISSISSIPPI C	MISSISSIPPI D	FLORIDA C	FLORIDA D	LOUISIANA C	LOUISIANA D	ARKANSAS C	ARKANSAS D	OKLAHOMA C	OKLAHOMA D
FILLS	W	**	**	N	**	**	**	**	**	**	**	**	**	**	100	1	50	2
	E	**	**	S	**	**	**	**	**	**	**	**	**	**	**	**	50	2
	ST		**			**		**		**		**		**		1		4
SHAFTS	W	56	32	N	66	35	82	61	75	49	63	36	43	33	51	31	53	34
	E	44	26	S	34	18	18	13	25	16	37	21	57	44	49	30	47	30
	ST		58			53		75		65		57		78		61		64
THILLS	W	60	1	N	**	**	**	**	**	**	**	**	**	**	100	1	**	**
	E	40	1	S	100	1	**	**	**	**	**	**	**	**	**	**	**	**
	ST		2			1		**		**		**		**		1		**
SHAVS	W	32	13	N	58	27	76	19	67	23	75	32	100	22	74	27	53	17
	E	68	27	S	42	19	24	6	33	12	25	11	**	**	26	10	47	15
	ST		40			46		25		35		43		22		37		32

FARM EQUIPMENT
BAR TO WHICH A SINGLE HORSE IS HITCHED

ITEM (43)
WORK SHEET (21)

		TENNESSEE A	TENNESSEE B		GEORGIA A	GEORGIA B	ALABAMA A	ALABAMA B	MISSISSIPPI A	MISSISSIPPI B	FLORIDA A	FLORIDA B	LOUISIANA A	LOUISIANA B	ARKANSAS A	ARKANSAS B	OKLAHOMA A	OKLAHOMA B
SINGLETREE	W	19	14	N	19	14	7	5	5	3	7	5	8	6	31	23	15	11
	E	23	17	S	12	9	2	2	2	1	3	2	3	3	26	19	16	12
	ST	43	31		32	23	9	7	7	5	10	8	12	9	57	42	31	23
SWINGLETREE	W	9	1	N	23	2	7	1	**	**	13	1	**	**	75	1	**	**
	E	27	2	S	17	1	**	**	1	.1	3	.2	**	**	**	**	25	.3
	ST	36	3		40	3	7	1	1	.1	16	1	**	**	75	1	25	.3
SWIVELTREE	W	14	.1	N	14	.1	**	**	**	**	**	**	**	**	25	.3	25	.3
	E	29	.2	S	29	.2	14	.1	**	**	**	**	**	**	**	**	50	1
	ST	43	.3		43	.3	14	.1	**	**	**	**	**	**	25	.3	75	1
WHIFFLETREE	W	50	.3	N	**	**	**	**	**	**	17	.1	**	**	67	1	**	**
	E	**	**	S	33	.2	**	**	**	**	**	**	**	**	33	.3	**	**
	ST	50	.3		33	.2	**	**	**	**	17	.1	**	**	100	1	**	**
SHIPPLETREE	W	**	**	N	20	.2	10	.1	**	**	10	.1	**	**	**	**	**	**
	E	30	.3	S	30	.3	**	**	**	**	**	**	**	**	**	**	100	.3
	ST	30	.3		50	1	10	.1	**	**	10	.1	**	**	**	**	100	.3

		TENNESSEE C	TENNESSEE D		GEORGIA C	GEORGIA D	ALABAMA C	ALABAMA D	MISSISSIPPI C	MISSISSIPPI D	FLORIDA C	FLORIDA D	LOUISIANA C	LOUISIANA D	ARKANSAS C	ARKANSAS D	OKLAHOMA C	OKLAHOMA D
SINGLETREE	W	46	41	N	61	52	75	67	70	69	70	60	71	71	55	52	48	44
	E	54	49	S	39	33	25	23	30	29	30	25	29	29	45	43	52	49
	ST		90			86		90		98		85		100		94		93
SWINGLETREE	W	24	2	N	57	6	100	7	**	**	82	10	**	**	100	2	**	**
	E	76	6	S	43	5	**	**	100	2	18	2	**	**	**	**	100	1
	ST		7			11		7		2		13		**		2		1
SWIVELTREE	W	33	.2	N	33	.3	**	**	**	**	**	**	**	**	100	1	33	1
	E	67	1	S	67	1	100	1	**	**	**	**	**	**	**	**	67	3
	ST		1			1		1		**		**		**		1		4
WHIFFLETREE	W	100	1	N	**	**	**	**	**	**	100	1	**	**	67	2	**	**
	E	**	**	S	100	1	**	**	**	**	**	**	**	**	33	1	**	**
	ST		1			1		**		**		1		**		2		**
SHIPPLETREE	W	**	**	N	40	1	100	1	**	**	100	1	**	**	**	**	**	**
	E	100	1	S	60	1	**	**	**	**	**	**	**	**	**	**	100	1
	ST		1			2		1		**		1		**		**		1

BAR FOR TWO HORSES

ITEM (43)
WORK SHEET (21)

		TENNESSEE A	TENNESSEE B		GEORGIA A	GEORGIA B	ALABAMA A	ALABAMA B	MISSISSIPPI A	MISSISSIPPI B	FLORIDA A	FLORIDA B	LOUISIANA A	LOUISIANA B	ARKANSAS A	ARKANSAS B	OKLAHOMA A	OKLAHOMA B
DOUBLE EVENER	W	67	.4	N	**	**	17	.1	**	**	**	**	**	**	**	**	**	**
	E	17	.1	S	**	**	**	**	**	**	**	**	**	**	**	**	100	1
	ST	83	1		**	**	17	.1	**	**	**	**	**	**	**	**	100	1
DOUBLE SINGLETREE	W	16	3	N	23	4	10	2	5	1	10	2	4	.3	33	3	11	1
	E	9	2	S	13	2	5	1	4	1	4	1	4	.3	26	3	22	2
	ST	25	4		36	6	15	3	9	2	14	2	7	1	59	6	33	3
DOUBLE SWINGLETREE	W	14	.4	N	14	.4	7	.2	3	.1	7	.2	17	.3	33	1	17	.3
	E	21	1	S	28	1	3	.1	**	**	3	.1	**	**	**	**	33	1
	ST	34	1		41	1	10	.3	3	.1	10	.3	17	.3	33	1	50	1
DOUBLETREE	W	19	10	N	21	12	6	3	4	2	6	4	9	5	32	19	17	10
	E	27	15	S	12	7	1	1	1	1	3	1	2	1	25	15	14	9
	ST	46	25		33	18	7	4	5	3	9	5	11	7	57	35	32	19
EVENER	W	29	.2	N	14	.1	**	**	**	**	**	**	25	.3	25	.3	**	**
	E	29	.2	S	29	.2	**	**	**	**	**	**	**	**	**	**	50	1
	ST	57	.4		43	.3	**	**	**	**	**	**	25	.3	25	.3	50	1
SPREADER	W	27	.3	N	**	**	**	**	**	**	9	.1	**	**	**	**	**	**
	E	55	1	S	**	**	**	**	9	.1	**	**	**	**	**	**	**	**
	ST	82	1		**	**	**	**	9	.1	9	.1	**	**	**	**	**	**

		TENNESSEE C	TENNESSEE D		GEORGIA C	GEORGIA D	ALABAMA C	ALABAMA D	MISSISSIPPI C	MISSISSIPPI D	FLORIDA C	FLORIDA D	LOUISIANA C	LOUISIANA D	ARKANSAS C	ARKANSAS D	OKLAHOMA C	OKLAHOMA D
DOUBLE EVENER	W	80	1	N	**	**	100	2	**	**	**	**	**	**	**	**	**	**
	E	20	.3	S	**	**	**	**	**	**	**	**	**	**	**	**	100	4
	ST		2			**		2		**		**		**		**		4
DOUBLE SINGLETREE	W	64	9	N	63	15	64	24	60	20	71	23	50	4	56	8	33	4
	E	36	5	S	37	9	36	14	40	13	29	9	50	4	44	6	67	9
	ST		13			24		38		33		32		9		14		13
DOUBLE SWINGLETREE	W	40	1	N	33	2	67	3	100	2	67	3	100	4	100	2	33	1
	E	60	2	S	67	3	33	2	**	**	33	1	**	**	**	**	67	3
	ST		3			5		5		2		4		4		2		4
DOUBLETREE	W	41	32	N	63	45	84	47	75	47	72	45	79	65	56	47	55	41
	E	59	46	S	37	26	16	9	25	16	28	17	21	17	44	37	45	34
	ST		78			70		56		62		63		83		83		76
EVENER	W	50	1	N	33	.3	**	**	**	**	**	**	100	4	100	1	**	**
	E	50	1	S	67	1	**	**	**	**	**	**	**	**	**	**	100	3
	ST		1			1		**		**		**		4		1		3
SPREADER	W	33	1	N	**	**	**	**	**	**	100	1	**	**	**	**	**	**
	E	67	2	S	**	**	**	**	100	2	**	**	**	**	**	**	**	**
	ST		3			**		**		2		1		**		**		**

ACTIVITIES
TRANSPORTING FIREWOOD IN A WAGON

ITEM (44)
WORK SHEET (21)

		TENNESSEE A	TENNESSEE B		GEORGIA A	GEORGIA B	ALABAMA A	ALABAMA B	MISSISSIPPI A	MISSISSIPPI B	FLORIDA A	FLORIDA B	LOUISIANA A	LOUISIANA B	ARKANSAS A	ARKANSAS B	OKLAHOMA A	OKLAHOMA B
CARRYING	W	23	1	N	9	1	13	1	4	.2	7	.4	5	.3	18	1	18	1
	E	23	1	S	9	1	2	.1	4	.2	7	.4	14	1	14	1	32	3
	ST	46	3		18	1	14	1	7	.4	14	1	18	1	32	3	50	4
CARTING	W	11	.2	N	11	.2	6	.1	11	.2	22	.4	**	**	25	.3	**	**
	E	22	.4	S	17	.3	**	**	**	**	**	**	**	**	**	**	75	1
	ST	33	1		28	1	6	.1	11	.2	22	.4	**	**	25	.3	75	1
DRAWING	W	6	.1	N	29	1	6	.1	**	**	**	**	**	**	**	**	**	**
	E	**	**	S	53	1	**	**	**	**	6	.1	**	**	**	**	**	**
	ST	6	.1		82	1	6	.1	**	**	6	.1	**	**	**	**	**	**
HAULING	W	19	15	N	18	14	7	6	4	3	7	6	8	6	30	24	12	10
	E	27	21	S	10	8	2	2	2	2	3	2	8	6	24	19	18	15
	ST	46	36		28	22	10	8	6	5	10	8	16	13	54	44	31	25
TEAMING	W	100	.1	N	**	**	**	**	**	**	**	**	**	**	**	**	**	**
					(NO RESPONSE)													
	ST	100	.1		**	**	**	**	**	**	**	**	**	**	**	**	**	**
TOTING	W	11	.3	N	11	.3	7	.2	7	.2	11	.3	**	**	**	**	**	**
	E	7	.2	S	33	1	**	**	7	.2	4	.1	**	**	50	.3	50	.3
	ST	19	1		44	1	7	.2	15	.4	15	.4	**	**	50	.3	50	.3

		TENNESSEE C	TENNESSEE D		GEORGIA C	GEORGIA D	ALABAMA C	ALABAMA D	MISSISSIPPI C	MISSISSIPPI D	FLORIDA C	FLORIDA D	LOUISIANA C	LOUISIANA D	ARKANSAS C	ARKANSAS D	OKLAHOMA C	OKLAHOMA D
CARRYING	W	50	3	N	50	2	88	8	50	3	50	4	25	3	57	3	36	5
	E	50	3	S	50	2	13	1	50	3	50	4	75	8	43	2	64	8
	ST		7			4		9		7		8		10		5		13
CARTING	W	33	1	N	40	1	100	1	100	3	100	4	**	**	100	1	**	**
	E	67	1	S	60	1	**	**	**	**	**	**	**	**	**	**	100	4
	ST		2			2		1		3		4		**		1		4
DRAWING	W	100	.2	N	36	2	100	1	**	**	**	**	**	**	**	**	**	**
	E	**	**	S	64	4	**	**	**	**	100	1	**	**	**	**	**	**
	ST		.2			6		1		**		1		**		**		**
HAULING	W	42	38	N	64	54	74	64	65	53	70	57	49	44	55	52	41	33
	E	58	52	S	36	30	26	22	35	29	30	25	51	46	45	42	59	49
	ST		90			84		86		83		82		90		93		82
TEAMING	W	100	.2	N	**	**	**	**	**	**	**	**	**	**	**	**	**	**
					(NO RESPONSE)													
	ST		.2			**		**		**		**		**		**		**
TOTING	W	60	1	N	25	1	100	2	50	3	75	3	**	**	**	**	**	**
	E	40	1	S	75	4	**	**	50	3	25	1	**	**	100	1	100	1
	ST		1			5		2		7		4		**		1		1

ITEM (45)
WORK SHEET (21)

FARM EQUIPMENT
IMPLEMENT WITH TEETH FOR BREAKING CLODS AFTER PLOWING

		TENNESSEE			GEORGIA		ALABAMA		MISSISSIPPI		FLORIDA		LOUISIANA		ARKANSAS		OKLAHOMA	
		A	B		A	B	A	B	A	B	A	B	A	B	A	B	A	B
DRAG	W	10	1	N	33	5	4	1	1	.2	2	.3	**	**	40	2	7	.3
	E	31	5	S	15	2	2	.3	1	.1	1	.1	7	.3	27	1	20	1
	ST	41	6		48	7	6	1	2	.3	3	.4	7	.3	67	4	27	1
HARROW	W	20	15	N	18	14	6	5	4	3	8	6	7	5	30	24	16	13
	E	25	20	S	11	9	2	2	2	1	4	3	5	4	24	19	18	15
	ST	44	35		30	23	9	7	6	5	11	9	12	9	54	43	35	28

		TENNESSEE			GEORGIA		ALABAMA		MISSISSIPPI		FLORIDA		LOUISIANA		ARKANSAS		OKLAHOMA	
		C	D		C	D	C	D	C	D	C	D	C	D	C	D	C	D
DRAG	W	24	4	N	69	16	67	8	67	4	75	3	**	**	60	5	25	1
	E	76	11	S	31	7	33	4	33	2	25	1	100	4	40	3	75	4
	ST		15			23		12		6		4		4		8		5
HARROW	W	44	38	N	61	47	74	65	73	69	68	65	58	56	55	51	47	44
	E	56	48	S	39	30	26	23	27	25	32	31	42	41	45	42	53	51
	ST		85			77		88		94		96		96		92		95

A UNIT OF MEASURE
THE AMOUNT OF WOOD YOU CAN CARRY IN BOTH ARMS

ITEM (46)
WORK SHEET (19)

		TENNESSEE			GEORGIA		ALABAMA		MISSISSIPPI		FLORIDA		LOUISIANA		ARKANSAS		OKLAHOMA	
		A	B		A	B	A	B	A	B	A	B	A	B	A	B	A	B
ARMFUL	W	20	9	N	21	10	6	3	5	2	5	3	8	2	25	6	12	3
	E	25	12	S	10	5	3	1	3	1	3	1	12	3	27	7	15	4
	ST	45	22		31	15	9	4	7	4	8	4	21	5	52	14	27	7
ARMLOAD	W	21	7	N	12	4	7	2	4	1	8	3	7	4	31	18	18	11
	E	32	11	S	7	2	2	1	2	1	4	2	4	2	20	12	22	13
	ST	54	19		19	7	9	3	6	2	12	4	10	6	50	30	40	24
CHANCE					(NO RESPONSE)													
					(NO RESPONSE)													
					(NO RESPONSE)													
LOAD	W	17	1	N	20	2	11	1	4	.3	4	.3	5	.3	21	1	5	.3
	E	31	2	S	7	1	3	.2	**	**	4	.3	21	1	37	3	11	1
	ST	48	4		27	2	13	1	4	.3	8	1	26	2	58	4	16	1
TURN	W	4	1	N	29	4	4	1	**	**	18	2	33	.3	**	**	33	.3
	E	2	.2	S	34	4	3	.3	3	.3	5	1	33	.3	**	**	**	**
	ST	6	1		62	8	7	1	3	.3	23	3	67	1	**	**	33	.3

		TENNESSEE			GEORGIA		ALABAMA		MISSISSIPPI		FLORIDA		LOUISIANA		ARKANSAS		OKLAHOMA	
		C	D		C	D	C	D	C	D	C	D	C	D	C	D	C	D
ARMFUL	W	43	21	N	67	32	70	33	65	37	66	22	40	15	47	14	45	10
	E	57	28	S	33	16	30	14	35	20	34	12	60	23	53	15	55	12
	ST		49			48		47		57		34		38		29		22
ARMLOAD	W	40	17	N	63	13	80	26	70	23	63	23	65	28	61	38	45	33
	E	60	25	S	38	8	20	7	30	10	37	13	35	15	39	25	55	40
	ST		41			21		33		33		37		44		63		73
CHANCE					(NO RESPONSE)													
					(NO RESPONSE)													
	ST		**			**		**		**		**		**		**		**
LOAD	W	36	3	N	75	5	80	9	100	5	50	3	20	3	36	3	33	1
	E	64	5	S	25	2	20	2	**	**	50	3	80	10	64	5	67	2
	ST		8			7		11		5		5		13		8		3
TURN	W	71	1	N	46	11	63	5	**	**	78	19	50	3	**	**	100	1
	E	29	.4	S	54	13	38	3	100	5	22	5	50	3	**	**	**	**
	ST		2			25		9		5		24		5		**		1

FARM EQUIPMENT
AN A-FRAME IMPLEMENT TO HOLD BOARDS TO SAW, USED BY CARPENTERS

ITEM (47)
WORK SHEET (22)

		TENNESSEE A	TENNESSEE B		GEORGIA A	GEORGIA B	ALABAMA A	ALABAMA B	MISSISSIPPI A	MISSISSIPPI B	FLORIDA A	FLORIDA B	LOUISIANA A	LOUISIANA B	ARKANSAS A	ARKANSAS B	OKLAHOMA A	OKLAHOMA B
HORSE(A)	W	28	7	N	13	3	9	2	4	1	2	1	4	1	25	6	3	1
	E	32	9	S	5	1	2	.4	4	1	2	.4	15	4	40	10	12	3
	ST	60	16		18	5	11	3	8	2	3	1	19	5	66	16	15	4
JACK(A)	W	13	.2	N	27	.4	13	.2	**	**	**	**	**	**	33	.3	**	**
	E	27	.4	S	7	.1	**	**	7	.1	7	.1	33	.3	33	.3	**	**
	ST	40	1		33	1	13	.2	7	.1	7	.1	33	.3	67	1	**	**
RACK(A)	W	26	1	N	9	.3	**	**	**	**	**	**	17	.3	50	1	**	**
	E	56	2	S	9	.3	**	**	**	**	**	**	**	**	33	1	**	**
	ST	82	3		18	1	**	**	**	**	**	**	17	.5	83	2	**	**
SAWBUCK(A)	W	10	1	N	13	.2	**	**	**	**	**	**	**	**	20	.3	**	**
	E	13	.2	S	27	.4	**	**	7	.1	**	**	20	.3	40	1	20	.3
	ST	53	1		40	1	**	**	7	.1	**	**	20	.3	60	1	20	.3
SAW HORSE(A)	W	13	7	N	20	12	7	4	5	3	10	6	8	5	31	18	20	12
	E	21	12	S	15	8	3	2	1	1	5	3	5	3	18	10	18	11
	ST	34	19		35	20	10	6	6	3	15	8	13	8	48	29	39	23
SAW JACK(A)	W	31	.4	N	15	.2	**	**	8	.1	**	**	**	**	**	**	**	**
	E	15	.2	S	8	.1	**	**	15	.2	8	.1	100	.3	**	**	**	**
	ST	46	1		23	.3	**	**	23	.3	8	.1	100	.3	**	**	**	**
TRESTLE(A)	W	42	2	N	5	.2	7	.3	2	.1	**	**	**	**	27	1	18	1
	E	40	2	S	**	**	**	**	5	.2	**	**	**	**	36	1	18	1
	ST	81	4		5	.2	7	.3	7	.3	**	**	**	**	64	3	36	1

(CONTINUED) AN A-FRAME IMPLEMENT TO HOLD BOARDS TO SAW, USED BY CARPENTERS

ITEM (47)		TENNESSEE			GEORGIA		ALABAMA		MISSISSIPPI		FLORIDA		LOUISIANA		ARKANSAS		OKLAHOMA	
		C	D		C	D	C	D	C	D	C	D	C	D	C	D	C	D
HORSE(A)	W	46	17	N	72	13	86	27	52	18	56	5	23	8	39	12	20	3
	E	54	20	S	28	5	14	4	48	16	44	4	77	26	61	19	80	10
	ST		36			18		31		34		10		34		31		13
JACK(A)	W	33	.4	N	80	2	100	2	**	**	**	**	**	**	50	1	**	**
	E	67	1	S	20	.3	**	**	100	2	100	1	100	3	50	1	**	**
	ST		1			2		2		2		1		3		1		**
RACK(A)	W	32	2	N	50	1	**	**	**	**	**	**	100	3	60	2	**	**
	E	68	4	S	50	1	**	**	**	**	**	**	**	**	40	1	**	**
	ST		7			2		**		**		**		3		4		**
SAWBUCK(A)	W	75	1	N	33	1	**	**	**	**	**	**	**	**	33	1	**	**
	E	25	.4	S	67	2	**	**	100	2	**	**	100	3	67	1	100	1
	ST		2			2		**		2		**		3		2		1
SAW HORSE(A)	W	39	17	N	58	43	70	44	79	42	69	61	62	34	63	36	52	42
	E	61	27	S	42	31	30	19	21	11	31	27	38	21	37	21	48	38
	ST		44			74		63		53		88		55		56		81
SAW JACK(A)	W	67	1	N	67	1	**	**	33	2	**	**	**	**	**	**	**	**
	E	33	.4	S	33	.3	**	**	67	3	100	1	100	3	**	**	**	**
	ST		1			1		**		5		1		3		**		**
TRESTLE(A)	W	51	4	N	100	1	100	3	33	2	**	**	**	**	43	2	50	3
	E	49	4	S	**	**	**	**	67	3	**	**	**	**	57	3	50	3
	ST		8			1		3		5		**		**		5		5

FARM EQUIPMENT
IMPLEMENT WITH AN X-FRAME FOR HOLDING FIREWOOD FOR SAWING

ITEM (47)
WORK SHEET (22)

		TENNESSEE A	TENNESSEE B		GEORGIA A	GEORGIA B	ALABAMA A	ALABAMA B	MISSISSIPPI A	MISSISSIPPI B	FLORIDA A	FLORIDA B	LOUISIANA A	LOUISIANA B	ARKANSAS A	ARKANSAS B	OKLAHOMA A	OKLAHOMA B
BUCK	W	13	.1	N	25	.2	**	**	**	**	**	**	14	.3	57	1	**	**
	E	25	.2	S	25	.2	**	**	**	**	13	.1	**	**	14	.3	14	.3
	ST	38	.3		50	.4	**	**	**	**	13	.1	14	.3	71	2	14	.3
HORSE(B)	W	30	2	N	14	1	8	1	1	.1	3	.2	9	.3	18	1	9	.3
	E	36	3	S	5	.4	1	.1	1	.1	**	**	36	1	9	.3	18	1
	ST	66	5		20	2	9	1	3	.2	3	.2	45	2	27	1	27	1
JACK(B)	W	7	.1	N	36	1	21	.3	21	.3	**	**	**	**	50	1	**	**
	E	14	.2	S	**	**	**	**	**	**	**	**	17	.3	33	1	**	**
	ST	21	.3		36	1	21	.3	21	.3	**	**	17	.3	83	2	**	**
RACK(B)	W	18	3	N	13	2	6	1	3	1	8	1	5	1	35	5	7	1
	E	30	[illegible]	S	10	3	1	.1	3	1	2	.4	7	1	28	4	19	3
	ST	47	0		31	5	7	1	6	1	10	2	12	2	63	10	26	4
SAWBUCK(B)	W	27	2	N	16	1	6	.4	4	.3	10	1	8	1	38	4	15	1
	E	21	1	S	4	.3	1	.1	3	.2	6	.4	4	.3	27	3	8	1
	ST	48	3		21	1	7	1	7	1	16	1	12	1	65	6	23	2
SAW HORSE(B)	W	16	5	N	25	8	7	2	3	1	6	2	7	2	34	10	15	4
	E	22	7	S	13	4	2	1	2	1	4	1	5	1	23	7	16	5
	ST	39	13		37	12	9	3	5	2	10	3	12	4	57	17	30	9
SAW JACK(B)	W	19	1	N	22	1	19	1	3	.1	13	.4	**	**	33	.3	33	.3
	E	13	.4	S	6	.2	3	.1	3	.1	**	**	**	**	**	**	33	.3
	ST	31	1		28	1	22	1	6	.2	13	.4	**	**	33	.3	67	1
TRESTLE(B)	W	25	.3	N	8	.1	**	**	25	.3	**	**	50	.3	50	.3	**	**
	E	25	.3	S	**	**	8	.1	**	**	8	.1	**	**	**	**	**	**
	ST	50	1		8	.1	8	.1	25	.3	8	.1	50	.3	50	.3	**	**
WOOD BUCK	W	31	.4	N	15	.2	15	.2	**	**	8	.1	**	**	100	.3	**	**
	E	15	.2	S	**	**	**	**	**	**	15	.2	**	**	**	**	**	**
	ST	46	1		15	.2	15	.2	**	**	23	.3	**	**	100	.3	**	**

(CONTINUED) IMPLEMENT WITH AN X-FRAME FOR HOLDING FIREWOOD FOR SAWING

ITEM (47)		TENNESSEE C	TENNESSEE D		GEORGIA C	GEORGIA D	ALABAMA C	ALABAMA D	MISSISSIPPI C	MISSISSIPPI D	FLORIDA C	FLORIDA D	LOUISIANA C	LOUISIANA D	ARKANSAS C	ARKANSAS D	OKLAHOMA C	OKLAHOMA D
BUCK	W	33	.3	N	50	1	**	**	**	**	**	**	100	4	80	4	**	**
	E	67	1	S	50	1	**	**	**	**	100	1	**	**	20	1	100	2
	ST		1			2		**		**		1		4		5		2
HORSE(B)	W	46	7	N	73	5	86	9	50	2	100	3	20	4	67	2	33	2
	E	54	9	S	27	2	14	2	50	2	**	**	80	15	33	1	67	4
	ST		16			7		11		5		3		19		3		6
JACK(B)	W	33	.3	N	100	2	100	5	100	7	**	**	**	**	60	3	**	**
	E	67	1	S	**	**	**	**	**	**	**	**	100	4	40	2	**	**
	ST		1			2		5		7		**		4		5		**
RACK(B)	W	39	10	N	42	10	91	16	50	12	76	18	40	8	56	14	27	6
	E	61	15	S	58	13	9	2	50	12	24	6	60	12	44	11	73	17
	ST		25			23		17		24		24		19		25		23
SAWBUCK(B)	W	56	6	N	79	5	80	6	60	7	64	10	67	8	59	9	67	8
	E	44	4	S	21	1	20	2	40	5	36	6	33	4	41	7	33	4
	ST		10			6		8		12		15		12		16		13
SAW HORSE(B)	W	42	17	N	66	36	79	34	69	27	61	28	60	23	60	26	48	25
	E	58	23	S	34	18	21	9	31	12	39	18	40	15	40	18	52	27
	ST		40			54		44		39		46		38		44		52
SAW JACK(B)	W	60	2	N	78	3	86	9	50	2	100	6	**	**	100	1	50	2
	E	40	1	S	22	1	14	2	50	2	**	**	**	**	**	**	50	2
	ST		3			4		11		5		6		**		1		4
TRESTLE(B)	W	50	1	N	100	.4	**	**	100	7	**	**	100	4	100	1	**	**
	E	50	1	S	**	**	100	2	**	**	100	1	**	**	**	**	**	**
	ST		2			.4		2		7		1		4		1		**
WOOD BUCK	W	67	1	N	100	1	100	3	**	**	33	1	**	**	100	1	**	**
	E	33	1	S	**	**	**	**	**	**	67	3	**	**	**	**	**	**
	ST		2			1		3		**		4		**		1		**

SOCIAL LIFE
PLAYGROUND EQUIPMENT

ITEM (48)
WORK SHEET (22)

		TENNESSEE A	TENNESSEE B		GEORGIA A	GEORGIA B	ALABAMA A	ALABAMA B	MISSISSIPPI A	MISSISSIPPI B	FLORIDA A	FLORIDA B	LOUISIANA A	LOUISIANA B	ARKANSAS A	ARKANSAS B	OKLAHOMA A	OKLAHOMA B
DANDLE	W	100	.1	N	**	**	**	**	**	**	**	**	**	**	**	**	**	**
					(NO RESPONSE)													
	ST	100	.1		**	**	**	**	**	**	**	**	**	**	**	**	**	**
RIDY HORSE(A)	W	13	1	N	19	1	8	1	**	**	14	1	20	.3	40	1	**	**
	E	19	1	S	19	1	2	.1	6	.4	2	.1	20	.3	20	.3	**	**
	ST	31	2		38	2	9	1	6	.4	16	1	40	1	60	1	**	**
SEESAW	W	19	17	N	18	15	7	6	4	4	7	6	7	6	29	23	10	8
	E	26	22	S	11	9	2	2	2	2	4	3	9	7	26	21	18	14
	ST	45	38		29	25	9	0	7	6	11	9	16	13	56	44	28	22
TEETER	W	13	.2	N	**	**	13	.2	**	**	**	**	6	.3	25	1	44	3
	E	38	1	S	13	.2	13	.2	6	.1	6	.1	**	**	6	.3	19	1
	ST	50	1		13	.2	25	.4	6	.1	6	.1	6	.3	31	2	63	4
TEETER BOARD	W	10	.3	N	10	.3	7	.2	7	.2	14	.4	**	**	33	1	33	1
	E	21	1	S	14	.4	7	.2	3	.1	7	.2	**	**	17	1	17	1
	ST	31	1		24	1	14	.4	10	.3	21	1	**	**	50	2	50	2
HICKY HORSE	W	25	.1	N	25	.1	**	**	**	**	25	.1	**	**	**	**	**	**
	E	**	**	S	25	.1	**	**	**	**	**	**	**	**	**	**	**	**
	ST	25	.1		50	.2	**	**	**	**	25	.1	**	**	**	**	**	**
COCK HORSE	W	25	.1	N	50	.2	**	**	**	**	**	**	**	**	**	**	100	.3
	E	25	.1	S	**	**	**	**	**	**	**	**	**	**	**	**	**	**
	ST	50	.2		50	.2	**	**	**	**	**	**	**	**	**	**	100	.3

(CONTINUED) PLAYGROUND EQUIPMENT

ITEM (48)		TENNESSEE C	TENNESSEE D		GEORGIA C	GEORGIA D	ALABAMA C	ALABAMA D	MISSISSIPPI C	MISSISSIPPI D	FLORIDA C	FLORIDA D	LOUISIANA C	LOUISIANA D	ARKANSAS C	ARKANSAS D	OKLAHOMA C	OKLAHOMA D
DANDLE	W	100	.2	N	**	**	**	**	**	**	**	**	**	**	**	**	**	**
					(NO RESPONSE)													
	ST		.2			**		**		**		**		**		**		**
RIDY HORSE(A)	W	40	2	N	50	4	83	6	**	**	90	8	50	3	67	1	**	**
	E	60	3	S	50	4	17	1	100	6	10	1	50	3	33	1	**	**
	ST		5			9		7		6		9		5		2		**
SEESAW	W	43	39	N	62	53	76	64	65	56	67	56	46	42	53	47	36	28
	E	57	51	S	38	33	24	20	35	31	33	27	54	50	47	42	64	50
	ST		90			87		84		87		83		92		90		78
TEETER	W	25	.4	N	**	**	50	2	**	**	**	**	100	3	80	3	70	9
	E	75	1	S	100	1	50	2	100	2	100	1	**	**	20	1	30	4
	ST		2			1		4		2		1		3		4		13
TEETER BOARD	W	33	1	N	43	1	50	2	67	3	67	4	**	**	67	3	67	5
	E	67	1	S	57	1	50	2	33	2	33	2	**	**	33	1	33	3
	ST		2			3		4		5		6		**		4		8
HICKY HORSE	W	100	.2	N	50	.3	**	**	**	**	100	1	**	**	**	**	**	**
	E	**	**	S	50	.3	**	**	**	**	**	**	**	**	**	**	**	**
	ST		.2			1		**		**		1		**		**		**
COCK HORSE	W	50	.2	N	100	1	**	**	**	**	**	**	**	**	**	**	100	1
	E	50	.2	S	**	**	**	**	**	**	**	**	**	**	**	**	**	**
	ST		.4			1		**		**		**		**		**		1

SOCIAL LIFE
HOME MADE MERRY-GO-ROUND

ITEM (49)
WORK SHEET (22)

		TENNESSEE A	TENNESSEE B		GEORGIA A	GEORGIA B	ALABAMA A	ALABAMA B	MISSISSIPPI A	MISSISSIPPI B	FLORIDA A	FLORIDA B	LOUISIANA A	LOUISIANA B	ARKANSAS A	ARKANSAS B	OKLAHOMA A	OKLAHOMA B
FLYING DUTCHMAN	W	11	.2	N	22	.4	6	.1	11	.2	**	**	8	.3	15	1	15	1
	E	39	1	S	**	**	**	**	**	**	11	.2	8	.3	8	.3	46	2
	ST	50	1		22	.4	6	.1	11	.2	11	.2	15	1	23	1	62	3
FLYING JENNY	W	11	.2	N	22	.4	6	.1	11	.2	**	**	8	.3	15	1	15	1
	E	39	1	S	**	**	**	**	**	**	11	.2	8	.3	8	.3	46	2
	ST	50	1		22	.4	6	.1	11	.2	11	.2	15	1	23	1	62	3
FLYING MARE	W	18	.2	N	18	.2	**	**	**	**	**	**	**	**	**	**	50	.3
	E	18	.2	S	27	.3	18	.2	**	**	**	**	**	**	50	.3	**	**
	ST	36	.4		45	1	18	.2	**	**	**	**	**	**	50	.3	50	.3
RIDY HORSE(B)	W	11	1	N	13	1	2	.1	2	.1	11	1	**	**	71	2	**	**
	E	33	2	S	16	1	**	**	7	.3	4	.2	14	.3	**	**	14	.3
	ST	44	2		29	1	2	.1	9	.4	16	1	14	.3	71	2	14	.3
WHIRLYGIG	W	10	.4	N	5	.2	5	.2	**	**	10	.4	11	1	32	2	37	3
	E	55	2	S	3	.1	5	.2	5	.2	3	.1	**	**	5	.3	16	1
	ST	65	3		8	.3	10	.4	5	.2	13	1	11	1	37	3	53	4
WHIRLYJIG	W	17	1	N	7	.2	7	.2	**	**	10	.3	**	**	**	**	50	1
	E	48	1	S	**	**	**	**	3	.1	7	.2	**	**	**	**	50	1
	ST	66	2		7	.2	7	.2	3	.1	17	1	**	**	**	**	100	1

		TENNESSEE C	TENNESSEE D		GEORGIA C	GEORGIA D	ALABAMA C	ALABAMA D	MISSISSIPPI C	MISSISSIPPI D	FLORIDA C	FLORIDA D	LOUISIANA C	LOUISIANA D	ARKANSAS C	ARKANSAS D	OKLAHOMA C	OKLAHOMA D
FLYING DUTCHMAN	W	22	2	N	100	13	100	9	100	18	**	**	50	14	67	11	25	6
	E	78	8	S	**	**	**	**	**	**	100	10	50	14	33	5	75	19
	ST		10			13		9		18		10		29		16		25
FLYING JENNY	W	22	2	N	100	13	100	9	100	18	**	**	50	14	67	11	25	6
	E	78	8	S	**	**	**	**	**	**	100	10	50	14	33	5	75	19
	ST		10			13		9		18		10		29		16		25
FLYING MARE	W	50	2	N	40	6	**	**	**	**	**	**	**	**	**	**	100	3
	E	50	2	S	60	10	100	18	**	**	**	**	**	**	100	5	**	**
	ST		5			16		18		**		**		**		5		3
RIDY HORSE(B)	W	25	6	N	46	19	100	9	25	9	71	24	**	**	100	26	**	**
	E	75	17	S	54	23	**	**	75	27	29	10	100	14	**	**	100	3
	ST		23			42		9		36		33		14		26		3
WHIRLYGIG	W	15	5	N	67	6	50	18	**	**	80	19	100	29	86	32	70	22
	E	85	25	S	33	3	50	18	100	18	20	5	**	**	14	5	30	9
	ST		30			10		36		18		24		29		37		31
WHIRLYJIG	W	26	6	N	100	6	100	18	**	**	60	14	**	**	**	**	50	6
	E	74	16	S	**	**	**	**	100	9	40	10	**	**	**	**	50	6
	ST		22			6		18		9		24		**		**		13

SOCIAL LIFE
IN PLAYING MARBLES

ITEM (50)
WORK SHEET (22)

		TENNESSEE A	TENNESSEE B		GEORGIA A	GEORGIA B	ALABAMA A	ALABAMA B	MISSISSIPPI A	MISSISSIPPI B	FLORIDA A	FLORIDA B	LOUISIANA A	LOUISIANA B	ARKANSAS A	ARKANSAS B	OKLAHOMA A	OKLAHOMA B
LAGGING LINE	W	19	1	N	13	1	17	1	7	.4	7	.4	13	1	23	3	13	1
	E	22	1	S	6	.3	6	.3	4	.2	**	**	17	2	7	1	27	3
	ST	41	2		19	1	22	1	11	1	7	.4	30	3	30	3	40	4
LAG LINE	W	20	1	N	10	1	8	.4	12	1	4	.2	7	1	14	1	50	5
	E	20	1	S	14	1	**	**	4	.2	6	.3	11	1	14	1	4	.3
	ST	41	2		24	1	8	.4	16	1	10	1	18	2	29	3	54	5
STARTING LINE	W	16	1	N	10	1	9	1	5	.4	5	.4	7	.3	29	1	21	1
	E	35	3	S	14	1	1	.1	1	.1	4	.3	7	.3	7	.3	29	1
	ST	51	4		24	2	10	1	6	1	9	1	14	1	36	2	50	3
TAW	W	15	5	N	22	7	7	2	4	1	7	2	6	1	21	5	6	1
	E	22	7	S	12	4	3	1	3	1	5	1	10	3	42	11	15	4
	ST	38	12		35	11	10	3	7	2	11	4	15	4	63	16	21	5
TAW LINE	W	15	4	N	31	8	4	1	1	.3	9	2	8	2	40	11	12	3
	E	18	4	S	13	3	1	.3	2	.4	4	1	1	.3	16	4	23	6
	ST	33	8		44	11	6	1	3	1	14	3	9	3	56	15	35	9

		TENNESSEE C	TENNESSEE D		GEORGIA C	GEORGIA D	ALABAMA C	ALABAMA D	MISSISSIPPI C	MISSISSIPPI D	FLORIDA C	FLORIDA D	LOUISIANA C	LOUISIANA D	ARKANSAS C	ARKANSAS D	OKLAHOMA C	OKLAHOMA D
LAGGING LINE	W	45	4	N	70	3	75	13	67	9	100	5	44	12	78	6	33	5
	E	55	4	S	30	1	25	4	33	4	**	**	56	15	22	2	67	11
	ST		8			4		18		13		5		26		8		16
LAG LINE	W	50	4	N	42	2	100	6	75	13	40	2	40	6	50	4	93	19
	E	50	4	S	58	3	**	**	25	4	60	4	60	9	50	4	7	1
	ST		7			5		6		17		6		15		7		20
STARTING LINE	W	32	5	N	42	3	88	10	80	9	57	5	50	3	80	4	43	4
	E	68	10	S	58	4	13	1	20	2	43	4	50	3	20	1	57	5
	ST		15			8		12		11		9		6		5		9
TAW	W	41	17	N	65	27	73	33	60	26	59	24	36	12	33	14	27	5
	E	59	25	S	35	15	27	12	40	17	41	17	64	21	67	28	73	15
	ST		42			42		45		43		41		32		41		20
TAW LINE	W	46	13	N	71	29	77	15	43	7	69	27	86	18	71	28	35	12
	E	54	15	S	29	12	23	4	57	9	31	12	14	3	29	11	65	23
	ST		28			41		19		15		39		21		39		35

HOUSEHOLD EQUIPMENT
A VESSEL FOR COAL

ITEM (51)
WORK SHEET (23)

		TENNESSEE A	TENNESSEE B		GEORGIA A	GEORGIA B	ALABAMA A	ALABAMA B	MISSISSIPPI A	MISSISSIPPI B	FLORIDA A	FLORIDA B	LOUISIANA A	LOUISIANA B	ARKANSAS A	ARKANSAS B	OKLAHOMA A	OKLAHOMA B
COAL BUCKET	W	11	4	N	11	4	5	2	2	1	7	3	9	5	26	14	18	10
	E	42	17	S	14	6	3	1	2	1	3	1	7	4	17	9	22	12
	ST	53	21		25	10	8	3	4	2	10	4	16	9	43	23	41	22
COAL HOD	W	22	1	N	15	.4	4	.1	**	**	7	.2	**	**	50	2	10	.3
	E	30	1	S	**	**	11	.3	**	**	11	.3	**	**	20	1	20	1
	ST	52	1		15	.4	15	.4	**	**	19	1	**	**	70	3	30	1
COAL PAIL	W	**	**	N	23	.3	8	.1	**	**	23	.3	14	.3	29	1	14	.3
	E	**	**	S	31	.4	8	.1	**	**	8	.1	**	**	29	1	14	.3
	ST	**	**		54	1	15	.2	**	**	31	.4	14	.3	57	1	29	1
COAL SCUTTLE	W	23	11	N	26	12	11	5	7	3	4	2	4	1	36	10	9	3
	E	16	8	S	10	5	2	1	2	1	1	1	5	1	32	9	13	4
	ST	39	19		36	17	12	6	9	4	5	2	9	3	69	19	22	6

		TENNESSEE C	TENNESSEE D		GEORGIA C	GEORGIA D	ALABAMA C	ALABAMA D	MISSISSIPPI C	MISSISSIPPI D	FLORIDA C	FLORIDA D	LOUISIANA C	LOUISIANA D	ARKANSAS C	ARKANSAS D	OKLAHOMA C	OKLAHOMA D
COAL BUCKET	W	20	11	N	44	15	60	20	40	11	71	39	54	41	60	30	45	33
	E	80	41	S	56	20	40	13	60	16	29	16	46	34	40	20	55	40
	ST		51			35		33		27		54		75		50		73
COAL HOD	W	43	2	N	100	1	25	1	**	**	40	3	**	**	71	4	33	1
	E	57	2	S	**	**	75	3	**	**	60	4	**	**	29	2	67	2
	ST		4			1		4		**		7		**		6		4
COAL PAIL	W	**	**	N	43	1	50	1	**	**	75	4	100	3	50	2	50	1
	E	**	**	S	57	1	50	1	**	**	25	1	**	**	50	2	50	1
	ST		**			3		2		**		6		3		3		2
COAL SCUTTLE	W	59	27	N	72	44	88	53	78	56	78	26	43	9	53	22	41	9
	E	41	18	S	28	17	13	8	23	16	22	7	57	13	47	20	59	12
	ST		45			61		61		73		33		22		42		21

ITEM (52)
WORK SHEET (23)

FARM EQUIPMENT
FLAT PIECE OF STONE TO SHARPEN KNIVES OR SCYTHES

		TENNESSEE A	TENNESSEE B		GEORGIA A	GEORGIA B	ALABAMA A	ALABAMA B	MISSISSIPPI A	MISSISSIPPI B	FLORIDA A	FLORIDA B	LOUISIANA A	LOUISIANA B	ARKANSAS A	ARKANSAS B	OKLAHOMA A	OKLAHOMA B
WHET	W	33	.2	N	17	.1	**	**	**	**	**	**	**	**	50	1	**	**
	E	50	.3	S	**	**	**	**	**	**	**	**	**	**	25	.3	25	.3
	ST	83	1		17	.1	**	**	**	**	**	**	**	**	75	1	25	.3
WHET ROCK	W	15	10	N	21	13	6	4	4	2	7	5	7	4	34	17	10	5
	E	27	18	S	14	9	2	1	2	1	3	2	4	2	25	13	20	10
	ST	42	28		35	23	8	5	5	4	10	7	11	6	59	30	30	15
WHET SEED	W	**	**	N	**	**	40	.2	**	**	**	**	**	**	**	**	**	**
	E	40	.2	S	**	**	20	.1	**	**	**	**	**	**	100	1	**	**
	ST	40	.2		**	**	60	.3	**	**	**	**	**	**	100	1	**	**
WHET STONE	W	20	5	N	13	4	9	2	5	1	10	3	4	1	25	10	22	9
	E	23	6	S	6	2	3	1	3	1	8	2	11	4	21	8	17	7
	ST	43	12		20	5	12	3	7	2	18	5	15	6	46	18	39	16
WHETTER	W	10	.1	N	20	.2	**	**	**	**	10	.1	**	**	**	**	**	**
	E	10	.1	S	40	.4	**	**	**	**	10	.1	**	**	**	**	**	**
	ST	20	.2		60	1	**	**	**	**	20	.2	**	**	**	**	**	**

		TENNESSEE C	TENNESSEE D		GEORGIA C	GEORGIA D	ALABAMA C	ALABAMA D	MISSISSIPPI C	MISSISSIPPI D	FLORIDA C	FLORIDA D	LOUISIANA C	LOUISIANA D	ARKANSAS C	ARKANSAS D	OKLAHOMA C	OKLAHOMA D
WHET	W	40	1	N	100	.3	**	**	**	**	**	**	**	**	67	1	**	**
	E	60	1	S	**	**	**	**	**	**	**	**	**	**	33	1	100	1
	ST		1			.3		**		**		**		**		2		1
WHET ROCK	W	35	24	N	59	46	78	45	71	45	75	42	63	31	57	34	33	16
	E	65	45	S	41	33	22	13	29	19	25	14	38	19	43	26	67	33
	ST		69			79		58		64		56		50		60		49
WHET SEED	W	**	**	N	**	**	67	2	**	**	**	**	**	**	**	**	**	**
	E	100	1	S	**	**	33	1	**	**	**	**	**	**	100	1	**	**
	ST		1			**		4		**		**		**		1		**
WHET STONE	W	46	13	N	67	13	72	27	63	23	57	24	25	13	54	20	56	28
	E	54	16	S	33	6	28	11	37	13	43	18	75	38	46	17	44	22
	ST		29			19		38		36		42		50		36		50
WHETTER	W	50	.2	N	33	1	**	**	**	**	50	1	**	**	**	**	**	**
	E	50	.2	S	67	1	**	**	**	**	50	1	**	**	**	**	**	**
	ST		1			2		**		**		2		**		**		**

ITEM (53)
WORK SHEET (24)

HOUSEHOLD EQUIPMENT
FUEL FOR LAMPS

		TENNESSEE			GEORGIA		ALABAMA		MISSISSIPPI		FLORIDA		LOUISIANA		ARKANSAS		OKLAHOMA	
		A	B		A	B	A	B	A	B	A	B	A	B	A	B	A	B
CARBON OIL	W	33	.4	N	**	**	8	.1	8	.1	**	**	**	**	50	1	**	**
	E	42	1	S	**	**	**	**	**	**	8	.1	**	**	25	.3	25	.3
	ST	75	1		**	**	8	.1	8	.1	8	.1	**	**	75	1	25	.3
COAL OIL	W	33	12	N	5	2	7	2	8	3	2	1	8	5	25	16	13	9
	E	35	13	S	1	.2	1	.3	5	2	4	1	8	5	25	16	19	12
	ST	68	25		5	2	8	3	13	5	6	2	17	11	51	32	33	21
KEROSENE	W	8	5	N	25	14	7	4	3	2	11	7	7	3	31	14	15	6
	E	18	11	S	18	10	3	2	2	1	5	3	7	3	20	9	22	10
	ST	26	15		43	25	11	6	4	3	16	.9	13	6	50	[illegible]	37	16
LAMP OIL	W	7	1	N	33	3	1	.1	4	.3	3	.2	**	**	25	.3	25	.3
	E	47	[illegible]	S	[illegible]	.4	**	**	**	**	**	**	**	**	25	.3	25	.3
	ST	54	4		38	3	1	.1	4	.3	3	.2	**	**	50	1	50	1

		TENNESSEE			GEORGIA		ALABAMA		MISSISSIPPI		FLORIDA		LOUISIANA		ARKANSAS		OKLAHOMA	
		C	D		C	D	C	D	C	D	C	D	C	D	C	D	C	D
CARBON OIL	W	44	1	N	**	**	100	1	100	1	**	**	**	**	67	1	**	**
	E	56	1	S	**	**	**	**	**	**	100	1	**	**	33	1	100	1
	ST		2			**		1		1		1		**		2		1
COAL OIL	W	48	26	N	89	6	89	27	61	37	38	7	50	33	50	29	41	23
	E	52	28	S	11	1	11	3	39	24	62	11	50	33	50	29	59	32
	ST		55			7		31		61		18		65		57		55
KEROSENE	W	31	10	N	59	49	69	47	60	20	71	56	50	17	61	24	40	17
	E	69	23	S	41	34	31	20	40	13	29	23	50	17	39	15	60	25
	ST		34			83		67		33		79		35		39		42
LAMP OIL	W	12	1	N	86	9	100	1	100	4	100	2	**	**	50	1	50	1
	E	88	8	S	14	1	**	**	**	**	**	**	**	**	50	1	50	1
	ST		9			10		1		4		2		**		1		2

HOUSEHOLD EQUIPMENT
A FANCY DAYTIME COVER FOR A BED

ITEM (54)
WORK SHEET (28)

		TENNESSEE A	TENNESSEE B		GEORGIA A	GEORGIA B	ALABAMA A	ALABAMA B	MISSISSIPPI A	MISSISSIPPI B	FLORIDA A	FLORIDA B	LOUISIANA A	LOUISIANA B	ARKANSAS A	ARKANSAS B	OKLAHOMA A	OKLAHOMA B
BEDSPREAD	W	16	11	N	18	12	7	5	4	3	8	5	6	5	28	22	17	13
	E	27	19	S	12	8	3	2	2	1	4	3	8	6	23	18	19	15
	ST	43	30		30	20	10	7	6	4	12	8	14	11	51	41	35	29
COUNTERPANE	W	23	3	N	18	3	10	1	6	1	11	2	4	.3	41	4	4	.3
	E	15	2	S	6	1	1	.2	5	1	4	1	7	1	26	3	19	2
	ST	38	6		25	4	11	2	11	2	15	2	11	1	67	6	22	2
COUNTERPIN	W	15	2	N	24	4	2	.3	4	1	8	1	15	1	25	2	**	**
	E	28	4	S	15	2	1	.1	1	.2	2	.3	5	.3	45	3	10	1
	ST	42	6		40	6	3	.4	6	1	10	1	20	1	70	5	10	1
COVERLET	W	19	1	N	15	.4	22	1	**	**	7	.2	8	.3	58	3	**	**
	E	19	1	S	7	.2	7	.2	4	.1	**	**	**	**	25	1	8	.3
	ST	37	1		22	1	30	1	4	.1	7	.2	8	.3	83	4	8	.3
COVERLID	W	14	1	N	16	1	5	.2	3	.1	**	**	**	**	100	1	**	**
	E	54	2	S	3	.1	**	**	5	.2	**	**	**	**	**	**	**	**
	ST	68	3		19	1	5	.2	8	.3	**	**	**	**	100	1	**	**

		TENNESSEE C	TENNESSEE D		GEORGIA C	GEORGIA D	ALABAMA C	ALABAMA D	MISSISSIPPI C	MISSISSIPPI D	FLORIDA C	FLORIDA D	LOUISIANA C	LOUISIANA D	ARKANSAS C	ARKANSAS D	OKLAHOMA C	OKLAHOMA D
BEDSPREAD	W	37	24	N	60	39	74	51	68	40	66	45	45	36	55	39	47	42
	E	63	42	S	40	26	26	18	32	18	34	23	55	44	45	32	53	48
	ST		66			65		68		58		68		79		72		90
COUNTERPANE	W	61	8	N	74	9	88	15	53	12	76	14	33	3	61	7	17	1
	E	39	5	S	26	3	13	2	47	11	24	4	67	5	39	4	83	6
	ST		12			12		17		23		18		8		11		7
COUNTERPIN	W	34	5	N	61	12	75	3	75	9	79	9	75	8	36	3	**	**
	E	66	9	S	39	7	25	1	25	3	21	3	25	3	64	6	100	2
	ST		14			19		4		12		12		10		9		2
COVERLET	W	50	1	N	67	1	75	6	**	**	100	2	100	3	70	4	**	**
	E	50	1	S	33	1	25	2	100	2	**	**	**	**	30	2	100	1
	ST		2			2		8		2		2		3		6		1
COVERLID	W	20	1	N	86	2	100	2	33	2	**	**	**	**	100	2	**	**
	E	80	5	S	14	.3	**	**	67	3	**	**	**	**	**	**	**	**
	ST		6			2		2		5		**		**		2		**

HOUSEHOLD EQUIPMENT
A BED COVER FILLED WITH COTTON, TIED, NOT QUILTED

ITEM (55)
WORK SHEET (29)

		TENNESSEE			GEORGIA		ALABAMA		MISSISSIPPI		FLORIDA		LOUISIANA		ARKANSAS		OKLAHOMA	
		A	B		A	B	A	B	A	B	A	B	A	B	A	B	A	B
COMFORT	W	16	10	N	20	12	6	4	3	2	8	5	6	4	30	19	15	9
	E	27	16	S	12	7	2	1	3	2	2	1	4	3	25	16	20	13
	ST	43	26		32	19	9	5	6	4	10	6	10	6	55	35	35	22
COMFORTABLE	W	**	**	N	**	**	**	**	50	.2	**	**	**	**	**	**	**	**
	E	25	.1	S	25	.1	**	**	**	**	**	**	**	**	**	**	**	**
	ST	25	.1		25	.1	**	**	50	.2	**	**	**	**	**	**	**	**
COMFORTER	W	11	2	N	16	3	7	1	7	1	10	2	4	1	35	7	22	4
	E	22	4	S	13	2	.4	1	1	.1	9	2	7	1	16	3	16	4
	ST	33	5		29	5	11	2	7	1	19	4	11	2	51	10	38	8
HAP	W	50	.1	N	**	**	**	**	50	.1	**	**	**	**	**	**	**	**
					(NO RESPONSE)													
	ST	50	.1		**	**	**	**	50	.1	**	**	**	**	**	**	**	**
TIED QUILT	W	13	1	N	15	1	9	1	8	.4	8	.4	**	**	60	1	**	**
	E	26	1	S	17	1	2	.1	**	**	2	.1	20	.3	**	**	20	.3
	ST	40	2		32	2	11	1	8	.4	9	1	20	.3	60	1	20	.3

		TENNESSEE			GEORGIA		ALABAMA		MISSISSIPPI		FLORIDA		LOUISIANA		ARKANSAS		OKLAHOMA	
		C	D		C	D	C	D	C	D	C	D	C	D	C	D	C	D
COMFORT	W	38	29	N	62	45	74	50	53	34	79	48	59	42	55	41	43	31
	E	62	48	S	38	28	26	18	47	30	21	13	41	29	45	34	57	42
	ST		77			74		68		64		61		71		76		73
COMFORTABLE	W	**	**	N	**	**	**	**	100	4	**	**	**	**	**	**	**	**
	E	100	.3	S	100	.4	**	**	**	**	**	**	**	**	**	**	**	**
	ST		.3			.4		**		4		**		**		**		**
COMFORTER	W	32	5	N	55	11	67	16	92	21	52	17	33	8	68	15	57	14
	E	68	11	S	45	9	33	8	8	2	48	16	67	17	32	7	43	11
	ST		16			19		24		23		33		25		22		25
HAP	W	100	.3	N	**	**	**	**	100	2	**	**	**	**	**	**	**	**
					(NO RESPONSE)													
	ST		.3			**		**		2		**		**		**		**
TIED QUILT	W	33	2	N	47	3	83	7	100	8	80	4	**	**	100	2	**	**
	E	67	4	S	53	4	17	1	**	**	20	1	100	4	**	**	100	1
	ST		6			7		8		8		5		4		2		1

ITEM (56)
WORK SHEET (29)

HOUSEHOLD EQUIPMENT
A BED ON THE FLOOR

		TENNESSEE			GEORGIA		ALABAMA		MISSISSIPPI		FLORIDA		LOUISIANA		ARKANSAS		OKLAHOMA	
		A	B		A	B	A	B	A	B	A	B	A	B	A	B	A	B
BUNK	W	15	1	N	10	.4	3	.1	**	**	8	.3	6	.3	29	2	**	**
	E	48	2	S	13	1	**	**	3	.1	3	.1	35	2	24	1	6	.3
	ST	63	3		23	1	3	.1	3	.1	10	.4	41	3	53	3	6	.3
LODGE	W	100	.2	N	**	**	**	**	**	**	**	**	**	**	**	**	**	**
	E	**	**	S	**	**	**	**	**	**	**	**	**	**	**	**	100	.3
	ST	100	.2		**	**	**	**	**	**	**	**	**	**	**	**	100	.3
PALLET	W	19	16	N	19	16	6	6	4	3	8	7	7	6	29	25	15	13
	E	24	21	S	12	10	3	2	2	2	4	3	5	4	24	20	20	17
	ST	43	37		30	26	9	8	6	5	11	10	12	10	53	44	35	30
SHAKEDOWN	W	50	.1	N	**	**	**	**	**	**	**	**	**	**	**	**	**	**
	E	50	.1	S	**	**	**	**	**	**	**	**	**	**	**	**	100	.3
	ST	100	.2		**	**	**	**	**	**	**	**	**	**	**	**	100	.3

		TENNESSEE			GEORGIA		ALABAMA		MISSISSIPPI		FLORIDA		LOUISIANA		ARKANSAS		OKLAHOMA	
		C	D		C	D	C	D	C	D	C	D	C	D	C	D	C	D
BUNK	W	24	2	N	44	2	100	1	**	**	75	3	14	3	56	4	**	**
	E	76	5	S	56	2	**	**	100	2	25	1	86	18	44	3	100	1
	ST		6			3		1		2		4		21		7		1
LODGE	W	100	1	N	**	**	**	**	**	**	**	**	**	**	**	**	**	**
	E	**	**	S	**	**	**	**	**	**	**	**	**	**	**	**	100	1
	ST		1			**		**		**		**		**		**		1
PALLET	W	44	41	N	62	60	72	71	65	63	67	64	59	47	55	52	43	41
	E	56	52	S	38	37	28	28	35	35	33	32	41	32	45	42	57	55
	ST		93			97		99		98		96		79		93		96
SHAKEDOWN	W	50	.2	N	**	**	**	**	**	**	**	**	**	**	**	**	**	**
	E	50	.2	S	**	**	**	**	**	**	**	**	**	**	**	**	100	1
	ST		1			**		**		**		**		**		**		1

ITEM (57)
WORK SHEET (29)

TOPOGRAPHY
LOW GROUND IN A RIVER VALLEY

		TENNESSEE A	TENNESSEE B		GEORGIA A	GEORGIA B	ALABAMA A	ALABAMA B	MISSISSIPPI A	MISSISSIPPI B	FLORIDA A	FLORIDA B	LOUISIANA A	LOUISIANA B	ARKANSAS A	ARKANSAS B	OKLAHOMA A	OKLAHOMA B
BOTTOM LAND	W	19	11	N	19	11	6	4	4	3	8	5	7	4	25	14	21	12
	E	23	13	S	13	7	3	2	2	1	3	2	4	2	18	10	25	14
	ST	41	24		31	18	9	5	7	4	11	7	11	6	43	24	46	25
BOTTOMS	W	22	7	N	22	7	8	3	4	1	4	1	6	2	35	13	7	3
	E	28	9	S	8	3	1	.3	2	1	1	.3	7	3	36	13	10	4
	ST	49	16		30	9	9	3	6	2	5	2	13	5	70	26	17	6
INTERVALE(A)	W	**	**	N	**	**	**	**	100	.1	**	**	**	**	**	**	**	**
					(NO RESPONSE)													
	ST	**	**		**	**	**	**	100	.1	**	**	**	**	**	**	**	**

		TENNESSEE C	TENNESSEE D		GEORGIA C	GEORGIA D	ALABAMA C	ALABAMA D	MISSISSIPPI C	MISSISSIPPI D	FLORIDA C	FLORIDA D	LOUISIANA C	LOUISIANA D	ARKANSAS C	ARKANSAS D	OKLAHOMA C	OKLAHOMA D
BOTTOM LAND	W	45	27	N	60	40	68	44	68	44	70	56	65	37	59	28	46	37
	E	55	33	S	40	26	32	21	32	21	30	24	35	20	41	20	54	44
	ST		61			66		65		65		80		57		48		80
BOTTOMS	W	44	17	N	72	24	89	31	68	23	81	16	46	20	49	26	41	8
	E	56	22	S	28	10	11	4	32	11	19	4	54	23	51	26	59	11
	ST		39			34		35		33		20		43		52		20
INTERVALE(A)	W	**	**	N	**	**	**	**	100	2	**	**	**	**	**	**	**	**
					(NO RESPONSE)													
	ST		**			**		**		2		**		**		**		**

TOPOGRAPHY
SWAMPY GROUND WITH A SMALL STREAM RUNNING THROUGH IT

ITEM (58)
WORK SHEET (29)

		TENNESSEE			GEORGIA		ALABAMA		MISSISSIPPI		FLORIDA		LOUISIANA		ARKANSAS		OKLAHOMA	
		A	B		A	B	A	B	A	B	A	B	A	B	A	B	A	B
BAYOU(A)	W	58	3	N	2	.1	4	.2	8	.4	8	.4	8	1	27	5	4	1
	E	8	.4	S	**	**	4	.2	8	.4	2	.1	17	3	33	6	12	2
	ST	65	4		2	.1	8	.4	15	1	10	1	25	5	60	11	15	3
BOG	W	29	1	N	8	.2	13	.3	**	**	4	.1	**	**	20	1	30	1
	E	4	.1	S	25	1	8	.2	**	**	8	.2	10	.3	**	**	40	1
	ST	33	1		33	1	21	1	**	**	13	.3	10	.3	20	1	70	3
DRAW(A)	W	33	.2	N	17	.1	**	**	**	**	**	**	**	**	16	1	32	2
	E	17	.1	S	33	.2	**	**	**	**	**	**	5	.3	11	1	37	3
	ST	50	.3		50	.3	**	**	**	**	**	**	5	.3	26	2	68	5
MARSH	W	12	2	N	20	3	12	2	3	.4	5	1	**	**	26	3	13	1
	E	22	3	S	11	1	4	1	4	1	8	1	19	2	19	2	23	3
	ST	35	5		31	4	15	2	7	1	12	2	19	2	45	5	35	4
SEEP(A)	W	20	.1	N	20	.1	20	.1	**	**	**	**	**	**	50	.3	**	**
	E	20	.1	S	**	**	**	**	20	.1	**	**	**	**	**	**	50	.3
	ST	40	.2		20	.1	20	.1	20	.1	**	**	**	**	50	.3	50	.3
SLOUGH	W	27	4	N	7	1	7	1	11	2	15	2	10	3	37	11	12	4
	E	11	2	S	13	2	1	.1	2	.2	6	1	4	1	23	7	15	4
	ST	38	5		20	3	8	1	13	2	21	3	13	4	60	18	27	8
SWALE(A)	W	40	.2	N	**	**	**	**	**	**	**	**	**	**	100	.3	**	**
	E	20	.1	S	**	**	20	.1	**	**	20	.1	**	**	**	**	**	**
	ST	60	.3		**	**	20	.1	**	**	20	.1	**	**	100	.3	**	**
SWAMP	W	16	10	N	22	13	7	4	3	2	7	4	7	3	26	9	11	4
	E	28	17	S	12	7	2	1	2	1	2	1	8	3	26	9	22	8
	ST	44	27		33	21	9	6	5	3	9	5	15	5	52	19	33	12

ITEM (58) (CONTINUED) SWAMPY GROUND WITH A SMALL STREAM RUNNING THROUGH IT

		TENNESSEE			GEORGIA		ALABAMA		MISSISSIPPI		FLORIDA		LOUISIANA		ARKANSAS		OKLAHOMA	
		C	D		C	D	C	D	C	D	C	D	C	D	C	D	C	D
BAYOU(A)	W	88	7	N	100	.3	50	2	50	6	80	4	31	9	45	9	25	2
	E	12	1	S	**	**	50	2	50	6	20	1	69	19	55	11	75	6
	ST		8			.3		4		13		5		28		20		8
BOG	W	88	2	N	25	1	60	3	**	**	33	1	**	**	100	1	43	3
	E	13	.2	S	75	2	40	2	**	**	67	2	100	2	**	**	57	4
	ST		2			3		5		**		3		2		1		7
DRAW(A)	W	67	.4	N	33	.3	**	**	**	**	**	**	**	**	60	2	46	6
	E	33	.2	S	67	1	**	**	**	**	**	**	100	2	40	1	54	7
	ST		1			1		**		**		**		2		3		14
MARSH	W	36	4	N	65	9	75	15	44	6	38	6	**	**	57	5	36	4
	E	64	7	S	35	5	25	7	56	8	63	9	100	13	43	4	64	7
	ST		11			14		21		14		15		13		9		12
SEEP(A)	W	50	.2	N	100	.3	100	1	**	**	**	**	**	**	100	1	**	**
	E	50	.2	S	**	**	**	**	100	2	**	**	**	**	**	**	100	1
	ST		.4			.3		1		2		**		**		1		1
SLOUGH	W	70	9	N	35	3	90	9	88	24	71	19	73	17	61	19	45	11
	E	30	4	S	65	6	10	1	12	3	29	8	27	6	39	12	55	13
	ST		12			9		10		27		26		23		32		23
SWALE(A)	W	67	.4	N	**	**	**	**	**	**	**	**	**	**	100	1	**	**
	E	33	.2	S	**	**	100	1	**	**	100	1	**	**	**	**	**	**
	ST		1			**		1		**		1		**		1		**
SWAMP	W	36	23	N	65	46	77	44	61	27	74	37	47	15	50	17	33	12
	E	64	41	S	35	25	23	13	39	17	26	13	53	17	50	17	67	23
	ST		65			72		58		44		50		32		34		35

ITEM (58)
WORK SHEET (30)

TOPOGRAPHY
A SLIGHT DEPRESSION, SOMETIMES WITH A LITTLE STREAM

		TENNESSEE			GEORGIA		ALABAMA		MISSISSIPPI		FLORIDA		LOUISIANA		ARKANSAS		OKLAHOMA	
		A	B		A	B	A	B	A	B	A	B	A	B	A	B	A	B
COULEE	W	12	.2	N	29	1	6	.1	12	.2	6	.1	9	.3	9	.3	**	**
	E	18	.3	S	6	.1	6	.1	6	.1	**	**	73	3	9	.3	**	**
	ST	29	1		35	1	12	.2	18	.3	6	.1	82	3	18	1	**	**
DRAW(B)	W	19	3	N	27	4	10	2	3	.4	4	1	4	2	33	14	25	10
	E	19	3	S	10	2	1	.2	3	.4	2	.3	3	1	13	5	22	9
	ST	39	6		38	6	12	2	6	1	6	1	7	3	46	19	47	19
SEEP(B)	W	22	5	N	18	4	5	1	3	1	4	1	7	1	56	5	7	1
	E	32	7	S	9	2	1	.3	3	1	1	.3	**	**	30	3	**	**
	ST	54	12		28	6	6	1	6	1	6	1	7	1	85	8	7	1
SWALE(B)	W	29	.4	N	7	.1	14	.2	**	**	**	**	**	**	20	.3	20	.3
	E	21	.3	S	7	.1	14	.2	**	**	7	.1	**	**	60	1	**	**
	ST	50	1		14	.2	29	.4	**	**	7	.1	**	**	80	1	20	.3

		TENNESSEE			GEORGIA		ALABAMA		MISSISSIPPI		FLORIDA		LOUISIANA		ARKANSAS		OKLAHOMA	
		C	D		C	D	C	D	C	D	C	D	C	D	C	D	C	D
COULEE	W	40	1	N	83	4	50	3	67	8	100	4	11	5	50	1	**	**
	E	60	2	S	17	1	50	3	33	4	**	**	89	42	50	1	**	**
	ST		3			5		5		13		4		47		2		**
DRAW(B)	W	50	15	N	72	32	88	41	50	17	67	26	63	26	72	46	54	51
	E	50	15	S	28	12	12	5	50	17	33	13	38	16	28	18	46	44
	ST		30			44		46		33		39		42		65		95
SEEP(B)	W	41	26	N	67	33	79	30	46	25	75	39	100	11	65	18	100	4
	E	59	38	S	33	16	21	8	54	29	25	13	**	**	35	10	**	**
	ST		63			49		38		54		52		11		28		4
SWALE(B)	W	57	2	N	50	1	50	5	**	**	**	**	**	**	25	1	100	2
	E	43	2	S	50	1	50	5	**	**	100	4	**	**	75	4	**	**
	ST		4			2		11		**		4		**		5		2

ITEM (58)
WORK SHEET (29)

TOPOGRAPHY
A LOW GRASSLAND

		TENNESSEE A	TENNESSEE B		GEORGIA A	GEORGIA B	ALABAMA A	ALABAMA B	MISSISSIPPI A	MISSISSIPPI B	FLORIDA A	FLORIDA B	LOUISIANA A	LOUISIANA B	ARKANSAS A	ARKANSAS B	OKLAHOMA A	OKLAHOMA B
BAYOU(B)	W	32	1	N	12	.3	4	.1	20	1	4	.1	8	.3	46	2	8	.3
	E	16	.4	S	**	**	**	**	12	.3	**	**	**	**	23	1	15	1
	ST	48	1		12	.3	4	.1	32	1	4	.1	8	.3	69	3	23	1
COULEE(B)					(NO RESPONSE)													
	E	**	**	S	**	**	**	**	**	**	**	**	100	.3	**	**	**	**
	ST	**	**		**	**	**	**	**	**	**	**	100	.3	**	**	**	**
SWALE(C)	W	25	.2	N	25	.2	**	**	**	**								
	E	25	.2	S	**	**	**	**	**	**	13	.1	**	**	**	**	**	**
											13	.1	**	**	50	1	50	1
	ST	50	.4		25	.2	**	**	**	**	25	.2	**	**	50	1	50	1
MEADOW	W	20	12	N	23	14	8	5	4	2	2	1	7	4	32	18	15	9
	E	30	18	S	9	6	2	1	2	1	1	1	4	3	22	13	19	11
	ST	49	31		32	20	10	6	6	3	3	2	11	6	55	31	34	19
INTERVALE(B)	W	67	.2	N	33	.1	**	**	**	**	**	**	**	**	**	**	**	**
					(NO RESPONSE)													
	ST	67	.2		33	.1	**	**	**	**	**	**	**	**	**	**	**	**
PRAIRIE	W	9	1	N	4	.3	9	1	3	.2	38	3	**	**	12	2	21	3
	E	6	1	S	10	1	1	.1	1	.1	19	2	12	2	19	3	37	6
	ST	15	1		14	1	10	1	4	.3	57	5	12	2	30	5	58	9
DAGO	W	100	.1	N	**	**	**	**	**	**	**	**	**	**	**	**	**	**
	E	**	**	S	**	**	**	**	**	**	**	**	**	**	**	**	100	.3
	ST	100	.1		**	**	**	**	**	**	**	**	**	**	**	**	100	.3

ITEM (58) (CONTINUED) A LOW GRASSLAND

ITEM (58)		TENNESSEE C	TENNESSEE D		GEORGIA C	GEORGIA D	ALABAMA C	ALABAMA D	MISSISSIPPI C	MISSISSIPPI D	FLORIDA C	FLORIDA D	LOUISIANA C	LOUISIANA D	ARKANSAS C	ARKANSAS D	OKLAHOMA C	OKLAHOMA D
BAYOU(B)	W	67	2	N	100	1	100	1	63	11	100	1	100	4	67	5	33	1
	E	33	1	S	**	**	**	**	38	7	**	**	**	**	33	3	67	2
	ST		4			1		1		18		1		4		8		4
COULEE(B)					(NO RESPONSE)													
	E	**	**	S	**	**	**	**	**	**	**	**	100	4	**	**	**	**
	ST		**			**		**		**		**		4		**		**
SWALE(C)	W	50	1	N	100	1	**	**	**	**	50	1	**	**	**	**	**	**
	E	50	1	S	**	**	**	**	**	**	50	1	**	**	100	2	100	2
	ST		1			1		**		**		3		**		2		2
MEADOW	W	40	36	N	71	65	77	67	67	50	70	21	65	46	59	46	44	28
	E	60	55	S	29	27	23	20	33	25	30	9	35	25	41	32	56	35
	ST		91			92		87		75		29		71		78		64
INTERVALE(B)	W	100	1	N	100	.4	**	**	**	**	**	**	**	**	**	**	**	**
					(NO RESPONSE)													
	ST		1			.4		**		**		**		**		**		**
PRAIRIE	W	58	2	N	27	1	88	10	67	5	67	44	**	**	38	5	36	11
	E	42	2	S	73	4	13	1	33	2	33	22	100	21	62	7	64	19
	ST		4			5		12		7		66		21		12		29
DAGO	W	100	.3	N	**	**	**	**	**	**	**	**	**	**	**	**	**	**
	E	**	**	S	**	**	**	**	**	**	**	**	**	**	**	**	100	1
	ST		.3			**		**		**		**		**		**		1

TOPOGRAPHY
A ROAD PAVED WITH CONCRETE

ITEM (59)
WORK SHEET (31)

		TENNESSEE A	TENNESSEE B		GEORGIA A	GEORGIA B	ALABAMA A	ALABAMA B	MISSISSIPPI A	MISSISSIPPI B	FLORIDA A	FLORIDA B	LOUISIANA A	LOUISIANA B	ARKANSAS A	ARKANSAS B	OKLAHOMA A	OKLAHOMA B
CEMENT ROAD	W	15	1	N	31	2	13	1	4	.2	6	.3	**	**	13	.3	**	**
	E	8	.4	S	8	.4	6	.3	4	.2	6	.3	25	1	**	**	63	2
	ST	23	1		38	2	19	1	8	.4	12	1	25	1	13	.3	63	2
CONCRETE ROAD	W	22	8	N	14	5	8	3	4	1	6	2	8	1	35	5	3	.3
	E	32	12	S	6	2	1	.4	3	1	5	2	8	1	22	3	24	3
	ST	54	19		20	7	9	3	7	2	10	4	16	2	57	8	27	4
HARD ROAD	W	10	1	N	8	.4	**	**	**	**	36	2	**	**	50	1	**	**
	E	14	1	S	20	1	**	**	**	**	12	1	**	**	50	1	**	**
	ST	24	1		28	1	**	**	**	**	48	2	**	**	100	1	**	**
HARD SURFACE ROAD(A)	W	43	3	N	11	1	3	.2	**	**	2	.1	**	**	50	3	11	1
	E	30	2	S	8	1	**	**	**	**	3	.2	**	**	28	2	11	1
	ST	72	5		20	1	3	.2	**	**	5	.3	**	**	78	5	22	1
PAVED ROAD	W	14	5	N	23	8	7	2	4	1	7	2	6	2	29	10	14	5
	E	19	7	S	17	6	4	1	4	1	2	1	14	5	24	8	13	4
	ST	33	11		40	14	11	4	8	3	9	3	20	7	53	18	27	9
PAVEMENT(A)	W	14	3	N	18	3	12	2	7	1	7	1	6	3	23	11	20	10
	E	21	4	S	14	3	4	1	3	1	2	.4	5	2	21	10	24	12
	ST	34	7		32	6	16	3	9	2	9	2	11	5	45	21	45	21
PAVE	W	50	.2	N	25	.1	**	**	**	**	**	**	40	1	**	**	**	**
	E	25	.1	S	**	**	**	**	**	**	**	**	40	1	**	**	20	.3
	ST	75	.3		25	.1	**	**	**	**	**	**	80	1	**	**	20	.3
PIKE	W	48	1	N	4	.1	4	.1	4	.1	**	**	**	**	25	.3	**	**
	E	37	1	S	**	**	**	**	**	**	4	.1	**	**	50	1	25	.3
	ST	85	2		4	.1	4	.1	4	.1	4	.1	**	**	75	1	25	.3
SLAB	W	75	1	N	6	.1	**	**	6	.1	**	**	**	**	50	3	14	1
	E	13	.2	S	**	**	**	**	**	**	**	**	**	**	7	.3	29	1
	ST	88	1		6	.1	**	**	6	.1	**	**	**	**	57	3	43	2

(CONTINUED) A ROAD PAVED WITH CONCRETE

ITEM (59)		TENNESSEE C	TENNESSEE D		GEORGIA C	GEORGIA D	ALABAMA C	ALABAMA D	MISSISSIPPI C	MISSISSIPPI D	FLORIDA C	FLORIDA D	LOUISIANA C	LOUISIANA D	ARKANSAS C	ARKANSAS D	OKLAHOMA C	OKLAHOMA D
CEMENT ROAD	W	67	2	N	80	5	70	6	50	3	50	3	**	**	100	1	**	**
	E	33	1	S	20	1	30	3	50	3	50	3	100	4	**	**	100	5
	ST		3			6		9		6		5		4		1		5
CONCRETE ROAD	W	40	16	N	68	15	87	24	58	19	56	17	50	7	62	8	10	1
	E	60	24	S	32	7	13	4	42	14	44	14	50	7	38	5	90	8
	ST		40			22		28		33		31		13		13		9
HARD ROAD	W	42	1	N	29	1	**	**	**	**	75	16	**	**	50	1	**	**
	E	58	1	S	71	3	**	**	**	**	25	5	**	**	50	1	**	**
	ST		3			5		**		**		21		**		3		**
HARD SURFACE ROAD(A)	W	59	6	N	58	2	100	2	**	**	33	1	**	**	64	6	50	2
	E	41	4	S	42	2	**	**	**	**	67	2	**	**	36	3	50	2
	ST		9			4		2		**		3		**		9		4
PAVED ROAD	W	43	10	N	58	25	64	21	52	18	77	20	32	13	54	17	52	12
	E	57	13	S	42	18	36	12	48	17	23	6	68	29	46	14	48	11
	ST		24			43		33		35		26		42		31		23
PAVEMENT(A)	W	40	5	N	57	11	76	20	71	17	75	10	57	18	53	19	46	24
	E	60	8	S	43	8	24	6	29	7	25	3	43	13	47	18	54	29
	ST		13			19		27		24		14		31		37		53
PAVE	W	67	.4	N	100	.3	**	**	**	**	**	**	50	4	**	**	**	**
	E	33	.2	S	**	**	**	**	**	**	**	**	50	4	**	**	100	1
	ST		1			.3		**		**		**		9		**		1
PIKE	W	57	3	N	100	.3	100	1	100	1	**	**	**	**	33	1	**	**
	E	43	2	S	**	**	**	**	**	**	100	1	**	**	67	1	100	1
	ST		5			.3		1		1		1		**		2		1
SLAB	W	86	3	N	100	.3	**	**	100	1	**	**	**	**	88	4	33	2
	E	14	.4	S	**	**	**	**	**	**	**	**	**	**	13	1	67	4
	ST		3			.3		**		1		**		**		5		5

QUALITIES
THE ROAD IS ______

ITEM (60)
WORK SHEET (31)

		TENNESSEE A	TENNESSEE B		GEORGIA A	GEORGIA B	ALABAMA A	ALABAMA B	MISSISSIPPI A	MISSISSIPPI B	FLORIDA A	FLORIDA B	LOUISIANA A	LOUISIANA B	ARKANSAS A	ARKANSAS B	OKLAHOMA A	OKLAHOMA B
SLICK	W	21	11	N	16	9	6	3	5	3	4	2	7	4	30	18	17	10
	E	29	16	S	12	7	2	1	3	1	2	1	3	2	23	13	20	12
	ST	50	27		28	15	8	4	8	4	6	3	10	6	53	31	37	22
SLIPPERY	W	17	6	N	19	7	9	3	3	1	11	4	8	3	26	8	11	4
	E	20	7	S	10	4	3	1	2	1	6	2	14	5	27	9	14	5
	ST	37	14		29	11	12	4	5	2	17	7	22	7	52	17	26	8

		TENNESSEE C	TENNESSEE D		GEORGIA C	GEORGIA D	ALABAMA C	ALABAMA D	MISSISSIPPI C	MISSISSIPPI D	FLORIDA C	FLORIDA D	LOUISIANA C	LOUISIANA D	ARKANSAS C	ARKANSAS D	OKLAHOMA C	OKLAHOMA D
SLICK	W	42	28	N	57	33	74	37	67	45	67	23	69	31	57	37	45	33
	E	58	39	S	43	25	26	13	33	22	33	11	31	14	43	28	55	40
	ST		66			59		50		67		34		44		65		72
SLIPPERY	W	46	16	N	65	27	72	36	53	17	65	43	35	19	49	17	43	12
	E	54	18	S	35	14	28	14	47	16	35	23	65	36	51	18	57	16
	ST		34			41		50		33		66		56		35		28

TOPOGRAPHY
A ROAD WITH A BITUMINOUS SURFACE

ITEM (61)
WORK SHEET (31)

		TENNESSEE			GEORGIA		ALABAMA		MISSISSIPPI		FLORIDA		LOUISIANA		ARKANSAS		OKLAHOMA	
		A	B		A	B	A	B	A	B	A	B	A	B	A	B	A	B
BLACKTOP	W	22	14	N	16	10	8	5	5	3	5	3	7	5	25	19	16	13
	E	31	20	S	7	5	3	2	2	2	2	1	9	7	23	18	20	15
	ST	53	34		23	15	11	7	7	5	6	4	15	12	49	38	36	28
OILED ROAD	W	20	1	N	11	1	7	.3	2	.1	7	.3	**	**	50	1	25	.3
	E	40	2	S	2	.1	2	.1	4	.2	4	.2	**	**	**	**	25	.3
	ST	60	3		13	1	9	.4	7	.3	11	1	**	**	50	1	50	1
PAVEMENT(B)	W	8	1	N	30	3	9	1	5	1	6	1	**	**	33	1	**	**
	E	8	1	S	25	3	4	.4	1	.1	6	1	**	**	33	1	33	1
	ST	15	2		55	6	13	1	6	1	12	1	**	**	67	1	33	1
HARD SURFACE ROAD(B)	W	15	1	N	24	2	9	1	2	.2	13	1	10	1	20	1	10	1
	E	9	1	S	14	1	1	.1	2	.2	11	1	5	.3	35	3	20	1
	ST	24	2		38	3	10	1	5	.4	24	2	15	1	55	4	30	2
SURFACE TREATED ROAD	W	13	.2	N	38	1	6	.1	**	**	6	.1	**	**	33	.3	33	.3
	E	**	**	S	25	.4	**	**	**	**	13	.2	**	**	33	.3	**	**
	ST	13	.2		63	1	6	.1	**	**	19	.3	**	**	67	1	33	.3
MACADAM ROAD	W	45	2	N	15	1	**	**	3	.1	3	.1	**	**	33	1	17	.3
	E	15	1	S	3	.1	3	.1	3	.1	9	.3	**	**	33	1	17	.3
	ST	61	2		18	1	3	.1	6	.2	12	.4	**	**	67	1	33	1
TARVIA					(NO RESPONSE)													
	E	100	.1	S	**	**	**	**	**	**	**	**	**	**	**	**	**	**
	ST	100	.1		**	**	**	**	**	**	**	**	**	**	**	**	**	**
TARVIA ROAD	W	**	**	N	50	.1	50	.1	**	**	**	**	**	**	**	**	**	**
					(NO RESPONSE)													
	ST	**	**		50	.1	50	.1	**	**	**	**	**	**	**	**	**	**

ITEM (61)

(CONTINUED) A ROAD WITH A BITUMINOUS SURFACE

		TENNESSEE			GEORGIA		ALABAMA		MISSISSIPPI		FLORIDA		LOUISIANA		ARKANSAS		OKLAHOMA	
		C	D		C	D	C	D	C	D	C	D	C	D	C	D	C	D
BLACKTOP	W	42	33	N	69	39	73	51	66	49	74	35	42	39	52	43	45	39
	E	58	46	S	31	17	27	19	34	25	26	12	58	53	48	39	55	47
	ST		79			56		69		75		46		92		82		86
OILED ROAD	W	33	2	N	83	2	75	3	33	2	60	4	**	**	100	2	50	1
	E	67	4	S	17	.3	25	1	67	3	40	2	**	**	**	**	50	1
	ST		6			2		4		5		6		**		2		2
PAVEMENT(B)	W	50	2	N	54	12	69	9	83	8	50	7	**	**	50	2	**	**
	E	50	2	S	46	10	31	4	17	2	50	7	**	**	50	2	100	2
	ST		4			22		14		10		14		**		3		2
HARD SURFACE ROAD(B)	W	62	3	N	64	8	89	8	50	3	52	13	67	6	36	3	33	3
	E	38	2	S	36	5	11	1	50	3	48	12	33	3	64	6	67	4
	ST		5			13		9		7		25		8		9		7
SURFACE TREATED ROAD	W	100	.4	N	60	2	100	1	**	**	33	1	**	**	50	1	100	1
	E	**	**	S	40	2	**	**	**	**	67	2	**	**	50	1	**	**
	ST		.4			4		1		**		4		**		2		1
MACADAM ROAD	W	75	4	N	83	2	**	**	50	2	25	1	**	**	50	2	50	1
	E	25	1	S	17	.3	100	1	50	2	75	4	**	**	50	2	50	1
	ST		5			2		1		3		5		**		3		2
TARVIA					(NO RESPONSE)													
	E	100	.2	S	**	**	**	**	**	**	**	**	**	**	**	**	**	**
	ST		.2			**		**		**		**		**		**		**
TARVIA ROAD	W	**	**	N	100	.3	100	1	**	**	**	**	**	**	**	**	**	**
					(NO RESPONSE)													
	ST		**			.3		1		**		**		**		**		**

ITEM (62)
WORK SHEET (31)

TOPOGRAPHY
GRASS STRIP BETWEEN SIDEWALK AND STREET

		TENNESSEE			GEORGIA		ALABAMA		MISSISSIPPI		FLORIDA		LOUISIANA		ARKANSAS		OKLAHOMA	
		A	B		A	B	A	B	A	B	A	B	A	B	A	B	A	B
BERM	W	50	.3	N	17	.1	17	.1	**	**	17	.1	**	**	100	.3	**	**
					(NO RESPONSE)													
	ST	50	.3		17	.1	17	.1	**	**	17	.1	**	**	100	.3	**	**
BOULEVARD	W	26	1	N	4	.2	12	1	8	.4	4	.2	**	**	25	1	6	.3
	E	24	1	S	6	.3	8	.4	4	.2	4	.2	31	2	25	1	13	1
	ST	50	3		10	1	20	1	12	1	8	.4	31	2	50	3	19	1
BOULEVARD STRIP	W	31	2	N	22	1	5	.3	5	.3	3	.2	14	1	33	3	14	1
	E	28	2	S	3	.2	**	**	3	.2	2	.1	**	**	24	2	14	1
	ST	58	4		25	2	5	.3	8	1	5	.3	14	1	57	4	29	2
PARKING	W	18	.2	N	18	.2	**	**	**	**	**	**	**	**	14	2	47	6
	E	27	.3	S	36	.4	**	**	**	**	**	**	**	**	3	.3	36	5
	ST	45	1		55	1	**	**	**	**	**	**	**	**	17	2	83	11
PARKING STRIP	W	30	2	N	18	1	6	.3	6	.3	6	.3	7	.3	64	3	14	1
	E	16	1	S	12	1	**	**	**	**	6	.3	**	**	7	.3	7	.3
	ST	46	2		30	2	6	.3	6	.3	12	1	7	.3	71	4	21	1
PARKWAY	W	16	2	N	17	2	9	1	3	.4	15	2	**	**	31	4	6	1
	E	17	2	S	14	2	3	.4	**	**	6	1	**	**	25	3	39	5
	ST	33	4		31	4	12	1	3	.4	21	2	**	**	56	7	44	6
SIDEWALK PLOT	W	21	3	N	24	4	7	1	5	1	1	.1	8	1	36	3	4	.3
	E	21	3	S	17	3	2	.3	3	.4	1	.1	12	1	36	3	4	.3
	ST	42	7		41	7	9	1	8	1	1	.2	20	2	72	6	8	1
TREE LAWN	W	18	1	N	23	1	13	1	**	**	13	1	11	.3	22	1	**	**
	E	13	1	S	15	1	3	.1	**	**	3	.1	11	.3	44	1	11	.3
	ST	31	1		38	2	15	1	**	**	15	1	22	1	67	2	11	.3

ITEM (62) (CONTINUED) GRASS STRIP BETWEEN SIDEWALK AND STREET

ITEM (62)		TENNESSEE C	TENNESSEE D		GEORGIA C	GEORGIA D	ALABAMA C	ALABAMA D	MISSISSIPPI C	MISSISSIPPI D	FLORIDA C	FLORIDA D	LOUISIANA C	LOUISIANA D	ARKANSAS C	ARKANSAS D	OKLAHOMA C	OKLAHOMA D
BERM	W	100	1	N	100	1	100	2	**	**	100	2	**	**	100	1	**	**
					(NO RESPONSE)													
	ST		1			1		2		**		2		**		1		**
BOULEVARD	W	52	6	N	40	1	60	12	67	13	50	4	**	**	50	5	33	2
	E	48	6	S	60	2	40	8	33	7	50	4	100	31	50	5	67	3
	ST		12			3		20		20		9		31		10		5
BOULEVARD STRIP	W	53	10	N	88	9	100	6	60	10	67	4	100	19	58	9	50	5
	E	47	9	S	13	1	**	**	40	7	33	2	**	**	42	6	50	5
	ST		18			10		6		17		7		19		15		10
PARKING	W	40	1	N	33	1	**	**	**	**	**	**	**	**	83	6	57	28
	E	60	1	S	67	3	**	**	**	**	**	**	**	**	17	1	43	21
	ST		2			4		**		**		**		**		7		49
PARKING STRIP	W	65	7	N	60	6	100	6	100	10	50	7	100	6	90	11	67	3
	E	35	4	S	40	4	**	**	**	**	50	7	**	**	10	1	33	2
	ST		11			9		6		10		13		6		12		5
PARKWAY	W	47	9	N	56	13	71	20	100	13	71	37	**	**	55	14	13	3
	E	53	10	S	44	10	29	8	**	**	29	15	**	**	45	11	88	23
	ST		18			23		27		13		52		**		25		26
SIDEWALK PLOT	W	50	16	N	58	24	79	22	67	27	50	2	40	13	50	11	50	2
	E	50	16	S	42	17	21	6	33	13	50	2	60	19	50	11	50	2
	ST		31			41		27		40		4		31		22		3
TREE LAWN	W	58	3	N	60	6	83	10	**	**	83	11	50	6	33	2	**	**
	E	42	2	S	40	4	17	2	**	**	17	2	50	6	67	5	100	2
	ST		6			9		12		**		13		13		7		2

TOPOGRAPHY
A DITCH BY THE SIDE OF A GRADED ROAD

ITEM (63)
WORK SHEET (31)

		TENNESSEE A	TENNESSEE B		GEORGIA A	GEORGIA B	ALABAMA A	ALABAMA B	MISSISSIPPI A	MISSISSIPPI B	FLORIDA A	FLORIDA B	LOUISIANA A	LOUISIANA B	ARKANSAS A	ARKANSAS B	OKLAHOMA A	OKLAHOMA B
BAR DITCH	W	60	.3	N	**	**	**	**	**	**	20	.1	**	**	4	1	39	7
	E	**	**	S	20	.1	**	**	**	**	**	**	**	**	4	1	53	9
	ST	60	.3		20	.1	**	**	**	**	20	.1	**	**	8	1	92	16
BAR PIT	W	17	1	N	6	.2	6	.2	29	1	3	.1	19	2	16	2	13	1
	E	3	.1	S	17	1	3	.1	17	1	**	**	3	.3	42	5	6	1
	ST	20	1		23	1	9	.3	46	2	3	.1	23	3	58	6	19	2
BARROW DITCH	W	**	**	N	33	.1	**	**	33	.1	**	**	**	**	50	.3	**	**
	E	**	**	S	**	**	**	**	33	.1	**	**	**	**	**	**	50	.3
	ST	**	**		33	.1	**	**	67	.2	**	**	**	**	50	.3	50	.3
BARROW PIT	W	17	.1	N	17	.1	17	.1	17	.1	**	**	17	.3	33	1	**	**
	E	17	.1	S	17	.1	**	**	**	**	**	**	33	1	17	.3	**	**
	ST	33	.2		33	.2	17	.1	17	.1	**	**	50	1	50	1	**	**
BORROW DITCH	W	67	.2	N	**	**	**	**	**	**	33	.1	**	**	**	**	**	**
					(NO RESPONSE)													
	ST	67	.2		**	**	**	**	**	**	33	.1	**	**	**	**	**	**
BORROW PIT	W	14	.1	N	14	.1	14	.1	14	.1	**	**	20	.3	40	1	20	.3
	E	14	.1	S	14	.1	**	**	14	.1	**	**	**	**	20	.3	**	**
	ST	29	.2		29	.2	14	.1	29	.2	**	**	20	.3	60	1	20	.3
DITCH	W	20	12	N	14	9	7	4	3	2	8	5	6	3	36	17	9	4
	E	30	19	S	9	6	3	2	2	1	4	3	12	6	26	12	11	5
	ST	50	31		23	14	10	6	5	3	12	8	19	9	61	29	20	9
GRADER DITCH	W	16	1	N	21	1	5	.3	3	.2	11	1	5	.3	32	2	26	2
	E	20	1	S	16	1	**	**	**	**	7	.4	**	**	21	1	16	1
	ST	36	2		38	2	5	.3	3	.2	18	1	5	.3	53	4	42	3
GUTTER(B)	W	19	3	N	30	4	10	1	3	.4	3	.4	**	**	29	1	**	**
	E	16	2	S	12	2	3	.4	1	.2	3	.4	21	1	21	1	29	1
	ST	35	5		41	6	13	2	4	1	6	1	21	1	50	3	29	1

ITEM (63) (CONTINUED) A DITCH BY THE SIDE OF A GRADED ROAD

		TENNESSEE			GEORGIA		ALABAMA		MISSISSIPPI		FLORIDA		LOUISIANA		ARKANSAS		OKLAHOMA	
		C	D		C	D	C	D	C	D	C	D	C	D	C	D	C	D
BAR DITCH	W	100	1	N	**	**	**	**	**	**	100	1	**	**	50	2	42	21
	E	**	**	S	100	.4	**	**	**	**	**	**	**	**	50	2	58	29
	ST		1			.4		**		**		1		**		3		49
BAR PIT	W	86	2	N	25	1	67	2	63	17	100	1	86	15	28	4	67	4
	E	14	.2	S	75	3	33	1	38	10	**	**	14	3	72	10	33	2
	ST		2			3		4		27		1		18		14		7
BARROW DITCH	W	**	**	N	100	.4	**	**	50	2	**	**	**	**	100	1	**	**
	E	**	**	S	**	**	**	**	50	2	**	**	**	**	**	**	100	1
	ST		**			.4		**		3		**		**		1		1
BARROW PIT	W	50	.2	N	50	.4	100	1	100	2	**	**	33	3	67	2	**	**
	E	50	.2	S	50	.4	**	**	**	**	**	**	67	5	33	1	**	**
	ST		1			1		1		2		**		8		2		**
BURROW DITCH	W	100	1	N	**	**	**	**	**	**	100	1	**	**	**	**	**	**
					(NO RESPONSE)													
	ST		1			**		**		**		1		**		**		**
BORROW PIT	W	50	.2	N	50	.4	100	1	50	2	**	**	100	3	67	2	100	1
	E	50	.2	S	50	.4	**	**	50	2	**	**	**	**	33	1	**	**
	ST		1			1		1		3		**		3		2		1
DITCH	W	39	31	N	59	36	71	49	63	32	67	52	33	21	58	37	46	13
	E	61	47	S	41	24	29	20	37	19	33	26	67	41	42	26	54	15
	ST		78			60		69		51		77		62		63		29
GRADER DITCH	W	45	3	N	57	6	100	4	100	3	64	7	100	3	60	5	63	5
	E	55	3	S	43	4	**	**	**	**	36	4	**	**	40	3	38	3
	ST		6			10		4		3		11		3		8		9
GUTTER(B)	W	55	7	N	71	17	78	17	67	7	50	4	**	**	57	3	**	**
	E	45	5	S	29	7	22	5	33	3	50	4	100	8	43	2	100	4
	ST		12			24		21		10		8		8		6		4

ITEM (64)
WORK SHEET (32)

ACTIVITIES
HE THREW A _____ AT THE DOG

		TENNESSEE A	TENNESSEE B		GEORGIA A	GEORGIA B	ALABAMA A	ALABAMA B	MISSISSIPPI A	MISSISSIPPI B	FLORIDA A	FLORIDA B	LOUISIANA A	LOUISIANA B	ARKANSAS A	ARKANSAS B	OKLAHOMA A	OKLAHOMA B
DONNICK	W	**	**	N	**	**	**	**	**	**	**	**	**	**	100	.3	**	**
	E	100	.1	S	**	**	**	**	**	**	**	**	**	**	**	**	**	**
	ST	100	.1		**	**	**	**	**	**	**	**	**	**	100	.3	**	**
DORNICK	W	75	.3	N	25	.1	**	**	**	**	**	**	**	**	100	1	**	**
					(NO RESPONSE)													
	ST	75	.3		25	.1	**	**	**	**	**	**	**	**	100	1	**	**
ROCK	W	19	16	N	18	15	7	5	4	3	7	6	5	4	27	22	17	14
	E	26	21	S	11	9	2	2	2	2	4	3	7	6	24	20	19	16
	ST	46	37		28	23	9	7	6	5	11	9	13	10	51	42	36	30
STONE	W	19	2	N	18	1	6	1	5	.4	11	1	5	.3	48	4	**	**
	E	20	2	S	11	1	3	.2	3	.2	4	.3	**	**	33	3	14	1
	ST	39	3		29	2	9	1	8	1	15	1	5	.3	81	6	14	1

		TENNESSEE C	TENNESSEE D		GEORGIA C	GEORGIA D	ALABAMA C	ALABAMA D	MISSISSIPPI C	MISSISSIPPI D	FLORIDA C	FLORIDA D	LOUISIANA C	LOUISIANA D	ARKANSAS C	ARKANSAS D	OKLAHOMA C	OKLAHOMA D
DONNICK	W	**	**	N	**	**	**	**	**	**	**	**	**	**	100	1	**	**
	E	100	.2	S	**	**	**	**	**	**	**	**	**	**	**	**	**	**
	ST		.2			**		**		**		**		**		1		**
DORNICK	W	100	1	N	100	.4	**	**	**	**	**	**	**	**	100	1	**	**
					(NO RESPONSE)													
	ST		1			.4		**		**		**		**		1		**
ROCK	W	43	39	N	63	57	73	67	65	58	66	58	41	40	53	45	46	45
	E	58	52	S	37	34	27	24	35	31	34	30	59	57	47	40	54	52
	ST		91			90		91		89		88		97		85		96
STONE	W	48	4	N	61	6	71	6	67	7	75	9	100	3	59	7	**	**
	E	52	4	S	39	4	29	3	33	4	25	3	**	**	41	5	100	4
	ST		8			9		9		11		12		3		13		4

ANIMALS
A WORTHLESS DOG

ITEM (65)
WORK SHEET (33)

		TENNESSEE A	TENNESSEE B		GEORGIA A	GEORGIA B	ALABAMA A	ALABAMA B	MISSISSIPPI A	MISSISSIPPI B	FLORIDA A	FLORIDA B	LOUISIANA A	LOUISIANA B	ARKANSAS A	ARKANSAS B	OKLAHOMA A	OKLAHOMA B
COMMON DOG	W	15	1	N	16	1	8	1	3	.2	18	1	6	.3	38	2	6	.3
	E	20	1	S	15	1	3	.2	2	.1	**	**	19	1	25	1	6	.3
	ST	34	2		31	2	11	1	5	.3	18	1	25	1	63	4	13	1
CUR	W	27	9	N	17	6	6	2	3	1	6	2	2	1	28	9	15	5
	E	21	7	S	7	2	2	1	4	1	6	2	6	2	31	10	17	6
	ST	48	16		24	8	8	3	7	2	12	4	9	3	59	20	32	11
CUR DOG	W	26	3	N	18	2	4	1	7	1	9	1	16	2	41	5	13	1
	E	18	2	S	11	1	1	.1	2	.2	4	1	9	1	16	2	6	1
	ST	44	5		29	4	5	1	9	1	13	2	25	3	56	6	19	2
FICE	W	7	.2	N	19	1	19	1	**	**	7	.2	**	**	**	**	**	**
	E	11	.3	S	15	.4	11	.3	7	.2	4	.1	**	**	100	.3	**	**
	ST	19	1		33	1	30	1	7	.2	11	.3	**	**	100	.3	**	**
FISTE	W	20	1	N	12	1	6	.3	6	.3	2	.1	10	.3	40	1	20	1
	E	40	2	S	6	.3	**	**	2	.1	6	.3	**	**	20	1	10	.3
	ST	60	3		18	1	6	.3	8	.4	8	.4	10	.3	60	2	30	1
MONGREL	W	18	4	N	16	3	11	2	4	1	6	1	4	1	14	4	23	7
	E	25	5	S	8	2	4	1	3	1	5	1	10	3	18	5	31	9
	ST	43	8		24	5	15	3	7	1	11	2	13	4	33	10	54	16
NO-COUNT	W	10	2	N	24	4	4	1	1	.1	8	1	7	1	43	5	7	1
	E	33	5	S	15	2	2	.3	3	.4	1	.1	10	1	20	2	13	1
	ST	43	6		39	6	6	1	3	1	8	1	17	2	63	7	20	2
SCRUB	W	15	1	N	31	1	3	.1	8	.3	3	.1	33	1	33	1	**	**
	E	21	1	S	15	1	**	**	3	.1	3	.1	**	**	**	**	33	1
	ST	36	1		46	2	3	.1	10	.4	5	.2	33	1	33	1	33	1
HEINZ	W	22	.4	N	11	.2	6	.1	6	.1	6	.1	33	1	17	.3	17	.3
	E	33	1	S	6	.1	**	**	**	**	11	.2	17	.3	**	**	17	.3
	ST	56	1		17	.3	6	.1	6	.1	17	.3	50	1	17	.3	33	1
SOONER	W	23	1	N	8	1	8	1	3	.2	16	1	**	**	40	1	**	**
	E	11	1	S	23	1	3	.2	**	**	5	.3	**	**	20	.3	40	1
	ST	34	2		31	2	11	1	3	.2	21	1	**	**	60	1	40	1

(CONTINUED) A WORTHLESS DOG

ITEM (65)		TENNESSEE C	TENNESSEE D		GEORGIA C	GEORGIA D	ALABAMA C	ALABAMA D	MISSISSIPPI C	MISSISSIPPI D	FLORIDA C	FLORIDA D	LOUISIANA C	LOUISIANA D	ARKANSAS C	ARKANSAS D	OKLAHOMA C	OKLAHOMA D
COMMON DOG	W	43	2	N	53	3	71	5	67	3	100	9	25	2	60	4	50	1
	E	57	3	S	47	3	29	2	33	1	**	**	75	7	40	3	50	1
	ST		5			7		7		4		9		9		7		2
CUR	W	56	19	N	71	19	70	20	42	15	51	16	25	5	47	18	47	14
	E	44	15	S	29	8	30	8	58	21	49	15	75	14	53	20	53	16
	ST		35			27		28		35		32		19		38		30
CUR DOG	W	59	7	N	62	7	83	5	80	12	67	8	63	12	72	9	67	4
	E	41	5	S	38	4	17	1	20	3	33	4	38	7	28	3	33	2
	ST		11			12		6		15		12		19		13		6
FICE	W	40	.4	N	56	2	63	5	**	**	67	2	**	**	**	**	**	**
	E	60	1	S	44	1	38	3	100	3	33	1	**	**	100	1	**	**
	ST		1			3		8		3		2		**		1		**
FISTE	W	33	2	N	67	2	100	3	75	4	25	1	100	2	67	3	67	2
	E	67	4	S	33	1	**	**	25	1	75	2	**	**	33	1	33	1
	ST		7			3		3		6		3		2		4		3
MONGREL	W	41	8	N	67	11	71	21	62	12	57	10	27	7	44	8	42	19
	E	59	11	S	33	5	29	8	38	7	43	7	73	19	56	10	58	26
	ST		18			16		29		19		17		26		19		45
NO-COUNT	W	24	3	N	61	12	67	6	20	1	92	9	40	5	68	9	33	2
	E	76	10	S	39	8	33	3	80	6	8	1	60	7	32	4	67	4
	ST		14			19		9		7		10		12		13		6
SCRUB	W	43	1	N	67	4	100	1	75	4	50	1	100	7	100	2	**	**
	E	57	2	S	33	2	**	**	25	1	50	1	**	**	**	**	100	3
	ST		3			6		1		6		2		7		2		3
HEINZ	W	40	1	N	67	1	100	1	100	1	33	1	67	5	100	1	50	1
	E	60	1	S	33	.3	**	**	**	**	67	2	33	2	**	**	50	1
	ST		2			1		1		1		2		7		1		2
SOONER	W	67	3	N	26	2	71	5	100	3	77	8	**	**	67	1	**	**
	E	33	2	S	74	5	29	2	**	**	23	2	**	**	33	1	100	2
	ST		5			7		7		3		11		**		2		2

ITEM (66)
WORK SHEET (36)

ANIMALS
NAME FOR SOUND MADE BY CALF BEING WEANED

		TENNESSEE			GEORGIA		ALABAMA		MISSISSIPPI		FLORIDA		LOUISIANA		ARKANSAS		OKLAHOMA	
		A	B		A	B	A	B	A	B	A	B	A	B	A	B	A	B
BAWL(A)	W	25	11	N	12	6	7	3	4	2	4	2	5	3	32	20	19	12
	E	40	18	S	3	2	1	1	1	.4	2	1	2	1	21	13	21	13
	ST	65	29		16	7	8	4	5	2	6	3	6	4	54	33	40	25
BELLER(A)	W	22	2	N	24	2	4	.3	1	.1	6	.4	6	.3	31	2	25	1
	E	24	2	S	12	1	1	.1	**	**	4	.3	6	.3	13	1	19	1
	ST	46	3		36	2	6	.4	1	.1	10	1	13	1	44	3	44	3
BELLOW(A)	W	16	1	N	14	1	8	1	1	.1	15	1	**	**	18	1	**	**
	E	18	1	S	21	2	4	.3	3	.2	1	.1	18	1	45	[illegible]	10	1
	ST	34	3		35	3	11	1	4	.3	16	1	18	1	64	3	18	1
BLARE	W	**	**	N	75	.3	25	.1	**	**	**	**	**	**	**	**	**	**
					(NO RESPONSE)													
	ST	**	**		75	.3	25	.1	**	**	**	**	**	**	**	**	**	**
BLART	W	**	**	N	**	**	**	**	**	**	100	.1	**	**	100	.3	**	**
					(NO RESPONSE)													
	ST	**	**		**	**	**	**	**	**	100	.1	**	**	100	.3	**	**
BLAT	W	26	1	N	32	1	11	.2	5	.1	5	.1	**	**	33	.3	**	**
	E	**	**	S	11	.2	**	**	5	.1	5	.1	**	**	67	1	**	**
	ST	26	1		42	1	11	.2	11	.2	11	.2	**	**	100	1	**	**
BLATE	W	8	1	N	26	4	7	1	4	1	13	2	36	2	14	1	**	**
	E	3	.4	S	26	4	4	1	5	1	4	1	7	.3	43	2	**	**
	ST	10	2		52	9	11	2	9	2	18	3	43	2	57	3	**	**
BLEAT	W	11	1	N	34	4	3	.4	5	1	10	1	20	1	25	2	5	.3
	F	3	.4	S	21	2	3	.3	4	1	5	1	25	2	20	1	5	.3
	ST	15	2		55	7	6	1	10	1	15	2	45	3	45	3	10	1

ITEM (66)

(CONTINUED) NAME FOR SOUND MADE BY CALF BEING WEANED

		TENNESSEE C	TENNESSEE D		GEORGIA C	GEORGIA D	ALABAMA C	ALABAMA D	MISSISSIPPI C	MISSISSIPPI D	FLORIDA C	FLORIDA D	LOUISIANA C	LOUISIANA D	ARKANSAS C	ARKANSAS D	OKLAHOMA C	OKLAHOMA D
BAWL(A)	W	38	29	N	78	19	86	42	82	33	67	19	73	27	60	44	47	41
	E	62	46	S	22	5	14	6	18	7	33	9	27	10	40	29	53	46
	ST		75			25		48		41		28		37		72		86
BELLER(A)	W	48	4	N	67	6	75	4	100	2	57	4	50	3	71	4	57	5
	E	52	4	S	33	3	25	1	**	**	43	3	50	3	29	2	43	4
	ST		8			9		5		2		7		7		6		9
BELLOW(A)	W	48	3	N	39	4	67	8	33	2	92	13	**	**	29	2	**	**
	E	52	4	S	61	6	33	4	67	4	8	1	100	7	71	4	100	3
	ST		7			10		12		6		14		7		6		3
BLARE	W	**	**	N	100	1	100	1	**	**	**	**	**	**	**	**	**	**
					(NO RESPONSE)													
	ST		**			1		1		**		**		**		**		**
BLART	W	**	**	N	**	**	**	**	**	**	100	1	**	**	100	1	**	**
					(NO RESPONSE)													
	ST		**			**		**		**		1		**		1		**
BLAT	W	100	1	N	75	2	100	3	50	2	50	1	**	**	33	1	**	**
	E	**	**	S	25	1	**	**	50	2	50	1	**	**	67	2	**	**
	ST		1			3		3		4		2		**		2		**
BLATE	W	75	3	N	49	15	65	14	47	13	75	22	83	17	25	2	**	**
	E	25	1	S	51	15	35	8	53	15	25	7	17	3	75	5	**	**
	ST		4			30		22		28		29		20		6		**
BLEAT	W	76	3	N	62	14	57	5	55	11	65	12	44	13	56	4	50	1
	E	24	1	S	38	9	43	4	45	9	35	6	56	17	44	3	50	1
	ST		4			23		9		20		18		30		7		3

ANIMALS
NAME FOR LOUD SOUND MADE BY A COW WHEN CALF IS TAKEN AWAY

ITEM (67)
WORK SHEET (36)

		TENNESSEE			GEORGIA		ALABAMA		MISSISSIPPI		FLORIDA		LOUISIANA		ARKANSAS		OKLAHOMA	
		A	B		A	B	A	B	A	B	A	B	A	B	A	B	A	B
BAWL(B)	W	25	9	N	13	4	9	3	4	1	1	.2	4	2	36	17	16	8
	E	41	15	S	3	1	.2	.1	2	1	3	1	1	.3	24	12	20	9
	ST	66	23		16	5	9	3	5	2	4	1	5	2	60	29	36	17
BELLER(B)	W	26	3	N	17	2	7	1	7	1	7	1	7	1	30	3	19	2
	E	21	2	S	7	1	5	1	1	.1	2	.2	11	1	11	1	22	2
	ST	47	5		24	2	12	1	8	1	9	1	19	2	41	4	41	4
BELLOW(B)	W	25	4	N	23	3	8	1	6	1	6	1	7	1	26	3	11	1
	E	15	2	S	11	2	2	.3	4	1	1	.1	11	1	37	4	7	1
	ST	40	6		34	5	11	2	9	1	6	1	19	2	63	6	19	2
CRY	W	14	.1	N	14	.1	**	**	14	.1	**	**	**	**	33	.3	33	.3
	E	43	.3	S	14	.1	**	**	**	**	**	**	**	**	33	.3	**	**
	ST	57	.4		29	.2	**	**	14	.1	**	**	**	**	67	1	33	.3
LOW(A)	W	8	2	N	25	5	4	1	2	1	15	3	23	2	23	2	5	.3
	E	2	1	S	29	6	3	1	3	1	7	1	9	1	27	2	14	1
	ST	10	2		54	11	8	2	6	1	22	5	32	3	50	4	18	1
LOO(A)	W	6	.2	N	33	1	3	.1	3	.1	12	.4	67	1	**	**	**	**
	E	**	**	S	30	1	3	.1	6	.2	3	.1	33	.3	**	**	**	**
	ST	6	.2		64	2	6	.2	9	.3	15	1	100	1	**	**	**	**
MEW(A)	W	25	.1	N	**	**	**	**	**	**	**	**	**	**	33	.3	**	**
	E	25	.1	S	50	.2	**	**	**	**	**	**	33	.3	33	.3	**	**
	ST	50	.2		50	.2	**	**	**	**	**	**	33	.3	67	1	**	**
MOO(A)	W	21	2	N	18	2	4	1	2	.2	12	1	8	1	16	2	16	2
	E	27	3	S	8	1	2	.2	2	.2	4	1	19	3	16	2	24	3
	ST	48	6		26	3	6	1	3	.4	17	2	27	4	32	4	41	5

ITEM (67)

(CONTINUED) NAME FOR LOUD SOUND MADE BY A COW WHEN CALF IS TAKEN AWAY

		TENNESSEE C	TENNESSEE D		GEORGIA C	GEORGIA D	ALABAMA C	ALABAMA D	MISSISSIPPI C	MISSISSIPPI D	FLORIDA C	FLORIDA D	LOUISIANA C	LOUISIANA D	ARKANSAS C	ARKANSAS D	OKLAHOMA C	OKLAHOMA D
BAWL(B)	W	38	21	N	81	15	97	35	67	20	15	2	83	14	59	35	45	25
	E	62	34	S	19	3	3	1	33	10	85	11	17	3	41	24	55	31
	ST		55			18		37		31		13		16		59		57
BELLER(B)	W	55	6	N	71	6	58	9	88	12	78	7	40	5	73	6	45	6
	E	45	5	S	29	2	42	6	13	2	22	2	60	8	27	2	55	7
	ST		11			8		15		14		9		14		8		13
BELLOW(B)	W	63	9	N	69	11	80	15	62	14	89	8	40	5	41	5	60	4
	E	37	5	S	31	5	20	4	38	8	11	1	60	8	59	7	40	2
	ST		14			17		18		22		9		14		13		6
CRY	W	25	.2	N	50	.3	**	**	100	2	**	**	**	**	50	1	100	1
	E	75	1	S	50	.3	**	**	**	**	**	**	**	**	50	1	**	**
	ST		1			1		**		2		**		**		1		1
LOW(A)	W	76	4	N	46	18	56	11	42	8	68	30	71	14	45	4	25	1
	E	24	1	S	54	20	44	9	58	12	32	14	29	5	55	4	75	4
	ST		5			38		20		20		44		19		8		5
LOO(A)	W	100	.4	N	52	4	50	1	33	2	80	4	67	5	**	**	**	**
	E	**	**	S	48	3	50	1	67	3	20	1	33	3	**	**	**	**
	ST		.4			7		2		5		5		8		**		**
MEW(A)	W	50	.2	N	**	**	**	**	**	**	**	**	**	**	50	1	**	**
	E	50	.2	S	100	1	**	**	**	**	**	**	100	3	50	1	**	**
	ST		.4			1		**		**		**		3		1		**
MOO(A)	W	44	6	N	70	7	71	6	50	3	74	14	30	8	50	4	40	7
	E	56	7	S	30	3	29	2	50	3	26	5	70	19	50	4	60	11
	ST		13			10		9		7		19		27		9		18

ITEM (67)
WORK SHEET (36)

ANIMALS
NAME FOR GENTLE SOUND MADE BY A COW AT FEEDING TIME

		TENNESSEE			GEORGIA		ALABAMA		MISSISSIPPI		FLORIDA		LOUISIANA		ARKANSAS		OKLAHOMA	
		A	B		A	B	A	B	A	B	A	B	A	B	A	B	A	B
BAWL(C)	W	20	1	N	15	1	11	1	4	.2	2	.1	5	.3	37	3	26	2
	E	44	2	S	2	.1	**	**	2	.1	2	.1	**	**	11	1	21	1
	ST	64	4		16	1	11	1	5	.3	4	.2	5	.3	47	3	47	3
BELLER(C)	W	11	.2	N	37	1	**	**	5	.1	16	.3	**	**	67	1	**	**
	E	16	.3	S	**	**	11	.2	5	.1	**	**	**	**	**	**	33	.3
	ST	26	1		37	1	11	.2	11	.2	16	.3	**	**	67	1	33	.3
BELLOW(C)	W	13	.4	N	23	1	**	**	10	.3	3	.1	**	**	100	1	**	**
	E	20	1	S	17	1	3	.1	3	.1	7	.2	**	**	**	**	**	**
	ST	33	1		40	1	3	.1	13	.4	10	.3	**	**	100	1	**	**
LOO(B)	W	14	1	N	27	1	8	.3	11	.4	16	1	63	2	25	1	**	**
	E	11	.4	S	5	.2	3	.1	3	.1	3	.1	13	.3	**	**	**	**
	ST	24	1		32	1	11	.4	14	1	19	1	75	2	25	1	**	**
LOW(B)	W	18	3	N	18	3	8	2	3	1	11	2	7	1	16	3	22	4
	E	13	2	S	15	3	3	1	4	1	6	1	11	2	29	6	15	3
	ST	31	6		34	6	11	2	7	1	17	3	18	4	45	9	36	7
HUM	W	13	.3	N	17	.4	4	.1	**	**	17	.4	**	**	50	.3	**	**
	E	8	.2	S	21	1	4	.1	**	**	17	.4	50	.3	**	**	**	**
	ST	21	1		38	1	8	.2	**	**	33	1	50	.3	50	.3	**	**
MEW(B)	W	8	.2	N	31	1	**	**	**	**	4	.1	33	.3	33	.3	**	**
	E	23	1	S	19	1	8	.2	**	**	8	.2	**	**	**	**	33	.3
	ST	31	1		50	1	8	.2	**	**	12	.3	33	.3	33	.3	33	.3
MOO(B)	W	19	9	N	17	8	7	3	5	2	7	3	5	3	34	17	15	8
	E	27	13	S	12	6	2	1	2	1	2	1	6	3	21	11	19	10
	ST	46	22		30	14	9	4	6	3	9	4	11	5	55	28	34	17

ITEM (67)

(CONTINUED) NAME FOR GENTLE SOUND MADE BY A COW AT FEEDING TIME

ITEM		TENNESSEE C	TENNESSEE D		GEORGIA C	GEORGIA D	ALABAMA C	ALABAMA D	MISSISSIPPI C	MISSISSIPPI D	FLORIDA C	FLORIDA D	LOUISIANA C	LOUISIANA D	ARKANSAS C	ARKANSAS D	OKLAHOMA C	OKLAHOMA D
BAWL(C)	W	31	3	N	89	3	100	8	67	4	50	1	100	3	78	6	56	6
	E	69	7	S	11	.3	**	**	33	2	50	1	**	**	22	2	44	5
	ST		10			3		8		5		2		3		8		11
BELLER(C)	W	40	1	N	100	3	**	**	50	2	100	3	**	**	100	2	**	**
	E	60	1	S	**	**	100	3	50	2	**	**	**	**	**	**	100	1
	ST		1			3		3		4		3		**		2		1
BELLOW(C)	W	40	1	N	58	3	**	**	75	5	33	1	**	**	100	2	**	**
	E	60	2	S	42	2	100	1	25	2	67	2	**	**	**	**	**	**
	ST		3			5		1		7		3		**		2		**
LOO(B)	W	56	1	N	83	4	75	4	80	7	86	6	83	15	100	2	**	**
	E	44	1	S	17	1	25	1	20	2	14	1	17	3	**	**	**	**
	ST		3			5		5		9		7		18		2		**
LOW(B)	W	57	9	N	54	13	75	19	46	11	65	20	40	12	36	8	60	15
	E	43	7	S	46	11	25	6	54	13	35	11	60	18	64	13	40	10
	ST		16			23		26		23		31		29		21		25
HUM	W	60	1	N	44	2	50	1	**	**	50	4	**	**	100	1	**	**
	E	40	1	S	56	2	50	1	**	**	50	4	100	3	**	**	**	**
	ST		1			3		3		**		8		3		1		**
MEW(B)	W	25	1	N	62	3	**	**	**	**	33	1	100	3	100	1	**	**
	E	75	2	S	38	2	100	3	**	**	67	2	**	**	**	**	100	1
	ST		2			5		3		**		3		3		1		1
MOO(B)	W	42	26	N	58	31	78	41	72	38	79	33	47	21	61	39	44	27
	E	58	36	S	42	22	22	12	28	14	21	9	53	24	39	25	56	34
	ST		63			53		53		52		42		44		65		61

ANIMALS
NAME FOR GENTLE SOUND MADE BY HORSES AT FEEDING TIME

ITEM (68)
WORK SHEET (36)

		TENNESSEE			GEORGIA		ALABAMA		MISSISSIPPI		FLORIDA		LOUISIANA		ARKANSAS		OKLAHOMA	
		A	B		A	B	A	B	A	B	A	B	A	B	A	B	A	B
LAUGH	W	25	.1	N	**	**	**	**	**	**	50	.2	**	**	**	**	**	**
	E	25	.1	S	**	**	**	**	**	**	**	**	**	**	**	**	**	**
	ST	50	.2		**	**	**	**	**	**	50	.2	**	**	**	**	**	**
NEIGH	W	25	5	N	20	4	8	2	5	1	6	1	9	1	21	3	9	1
	E	18	4	S	12	3	1	.3	1	.2	3	1	14	2	26	4	21	3
	ST	43	9		32	7	10	2	6	1	10	2	23	4	47	7	30	5
NICKER	W	24	8	N	23	8	7	3	3	1	1	1	6	3	43	19	13	6
	E	34	12	S	3	1	1	.3	1	1	3	1	2	1	23	10	14	6
	ST	58	20		26	9	8	3	4	2	4	1	7	3	66	30	27	12
WHICKER	W	3	.3	N	16	2	4	.4	**	**	22	2	33	1	**	**	50	1
	E	3	.3	S	41	4	3	.3	3	.3	4	.4	**	**	**	**	17	.3
	ST	6	1		57	5	8	1	3	.3	26	2	33	1	**	**	67	1
WHINKER	W	4	.1	N	12	.3	4	.1	**	**	20	1	**	**	**	**	**	**
	E	4	.1	S	40	1	12	.3	**	**	4	.1	**	**	**	**	**	**
	ST	8	.2		52	1	16	.4	**	**	24	1	**	**	**	**	**	**
WHINNY	W	19	5	N	14	3	5	1	7	2	9	2	9	3	14	4	22	6
	E	26	6	S	11	3	2	.4	3	1	4	1	9	3	18	5	27	8
	ST	45	11		25	6	7	2	11	3	13	3	18	5	32	9	49	14
WHINNER	W	20	.1	N	**	**	**	**	**	**	20	.1	**	**	**	**	**	**
	E	20	.1	S	20	.1	**	**	**	**	20	.1	**	**	100	.3	**	**
	ST	40	.2		20	.1	**	**	**	**	40	.2	**	**	100	.3	**	**

ITEM (68) (CONTINUED) NAME FOR GENTLE SOUND MADE BY HORSES AT FEEDING TIME

		TENNESSEE C	TENNESSEE D		GEORGIA C	GEORGIA D	ALABAMA C	ALABAMA D	MISSISSIPPI C	MISSISSIPPI D	FLORIDA C	FLORIDA D	LOUISIANA C	LOUISIANA D	ARKANSAS C	ARKANSAS D	OKLAHOMA C	OKLAHOMA D
LAUGH	W	50	.2	N	**	**	**	**	**	**	100	2	**	**	**	**	**	**
	E	50	.2	S	**	**	**	**	**	**	**	**	**	**	**	**	**	**
	ST		1			**		**		**		2		**		**		**
NEIGH	W	59	13	N	62	14	85	23	83	18	65	13	40	11	45	7	31	5
	E	41	9	S	38	9	15	4	17	4	35	7	60	17	55	9	69	10
	ST		22			23		27		22		21		29		16		15
NICKER	W	41	20	N	88	28	89	33	67	18	36	5	78	20	65	41	48	18
	E	59	29	S	13	4	11	4	33	9	64	9	22	6	35	23	52	19
	ST		49			32		37		27		14		26		64		38
WHICKER	W	50	1	N	28	5	57	5	**	**	83	21	100	6	**	**	75	3
	E	50	1	S	72	14	43	4	100	5	17	4	**	**	**	**	25	1
	ST		2			19		9		5		25		6		**		5
WHINKER	W	50	.2	N	23	1	25	1	**	**	83	5	**	**	**	**	**	**
	E	50	.2	S	77	4	75	4	**	**	17	1	**	**	**	**	**	**
	ST		1			5		5		**		6		**		**		**
WHINNY	W	43	11	N	56	12	75	16	68	31	69	21	50	20	44	9	45	19
	E	57	15	S	44	9	25	5	32	15	31	9	50	20	56	11	55	24
	ST		26			21		21		45		30		40		20		43
WHINNER	W	50	.2	N	**	**	**	**	**	**	50	1	**	**	**	**	**	**
	E	50	.2	S	100	.3	**	**	**	**	50	1	**	**	100	1	**	**
	ST		1			.3		**		**		2		**		1		**

FOOD
A BONE FROM CHICKEN BREAST

ITEM (69)
WORK SHEET (37)

		TENNESSEE			GEORGIA		ALABAMA		MISSISSIPPI		FLORIDA		LOUISIANA		ARKANSAS		OKLAHOMA	
		A	B		A	B	A	B	A	B	A	B	A	B	A	B	A	B
BREAKBONE	W	30	1	N	5	.1	**	**	5	.1	10	.2	33	.3	**	**	33	.3
	E	40	1	S	10	.2	**	**	**	**	**	**	**	**	**	**	33	.3
	ST	70	1		15	.3	**	**	5	.1	10	.2	33	.3	**	**	67	1
LUCKY BONE	W	75	.3	N	**	**	**	**	**	**	**	**	**	**	**	**	**	**
	E	**	**	S	25	.1	**	**	**	**	**	**	**	**	50	.3	50	.3
	ST	75	.3		25	.1	**	**	**	**	**	**	**	**	50	.3	50	.3
PULL BONE	W	18	1	N	18	1	4	.1	**	**	11	.3	**	**	50	.3	**	**
	E	18	1	S	18	1	**	**	7	.2	7	.2	**	**	50	.3	**	**
	ST	36	1		36	1	4	.1	7	.2	18	1	**	**	100	1	**	**
PULLY BONE	W	19	13	N	19	14	0	3	4	3	6	5	8	5	28	19	14	9
	E	27	19	S	12	9	2	2	2	1	2	2	3	2	28	19	20	13
	ST	46	33		31	22	9	6	6	4	9	6	10	7	56	38	34	22
PULLING BONE	W	14	.2	N	14	.2	7	.1	**	**	7	.1	**	**	25	.3	**	**
	E	43	1	S	14	.2	**	**	**	**	**	**	**	**	25	.3	50	1
	ST	57	1		29	.4	7	.1	**	**	7	.1	**	**	50	1	50	1
WISHBONE	W	22	7	N	16	5	7	2	3	1	9	3	7	3	22	9	19	8
	E	20	7	S	9	3	3	1	3	1	7	2	14	5	20	8	19	8
	ST	42	14		25	8	11	4	6	2	16	5	21	8	41	17	38	15

		TENNESSEE			GEORGIA		ALABAMA		MISSISSIPPI		FLORIDA		LOUISIANA		ARKANSAS		OKLAHOMA	
		C	D		C	D	C	D	C	D	C	D	C	D	C	D	C	D
BREAKBONE	W	43	1	N	33	.3	**	**	100	2	100	2	100	2	**	**	50	1
	E	57	2	S	67	1	**	**	**	**	**	**	**	**	**	**	50	1
	ST		3			1		**		2		2		2		**		2
LUCKY BONE	W	100	1	N	**	**	**	**	**	**	**	**	**	**	**	**	**	**
	E	**	**	S	100	.3	**	**	**	**	**	**	**	**	100	1	100	1
	ST		1			.3		**		**		**		**		1		1
PULL BONE	W	50	1	N	50	2	100	1	**	**	60	3	**	**	50	1	**	**
	E	50	1	S	50	2	**	**	100	3	40	2	**	**	50	1	**	**
	ST		2			3		1		3		4		**		1		**
PULLY BONE	W	41	27	N	61	42	75	46	71	48	75	38	74	33	50	34	40	23
	E	59	39	S	39	27	25	16	29	19	25	13	26	12	50	34	60	34
	ST		65			69		62		67		50		44		67		57
PULLING BONE	W	25	.4	N	50	1	100	1	**	**	100	1	**	**	50	1	**	**
	E	75	1	S	50	1	**	**	**	**	**	**	**	**	50	1	100	2
	ST		2			1		1		**		1		**		1		2
WISHBONE	W	52	14	N	65	16	68	24	50	14	57	24	35	19	52	15	50	19
	E	48	13	S	35	9	32	12	50	14	43	18	65	35	48	14	50	19
	ST		27			25		36		29		43		53		30		39

TIME
TIME WHEN FARM ANIMALS ARE ATTENDED TO

ITEM (70)
WORK SHEET (37)

		TENNESSEE A	TENNESSEE B		GEORGIA A	GEORGIA B	ALABAMA A	ALABAMA B	MISSISSIPPI A	MISSISSIPPI B	FLORIDA A	FLORIDA B	LOUISIANA A	LOUISIANA B	ARKANSAS A	ARKANSAS B	OKLAHOMA A	OKLAHOMA B
CHORE TIME	W	28	1	N	17	1	9	.4	4	.2	11	1	1	.3	23	6	39	10
	E	21	1	S	4	.2	2	.1	2	.1	2	.1	3	1	13	3	20	5
	ST	49	2		21	1	11	1	6	.3	13	1	4	1	36	9	59	15
FEEDING TIME	W	19	10	N	19	10	8	4	5	2	6	3	11	5	26	12	7	3
	E	27	14	S	10	5	3	1	1	1	3	1	8	4	29	13	20	9
	ST	46	24		29	15	10	5	6	3	8	4	19	9	55	25	27	12
FEED TIME	W	15	2	N	23	3	4	.4	1	.1	10	1	**	**	56	3	19	1
	E	19	2	S	17	2	**	**	5	1	7	1	**	**	6	.3	19	1
	ST	33	4		40	4	4	.4	6	1	18	2	**	**	63	4	38	2
TIME TO FEED	W	18	4	N	18	4	5	1	3	1	8	2	4	1	41	7	8	1
	E	27	6	S	14	3	2	1	2	.4	3	1	6	1	24	4	16	3
	ST	45	11		32	8	7	2	5	1	11	2	10	2	65	12	24	4

		TENNESSEE C	TENNESSEE D		GEORGIA C	GEORGIA D	ALABAMA C	ALABAMA D	MISSISSIPPI C	MISSISSIPPI D	FLORIDA C	FLORIDA D	LOUISIANA C	LOUISIANA D	ARKANSAS C	ARKANSAS D	OKLAHOMA C	OKLAHOMA D
CHORE TIME	W	57	3	N	80	3	80	5	67	4	83	5	33	3	64	12	66	29
	E	43	3	S	20	1	20	1	33	2	17	1	67	6	36	7	34	15
	ST		6			4		6		6		7		9		18		44
FEEDING TIME	W	42	25	N	64	35	74	50	77	47	69	32	58	44	47	24	26	10
	E	58	35	S	36	19	26	18	23	14	31	14	42	31	53	27	74	27
	ST		59			54		68		61		46		75		51		37
FEED TIME	W	44	4	N	58	9	100	5	17	2	58	12	**	**	90	7	50	3
	E	56	5	S	42	7	**	**	83	10	42	9	**	**	10	1	50	3
	ST		9			16		5		12		21		**		7		6
TIME TO FEED	W	40	10	N	56	15	69	14	64	14	75	20	40	6	63	15	33	4
	E	60	15	S	44	12	31	6	36	8	25	7	60	9	38	9	67	9
	ST		26			27		21		22		26		16		23		13

ANIMALS
A CALL TO COWS TO GET THEM IN FROM PASTURE

ITEM (71)
WORK SHEET (37)

		TENNESSEE A	TENNESSEE B		GEORGIA A	GEORGIA B	ALABAMA A	ALABAMA B	MISSISSIPPI A	MISSISSIPPI B	FLORIDA A	FLORIDA B	LOUISIANA A	LOUISIANA B	ARKANSAS A	ARKANSAS B	OKLAHOMA A	OKLAHOMA B
BOSS(IE)(A)	W	40	.2	N	20	.1	**	**	**	**	**	**	**	**	**	**	**	**
	E	40	.2	S	**	**	**	**	**	**	**	**	**	**	**	**	100	1
	ST	80	.4		20	.1	**	**	**	**	**	**	**	**	**	**	100	1
CO-BOSS(IE)	W	4	.2	N	6	.3	2	.1	2	.1	34	2	**	**	40	1	20	.3
	E	2	.1	S	19	1	8	.4	**	**	25	1	**	**	40	1	**	**
	ST	6	.3		25	1	9	1	2	.1	58	3	**	**	80	1	20	.3
COME BOSS(IE)	W	15	.2	N	8	.1	8	.1	15	.2	23	.3	13	.3	13	.3	50	1
	E	8	.1	S	8	.1	8	.1	8	.1	**	**	**	**	**	**	25	1
	ST	23	.3		15	.2	15	.2	23	.3	23	.3	13	.3	13	.3	75	2
CO-EE	W	2	.1	N	33	2	3	.2	2	.1	9	1	29	1	**	**	**	**
	E	**	**	S	47	3	3	.2	**	**	2	.1	29	1	14	.3	29	1
	ST	2	.1		79	5	7	.4	2	.1	10	1	57	1	14	.3	29	1
CO-WENCH	W	2	1	N	6	.3	**	**	**	**	40	2	**	**	**	**	**	**
	E	**	**	S	45	2	**	**	2	.1	4	.2	**	**	**	**	100	.3
	ST	2	.1		51	2	**	**	2	.1	45	2	**	**	**	**	100	.3
HERE BOSS(IE)	W	33	1	N	13	.2	13	.2	27	.4	7	.1	14	1	14	1	29	1
	E	**	**	S	**	**	7	.1	**	**	**	**	7	.3	14	1	21	1
	ST	33	1		13	.2	20	.3	27	.4	7	.1	21	1	29	1	50	3
SOO(A)	W	29	1	N	15	1	9	.3	12	.4	**	**	14	1	24	2	10	1
	E	26	1	S	**	**	6	.2	3	.1	**	**	5	.3	24	2	24	2
	ST	56	2		15	1	15	1	15	1	**	**	19	1	48	4	33	3
SOOK(IE)	W	25	3	N	14	1	6	1	5	1	2	.2	6	1	39	4	13	1
	E	37	4	S	7	1	2	.2	**	**	2	.2	3	.3	10	1	29	3
	ST	63	7		21	2	8	1	5	1	4	.4	10	1	48	5	42	5
SOOK BOSS(IE)	W	16	1	N	16	1	8	.3	5	.2	**	**	**	**	31	3	35	3
	E	49	2	S	3	.1	**	**	**	**	3	.1	4	.3	15	1	15	1
	ST	65	2		19	1	8	.3	5	.2	3	.1	4	.3	46	4	50	5
SOOK COW	W	26	10	N	19	8	9	4	4	2	2	1	10	4	33	15	13	6
	E	32	13	S	3	1	1	.4	3	1	**	**	5	2	25	11	15	7
	ST	58	23		23	9	10	4	8	3	2	1	14	6	58	26	28	13

(CONTINUED) A CALL TO COWS TO GET THEM IN FROM PASTURE

ITEM (71)		TENNESSEE C	TENNESSEE D		GEORGIA C	GEORGIA D	ALABAMA C	ALABAMA D	MISSISSIPPI C	MISSISSIPPI D	FLORIDA C	FLORIDA D	LOUISIANA C	LOUISIANA D	ARKANSAS C	ARKANSAS D	OKLAHOMA C	OKLAHOMA D
BOSS(IE)(A)	W	50	1	N	100	.4	**	**	**	**	**	**	**	**	**	**	**	**
	E	50	1	S	**	**	**	**	**	**	**	**	**	**	**	**	100	2
	ST		1			.4		**		**		**		**		**		2
CO-BOSS(IE)	W	67	1	N	23	1	20	1	100	2	58	25	**	**	50	2	100	1
	E	33	.2	S	77	5	80	6	**	**	42	18	**	**	50	2	**	**
	ST		1			6		7		2		42		**		3		1
COME BOSS(IE)	W	67	1	N	50	.4	50	1	67	4	100	4	100	3	100	1	67	5
	E	33	.2	S	50	.4	50	1	33	2	**	**	**	**	**	**	33	2
	ST		1			1		3		6		4		3		1		7
CO-EE	W	100	.2	N	41	9	50	3	100	2	83	7	50	6	**	**	**	**
	E	**	**	S	59	13	50	3	**	**	17	1	50	6	100	1	100	2
	ST		.2			22		6		2		8		12		1		2
CO-WENCH	W	100	.2	N	13	1	**	**	**	**	90	26	**	**	**	**	**	**
	E	**	**	S	88	10	**	**	100	2	10	3	**	**	**	**	100	1
	ST		.2			12		**		2		29		**		**		1
HERE BOSS(IE)	W	100	1	N	100	1	67	3	100	8	100	1	67	6	50	2	57	5
	E	**	**	S	**	**	33	1	**	**	**	**	33	3	50	2	43	3
	ST		1			1		4		8		1		9		3		8
SOO(A)	W	53	3	N	100	2	60	4	80	8	**	**	75	9	50	4	29	2
	E	47	3	S	**	**	40	3	20	2	**	**	25	3	50	4	71	6
	ST		5			2		7		10		**		12		8		8
SOOK(IE)	W	41	7	N	67	7	75	9	100	10	50	3	67	6	80	10	31	5
	E	59	11	S	33	3	25	3	**	**	50	3	33	3	20	3	69	10
	ST		18			10		12		10		5		9		13		15
SOOK BOSS(IE)	W	25	2	N	86	3	100	4	100	4	**	**	**	**	67	7	69	10
	E	75	5	S	14	.4	**	**	**	**	100	1	100	3	33	3	31	5
	ST		7			3		4		4		1		3		10		15
SOOK COW	W	45	29	N	86	36	90	51	57	33	100	8	67	35	58	35	46	18
	E	55	36	S	14	6	10	6	43	25	**	**	33	18	42	26	54	22
	ST		64			42		57		58		8		53		61		40

ANIMALS
A CALL TO COWS TO MAKE THEM STAND STILL AT MILKING TIME

ITEM (72)
WORK SHEET (37)

		TENNESSEE			GEORGIA		ALABAMA		MISSISSIPPI		FLORIDA		LOUISIANA		ARKANSAS		OKLAHOMA	
		A	B		A	B	A	B	A	B	A	B	A	B	A	B	A	B
HERE	W	24	.4	N	6	.1	18	.3	**	**	6	.1	**	**	25	.3	**	**
	E	35	1	S	6	.1	6	.1	**	**	**	**	**	**	25	.3	50	1
	ST	59	1		12	.2	24	.4	**	**	6	.1	**	**	50	1	50	1
HISTE	W	**	**	N	**	**	**	**	**	**	**	**	**	**	**	**	67	1
	E	**	**	S	**	**	**	**	**	**	**	**	**	**	**	**	33	.3
	ST	**	**		**	**	**	**	**	**	**	**	**	**	**	**	100	1
SAH	W	12	3	N	30	7	7	2	2	1	5	1	4	1	38	6	11	2
	E	25	5	S	13	3	3	1	2	.4	1	.2	4	1	26	4	17	3
	ST	37	8		43	9	10	2	4	1	6	1	9	1	64	11	28	5
SAW	W	27	9	N	19	6	6	2	4	1	3	1	12	4	34	11	10	3
	E	26	8	S	10	3	1	.4	2	1	2	1	3	1	27	9	13	4
	ST	53	17		29	9	8	2	6	2	4	1	16	5	61	20	23	8
SAW BOSS(IE)	W	21	2	N	19	1	5	.4	7	1	3	.2	**	**	34	4	25	3
	E	32	2	S	8	1	3	.2	1	.1	1	.1	3	.3	16	2	22	3
	ST	53	4		27	2	8	1	8	1	4	.3	3	.3	50	6	47	5
SO	W	6	.4	N	10	1	3	.2	3	.2	27	2	**	**	14	.3	29	1
	E	10	1	S	24	2	3	.2	**	**	13	1	14	.3	14	.3	29	1
	ST	16	1		34	2	6	.4	3	.2	40	3	14	.3	29	1	57	1
SO-BOSS(IE)	W	11	1	N	8	1	6	.4	2	.1	27	2	**	**	23	2	35	3
	E	21	1	S	16	1	3	.2	**	**	6	.4	8	1	19	2	15	1
	ST	32	2		24	2	10	1	2	.1	33	2	8	1	42	4	50	5
SO-WENCH	W	43	.3	N	14	.1	**	**	**	**	14	.1	**	**	100	.3	**	**
	E	**	**	S	14	.1	14	.1	**	**	**	**	**	**	**	**	**	**
	ST	43	.3		29	.2	14	.1	**	**	14	.1	**	**	100	.3	**	**

(CONTINUED) A CALL TO COWS TO MAKE THEM STAND STILL AT MILKING TIME

ITEM (72)		TENNESSEE C	TENNESSEE D		GEORGIA C	GEORGIA D	ALABAMA C	ALABAMA D	MISSISSIPPI C	MISSISSIPPI D	FLORIDA C	FLORIDA D	LOUISIANA C	LOUISIANA D	ARKANSAS C	ARKANSAS D	OKLAHOMA C	OKLAHOMA D
HERE	W	40	1	N	50	.4	75	5	**	**	100	1	**	**	50	1	**	**
	E	60	2	S	50	.4	25	2	**	**	**	**	**	**	50	1	100	3
	ST		3			1		6		**		1		**		2		3
HISTE	W	**	**	N	**	**	**	**	**	**	**	**	**	**	**	**	67	3
	E	**	**	S	**	**	**	**	**	**	**	**	**	**	**	**	33	1
	ST		**			**		**		**		**		**		**		4
SAH	W	33	8	N	69	26	71	23	56	14	83	13	50	9	60	15	38	7
	E	67	16	S	31	11	29	9	44	11	17	3	50	9	40	10	62	11
	ST		24			37		32		25		15		18		26		18
SAW	W	51	26	N	66	25	83	30	67	33	62	10	79	50	56	26	43	13
	E	49	25	S	34	13	17	6	33	17	38	6	21	14	44	21	57	17
	ST		51			37		36		50		17		64		47		30
SAW BOSS(IE)	W	40	5	N	70	6	67	6	83	14	67	3	**	**	69	9	53	11
	E	60	7	S	30	2	33	3	17	3	33	1	100	5	31	4	47	10
	ST		12			8		9		17		4		5		14		21
SO	W	36	1	N	30	3	50	3	100	6	67	23	**	**	50	1	50	3
	E	64	2	S	70	7	50	3	**	**	33	12	100	5	50	1	50	3
	ST		3			9		6		6		35		5		2		6
SO-BOSS(IE)	W	35	2	N	33	2	67	6	100	3	81	22	**	**	55	5	69	13
	E	65	4	S	67	4	33	3	**	**	19	5	100	9	45	4	31	6
	ST		6			6		9		3		27		9		9		18
SO-WENCH	W	100	1	N	50	.4	**	**	**	**	100	1	**	**	100	1	**	**
	E	**	**	S	50	.4	100	2	**	**	**	**	**	**	**	**	**	**
	ST		1			1		2		**		1		**		1		**

ANIMALS
A CALL TO CALVES

ITEM (73)
WORK SHEET (37)

		TENNESSEE A	TENNESSEE B		GEORGIA A	GEORGIA B	ALABAMA A	ALABAMA B	MISSISSIPPI A	MISSISSIPPI B	FLORIDA A	FLORIDA B	LOUISIANA A	LOUISIANA B	ARKANSAS A	ARKANSAS B	OKLAHOMA A	OKLAHOMA B
BOSS(IE)(B)	W	22	.2	N	11	.1	**	**	**	**	11	.1	**	**	**	**	**	**
	E	33	.3	S	22	.2	**	**	**	**	**	**	**	**	100	.3	**	**
	ST	56	1		33	.3	**	**	**	**	11	.1	**	**	100	.3	**	**
CO-CALF(IE)	W	5	.2	N	11	.4	8	.3	3	.1	32	1	20	.3	60	1	20	.3
	E	13	1	S	21	1	5	.2	**	**	3	.1	**	**	**	**	**	**
	ST	18	1		32	1	13	1	3	.1	34	1	20	.3	60	1	20	.3
COME BOSS(IE)	W	29	.2	N	**	**	**	**	**	**	**	**	**	**	**	**	**	**
	E	14	.1	S	29	.2	**	**	**	**	29	.2	**	**	**	**	**	**
	ST	43	.3		29	.2	**	**	**	**	29	.2	**	**	**	**	**	**
COME CALF(IE)	W	13	.4	N	16	1	3	.1	6	.2	9	.3	**	**	33	1	50	1
	E	28	1	S	16	1	6	[illegible]	**	**	3	.1	17	.3	**	**	**	**
	ST	41	1		31	1	9	.3	6	.2	13	.4	17	.3	33	1	50	1
COSSIE	W	100	.1	N	**	**	**	**	**	**	**	**	**	**	**	**	67	1
	E	**	**	S	**	**	**	**	**	**	**	**	**	**	33	.3	**	**
	ST	100	.1		**	**	**	**	**	**	**	**	**	**	33	.3	67	1
CUSSIE	W	**	**	N	**	**	**	**	50	.1	50	.1	**	**	**	**	**	**
					(NO RESPONSE)													
	ST	**	**		**	**	**	**	50	.1	50	.1	**	**	**	**	**	**
CUBBIE					(NO RESPONSE)													
					(NO RESPONSE)													
					(NO RESPONSE)													
SOO(B)	W	18	.3	N	12	.2	6	.1	**	**	6	.1	25	.3	25	.3	**	**
	E	24	.4	S	6	.1	6	.1	6	.1	18	.3	**	**	25	.3	25	.3
	ST	41	1		18	.3	12	.2	6	.1	24	.4	25	.3	50	1	25	.3
SOOK CALF(IE)	W	21	10	N	24	11	6	3	4	2	3	2	6	3	35	18	12	6
	E	28	14	S	11	5	1	.4	1	1	1	1	4	2	25	13	18	9
	ST	49	24		35	17	7	3	5	2	5	2	10	5	60	31	30	16
SOOK	W	27	2	N	15	1	11	1	1	.1	3	.2	**	**	18	1	27	1
	E	27	2	S	8	1	3	.2	1	.1	3	.2	**	**	36	1	18	1
	ST	55	4		23	2	14	1	3	.2	5	.4	**	**	55	2	45	2
SEOK	W	33	.2	N	17	.1	33	.2	**	**	**	**	**	**	**	**	50	.3
	E	17	.1	S	**	**	**	**	**	**	**	**	**	**	**	**	50	.3
	ST	50	.3		17	.1	33	.2	**	**	**	**	**	**	**	**	100	1
SOOKIE, SOOKIE	W	14	1	N	17	2	6	1	4	.4	12	1	12	1	35	2	18	1
	E	12	1	S	28	3	2	.2	3	.3	2	.2	12	1	6	.3	18	1
	ST	25	2		45	4	8	1	7	1	14	1	24	1	41	3	35	2

ITEM (73) (CONTINUED) A CALL TO CALVES

ITEM		TENNESSEE C	TENNESSEE D		GEORGIA C	GEORGIA D	ALABAMA C	ALABAMA D	MISSISSIPPI C	MISSISSIPPI D	FLORIDA C	FLORIDA D	LOUISIANA C	LOUISIANA D	ARKANSAS C	ARKANSAS D	OKLAHOMA C	OKLAHOMA D
BOSS(IE)(B)	W	40	1	N	33	.3	**	**	**	**	100	2	**	**	**	**	**	**
	E	60	1	S	67	1	**	**	**	**	**	**	**	**	100	1	**	**
	ST		2			1		**		**		2		**		1		**
CO-CALF(IE)	W	29	1	N	33	2	60	5	100	3	92	19	100	5	100	3	100	2
	E	71	2	S	67	3	40	3	**	**	8	2	**	**	**	**	**	**
	ST		2			5		8		3		20		5		3		2
COME BOSS(IE)	W	67	1	N	**	**	**	**	**	**	**	**	**	**	**	**	**	**
	E	33	.3	S	100	1	**	**	**	**	100	3	**	**	**	**	**	**
	ST		1			1		**		**		3		**		**		**
COME CALF(IE)	W	31	1	N	50	2	33	2	100	5	75	5	**	**	100	2	100	5
	E	69	3	S	50	2	67	3	**	**	25	2	100	5	**	**	**	**
	ST		4			4		5		5		6		5		2		5
COSSIE	W	100	.3	N	**	**	**	**	**	**	**	**	**	**	**	**	100	3
	E	**	**	S	**	**	**	**	**	**	**	**	**	**	100	1	**	**
	ST		.3			**		**		**		**		**		1		3
CUSSIE	W	**	**	N	**	**	**	**	100	3	100	2	**	**	**	**	**	**
					(NO RESPONSE)													
	ST		**			**		**		3		2		**		**		**
CUBBIE					(NO RESPONSE)													
					(NO RESPONSE)													
	ST		**			**		**		**		**		**		**		**
SOO(B)	W	43	1	N	67	1	50	2	**	**	25	2	100	5	50	1	**	**
	E	57	1	S	33	.3	50	2	100	3	75	5	**	**	50	1	100	2
	ST		2			1		3		3		6		5		2		2
SOOK CALF(IE)	W	43	29	N	69	44	87	44	74	46	73	25	60	41	59	47	40	27
	E	57	40	S	31	20	13	7	26	16	27	9	40	27	41	33	60	41
	ST		69			64		51		62		34		68		80		68
SOOK	W	50	6	N	65	4	80	13	50	3	50	3	**	**	33	2	60	5
	E	50	6	S	35	2	20	3	50	3	50	3	**	**	67	4	40	3
	ST		12			7		16		5		6		**		6		8
SEOK	W	67	1	N	100	.3	100	3	**	**	**	**	**	**	**	**	50	2
	E	33	.3	S	**	**	**	**	**	**	**	**	**	**	**	**	50	2
	ST		1			.3		3		**		**		**		**		3
SOOKIE, SOOKIE	W	54	4	N	37	6	75	10	57	11	85	17	50	9	86	6	50	5
	E	46	3	S	63	11	25	3	43	8	15	3	50	9	14	1	50	5
	ST		[illegible]			[illegible]		13		19		20		18		6		10

A CALL TO HORSES TO GET THEM IN FROM PASTURE

ITEM (74)
WORK SHEET (38)

		TENNESSEE			GEORGIA		ALABAMA		MISSISSIPPI		FLORIDA		LOUISIANA		ARKANSAS		OKLAHOMA	
		A	B		A	B	A	B	A	B	A	B	A	B	A	B	A	B
CALL BY NAME	W	23	5	N	18	4	2	1	6	1	10	2	6	1	34	8	19	4
	E	19	4	S	13	3	2	.4	2	.4	4	1	8	2	17	4	16	4
	ST	42	9		31	7	4	1	8	2	15	3	14	3	52	12	34	8
CO-JACK	W	30	1	N	11	.3	11	.3	**	**	**	**	**	**	25	.3	25	.3
	E	19	1	S	22	1	**	**	4	.1	4	.1	25	.3	25	.3	**	**
	ST	48	1		33	1	11	.3	4	.1	4	.1	25	.3	50	1	25	.3
COME	W	9	.1	N	**	**	18	.2	9	.1	18	.2	**	**	100	.3	**	**
	E	9	.1	S	27	.3	**	**	9	.1	**	**	**	**	**	**	**	**
	ST	18	.2		27	.3	18	.2	18	.2	18	.2	**	**	100	.3	**	**
COME UP	W	**	**	N	36	.4	**	**	9	.1	9	.1	**	**	25	.3	**	**
	E	18	.2	S	27	.3	**	**	**	**	**	**	**	**	**	**	75	1
	ST	18	.2		64	1	**	**	9	.1	9	.1	**	**	25	.3	75	1
KOPE	W	16	3	N	19	4	6	1	2	.3	3	1	11	1	46	5	7	1
	E	38	7	S	9	2	1	.2	2	.3	4	1	7	1	14	1	14	1
	ST	54	10		28	5	7	1	3	1	7	1	18	2	61	6	21	2
WHISTLE	W	19	7	N	24	9	8	3	4	2	5	2	8	3	35	15	15	6
	E	24	9	S	10	4	2	1	2	1	2	1	4	2	23	10	15	6
	ST	43	16		34	12	10	4	6	2	7	3	12	5	58	25	30	13

		TENNESSEE			GEORGIA		ALABAMA		MISSISSIPPI		FLORIDA		LOUISIANA		ARKANSAS		OKLAHOMA	
		C	D		C	D	C	D	C	D	C	D	C	D	C	D	C	D
CALL BY NAME	W	54	13	N	57	14	56	8	75	25	70	29	44	14	67	18	55	18
	E	46	11	S	43	11	44	6	25	8	30	12	56	17	33	9	45	15
	ST		24			25		15		33		41		31		27		33
CO-JACK	W	62	2	N	33	1	100	5	**	**	**	**	**	**	50	1	100	1
	E	38	1	S	67	2	**	**	100	2	100	1	100	3	50	1	**	**
	ST		4			4		5		2		1		3		2		1
COME	W	50	.2	N	**	**	100	3	50	2	100	3	**	**	100	1	**	**
	E	50	.2	S	100	1	**	**	50	2	**	**	**	**	**	**	**	**
	ST		1			1		3		4		3		**		1		**
COME UP	W	**	**	N	57	2	**	**	100	2	100	1	**	**	100	1	**	**
	E	100	1	S	43	1	**	**	**	**	**	**	**	**	**	**	100	4
	ST		1			3		**		2		1		**		1		4
KOPE	W	30	8	N	68	14	85	18	50	6	43	8	60	10	76	11	33	3
	E	70	20	S	32	7	15	3	50	6	57	11	40	7	24	3	67	6
	ST		29			21		21		13		19		17		14		9
WHISTLE	W	45	19	N	71	33	83	47	68	31	76	26	64	31	60	34	49	25
	E	55	23	S	29	14	17	10	32	15	24	8	36	17	40	22	51	27
	ST		43			47		56		46		34		48		56		52

ITEM (75)
WORK SHEET (38)

ANIMALS
A CALL TO HORSES TO URGE THEM ON

		TENNESSEE A	TENNESSEE B		GEORGIA A	GEORGIA B	ALABAMA A	ALABAMA B	MISSISSIPPI A	MISSISSIPPI B	FLORIDA A	FLORIDA B	LOUISIANA A	LOUISIANA B	ARKANSAS A	ARKANSAS B	OKLAHOMA A	OKLAHOMA B
C L U C K	W	21	5	N	20	5	8	2	4	1	8	2	7	1	42	8	15	3
	E	17	4	S	15	3	3	1	3	1	3	1	**	**	18	4	18	4
	ST	37	9		35	8	11	3	6	1	11	2	7	1	60	12	33	6
GEE-UP	W	23	1	N	13	.4	10	.3	13	.4	6	.2	17	.3	**	**	17	.3
	E	13	.4	S	6	.2	6	.2	3	.1	6	.2	17	.3	17	.3	33	1
	ST	35	1		19	1	16	1	16	1	13	.4	33	1	17	.3	50	1
GET UP	W	20	10	N	19	10	6	3	3	2	8	4	9	4	30	12	12	5
	E	27	14	S	11	6	1	1	2	1	3	1	2	1	33	13	15	6
	ST	47	24		31	15	7	4	6	3	10	5	11	4	63	25	26	10
GIDDAP	W	23	3	N	19	2	7	1	3	.4	8	1	5	1	33	5	19	3
	E	21	3	S	12	2	1	.1	4	1	2	.3	12	2	16	3	16	3
	ST	44	6		31	4	8	1	7	1	10	1	16	3	49	8	35	5
GIDDY-AP	W	17	.3	N	6	.1	**	**	11	.2	22	.4	**	**	35	2	6	.3
	E	22	.4	S	**	**	11	.2	**	**	11	.2	18	1	18	1	24	1
	ST	39	1		6	.1	11	.2	11	.2	33	1	18	1	53	3	29	2
GIDDY-UP	W	16	2	N	14	1	8	1	5	1	6	1	5	1	26	4	23	3
	E	28	3	S	11	1	4	.4	**	**	7	1	13	2	5	1	28	4
	ST	44	4		25	2	13	1	5	1	14	1	18	3	31	4	51	7

		TENNESSEE C	TENNESSEE D		GEORGIA C	GEORGIA D	ALABAMA C	ALABAMA D	MISSISSIPPI C	MISSISSIPPI D	FLORIDA C	FLORIDA D	LOUISIANA C	LOUISIANA D	ARKANSAS C	ARKANSAS D	OKLAHOMA C	OKLAHOMA D
C L U C K	W	55	11	N	58	15	72	20	57	13	75	16	100	11	70	16	44	9
	E	45	9	S	42	11	28	8	43	10	25	5	**	**	30	7	56	11
	ST		19			26		28		23		22		11		23		20
GEE-UP	W	64	2	N	67	1	60	3	80	6	50	2	50	3	**	**	33	1
	E	36	1	S	33	1	40	2	20	2	50	2	50	3	100	1	67	2
	ST		3			2		6		8		4		6		1		3
GET UP	W	42	22	N	63	32	82	32	63	27	74	34	83	29	48	23	45	14
	E	58	31	S	37	18	18	7	37	16	26	12	17	6	52	25	55	18
	ST		54			50		39		44		45		34		48		32
GIDDAP	W	53	7	N	62	8	90	10	44	6	77	9	29	6	67	10	53	9
	E	47	6	S	38	5	10	1	56	8	23	3	71	14	33	5	47	8
	ST		13			13		11		15		12		20		14		17
GIDDY-AP	W	43	1	N	100	.3	**	**	100	3	67	4	**	**	67	4	20	1
	E	57	1	S	**	**	100	2	**	**	33	2	100	9	33	2	80	4
	ST		2			.3		2		3		5		9		6		6
GIDDY-UP	W	36	4	N	54	4	67	9	100	8	46	5	29	6	83	7	45	10
	E	64	6	S	46	4	33	5	**	**	54	6	71	14	17	1	55	12
						[illegible]		14		8		12		20		8		22

ITEM (76)
WORK SHEET (38)

ANIMALS
A CALL TO HOGS AT FEEDING TIME

		TENNESSEE A	TENNESSEE B		GEORGIA A	GEORGIA B	ALABAMA A	ALABAMA B	MISSISSIPPI A	MISSISSIPPI B	FLORIDA A	FLORIDA B	LOUISIANA A	LOUISIANA B	ARKANSAS A	ARKANSAS B	OKLAHOMA A	OKLAHOMA B
CHOOK, CHOOK	W	33	.1	N	**	**	**	**	33	.1	**	**	**	**	33	.3	**	**
	E	33	.1	S	**	**	**	**	**	**	**	**	67	1	**	**	**	**
	ST	67	.2		**	**	**	**	33	.1	**	**	67	1	33	.3	**	**
HOO-EE	W	40	3	N	13	1	7	1	1	.1	7	1	8	.3	15	1	8	.3
	E	9	1	S	20	1	1	.1	**	**	1	.1	15	1	38	2	15	1
	ST	49	4		33	2	9	1	1	.1	9	1	23	1	54	3	23	1
PIGGY, PIGGY	W	14	5	N	24	9	8	3	4	1	6	2	9	3	36	10	13	4
	E	26	9	S	12	4	2	1	2	1	2	1	4	1	23	6	16	5
	ST	40	14		37	13	9	3	6	2	9	3	13	4	59	17	29	8
PIGOO-WEE	W	17	2	N	15	2	5	1	1	.1	5	1	9	1	52	4	9	1
	E	45	6	S	12	2	**	**	1	.1	**	**	**	**	22	2	9	1
	ST	61	9		27	4	5	1	1	.2	5	1	9	1	74	6	17	1
POO-WEE	W	14	.1	N	14	.1	**	**	**	**	**	**	**	**	25	.3	50	1
	E	29	.2	S	29	.2	14	.1	**	**	**	**	**	**	**	**	25	.3
	ST	43	.3		43	.3	14	.1	**	**	**	**	**	**	25	.3	75	1
SOO-PIG	W	19	3	N	13	2	7	1	10	2	11	2	7	2	27	7	15	4
	E	17	3	S	9	1	3	1	5	1	3	1	5	1	26	7	19	5
	ST	37	6		23	4	11	2	15	2	14	2	12	3	53	14	34	9
SOO-WEE	W	17	1	N	27	2	11	1	3	.2	3	.2	10	1	24	3	21	2
	E	23	2	S	3	.2	5	.3	3	.2	6	.4	7	1	10	1	28	3
	ST	39	3		30	2	15	1	6	.4	9	1	17	2	34	4	48	5
WOO-EE	W	37	1	N	13	.4	3	.1	**	**	7	.2	**	**	23	1	8	.3
	E	13	.4	S	17	1	**	**	**	**	10	.3	8	.3	38	2	23	1
	ST	50	2		30	1	3	.1	**	**	17	1	8	.3	62	3	31	1

ITEM (76) (CONTINUED) A CALL TO HOGS AT FEEDING TIME

ITEM (76)		TENNESSEE C	TENNESSEE D		GEORGIA C	GEORGIA D	ALABAMA C	ALABAMA D	MISSISSIPPI C	MISSISSIPPI D	FLORIDA C	FLORIDA D	LOUISIANA C	LOUISIANA D	ARKANSAS C	ARKANSAS D	OKLAHOMA C	OKLAHOMA D
CHOOK, CHOOK	W	50	.2	N	**	**	**	**	100	2	**	**	**	**	100	1	**	**
	E	50	.2	S	**	**	**	**	**	**	**	**	100	6	**	**	**	**
	ST		1			**		**		2		**		6		1		**
HOO-EE	W	82	8	N	39	4	83	7	100	2	83	7	33	3	29	2	33	1
	E	18	2	S	61	6	17	1	**	**	17	1	67	6	71	4	67	3
	ST		9			9		8		2		8		9		5		4
PIGGY, PIGGY	W	36	14	N	67	33	81	36	68	26	73	29	70	22	62	22	43	13
	E	64	25	S	33	17	19	8	32	12	27	11	30	9	38	14	57	17
	ST		39			50		44		38		40		31		36		30
PIGOO-WEE	W	27	6	N	55	8	100	10	50	2	100	9	100	6	71	9	50	3
	E	73	17	S	45	7	**	**	50	2	**	**	**	**	29	4	50	3
	ST		24			15		10		4		9		6		13		5
POO-WEE	W	33	.2	N	33	.3	**	**	**	**	**	**	**	**	100	1	67	3
	E	67	1	S	67	1	100	1	**	**	**	**	**	**	**	**	33	1
	ST		1			1		1		**		**		**		1		4
SOO-PIG	W	53	8	N	59	8	69	15	65	30	76	21	56	16	51	15	44	14
	E	47	7	S	41	6	31	7	35	16	24	7	44	13	49	15	56	18
	ST		15			13		22		46		28		28		30		33
SOO-WEE	W	42	3	N	90	7	70	10	50	4	33	3	60	9	70	5	43	8
	E	58	4	S	10	1	30	4	50	4	67	5	40	6	30	2	57	11
	ST		7			8		14		8		8		16		8		18
WOO-EE	W	73	3	N	44	2	100	1	**	**	40	3	**	**	38	2	25	1
	E	27	1	S	56	2	**	**	**	**	60	4	100	3	63	4	75	4
	ST		4			4		1		**		7		3		6		5

ITEM (77)
WORK SHEET (38)

ANIMALS
A CALL TO SHEEP TO GET THEM IN FROM PASTURE

		TENNESSEE A	TENNESSEE B		GEORGIA A	GEORGIA B	ALABAMA A	ALABAMA B	MISSISSIPPI A	MISSISSIPPI B	FLORIDA A	FLORIDA B	LOUISIANA A	LOUISIANA B	ARKANSAS A	ARKANSAS B	OKLAHOMA A	OKLAHOMA B
CADE	W	**	**	N	33	.1	**	**	**	**	33	.1	**	**	**	**	**	**
	E	33	.1	S	**	**	**	**	**	**	**	**	**	**	**	**	100	.3
	ST	33	.1		33	.1	**	**	**	**	33	.1	**	**	**	**	100	.3
CO-DACK	W	100	.3	N	**	**	**	**	**	**	**	**	**	**	**	**	**	**
					(NO RESPONSE)													
	ST	100	.3		**	**	**	**	**	**	**	**	**	**	**	**	**	**
CO-DAY					(NO RESPONSE)													
	E	50	.1	S	50	.1	**	**	**	**	**	**	**	**	**	**	**	**
	ST	50	.1		50	.1	**	**	**	**	**	**	**	**	**	**	**	**
CO-DICK	W	100	.1	N	**	**	**	**	**	**	**	**	**	**	**	**	**	**
					(NO RESPONSE)													
	ST	100	.1		**	**	**	**	**	**	**	**	**	**	**	**	**	**
COME NAN(NIE)	W	9	.2	N	35	1	9	.2	4	.1	**	**	**	**	56	2	22	1
	E	22	1	S	17	.4	**	**	4	.1	**	**	**	**	11	.3	11	.3
	ST	30	1		52	1	9	.2	9	.2	**	**	**	**	67	2	33	1
CO-NIN(NIE)	W	8	.1	N	17	.2	**	**	**	**	**	**	**	**	33	.3	67	1
	E	8	.1	S	67	1	**	**	**	**	**	**	**	**	**	**	**	**
	ST	17	.2		83	1	**	**	**	**	**	**	**	**	33	.3	67	1
COO-SHEEP	W	28	6	N	21	5	7	2	4	1	3	1	13	2	33	5	**	**
	E	26	6	S	7	2	.4	.1	2	1	**	**	3	.3	43	6	10	1
	ST	55	12		29	6	7	2	6	1	3	1	15	2	75	11	10	1
CO-SHEEP	W	9	.4	N	21	1	7	.3	7	.3	**	**	**	**	40	1	**	**
	E	35	2	S	14	1	**	**	**	**	7	.3	**	**	60	2	**	**
	ST	44	2		35	2	7	.3	7	.3	7	.3	**	**	100	4	**	**
NAN(NIE)	W	33	.2	N	**	**	33	.2	**	**	**	**	**	**	33	.3	**	**
	E	**	**	S	33	.2	**	**	**	**	**	**	33	.3	**	**	33	.3
	ST	33	.2		33	.2	33	.2	**	**	**	**	33	.3	33	.3	33	.3
SHEEP	W	43	1	N	19	.4	5	.1	**	**	5	.1	**	**	33	.3	**	**
	E	19	.4	S	5	.1	**	**	5	.1	**	**	33	.3	**	**	33	.3
	ST	62	1		24	1	5	.1	5	.1	5	.1	33	.3	33	.3	33	.3
SHEEPIE	W	21	2	N	17	1	2	.2	1	.1	5	.4	6	.3	39	3	11	1
	E	42	4	S	4	.3	2	.2	4	.3	1	.1	6	.3	17	1	22	1
	ST	63	5		21	2	5	.4	5	.4	6	1	11	1	56	4	33	2

(CONTINUED) A CALL TO SHEEP TO GET THEM IN FROM PASTURE

ITEM (77)		TENNESSEE C	TENNESSEE D		GEORGIA C	GEORGIA D	ALABAMA C	ALABAMA D	MISSISSIPPI C	MISSISSIPPI D	FLORIDA C	FLORIDA D	LOUISIANA C	LOUISIANA D	ARKANSAS C	ARKANSAS D	OKLAHOMA C	OKLAHOMA D
CADE	W	**	**	N	100	1	**	**	**	**	100	6	**	**	**	**	**	**
	E	100	.4	S	**	**	**	**	**	**	**	**	**	**	**	**	100	6
	ST		.4			1		**		**		6		**		**		6
CO-DACK	W	100	1	N	**	**	**	**	**	**	**	**	**	**	**	**	**	**
					(NO RESPONSE)													
	ST		1			**		**		**		**		**		**		**
CO-DAY					(NO RESPONSE)													
	E	100	.4	S	100	1	**	**	**	**	**	**	**	**	**	**	**	**
	ST		.4			1		**		**		**		**		**		**
CO-DICK	W	100	.4	N	**	**	**	**	**	**	**	**	**	**	**	**	**	**
					(NO RESPONSE)													
	ST		.4			**		**		**		**		**		**		**
COME NAN(NIE)	W	29	1	N	67	6	100	7	50	4	**	**	**	**	83	8	67	11
	E	71	2	S	33	3	**	**	50	4	**	**	**	**	17	2	33	6
	ST		3			10		7		8		**		**		10		17
CO-NIN(NIE)	W	50	.4	N	20	2	**	**	**	**	**	**	**	**	100	2	100	11
	E	50	.4	S	80	6	**	**	**	**	**	**	**	**	**	**	**	**
	ST		1			8		**		**		**		**		2		11
COO-SHEEP	W	52	28	N	74	37	94	54	64	38	100	38	83	50	43	22	**	**
	E	48	26	S	26	13	6	4	36	21	**	**	17	10	57	29	100	22
	ST		54			50		57		58		38		60		51		22
CO-SHEEP	W	21	2	N	60	7	100	11	100	13	**	**	**	**	40	7	**	**
	E	79	7	S	40	5	**	**	**	**	100	19	**	**	60	10	**	**
	ST		9			12		11		13		19		**		17		**
NAN(NIE)	W	100	1	N	**	**	100	7	**	**	**	**	**	**	100	2	**	**
	E	**	**	S	100	2	**	**	**	**	**	**	100	10	**	**	100	6
	ST		1			2		7		**		**		10		2		6
SHEEP	W	69	4	N	80	3	100	4	**	**	100	6	**	**	100	2	**	**
	E	31	2	S	20	1	**	**	100	4	**	**	100	10	**	**	100	6
	ST		6			4		4		4		6		10		2		6
SHEEPIE	W	33	8	N	82	11	50	7	25	4	80	25	50	10	70	12	33	11
	E	67	16	S	18	2	50	7	75	13	20	6	50	10	30	5	67	22
	ST		23			14		14		17		31		20		17		33

ITEM (78)
WORK SHEET (38)

ANIMALS
A CALL TO CHICKENS

		TENNESSEE A	TENNESSEE B		GEORGIA A	GEORGIA B	ALABAMA A	ALABAMA B	MISSISSIPPI A	MISSISSIPPI B	FLORIDA A	FLORIDA B	LOUISIANA A	LOUISIANA B	ARKANSAS A	ARKANSAS B	OKLAHOMA A	OKLAHOMA B
BEE	W	50	.1	N	**	**	**	**	**	**	**	**	**	**	**	**	**	**
	E	**	**	S	50	.1	**	**	**	**	**	**	**	**	**	**	**	**
	ST	50	.1		50	.1	**	**	**	**	**	**	**	**	**	**	**	**
BIDDIE	W	6	.2	N	19	1	13	.4	6	.2	3	.1	25	1	38	1	**	**
	E	**	**	S	42	1	3	.1	3	.1	3	.1	**	**	13	.3	25	1
	ST	6	.2		61	2	16	1	10	.3	6	.2	25	1	50	1	25	1
CHICK, CHICK	W	20	10	N	18	9	6	3	5	3	9	4	7	4	27	13	17	9
	E	20	10	S	13	6	3	1	2	1	5	2	8	4	25	13	16	8
	ST	40	20		31	15	9	4	7	4	14	7	15	8	52	26	33	17
CHICKIE, CHICKIE	W	17	6	N	24	8	6	2	2	1	7	2	5	1	36	11	12	4
	E	32	11	S	7	3	1	1	2	1	2	1	2	1	19	6	25	8
	ST	49	17		31	11	7	2	4	1	9	3	7	2	55	17	37	11
CHUCK, CHUCK	W	38	.3	N	**	**	13	.1	**	**	**	**	**	**	**	**	**	**
	E	13	.1	S	13	.1	25	.2	**	**	**	**	**	**	**	**	**	**
	ST	50	.4		13	.1	38	.3	**	**	**	**	**	**	**	**	**	**
CO-CHEE	W	50	.2	N	**	**	**	**	**	**	**	**	50	.3	**	**	**	**
	E	25	.1	S	25	.1	**	**	**	**	**	**	**	**	**	**	50	.3
	ST	75	.3		25	.1	**	**	**	**	**	**	50	.3	**	**	50	.3
COO-CHICK	W	53	1	N	**	**	7	.1	**	**	13	.2	**	**	50	1	**	**
	E	13	.2	S	13	.2	**	**	**	**	**	**	**	**	50	1	**	**
	ST	67	1		13	.2	7	.1	**	**	13	.2	**	**	100	1	**	**
KIP, KIP	W	**	**	N	50	.1	**	**	**	**	**	**	**	**	**	**	**	**
	E	**	**	S	50	.1	**	**	**	**	**	**	**	**	**	**	**	**
	ST	**	**		100	.2	**	**	**	**	**	**	**	**	**	**	**	**
KIT, KIT					(NO RESPONSE)													
	E	**	**	S	**	**	**	**	**	**	**	**	100	1	**	**	**	**
	ST	**	**		**	**	**	**	**	**	**	**	100	1	**	**	**	**
KUT, KUT	W	22	.2	N	22	.2	**	**	22	.2	**	**	50	.3	**	**	**	**
	E	11	.1	S	22	.2	**	**	**	**	**	**	**	**	**	**	50	.3
	ST	33	.3		44	.4	**	**	22	.2	**	**	50	.3	**	**	50	.3
WIDDIE	W	67	.2	N	**	**	**	**	**	**	**	**	50	.3	**	**	**	**
	E	**	**	S	33	.1	**	**	**	**	**	**	**	**	**	**	50	.3
	ST	67	.2		33	.1	**	**	**	**	**	**	50	.3	**	**	50	.3

(CONTINUED) A CALL TO CHICKENS

ITEM (78)		TENNESSEE C	TENNESSEE D		GEORGIA C	GEORGIA D	ALABAMA C	ALABAMA D	MISSISSIPPI C	MISSISSIPPI D	FLORIDA C	FLORIDA D	LOUISIANA C	LOUISIANA D	ARKANSAS C	ARKANSAS D	OKLAHOMA C	OKLAHOMA D
BEE	W	100	.2	N	**	**	**	**	**	**	**	**	**	**	**	**	**	**
	E	**	**	S	100	.3	**	**	**	**	**	**	**	**	**	**	**	**
	ST		.2			.3		**		**		**		**		**		**
BIDDIE	W	100	1	N	32	2	80	5	67	4	50	1	100	6	75	2	**	**
	E	**	**	S	68	5	20	1	33	2	50	1	**	**	25	1	100	2
	ST		1			7		7		6		2		6		3		2
CHICK, CHICK	W	50	25	N	58	30	71	40	71	46	65	42	48	29	51	29	52	29
	E	50	25	S	42	22	29	16	29	19	35	23	52	31	49	28	48	27
	ST		49			52		56		65		65		60		57		56
CHICKIE, CHICKIE	W	35	15	N	76	29	79	25	50	13	77	24	67	11	65	24	32	12
	E	65	29	S	24	9	21	7	50	13	23	7	33	6	35	13	68	26
	ST		44			37		32		26		31		17		37		38
CHUCK, CHUCK	W	75	1	N	**	**	33	1	**	**	**	**	**	**	**	**	**	**
	E	25	.2	S	100	.3	67	3	**	**	**	**	**	**	**	**	**	**
	ST		1			.3		4		**		**		**		**		**
CO-CHEE	W	67	1	N	**	**	**	**	**	**	**	**	100	3	**	**	**	**
	E	33	.2	S	100	.3	**	**	**	**	**	**	**	**	**	**	100	1
	ST		1			.3		**		**		**		3		**		1
COO-CHICK	W	80	2	N	**	**	100	1	**	**	100	2	**	**	50	2	**	**
	E	20	1	S	100	1	**	**	**	**	**	**	**	**	50	2	**	**
	ST		3			1		1		**		2		**		3		**
KIP, KIP	W	**	**	N	50	.3	**	**	**	**	**	**	**	**	**	**	**	**
	E	**	**	S	50	.3	**	**	**	**	**	**	**	**	**	**	**	**
	ST		**			1		**		**		**		**		**		**
KIT, KIT					(NO RESPONSE)													
	E	**	**	S	**	**	**	**	**	**	**	**	100	9	**	**	**	**
	ST		**			**		**		**		**		9		**		**
KUT, KUT	W	67	1	N	50	1	**	**	100	4	**	**	100	3	**	**	**	**
	E	33	.2	S	50	1	**	**	**	**	**	**	**	**	**	**	100	1
	ST		1			1		**		4		**		3		**		1
WIDDIE	W	100	1	N	**	**	**	**	**	**	**	**	100	3	**	**	**	**
	E	**	**	S	100	.3	**	**	**	**	**	**	**	**	**	**	100	1
	ST		1			.3		**		**		**		3		**		1

ITEM (79)
WORK SHEET (39)

ANIMALS
THE HORSE ON THE LEFT SIDE IN PLOWING OR HAULING

		TENNESSEE A	TENNESSEE B		GEORGIA A	GEORGIA B	ALABAMA A	ALABAMA B	MISSISSIPPI A	MISSISSIPPI B	FLORIDA A	FLORIDA B	LOUISIANA A	LOUISIANA B	ARKANSAS A	ARKANSAS B	OKLAHOMA A	OKLAHOMA B
LEADER	W	27	2	N	30	2	**	**	2	.1	8	1	**	**	42	2	8	.3
	E	25	2	S	7	.4	**	**	2	.1	**	**	**	**	25	1	25	1
	ST	52	3		37	2	**	**	3	.2	8	1	**	**	67	3	33	1
LEAD HORSE	W	23	8	N	22	8	6	2	3	1	4	1	2	1	49	16	8	3
	E	28	10	S	9	3	1	.2	1	1	2	1	5	1	19	6	17	5
	ST	51	18		31	11	6	2	5	2	6	2	7	2	68	22	25	8
LINE HORSE	W	19	1	N	8	.3	14	1	**	**	5	.2	**	**	50	1	13	.3
	E	30	1	S	19	1	3	.1	**	**	3	.1	25	1	13	.3	**	**
	ST	49	2		27	1	16	1	**	**	8	.3	25	1	63	2	13	.3
NEAR HORSE	W	13	.3	N	22	1	17	.4	**	**	**	**	13	1	7	.3	33	2
	E	26	1	S	**	**	9	.2	9	.2	4	.1	13	1	27	1	7	.3
	ST	39	1		22	1	26	1	9	.2	4	.1	27	1	33	2	40	2
NEAR-SIDE HORSE	W	25	.1	N	**	**	**	**	**	**	25	.1	**	**	25	.3	50	1
	E	50	.2	S	**	**	**	**	**	**	**	**	**	**	25	.3	**	**
	ST	75	.3		**	**	**	**	**	**	25	.1	**	**	50	1	50	1
NIGH HORSE	W	44	.4	N	**	**	11	.1	**	**	22	.2	33	.3	**	**	**	**
	E	11	.1	S	11	.1	**	**	**	**	**	**	**	**	33	.3	33	.3
	ST	56	1		11	.1	11	.1	**	**	22	.2	33	.3	33	.3	33	.3
SADDLE HORSE	W	21	1	N	14	1	5	.2	5	.2	5	.2	67	1	**	**	33	.3
	E	19	1	S	29	1	**	**	**	**	2	.1	**	**	**	**	**	**
	ST	40	2		43	2	5	.2	5	.2	7	.3	67	1	**	**	33	.3
WHEEL HORSE	W	28	2	N	21	1	9	1	10	1	**	**	13	1	20	1	13	1
	E	13	1	S	18	1	1	.1	**	**	**	**	**	**	33	2	20	1
	ST	41	3		38	3	10	1	10	1	**	**	13	1	53	3	33	2

(CONTINUED) THE HORSE ON THE LEFT SIDE IN PLOWING OR HAULING

ITEM (79)		TENNESSEE C	TENNESSEE D		GEORGIA C	GEORGIA D	ALABAMA C	ALABAMA D	MISSISSIPPI C	MISSISSIPPI D	FLORIDA C	FLORIDA D	LOUISIANA C	LOUISIANA D	ARKANSAS C	ARKANSAS D	OKLAHOMA C	OKLAHOMA D
LEADER	W	52	6	N	82	9	**	**	50	3	100	14	**	**	63	6	25	2
	E	48	5	S	18	2	**	**	50	3	**	**	**	**	38	3	75	7
	ST		11			12		**		7		14		**		9		10
LEAD HORSE	W	45	27	N	70	40	91	45	71	40	67	39	33	12	72	48	32	17
	E	55	34	S	30	17	9	5	29	17	33	19	67	24	28	19	68	36
	ST		61			57		50		57		58		35		67		52
LINE HORSE	W	39	2	N	30	2	83	11	**	**	67	6	**	**	80	4	100	2
	E	61	4	S	70	4	17	2	**	**	33	3	100	12	20	1	**	**
	ST		6			5		14		**		8		12		6		2
NEAR HORSE	W	33	1	N	100	3	67	9	**	**	**	**	50	12	20	1	83	12
	E	67	2	S	**	**	33	5	100	7	100	3	50	12	80	4	17	2
	ST		3			3		14		7		3		24		6		14
NEAR-SIDE HORSE	W	33	.3	N	**	**	**	**	**	**	100	3	**	**	50	1	100	5
	E	67	1	S	**	**	**	**	**	**	**	**	**	**	50	1	**	**
	ST		1			**		**		**		3		**		2		5
NIGH HORSE	W	80	1	N	**	**	100	2	**	**	100	6	100	6	**	**	**	**
	E	20	.3	S	100	1	**	**	**	**	**	**	**	**	100	1	100	2
	ST		2			1		2		**		6		6		1		2
SADDLE HORSE	W	53	3	N	33	3	100	5	100	7	67	6	100	12	**	**	100	2
	E	47	3	S	67	6	**	**	**	**	33	3	**	**	**	**	**	**
	ST		6			9		5		7		8		12		**		2
WHEEL HORSE	W	68	7	N	54	7	86	14	100	23	**	**	100	12	38	3	40	5
	E	32	3	S	46	6	14	2	**	**	**	**	**	**	63	6	60	7
	ST		10			14		16		23		**		12		9		12

ITEM (80)
WORK SHEET (39)

A UNIT OF MEASURE
A SHORT DISTANCE

		TENNESSEE A	TENNESSEE B		GEORGIA A	GEORGIA B	ALABAMA A	ALABAMA B	MISSISSIPPI A	MISSISSIPPI B	FLORIDA A	FLORIDA B	LOUISIANA A	LOUISIANA B	ARKANSAS A	ARKANSAS B	OKLAHOMA A	OKLAHOMA B
A WAYS	W	21	.3	N	14	.2	21	.3	**	**	**	**	**	**	20	.3	20	.3
	E	29	.4	S	7	.1	7	.1	**	**	**	**	**	**	20	.3	40	1
	ST	50	1		21	.3	29	.4	**	**	**	**	**	**	40	1	60	1
A LITTLE PIECE	W	20	8	N	20	8	5	2	5	2	3	1	18	4	33	7	11	3
	E	29	12	S	12	5	2	1	2	1	2	1	16	4	11	3	10	2
	ST	48	20		32	13	7	3	7	3	5	2	34	8	44	10	21	5
A LITTLE WAY	W	20	7	N	17	6	8	3	4	1	8	3	4	1	27	11	16	6
	E	21	7	S	11	4	3	1	2	1	5	2	2	1	30	12	21	8
	ST	41	14		28	9	11	4	6	2	14	5	5	2	57	23	37	15
A LITTLE WAYS	W	15	3	N	18	4	7	1	3	1	11	2	6	2	27	8	19	6
	E	24	5	S	14	3	3	1	3	1	2	1	7	2	19	6	22	7
	ST	39	8		32	7	10	2	6	1	13	3	13	4	46	14	41	13
A PIECE	W	20	1	N	14	1	**	**	6	.3	14	1	**	**	**	**	43	1
	E	31	2	S	6	.3	6	.3	2	.1	**	**	29	1	14	.3	14	.3
	ST	51	3		20	1	6	.3	8	.4	14	1	29	1	14	.3	57	1

		TENNESSEE C	TENNESSEE D		GEORGIA C	GEORGIA D	ALABAMA C	ALABAMA D	MISSISSIPPI C	MISSISSIPPI D	FLORIDA C	FLORIDA D	LOUISIANA C	LOUISIANA D	ARKANSAS C	ARKANSAS D	OKLAHOMA C	OKLAHOMA D
A WAYS	W	43	1	N	67	1	75	3	**	**	**	**	**	**	50	1	33	1
	E	57	1	S	33	.3	25	1	**	**	**	**	**	**	50	1	67	2
	ST		2			1		4		**		**		**		2		3
A LITTLE PIECE	W	40	18	N	63	27	72	23	67	29	65	13	52	28	74	15	54	7
	E	60	26	S	37	16	28	9	33	14	35	7	48	25	26	5	46	6
	ST		44			43		32		43		20		53		20		14
A LITTLE WAY	W	48	15	N	62	19	71	27	68	21	61	28	67	10	48	23	44	19
	E	52	16	S	38	12	29	11	32	10	39	17	33	5	52	25	56	24
	ST		30			30		38		30		45		15		48		43
A LITTLE WAYS	W	39	7	N	56	13	67	15	54	11	81	22	45	13	59	17	46	17
	E	61	11	S	44	10	33	8	46	10	19	5	55	15	41	12	54	20
	ST		18			22		23		21		28		28		30		36
A PIECE	W	40	2	N	70	2	**	**	75	5	100	7	**	**	**	**	75	3
	E	60	3	S	30	1	100	3	25	2	**	**	100	5	100	1	25	1
	ST		6			3		3		6		7		5		1		4

CROPS
A SECOND GROWTH OF HAY OR CLOVER

ITEM (81)
WORK SHEET (41)

		TENNESSEE A	TENNESSEE B		GEORGIA A	GEORGIA B	ALABAMA A	ALABAMA B	MISSISSIPPI A	MISSISSIPPI B	FLORIDA A	FLORIDA B	LOUISIANA A	LOUISIANA B	ARKANSAS A	ARKANSAS B	OKLAHOMA A	OKLAHOMA B
AFTERMATH	W	40	.2	N	**	**	60	.3	**	**	**	**	**	**	**	**	**	**
					(NO RESPONSE)													
	ST	40	.2		**	**	60	.3	**	**	**	**	**	**	**	**	**	**
LATTERMATH					(NO RESPONSE)													
					(NO RESPONSE)													
					(NO RESPONSE)													
ROWEN	W	**	**	N	50	.1	**	**	**	**	**	**	**	**	**	**	**	**
	E	**	**	S	50	.1	**	**	**	**	**	**	**	**	100	.3	**	**
	ST	**	**		100	.2	**	**	**	**	**	**	**	**	100	.3	**	**
SECOND CROP	W	23	9	N	16	6	6	2	4	2	7	3	9	3	38	13	5	2
	E	22	9	S	15	6	2	1	2	1	3	1	5	2	24	8	18	6
	ST	45	18		31	12	8	3	6	2	10	4	14	5	63	21	23	8
SECOND CUTTING	W	21	6	N	25	7	5	1	5	1	3	1	7	3	29	10	23	8
	E	30	8	S	8	2	1	.3	2	.4	.3	.1	2	1	22	8	16	6
	ST	50	14		33	9	6	2	6	2	4	1	9	3	52	18	39	14
VOLUNTEER (CROP)	W	18	2	N	22	3	9	1	5	1	10	1	**	**	20	2	32	3
	E	16	2	S	13	2	4	1	1	.1	3	.4	**	**	24	2	24	2
	ST	34	4		35	5	13	2	6	1	13	2	**	**	44	4	56	5

		TENNESSEE C	TENNESSEE D		GEORGIA C	GEORGIA D	ALABAMA C	ALABAMA D	MISSISSIPPI C	MISSISSIPPI D	FLORIDA C	FLORIDA D	LOUISIANA C	LOUISIANA D	ARKANSAS C	ARKANSAS D	OKLAHOMA C	OKLAHOMA D
AFTERMATH	W	100	1	N	**	**	100	4	**	**	**	**	**	**	**	**	**	**
					(NO RESPONSE)													
	ST		1			**		4		**		**		**		**		**
LATTERMATH					(NO RESPONSE)													
					(NO RESPONSE)													
	ST		**			**		**		**		**		**		**		**
ROWEN	W	**	**	N	50	.3	**	**	**	**	**	**	**	**	**	**	**	**
	E	**	**	S	50	.3	**	**	**	**	**	**	**	**	100	1	**	**
	ST		**			1		**		**		**		**		1		**
SECOND CROP	W	52	26	N	52	24	72	34	63	32	70	41	62	36	61	29	24	7
	E	48	24	S	48	23	28	13	38	19	30	17	38	23	39	18	76	22
	ST		50			47		47		51		59		59		48		28
SECOND CUTTING	W	41	15	N	76	26	82	21	75	26	90	14	78	32	57	24	59	31
	E	59	22	S	24	8	18	4	25	9	10	2	22	9	43	18	41	22
	ST		38			35		25		34		16		41		43		53
VOLUNTEER	W	52	6	N	64	11	69	16	86	13	75	19	**	**	45	4	57	11
	[illegible]	[illegible]	[illegible]	S	[illegible]	[illegible]	31	7	14	2	25	6	**	**	55	5	43	8
	[illegible]		[illegible]			[illegible]		[illegible]		[illegible]		[illegible]		**		9		19

ITEM (82)
WORK SHEET (41)

CROPS
WHEAT THAT HAS BEEN GATHERED AND BOUND

		TENNESSEE A	TENNESSEE B		GEORGIA A	GEORGIA B	ALABAMA A	ALABAMA B	MISSISSIPPI A	MISSISSIPPI B	FLORIDA A	FLORIDA B	LOUISIANA A	LOUISIANA B	ARKANSAS A	ARKANSAS B	OKLAHOMA A	OKLAHOMA B
BIND	W	13	1	N	15	1	13	1	4	.2	7	.3	17	.3	50	1	17	.3
	E	37	2	S	7	.3	**	**	2	.1	2	.1	**	**	**	**	17	.3
	ST	50	2		22	1	13	1	7	.3	9	.4	17	.3	50	1	33	1
BUNDLE	W	17	9	N	24	13	6	3	3	2	7	4	2	1	34	16	19	9
	E	25	14	S	14	8	2	1	1	1	2	1	3	1	21	10	20	9
	ST	43	23		38	20	8	4	4	2	8	4	6	3	55	25	39	18
SHAFE	W	13	.1	N	25	.2	13	.1	**	**	**	**	**	**	**	**	**	**
	E	25	.2	S	13	.1	**	**	13	.1	**	**	25	.3	25	.3	50	1
	ST	38	.3		38	.3	13	.1	13	.1	**	**	25	.3	25	.3	50	1
SHEAF	W	30	4	N	15	2	8	1	4	1	4	1	8	1	31	5	21	4
	E	23	3	S	8	1	2	.3	2	.3	3	1	4	1	21	4	15	3
	ST	53	0		23	3	10	2	6	1	8	1	13	2	52	9	35	6

		TENNESSEE C	TENNESSEE D		GEORGIA C	GEORGIA D	ALABAMA C	ALABAMA D	MISSISSIPPI C	MISSISSIPPI D	FLORIDA C	FLORIDA D	LOUISIANA C	LOUISIANA D	ARKANSAS C	ARKANSAS D	OKLAHOMA C	OKLAHOMA D
BIND	W	26	2	N	70	3	100	10	67	6	75	5	100	7	100	3	50	1
	E	74	5	S	30	1	**	**	33	3	25	2	**	**	**	**	50	1
	ST		7			4		10		9		7		7		3		3
BUNDLE	W	41	28	N	62	51	78	51	75	45	81	60	43	20	61	43	48	34
	E	59	40	S	38	30	22	14	25	15	19	14	57	27	39	27	52	37
	ST		69			81		65		61		74		47		71		70
SHAFE	W	33	.3	N	67	1	100	2	**	**	**	**	**	**	**	**	**	**
	E	67	1	S	33	.4	**	**	100	3	**	**	100	7	100	1	100	3
	ST		1			1		2		3		**		7		1		3
SHEAF	W	57	13	N	67	9	80	19	67	18	55	11	67	27	60	15	59	14
	E	43	10	S	33	5	20	5	33	9	45	9	33	13	40	10	41	10
	ST		23			14		24		27		19		40		25		24

FOOD
BREAD IN LOAVES, MADE OF WHITE FLOUR

ITEM (83)
WORK SHEET (44)

		TENNESSEE			GEORGIA		ALABAMA		MISSISSIPPI		FLORIDA		LOUISIANA		ARKANSAS		OKLAHOMA	
		A	B		A	B	A	B	A	B	A	B	A	B	A	B	A	B
BREAD	W	23	3	N	8	1	8	1	6	1	6	1	4	1	21	4	18	4
	E	29	4	S	6	1	4	1	5	1	6	1	14	3	25	5	18	4
	ST	52	7		13	2	12	2	10	1	13	2	18	4	46	9	36	7
LIGHT-BREAD	W	20	12	N	12	7	5	3	5	3	8	5	7	4	31	19	15	9
	E	30	18	S	13	8	2	1	3	2	3	2	5	3	23	14	19	12
	ST	50	30		24	15	7	4	7	4	11	7	13	8	54	32	34	21
LOAF BREAD	W	15	4	N	38	9	13	3	3	1	3	1	5	.3	50	4	9	1
	E	13	3	S	10	2	2	.4	1	.3	1	.3	5	.3	27	2	5	.3
	ST	28	7		48	11	15	4	5	1	4	1	9	1	77	6	14	1
WHEAT BREAD	W	20	.2	N	30	.3	10	.1	**	**	10	.1	**	**	100	.3	**	**
	E	20	.2	S	10	.1	**	**	**	**	**	**	**	**	**	**	**	**
	ST	40	.4		40	.4	10	.1	**	**	10	.1	**	**	100	.3	**	**
WHITE BREAD	W	14	1	N	7	.4	13	1	**	**	18	1	6	1	26	3	14	2
	E	27	2	S	5	.3	4	.2	4	.2	9	1	14	2	17	2	23	3
	ST	41	2		13	1	16	1	4	.2	27	2	20	3	43	5	37	5
YEAST BREAD	W	30	1	N	**	**	5	.1	5	.1	15	.3	**	**	20	.3	**	**
	E	20	.4	S	15	.3	**	**	**	**	10	.2	**	**	40	1	40	1
	ST	50	1		15	.3	5	.1	5	.1	25	1	**	**	60	1	40	1
RIZ BREAD	W	50	.2	N	**	**	**	**	**	**	**	**	**	**	100	.3	**	**
	E	**	**	S	25	.1	**	**	**	**	25	.1	**	**	**	**	**	**
	ST	50	.2		25	.1	**	**	**	**	25	.1	**	**	100	.3	**	**

ITEM (83)

(CONTINUED) BREAD IN LOAVES, MADE OF WHITE FLOUR

		TENNESSEE C	TENNESSEE D		GEORGIA C	GEORGIA D	ALABAMA C	ALABAMA D	MISSISSIPPI C	MISSISSIPPI D	FLORIDA C	FLORIDA D	LOUISIANA C	LOUISIANA D	ARKANSAS C	ARKANSAS D	OKLAHOMA C	OKLAHOMA D
BREAD	W	44	6	N	59	4	67	10	54	10	50	7	20	5	46	8	50	11
	E	56	8	S	41	2	33	5	46	9	50	7	80	20	54	9	50	11
	ST		14			6		15		19		14		25		17		21
LIGHT-BREAD	W	40	25	N	48	24	72	28	60	37	73	42	57	30	58	34	44	26
	E	60	38	S	52	26	28	11	40	24	27	15	43	23	42	25	56	34
	ST		63			50		39		61		57		53		59		60
LOAF BREAD	W	54	8	N	80	31	89	31	73	11	70	6	50	3	65	7	67	2
	E	46	7	S	20	8	11	4	27	4	30	3	50	3	35	4	33	1
	ST		14			39		35		16		9		5		11		5
WHEAT BREAD	W	50	.4	N	75	1	100	1	**	**	100	1	**	**	100	1	**	**
	E	50	.4	S	25	.3	**	**	**	**	**	**	**	**	**	**	**	**
	ST		1			1		1		**		1		**		1		**
WHITE BREAD	W	35	2	N	57	1	78	7	**	**	67	9	29	5	60	6	38	5
	E	65	3	S	43	1	22	2	100	3	33	4	71	13	40	4	62	8
	ST		5			2		9		3		13		18		10		14
YEAST BREAD	W	60	1	N	**	**	100	1	100	1	60	3	**	**	33	1	**	**
	E	40	1	S	100	1	**	**	**	**	40	2	**	**	67	1	100	2
	ST		2			1		1		1		4		**		2		2
RIZ BREAD	W	100	.4	N	**	**	**	**	**	**	**	**	**	**	100	1	**	**
	E	**	**	S	100	.3	**	**	**	**	100	1	**	**	**	**	**	**
	ST		.4			.3		**		**		1		**		1		**

ITEM (84)
WORK SHEET (44)

FOOD
BREAD MADE OF CORN MEAL

		TENNESSEE A	TENNESSEE B		GEORGIA A	GEORGIA B	ALABAMA A	ALABAMA B	MISSISSIPPI A	MISSISSIPPI B	FLORIDA A	FLORIDA B	LOUISIANA A	LOUISIANA B	ARKANSAS A	ARKANSAS B	OKLAHOMA A	OKLAHOMA B
CORN BREAD	W	18	15	N	18	15	7	6	4	3	7	6	5	4	29	25	16	13
	E	26	22	S	11	9	2	2	2	2	3	3	8	7	24	20	18	16
	ST	45	37		29	24	10	8	6	5	11	9	13	11	53	45	34	29
CORN DODGER(S)	W	25	2	N	6	.4	1	.1	1	.1	7	1	**	**	44	1	11	.3
	E	30	2	S	19	1	**	**	3	.2	6	.4	**	**	22	1	22	1
	ST	55	4		25	2	1	.1	4	.3	13	1	**	**	67	2	33	1
CORN PONE	W	26	2	N	14	1	9	1	1	.1	12	1	23	1	31	1	8	.3
	E	22	2	S	7	1	4	.3	1	.1	3	.2	**	**	15	1	23	1
	ST	48	3		22	2	13	1	3	.2	14	1	23	1	46	2	31	1
HOE CAKE(S)	W	27	4	N	9	1	5	1	4	1	11	1	**	**	58	3	**	**
	E	18	2	S	17	2	2	.2	4	1	5	1	8	.3	17	1	17	1
	ST	45	6		26	3	6	1	8	1	16	2	8	.3	75	3	17	1
JOHNNY CAKE	W	33	.4	N	17	.2	8	.1	**	**	**	**	**	**	75	1	**	**
	E	17	.2	S	17	.2	**	**	**	**	8	.1	**	**	25	.3	**	**
	ST	50	1		33	.4	8	.1	**	**	8	.1	**	**	100	1	**	**
PONE BREAD	W	29	2	N	12	1	6	.3	**	**	4	.2	25	1	38	1	**	**
	E	13	1	S	25	1	6	.3	2	.1	4	.2	13	.3	13	.3	13	.3
	ST	42	2		37	2	12	1	2	.1	8	.4	38	1	50	1	13	.3

		TENNESSEE C	TENNESSEE D		GEORGIA C	GEORGIA D	ALABAMA C	ALABAMA D	MISSISSIPPI C	MISSISSIPPI D	FLORIDA C	FLORIDA D	LOUISIANA C	LOUISIANA D	ARKANSAS C	ARKANSAS D	OKLAHOMA C	OKLAHOMA D
CORN BREAD	W	41	29	N	63	46	74	56	65	49	69	45	39	32	55	45	46	41
	E	59	41	S	37	27	26	19	35	27	31	21	61	50	45	36	54	48
	ST		70			73		76		76		66		82		81		89
CORN DODGER(S)	W	46	3	N	24	1	100	1	33	1	56	4	**	**	67	3	33	1
	E	54	4	S	76	4	**	**	67	3	44	3	**	**	33	1	67	2
	ST		7			5		1		4		7		**		4		3
CORN PONE	W	55	3	N	67	3	67	6	50	1	80	6	100	8	67	3	25	1
	E	45	3	S	33	2	33	3	50	1	20	2	**	**	33	1	75	3
	ST		6			5		9		3		8		8		4		4
HOE CAKE(S)	W	60	7	N	33	3	75	6	50	7	70	11	**	**	78	5	**	**
	E	40	4	S	67	7	25	2	50	7	30	5	100	3	22	1	100	2
	ST		11			10		8		15		15		3		6		2
JOHNNY CAKE	W	67	1	N	50	1	100	1	**	**	**	**	**	**	75	2	**	**
	E	33	.3	S	50	1	**	**	**	**	100	1	**	**	25	1	**	**
	ST		1			1		1		**		1		**		3		**
PONE BREAD	W	68	3	N	32	2	50	3	**	**	50	2	67	5	75	2	**	**
	E	32	1	S	68	4	50	3	100	1	50	2	33	3	25	1	100	1
	ST		4			6		6		1		3		8		3		1

ITEM (84)
WORK SHEET (44)

FOOD
CORN BREAD BAKED IN ASHES

		TENNESSEE			GEORGIA		ALABAMA		MISSISSIPPI		FLORIDA		LOUISIANA		ARKANSAS		OKLAHOMA	
		A	B		A	B	A	B	A	B	A	B	A	B	A	B	A	B
ASH BREAD	W	23	2	N	16	2	10	1	5	1	4	.4	4	.3	32	3	8	1
	E	27	3	S	10	1	1	.1	1	.1	4	.4	8	1	28	3	20	2
	ST	50	5		26	3	11	1	6	1	8	1	12	1	60	5	28	3
ASH CAKE	W	19	5	N	36	9	7	2	2	1	3	1	16	1	40	4	4	.3
	E	18	4	S	11	3	2	.4	1	.3	2	.4	4	.3	32	3	4	.3
	ST	37	9		46	12	8	2	4	1	5	1	20	2	72	6	8	1
ASH PONE	W	21	2	N	16	2	3	.4	5	1	8	1	10	1	46	7	10	1
	E	25	3	S	10	1	3	.3	4	1	4	1	5	1	24	4	5	1
	ST	46	5		26	3	6	1	10	1	12	1	15	2	71	10	15	2
		TENNESSEE			GEORGIA		ALABAMA		MISSISSIPPI		FLORIDA		LOUISIANA		ARKANSAS		OKLAHOMA	
		C	D		C	D	C	D	C	D	C	D	C	D	C	D	C	D
ASH BREAD	W	46	12	N	63	10	91	26	83	19	50	12	33	7	53	13	29	13
	E	54	14	S	37	6	9	3	17	4	50	12	67	14	47	11	71	33
	ST		27			16		29		23		24		21		24		47
ASH CAKE	W	52	24	N	77	51	80	42	67	23	64	21	80	29	56	16	50	7
	E	48	22	S	23	15	20	11	33	12	36	12	20	7	44	13	50	7
	ST		46			66		53		35		33		36		29		13
ASH PONE	W	45	12	N	60	11	57	11	55	23	64	27	67	29	66	31	67	27
	E	55	15	S	40	7	43	8	45	19	36	15	33	14	34	16	33	13
	ST		27			18		18		42		42		43		47		40

TABLE I

FOOD
SOFT, MUSHY CORN BREAD SERVED WITH A SPOON

ITEM (84)
WORK SHEET (44)

		TENNESSEE A	TENNESSEE B		GEORGIA A	GEORGIA B	ALABAMA A	ALABAMA B	MISSISSIPPI A	MISSISSIPPI B	FLORIDA A	FLORIDA B	LOUISIANA A	LOUISIANA B	ARKANSAS A	ARKANSAS B	OKLAHOMA A	OKLAHOMA B
AWENDAW	W	67	.2	N	**	**	33	.1	**	**	**	**	**	**	**	**	**	**
					(NO RESPONSE)													
	ST	67	.2		**	**	33	.1	**	**	**	**	**	**	**	**	**	**
BATTER BREAD	W	12	2	N	26	3	6	1	2	.2	8	1	12	1	59	4	6	.3
	E	33	4	S	11	1	1	.1	2	.3	**	**	6	.3	12	1	6	.3
	ST	45	6		37	5	7	1	4	1	8	1	18	1	71	4	12	1
SPOON BREAD	W	22	10	N	18	8	7	3	5	2	7	3	7	3	29	13	17	8
	E	23	11	S	10	5	3	1	2	1	4	2	6	3	26	12	15	7
	ST	45	21		28	13	9	4	7	3	11	5	13	6	55	25	31	14

		TENNESSEE C	TENNESSEE D		GEORGIA C	GEORGIA D	ALABAMA C	ALABAMA D	MISSISSIPPI C	MISSISSIPPI D	FLORIDA C	FLORIDA D	LOUISIANA C	LOUISIANA D	ARKANSAS C	ARKANSAS D	OKLAHOMA C	OKLAHOMA D
AWENDAW	W	100	1	N	**	**	100	2	**	**	**	**	**	**	**	**	**	**
					(NO RESPONSE)													
	ST		1			**		2		**		**		**		**		**
BATTER BREAD	W	26	6	N	70	19	89	16	40	5	100	18	67	10	83	12	50	2
	E	74	16	S	30	8	11	2	60	8	**	**	33	5	17	2	50	2
	ST		22			28		18		13		18		15		15		5
SPOON BREAD	W	48	37	N	64	46	71	57	73	63	62	51	53	45	53	45	53	50
	E	52	40	S	36	26	29	24	27	24	38	32	47	40	47	40	48	45
	ST		77			72		80		87		82		85		85		95

ITEM (85)
WORK SHEET (45)

FOOD
A ROUND FLAT CONFECTION WITH HOLE IN CENTER, MADE WITH BAKING POWDER

		TENNESSEE			GEORGIA		ALABAMA		MISSISSIPPI		FLORIDA		LOUISIANA		ARKANSAS		OKLAHOMA	
		A	B		A	B	A	B	A	B	A	B	A	B	A	B	A	B
CRULL(A)					(NO RESPONSE)													
	E	**	**	S	50	.1	**	**	**	**	50	.1	**	**	**	**	**	**
	ST	**	**		50	.1	**	**	**	**	50	.1	**	**	**	**	**	**
CRULLER(A)	W	35	1	N	12	.2	6	.1	12	.2	12	.2	17	.3	33	1	17	.3
	E	12	.2	S	**	**	6	.1	**	**	6	.1	**	**	33	1	**	**
	ST	47	1		12	.2	12	.2	12	.2	18	.3	17	.3	67	1	17	.3
DOUGHNUT(A)	W	19	15	N	19	15	7	5	4	3	7	6	7	5	30	24	14	11
	E	26	21	S	11	9	2	2	2	2	3	3	8	6	24	19	17	14
	ST	45	36		30	24	9	7	6	5	10	8	15	12	54	43	31	25
FAT CAKE(A)	W	**	**	N	**	**	33	.1	**	**	**	**	25	.3	25	.3	50	1
	E	**	**	S	33	.1	**	**	33	.1	**	**	**	**	**	**	**	**
	ST	**	**		33	.1	33	.1	33	.1	**	**	25	.3	25	.3	50	1
FRIED CAKE(A)	W	7	.1	N	14	.2	14	.2	**	**	7	.1	**	**	20	.3	**	**
	E	21	.3	S	14	.2	7	.1	7	.1	7	.1	20	.3	40	1	20	.3
	ST	29	.4		29	.4	21	.3	7	.1	14	.2	20	.3	60	1	20	.3
CAKE DOUGHNUT	W	11	.3	N	11	.3	7	.2	11	.3	11	.3	**	**	38	3	17	1
	E	29	1	S	11	.3	4	.1	4	.1	4	.1	**	**	17	1	29	3
	ST	39	1		21	1	11	.3	14	.4	14	.4	**	**	54	5	46	4
RAISED DOUGHNUT(A)	W	17	.3	N	22	.4	11	.2	6	.1	11	.2	**	**	67	1	**	**
	E	6	.1	S	17	.3	**	**	**	**	11	.2	**	**	**	**	33	.3
	ST	22	.4		39	1	11	.2	6	.1	22	.4	**	**	67	1	33	.3

(CONTINUED) A ROUND FLAT CONFECTION WITH HOLE IN CENTER, MADE WITH BAKING POWDER

ITEM (85)		TENNESSEE C	TENNESSEE D		GEORGIA C	GEORGIA D	ALABAMA C	ALABAMA D	MISSISSIPPI C	MISSISSIPPI D	FLORIDA C	FLORIDA D	LOUISIANA C	LOUISIANA D	ARKANSAS C	ARKANSAS D	OKLAHOMA C	OKLAHOMA D
CRULL(A)					(NO RESPONSE)													
	E	**	**	S	100	.3	**	**	**	**	100	1	**	**	**	**	**	**
	ST		**			.3		**		**		1		**		**		**
CRULLER(A)	W	75	2	N	100	1	50	1	100	4	67	2	100	3	50	1	100	1
	E	25	1	S	**	**	50	1	**	**	33	1	**	**	50	1	**	**
	ST		2			1		3		4		3		3		3		1
DOUGHNUT(A)	W	42	39	N	63	58	75	65	67	56	69	59	45	42	56	47	45	36
	E	58	53	S	37	34	25	22	33	27	31	26	55	50	44	37	55	45
	ST		93			92		86		84		85		92		84		81
FAT CAKE(A)	W	**	**	N	**	**	100	1	**	**	**	**	100	3	100	1	100	2
	E	**	**	S	100	.3	**	**	100	2	**	**	**	**	**	**	**	**
	ST		**			.3		1		2		**		3		1		2
FRIED CAKE(A)	W	25	.2	N	50	1	67	3	**	**	50	1	**	**	33	1	**	**
	E	75	1	S	50	1	33	1	100	2	50	1	100	3	67	1	100	1
	ST		1			2		4		2		2		3		2		1
CAKE DOUGHNUT	W	27	1	N	50	1	67	3	75	5	75	3	**	**	69	6	36	5
	E	73	2	S	50	1	33	1	25	2	25	1	**	**	31	3	64	8
	ST		3			2		4		7		4		**		9		13
RAISED DOUGHNUT(A)	W	75	1	N	57	2	100	3	100	2	50	2	**	**	100	1	**	**
	E	25	.2	S	43	1	**	**	**	**	50	2	**	**	**	**	100	1
	ST		1			3		3		2		4		**		1		1

ITEM (85)
WORK SHEET (45)

FOOD
SIMILAR CONFECTION, MADE WITH YEAST

		TENNESSEE A	TENNESSEE B		GEORGIA A	GEORGIA B	ALABAMA A	ALABAMA B	MISSISSIPPI A	MISSISSIPPI B	FLORIDA A	FLORIDA B	LOUISIANA A	LOUISIANA B	ARKANSAS A	ARKANSAS B	OKLAHOMA A	OKLAHOMA B
COOKIE	W	25	4	N	16	2	7	1	4	1	5	1	9	1	39	3	**	**
	E	25	4	S	12	2	2	.3	3	1	1	.1	**	**	30	3	22	2
	ST	50	8		28	4	9	1	7	1	5	1	9	1	70	6	22	2
CRULL(B)					(NO RESPONSE)													
	E	**	**	S	**	**	**	**	100	.1	**	**	**	**	**	**	**	**
	ST	**	**		**	**	**	**	100	.1	**	**	**	**	**	**	**	**
CRULLER(B)	W	52	1	N	14	.3	5	.1	5	.1	5	.1	**	**	100	1	**	**
	E	5	.1	S	5	.1	5	.1	**	**	5	.1	**	**	**	**	**	**
	ST	57	1		19	.4	10	.2	5	.1	10	.2	**	**	100	1	**	**
DOUGHNUT(B)	W	19	5	N	14	4	9	3	4	1	8	2	7	3	31	10	15	5
	E	29	8	S	9	2	3	1	1	.3	5	1	4	1	19	6	24	8
	ST	47	13		23	7	12	4	5	1	12	4	12	4	49	17	39	13
FAT CAKE(B)	W	25	.1	N	50	.2	**	**	**	**	25	.1	**	**	100	.3	**	**
					(NO RESPONSE)													
	ST	25	.1		50	.2	**	**	**	**	25	.1	**	**	100	.3	**	**
FRIED CAKE(B)	W	19	.3	N	31	1	13	.2	13	.2	**	**	50	.3	**	**	**	**
	E	13	.2	S	**	**	**	**	6	.1	6	.1	**	**	**	**	50	.3
	ST	31	1		31	1	13	.2	19	.3	6	.1	50	.3	**	**	50	.3
NUT CAKE	W	31	.4	N	8	.1	15	.2	**	**	**	**	**	**	**	**	**	**
	E	15	.2	S	23	.3	**	**	8	.1	**	**	**	**	**	**	**	**
	ST	46	1		31	.4	15	.2	8	.1	**	**	**	**	**	**	**	**
RAISED DOUGHNUT(B)	W	12	2	N	26	4	4	1	2	.3	8	1	5	1	28	8	24	7
	E	26	4	S	14	2	3	1	1	.2	5	1	5	1	22	6	16	5
	ST	38	7		40	7	7	1	3	1	13	2	10	3	49	14	41	12
BREAD DOUGHNUT	W	33	2	N	22	1	6	.3	8	.4	**	**	5	.3	48	4	19	1
	E	14	1	S	14	1	**	**	**	**	4	.2	19	1	**	**	10	1
	ST	47	2		35	2	6	.3	8	.4	4	.2	24	2	48	4	29	2

(CONTINUED) SIMILAR CONFECTION, MADE WITH YEAST

ITEM (85)		TENNESSEE C	TENNESSEE D		GEORGIA C	GEORGIA D	ALABAMA C	ALABAMA D	MISSISSIPPI C	MISSISSIPPI D	FLORIDA C	FLORIDA D	LOUISIANA C	LOUISIANA D	ARKANSAS C	ARKANSAS D	OKLAHOMA C	OKLAHOMA D
COOKIE	W	50	12	N	57	12	79	16	55	15	88	10	100	7	56	8	**	**
	E	50	12	S	43	9	21	4	45	13	13	1	**	**	44	6	100	6
	ST		23			20		21		28		11		7		14		6
CRULL(B)					(NO RESPONSE)													
	E	**	**	S	**	**	**	**	100	3	**	**	**	**	**	**	**	**
	ST		**			**		**		3		**		**		**		**
CRULLER(B)	W	92	3	N	75	1	50	1	100	3	50	1	**	**	100	2	**	**
	E	8	.3	S	25	.4	50	1	**	**	50	1	**	**	**	**	**	**
	ST		4			2		3		3		3		**		2		**
DOUGHNUT(B)	W	39	16	N	62	19	74	37	79	28	62	30	64	26	62	25	38	17
	E	61	25	S	38	12	26	13	21	8	38	19	36	15	38	16	62	28
	ST		41			31		50		35		49		41		41		46
FAT CAKE(B)	W	100	.3	N	100	1	**	**	**	**	100	1	**	**	100	1	**	**
					(NO RESPONSE)													
	ST		.3			1		**		**		1		**		1		**
FRIED CAKE(B)	W	60	1	N	100	2	100	3	67	5	**	**	100	4	**	**	**	**
	E	40	1	S	**	**	**	**	33	3	100	1	**	**	**	**	100	1
	ST		2			2		3		8		1		4		**		1
NUT CAKE	W	67	1	N	25	.4	100	3	**	**	**	**	**	**	**	**	**	**
	E	33	1	S	75	1	**	**	100	3	**	**	**	**	**	**	**	**
	ST		2			2		3		3		**		**		**		**
RAISED DOUGHNUT(B)	W	32	6	N	64	21	55	9	60	8	64	20	50	15	56	19	59	23
	E	68	14	S	36	12	45	7	40	5	36	11	50	15	44	15	41	16
	ST		20			33		16		13		31		30		34		40
BREAD DOUGHNUT	W	71	5	N	61	5	100	4	100	10	**	**	20	4	100	9	67	5
	E	29	2	S	39	3	**	**	**	**	100	3	80	15	**	**	33	2
	ST		8			9		4		10		3		19		9		7

FOOD
FRIED, ROUND, FLAT CAKES MADE WITH WHITE FLOUR

ITEM (86)
WORK SHEET (45)

		TENNESSEE			GEORGIA		ALABAMA		MISSISSIPPI		FLORIDA		LOUISIANA		ARKANSAS		OKLAHOMA	
		A	B		A	B	A	B	A	B	A	B	A	B	A	B	A	B
BATTER CAKES	W	22	6	N	22	6	7	2	4	1	6	2	15	1	27	3	**	**
	E	14	4	S	15	4	3	1	4	1	3	1	15	1	42	4	**	**
	ST	36	10		37	10	9	3	8	2	9	3	31	3	69	6	**	**
FLANNEL CAKES	W	40	.4	N	10	.1	10	.1	**	**	10	.1	**	**	**	**	**	**
	E	20	.2	S	**	**	**	**	10	.1	**	**	**	**	**	**	**	**
	ST	60	1		10	.1	10	.1	10	.1	10	.1	**	**	**	**	**	**
FLAPJACKS	W	27	4	N	17	2	5	1	5	1	6	1	12	2	23	4	7	1
	E	17	2	S	13	2	3	.4	4	1	4	1	2	.3	33	5	23	4
	ST	44	6		30	4	8	1	8	1	10	1	14	2	56	9	30	5
FLITTERS	W	17	1	N	20	2	5	.4	1	.1	**	**	**	**	67	1	**	**
	E	36	3	S	13	1	1	.1	4	.3	3	.2	17	.3	**	**	17	.3
	ST	53	4		33	3	7	1	5	.4	3	.2	17	.3	67	1	17	.3
FRITTERS	W	22	1	N	22	1	9	.3	**	**	9	.3	33	1	22	1	**	**
	E	25	1	S	13	.4	**	**	**	**	**	**	**	**	44	1	**	**
	ST	47	2		34	1	9	.3	**	**	9	.3	33	1	67	2	**	**
GRIDDLE CAKES	W	30	1	N	13	.3	9	.2	4	.1	4	.1	**	**	44	1	22	1
	E	22	1	S	4	.1	4	.1	4	.1	4	.1	11	.3	11	.3	11	.3
	ST	52	1		17	.4	13	.3	9	.2	9	.2	11	.3	56	2	33	1
HOT CAKES	W	21	4	N	23	5	5	1	4	1	9	2	9	3	27	9	9	3
	E	16	3	S	12	2	3	1	3	1	3	1	4	1	21	7	29	9
	ST	38	7		35	7	8	2	7	1	13	2	13	4	48	16	38	12
PANCAKES	W	17	9	N	16	8	7	4	4	2	7	4	6	4	30	19	19	12
	E	30	15	S	10	5	2	1	1	1	4	2	8	5	19	12	18	12
	ST	47	24		26	13	10	5	5	3	11	6	14	9	49	31	38	24
SLAPJACKS	W	13	.2	N	19	.3	6	.1	**	**	13	.2	**	**	80	1	**	**
	E	19	.3	S	19	.3	6	.1	6	.1	**	**	**	**	**	**	20	.3
	ST	31	1		38	1	13	.2	6	.1	13	.2	**	**	80	1	20	.3
WHEAT CAKES	W	40	.2	N	20	.1	**	**	**	**	**	**	**	**	**	**	50	.3
	E	40	.2	S	**	**	**	**	**	**	**	**	**	**	**	**	50	.3
	ST	80	.4		20	.1	**	**	**	**	**	**	**	**	**	**	100	1

(CONTINUED) FRIED, ROUND, FLAT CAKES MADE WITH WHITE FLOUR

ITEM (86)		TENNESSEE C	TENNESSEE D		GEORGIA C	GEORGIA D	ALABAMA C	ALABAMA D	MISSISSIPPI C	MISSISSIPPI D	FLORIDA C	FLORIDA D	LOUISIANA C	LOUISIANA D	ARKANSAS C	ARKANSAS D	OKLAHOMA C	OKLAHOMA D
BATTER CAKES	W	60	11	N	59	15	72	16	45	12	64	13	50	7	39	4	**	**
	E	40	7	S	41	11	28	6	55	15	36	7	50	7	61	6	**	**
	ST		18			26		22		27		20		15		10		**
FLANNEL CAKES	W	67	1	N	100	.2	100	1	**	**	100	1	**	**	**	**	**	**
	E	33	.3	S	**	**	**	**	100	1	**	**	**	**	**	**	**	**
	ST		1			.2		1		1		1		**		**		**
FLAPJACKS	W	61	6	N	56	6	60	5	55	7	62	6	83	9	42	5	23	3
	E	39	4	S	44	4	40	4	45	6	38	4	17	2	58	7	77	8
	ST		11			10		9		14		10		11		13		11
FLITTERS	W	33	2	N	60	4	80	4	25	1	**	**	**	**	100	2	**	**
	E	68	5	S	40	3	20	1	75	4	100	2	100	2	**	**	100	1
	ST		7			7		4		5		2		2		2		1
FRITTERS	W	47	1	N	64	2	100	3	**	**	100	2	100	5	33	1	**	**
	E	53	1	S	36	1	**	**	**	**	**	**	**	**	67	2	**	**
	ST		3			3		3		**		2		5		3		**
GRIDDLE CAKES	W	58	1	N	75	1	67	2	50	1	50	1	**	**	80	2	67	2
	E	42	1	S	25	.2	33	1	50	1	50	1	100	2	20	1	33	1
	ST		2			1		3		2		2		2		3		3
HOT CAKES	W	57	8	N	67	11	63	9	62	10	75	14	67	15	56	13	24	7
	E	43	6	S	33	6	38	5	38	6	25	5	33	7	44	10	76	22
	ST		13			17		14		16		19		22		23		28
PANCAKES	W	36	16	N	61	21	77	32	74	25	65	28	42	18	61	28	52	28
	E	64	27	S	39	13	23	10	26	9	35	15	58	25	39	17	48	27
	ST		43			34		42		33		43		44		45		55
SLAPJACKS	W	40	.3	N	50	1	50	1	**	**	100	2	**	**	100	2	**	**
	E	60	1	S	50	1	50	1	100	1	**	**	**	**	**	**	100	1
	ST		1			2		2		1		2		**		2		1
WHEAT CAKES	W	50	.3	N	100	.2	**	**	**	**	**	**	**	**	**	**	50	1
	E	50	.3	S	**	**	**	**	**	**	**	**	**	**	**	**	50	1
	ST		1			.2		**		**		**		**		**		2

FOOD
MEAT FROM SIDES OF HOG, SALTED BUT NOT SMOKED

ITEM (87)
WORK SHEET (46)

		TENNESSEE			GEORGIA		ALABAMA		MISSISSIPPI		FLORIDA		LOUISIANA		ARKANSAS		OKLAHOMA	
		A	B		A	B	A	B	A	B	A	B	A	B	A	B	A	B
BACON	W	18	4	N	16	3	7	1	3	1	9	2	5	1	19	4	20	4
	E	29	6	S	8	2	2	.3	3	1	7	1	8	2	17	4	31	6
	ST	47	9		24	5	8	2	5	1	15	3	14	3	36	8	51	11
FLITCH	W	**	**	N	25	.1	**	**	**	**	**	**	**	**	**	**	**	**
	E	50	.2	S	25	.1	**	**	**	**	**	**	**	**	**	**	**	**
	ST	50	.2		50	.2	**	**	**	**	**	**	**	**	**	**	**	**
MIDDLIN(S)	W	20	4	N	19	4	5	1	4	1	7	1	12	1	45	5	**	**
	E	30	6	S	9	2	3	1	2	.4	1	.2	6	1	24	3	12	1
	ST	49	9		28	5	8	2	7	1	8	1	18	2	70	8	12	1
MIDDLIN MEAT	W	22	3	N	30	4	2	.3	2	.2	2	.3	9	.3	55	2	**	**
	E	26	3	S	14	2	**	**	2	.3	**	**	**	**	36	1	**	**
	ST	47	6		44	6	2	.3	4	1	2	.3	9	.3	91	4	**	**
SALT PORK	W	27	4	N	3	.4	11	2	5	1	13	2	6	3	25	10	17	7
	E	14	2	S	5	1	6	1	5	1	11	1	2	1	24	9	25	10
	ST	41	6		8	1	17	2	10	1	23	3	8	3	49	19	43	17
SIDE PORK	W	21	1	N	6	.2	3	.1	3	.1	18	1	**	**	35	2	41	3
	E	26	1	S	12	.4	3	.1	9	.3	**	**	6	.3	12	1	6	.3
	ST	47	2		18	1	6	.2	12	.4	18	1	6	.3	47	3	47	3
SIDE MEAT	W	22	6	N	23	6	6	2	4	1	3	1	3	.3	49	7	10	1
	E	22	6	S	15	4	4	1	1	.3	**	**	5	1	23	3	10	1
	ST	44	12		38	10	11	3	5	1	3	1	8	1	72	10	21	3
SOWBELLY	W	17	1	N	14	1	10	1	7	1	14	1	11	1	46	5	4	.3
	E	13	1	S	16	1	**	**	3	.2	6	.4	4	.3	18	2	18	2
	ST	30	2		30	2	10	1	10	1	20	1	14	1	64	6	21	2
FATBACK	W	7	1	N	33	4	10	1	3	.4	4	1	11	.3	78	3	**	**
	E	30	4	S	11	1	**	**	1	.1	1	.1	**	**	11	.3	**	**
	ST	37	5		44	5	10	1	4	1	5	1	11	.3	89	3	**	**

(CONTINUED) MEAT FROM SIDES OF HOG, SALTED BUT NOT SMOKED

ITEM (87)		TENNESSEE C	TENNESSEE D		GEORGIA C	GEORGIA D	ALABAMA C	ALABAMA D	MISSISSIPPI C	MISSISSIPPI D	FLORIDA C	FLORIDA D	LOUISIANA C	LOUISIANA D	ARKANSAS C	ARKANSAS D	OKLAHOMA C	OKLAHOMA D
BACON	W	38	7	N	67	9	81	12	50	7	57	15	38	9	52	6	40	12
	E	62	12	S	33	4	19	3	50	7	43	12	63	15	48	6	60	17
	ST		19			13		15		14		27		24		12		29
FLITCH	W	**	**	N	50	.2	**	**	**	**	**	**	**	**	**	**	**	**
	E	100	.4	S	50	.2	**	**	**	**	**	**	**	**	**	**	**	**
	ST		.4			1		**		**		**		**		**		**
MIDDLIN(S)	W	40	7	N	67	10	67	10	67	12	86	11	67	12	65	9	**	**
	E	60	11	S	33	5	33	5	33	6	14	2	33	6	35	5	100	4
	ST		18			15		14		17		13		18		14		4
MIDDLIN MEAT	W	46	5	N	69	11	100	3	40	3	100	3	100	3	60	4	**	**
	E	54	7	S	31	5	**	**	60	4	**	**	**	**	40	2	**	**
	ST		12			16		3		7		3		3		6		**
SALT PORK	W	65	7	N	36	1	65	14	54	10	55	15	78	21	52	16	40	18
	E	35	4	S	64	2	35	8	46	9	45	13	22	6	48	15	60	27
	ST		11			3		22		19		28		27		32		46
SIDE PORK	W	44	1	N	33	1	50	1	25	1	100	5	**	**	75	4	88	7
	E	56	2	S	67	1	50	1	75	4	**	**	100	3	25	1	13	1
	ST		3			2		2		6		5		3		5		8
SIDE MEAT	W	50	11	N	60	17	59	15	77	14	100	7	33	3	68	11	50	4
	E	50	11	S	40	11	41	10	23	4	**	**	67	6	32	5	50	4
	ST		23			28		26		19		7		9		16		8
SOWBELLY	W	57	2	N	48	3	100	7	71	7	71	9	75	9	72	8	17	1
	E	43	2	S	52	3	**	**	29	3	29	4	25	3	28	3	83	5
	ST		4			6		7		10		13		12		11		6
FATBACK	W	18	2	N	75	12	100	11	80	6	83	4	100	3	88	4	**	**
	E	82	7	S	25	4	**	**	20	1	17	1	**	**	13	1	**	**
	ST		9			16		11		7		5		3		5		**

ITEM (88)
WORK SHEET (46)

FOOD
TOUGH COVERING OF BACON

		TENNESSEE			GEORGIA		ALABAMA		MISSISSIPPI		FLORIDA		LOUISIANA		ARKANSAS		OKLAHOMA	
		A	B		A	B	A	B	A	B	A	B	A	B	A	B	A	B
RIND	W	24	11	N	16	8	8	4	5	2	8	4	6	4	26	18	18	13
	E	21	10	S	7	4	3	2	3	1	5	2	5	3	23	16	22	15
	ST	45	22		23	11	11	6	8	4	13	6	11	8	49	34	40	28
RINN	W	16	.4	N	4	.1	12	.3	4	.1	12	.3	**	**	56	4	17	1
	E	40	1	S	8	.2	**	**	4	.1	**	**	**	**	17	1	11	1
	ST	56	1		12	.3	12	.3	8	.2	12	.3	**	**	72	5	28	2
SKIN	W	15	6	N	21	9	5	2	2	1	7	3	13	2	41	6	**	**
	E	27	11	S	16	7	2	1	1	1	2	1	18	3	21	3	8	1
	ST	42	18		38	16	6	3	4	2	10	4	31	4	63	9	8	1

		TENNESSEE			GEORGIA		ALABAMA		MISSISSIPPI		FLORIDA		LOUISIANA		ARKANSAS		OKLAHOMA	
		C	D		C	D	C	D	C	D	C	D	C	D	C	D	C	D
RIND	W	53	28	N	69	28	72	47	64	43	61	36	57	36	52	37	45	41
	E	47	25	S	31	13	28	18	36	24	39	23	43	27	48	34	55	49
	ST		53			41		65		67		59		64		72		91
RINN	W	29	1	N	33	.3	100	4	50	2	100	3	**	**	77	8	60	4
	E	71	3	S	67	1	**	**	50	2	**	**	**	**	23	2	40	2
	ST		4			1		4		4		3		**		10		6
SKIN	W	35	15	N	56	33	73	23	63	19	74	28	42	15	67	12	**	**
	E	65	28	S	44	25	27	8	38	11	26	10	58	21	33	6	100	4
	ST		43			58		31		30		38		36		18		4

FOOD
(NO TEXT)

ITEM (89)
WORK SHEET (46)

		TENNESSEE			GEORGIA		ALABAMA		MISSISSIPPI		FLORIDA		LOUISIANA		ARKANSAS		OKLAHOMA	
		A	B		A	B	A	B	A	B	A	B	A	B	A	B	A	B
CHIPPED BEEF	W	21	4	N	14	3	9	2	3	1	7	2	2	.3	19	4	21	5
	E	30	6	S	7	2	2	.4	2	1	4	1	5	1	32	7	22	5
	ST	50	11		22	5	11	2	5	1	12	2	6	1	51	12	43	10
DRIED BEEF	W	17	8	N	19	9	5	2	3	2	8	4	4	1	28	9	25	8
	E	28	13	S	12	6	2	1	2	1	4	2	2	1	20	7	20	7
	ST	45	20		31	14	7	3	5	2	12	5	6	2	48	16	45	15
JERKED BEEF	W	13	.2	N	13	.2	13	.2	**	**	20	.3	**	**	50	1	**	**
	E	7	.1	S	20	.3	**	**	**	**	13	.2	17	.3	33	1	**	**
	ST	20	.3		33	1	13	.2	**	**	33	1	17	.3	83	2	**	**
JERKY	W	21	.3	N	**	**	**	**	7	.1	7	.1	17	.3	**	**	33	1
	E	29	.4	S	14	.2	**	**	7	.1	14	.2	**	**	**	**	50	1
	ST	50	1		14	.2	**	**	14	.2	21	.3	17	.3	**	**	83	2

		TENNESSEE			GEORGIA		ALABAMA		MISSISSIPPI		FLORIDA		LOUISIANA		ARKANSAS		OKLAHOMA	
		C	D		C	D	C	D	C	D	C	D	C	D	C	D	C	D
CHIPPED BEEF	W	41	14	N	66	15	82	33	55	17	63	18	25	8	38	15	48	18
	E	59	20	S	34	8	18	7	45	14	38	11	75	25	63	24	52	19
	ST		33			23		40		31		29		33		39		36
DRIED BEEF	W	37	23	N	61	44	68	38	68	43	69	42	67	33	58	32	55	31
	E	63	40	S	39	29	32	18	32	20	31	19	33	17	42	23	45	26
	ST		64			73		56		63		61		50		55		57
JERKED BEEF	W	67	1	N	40	1	100	4	**	**	60	4	**	**	60	4	**	**
	E	33	.3	S	60	2	**	**	**	**	40	2	100	8	40	2	**	**
	ST		1			3		4		**		6		8		6		**
JERKY	W	43	1	N	**	**	**	**	50	3	33	1	100	8	**	**	40	3
	E	57	1	S	100	1	**	**	50	3	67	2	**	**	**	**	60	4
	ST		2			1		**		6		4		8		**		7

ITEM (90)
WORK SHEET (46)

FOOD
MADE OF CORN MEAL, MEAT JUICE, AND SCRAPS

		TENNESSEE A	TENNESSEE B		GEORGIA A	GEORGIA B	ALABAMA A	ALABAMA B	MISSISSIPPI A	MISSISSIPPI B	FLORIDA A	FLORIDA B	LOUISIANA A	LOUISIANA B	ARKANSAS A	ARKANSAS B	OKLAHOMA A	OKLAHOMA B
CRIPPLE	W	**	**	N	25	1	10	.2	15	.3	5	.1	**	**	40	1	40	1
	E	25	1	S	15	.3	5	.1	**	**	**	**	**	**	20	.3	**	**
	ST	25	1		40	1	15	.3	15	.3	5	.1	**	**	60	1	40	1
PONHAWS	W	23	.3	N	15	.2	23	.3	**	**	**	**	25	.3	25	.3	50	1
	E	23	.3	S	15	.2	**	**	**	**	**	**	**	**	**	**	**	**
	ST	46	1		31	.4	23	.3	**	**	**	**	25	.3	25	.3	50	1
PONHOSS	W	8	.1	N	58	1	**	**	**	**	**	**	**	**	60	1	**	**
	E	17	.2	S	17	.2	**	**	**	**	**	**	**	**	20	.3	20	.3
	ST	25	.3		75	1	**	**	**	**	**	**	**	**	80	1	20	.3
SCRAPPLE	W	19	6	N	27	8	5	2	3	1	7	2	2	1	42	13	17	5
	E	22	7	S	9	3	2	1	2	1	4	1	2	1	22	6	14	4
	ST	41	13		37	11	7	2	5	1	11	3	5	1	64	19	31	9

		TENNESSEE C	TENNESSEE D		GEORGIA C	GEORGIA D	ALABAMA C	ALABAMA D	MISSISSIPPI C	MISSISSIPPI D	FLORIDA C	FLORIDA D	LOUISIANA C	LOUISIANA D	ARKANSAS C	ARKANSAS D	OKLAHOMA C	OKLAHOMA D
CRIPPLE	W	**	**	N	63	4	67	8	100	18	100	3	**	**	67	3	100	6
	E	100	4	S	38	2	33	4	**	**	**	**	**	**	33	2	**	**
	ST		4			6		12		18		3		**		5		6
PONHAWS	W	50	2	N	50	2	100	12	**	**	**	**	100	20	100	2	100	6
	E	50	2	S	50	2	**	**	**	**	**	**	**	**	**	**	**	**
	ST		4			3		12		**		**		20		2		6
PONHOSS	W	33	1	N	78	5	**	**	**	**	**	**	**	**	75	5	**	**
	E	67	1	S	22	2	**	**	**	**	**	**	**	**	25	2	100	3
	ST		2			7		**		**		**		**		/		3
SCRAPPLE	W	47	42	N	75	63	75	58	64	53	63	61	50	40	66	57	54	45
	E	53	47	S	25	21	25	19	36	29	38	36	50	40	34	30	46	39
	ST		90			84		77		82		97		80		87		84

ITEM (91)
WORK SHEET (47)

FOOD
PRESSED MEAT LOAF MADE OF HOGS JOWLS, HEAD, ETC.

		TENNESSEE A	TENNESSEE B		GEORGIA A	GEORGIA B	ALABAMA A	ALABAMA B	MISSISSIPPI A	MISSISSIPPI B	FLORIDA A	FLORIDA B	LOUISIANA A	LOUISIANA B	ARKANSAS A	ARKANSAS B	OKLAHOMA A	OKLAHOMA B
HEAD CHEESE	W	20	1	N	12	1	2	.1	4	.2	14	1	1	.3	33	8	31	8
	E	20	1	S	14	1	**	**	**	**	12	1	3	1	10	3	21	5
	ST	41	2		27	1	2	.1	4	.2	27	1	4	1	43	11	53	13
HOG(S) HEAD CHEESE	W	13	2	N	8	1	2	.2	3	.4	32	4	17	3	21	4	8	1
	E	5	1	S	15	2	5	1	4	1	14	2	26	5	15	3	13	3
	ST	18	2		23	3	7	1	7	1	45	6	43	8	36	7	21	4
SOUSE	W	23	14	N	14	9	7	4	5	3	5	3	7	4	35	17	9	5
	E	28	17	S	12	8	2	1	2	1	2	1	2	1	30	15	16	8
	ST	50	31		27	16	9	6	8	5	6	4	9	5	65	32	25	13
PRESSED MEAT	W	8	1	N	60	9	12	2	1	.2	**	**	**	**	33	1	17	1
	E	7	1	S	10	1	**	**	1	.1	1	.1	**	**	33	1	17	1
	ST	16	2		69	11	12	2	2	.3	1	.1	**	**	67	3	33	1

		TENNESSEE C	TENNESSEE D		GEORGIA C	GEORGIA D	ALABAMA C	ALABAMA D	MISSISSIPPI C	MISSISSIPPI D	FLORIDA C	FLORIDA D	LOUISIANA C	LOUISIANA D	ARKANSAS C	ARKANSAS D	OKLAHOMA C	OKLAHOMA D
HEAD CHEESE	W	50	3	N	46	2	100	1	100	3	54	6	33	3	77	16	59	25
	E	50	3	S	54	2	**	**	**	**	46	5	67	5	23	5	41	17
	ST		5			4		1		3		12		8		20		43
HOG(S) HEAD CHEESE	W	71	5	N	33	3	22	2	44	7	70	38	39	23	58	7	36	5
	E	29	2	S	67	7	78	9	56	8	30	16	61	36	42	5	64	8
	ST		7			10		11		15		54		59		13		13
SOUSE	W	45	37	N	54	28	76	50	69	53	76	25	77	26	53	33	37	15
	E	55	45	S	46	24	24	16	31	24	24	8	23	8	47	29	63	25
	ST		82			52		66		76		33		33		61		40
PRESSED MEAT	W	52	3	N	86	29	100	22	67	3	**	**	**	**	50	3	50	2
	E	48	3	S	14	5	**	**	33	2	100	1	**	**	50	3	50	2
	ST		6			34		22		5		1		**		5		5

ITEM (92)
WORK SHEET (48)

FOOD
A SWEET LIQUID SERVED WITH PUDDING

		TENNESSEE A	TENNESSEE B		GEORGIA A	GEORGIA B	ALABAMA A	ALABAMA B	MISSISSIPPI A	MISSISSIPPI B	FLORIDA A	FLORIDA B	LOUISIANA A	LOUISIANA B	ARKANSAS A	ARKANSAS B	OKLAHOMA A	OKLAHOMA B
DIP	W	13	1	N	17	1	1	.1	**	**	**	**	**	**	78	6	13	1
	E	66	5	S	1	.1	**	**	**	**	1	.1	**	**	4	.3	4	.3
	ST	79	6		19	1	1	.1	**	**	1	.1	**	**	83	7	17	1
DOPE	W	**	**	N	40	.2	**	**	20	.1	**	**	**	**	**	**	**	**
	E	40	.2	S	**	**	**	**	**	**	**	**	**	**	**	**	100	.3
	ST	40	.2		40	.2	**	**	20	.1	**	**	**	**	**	**	100	.3
DRESSING GRAVY	W	17	1	N	17	1	10	1	**	**	2	.1	11	.3	56	2	**	**
	E	28	2	S	22	1	**	**	3	.2	2	.1	11	.3	11	.3	11	.3
	ST	45	3		38	2	10	1	3	.2	3	.2	22	1	67	2	11	.3
SAUCE	W	20	13	N	18	12	7	5	5	3	9	6	8	5	23	16	16	11
	E	21	14	S	12	8	3	2	2	2	4	3	8	5	27	18	18	12
	ST	41	27		29	20	10	7	7	5	13	9	16	11	50	34	34	23

		TENNESSEE C	TENNESSEE D		GEORGIA C	GEORGIA D	ALABAMA C	ALABAMA D	MISSISSIPPI C	MISSISSIPPI D	FLORIDA C	FLORIDA D	LOUISIANA C	LOUISIANA D	ARKANSAS C	ARKANSAS D	OKLAHOMA C	OKLAHOMA D
DIP	W	16	3	N	92	5	100	1	**	**	**	**	**	**	95	15	75	4
	E	84	13	S	8	.4	**	**	**	**	100	1	**	**	5	1	25	1
	ST		16			6		1		**		1		**		16		6
DOPE	W	**	**	N	100	1	**	**	100	2	**	**	**	**	**	**	**	**
	E	100	1	S	**	**	**	**	**	**	**	**	**	**	**	**	100	1
	ST		1			1		**		2		**		**		**		1
DRESSING GRAVY	W	37	3	N	43	4	100	8	**	**	50	1	50	3	83	4	**	**
	E	63	5	S	57	6	**	**	100	4	50	1	50	3	17	1	100	1
	ST		8			10		8		4		2		6		5		1
SAUCE	W	49	37	N	60	50	73	66	67	63	67	65	50	47	46	36	48	44
	E	51	39	S	40	33	27	24	33	31	33	32	50	47	54	43	52	47
	ST		76			83		91		94		97		94		79		91

TABLE I

ITEM (93)
WORK SHEET (47)

FOOD
THICK, SOUR MILK

		TENNESSEE A	TENNESSEE B		GEORGIA A	GEORGIA B	ALABAMA A	ALABAMA B	MISSISSIPPI A	MISSISSIPPI B	FLORIDA A	FLORIDA B	LOUISIANA A	LOUISIANA B	ARKANSAS A	ARKANSAS B	OKLAHOMA A	OKLAHOMA B
CLABBER	W	18	10	N	20	11	6	3	4	2	12	6	9	4	17	8	13	6
	E	9	5	S	19	10	3	2	3	1	5	3	11	5	35	17	15	7
	ST	27	15		39	21	10	5	7	4	17	9	20	10	52	25	28	13
CLABBER MILK	W	20	3	N	11	2	10	2	4	1	1	.1	2	1	26	8	16	5
	E	44	7	S	3	1	2	.4	2	.4	2	.4	5	1	20	6	31	9
	ST	65	11		14	2	12	2	6	1	3	1	7	2	46	13	47	14
CLABBERED MILK	W	20	4	N	15	3	6	1	4	1	2	.4	5	1	50	8	11	2
	E	47	10	S	4	1	2	.3	1	.1	1	.1	5	1	9	1	20	3
	ST	67	14		19	4	7	1	5	1	3	1	9	1	59	9	32	5
CRUDDLED MILK	W	**	**	N	**	**	25	.1	25	.1	**	**	25	.3	**	**	**	**
	E	50	.2	S	**	**	**	**	**	**	**	**	**	**	25	.3	50	1
	ST	50	.2		**	**	25	.1	25	.1	**	**	25	.3	25	.3	50	1
CURDLED MILK	W	27	1	N	23	1	12	.3	**	**	**	**	**	**	22	1	44	1
	E	31	1	S	4	.1	4	.1	**	**	**	**	**	**	11	.3	22	1
	ST	58	2		27	1	15	.4	**	**	**	**	**	**	33	1	67	2
BONNY CLABBER	W	60	.3	N	20	.1	**	**	**	**	**	**	**	**	**	**	**	**
	E	20	.1	S	**	**	**	**	**	**	**	**	**	**	**	**	**	**
	ST	80	.4		20	.1	**	**	**	**	**	**	**	**	**	**	**	**
LOBBERED MILK	W	**	**	N	33	.1	33	.1	**	**	**	**	**	**	75	1	**	**
	E	**	**	S	**	**	**	**	33	.1	**	**	**	**	25	.3	**	**
	ST	**	**		33	.1	33	.1	33	.1	**	**	**	**	100	1	**	**
LOPPERED MILK					(NO RESPONSE)													
					(NO RESPONSE)													
					(NO RESPONSE)													
THICK MILK	W	**	**	N	33	.1	**	**	**	**	**	**	**	**	50	.3	**	**
	E	67	.2	S	**	**	**	**	**	**	**	**	**	**	50	.3	**	**
	ST	67	.2		33	.1	**	**	**	**	**	**	**	**	100	1	**	**
BONNY CLAPPER					(NO RESPONSE)													
	E	100	.1	S	**	**	**	**	**	**	**	**	**	**	**	**	**	**
	ST	100	.1		**	**	**	**	**	**	**	**	**	**	**	**	**	**

ITEM (93) (CONTINUED) THICK, SOUR MILK

		TENNESSEE C	TENNESSEE D		GEORGIA C	GEORGIA D	ALABAMA C	ALABAMA D	MISSISSIPPI C	MISSISSIPPI D	FLORIDA C	FLORIDA D	LOUISIANA C	LOUISIANA D	ARKANSAS C	ARKANSAS D	OKLAHOMA C	OKLAHOMA D
CLABBER	W	67	23	N	52	39	64	36	62	40	68	61	44	32	33	16	46	18
	E	33	12	S	48	36	36	20	38	24	32	29	56	39	67	33	54	21
	ST		35			74		56		64		90		71		49		38
CLABBER MILK	W	32	8	N	77	6	80	18	60	10	20	1	33	5	57	15	34	13
	E	68	18	S	23	2	20	4	40	7	80	4	67	11	43	11	66	26
	ST		26			8		22		17		5		16		26		39
CLABBERED MILK	W	30	10	N	79	11	79	12	89	14	80	4	50	5	85	15	36	5
	E	70	23	S	21	3	21	3	11	2	20	1	50	5	15	3	64	9
	ST		33			14		16		16		5		11		18		14
CRUDDLED MILK	W	**	**	N	**	**	100	1	100	2	**	**	100	3	**	**	**	**
	E	100	.4	S	**	**	**	**	**	**	**	**	**	**	100	1	100	2
	ST		.4			**		1		2		**		3		1		2
CURDLED MILK	W	47	2	N	86	2	75	3	**	**	**	**	**	**	67	1	67	4
	E	53	2	S	14	.3	25	1	**	**	**	**	**	**	33	1	33	2
	ST		4			3		4		**		**		**		2		6
BONNY CLABBER	W	75	1	N	100	.3	**	**	**	**	**	**	**	**	**	**	**	**
	E	25	.2	S	**	**	**	**	**	**	**	**	**	**	**	**	**	**
	ST		1			.3		**		**		**		**		**		**
LOBBERED MILK	W	**	**	N	100	.3	100	1	**	**	**	**	**	**	75	2	**	**
	E	**	**	S	**	**	**	**	100	2	**	**	**	**	25	1	**	**
	ST		**			.3		1		2		**		**		3		**
LOPPERED MILK					(NO RESPONSE)													
					(NO RESPONSE)													
	ST		**			**		**		**		**		**		**		**
THICK MILK	W	**	**	N	100	.3	**	**	**	**	**	**	**	**	50	1	**	**
	E	100	.4	S	**	**	**	**	**	**	**	**	**	**	50	1	**	**
	ST		.4			.3		**		**		**		**		1		**
BONNY CLAPPER					(NO RESPONSE)													
	E	100	.2	S	**	**	**	**	**	**	**	**	**	**	**	**	**	**
	ST		.2			**		**		**		**		**		**		**

TABLE I

FOOD
HOME MADE CHEESE

ITEM (94)
WORK SHEET (47)

		TENNESSEE A	TENNESSEE B		GEORGIA A	GEORGIA B	ALABAMA A	ALABAMA B	MISSISSIPPI A	MISSISSIPPI B	FLORIDA A	FLORIDA B	LOUISIANA A	LOUISIANA B	ARKANSAS A	ARKANSAS B	OKLAHOMA A	OKLAHOMA B
CLABBER	W	22	1	N	24	1	4	.2	6	.3	8	.4	**	**	33	2	22	1
CHEESE	E	20	1	S	6	.3	4	.2	6	.3	2	.1	11	1	17	1	17	1
	ST	41	2		29	2	8	.4	12	1	10	1	11	1	50	3	39	3
COTTAGE	W	18	10	N	19	10	5	3	4	2	6	3	7	4	29	17	16	10
CHEESE	E	31	16	S	9	5	1	1	2	1	5	2	3	2	26	16	19	11
	ST	49	26		28	15	7	4	5	3	10	6	10	6	55	33	35	21
CURD CHEESE	W	8	.3	N	22	1	3	.1	8	.3	14	1	14	.3	43	1	**	**
	E	16	1	S	19	1	**	**	**	**	11	.4	**	**	29	1	14	.3
	ST	24	1		41	2	3	.1	8	.3	24	1	14	.3	71	2	14	.3
CURD(S)	W	5	.2	N	14	1	11	.4	**	**	41	2	**	**	100	.3	**	**
	E	3	.1	S	8	.3	3	.1	**	**	16	1	**	**	**	**	**	**
	ST	8	.3		22	1	14	1	**	**	57	2	**	**	100	.3	**	**
DUTCH CHEESE	W	25	.1	N	25	.1	**	**	**	**	**	**	**	**	**	**	**	**
	E	25	.1	S	25	.1	**	**	**	**	**	**	**	**	100	.3	**	**
	ST	50	.2		50	.2	**	**	**	**	**	**	**	**	100	.3	**	**
HOME MADE	W	21	4	N	16	3	13	2	3	.4	4	1	8	1	40	6	13	2
CHEESE	E	20	3	S	19	3	4	1	1	.2	1	.1	18	3	5	1	18	3
	ST	41	7		34	6	16	3	4	1	4	1	25	4	45	6	30	4
POT CHEESE					(NO RESPONSE)													
	E	50	.1	S	**	**	**	**	50	.1	**	**	**	**	**	**	**	**
	ST	50	.1		**	**	**	**	50	.1	**	**	**	**	**	**	**	**
SMEARCASE	W	67	1	N	**	**	**	**	6	.1	6	.1	**	**	50	2	20	1
	E	22	.4	S	**	**	**	**	**	**	**	**	**	**	10	.3	20	1
	ST	89	2		**	**	**	**	6	.1	6	.1	**	**	60	2	40	1

ITEM (94)

(CONTINUED) HOME MADE CHEESE

		TENNESSEE C	TENNESSEE D		GEORGIA C	GEORGIA D	ALABAMA C	ALABAMA D	MISSISSIPPI C	MISSISSIPPI D	FLORIDA C	FLORIDA D	LOUISIANA C	LOUISIANA D	ARKANSAS C	ARKANSAS D	OKLAHOMA C	OKLAHOMA D
CLABBER CHEESE	W	52	3	N	80	5	50	3	50	7	80	4	**	**	67	5	57	5
	E	48	3	S	20	1	50	3	50	7	20	1	100	7	33	2	43	4
	ST		6			6		6		13		5		7		7		9
COTTAGE CHEESE	W	38	26	N	68	41	79	39	71	44	56	31	71	40	52	36	47	33
	E	62	43	S	32	19	21	10	29	18	44	25	29	17	48	33	53	38
	ST		68			61		49		62		56		57		70		71
CURD CHEESE	W	33	1	N	53	3	100	1	100	7	56	5	100	3	60	2	**	**
	E	67	2	S	47	3	**	**	**	**	44	4	**	**	40	2	100	1
	ST		2			6		1		7		9		3		4		1
CURD(S)	W	67	1	N	63	2	80	6	**	**	71	15	**	**	100	1	**	**
	E	33	.2	S	30	1	20	1	**	**	29	6	**	**	**	**	**	**
	ST		1			3		7		**		22		**		1		**
DUTCH CHEESE	W	50	.2	N	50	.4	**	**	**	**	**	**	**	**	**	**	**	**
	E	50	.2	S	50	.4	**	**	**	**	**	**	**	**	100	1	**	**
	ST		1			1		**		**		**		**		1		**
HOME MADE CHEESE	W	52	9	N	45	10	77	29	67	9	86	6	30	10	89	12	42	6
	E	48	9	S	55	12	23	9	33	4	14	1	70	23	11	2	58	9
	ST		18			23		37		13		7		33		14		15
POT CHEESE					(NO RESPONSE)													
	E	100	.2	S	**	**	**	**	100	2	**	**	**	**	**	**	**	**
	ST		.2			**		**		2		**		**		**		**
SMEARCASE	W	75	3	N	**	**	**	**	100	2	100	1	**	**	83	4	50	2
	E	25	1	S	**	**	**	**	**	**	**	**	**	**	17	1	50	2
	ST		4			**		**		2		1		**		5		5

ITEM (95)
WORK SHEET (48)

FOOD
FOOD EATEN BETWEEN REGULAR MEALS

		TENNESSEE			GEORGIA		ALABAMA		MISSISSIPPI		FLORIDA		LOUISIANA		ARKANSAS		OKLAHOMA	
		A	B		A	B	A	B	A	B	A	B	A	B	A	B	A	B
A BITE	W	19	2	N	15	2	6	1	3	.3	5	1	7	1	37	4	7	1
	E	22	2	S	17	2	4	.4	4	.4	5	1	13	1	17	2	20	2
	ST	41	5		33	4	10	1	6	1	10	1	20	2	53	6	27	3
LUNCH	W	29	1	N	20	1	7	.3	**	**	17	1	22	1	33	1	11	.3
	E	12	1	S	10	.4	**	**	5	.2	**	**	11	.3	11	.3	11	.3
	ST	41	2		29	1	7	.3	5	.2	17	1	33	1	44	1	22	1
A PIECE	W	10	.1	N	10	.1	**	**	**	**	**	**	**	**	**	**	100	3
	E	40	.4	S	10	.1	10	.1	**	**	20	.2	**	**	**	**	**	**
	ST	50	1		20	.2	10	.1	**	**	20	.2	**	**	**	**	100	3
PIECE MEAL	W	14	.2	N	7	.1	7	.1	**	**	14	.2	**	**	60	1	20	.3
	E	36	1	S	14	.2	7	.1	**	**	**	**	**	**	**	**	20	.3
	ST	50	1		21	.3	14	.2	**	**	14	.2	**	**	60	1	40	1
A SNACK	W	19	14	N	18	14	7	5	5	4	7	5	7	5	27	21	16	12
	E	26	20	S	11	8	2	2	2	1	4	3	7	6	25	19	18	14
	ST	45	34		29	22	9	7	7	5	11	8	14	11	52	40	34	26

		TENNESSEE			GEORGIA		ALABAMA		MISSISSIPPI		FLORIDA		LOUISIANA		ARKANSAS		OKLAHOMA	
		C	D		C	D	C	D	C	D	C	D	C	D	C	D	C	D
A BITE	W	47	5	N	47	6	64	8	43	5	45	5	33	5	69	8	25	2
	E	53	6	S	53	7	36	5	57	7	55	6	67	10	31	4	75	6
	ST		11			14		13		12		11		15		12		9
LUNCH	W	71	3	N	67	3	100	4	**	**	100	7	67	5	75	2	50	1
	E	29	1	S	33	2	**	**	100	3	**	**	33	3	25	1	50	1
	ST		4			5		4		3		7		8		3		2
A PIECE	W	20	.2	N	50	.3	**	**	**	**	**	**	**	**	**	**	100	9
	E	80	1	S	50	.3	100	1	**	**	100	2	**	**	**	**	**	**
	ST		1			1		1		**		2		**		**		9
PIECE MEAL	W	29	.4	N	33	.3	50	1	**	**	100	2	**	**	100	2	50	1
	E	71	1	S	67	1	50	1	**	**	**	**	**	**	**	**	50	1
	ST		2			1		2		**		2		**		2		2
A SNACK	W	42	34	N	64	51	75	60	71	60	64	50	47	36	52	43	47	37
	E	58	48	S	36	29	25	20	29	24	36	28	53	41	48	40	53	42
	ST		82			80		80		84		78		77		83		78

THE HOUSE AND ITS ENVIRONS
A SMALL GARDEN FOR TABLE USE

ITEM (96)
WORK SHEET (50)

		TENNESSEE			GEORGIA		ALABAMA		MISSISSIPPI		FLORIDA		LOUISIANA		ARKANSAS		OKLAHOMA	
		A	B		A	B	A	B	A	B	A	B	A	B	A	B	A	B
FAMILY GARDEN	W	18	1	N	34	2	2	.1	4	.2	2	.1	**	**	62	3	8	.3
	E	18	1	S	18	1	**	**	**	**	5	.3	**	**	15	1	15	1
	ST	36	2		52	3	2	.1	4	.2	7	.4	**	**	77	4	23	1
GARDEN PATCH	W	23	2	N	8	1	3	.2	3	.2	14	1	6	.3	38	2	19	1
	E	29	2	S	9	1	5	.3	3	.2	3	.2	**	**	6	.3	31	2
	ST	52	4		17	1	8	1	6	.4	17	1	6	.3	44	3	50	3
GARDEN	W	18	9	N	18	9	8	4	4	2	6	3	7	4	27	14	17	9
	E	26	13	S	13	6	2	1	2	1	3	1	7	4	26	14	17	9
	ST	44	22		31	15	10	5	6	3	9	4	14	8	52	28	34	18
KITCHEN GARDEN	W	26	1	N	5	.1	5	.1	5	.1	11	.2	**	**	**	**	100	.3
	E	26	1	S	11	.2	**	**	**	**	11	.2	**	**	**	**	**	**
	ST	53	1		16	.3	5	.1	5	.1	21	.4	**	**	**	**	100	.3
VEGETABLE GARDEN	W	19	6	N	20	7	8	3	4	1	9	3	9	3	28	8	13	4
	E	22	7	S	9	3	3	1	2	1	4	1	11	3	21	6	18	5
	ST	41	14		29	10	11	4	7	2	13	4	20	6	49	14	32	9

		TENNESSEE			GEORGIA		ALABAMA		MISSISSIPPI		FLORIDA		LOUISIANA		ARKANSAS		OKLAHOMA	
		C	D		C	D	C	D	C	D	C	D	C	D	C	D	C	D
FAMILY GARDEN	W	50	2	N	66	7	100	1	100	4	25	1	**	**	80	6	33	1
	E	50	2	S	34	4	**	**	**	**	75	3	**	**	20	1	67	2
	ST		5			10		1		4		4		**		7		3
GARDEN PATCH	W	44	4	N	45	2	40	2	50	4	02	9	100	3	86	4	38	3
	E	56	5	S	55	2	60	3	50	4	18	2	**	**	14	1	63	6
	ST		8			4		5		7		11		3		5		9
GARDEN	W	42	22	N	58	31	78	41	67	33	70	29	52	29	51	30	50	28
	E	50	30	S	42	22	22	12	33	16	30	13	48	26	49	28	50	28
	ST		52			52		53		49		42		55		58		57
KITCHEN GARDEN	W	50	1	N	33	.3	100	1	100	2	50	2	**	**	**	**	100	1
	E	50	1	S	67	1	**	**	**	**	50	2	**	**	**	**	**	**
	ST		2			1		1		2		4		**		**		1
VEGETABLE GARDEN	W	47	15	N	70	23	72	28	67	25	68	27	44	18	58	17	42	13
	E	53	17	S	30	10	28	11	33	13	32	13	56	24	43	13	58	17
	ST		32			33		39		38		40		42		30		30

TABLE I

CROPS
THE CENTER OF A CHERRY

ITEM (97)
WORK SHEET (54)

		TENNESSEE A	TENNESSEE B		GEORGIA A	GEORGIA B	ALABAMA A	ALABAMA B	MISSISSIPPI A	MISSISSIPPI B	FLORIDA A	FLORIDA B	LOUISIANA A	LOUISIANA B	ARKANSAS A	ARKANSAS B	OKLAHOMA A	OKLAHOMA B
PIT(A)	W	22	6	N	18	5	8	2	6	2	7	2	1	.3	26	9	21	7
	E	20	5	S	11	3	3	1	1	.3	6	1	11	4	26	9	15	5
	ST	41	11		28	7	11	3	7	2	12	3	12	4	53	18	36	12
SEED(A)	W	19	10	N	19	10	6	3	3	2	6	3	10	5	32	18	14	8
	E	29	16	S	11	6	2	1	2	1	3	1	5	3	20	11	19	10
	ST	48	26		29	16	8	4	5	3	9	5	15	8	52	29	33	18
STONE(A)	W	28	2	N	13	1	7	1	2	.2	5	.4	5	.3	38	3	5	.3
	E	27	2	S	6	1	1	.1	4	.3	6	1	14	1	14	1	24	2
	ST	55	5		20	2	9	1	6	1	11	1	19	1	52	4	29	2
KERNEL(A)	W	19	1	N	29	1	7	.3	5	.2	17	1	**	**	50	.3	**	**
	E	5	.2	S	19	1	**	**	**	**	**	**	**	**	50	.3	**	**
	ST	24	1		48	2	7	.3	5	.2	17	1	**	**	100	1	**	**
HEART(A)	W	22	.4	N	6	.1	17	.3	6	.1	11	.2	**	**	**	**	50	.3
	E	17	.3	S	6	.1	11	.2	**	**	6	.1	**	**	**	**	50	.3
	ST	39	1		11	.2	28	1	6	.1	17	.3	**	**	**	**	100	1

		TENNESSEE C	TENNESSEE D		GEORGIA C	GEORGIA D	ALABAMA C	ALABAMA D	MISSISSIPPI C	MISSISSIPPI D	FLORIDA C	FLORIDA D	LOUISIANA C	LOUISIANA D	ARKANSAS C	ARKANSAS D	OKLAHOMA C	OKLAHOMA D
PIT(A)	W	52	13	N	63	17	71	23	83	28	55	18	9	3	50	18	59	22
	E	48	12	S	38	10	29	9	17	6	45	14	91	26	50	18	41	15
	ST		25			27		33		34		32		29		35		37
SEED(A)	W	39	24	N	63	37	72	36	63	32	70	34	65	39	62	35	43	24
	E	61	37	S	37	21	28	14	37	19	30	14	35	21	38	21	57	31
	ST		61			59		50		51		48		61		56		55
STONE(A)	W	51	5	N	69	4	86	7	40	4	44	4	25	3	73	6	17	1
	E	49	5	S	31	2	14	1	60	6	56	5	75	8	27	2	83	5
	ST		11			6		8		9		9		11		8		6
KERNEL(A)	W	80	2	N	60	5	100	3	100	4	100	7	**	**	50	1	**	**
	E	20	.4	S	40	3	**	**	**	**	**	**	**	**	50	1	**	**
	ST		2			8		3		4		7		**		1		**
HEART(A)	W	57	1	N	50	.3	60	3	100	2	67	2	**	**	**	**	50	1
	E	43	1	S	50	.3	40	2	**	**	33	1	**	**	**	**	50	1
	ST		2			1		6		2		3		**		**		2

ITEM (97)
WORK SHEET (54)

CROPS
THE CENTER OF A PEACH

		TENNESSEE			GEORGIA		ALABAMA		MISSISSIPPI		FLORIDA		LOUISIANA		ARKANSAS		OKLAHOMA	
		A	B		A	B	A	B	A	B	A	B	A	B	A	B	A	B
PIT(B)	W	22	1	N	13	1	6	.4	3	.2	2	.1	**	**	31	2	25	1
	E	27	2	S	14	1	2	.1	**	**	13	1	19	1	19	1	6	.3
	ST	48	3		27	2	8	1	3	.2	14	1	19	1	50	3	31	2
SEED(B)	W	19	13	N	18	12	7	5	5	3	8	6	8	5	30	20	17	11
	E	25	18	S	12	8	2	1	2	1	3	2	3	2	23	15	19	13
	ST	44	31		30	21	9	6	6	4	11	7	11	7	53	35	36	24
STONE(B)	W	26	3	N	16	2	5	1	2	.2	5	1	5	1	20	3	18	3
	E	23	3	S	8	1	5	1	4	1	6	1	27	4	18	3	11	2
	ST	49	6		23	3	10	1	6	1	11	1	32	5	39	6	30	5
KERNEL(B)	W	13	1	N	35	3	7	1	**	**	8	1	9	.3	36	1	**	**
	E	10	1	S	21	2	3	.2	**	**	4	.3	9	.3	45	2	**	**
	ST	22	2		56	4	10	1	**	**	13	1	18	1	82	3	**	**
HEART(B)	W	10	.1	N	10	.1	**	**	10	.1	**	**	**	**	33	.3	**	**
	E	30	.3	S	**	**	20	.2	10	.1	10	.1	**	**	67	1	**	**
	ST	40	.4		10	.1	20	.2	20	.2	10	.1	**	**	100	1	**	**

		TENNESSEE			GEORGIA		ALABAMA		MISSISSIPPI		FLORIDA		LOUISIANA		ARKANSAS		OKLAHOMA	
		C	D		C	D	C	D	C	D	C	D	C	D	C	D	C	D
PIT(B)	W	45	3	N	47	3	80	5	100	4	11	1	**	**	63	4	80	5
	E	55	4	S	53	3	20	1	**	**	89	8	100	8	38	2	20	1
	ST		8			6		6		4		9		8		6		6
SEED(B)	W	43	31	N	60	42	77	53	72	57	75	52	70	36	57	41	46	36
	E	57	42	S	40	28	23	16	28	22	25	17	30	15	43	31	54	42
	ST		74			70		70		80		69		51		73		79
STONE(B)	W	53	7	N	67	6	50	7	29	4	46	6	14	5	53	7	62	9
	E	47	7	S	33	3	50	7	71	9	54	7	86	31	47	6	38	6
	ST		14			9		14		13		13		36		13		15
KERNEL(B)	W	56	2	N	63	9	71	6	**	**	67	6	50	3	44	3	**	**
	E	44	2	S	38	5	29	2	**	**	33	3	50	3	56	4	**	**
	ST		4			14		8		**		9		5		7		**
HEART(B)	W	25	.2	N	100	.3	**	**	50	2	**	**	**	**	33	1	**	**
	E	75	1	S	**	**	100	2	50	2	100	1	**	**	67	1	**	**
	ST		1			.3		2		4		1		**		2		**

CROPS
A PEACH WHOSE MEAT STICKS TO THE SEED

ITEM (98)
WORK SHEET (54)

		TENNESSEE A	TENNESSEE B		GEORGIA A	GEORGIA B	ALABAMA A	ALABAMA B	MISSISSIPPI A	MISSISSIPPI B	FLORIDA A	FLORIDA B	LOUISIANA A	LOUISIANA B	ARKANSAS A	ARKANSAS B	OKLAHOMA A	OKLAHOMA B
CLING	W	21	2	N	13	2	13	2	3	.4	6	1	2	1	26	8	27	8
	E	24	3	S	10	1	3	.3	**	**	7	1	6	2	16	5	23	7
	ST	45	5		23	3	16	2	3	.4	13	2	9	3	41	12	50	15
CLING PEACH	W	21	3	N	16	2	7	1	7	1	9	1	13	3	30	6	20	4
	E	21	3	S	11	2	3	1	1	.2	3	1	5	1	16	3	16	3
	ST	42	7		27	4	10	2	9	1	12	2	18	4	46	9	36	7
CLINGSTONE	W	22	6	N	23	7	4	1	3	1	9	3	3	1	29	7	8	2
	E	25	7	S	7	2	1	.3	2	1	4	1	9	2	32	8	18	4
	ST	47	13		30	9	5	1	5	1	13	4	12	3	62	14	26	6
CLINGSTONE PEACH	W	19	2	N	20	2	7	1	4	.4	7	1	11	1	41	4	7	1
	E	29	3	S	6	1	3	.3	3	.3	4	.4	7	1	22	2	11	1
	ST	48	5		25	3	9	1	7	1	10	1	19	2	63	6	19	2
HARD PEACH	W	10	.3	N	7	.2	17	1	3	.1	10	.3	**	**	**	**	**	**
	E	28	1	S	7	.2	10	.3	7	.2	**	**	**	**	**	**	**	**
	ST	38	1		14	.4	28	1	10	.3	10	.3	**	**	**	**	**	**
PLUM PEACH	W	27	5	N	27	5	10	2	6	1	**	**	**	**	56	5	4	.3
	E	29	5	S	2	.4	**	**	**	**	**	**	**	**	36	3	4	.3
	ST	56	10		29	5	10	2	6	1	**	**	**	**	92	8	8	1
PRESS PEACH	W	1	.1	N	13	1	2	.2	1	.1	15	2	67	2	**	**	**	**
	E	**	**	S	58	6	4	.4	6	1	**	**	**	**	33	1	**	**
	ST	1	.1		71	8	6	1	7	1	15	2	67	2	33	1	**	**

ITEM (98)

(CONTINUED) A PEACH WHOSE MEAT STICKS TO THE SEED

		TENNESSEE			GEORGIA		ALABAMA		MISSISSIPPI		FLORIDA		LOUISIANA		ARKANSAS		OKLAHOMA	
		C	D		C	D	C	D	C	D	C	D	C	D	C	D	C	D
CLING	W	46	6	N	58	5	83	17	100	7	47	7	29	6	62	15	54	26
	E	54	7	S	42	4	17	3	**	**	53	8	71	14	38	9	46	22
	ST		13			8		21		7		15		19		24		48
CLING PEACH	W	51	8	N	59	8	67	11	85	19	72	13	70	19	65	12	55	13
	E	49	8	S	41	6	33	6	15	3	28	5	30	8	35	6	45	11
	ST		16			13		17		22		18		28		18		24
CLINGSTONE	W	48	15	N	76	21	77	11	57	14	68	25	25	6	48	13	29	6
	E	52	17	S	24	7	23	3	43	10	32	12	75	17	53	15	71	14
	ST		32			27		15		24		37		22		28		20
CLINGSTONE PEACH	W	39	5	N	78	7	70	8	57	7	64	7	60	8	65	8	40	2
	F	61	8	S	22	2	30	3	43	5	36	4	40	6	35	4	60	4
	ST		13			9		11		12		11		14		12		6
HARD PEACH	W	27	1	N	50	1	63	6	33	2	100	3	**	**	**	**	**	**
	E	73	2	S	50	1	38	3	67	3	**	**	**	**	**	**	**	**
	ST		3			1		9		5		3		**		**		**
PLUM PEACH	W	48	12	N	92	15	100	20	100	17	**	**	**	**	61	10	50	1
	E	52	13	S	8	1	**	**	**	**	**	**	**	**	39	6	50	1
	ST		24			17		20		17		**		**		16		2
PRESS PEACH	W	100	.2	N	19	5	33	2	14	2	100	16	10C	17	**	**	**	**
	E	**	**	S	81	20	67	5	86	10	**	**	**	**	100	2	**	**
	ST		.2			24		7		12		16		17		2		**

CROPS
A PEACH WHOSE MEAT EASILY SEPARATES FROM THE SEED

ITEM (99)
WORK SHEET (54)

		TENNESSEE A	TENNESSEE B		GEORGIA A	GEORGIA B	ALABAMA A	ALABAMA B	MISSISSIPPI A	MISSISSIPPI B	FLORIDA A	FLORIDA B	LOUISIANA A	LOUISIANA B	ARKANSAS A	ARKANSAS B	OKLAHOMA A	OKLAHOMA B
CLEAR SEED	W	6	2	N	32	9	11	3	6	2	11	3	27	3	12	1	4	.3
	E	1	.2	S	27	7	2	1	3	1	2	.4	**	**	58	5	**	**
	ST	7	2		60	16	13	3	8	2	12	3	27	3	69	6	4	.3
CLEARSEED PEACH	W	10	1	N	27	2	15	1	5	.4	8	1	43	2	21	1	**	**
	E	6	1	S	18	2	7	1	4	.3	**	**	**	**	36	2	**	**
	ST	15	1		45	4	23	2	8	1	8	1	43	2	57	3	**	**
CLEARSTONE	W	11	1	N	43	3	6	.4	6	.4	13	1	8	.3	8	.3	8	.3
	E	3	.2	S	5	.3	**	**	3	.2	10	1	15	1	54	3	8	.3
	ST	14	1		48	3	6	.4	10	1	22	1	23	1	62	3	15	1
CLEAVESTONE	W	33	.1	N	33	.1	**	**	**	**	**	**	**	**	**	**	**	**
	E	**	**	S	33	.1	**	**	**	**	**	**	**	**	**	**	**	**
	ST	33	.1		67	.2	**	**	**	**	**	**	**	**	**	**	**	**
FREE PEACH	W	50	.3	N	17	.1	**	**	17	.1	**	**	**	**	**	**	**	**
	E	17	.1	S	**	**	**	**	**	**	**	**	**	**	**	**	100	.3
	ST	67	.4		17	.1	**	**	17	.1	**	**	**	**	**	**	100	.3
FREESTONE	W	29	8	N	8	2	6	2	4	1	6	2	1	.3	34	14	17	7
	E	37	10	S	1	.2	1	.3	2	.4	7	2	8	3	20	8	21	9
	ST	66	17		9	2	7	2	6	1	13	3	9	4	54	22	37	16
FREESTONE PEACH	W	33	5	N	9	1	3	1	3	1	4	1	8	2	40	9	14	3
	E	36	6	S	5	1	2	.3	3	1	1	.2	8	2	17	4	14	3
	ST	69	11		14	2	5	1	6	1	6	1	15	4	57	13	28	6
OPEN PEACH	W	20	.1	N	20	.1	**	**	**	**	**	**	25	.3	**	**	50	1
	E	60	.3	S	**	**	**	**	**	**	**	**	**	**	**	**	25	.3
	ST	80	.4		20	.1	**	**	**	**	**	**	25	.3	**	**	75	1
OPEN SEED	W	**	**	N	**	**	**	**	**	**	**	**	**	**	**	**	100	.3
	E	75	.3	S	**	**	25	.1	**	**	**	**	**	**	**	**	**	**
	ST	75	.3		**	**	25	.1	**	**	**	**	**	**	**	**	100	.3
OPEN SEED PEACH	W	**	**	N	**	**	**	**	**	**	**	**	**	**	**	**	50	.3
	E	100	.1	S	**	**	**	**	**	**	**	**	**	**	50	.3	**	**
	ST	100	.1		**	**	**	**	**	**	**	**	**	**	50	.3	50	.3
OPEN STONE	W	10	.3	N	17	1	**	**	**	**	**	**	**	**	**	**	**	**
	E	73	2	S	**	**	**	**	**	**	**	**	**	**	**	**	**	**
	ST	83	3		17	1	**	**	**	**	**	**	**	**	**	**	**	**
OPEN STONE PEACH	W	15	.2	N	8	.1	**	**	**	**	**	**	**	**	**	**	**	**
	E	77	1	S	**	**	**	**	**	**	**	**	**	**	**	**	100	.3
	ST	92	1		8	.1	**	**	**	**	**	**	**	**	**	**	100	.3
SOFT PEACH	W	44	3	N	8	1	3	.2	3	.2	8	1	**	**	27	1	9	.3
	E	25	2	S	7	1	1	.1	**	**	**	**	**	**	18	1	45	2
	ST	69	5		15	1	4	.3	3	.2	8	1	**	**	45	2	55	2

ITEM (99) (CONTINUED) A PEACH WHOSE MEAT EASILY SEPARATES FROM THE SEED

		TENNESSEE			GEORGIA		ALABAMA		MISSISSIPPI		FLORIDA		LOUISIANA		ARKANSAS		OKLAHOMA	
		C	D		C	D	C	D	C	D	C	D	C	D	C	D	C	D
CLEAR SEED	W	89	4	N	54	29	85	33	68	24	88	28	100	19	17	2	100	1
	E	11	.4	S	46	25	15	6	32	11	13	4	**	**	83	11	**	**
	ST		4			54		38		35		32		19		13		1
CLEARSEED PEACH	W	62	2	N	61	8	68	15	57	6	100	7	100	16	38	2	**	**
	E	38	1	S	39	5	32	7	43	5	**	**	**	**	63	4	**	**
	ST		3			13		22		11		7		16		6		**
CLEARSTONE	W	78	2	N	90	9	100	5	67	6	57	8	33	3	13	1	50	1
	E	22	.4	S	10	1	**	**	33	3	43	6	67	5	88	5	50	1
	ST		2			10		5		10		14		8		6		3
CLEAVESTONE	W	100	.2	N	50	.3	**	**	**	**	**	**	**	**	**	**	**	**
	E	**	**	S	50	.3	**	**	**	**	**	**	**	**	**	**	**	**
	ST		.2			1		**		**		**		**		**		**
FREE PEACH	W	75	1	N	100	.3	**	**	100	2	**	**	**	**	**	**	**	**
	E	25	.2	S	**	**	**	**	**	**	**	**	**	**	**	**	100	1
	ST		1			.3		**		2		**		**		**		1
FREESTONE	W	44	18	N	91	7	83	17	71	16	47	15	10	3	63	28	44	25
	E	56	23	S	9	1	17	3	29	6	53	17	90	24	37	17	56	31
	ST		40			8		21		23		32		27		45		56
FREESTONE PEACH	W	47	13	N	64	5	63	6	50	8	78	7	50	14	70	19	50	12
	E	53	14	S	36	3	38	3	50	8	22	2	50	14	30	8	50	12
	ST		26			8		9		16		9		27		27		23
OPEN PEACH	W	25	.2	N	100	.3	**	**	**	**	**	**	100	3	**	**	67	3
	E	75	1	S	**	**	**	**	**	**	**	**	**	**	**	**	33	1
	ST		1			.3		**		**		**		3		**		4
OPEN SEED	W	**	**	N	**	**	**	**	**	**	**	**	**	**	**	**	100	1
	E	100	1	S	**	**	100	1	**	**	**	**	**	**	**	**	**	**
	ST		1			**		1		**		**		**		**		1
OPEN SEED PEACH	W	**	**	N	**	**	**	**	**	**	**	**	**	**	**	**	100	1
	E	100	.2	S	**	**	**	**	**	**	**	**	**	**	100	1	**	**
	ST		.2			**		**		**		**		**		1		1
OPEN STONE	W	12	1	N	100	2	**	**	**	**	**	**	**	**	**	**	**	**
	E	88	5	S	**	**	**	**	**	**	**	**	**	**	**	**	**	**
	ST		6			2		**		**		**		**		**		**
OPEN STONE PEACH	W	17	.4	N	100	.3	**	**	**	**	**	**	**	**	**	**	**	**
	E	83	2	S	**	**	**	**	**	**	**	**	**	**	**	**	100	1
	ST		3			.3		**		**		**		**		**		1
SOFT PEACH	W	63	7	N	55	2	67	2	100	3	100	6	**	**	60	2	17	1
	E	37	4	S	45	2	33	1	**	**	**	**	**	**	40	1	83	6
	ST		12			4		3		3		6		**		4		8

CROPS
THE HARD INNER COVER OF A WALNUT

ITEM (100)
WORK SHEET (54)

		TENNESSEE A	TENNESSEE B		GEORGIA A	GEORGIA B	ALABAMA A	ALABAMA B	MISSISSIPPI A	MISSISSIPPI B	FLORIDA A	FLORIDA B	LOUISIANA A	LOUISIANA B	ARKANSAS A	ARKANSAS B	OKLAHOMA A	OKLAHOMA B
HULL(A)	W	17	5	N	20	6	6	2	4	1	6	2	8	2	35	8	12	3
	E	26	8	S	14	4	2	1	2	1	3	1	11	3	23	5	11	3
	ST	43	14		34	11	8	2	7	2	8	3	18	4	58	14	23	5
HUSK(A)	W	14	1	N	16	1	5	.3	2	.1	23	1	12	1	12	1	12	1
	E	7	.4	S	16	1	4	.2	5	.3	7	.4	18	1	18	1	29	2
	ST	21	1		32	2	9	1	7	.4	30	2	29	2	29	2	41	3
SHELL(A)	W	22	11	N	18	9	7	4	4	2	5	3	6	3	31	15	16	8
	E	27	14	S	9	4	2	1	1	1	4	2	5	3	24	12	18	9
	ST	49	25		27	14	9	5	5	3	9	5	11	5	54	27	35	17
SHUCK(A)	W	**	**	N	20	.2	**	**	**	**	10	.1	**	**	33	.3	67	1
	E	20	.2	S	40	.4	10	.1	**	**	**	**	**	**	**	**	**	**
	ST	20	.2		60	1	10	.1	**	**	10	.1	**	**	33	.3	67	1

		TENNESSEE C	TENNESSEE D		GEORGIA C	GEORGIA D	ALABAMA C	ALABAMA D	MISSISSIPPI C	MISSISSIPPI D	FLORIDA C	FLORIDA D	LOUISIANA C	LOUISIANA D	ARKANSAS C	ARKANSAS D	OKLAHOMA C	OKLAHOMA D
HULL(A)	W	40	14	N	58	23	79	25	65	25	68	19	42	16	61	19	53	11
	E	60	20	S	42	17	21	7	35	14	32	9	58	22	39	13	47	10
	ST		34			40		32		39		28		38		32		21
HUSK(A)	W	67	2	N	50	3	60	4	25	2	76	15	40	6	40	2	29	3
	E	33	1	S	50	3	40	3	75	6	24	5	60	9	60	3	71	7
	ST		3			7		7		8		19		16		4		10
SHELL(A)	W	45	28	N	67	34	78	47	78	41	58	30	53	25	57	36	47	31
	E	55	34	S	33	17	22	13	22	12	42	22	47	22	43	27	53	35
	ST		62			51		61		53		51		47		63		66
SHUCK(A)	W	**	**	N	33	1	**	**	**	**	100	1	**	**	100	1	100	3
	E	100	1	S	67	2	100	1	**	**	**	**	**	**	**	**	**	**
	ST		1			2		1		**		1		**		1		3

ITEM (100)
WORK SHEET (54)

CROPS
THE GREEN OUTER COVER OF A WALNUT

		TENNESSEE A	TENNESSEE B		GEORGIA A	GEORGIA B	ALABAMA A	ALABAMA B	MISSISSIPPI A	MISSISSIPPI B	FLORIDA A	FLORIDA B	LOUISIANA A	LOUISIANA B	ARKANSAS A	ARKANSAS B	OKLAHOMA A	OKLAHOMA B
HULL(B)	W	20	12	N	20	12	7	4	3	2	6	4	7	4	32	17	13	7
	E	28	17	S	11	6	2	1	1	1	2	1	5	3	23	13	19	10
	ST	48	29		31	18	9	5	5	3	8	5	12	6	56	30	32	17
HUSK(B)	W	20	2	N	23	2	6	1	10	1	6	1	9	1	35	3	17	1
	E	15	1	S	12	1	2	.2	4	.3	2	.2	**	**	22	2	17	1
	ST	36	3		35	3	8	1	13	1	8	1	9	1	57	5	35	3
SHELL(B)	W	14	2	N	9	1	8	1	5	1	13	2	3	.3	14	2	27	4
	E	24	3	S	11	2	4	1	5	1	7	1	24	3	14	2	19	3
	ST	38	5		20	3	12	2	10	1	20	3	27	4	27	4	46	6
SHUCK(B)	W	7	.2	N	37	1	7	.2	**	**	11	.3	**	**	25	.3	**	**
	E	7	.2	S	22	1	**	**	4	.1	4	.1	**	**	50	1	25	.3
	ST	15	.4		59	2	7	.2	4	.1	15	.4	**	**	75	1	25	.3

		TENNESSEE C	TENNESSEE D		GEORGIA C	GEORGIA D	ALABAMA C	ALABAMA D	MISSISSIPPI C	MISSISSIPPI D	FLORIDA C	FLORIDA D	LOUISIANA C	LOUISIANA D	ARKANSAS C	ARKANSAS D	OKLAHOMA C	OKLAHOMA D
HULL(B)	W	42	33	N	65	46	82	54	70	36	78	43	61	37	58	44	40	26
	E	58	44	S	35	25	18	12	30	15	22	12	39	23	42	32	60	39
	ST		77			71		66		51		55		60		76		65
HUSK(B)	W	57	5	N	66	8	71	7	73	15	71	6	100	7	62	7	50	5
	E	43	4	S	34	4	29	3	27	6	29	2	**	**	38	5	50	5
	ST		8			12		9		21		8		7		12		11
SHELL(B)	W	37	5	N	44	5	69	15	50	13	67	21	10	3	50	5	59	14
	E	63	9	S	56	6	31	7	50	13	33	11	90	30	50	5	41	9
	ST		14			11		22		26		32		33		9		23
SHUCK(B)	W	50	1	N	63	4	100	3	**	**	75	4	**	**	33	1	**	**
	E	50	1	S	38	2	**	**	100	2	25	1	**	**	67	2	100	1
	ST		1			6		3		2		5		**		3		1

CROPS
EARLY ONIONS WITH AN EDIBLE STEM

ITEM (101)
WORK SHEET (55)

		TENNESSEE			GEORGIA		ALABAMA		MISSISSIPPI		FLORIDA		LOUISIANA		ARKANSAS		OKLAHOMA	
		A	B		A	B	A	B	A	B	A	B	A	B	A	B	A	B
GREEN ONIONS	W	20	9	N	11	5	7	4	3	1	6	3	6	4	31	19	17	10
	E	36	17	S	7	3	3	1	1	1	5	3	6	4	18	11	22	13
	ST	56	26		19	9	10	5	4	2	11	5	12	7	49	30	39	23
LIVE FOREVERS	W	33	.1	N	**	**	**	**	**	**	**	**	**	**	**	**	50	.3
	E	33	.1	S	33	.1	**	**	**	**	**	**	50	.3	**	**	**	**
	ST	67	.2		33	.1	**	**	**	**	**	**	50	.3	**	**	50	.3
MULTIPLIERS	W	17	1	N	18	1	4	.3	4	.3	14	1	21	1	21	1	21	1
	E	11	1	S	24	2	1	.1	7	1	**	**	**	**	21	1	14	1
	ST	28	2		42	3	6	.4	11	1	14	1	21	1	43	2	36	2
POTATO ONIONS	W	20	.2	N	**	**	**	**	**	**	**	**	**	**	**	**	**	**
	E	80	1	S	**	**	**	**	**	**	**	**	**	**	100	.3	**	**
	ST	100	1		**	**	**	**	**	**	**	**	**	**	100	.3	**	**
RARE RIPES	W	**	**	N	50	.1	**	**	**	**	**	**	**	**	100	.3	**	**
	E	50	.1	S	**	**	**	**	**	**	**	**	**	**	**	**	**	**
	ST	50	.1		50	.1	**	**	**	**	**	**	**	**	100	.3	**	**
SCALLION(S)	W	5	.2	N	30	1	5	.2	2	.1	16	1	14	.3	43	1	14	.3
	E	21	1	S	7	.3	**	**	5	.2	9	.4	**	**	29	1	**	**
	ST	26	1		37	2	5	.2	7	.3	26	1	14	.3	71	2	14	.3
SHALLOTS	W	26	4	N	35	5	9	1	7	1	1	.2	14	2	30	5	2	.3
	E	7	1	S	7	1	2	.3	4	1	1	.1	18	3	32	5	5	1
	ST	34	5		42	6	11	2	11	2	2	.3	32	5	61	10	7	1
SHELL OATS	W	**	**	N	33	1	5	.1	10	.2	19	.4	50	.3	50	.3	**	**
	E	5	.1	S	19	.4	**	**	10	.2	**	**	**	**	**	**	**	**
	ST	5	.1		52	1	5	.1	19	.4	19	.4	50	.3	50	.3	**	**
SPRING ONIONS	W	22	6	N	22	6	6	2	4	1	11	3	**	**	34	5	11	2
	E	12	3	S	18	5	2	1	2	1	2	1	**	**	39	6	16	3
	ST	33	9		40	11	8	2	6	2	13	4	**	**	73	12	27	4
YOUNG ONIONS	W	17	1	N	12	1	4	.3	4	.3	9	1	13	.3	50	1	13	.3
	E	30	2	S	13	1	4	.3	1	.1	4	.3	**	**	13	.3	13	.3
	ST	48	3		25	2	9	1	6	.4	13	1	13	.3	63	2	25	1

ITEM (101) (CONTINUED) EARLY ONIONS WITH AN EDIBLE STEM

ITEM (101)		TENNESSEE C	TENNESSEE D		GEORGIA C	GEORGIA D	ALABAMA C	ALABAMA D	MISSISSIPPI C	MISSISSIPPI D	FLORIDA C	FLORIDA D	LOUISIANA C	LOUISIANA D	ARKANSAS C	ARKANSAS D	OKLAHOMA C	OKLAHOMA D
GREEN ONIONS	W	36	19	N	61	16	72	35	68	18	51	21	50	24	63	33	43	31
	E	64	35	S	39	10	28	13	32	8	49	20	50	24	37	19	57	42
	ST		54			26		48		26		42		49		51		73
LIVE FOREVERS	W	50	.2	N	**	**	**	**	**	**	**	**	**	**	**	**	100	1
	E	50	.2	S	100	.3	**	**	**	**	**	**	100	2	**	**	**	**
	ST		.4			.3		**		**		**		2		**		1
MULTIPLIERS	W	60	3	N	43	4	75	3	38	4	100	8	100	7	50	2	60	3
	E	40	2	S	57	5	25	1	63	7	**	**	**	**	50	2	40	2
	ST		4			9		4		11		8		7		4		6
POTATO ONIONS	W	20	.4	N	**	**	**	**	**	**	**	**	**	**	**	**	**	**
	E	80	2	S	**	**	**	**	**	**	**	**	**	**	100	1	**	**
	ST		2			**		**		**		**		**		1		**
RARE RIPES	W	**	**	N	100	.3	**	**	**	**	**	**	**	**	100	1	**	**
	E	100	.2	S	**	**	**	**	**	**	**	**	**	**	**	**	**	**
	ST		.2			.3		**		**		**		**		1		**
SCALLION(S)	W	18	.4	N	81	4	100	2	33	1	64	6	100	2	60	2	100	1
	E	82	2	S	19	1	**	**	67	3	36	3	**	**	40	1	**	**
	ST		2			5		2		4		9		2		3		1
SHALLOTS	W	78	8	N	84	16	81	13	65	15	67	2	43	15	48	8	33	1
	E	22	2	S	16	3	19	3	35	8	33	1	57	20	52	9	67	2
	ST		11			19		16		24		2		34		17		3
SHELL OATS	W	**	**	N	64	2	100	1	50	3	100	3	100	2	100	1	**	**
	E	100	.2	S	36	1	**	**	50	3	**	**	**	**	**	**	**	**
	ST		.2			3		1		6		3		2		1		**
SPRING ONIONS	W	65	12	N	55	18	76	16	71	17	85	24	**	**	47	9	42	6
	E	35	7	S	45	15	24	5	29	7	15	4	**	**	53	11	58	8
	ST		19			32		22		24		28		**		20		13
YOUNG ONIONS	W	36	3	N	47	2	50	3	75	4	67	5	100	2	80	3	50	1
	E	64	4	S	53	3	50	3	25	1	33	2	**	**	20	1	50	1
	ST		7			5		6		6		7		2		3		2

ACTIVITIES
OF BEANS

ITEM (102)
WORK SHEET (55)

		TENNESSEE A	TENNESSEE B		GEORGIA A	GEORGIA B	ALABAMA A	ALABAMA B	MISSISSIPPI A	MISSISSIPPI B	FLORIDA A	FLORIDA B	LOUISIANA A	LOUISIANA B	ARKANSAS A	ARKANSAS B	OKLAHOMA A	OKLAHOMA B
TO HULL(C)	W	29	2	N	10	1	4	.3	2	.2	7	1	**	**	42	5	3	.3
	E	37	3	S	4	.3	1	.1	2	.2	4	.3	6	1	12	1	36	4
	ST	66	6		13	1	5	.4	5	.4	11	1	6	1	55	6	39	5
TO POD	W	13	.2	N	33	1	**	**	13	.2	**	**	**	**	50	.3	50	.3
	E	27	.4	S	7	.1	**	**	7	.1	**	**	**	**	**	**	**	**
	ST	40	1		40	1	**	**	20	.3	**	**	**	**	50	.3	50	.3
TO SHELL(C)	W	19	15	N	19	15	7	5	4	3	7	5	7	6	27	21	15	12
	E	25	20	S	12	10	2	2	2	2	4	3	8	6	25	19	18	14
	ST	43	35		31	25	9	7	6	5	11	9	15	12	52	40	33	25
TO SHUCK(C)	W	33	.4	N	8	.1	**	**	8	.1	**	**	**	**	25	.3	25	.3
	E	25	.3	S	8	.1	8	.1	8	.1	**	**	25	.3	25	.3	**	**
	ST	58	1		17	.2	8	.1	17	.2	**	**	25	.3	50	1	25	.3

		TENNESSEE C	TENNESSEE D		GEORGIA C	GEORGIA D	ALABAMA C	ALABAMA D	MISSISSIPPI C	MISSISSIPPI D	FLORIDA C	FLORIDA D	LOUISIANA C	LOUISIANA D	ARKANSAS C	ARKANSAS D	OKLAHOMA C	OKLAHOMA D
TO HULL(C)	W	44	6	N	73	3	75	4	50	4	67	7	**	**	78	11	8	1
	E	56	7	S	27	1	25	1	50	4	33	3	100	6	22	3	92	14
	ST		13			4		5		7		10		6		14		15
TO POD	W	33	.4	N	83	2	**	**	67	4	**	**	**	**	100	1	100	1
	E	67	1	S	17	.3	**	**	33	2	**	**	**	**	**	**	**	**
	ST		1			2		**		6		**		**		1		1
TO SHELL(C)	W	43	36	N	62	57	75	70	64	54	64	58	48	44	52	44	46	38
	E	57	47	S	38	35	25	24	36	30	36	33	52	47	48	41	54	45
	ST		83			93		93		83		90		92		84		82
TO SHUCK(C)	W	57	1	N	50	.3	**	**	50	2	**	**	**	**	50	1	100	1
	E	43	1	S	50	.3	100	1	50	2	**	**	100	3	50	1	**	**
	ST		2			1		1		4		**		3		2		1

CROPS
BEANS EATEN IN PODS

ITEM (103)
WORK SHEET (55)

		TENNESSEE A	TENNESSEE B		GEORGIA A	GEORGIA B	ALABAMA A	ALABAMA B	MISSISSIPPI A	MISSISSIPPI B	FLORIDA A	FLORIDA B	LOUISIANA A	LOUISIANA B	ARKANSAS A	ARKANSAS B	OKLAHOMA A	OKLAHOMA B
GREEN BEANS	W	22	8	N	13	5	6	2	2	1	4	1	3	1	29	14	21	10
	E	47	18	S	2	1	1	.3	1	.4	2	1	5	2	14	6	29	14
	ST	69	27		15	6	7	3	3	1	6	2	8	4	43	20	50	23
SALLET BEANS	W	17	.1	N	17	.1	**	**	**	**	**	**	**	**	100	.3	**	**
	E	50	.3	S	**	**	**	**	17	.1	**	**	**	**	**	**	**	**
	ST	67	.4		17	.1	**	**	17	.1	**	**	**	**	100	.3	**	**
SNAP BEANS	W	22	8	N	15	5	6	2	7	2	9	3	13	4	26	8	6	2
	E	6	2	S	21	8	4	1	4	2	5	2	23	6	25	7	8	2
	ST	27	10		37	13	10	4	11	4	14	5	35	10	51	15	14	4
SNAPS	W	20	.4	N	5	.1	5	.1	**	**	25	1	25	.3	**	**	**	**
	E	**	**	S	25	1	10	.2	**	**	10	.2	**	**	25	.3	50	1
	ST	20	.4		30	1	15	.3	**	**	35	1	25	.3	25	.3	50	1
STRING BEANS	W	18	8	N	22	10	9	4	5	2	8	4	9	4	31	13	9	4
	E	16	7	S	13	6	3	1	2	1	4	2	4	2	26	11	21	9
	ST	33	15		36	16	12	5	6	3	13	6	13	5	57	24	30	13
BEANS	W	17	1	N	17	1	9	.3	3	.1	6	.2	**	**	14	.3	14	.3
	E	29	1	S	11	.4	6	.2	**	**	3	.1	**	**	43	1	29	1
	ST	46	2		29	1	14	1	3	.1	9	.3	**	**	57	1	43	1

		TENNESSEE C	TENNESSEE D		GEORGIA C	GEORGIA D	ALABAMA C	ALABAMA D	MISSISSIPPI C	MISSISSIPPI D	FLORIDA C	FLORIDA D	LOUISIANA C	LOUISIANA D	ARKANSAS C	ARKANSAS D	OKLAHOMA C	OKLAHOMA D
GREEN BEANS	W	32	16	N	87	14	88	19	69	11	67	10	40	7	68	22	42	23
	E	68	34	S	13	2	12	3	31	5	33	5	60	11	32	11	58	33
	ST		50			16		22		16		16		19		33		56
SALLET BEANS	W	25	.1	N	100	.2	**	**	**	**	**	**	**	**	100	1	**	**
	E	75	1	S	**	**	**	**	100	1	**	**	**	**	**	**	**	**
	ST		1			.2		**		1		**		**		1		**
SNAP BEANS	W	80	14	N	42	15	61	18	62	30	63	23	36	19	51	12	45	4
	E	20	4	S	58	21	39	12	38	19	37	13	64	33	49	12	55	5
	ST		18			36		30		48		36		52		24		9
SNAPS	W	100	1	N	17	.2	33	1	**	**	71	4	100	2	**	**	**	**
	E	**	**	S	83	1	67	2	**	**	29	1	**	**	100	1	100	2
	ST		1			2		3		**		5		2		1		2
STRING BEANS	W	54	15	N	62	27	76	31	74	25	65	27	67	19	55	21	31	9
	E	46	13	S	38	16	24	10	26	9	35	14	33	9	45	18	69	21
	ST		28			43		41		33		41		28		39		30
BEANS	W	38	1	N	60	2	60	3	100	1	67	1	**	**	25	1	33	1
	E	63	2	S	40	1	40	2	**	**	33	1	**	**	75	2	67	2
	ST		3			3		4		1		2		**		2		3

ITEM (104)
WORK SHEET (55)

CROPS
EDIBLE TOPS OF TURNIPS, BEETS, ETC.

		TENNESSEE			GEORGIA		ALABAMA		MISSISSIPPI		FLORIDA		LOUISIANA		ARKANSAS		OKLAHOMA	
		A	B		A	B	A	B	A	B	A	B	A	B	A	B	A	B
GREENS	W	17	12	N	14	10	7	5	4	3	9	7	7	6	28	23	16	13
	E	26	19	S	12	9	3	2	2	2	4	3	8	7	22	18	19	15
	ST	43	31		26	19	10	7	7	5	14	10	15	13	50	41	34	28
SALAD	W	19	2	N	27	3	4	.4	3	.3	5	1	8	.3	23	1	8	.3
	E	12	1	S	23	2	1	.1	3	.3	1	.1	**	**	38	2	23	1
	ST	31	3		51	5	5	1	7	1	7	1	8	.3	62	3	31	1
SALLET	W	37	6	N	28	4	3	1	1	.2	1	.1	**	**	64	3	**	**
	E	28	4	S	1	.2	**	**	**	**	**	**	**	**	29	1	7	.3
	ST	65	10		29	5	3	1	1	.2	1	.1	**	**	93	5	7	.3

		TENNESSEE			GEORGIA		ALABAMA		MISSISSIPPI		FLORIDA		LOUISIANA		ARKANSAS		OKLAHOMA	
		C	D		C	D	C	D	C	D	C	D	C	D	C	D	C	D
GREENS	W	40	28	N	55	37	72	63	65	55	67	63	46	44	55	47	46	43
	E	60	42	S	45	30	28	24	35	30	33	30	54	53	45	38	54	51
	ST		70			67		87		86		93		97		84		94
SALAD	W	61	4	N	54	9	80	5	50	5	83	5	100	3	38	2	25	1
	E	39	3	S	46	8	20	1	50	5	17	1	**	**	63	4	75	4
	ST		7			17		6		11		6		3		6		5
SALLET	W	57	13	N	95	15	100	6	100	4	100	1	**	**	69	7	**	**
	E	43	10	S	5	1	**	**	**	**	**	**	**	**	31	3	100	1
	ST		23			16		6		4		1		**		10		1

CROPS
(NO TEXT)

ITEM (105)
WORK SHEET (54)

		TENNESSEE A	TENNESSEE B		GEORGIA A	GEORGIA B	ALABAMA A	ALABAMA B	MISSISSIPPI A	MISSISSIPPI B	FLORIDA A	FLORIDA B	LOUISIANA A	LOUISIANA B	ARKANSAS A	ARKANSAS B	OKLAHOMA A	OKLAHOMA B
GOOBERS	W	24	3	N	25	3	5	1	8	1	3	.4	12	1	32	3	28	3
	E	27	4	S	4	1	2	.2	2	.3	1	.1	4	.3	16	1	8	1
	ST	51	7		29	4	6	1	10	1	4	1	16	1	48	4	36	3
GROUND PEAS	W	5	.2	N	32	1	8	.3	**	**	14	1	**	**	**	**	**	**
	E	**	**	S	41	2	**	**	**	**	**	**	**	**	**	**	**	**
	ST	5	.2		73	3	8	.3	**	**	14	1	**	**	**	**	**	**
GROUND NUTS	W	29	.2	N	14	.1	14	.1	**	**	**	**	**	**	100	.3	**	**
	E	43	.3	S	**	**	**	**	**	**	**	**	**	**	**	**	**	**
	ST	71	1		14	.1	14	.1	**	**	**	**	**	**	100	.3	**	**
PEANUTS	W	19	13	N	19	14	7	5	4	3	8	5	6	5	28	22	16	13
	E	25	18	S	11	0	2	2	2	2	4	3	7	6	25	19	17	13
	ST	43	31		30	21	10	7	6	4	12	8	13	10	53	41	33	26
PINDERS	W	2	.1	N	7	.4	2	.1	2	.1	30	2	25	.3	25	.3	25	.3
	E	**	**	S	36	2	4	.2	11	1	7	.4	25	.3	**	**	**	**
	ST	2	.1		43	2	5	.3	13	1	38	2	50	1	25	.3	25	.3

		TENNESSEE C	TENNESSEE D		GEORGIA C	GEORGIA D	ALABAMA C	ALABAMA D	MISSISSIPPI C	MISSISSIPPI D	FLORIDA C	FLORIDA D	LOUISIANA C	LOUISIANA D	ARKANSAS C	ARKANSAS D	OKLAHOMA C	OKLAHOMA D
GOOBERS	W	47	8	N	86	11	75	7	77	16	80	4	75	9	67	6	78	9
	E	53	9	S	14	2	25	2	23	5	20	1	25	3	33	3	22	2
	ST		17			12		10		21		5		11		9		11
GROUND PEAS	W	100	1	N	44	4	100	4	**	**	100	5	**	**	**	**	**	**
	E	**	**	S	56	5	**	**	**	**	**	**	**	**	**	**	**	**
	ST		1			9		4		**		5		**		**		**
GROUND NUTS	W	40	1	N	100	.3	100	1	**	**	**	**	**	**	100	1	**	**
	E	60	1	S	**	**	**	**	**	**	**	**	**	**	**	**	**	**
	ST		1			.3		1		**		**		**		1		**
PEANUTS	W	43	35	N	64	45	74	60	64	44	66	48	45	37	54	48	49	43
	E	57	46	S	36	25	26	21	36	24	34	24	55	46	46	41	51	45
	ST		81			70		81		68		72		83		89		88
PINDERS	W	100	.2	N	17	1	33	1	14	2	81	15	50	3	100	1	100	1
	E	**	**	S	83	7	67	2	86	10	19	4	50	3	**	**	**	**
	ST		.2			8		4		11		19		6		1		1

CROPS
LARGE, FLAT, YELLOWISH BEANS, NOT IN PODS

ITEM (106)
WORK SHEET (55)

		TENNESSEE			GEORGIA		ALABAMA		MISSISSIPPI		FLORIDA		LOUISIANA		ARKANSAS		OKLAHOMA	
		A	B		A	B	A	B	A	B	A	B	A	B	A	B	A	B
BUTTER BEANS	W	21	14	N	20	13	7	4	4	3	6	4	6	4	28	19	17	12
	E	24	15	S	11	7	2	1	2	1	3	2	8	5	21	14	19	13
	ST	45	29		30	20	9	6	6	4	10	6	14	10	49	34	36	25
LIMA BEANS	W	17	6	N	16	5	8	3	2	1	7	2	7	3	30	12	15	6
	E	29	10	S	13	4	3	1	2	1	4	1	7	3	22	9	18	7
	ST	46	15		29	10	10	4	4	1	11	4	15	6	52	21	34	13
SEWEE BEANS	W	25	.1	N	25	.1	**	**	**	**	**	**	**	**	**	**	**	**
	E	**	**	S	50	.2	**	**	**	**	**	**	100	1	**	**	**	**
	ST	25	.1		75	.3	**	**	**	**	**	**	100	1	**	**	**	**
SIVVY BEANS					(NO RESPONSE)													
	E	50	.1	S	50	.1	**	**	**	**	**	**	83	2	17	.3	**	**
	ST	50	.1		50	.1	**	**	**	**	**	**	83	2	17	.3	**	**

		TENNESSEE			GEORGIA		ALABAMA		MISSISSIPPI		FLORIDA		LOUISIANA		ARKANSAS		OKLAHOMA	
		C	D		C	D	C	D	C	D	C	D	C	D	C	D	C	D
BUTTER BEANS	W	47	30	N	65	43	78	48	66	48	64	40	44	24	57	36	48	31
	E	53	34	S	35	23	22	13	34	25	36	22	56	30	43	26	52	34
	ST		65			66		62		73		61		54		62		65
LIMA BEANS	W	37	13	N	54	18	74	28	50	13	65	25	50	16	58	22	46	16
	E	63	22	S	46	15	26	10	50	13	35	14	50	16	42	16	54	19
	ST		35			33		38		27		39		32		38		35
SEWEE BEANS	W	100	.2	N	33	.3	**	**	**	**	**	**	**	**	**	**	**	**
	E	**	**	S	67	1	**	**	**	**	**	**	100	4	**	**	**	**
	ST		.2			1		**		**		**		4		**		**
SIVVY BEANS					(NO RESPONSE)													
	E	100	.2	S	100	.3	**	**	**	**	**	**	100	10	100	1	**	**
	ST		.2			.3		**		**		**		10		1		**

ITEM (107)
WORK SHEET (56)

CROPS
GREEN, LEAFY COVER OF AN EAR OF CORN

		TENNESSEE A	TENNESSEE B		GEORGIA A	GEORGIA B	ALABAMA A	ALABAMA B	MISSISSIPPI A	MISSISSIPPI B	FLORIDA A	FLORIDA B	LOUISIANA A	LOUISIANA B	ARKANSAS A	ARKANSAS B	OKLAHOMA A	OKLAHOMA B
CAP	W	50	.1	N	**	**	**	**	**	**	**	**	**	**	**	**	100	.3
	E	**	**	S	**	**	**	**	50	.1	**	**	**	**	**	**	**	**
	ST	50	.1		**	**	**	**	50	.1	**	**	**	**	**	**	100	.3
HUSK(C)	W	19	1	N	8	1	2	.1	5	.3	10	1	**	**	18	3	41	6
	E	38	2	S	**	**	5	.3	3	.2	11	1	10	1	10	1	21	3
	ST	57	4		8	1	6	.4	8	1	21	1	10	1	28	4	62	9
SHUCK(D)	W	18	15	N	19	16	7	6	4	4	7	6	8	6	32	24	11	8
	E	24	20	S	12	10	2	2	2	2	3	3	8	6	26	19	17	13
	ST	43	36		32	27	9	8	6	5	10	9	15	12	57	43	27	21

		TENNESSEE C	TENNESSEE D		GEORGIA C	GEORGIA D	ALABAMA C	ALABAMA D	MISSISSIPPI C	MISSISSIPPI D	FLORIDA C	FLORIDA D	LOUISIANA C	LOUISIANA D	ARKANSAS C	ARKANSAS D	OKLAHOMA C	OKLAHOMA D
CAP	W	100	.2	N	**	**	**	**	**	**	**	**	**	**	**	**	100	1
	E	**	**	S	**	**	**	**	100	2	**	**	**	**	**	**	**	**
	ST		.2			**		**		2		**		**		**		1
HUSK(C)	W	33	3	N	100	2	25	1	60	5	46	6	**	**	64	5	67	20
	E	67	6	S	**	**	75	4	40	4	54	7	100	11	36	3	33	10
	ST		9			2		5		9		13		11		8		29
SHUCK(D)	W	43	39	N	61	60	77	73	67	60	71	61	50	44	55	50	39	27
	E	57	51	S	39	38	23	22	33	30	29	26	50	44	45	41	61	43
	ST		90			98		95		89		87		89		92		70

CROPS
CORN EATEN ON THE COB

ITEM (108)
WORK SHEET (56)

		TENNESSEE A	TENNESSEE B		GEORGIA A	GEORGIA B	ALABAMA A	ALABAMA B	MISSISSIPPI A	MISSISSIPPI B	FLORIDA A	FLORIDA B	LOUISIANA A	LOUISIANA B	ARKANSAS A	ARKANSAS B	OKLAHOMA A	OKLAHOMA B
CORN ON THE COB	W	19	12	N	17	11	8	5	4	3	7	4	6	4	24	15	16	10
	E	23	14	S	12	8	3	2	2	1	4	3	9	5	22	14	23	14
	ST	42	26		30	18	11	7	6	4	11	7	15	9	47	29	38	24
GARDEN CORN	W	67	.4	N	**	**	**	**	**	**	**	**	**	**	**	**	**	**
	E	17	.1	S	17	.1	**	**	**	**	**	**	**	**	100	.3	**	**
	ST	83	1		17	.1	**	**	**	**	**	**	**	**	100	.3	**	**
GREEN CORN	W	36	.4	N	9	.1	**	**	**	**	36	.4	**	**	**	**	**	**
	E	**	**	S	18	.2	**	**	**	**	**	**	**	**	**	**	**	**
	ST	36	.4		27	.3	**	**	**	**	36	.4	**	**	**	**	**	**
MUTTON CORN	W	**	**	N	**	**	**	**	**	**	75	.3	**	**	**	**	**	**
	E	**	**	S	25	.1	**	**	**	**	**	**	**	**	**	**	**	**
	ST	**	**		25	.1	**	**	**	**	75	.3	**	**	**	**	**	**
ROASTING EARS	W	20	8	N	19	7	5	2	4	1	7	3	11	5	29	13	18	8
	E	30	11	S	9	4	1	.4	2	1	2	1	3	1	21	9	18	8
	ST	50	19		29	11	6	2	6	2	9	4	14	6	50	22	36	16
SUGAR CORN	W	**	**	N	50	.2	**	**	**	**	**	**	**	**	**	**	**	**
	E	**	**	S	25	.1	**	**	25	.1	**	**	**	**	100	.3	**	**
	ST	**	**		75	.3	**	**	25	.1	**	**	**	**	100	.3	**	**
SWEET CORN	W	21	1	N	8	.4	6	.3	2	.1	4	.2	7	1	27	3	13	1
	E	38	2	S	8	.4	**	**	2	.1	10	1	3	.3	30	3	20	2
	ST	58	3		17	1	6	.3	4	.2	15	1	10	1	57	6	33	4

ITEM (108) (CONTINUED) CORN EATEN ON THE COB

		TENNESSEE C	TENNESSEE D		GEORGIA C	GEORGIA D	ALABAMA C	ALABAMA D	MISSISSIPPI C	MISSISSIPPI D	FLORIDA C	FLORIDA D	LOUISIANA C	LOUISIANA D	ARKANSAS C	ARKANSAS D	OKLAHOMA C	OKLAHOMA D
CORN ON THE COB	W	46	24	N	59	35	73	52	68	40	63	37	42	24	53	26	41	23
	E	54	29	S	41	24	27	20	32	19	37	21	58	33	48	24	59	33
	ST		53			59		72		60		58		57		50		55
GARDEN CORN	W	80	1	N	**	**	**	**	**	**	**	**	**	**	**	**	**	**
	E	20	.2	S	100	.3	**	**	**	**	**	**	**	**	100	1	**	**
	ST		1			.3		**		**		**		**		1		**
GREEN CORN	W	100	1	N	33	.3	**	**	**	**	100	3	**	**	**	**	**	**
	E	**	**	S	67	1	**	**	**	**	**	**	**	**	**	**	**	**
	ST		1			1		**		**		3		**		**		**
MUTTON CORN	W	**	**	N	**	**	**	**	**	**	100	3	**	**	**	**	**	**
	E	**	**	S	100	.3	**	**	**	**	**	**	**	**	**	**	**	**
	ST		**			[illegible]		**		**		3		**		**		**
ROASTING EARS	W	40	15	N	67	24	83	21	64	23	77	23	76	28	58	22	50	18
	E	60	24	S	33	12	17	4	36	13	23	7	24	9	42	16	50	18
	ST		39			35		25		35		30		37		39		37
SUGAR CORN	W	**	**	N	67	1	**	**	**	**	**	**	**	**	**	**	**	**
	E	**	**	S	33	.3	**	**	100	2	**	**	**	**	100	1	**	**
	ST		**			1		**		2		**		**		1		**
SWEET CORN	W	36	2	N	50	1	100	3	50	2	29	2	67	4	47	5	40	3
	E	64	4	S	50	1	**	**	50	2	71	4	33	2	53	6	60	5
	ST		6			3		3		3		6		7		11		8

ITEM (109)
WORK SHEET (57)

VEGETATION
POISONOUS PLANT

		TENNESSEE			GEORGIA		ALABAMA		MISSISSIPPI		FLORIDA		LOUISIANA		ARKANSAS		OKLAHOMA	
		A	B		A	B	A	B	A	B	A	B	A	B	A	B	A	B
FROGSTOOL	W	28	1	N	28	1	2	.1	7	.3	2	.1	50	.3	50	.3	**	**
	E	15	1	S	11	1	2	.1	2	.1	2	.1	**	**	**	**	**	**
	ST	43	2		39	2	4	.2	9	.4	4	.2	50	.3	50	.3	**	**
TOADSTOOL	W	18	14	N	18	14	7	5	4	3	7	6	7	6	28	23	17	14
	E	25	20	S	11	9	3	2	2	2	4	3	8	7	22	18	17	14
	ST	43	34		29	23	10	7	6	5	11	9	16	13	50	41	34	27

		TENNESSEE			GEORGIA		ALABAMA		MISSISSIPPI		FLORIDA		LOUISIANA		ARKANSAS		OKLAHOMA	
		C	D		C	D	C	D	C	D	C	D	C	D	C	D	C	D
FROGSTOOL	W	65	4	N	72	5	50	1	75	6	50	1	100	3	100	1	**	**
	E	35	2	S	28	2	50	1	25	2	50	1	**	**	**	**	**	**
	ST		6			8		3		8		2		3		1		**
TOADSTOOL	W	42	39	N	61	57	72	70	65	60	65	64	46	44	56	55	50	50
	E	58	55	S	39	36	28	27	35	32	35	34	54	53	44	44	50	50
	ST		94			92		97		92		98		97		99		100

ANIMALS
A SMALL SQUIRREL-LIKE ANIMAL THAT RUNS ALONG THE GROUND

ITEM (110)
WORK SHEET (59)

		TENNESSEE			GEORGIA		ALABAMA		MISSISSIPPI		FLORIDA		LOUISIANA		ARKANSAS		OKLAHOMA	
		A	B		A	B	A	B	A	B	A	B	A	B	A	B	A	B
CHIPMUNK	W	25	7	N	15	4	8	2	4	1	5	1	6	2	24	8	20	6
	E	27	7	S	10	3	2	1	4	1	2	1	8	3	23	7	19	6
	ST	51	14		24	6	10	3	8	2	7	2	14	4	47	15	40	13
GRINNIE	W	50	.2	N	25	.1	**	**	**	**	**	**	**	**	**	**	**	**
	E	25	.1	S	**	**	**	**	**	**	**	**	**	**	**	**	**	**
	ST	75	.3		25	.1	**	**	**	**	**	**	**	**	**	**	**	**
GROUND SQUIRREL	W	17	10	N	23	13	7	4	4	2	6	3	5	3	35	17	16	8
	E	28	15	S	9	5	2	1	1	1	3	1	6	3	17	8	21	10
	ST	45	25		32	18	10	5	5	3	8	5	11	5	52	25	37	18

		TENNESSEE			GEORGIA		ALABAMA		MISSISSIPPI		FLORIDA		LOUISIANA		ARKANSAS		OKLAHOMA	
		C	D		C	D	C	D	C	D	C	D	C	D	C	D	C	D
CHIPMUNK	W	48	17	N	60	16	80	26	55	22	71	20	42	19	51	19	51	21
	E	52	18	S	40	11	20	6	45	18	29	8	58	26	49	18	49	20
	ST		35			26		32		41		28		44		37		42
GRINNIE	W	67	1	N	100	.4	**	**	**	**	**	**	**	**	**	**	**	**
	E	33	.2	S	**	**	**	**	**	**	**	**	**	**	**	**	**	**
	ST		1			.4		**		**		**		**		**		**
GROUND SQUIRREL	W	38	25	N	71	52	75	51	72	43	68	49	47	26	67	42	43	25
	E	62	40	S	29	22	25	17	28	16	32	23	53	30	33	21	57	33
	ST		64			73		68		59		72		56		63		58

ITEM (111)
WORK SHEET (59)

ANIMALS
AN ANIMAL WITH A STRONG ODOR

		TENNESSEE			GEORGIA		ALABAMA		MISSISSIPPI		FLORIDA		LOUISIANA		ARKANSAS		OKLAHOMA	
		A	B		A	B	A	B	A	B	A	B	A	B	A	B	A	B
POLECAT	W	17	9	N	20	11	6	3	3	2	9	5	13	4	29	9	12	4
	E	24	13	S	13	7	2	1	3	2	4	2	6	2	23	7	18	5
	ST	41	22		33	18	8	4	6	3	12	7	19	6	51	16	30	9
SKUNK	W	19	11	N	16	9	8	4	4	2	7	4	6	5	27	19	18	13
	E	27	15	S	9	5	3	2	2	1	5	3	7	5	22	16	19	14
	ST	46	26		25	14	10	6	7	4	12	6	14	10	49	35	38	27

		TENNESSEE			GEORGIA		ALABAMA		MISSISSIPPI		FLORIDA		LOUISIANA		ARKANSAS		OKLAHOMA	
		C	D		C	D	C	D	C	D	C	D	C	D	C	D	C	D
POLECAT	W	41	19	N	60	34	74	32	53	25	69	35	69	25	56	17	40	10
	E	59	27	S	40	22	26	11	47	22	31	16	31	11	44	13	60	15
	ST		46			56		43		48		51		36		30		25
SKUNK	W	41	22	N	62	27	73	41	69	36	60	29	46	30	55	38	49	37
	E	59	32	S	38	17	27	15	31	16	40	20	54	34	45	31	51	39
	ST		54			44		57		52		49		64		70		75

ANIMALS
A HOPPING ANIMAL

ITEM (112)
WORK SHEET (60)

		TENNESSEE A	TENNESSEE B		GEORGIA A	GEORGIA B	ALABAMA A	ALABAMA B	MISSISSIPPI A	MISSISSIPPI B	FLORIDA A	FLORIDA B	LOUISIANA A	LOUISIANA B	ARKANSAS A	ARKANSAS B	OKLAHOMA A	OKLAHOMA B
DRY-LAND FROG	W	**	**	N	33	.2	**	**	**	**	**	**	**	**	**	**	**	**
	E	33	.2	S	17	.1	**	**	**	**	17	.1	**	**	**	**	**	**
	ST	33	.2		50	.3	**	**	**	**	17	.1	**	**	**	**	**	**
GREY FROG	W	75	.3	N	**	**	**	**	**	**	**	**	**	**	**	**	**	**
	E	**	**	S	**	**	**	**	25	.1	**	**	100	.3	**	**	**	**
	ST	75	.3		**	**	**	**	25	.1	**	**	100	.3	**	**	**	**
HOP TOAD	W	23	1	N	**	**	4	.1	4	.1	**	**	**	**	17	1	67	6
	E	35	1	S	8	.2	**	**	8	.2	19	1	**	**	**	**	17	1
	ST	58	2		8	.2	4	.1	12	.3	19	1	**	**	17	1	83	7
TOAD	W	21	4	N	13	3	9	2	3	1	8	2	4	1	21	5	24	6
	E	29	6	S	8	[illegible]	3	1	2	.3	6	1	8	2	18	5	24	6
	ST	50	10		21	4	12	2	5	1	13	3	13	3	39	10	48	12
TOAD FROG	W	18	13	N	20	14	6	4	4	3	8	5	8	5	31	21	8	5
	E	24	18	S	13	9	3	2	2	2	3	2	9	6	28	19	17	12
	ST	42	30		33	24	8	6	6	5	11	8	16	11	59	40	25	17
WART FROG	W	25	.1	N	**	**	50	.2	**	**	**	**	**	**	100	.3	**	**
	E	**	**	S	**	**	**	**	25	.1	**	**	**	**	**	**	**	**
	ST	25	.1		**	**	50	.2	25	.1	**	**	**	**	100	.3	**	**
WARTY TOAD	W	**	**	N	**	**	**	**	**	**	50	.1	**	**	100	.3	**	**
	E	**	**	S	50	.1	**	**	**	**	**	**	**	**	**	**	**	**
	ST	**	**		50	.1	**	**	**	**	50	.1	**	**	100	.3	**	**

ITEM (112) (CONTINUED) A HOPPING ANIMAL

		TENNESSEE			GEORGIA		ALABAMA		MISSISSIPPI		FLORIDA		LOUISIANA		ARKANSAS		OKLAHOMA	
		C	D		C	D	C	D	C	D	C	D	C	D	C	D	C	D
DRY-LAND FROG	W	**	**	N	67	1	**	**	**	**	**	**	**	**	**	**	**	**
	E	100	.4	S	33	.3	**	**	**	**	100	1	**	**	**	**	**	**
	ST		.4			1		**		**		1		**		**		**
GREY FROG	W	100	1	N	**	**	**	**	**	**	**	**	**	**	**	**	**	**
	E	**	**	S	**	**	**	**	100	2	**	**	100	3	**	**	**	**
	ST		1			**		**		2		**		3		**		**
HOP TOAD	W	40	1	N	**	**	100	1	33	2	**	**	**	**	100	3	80	16
	E	60	2	S	100	1	**	**	67	3	100	5	**	**	**	**	20	4
	ST		4			1		1		5		5		**		3		20
TOAD	W	41	10	N	62	9	78	21	67	10	58	14	33	8	54	10	50	17
	E	59	14	S	38	6	22	6	33	5	42	10	67	15	46	9	50	17
	ST		24			15		27		15		24		23		19		34
TOAD FROG	W	42	30	N	61	51	69	48	64	49	71	49	47	35	53	40	30	14
	E	58	41	S	39	32	31	21	36	27	29	20	53	40	47	36	70	32
	ST		71			83		69		76		69		75		76		46
WART FROG	W	100	.2	N	**	**	100	2	**	**	**	**	**	**	100	1	**	**
	E	**	**	S	**	**	**	**	100	2	**	**	**	**	**	**	**	**
	ST		.2			**		2		2		**		**		1		**
WARTY TOAD	W	**	**	N	**	**	**	**	**	**	100	1	**	**	100	1	**	**
	E	**	**	S	100	.3	**	**	**	**	**	**	**	**	**	**	**	**
	ST		**			.3		**		**		1		**		1		**

ANIMALS
A WORM USED FOR BAIT IN FISHING

ITEM (113)
WORK SHEET (60)

		TENNESSEE			GEORGIA		ALABAMA		MISSISSIPPI		FLORIDA		LOUISIANA		ARKANSAS		OKLAHOMA	
		A	B		A	B	A	B	A	B	A	B	A	B	A	B	A	B
ANGLEDOG	W	50	.1	N	**	**	**	**	**	**	**	**	**	**	**	**	**	**
	E	50	.1	S	**	**	**	**	**	**	**	**	**	**	**	**	**	**
	ST	100	.2		**	**	**	**	**	**	**	**	**	**	**	**	**	**
ANGLEWORM	W	30	1	N	14	1	5	.2	**	**	9	.4	**	**	29	2	35	2
	E	16	1	S	9	.4	2	.1	7	.3	7	.3	6	.3	12	1	18	1
	ST	47	2		23	1	7	.3	7	.3	16	1	6	.3	41	3	53	3
BAIT WORM	W	31	1	N	16	1	3	.1	6	.2	13	.4	**	**	14	.3	14	.3
	E	22	1	S	6	.2	**	**	**	**	3	.1	29	1	**	**	43	1
	ST	53	2		22	1	3	.1	6	.2	16	1	29	1	14	.3	57	1
EACEWORM					(NO RESPONSE)													
					(NO RESPONSE)													
					(NO RESPONSE)													
EARTHWORM	W	8	2	N	21	6	8	2	4	1	16	4	13	4	21	6	15	5
	E	12	3	S	15	4	5	1	3	1	6	2	9	3	22	7	20	6
	ST	20	5		37	10	13	4	8	2	22	6	22	7	43	13	35	11
EEL WORM	W	7	.2	N	25	1	4	.1	**	**	14	.4	**	**	**	**	**	**
	E	**	**	S	50	1	**	**	**	**	**	**	**	**	100	.3	**	**
	ST	7	.2		75	2	4	.1	**	**	14	.4	**	**	100	.3	**	**
FISH BAIT	W	5	1	N	32	5	8	1	1	.2	9	1	17	1	26	2	13	1
	E	6	1	S	33	5	3	1	1	.2	1	.2	13	1	13	1	17	1
	ST	11	2		64	10	12	2	3	.4	10	2	30	3	39	3	30	3
FISHING WORM	W	49	10	N	9	2	6	1	7	1	3	1	4	1	26	5	16	3
	E	19	4	S	4	1	1	.2	**	**	4	1	10	2	28	5	16	3
	ST	68	14		12	2	7	1	7	1	6	1	14	3	54	10	32	6
FISHWORM	W	19	1	N	11	1	9	1	4	.2	7	.4	**	**	22	3	41	5
	E	26	2	S	7	.4	9	1	2	.1	7	.4	**	**	6	1	31	4
	ST	46	3		18	1	18	1	5	.3	14	1	**	**	28	3	72	8
MUDWORM	W	**	**	N	67	.2	**	**	**	**	**	**	**	**	**	**	**	**
	E	**	**	S	33	.1	**	**	**	**	**	**	100	.3	**	**	**	**
	ST	**	**		100	.3	**	**	**	**	**	**	100	.3	**	**	**	**
RAINWORM	W	**	**	N	33	.1	33	.1	**	**	**	**	**	**	**	**	**	**
	E	33	.1	S	**	**	**	**	**	**	**	**	**	**	**	**	**	**
	ST	33	.1		33	.1	33	.1	**	**	**	**	**	**	**	**	**	**
RED WORM	W	14	4	N	17	5	7	2	4	1	1	.2	5	2	43	15	6	2
	E	50	15	S	5	2	1	.4	1	.4	**	**	2	1	28	10	16	5
	ST	64	20		22	7	8	2	5	2	1	.2	7	3	71	25	22	8

ITEM (113)

(CONTINUED) A WORM USED FOR BAIT IN FISHING

ITEM		TENNESSEE C	TENNESSEE D		GEORGIA C	GEORGIA D	ALABAMA C	ALABAMA D	MISSISSIPPI C	MISSISSIPPI D	FLORIDA C	FLORIDA D	LOUISIANA C	LOUISIANA D	ARKANSAS C	ARKANSAS D	OKLAHOMA C	OKLAHOMA D
ANGLEDOG	W	50	.2	N	**	**	**	**	**	**	**	**	**	**	**	**	**	**
	E	50	.2	S	**	**	**	**	**	**	**	**	**	**	**	**	**	**
	ST		.4			**		**		**		**		**		**		**
ANGLEWORM	W	65	3	N	60	2	67	2	**	**	57	4	**	**	71	3	67	5
	E	35	2	S	40	1	33	1	100	5	43	3	100	2	29	1	33	3
	ST		4			3		3		5		6		2		4		8
BAIT WORM	W	59	2	N	71	1	100	1	100	3	80	4	**	**	100	1	25	1
	E	41	2	S	29	1	**	**	**	**	20	1	100	5	**	**	75	3
	ST		4			2		1		3		4		5		1		4
EACEWORM					(NO RESPONSE)													
					(NO RESPONSE)													
	ST		**			**		**		**		**		**		**		**
EARTHWORM	W	42	5	N	58	17	61	21	57	19	71	38	58	25	49	11	43	12
	E	58	7	S	42	12	39	13	43	15	29	15	42	18	51	12	57	15
	ST		11			29		34		34		53		43		23		27
EEL WORM	W	100	.4	N	33	2	100	1	**	**	100	4	**	**	**	**	**	**
	E	**	**	S	67	4	**	**	**	**	**	**	**	**	100	1	**	**
	ST		.4			6		1		**		4		**		1		**
FISH BAIT	W	44	2	N	49	14	71	11	50	3	87	12	57	9	67	4	43	3
	E	56	2	S	51	14	29	5	50	3	13	2	43	7	33	2	57	4
	ST		3			28		16		6		13		16		6		6
FISHING WORM	W	71	21	N	71	5	85	10	100	21	42	4	29	5	48	8	50	7
	E	29	8	S	29	2	15	2	**	**	58	6	71	11	52	9	50	7
	ST		29			7		12		21		11		16		17		15
FISHWORM	W	42	2	N	60	2	50	5	67	3	50	4	**	**	78	4	57	12
	E	58	3	S	40	1	50	5	33	2	50	4	**	**	22	1	43	9
	ST		6			3		9		5		7		**		6		21
MUDWORM	W	**	**	N	67	1	**	**	**	**	**	**	**	**	**	**	**	**
	E	**	**	S	33	.2	**	**	**	**	**	**	100	2	**	**	**	**
	ST		**			1		**		**		**		2		**		**
RAINWORM	W	**	**	N	100	.2	100	1	**	**	**	**	**	**	**	**	**	**
	E	100	.2	S	**	**	**	**	**	**	**	**	**	**	**	**	**	**
	ST		.2			.2		1		**		**		**		**		**
RED WORM	W	21	9	N	76	15	83	19	75	19	100	2	71	11	60	26	29	5
	[illegible]	[illegible]	[illegible]	[illegible]	[illegible]	5	17	4	25	6	**	**	29	5	40	17	71	14
	[illegible]		[illegible]			[illegible]		[illegible]		[illegible]		[illegible]		[illegible]		43		19

ITEM (113)
WORK SHEET (60)

ANIMALS
A LARGE WORM USED FOR BAIT

		TENNESSEE A	TENNESSEE B		GEORGIA A	GEORGIA B	ALABAMA A	ALABAMA B	MISSISSIPPI A	MISSISSIPPI B	FLORIDA A	FLORIDA B	LOUISIANA A	LOUISIANA B	ARKANSAS A	ARKANSAS B	OKLAHOMA A	OKLAHOMA B
DEW WORM	W	61	1	N	4	.1	**	**	**	**	9	.2	**	**	**	**	67	1
	E	22	1	S	**	**	4	.1	**	**	**	**	**	**	**	**	33	.3
	ST	83	2		4	.1	4	.1	**	**	9	.2	**	**	**	**	100	1
NIGHT CRAWLER	W	17	4	N	9	2	5	1	7	2	6	1	13	3	33	8	16	4
	E	46	10	S	2	1	2	.4	1	.3	3	1	6	1	20	5	12	3
	ST	64	14		12	3	7	2	8	2	9	2	19	5	54	13	28	7
NIGHT WALKER	W	33	.3	N	22	.2	11	.1	**	**	11	.1	**	**	**	**	**	**
	E	11	.1	S	**	**	**	**	**	**	11	.1	100	.3	**	**	**	**
	ST	44	.4		22	.2	11	.1	**	**	22	.2	100	.3	**	**	**	**
(GEORGIA) WIGGLER	W	4	1	N	40	10	6	2	1	.3	10	3	8	1	28	3	4	.3
	E	3	1	S	26	7	3	1	2	1	3	1	12	1	40	4	8	1
	ST	8	2		66	17	10	2	4	1	13	3	20	2	68	6	12	1
TOWN WORM	W	56	1	N	11	.1	**	**	**	**	**	**	**	**	100	.3	**	**
	E	**	**	S	22	.2	11	.1	**	**	**	**	**	**	**	**	**	**
	ST	56	1		33	.3	11	.1	**	**	**	**	**	**	100	.3	**	**

		TENNESSEE C	TENNESSEE D		GEORGIA C	GEORGIA D	ALABAMA C	ALABAMA D	MISSISSIPPI C	MISSISSIPPI D	FLORIDA C	FLORIDA D	LOUISIANA C	LOUISIANA D	ARKANSAS C	ARKANSAS D	OKLAHOMA C	OKLAHOMA D
DEW WORM	W	74	8	N	100	1	**	**	**	**	100	4	**	**	**	**	67	8
	E	26	3	S	**	**	100	2	**	**	**	**	**	**	**	**	33	4
	ST		10			1		2		**		4		**		**		12
NIGHT CRAWLER	W	27	20	N	80	10	73	26	83	56	65	23	69	47	62	42	58	44
	E	73	54	S	20	3	27	10	17	11	35	13	31	21	38	25	42	32
	ST		74			13		36		67		36		68		67		76
NIGHT WALKER	W	75	2	N	100	1	100	2	**	**	50	2	**	**	**	**	**	**
	E	25	1	S	**	**	**	**	**	**	50	2	100	5	**	**	**	**
	ST		2			1		2		**		4		5		**		**
(GEORGIA) WIGGLER	W	58	6	N	60	51	67	38	33	11	78	45	40	11	41	13	33	4
	E	42	4	S	40	34	33	19	67	22	22	13	60	16	59	18	67	8
	ST		10			84		57		33		57		26		31		12
TOWN WORM	W	100	3	N	33	1	**	**	**	**	**	**	**	**	100	2	**	**
	E	**	**	S	67	1	100	2	**	**	**	**	**	**	**	**	**	**
	ST		3			2		2		**		**		**		2		**

INSECTS
AN INSECT THAT GLOWS AT NIGHT

ITEM (114)
WORK SHEET (60)

		TENNESSEE			GEORGIA		ALABAMA		MISSISSIPPI		FLORIDA		LOUISIANA		ARKANSAS		OKLAHOMA	
		A	B		A	B	A	B	A	B	A	B	A	B	A	B	A	B
FIRE BUG	W	13	.2	N	6	.1	13	.2	6	.1	13	.2	**	**	25	.3	**	**
	E	13	.2	S	13	.2	6	.1	19	.3	**	**	25	.3	50	1	**	**
	ST	25	.4		19	.3	19	.3	25	.4	13	.2	25	.3	75	1	**	**
FIREFLY	W	20	2	N	13	1	13	1	2	.2	9	1	5	1	25	4	28	4
	F	24	2	S	7	1	2	.2	2	.2	8	1	3	.3	15	2	25	4
	ST	44	4		19	2	15	1	5	.4	17	2	8	1	40	6	53	8
GLOW WORM	W	29	1	N	19	1	2	.1	2	.1	4	.2	**	**	45	2	18	1
	E	29	1	S	4	.2	2	.1	2	.1	6	.3	**	**	18	1	18	1
	ST	58	3		23	1	4	.2	4	.2	10	1	**	**	64	3	36	1
JUNE BUG	W	50	1	N	8	.1	**	**	**	**	8	.1	**	**	40	1	**	**
	E	8	.1	S	8	.1	**	**	8	.1	8	.1	**	**	40	1	20	.3
	ST	58	1		17	.2	**	**	8	.1	17	.2	**	**	80	1	20	.3
LIGHTNING BUG	W	19	16	N	19	16	6	5	4	4	8	7	7	6	28	23	14	12
	E	26	22	S	11	10	2	2	2	2	3	3	9	7	23	19	18	15
	ST	44	38		30	26	9	7	6	6	11	9	16	13	52	43	33	27

		TENNESSEE			GEORGIA		ALABAMA		MISSISSIPPI		FLORIDA		LOUISIANA		ARKANSAS		OKLAHOMA	
		C	D		C	D	C	D	C	D	C	D	C	D	C	D	C	D
FIRE BUG	W	50	.4	N	33	.3	67	2	25	2	100	2	**	**	33	1	**	**
	E	50	.4	S	67	1	33	1	75	5	**	**	100	3	67	1	**	**
	ST		1			1		3		6		2		3		2		**
FIREFLY	W	46	4	N	65	4	85	12	50	3	53	7	67	5	63	7	52	11
	E	54	5	S	35	2	15	2	50	3	47	6	33	3	38	4	48	10
	ST		9			6		14		6		13		8		11		21
GLOW WORM	W	50	3	N	82	3	50	1	50	2	40	2	**	**	71	3	50	2
	E	50	3	S	18	1	50	1	50	2	60	3	**	**	29	1	50	2
	ST		6			4		2		3		4		**		5		4
JUNE BUG	W	86	1	N	50	.3	**	**	**	**	50	1	**	**	50	1	**	**
	E	14	.2	S	50	.3	**	**	100	2	50	1	**	**	50	1	100	1
	ST		2			1		**		2		2		**		3		1
LIGHTNING BUG	W	42	35	N	62	55	74	59	65	54	71	56	44	40	55	44	44	33
	E	58	48	S	38	33	26	21	35	29	29	23	56	50	45	36	56	42
	ST		83			88		80		83		79		90		80		74

ITEM (115)
WORK SHEET (60)

INSECTS
A LARGE WINGED INSECT SEEN AROUND WATER

		TENNESSEE A	TENNESSEE B		GEORGIA A	GEORGIA B	ALABAMA A	ALABAMA B	MISSISSIPPI A	MISSISSIPPI B	FLORIDA A	FLORIDA B	LOUISIANA A	LOUISIANA B	ARKANSAS A	ARKANSAS B	OKLAHOMA A	OKLAHOMA B
DARNING NEEDLE	W	33	.2	N	**	**	**	**	**	**	17	.1	**	**	20	.3	80	1
	E	33	.2	S	**	**	17	.1	**	**	**	**	**	**	**	**	**	**
	ST	67	.4		**	**	17	.1	**	**	17	.1	**	**	20	.3	80	1
DEVILS DARNING NEEDLE	W	38	1	N	8	.1	**	**	**	**	8	.1	**	**	20	1	60	2
	E	31	.4	S	**	**	**	**	15	.2	**	**	**	**	10	.3	10	.3
	ST	69	1		8	.1	**	**	15	.2	8	.1	**	**	30	1	70	3
DRAGON FLY	W	22	5	N	15	4	10	3	2	1	5	1	6	2	27	8	21	6
	E	28	7	S	7	2	5	1	.4	.1	4	1	2	1	16	5	28	8
	ST	50	12		23	6	15	4	3	1	9	2	9	3	43	13	49	14
CAR SEWER					(NO RESPONSE)													
	E	50	.1	S	50	.1	**	**	**	**	**	**	**	**	**	**	**	**
	ST	50	.1		50	.1	**	**	**	**	**	**	**	**	**	**	**	**
MOSQUITO HAWK	W	3	1	N	9	2	6	1	1	.2	23	5	19	5	15	4	**	**
	E	1	.3	S	36	8	4	1	6	1	11	3	27	6	37	9	1	.3
	ST	4	1		45	10	10	2	7	2	34	8	46	11	52	13	1	.3
SEWING NEEDLE	W	**	**	N	**	**	63	1	13	.1	**	**	**	**	**	**	100	.3
	E	**	**	S	**	**	25	.2	**	**	**	**	**	**	**	**	**	**
	ST	**	**		**	**	88	1	13	.1	**	**	**	**	**	**	100	.3
SNAKE DOCTOR	W	35	12	N	32	12	8	3	8	3	1	.2	1	.3	43	16	13	5
	E	10	3	S	4	1	1	.3	2	1	**	**	1	.3	20	7	22	8
	ST	44	16		36	13	9	3	10	4	1	.2	2	1	63	23	35	13
SNAKE FEEDER	W	5	1	N	7	1	1	.2	**	**	**	**	**	**	47	3	29	2
	E	86	15	S	1	.1	**	**	**	**	**	**	**	**	18	1	6	.3
	ST	91	16		8	1	1	.2	**	**	**	**	**	**	65	4	35	2

(CONTINUED) A LARGE WINGED INSECT SEEN AROUND WATER

ITEM (115)		TENNESSEE C	TENNESSEE D		GEORGIA C	GEORGIA D	ALABAMA C	ALABAMA D	MISSISSIPPI C	MISSISSIPPI D	FLORIDA C	FLORIDA D	LOUISIANA C	LOUISIANA D	ARKANSAS C	ARKANSAS D	OKLAHOMA C	OKLAHOMA D
DARNING NEEDLE	W	50	.4	N	**	**	**	**	**	**	100	1	**	**	100	1	100	4
	E	50	.4	S	**	**	100	1	**	**	**	**	**	**	**	**	**	**
	ST		1			**		1		**		1		**		1		4
DEVILS DARNING NEEDLE	W	56	1	N	100	.3	**	**	**	**	100	1	**	**	67	1	86	6
	E	44	1	S	**	**	**	**	100	3	**	**	**	**	33	1	14	1
	ST		2			.3		**		3		1		**		2		7
DRAGON FLY	W	43	12	N	67	13	68	25	86	10	59	13	71	13	63	15	43	18
	E	57	15	S	33	6	32	12	14	2	41	9	29	5	37	9	58	24
	ST		27			19		37		11		22		18		24		43
EAR SEWER					(NO RESPONSE)													
	E	100	.2	S	100	.3	**	**	**	**	**	**	**	**	**	**	**	**
	ST		.2			.3		**		**		**		**		**		**
MOSQUITO HAWK	W	67	1	N	20	7	62	13	13	3	67	50	42	33	29	7	**	**
	E	33	1	S	80	27	38	8	88	23	33	25	58	45	71	17	100	1
	ST		2			33		21		26		74		78		24		1
SEWING NEEDLE	W	**	**	N	**	**	71	5	100	2	**	**	**	**	**	**	100	1
	E	**	**	S	**	**	29	2	**	**	**	**	**	**	**	**	**	**
	ST		**			**		7		2		**		**		**		1
SNAKE DOCTOR	W	79	27	N	90	38	90	28	80	46	100	2	50	3	68	29	37	14
	E	21	7	S	10	4	10	3	20	11	**	**	50	3	32	14	63	23
	ST		34			43		31		57		2		5		43		37
SNAKE FEEDER	W	5	2	N	92	4	100	2	**	**	**	**	**	**	73	5	83	5
	E	95	33	S	8	.3	**	**	**	**	**	**	**	**	27	2	17	1
	ST		34			4		2		**		**		**		7		6

ITEM (116)
WORK SHEET (60)

ANIMALS
A FRESHWATER SHELLFISH WITH CLAWS, THAT SWIMS BACKWARD

		TENNESSEE			GEORGIA		ALABAMA		MISSISSIPPI		FLORIDA		LOUISIANA		ARKANSAS		OKLAHOMA	
		A	B		A	B	A	B	A	B	A	B	A	B	A	B	A	B
CRABS	W	18	1	N	15	1	1	.1	1	.1	16	1	**	**	14	1	**	**
	E	15	1	S	15	1	5	.4	3	.2	11	1	29	1	36	2	21	1
	ST	32	2		30	2	7	1	4	.3	27	2	29	1	50	3	21	1
CRAWS	W	**	**	N	**	**	14	.1	**	**	14	.1	**	**	**	**	**	**
	E	29	.2	S	**	**	14	.1	14	.1	14	.1	**	**	**	**	**	**
	ST	29	.2		**	**	29	.2	14	.1	29	.2	**	**	**	**	**	**
CRAWDAD(DIE)S	W	26	2	N	1	.1	4	.3	3	.2	4	.3	3	1	37	15	23	9
	E	49	3	S	**	**	3	.2	3	.2	6	.4	**	**	12	5	26	10
	ST	75	5		1	.1	7	1	6	.4	10	1	3	1	49	19	49	19
CRAWFISH	W	19	13	N	20	14	6	5	4	3	6	4	11	5	25	12	6	3
	E	24	17	S	12	9	3	2	3	2	3	2	14	6	32	15	12	6
	ST	43	30		32	23	9	6	7	5	9	6	24	12	57	27	18	9
CRAYFISH	W	15	1	N	14	1	10	1	9	1	9	1	18	1	24	1	12	1
	E	32	3	S	8	1	**	**	**	**	3	.2	12	1	24	1	12	1
	ST	47	4		22	2	10	1	9	1	12	1	29	2	47	3	24	1

		TENNESSEE			GEORGIA		ALABAMA		MISSISSIPPI		FLORIDA		LOUISIANA		ARKANSAS		OKLAHOMA	
		C	D		C	D	C	D	C	D	C	D	C	D	C	D	C	D
CRABS	W	54	3	N	50	4	20	1	33	2	60	12	**	**	29	1	**	**
	E	46	3	S	50	4	80	5	67	3	40	8	100	9	71	3	100	4
	ST		6			8		6		5		20		9		5		4
CRAWS	W	**	**	N	**	**	50	1	**	**	50	1	**	**	**	**	**	**
	E	100	.4	S	**	**	50	1	100	2	50	1	**	**	**	**	**	**
	ST		.4			**		3		2		2		**		**		**
CRAWDAD(DIE)S	W	35	4	N	100	.3	60	4	50	3	43	3	100	7	76	28	48	31
	E	65	8	S	**	**	40	3	50	3	57	4	**	**	24	9	52	33
	ST		13			.3		6		6		7		7		38		64
CRAWFISH	W	44	32	N	62	53	73	55	59	45	66	40	44	32	44	23	33	9
	E	56	40	S	38	32	27	20	41	31	34	21	56	41	56	29	67	19
	ST		72			85		75		77		62		73		52		28
CRAYFISH	W	32	3	N	65	4	100	10	100	11	78	7	60	7	50	3	50	2
	E	68	6	S	35	2	**	**	**	**	22	2	40	5	50	3	50	2
	ST		9			7		10		11		9		11		6		5

INSECTS
A WEB INDOORS

ITEM (117)
WORK SHEET (61)

		TENNESSEE A	TENNESSEE B		GEORGIA A	GEORGIA B	ALABAMA A	ALABAMA B	MISSISSIPPI A	MISSISSIPPI B	FLORIDA A	FLORIDA B	LOUISIANA A	LOUISIANA B	ARKANSAS A	ARKANSAS B	OKLAHOMA A	OKLAHOMA B
COBWEB(A)	W	22	11	N	17	8	8	4	4	2	8	4	6	4	25	16	17	11
	E	24	12	S	8	4	3	1	3	1	4	2	9	6	24	15	18	12
	ST	46	23		24	12	10	5	7	4	12	6	16	10	49	31	36	22
DUST WEB	W	33	.3	N	11	.1	**	**	11	.1	**	**	**	**	**	**	**	**
	E	22	.2	S	22	.2	**	**	**	**	**	**	50	.3	50	.3	**	**
	ST	56	1		33	.3	**	**	11	.1	**	**	50	.3	50	.3	**	**
SPIDERS WEB(A)	W	27	3	N	18	2	3	.4	4	1	7	1	7	1	37	4	4	.3
	E	22	3	S	11	1	2	.2	**	**	5	1	**	**	30	3	22	2
	ST	49	6		30	4	5	1	4	1	12	1	7	1	67	6	26	3
SPIDER WEB(A)	W	17	7	N	17	7	7	3	3	1	9	4	9	3	27	9	10	3
	E	25	10	S	14	6	2	1	2	1	3	1	10	3	28	9	17	5
	ST	42	17		32	13	10	4	5	2	11	5	19	6	54	18	27	9
WEB(A)	W	22	.4	N	22	.4	6	.1	**	**	11	.2	**	**	56	2	**	**
	E	33	1	S	**	**	**	**	**	**	6	.1	**	**	**	**	44	1
	ST	56	1		22	.4	6	.1	**	**	17	.3	**	**	56	2	44	1

		TENNESSEE C	TENNESSEE D		GEORGIA C	GEORGIA D	ALABAMA C	ALABAMA D	MISSISSIPPI C	MISSISSIPPI D	FLORIDA C	FLORIDA D	LOUISIANA C	LOUISIANA D	ARKANSAS C	ARKANSAS D	OKLAHOMA C	OKLAHOMA D
COBWEB(A)	W	48	23	N	69	28	75	39	61	35	65	31	41	23	52	28	48	31
	E	52	25	S	31	13	25	13	39	22	35	17	59	34	48	26	52	33
	ST		49			41		53		57		48		57		54		64
DUST WEB	W	60	1	N	33	.3	**	**	100	2	**	**	**	**	**	**	**	**
	E	40	.4	S	67	1	**	**	**	**	**	**	100	2	100	1	**	**
	ST		1			1		**		2		**		2		1		**
SPIDERS WEB(A)	W	55	7	N	62	7	67	4	100	8	57	7	100	4	56	6	14	1
	E	45	5	S	38	5	33	2	**	**	43	5	**	**	44	5	86	6
	ST		12			12		6		8		12		4		11		7
SPIDER WEB(A)	W	41	15	N	55	24	74	30	52	17	76	29	47	17	49	15	38	9
	E	59	21	S	45	20	26	10	48	16	24	9	53	19	51	16	63	15
	ST		36			44		40		33		38		36		31		25
WEB(A)	W	40	1	N	100	1	100	1	**	**	67	2	**	**	100	3	**	**
	E	60	1	S	**	**	**	**	**	**	33	1	**	**	**	**	100	4
	ST		2			1		1		**		3		**		3		4

A WEB OUTDOORS

ITEM (117)
WORK SHEET (61)

		TENNESSEE A	TENNESSEE B		GEORGIA A	GEORGIA B	ALABAMA A	ALABAMA B	MISSISSIPPI A	MISSISSIPPI B	FLORIDA A	FLORIDA B	LOUISIANA A	LOUISIANA B	ARKANSAS A	ARKANSAS B	OKLAHOMA A	OKLAHOMA B
COBWEB(B)	W	21	4	N	18	3	10	2	5	1	8	2	5	1	24	5	10	2
	E	18	3	S	12	2	3	1	2	.4	3	1	14	3	30	7	17	4
	ST	39	7		30	6	13	2	7	1	11	2	19	4	54	12	27	6
DEW WEB	W	30	1	N	22	1	4	.1	**	**	4	.1	**	**	50	.3	**	**
	E	22	1	S	4	.1	4	.1	**	**	9	.2	**	**	**	**	50	.3
	ST	52	1		26	1	9	.2	**	**	13	.3	**	**	50	.3	50	.3
SPIDER NEST	W	27	1	N	27	1	**	**	3	.1	3	.1	14	.3	57	1	**	**
	E	20	1	S	13	.4	**	**	**	**	7	.2	**	**	**	**	29	1
	ST	47	1		40	1	**	**	3	.1	10	.3	14	.3	57	1	29	1
SPIDERS WEB(B)	W	20	4	N	15	3	6	1	4	1	8	2	[illegible]	1	29	5	20	3
	E	28	6	S	10	2	1	[illegible]	[illegible]	1	3	1	**	**	22	4	24	4
	ST	[illegible]	10		26	5	6	1	8	2	12	2	4	1	51	8	44	7
SPIDER WEB(B)	W	20	10	N	19	9	8	4	4	2	6	3	10	5	26	13	17	9
	E	24	12	S	11	5	3	2	2	1	3	1	10	5	21	11	17	9
	ST	45	22		29	14	11	5	6	3	9	4	20	10	46	24	34	18
WEB(B)	W	21	1	N	18	1	14	.4	4	.1	7	.2	**	**	40	1	10	.3
	E	18	1	S	14	.4	4	.1	**	**	**	**	**	**	10	.3	40	1
	ST	39	1		32	1	18	1	4	.1	7	.2	**	**	50	2	50	2

		TENNESSEE C	TENNESSEE D		GEORGIA C	GEORGIA D	ALABAMA C	ALABAMA D	MISSISSIPPI C	MISSISSIPPI D	FLORIDA C	FLORIDA D	LOUISIANA C	LOUISIANA D	ARKANSAS C	ARKANSAS D	OKLAHOMA C	OKLAHOMA D
COBWEB(B)	W	54	9	N	59	12	78	19	69	15	75	16	25	7	44	11	35	6
	E	46	8	S	41	8	22	5	31	7	25	5	75	20	56	14	65	12
	ST		17			20		24		22		22		27		25		18
DEW WEB	W	58	2	N	83	2	50	1	**	**	33	1	**	**	100	1	**	**
	E	42	1	S	17	.3	50	1	**	**	67	2	**	**	**	**	100	1
	ST		3			2		2		**		3		**		1		1
SPIDER NEST	W	57	2	N	67	3	**	**	100	2	33	1	100	2	100	3	**	**
	E	43	1	S	33	1	**	**	**	**	67	2	**	**	**	**	100	2
	ST		3			4		**		2		3		2		3		2
SPIDERS WEB(B)	W	42	9	N	59	11	92	12	53	13	73	17	100	5	57	10	45	10
	E	58	13	S	41	7	8	1	47	12	27	7	**	**	43	7	55	12
	ST		23			18		13		25		24		5		17		21
SPIDER WEB(B)	W	45	23	N	63	33	71	39	67	33	71	33	48	32	55	28	49	26
	E	55	28	S	37	19	29	16	33	17	29	13	52	34	45	22	51	27
	ST		52			52		55		50		46		66		50		52
WEB(B)	W	55	1	N	56	2	80	4	100	2	100	2	**	**	80	3	20	1
	E	45	1	S	44	1	20	1	**	**	**	**	**	**	20	1	80	4
	ST		3			3		5		2		2		**		4		5

VEGETATION
A TREE THAT PRODUCES SUGAR AND SYRUP

ITEM (118)
WORK SHEET (61)

		TENNESSEE A	TENNESSEE B		GEORGIA A	GEORGIA B	ALABAMA A	ALABAMA B	MISSISSIPPI A	MISSISSIPPI B	FLORIDA A	FLORIDA B	LOUISIANA A	LOUISIANA B	ARKANSAS A	ARKANSAS B	OKLAHOMA A	OKLAHOMA B
HARD MAPLE	W	38	.3	N	**	**	**	**	**	**	**	**	**	**	67	1	**	**
	E	13	.1	S	25	.2	**	**	13	.1	13	.1	17	.3	17	.3	**	**
	ST	50	.4		25	.2	**	**	13	.1	13	.1	17	.3	83	2	**	**
ROCK MAPLE	W	**	**	N	22	.2	11	.1	**	**	22	.2	**	**	**	**	**	**
	E	22	.2	S	11	.1	**	**	11	.1	**	**	**	**	**	**	**	**
	ST	22	.2		33	.3	11	.1	11	.1	22	.2	**	**	**	**	**	**
SUGAR MAPLE	W	20	11	N	24	13	8	4	4	2	5	3	7	4	32	18	13	8
	E	23	12	S	11	6	2	1	2	1	3	2	4	3	28	16	15	9
	ST	42	23		35	19	10	5	5	3	8	5	12	6	60	34	29	16
SUGAR TREE	W	38	6	N	3	.4	5	1	5	1	**	**	**	**	50	3	14	1
	E	46	7	S	3	1	1	.1	**	**	**	**	**	**	14	1	21	1
	ST	85	14		6	1	5	1	5	1	**	**	**	**	64	3	36	2

		TENNESSEE C	TENNESSEE D		GEORGIA C	GEORGIA D	ALABAMA C	ALABAMA D	MISSISSIPPI C	MISSISSIPPI D	FLORIDA C	FLORIDA D	LOUISIANA C	LOUISIANA D	ARKANSAS C	ARKANSAS D	OKLAHOMA C	OKLAHOMA D
HARD MAPLE	W	75	1	N	**	**	**	**	**	**	**	**	**	**	80	4	**	**
	E	25	.2	S	100	1	**	**	100	3	100	2	100	5	20	1	**	**
	ST		1			1		**		3		2		5		5		**
ROCK MAPLE	W	**	**	N	67	1	100	2	**	**	100	4	**	**	**	**	**	**
	E	100	1	S	33	1	**	**	100	3	**	**	**	**	**	**	**	**
	ST		1			2		2		3		4		**		**		**
SUGAR MAPLE	W	46	29	N	68	63	81	69	70	53	66	62	61	58	54	47	47	42
	E	54	33	S	32	29	19	16	30	22	34	32	39	37	46	40	53	48
	ST		62			93		85		75		94		95		87		90
SUGAR TREE	W	45	16	N	44	2	88	11	100	19	**	**	**	**	78	7	40	4
	E	55	20	S	56	3	13	2	**	**	**	**	**	**	22	2	60	6
	ST		36			5		13		19		**		**		8		10

VEGETATION
A PLACE WHERE SAP IS GATHERED

ITEM (119)
WORK SHEET (61)

		TENNESSEE			GEORGIA		ALABAMA		MISSISSIPPI		FLORIDA		LOUISIANA		ARKANSAS		OKLAHOMA	
		A	B		A	B	A	B	A	B	A	B	A	B	A	B	A	B
MAPLE GROVE	W	25	2	N	25	2	10	1	3	.3	2	.2	3	.3	36	5	8	1
	E	18	2	S	12	1	2	.2	1	.1	1	.1	8	1	25	3	19	3
	ST	43	4		37	3	12	1	4	.4	3	.3	11	1	61	8	28	4
MAPLE ORCHARD	W	20	1	N	18	1	2	.1	4	.2	9	1	**	**	38	2	15	1
	E	27	2	S	9	1	4	.2	2	.1	7	.4	**	**	23	1	23	1
	ST	46	3		27	2	5	.3	5	.3	16	1	**	**	62	3	38	2
SAP BUSH	W	17	.1	N	17	.1	33	.2	**	**	17	.1	**	**	100	.3	**	**
	E	**	**	S	17	.1	**	**	**	**	**	**	**	**	**	**	**	**
	ST	17	.1		33	.2	33	.2	**	**	17	.1	**	**	100	.3	**	**
SAP ORCHARD	W	6	.1	N	22	.4	11	.2	11	.2	**	**	**	**	67	1	**	**
	E	44	1	S	6	.1	**	**	**	**	**	**	33	.3	**	**	**	**
	ST	50	1		28	1	11	.2	11	.2	**	**	33	.3	67	1	**	**
SUGAR BUSH	W	25	.4	N	13	.2	6	.1	**	**	6	.1	**	**	100	.3	**	**
	E	31	1	S	**	**	6	.1	13	.2	**	**	**	**	**	**	**	**
	ST	56	1		13	.2	13	.2	13	.2	6	.1	**	**	100	.3	**	**
SUGAR CAMP	W	24	1	N	5	.1	19	.4	5	.1	**	**	13	.3	63	2	**	**
	E	48	1	S	**	**	**	**	**	**	**	**	13	.3	**	**	13	.3
	ST	71	2		5	.1	19	.4	5	.1	**	**	25	1	63	2	13	.3
SUGAR GROVE	W	35	1	N	9	.3	3	.1	**	**	**	**	**	**	67	1	**	**
	E	44	2	S	6	.2	3	.1	**	**	**	**	**	**	**	**	33	1
	ST	79	3		15	1	6	.2	**	**	**	**	**	**	67	1	33	1
SUGAR LOT	W	20	.1	N	**	**	20	.1	**	**	**	**	**	**	**	**	**	**
	E	60	.3	S	**	**	**	**	**	**	**	**	**	**	**	**	**	**
	ST	80	.4		**	**	20	.1	**	**	**	**	**	**	**	**	**	**
SUGAR MAPLE GROVE	W	20	2	N	31	3	10	1	2	.2	1	.1	8	1	52	5	16	1
	E	20	2	S	11	1	2	.2	1	.1	1	.1	**	**	20	2	4	.3
	ST	40	3		42	4	12	1	4	.3	2	.2	8	1	72	6	20	2
SUGAR ORCHARD	W	13	.4	N	13	.4	3	.1	3	.1	3	.1	**	**	100	.3	**	**
	E	50	2	S	7	.2	**	**	3	.1	3	.1	**	**	**	**	**	**
	ST	63	2		20	1	3	.1	7	.2	7	.2	**	**	100	.3	**	**
SUGAR PLACE	W	40	.2	N	**	**	20	.1	**	**	**	**	**	**	**	**	**	**
	E	**	**	S	20	.1	**	**	20	.1	**	**	**	**	100	.3	**	**
	ST	40	.2		20	.1	20	.1	20	.1	**	**	**	**	100	.3	**	**
SUGAR TREE GROVE	W	36	2	N	9	1	3	.2	3	.2	2	.1	**	**	67	1	17	.3
	E	42	3	S	5	.3	**	**	**	**	**	**	**	**	17	.3	**	**
	ST	78	5		14	1	3	.2	3	.2	2	.1	**	**	83	2	17	.3

(CONTINUED) A PLACE WHERE SAP IS GATHERED

ITEM (119)		TENNESSEE C	TENNESSEE D		GEORGIA C	GEORGIA D	ALABAMA C	ALABAMA D	MISSISSIPPI C	MISSISSIPPI D	FLORIDA C	FLORIDA D	LOUISIANA C	LOUISIANA D	ARKANSAS C	ARKANSAS D	OKLAHOMA C	OKLAHOMA D
MAPLE GROVE	W	58	9	N	67	19	82	22	75	15	67	11	25	11	59	19	30	13
	E	42	7	S	33	10	18	5	25	5	33	5	75	33	41	13	70	29
	ST		16			29		27		20		16		44		32		42
MAPLE ORCHARD	W	42	5	N	67	9	33	2	67	10	56	26	**	**	63	7	40	8
	E	58	6	S	33	4	67	5	33	5	44	21	**	**	38	4	60	13
	ST		11			13		7		15		47		**		12		21
SAP BUSH	W	100	.4	N	50	1	100	5	**	**	100	5	**	**	100	1	**	**
	E	**	**	S	50	1	**	**	**	**	**	**	**	**	**	**	**	**
	ST		.4			2		5		**		5		**		1		**
SAP ORCHARD	W	11	.4	N	80	4	100	5	100	10	**	**	**	**	100	3	**	**
	E	89	3	S	20	1	**	**	**	**	**	**	100	11	**	**	**	**
	ST		4			4		5		10		**		11		3		**
SUGAR BUSH	W	44	2	N	100	2	50	2	**	**	100	5	**	**	100	1	**	**
	E	56	2	S	**	**	50	2	100	10	**	**	**	**	**	**	**	**
	ST		4			2		5		10		5		**		1		**
SUGAR CAMP	W	33	2	N	100	1	100	10	100	5	**	**	50	11	100	7	**	**
	E	67	4	S	**	**	**	**	**	**	**	**	50	11	**	**	100	4
	ST		6			1		10		5		**		22		7		4
SUGAR GROVE	W	44	5	N	60	3	50	2	**	**	**	**	**	**	100	6	**	**
	E	56	6	S	40	2	50	2	**	**	**	**	**	**	**	**	100	8
	ST		12			4		5		**		**		**		6		8
SUGAR LOT	W	25	.4	N	**	**	100	2	**	**	**	**	**	**	**	**	**	**
	E	75	1	S	**	**	**	**	**	**	**	**	**	**	**	**	**	**
	ST		2			**		2		**		**		**		**		**
SUGAR MAPLE GROVE	W	50	7	N	74	22	80	20	67	10	50	5	100	22	72	19	80	17
	E	50	7	S	26	8	20	5	33	5	50	5	**	**	28	7	20	4
	ST		14			30		24		15		11		22		26		21
SUGAR ORCHARD	W	21	2	N	67	4	100	2	50	5	50	5	**	**	100	1	**	**
	E	79	6	S	33	2	**	**	50	5	50	5	**	**	**	**	**	**
	ST		8			5		2		10		11		**		1		**
SUGAR PLACE	W	100	1	N	**	**	100	2	**	**	**	**	**	**	**	**	**	**
	E	**	**	S	100	1	**	**	100	5	**	**	**	**	100	1	**	**
	ST		1			1		2		5		**		**		1		**
SUGAR TREE	W	46	10	N	67	5	100	5	100	10	100	5	**	**	80	6	100	4
	E	54	12	S	33	3	**	**	**	**	**	**	**	**	20	1	**	**
										10		5		**		7		4

ITEM (120)
WORK SHEET (62)

VEGETATION
A BUNCH OF TREES GROWING IN OPEN COUNTRY, PARTICULARLY ON A HILL

		TENNESSEE A	TENNESSEE B		GEORGIA A	GEORGIA B	ALABAMA A	ALABAMA B	MISSISSIPPI A	MISSISSIPPI B	FLORIDA A	FLORIDA B	LOUISIANA A	LOUISIANA B	ARKANSAS A	ARKANSAS B	OKLAHOMA A	OKLAHOMA B
MOTTE	W	**	**	N	50	.1	**	**	**	**	**	**	**	**	**	**	**	**
	E	50	.1	S	**	**	**	**	**	**	**	**	**	**	**	**	**	**
	ST	50	.1		50	.1	**	**	**	**	**	**	**	**	**	**	**	**
CLUMP	W	19	6	N	17	5	7	2	4	1	8	3	9	3	26	9	16	5
	E	22	7	S	11	4	3	1	2	1	6	2	11	4	22	7	17	6
	ST	42	13		28	9	10	3	6	2	14	5	19	6	47	16	33	11
GROVE	W	23	10	N	18	8	8	4	5	2	5	2	7	4	31	18	14	8
	E	24	11	S	12	5	3	1	2	1	1	.4	6	4	20	12	11	12
	ST	46	21		30	14	11	5	7	3	[illegible]	[illegible]	[illegible]	8	51	29	36	21
BLUFF	W	[illegible]	2	N	27	2	3	.3	1	.1	7	1	14	.3	14	.3	**	**
	E	28	2	S	9	1	1	.1	2	.2	1	.1	**	**	43	1	29	1
	ST	48	4		36	3	5	.4	3	.3	8	1	14	.3	57	1	29	1

		TENNESSEE C	TENNESSEE D		GEORGIA C	GEORGIA D	ALABAMA C	ALABAMA D	MISSISSIPPI C	MISSISSIPPI D	FLORIDA C	FLORIDA D	LOUISIANA C	LOUISIANA D	ARKANSAS C	ARKANSAS D	OKLAHOMA C	OKLAHOMA D
MOTTE	W	**	**	N	100	.3	**	**	**	**	**	**	**	**	**	**	**	**
	E	100	.2	S	**	**	**	**	**	**	**	**	**	**	**	**	**	**
	ST		.2			.3		**		**		**		**		**		**
CLUMP	W	46	16	N	61	21	74	28	65	25	59	33	44	20	55	19	48	17
	E	54	19	S	39	14	26	10	35	13	41	23	56	25	45	16	52	18
	ST		35			35		38		38		56		45		34		34
GROVE	W	49	26	N	61	32	74	43	69	38	85	29	52	28	60	38	40	26
	E	51	28	S	39	20	26	15	31	17	15	5	48	25	40	25	60	38
	ST		54			53		57		56		35		53		63		63
BLUFF	W	41	5	N	74	9	75	4	33	2	[illegible]	8	100	3	25	1	**	**
	E	59	6	S	26	3	25	1	67	4	14	1	**	**	75	2	100	2
	ST		11			12		5		6		9		3		3		2

VEGETATION
(NO TEXT)

ITEM (121)
WORK SHEET (62)

		TENNESSEE A	TENNESSEE B		GEORGIA A	GEORGIA B	ALABAMA A	ALABAMA B	MISSISSIPPI A	MISSISSIPPI B	FLORIDA A	FLORIDA B	LOUISIANA A	LOUISIANA B	ARKANSAS A	ARKANSAS B	OKLAHOMA A	OKLAHOMA B
POISON IVY	W	16	8	N	15	8	8	4	3	2	10	5	5	3	24	15	22	13
	E	24	12	S	14	7	3	2	2	1	5	2	9	5	19	12	22	13
	ST	40	21		29	15	11	6	5	3	15	8	14	9	43	27	43	27
POISON IVORY	W	25	1	N	19	1	11	.4	6	.2	8	.3	**	**	33	.3	**	**
	E	11	.4	S	11	.4	**	**	3	.1	6	.2	33	.3	33	.3	**	**
	ST	36	1		31	1	11	.4	8	.3	14	1	33	.3	67	1	**	**
POISON OAK	W	25	12	N	23	11	10	5	4	2	6	3	9	4	32	16	11	5
	E	16	8	S	10	5	2	1	3	1	1	.4	7	3	26	12	16	8
	ST	41	20		33	16	13	6	7	4	7	3	16	8	58	28	26	13
POISON VINE	W	12	1	N	3	.3	**	**	**	**	4	.4	**	**	50	1	**	**
	E	75	8	S	4	.4	**	**	**	**	2	.2	13	.3	38	1	**	**
	ST	88	9		7	1	**	**	**	**	6	1	13	.3	88	3	**	**

		TENNESSEE C	TENNESSEE D		GEORGIA C	GEORGIA D	ALABAMA C	ALABAMA D	MISSISSIPPI C	MISSISSIPPI D	FLORIDA C	FLORIDA D	LOUISIANA C	LOUISIANA D	ARKANSAS C	ARKANSAS D	OKLAHOMA C	OKLAHOMA D
POISON IVY	W	41	16	N	53	24	70	32	58	24	68	43	38	19	55	26	50	34
	E	59	24	S	47	22	30	14	42	17	32	21	63	32	45	21	50	34
	ST		40			46		46		41		64		51		46		68
POISON IVORY	W	69	2	N	64	2	100	3	67	3	60	3	**	**	50	1	**	**
	E	31	1	S	36	1	**	**	33	2	40	2	100	2	50	1	**	**
	ST		3			4		3		5		4		2		1		**
POISON OAK	W	62	24	N	70	34	81	41	59	32	87	23	57	26	56	27	40	13
	E	38	15	S	30	14	19	9	41	22	13	3	43	19	44	21	60	19
	ST		38			48		50		54		27		45		48		32
POISON VINE	W	14	3	N	43	1	**	**	**	**	67	3	**	**	57	3	**	**
	E	86	16	S	57	1	**	**	**	**	33	2	100	2	43	2	**	**
	ST		19			2		**		**		5		2		4		**

ITEM (122)
WORK SHEET (63)

RELATIONSHIPS
FAMILY WORD FOR FATHER

		TENNESSEE A	TENNESSEE B		GEORGIA A	GEORGIA B	ALABAMA A	ALABAMA B	MISSISSIPPI A	MISSISSIPPI B	FLORIDA A	FLORIDA B	LOUISIANA A	LOUISIANA B	ARKANSAS A	ARKANSAS B	OKLAHOMA A	OKLAHOMA B
DAD	W	24	4	N	14	2	7	1	2	.3	7	1	5	1	22	6	25	7
	E	29	5	S	9	2	2	.4	2	.4	4	1	5	1	14	4	29	8
	ST	53	9		23	4	10	2	4	1	11	2	10	3	35	10	54	16
DADDY	W	18	9	N	16	8	8	4	5	2	7	3	7	3	26	12	13	6
	E	26	13	S	13	6	3	1	2	1	3	1	7	3	26	12	22	10
	ST	44	21		29	14	10	5	6	3	10	5	14	6	52	24	34	16
FATHER	W	23	2	N	21	2	13	1	2	.2	4	.4	3	.3	27	3	13	1
	E	22	2	S	5	1	1	.1	3	.3	4	.4	3	.3	27	3	[illegible]	[illegible]
	ST	45	4		26	2	14	1	5	1	9	1	[illegible]	1	53	6	40	[illegible]
PA	W	11	1	N	[illegible]	[illegible]	8	1	1	.1	8	1	**	**	71	4	7	.3
	E	[illegible]	3	S	14	1	1	.1	3	.3	3	.3	7	.3	7	.3	7	.3
	ST	40	4		36	4	9	1	4	.4	11	1	7	.3	79	4	14	1
PAPA	W	20	5	N	25	6	6	1	6	1	9	2	10	3	33	8	14	4
	E	15	4	S	8	2	2	.4	4	1	5	1	13	3	19	5	11	3
	ST	35	8		33	8	8	2	10	2	14	3	23	6	51	13	26	6
PAPPY	W	37	1	N	3	.1	**	**	**	**	6	.2	25	.3	25	.3	**	**
	E	46	2	S	9	.3	**	**	**	**	**	**	**	**	25	.3	25	.3
	ST	83	3		11	.4	**	**	**	**	6	.2	25	.3	50	1	25	.3
PAW	W	26	1	N	13	1	3	.1	3	.1	**	**	17	1	50	2	8	.3
	E	33	1	S	13	1	**	**	3	.1	8	.3	8	.3	17	1	**	**
	ST	59	2		26	1	3	.1	5	.2	8	.3	25	1	67	3	8	.3
POP	W	24	1	N	24	1	7	.2	**	**	7	.2	10	.3	20	1	30	1
	E	21	1	S	7	.2	**	**	3	.1	7	.2	20	1	10	.3	10	.3
	ST	45	1		31	1	7	.2	3	.1	14	.4	30	1	30	1	40	1

ITEM (122) (CONTINUED) FAMILY WORD FOR FATHER

ITEM		TENNESSEE C	TENNESSEE D		GEORGIA C	GEORGIA D	ALABAMA C	ALABAMA D	MISSISSIPPI C	MISSISSIPPI D	FLORIDA C	FLORIDA D	LOUISIANA C	LOUISIANA D	ARKANSAS C	ARKANSAS D	OKLAHOMA C	OKLAHOMA D
DAD	W	46	8	N	61	7	75	11	43	4	61	9	50	8	61	10	47	16
	E	54	9	S	39	5	25	4	57	6	39	6	50	8	39	6	53	18
	ST		17			11		15		10		15		15		16		34
DADDY	W	41	16	N	55	23	74	33	73	31	72	27	50	17	50	19	36	13
	E	59	24	S	45	19	26	11	27	11	28	10	50	17	50	19	64	22
	ST		40			41		44		42		37		35		39		35
FATHER	W	51	4	N	79	6	92	11	40	3	50	3	50	2	50	5	33	3
	E	49	4	S	21	2	8	1	60	4	50	3	50	2	50	5	67	6
	ST		8			7		12		7		6		4		9		10
PA	W	28	2	N	60	6	89	8	25	1	73	6	**	**	91	6	50	1
	E	72	5	S	40	4	11	1	75	4	27	2	100	2	9	1	50	1
	ST		8			11		8		6		9		2		6		2
PAPA	W	57	9	N	77	17	78	13	59	18	66	17	44	13	64	14	56	8
	E	43	7	S	23	5	22	4	41	13	34	9	56	17	36	8	44	6
	ST		15			22		17		31		26		31		21		14
PAPPY	W	45	3	N	25	.3	**	**	**	**	100	2	100	2	50	1	**	**
	E	55	3	S	75	1	**	**	**	**	**	**	**	**	50	1	100	1
	ST		6			1		**		**		2		2		1		1
PAW	W	43	2	N	50	2	100	1	50	1	**	**	67	4	75	4	100	1
	E	57	3	S	50	2	**	**	50	1	100	2	33	2	25	1	**	**
	ST		4			3		1		3		2		6		5		1
POP	W	54	1	N	78	2	100	2	**	**	50	2	33	2	67	1	75	2
	E	46	1	S	22	1	**	**	100	1	50	2	67	4	33	1	25	1
	ST		3			3		2		1		3		6		2		3

ITEM (123)
WORK SHEET (63)

RELATIONSHIPS
FAMILY WORD FOR MOTHER

		TENNESSEE			GEORGIA		ALABAMA		MISSISSIPPI		FLORIDA		LOUISIANA		ARKANSAS		OKLAHOMA	
		A	B		A	B	A	B	A	B	A	B	A	B	A	B	A	B
MA	W	13	1	N	22	2	5	1	1	.1	8	1	7	.3	43	2	7	.3
	E	28	3	S	16	2	1	.1	2	.2	3	.3	14	1	7	.3	21	1
	ST	41	4		38	4	7	1	3	.3	11	1	21	1	50	3	29	1
MAMA	W	17	7	N	21	9	8	3	5	2	10	4	9	4	25	12	11	5
	E	19	8	S	12	5	4	2	3	1	4	2	10	5	27	13	18	9
	ST	35	15		32	14	11	5	7	3	14	6	19	9	52	25	29	14
MAMMY	W	28	1	N	7	.3	7	.3	2	.1	2	.1	**	**	50	1	**	**
	E	41	2	S	7	.3	2	.1	**	**	4	.2	**	**	17	.3	**	1
	ST	70	3		13	1	9	.4	2	.1	7	.3	**	**	67	1	33	1
MAW	W	17	1	N	13	1	**	**	2	.1	4	.2	10	.3	70	3	10	.3
	E	30	1	S	24	1	**	**	2	.1	7	.3	10	.3	**	**	**	**
	ST	48	2		37	2	**	**	4	.2	11	1	20	1	70	3	10	.3
MOM	W	22	2	N	21	2	9	1	3	.2	6	1	2	.3	25	4	32	5
	E	27	2	S	8	1	**	**	1	.1	3	.2	16	3	7	1	18	3
	ST	49	4		29	2	9	1	4	.3	9	1	18	3	32	5	50	8
MOMMER	W	33	1	N	19	.4	14	.3	5	.1	**	**	33	.3	33	.3	**	**
	E	10	.2	S	14	.3	**	**	**	**	5	.1	**	**	33	.3	**	**
	ST	43	1		33	1	14	.3	5	.1	5	.1	33	.3	67	1	**	**
MOMMY	W	31	1	N	16	1	**	**	6	.2	3	.1	10	.3	30	1	20	1
	E	22	1	S	22	1	**	**	**	**	**	**	20	1	20	1	**	**
	ST	53	2		38	1	**	**	6	.2	3	.1	30	1	50	2	20	1
MOTHER	W	21	9	N	16	7	8	3	5	2	7	3	2	1	27	12	19	8
	E	29	12	S	9	4	2	1	2	1	2	1	5	2	23	10	24	11
	ST	50	22		25	11	9	4	6	3	9	4	7	3	50	22	43	19

ITEM (123) (CONTINUED) FAMILY WORD FOR MOTHER

		TENNESSEE			GEORGIA		ALABAMA		MISSISSIPPI		FLORIDA		LOUISIANA		ARKANSAS		OKLAHOMA	
		C	D		C	D	C	D	C	D	C	D	C	D	C	D	C	D
MA	W	32	2	N	57	6	83	5	33	1	70	6	33	2	86	4	25	1
	E	68	5	S	43	4	17	1	67	3	30	2	67	4	14	1	75	2
	ST		7			10		6		4		8		6		4		3
MAMA	W	48	14	N	64	26	69	31	61	28	70	33	48	24	48	19	37	11
	E	52	15	S	36	14	31	14	39	17	30	14	52	25	52	21	63	20
	ST		29			40		45		45		47		49		41		31
MAMMY	W	41	3	N	50	1	75	3	100	1	33	1	**	**	75	2	**	**
	E	59	4	S	50	1	25	1	**	**	67	2	**	**	25	1	100	2
	ST		6			2		4		1		2		**		2		2
MAW	W	36	2	N	35	2	**	**	50	1	40	2	50	2	100	4	100	1
	E	64	3	S	65	3	**	**	50	1	60	2	50	2	**	**	**	**
	ST		4			5		**		3		4		4		4		1
MOM	W	45	3	N	73	5	100	7	67	3	71	4	13	2	79	6	64	11
	E	55	4	S	27	2	**	**	33	1	29	2	88	14	21	2	36	7
	ST		7			6		7		4		6		16		8		18
MOMMER	W	78	1	N	57	1	100	3	100	1	**	**	100	2	50	1	**	**
	E	22	.3	S	43	1	**	**	**	**	100	1	**	**	50	1	**	**
	ST		2			2		3		1		1		2		1		**
MOMMY	W	59	2	N	42	1	**	**	100	3	100	1	33	2	60	2	100	2
	E	41	1	S	58	2	**	**	**	**	**	**	67	4	40	1	**	**
	ST		3			4		**		3		1		6		3		2
MOTHER	W	42	17	N	65	20	82	30	73	28	73	22	33	6	53	19	43	19
	E	58	24	S	35	11	18	7	27	10	27	8	67	12	47	17	57	25
	ST		41			31		36		38		31		18		36		43

RELATIONSHIPS
THE IMMEDIATE FAMILY

ITEM (124)
WORK SHEET (66)

		TENNESSEE			GEORGIA		ALABAMA		MISSISSIPPI		FLORIDA		LOUISIANA		ARKANSAS		OKLAHOMA	
		A	B		A	B	A	B	A	B	A	B	A	B	A	B	A	B
MY FAMILY(A)	W	18	8	N	17	8	8	4	5	2	10	4	7	4	29	15	13	6
	E	24	11	S	12	5	3	1	2	1	3	1	9	5	24	12	17	9
	ST	42	20		28	13	11	5	7	3	12	6	16	8	54	27	30	15
MY FOLKS(A)	W	19	5	N	18	5	5	1	5	1	5	1	5	1	25	7	22	6
	E	26	7	S	12	3	2	.4	3	1	6	2	4	1	14	4	29	8
	ST	45	12		30	8	7	2	8	2	11	3	9	3	39	11	51	14
MY PARENTS	W	21	3	N	18	2	10	1	3	.4	5	1	6	1	22	4	16	3
	E	25	3	S	10	1	3	.4	2	.2	3	.4	6	1	26	5	24	4
	ST	46	6		28	4	13	2	5	1	8	1	12	2	48	9	40	7
MY PEOPLE(A)	W	32	2	N	7	.4	7	.4	**	**	5	.3	25	1	38	1	**	**
	E	30	2	S	9	1	4	.2	5	.3	**	**	13	.3	13	.3	13	.3
	ST	63	4		16	1	11	1	5	.3	5	.3	38	1	50	1	13	.3
MY RELATIONS(A)	W	45	1	N	27	.3	**	**	**	**	9	.1	**	**	**	**	**	**
	E	18	.2	S	**	**	**	**	**	**	**	**	**	**	**	**	100	.3
	ST	64	1		27	.3	**	**	**	**	9	.1	**	**	**	**	100	.3
MY RELATIVES(A)	W	25	2	N	16	1	13	1	1	.1	6	1	**	**	27	1	**	**
	E	23	2	S	6	1	**	**	4	.3	5	.4	**	**	53	3	20	1
	ST	48	4		22	2	13	1	5	.4	12	1	**	**	80	4	20	1

		TENNESSEE			GEORGIA		ALABAMA		MISSISSIPPI		FLORIDA		LOUISIANA		ARKANSAS		OKLAHOMA	
		C	D		C	D	C	D	C	D	C	D	C	D	C	D	C	D
MY FAMILY(A)	W	42	18	N	59	28	72	36	70	33	78	41	43	26	55	28	43	17
	E	58	25	S	41	19	28	14	30	14	22	11	57	33	45	23	57	23
	ST		43			47		50		48		52		59		52		40
MY FOLKS(A)	W	42	11	N	61	18	78	14	65	21	43	11	57	10	63	13	44	16
	E	58	16	S	39	11	22	4	35	11	57	15	43	8	37	8	56	21
	ST		27			29		18		32		26		18		21		37
MY PARENTS	W	45	6	N	66	9	76	13	67	6	60	6	50	8	46	8	40	8
	E	55	7	S	34	4	24	4	33	3	40	4	50	8	54	9	60	11
	ST		13			13		17		10		9		15		17		19
MY PEOPLE(A)	W	51	4	N	44	1	67	4	**	**	100	3	67	5	75	2	**	**
	E	49	4	S	56	2	33	2	100	5	**	**	33	3	25	1	100	1
	ST		8			3		6		5		3		8		3		1
MY RELATIONS(A)	W	71	1	N	100	1	**	**	**	**	100	1	**	**	**	**	**	**
	E	29	.4	S	**	**	**	**	**	**	**	**	**	**	**	**	100	1
	ST		2			1		**		**		1		**		**		1
MY RELATIVES(A)	W	51	4	N	71	4	100	10	25	2	56	5	**	**	33	3	**	**
	E	49	4	S	29	2	**	**	75	5	44	4	**	**	67	6	100	3
	ST		8			6		10		6		8		**		8		3

RELATIONSHIPS
OTHERS RELATED BY BLOOD

ITEM (124)
WORK SHEET (66)

		TENNESSEE A	TENNESSEE B		GEORGIA A	GEORGIA B	ALABAMA A	ALABAMA B	MISSISSIPPI A	MISSISSIPPI B	FLORIDA A	FLORIDA B	LOUISIANA A	LOUISIANA B	ARKANSAS A	ARKANSAS B	OKLAHOMA A	OKLAHOMA B
MY FAMILY(B)	W	17	2	N	18	2	4	.4	4	.4	12	1	5	.3	24	2	5	.3
	E	29	3	S	8	1	3	.3	**	**	4	.4	10	1	38	3	19	1
	ST	46	4		26	2	8	1	4	.4	17	2	14	1	62	5	24	2
MY FOLKS(B)	W	20	2	N	18	1	9	1	5	.4	7	1	**	**	19	1	31	2
	E	22	2	S	12	1	**	**	5	.4	1	.1	**	**	13	1	38	2
	ST	42	3		30	2	9	1	11	1	8	1	**	**	31	2	69	4
MY KIN	W	37	1	N	9	.3	6	.2	3	.1	3	.1	**	**	60	1	**	**
	E	23	1	S	6	.2	3	.1	3	.1	9	.3	20	.3	**	**	20	.3
	ST	60	2		14	1	9	.3	6	.2	11	.4	20	.3	60	1	20	.3
MY KINFOLKS	W	18	9	N	18	8	6	3	4	2	7	3	7	3	32	12	11	4
	E	28	13	S	12	6	1	1	2	1	4	2	7	3	22	9	21	8
	ST	46	22		30	14	7	3	6	3	11	5	14	5	54	21	32	12
MY PEOPLE(B)	W	29	1	N	22	1	7	.3	**	**	5	.2	25	1	**	**	38	1
	E	22	1	S	7	.3	2	.1	**	**	5	.2	**	**	25	1	13	.3
	ST	51	2		29	1	10	.4	**	**	10	.4	25	1	25	1	50	1
MY RELATION	W	55	1	N	18	.2	**	**	**	**	**	**	**	**	20	.3	20	.3
	E	9	.1	S	9	.1	**	**	**	**	9	.1	20	.3	**	**	40	1
	ST	64	1		27	.3	**	**	**	**	9	.1	20	.3	20	.3	60	1
MY RELATIONS(B)	W	17	1	N	10	.3	13	.4	7	.2	13	.4	**	**	18	1	27	1
	E	33	1	S	**	**	3	.1	3	.1	**	**	27	1	9	.3	18	1
	ST	50	2		10	.3	17	1	10	.3	13	.4	27	1	27	1	45	2
MY RELATIVES(B)	W	19	7	N	16	6	9	3	4	2	8	3	7	3	29	14	20	10
	E	23	8	S	11	4	3	1	3	1	3	1	4	2	23	11	17	8
	ST	43	15		27	10	12	4	7	3	11	4	11	5	52	25	37	18

ITEM (124) (CONTINUED) OTHERS RELATED BY BLOOD

ITEM (124)		TENNESSEE C	TENNESSEE D		GEORGIA C	GEORGIA D	ALABAMA C	ALABAMA D	MISSISSIPPI C	MISSISSIPPI D	FLORIDA C	FLORIDA D	LOUISIANA C	LOUISIANA D	ARKANSAS C	ARKANSAS D	OKLAHOMA C	OKLAHOMA D
MY FAMILY(B)	W	37	3	N	70	5	57	4	100	6	73	9	33	3	38	3	20	1
	E	63	5	S	30	2	43	3	**	**	27	3	67	5	62	5	80	4
	ST		8			8		7		6		12		8		8		4
MY FOLKS(B)	W	48	3	N	59	4	100	7	50	6	83	4	**	**	60	2	45	4
	E	52	3	S	41	3	**	**	50	6	17	1	**	**	40	1	55	5
	ST		6			7		7		11		5		**		3		10
MY KIN	W	62	3	N	60	1	67	2	50	1	25	1	**	**	100	2	**	**
	E	38	2	S	40	1	33	1	50	1	75	2	100	3	**	**	100	1
	ST		4			2		3		3		3		3		2		1
MY KINFOLKS	W	40	17	N	59	27	85	28	64	26	63	26	47	18	59	22	35	11
	E	60	26	S	41	19	15	5	36	14	37	15	53	20	41	15	65	19
	ST		43			46		33		40		40		38		37		30
MY PEOPLE(B)	W	57	2	N	75	3	75	3	**	**	50	2	100	5	**	**	75	3
	E	43	2	S	25	1	25	1	**	**	50	2	**	**	100	1	25	1
	ST		4			4		4		**		3		5		1		4
MY RELATION	W	86	1	N	67	1	**	**	**	**	**	**	**	**	100	1	33	1
	E	14	.2	S	33	.3	**	**	**	**	100	1	100	3	**	**	67	2
	ST		1			1		**		**		1		3		1		3
MY RELATIONS(B)	W	33	1	N	100	1	80	4	67	3	100	3	**	**	67	1	60	3
	E	67	2	S	**	**	20	1	33	1	**	**	100	8	33	1	40	2
	ST		3			1		5		4		3		8		2		4
MY RELATIVES(B)	W	46	14	N	59	18	73	30	60	21	71	22	60	23	56	25	54	24
	E	54	16	S	41	13	27	11	40	14	29	9	40	15	44	20	46	20
	ST		30			31		41		36		31		38		45		44

HOUSEHOLD EQUIPMENT
A VEHICLE FOR A SMALL BABY

ITEM (125)
WORK SHEET (64)

		TENNESSEE			GEORGIA		ALABAMA		MISSISSIPPI		FLORIDA		LOUISIANA		ARKANSAS		OKLAHOMA	
		A	B		A	B	A	B	A	B	A	B	A	B	A	B	A	B
BABY BUGGY	W	29	16	N	8	4	7	4	6	3	4	2	7	5	27	22	16	13
	E	32	17	S	5	3	3	2	3	2	2	1	6	5	24	19	19	15
	ST	62	33		13	7	10	5	9	5	6	3	13	10	51	41	35	28
BABY CAB	W	50	.1	N	50	.1	**	**	**	**	**	**	**	**	**	**	**	**
	E	**	**	S	**	**	**	**	**	**	**	**	**	**	50	.3	50	.3
	ST	50	.1		50	.1	**	**	**	**	**	**	**	**	50	.3	50	.3
BABY CARRIAGE	W	8	4	N	30	13	7	3	1	1	12	5	6	1	35	7	15	3
	E	17	7	S	17	8	2	1	1	1	4	2	17	3	15	3	13	3
	ST	25	11		47	21	9	4	3	1	16	7	22	4	50	10	28	5
BABY COACH					(NO RESPONSE)													
					(NO RESPONSE)													
					(NO RESPONSE)													

		TENNESSEE			GEORGIA		ALABAMA		MISSISSIPPI		FLORIDA		LOUISIANA		ARKANSAS		OKLAHOMA	
		C	D		C	D	C	D	C	D	C	D	C	D	C	D	C	D
BABY BUGGY	W	47	36	N	59	15	72	42	63	51	61	19	52	37	53	43	46	38
	E	53	39	S	41	10	28	16	37	30	39	12	48	34	47	38	54	45
	ST		75			25		58		81		31		71		80		83
BABY CAB	W	100	.2	N	100	.3	**	**	**	**	**	**	**	**	**	**	**	**
	E	**	**	S	**	**	**	**	**	**	**	**	**	**	100	1	100	1
	ST		.2			.3		**		**		**		**		1		1
BABY CARRIAGE	W	32	8	N	63	47	76	32	55	11	74	51	25	7	70	13	53	9
	E	68	17	S	37	27	24	10	45	9	26	18	75	22	30	6	47	7
	ST		25			74		42		19		69		29		19		16
BABY COACH					(NO RESPONSE)													
					(NO RESPONSE)													
	ST		**			**		**		**		**		**		**		**

ITEM (126)
WORK SHEET (65)

ACTIVITIES
OF A CHILD, ______ HIS MOTHER

		TENNESSEE			GEORGIA		ALABAMA		MISSISSIPPI		FLORIDA		LOUISIANA		ARKANSAS		OKLAHOMA	
		A	B		A	B	A	B	A	D	A	B	A	B	A	B	A	B
FAVORS	W	21	5	N	18	4	10	2	5	1	5	1	11	3	26	7	11	3
	E	23	5	S	13	3	4	1	.4	.1	2	1	9	3	19	5	24	6
	ST	43	10		31	7	14	3	5	1	7	2	20	5	45	12	35	9
FEATURES	W	26	1	N	11	.2	**	**	**	**	11	.2	**	**	**	**	**	**
	E	26	1	S	11	.2	5	.1	**	**	11	.2	**	**	100	1	**	**
	ST	53	1		21	.4	5	.1	**	**	21	.4	**	**	100	1	**	**
LOOKS LIKE	W	18	8	N	14	6	7	3	4	2	7	3	6	3	24	11	20	9
	E	29	13	S	12	5	2	1	3	1	4	2	7	3	23	10	19	9
	ST	47	20		27	11	9	4	6	3	11	5	14	6	47	21	40	18
RESEMBLES	W	16	4	N	21	5	11	3	4	1	8	2	6	1	34	9	15	4
	E	[illegible]	[illegible]	S	10	[illegible]	2	.4	2	.4	4	1	4	1	27	7	14	4
	ST	30	9		32	8	13	3	6	1	12	3	10	3	61	16	30	8
TAKES AFTER	W	21	4	N	18	4	5	1	3	1	7	2	11	2	21	4	12	3
	E	22	5	S	10	2	2	1	5	1	4	1	12	3	21	4	23	5
	ST	44	9		29	6	7	2	8	2	11	2	23	5	42	9	35	7

		TENNESSEE			GEORGIA		ALABAMA		MISSISSIPPI		FLORIDA		LOUISIANA		ARKANSAS		OKLAHOMA	
		C	D		C	D	C	D	C	D	C	D	C	D	C	D	C	D
FAVORS	W	48	10	N	57	12	70	19	91	15	69	9	53	15	58	12	31	7
	E	52	10	S	43	9	30	8	9	1	31	4	47	13	42	9	69	16
	ST		20			22		27		16		14		29		21		22
FEATURES	W	50	1	N	50	1	**	**	**	**	50	2	**	**	**	**	**	**
	E	50	1	S	50	1	100	1	**	**	50	2	**	**	100	1	**	**
	ST		2			1		1		**		3		**		1		**
LOOKS LIKE	W	37	15	N	54	19	75	24	58	22	65	26	47	15	52	19	51	22
	E	63	26	S	46	16	25	8	42	16	35	14	53	17	48	18	49	21
	ST		41			35		32		39		39		33		36		42
RESEMBLES	W	43	8	N	67	16	86	23	69	13	64	15	57	8	56	15	52	9
	E	57	10	S	33	8	14	4	31	6	36	9	43	6	44	12	48	9
	ST		18			23		26		19		24		13		27		18
TAKES AFTER	W	49	9	N	64	12	67	9	41	10	65	13	46	12	50	8	35	6
	E	51	9	S	36	7	33	5	59	15	35	7	54	13	50	8	65	11
	ST		18			18		14		25		20		25		15		17

CHARACTERISTICS
A WOMAN WHO HELPS AT CHILDBIRTH

ITEM (127)
WORK SHEET (65)

		TENNESSEE A	TENNESSEE B		GEORGIA A	GEORGIA B	ALABAMA A	ALABAMA B	MISSISSIPPI A	MISSISSIPPI B	FLORIDA A	FLORIDA B	LOUISIANA A	LOUISIANA B	ARKANSAS A	ARKANSAS B	OKLAHOMA A	OKLAHOMA B
GODMOTHER	W	22	1	N	19	1	15	.4	4	.1	4	.1	10	.3	10	.3	**	**
	E	33	1	S	4	.1	**	**	**	**	**	**	20	1	20	1	40	1
	ST	56	2		22	1	15	.4	4	.1	4	.1	30	1	30	1	40	1
GRANNY	W	20	2	N	19	2	5	1	4	.4	9	1	11	.3	11	.3	11	.3
	E	20	2	S	16	2	1	.1	3	.3	3	.3	11	.3	56	2	**	**
	ST	40	4		35	4	6	1	7	1	12	1	22	1	67	2	11	.3
GRANNY DOCTOR	W	17	1	N	7	.2	**	**	10	.3	3	.1	33	.3	33	.3	**	**
	E	34	1	S	21	1	**	**	3	.1	3	.1	**	**	33	.3	**	**
	ST	52	2		28	1	**	**	14	.4	7	.2	33	.3	67	1	**	**
GRANNY WOMAN	W	17	2	N	18	2	3	.3	1	.1	3	.3	8	.3	67	3	**	**
	E	39	4	S	16	2	1	.1	**	**	1	.1	**	**	17	1	8	.3
	ST	56	6		35	4	4	.4	1	.1	4	.4	8	.3	83	4	8	.3
MIDWIFE	W	18	12	N	20	13	7	5	4	3	9	6	7	5	30	22	15	11
	E	22	15	S	12	8	2	2	2	2	4	3	8	6	25	18	16	12
	ST	40	27		32	21	9	6	6	4	13	9	15	11	54	40	31	23

		TENNESSEE C	TENNESSEE D		GEORGIA C	GEORGIA D	ALABAMA C	ALABAMA D	MISSISSIPPI C	MISSISSIPPI D	FLORIDA C	FLORIDA D	LOUISIANA C	LOUISIANA D	ARKANSAS C	ARKANSAS D	OKLAHOMA C	OKLAHOMA D
GODMOTHER	W	40	2	N	83	2	100	5	100	2	100	1	33	3	33	1	**	**
	E	60	2	S	17	.3	**	**	**	**	**	**	67	5	67	2	100	6
	ST		4			2		5		2		1		8		2		6
GRANNY	W	50	5	N	54	7	83	7	57	7	75	9	50	3	17	1	100	1
	E	50	5	S	46	6	17	1	43	5	25	3	50	3	83	4	**	**
	ST		10			12		8		13		11		5		5		1
GRANNY DOCTOR	W	33	1	N	25	1	**	**	75	5	50	1	100	3	50	1	**	**
	E	67	3	S	75	2	**	**	25	2	50	1	**	**	50	1	**	**
	ST		4			3		**		7		2		3		2		**
GRANNY WOMAN	W	31	4	N	53	6	75	4	100	2	75	3	100	3	80	6	**	**
	E	69	10	S	47	6	25	1	**	**	25	1	**	**	20	2	100	1
	ST		14			12		5		2		4		3		8		1
MIDWIFE	W	45	30	N	63	45	74	61	64	49	69	56	47	38	55	46	49	45
	E	55	37	S	37	27	26	21	36	27	31	26	53	43	45	38	51	46
	ST		68			71		82		76		82		81		84		91

CHARACTERISTICS
AN UNPROFESSIONAL, PART-TIME LAY PREACHER

ITEM (129)
WORK SHEET (67)

		TENNESSEE A	TENNESSEE B		GEORGIA A	GEORGIA B	ALABAMA A	ALABAMA B	MISSISSIPPI A	MISSISSIPPI B	FLORIDA A	FLORIDA B	LOUISIANA A	LOUISIANA B	ARKANSAS A	ARKANSAS B	OKLAHOMA A	OKLAHOMA B
BIBLE BANGER	W	80	.4	N	**	**	**	**	**	**	**	**	**	**	**	**	**	**
	E	20	.1	S	**	**	**	**	**	**	**	**	**	**	**	**	**	**
	ST	100	1		**	**	**	**	**	**	**	**	**	**	**	**	**	**
BROTHER SO-AND-SO	W	19	3	N	12	2	10	2	7	1	10	2	6	1	35	8	21	5
	E	22	4	S	13	2	4	1	2	.3	2	.3	5	1	17	4	17	4
	ST	41	7		25	4	13	2	9	2	12	2	11	3	52	12	38	9
CHAIR BACKER	W	100	.2	N	**	**	**	**	**	**	**	**	**	**	**	**	**	**
	E	**	**	S	**	**	**	**	**	**	**	**	**	**	**	**	100	.3
	ST	100	.2		**	**	**	**	**	**	**	**	**	**	**	**	100	.3
JACKLEG PREACHER	W	21	6	N	23	7	5	1	3	1	4	1	6	1	47	8	9	1
	E	28	8	S	12	3	1	.4	1	.3	2	1	4	1	21	4	13	2
	ST	48	14		35	10	6	2	4	1	6	2	11	2	68	12	21	4
DOMINIE	W	100	.1	N	**	**	**	**	**	**	**	**	**	**	**	**	**	**
					(NO RESPONSE)													
	ST	100	.1		**	**	**	**	**	**	**	**	**	**	**	**	**	**
LOCAL PREACHER	W	18	3	N	26	5	7	1	2	.4	6	1	2	.3	40	6	16	3
	E	22	4	S	11	2	1	.2	1	.2	4	1	4	1	27	4	11	2
	ST	40	7		38	7	8	1	4	1	11	2	7	1	67	11	27	4
PARSON	W	22	1	N	18	1	9	.4	4	.2	7	.3	40	1	40	1	**	**
	E	22	1	S	7	.3	**	**	4	.2	7	.3	**	**	**	**	20	1
	ST	44	2		24	1	9	.4	9	.4	13	1	40	1	40	1	20	1
THE REVEREND	W	26	1	N	19	1	4	.1	**	**	7	.2	**	**	50	1	**	**
	E	22	1	S	15	.4	**	**	4	.1	4	.1	**	**	25	.3	25	.3
	ST	48	1		33	1	4	.1	4	.1	11	.3	**	**	75	1	25	.3
YARD-AX	W	**	**	N	**	**	**	**	**	**	**	**	**	**	100	.3	**	**
	E	100	.1	S	**	**	**	**	**	**	**	**	**	**	**	**	**	**
	ST	100	.1		**	**	**	**	**	**	**	**	**	**	100	.3	**	**

ITEM (129)

(CONTINUED) AN UNPROFESSIONAL, PART-TIME LAY PREACHER

		TENNESSEE			GEORGIA		ALABAMA		MISSISSIPPI		FLORIDA		LOUISIANA		ARKANSAS		OKLAHOMA	
		C	D		C	D	C	D	C	D	C	D	C	D	C	D	C	D
BIBLE BANGER	W	80	1	N	**	**	**	**	**	**	**	**	**	**	**	**	**	**
	E	20	.3	S	**	**	**	**	**	**	**	**	**	**	**	**	**	**
	ST		2			**		**		**		**		**		**		**
BROTHER	W	46	10	N	49	9	73	27	80	32	85	27	57	21	68	22	56	27
SO-AND-SO	E	54	12	S	51	9	27	10	20	8	15	5	43	16	32	11	44	22
	ST		22			18		37		41		31		37		33		49
CHAIR BACKER	W	100	1	N	**	**	**	**	**	**	**	**	**	**	**	**	**	**
	E	**	**	S	**	**	**	**	**	**	**	**	**	**	**	**	100	2
	ST		1			**		**		**		**		**		**		2
JACKLEG	W	43	18	N	67	29	78	24	73	22	65	17	60	16	69	21	40	8
PREACHER	E	57	25	S	33	14	22	7	27	8	35	9	40	11	31	10	60	12
	ST		43			44		31		30		27		26		31		20
DOMINIE	W	100	.3	N	**	**	**	**	**	**	**	**	**	**	**	**	**	**
					(NO RESPONSE)													
	ST		.3			**		**		**		**		**		**		**
LOCAL PREACHER	W	44	10	N	70	20	86	20	67	11	61	17	33	5	60	17	58	14
	E	56	12	S	30	9	14	3	33	5	39	11	67	11	40	12	42	10
	ST		22			29		24		16		28		16		29		24
PARSON	W	50	3	N	73	4	100	7	50	5	50	5	100	21	100	4	**	**
	E	50	3	S	27	1	**	**	50	5	50	5	**	**	**	**	100	4
	ST		6			5		7		11		9		21		4		4
THE REVEREND	W	54	2	N	56	2	100	2	**	**	67	3	**	**	67	2	**	**
	E	46	2	S	44	2	**	**	100	3	33	2	**	**	33	1	100	2
	ST		4			4		2		3		5		**		3		2
YARD-AX	W	**	**	N	**	**	**	**	**	**	**	**	**	**	100	1	**	**
	E	100	.3	S	**	**	**	**	**	**	**	**	**	**	**	**	**	**
	ST		.3			**		**		**		**		**		1		**

CHARACTERISTICS
A RUSTIC

ITEM (130)
WORK SHEET (69)

		TENNESSEE A	TENNESSEE B		GEORGIA A	GEORGIA B	ALABAMA A	ALABAMA B	MISSISSIPPI A	MISSISSIPPI B	FLORIDA A	FLORIDA B	LOUISIANA A	LOUISIANA B	ARKANSAS A	ARKANSAS B	OKLAHOMA A	OKLAHOMA B
BACKWOODSMAN	W	15	1	N	19	2	9	1	3	.3	11	1	7	.3	20	1	20	1
	E	20	2	S	12	1	3	.3	3	.3	3	.3	**	**	27	1	27	1
	ST	35	3		31	3	12	1	7	1	15	1	7	.3	47	3	47	3
CLODHOPPER	W	29	5	N	14	2	6	1	2	.3	5	1	7	1	34	5	20	3
	E	33	5	S	5	1	2	.3	2	.3	1	.2	2	.3	9	1	27	4
	ST	62	10		19	3	8	1	4	1	7	1	9	1	43	7	48	8
COUNTRY GENTLEMAN	W	29	1	N	25	1	4	.1	4	.1	**	**	13	.3	63	2	**	**
	E	21	1	S	13	.3	4	.1	**	**	**	**	**	**	25	1	11	**
	ST	50	1		38	1	8	.2	4	.1	**	**	13	.3	00	3	**	**
COUNTRY JAKE	W	38	2	N	[illegible]	[illegible]	13	1	6	.3	2	.1	**	**	35	2	6	.3
	E	21	1	S	**	**	4	.2	9	.4	**	**	6	.3	18	1	35	2
	ST	60	3		6	.3	17	1	15	1	2	.1	6	.3	53	3	41	3
COUNTRY MAN	W	20	3	N	20	3	10	1	7	1	3	.4	18	1	47	3	6	.3
	E	20	3	S	8	1	4	1	2	.3	4	1	6	.3	24	1	**	**
	ST	41	5		28	4	14	2	10	1	7	1	24	1	71	4	6	.3
HAYSEED	W	36	2	N	20	1	9	.4	2	.1	4	.2	4	.3	12	1	20	2
	E	20	1	S	7	.3	**	**	**	**	2	.1	**	**	24	2	40	4
	ST	56	3		27	1	9	.4	2	.1	7	.3	4	.3	36	3	60	5
HICK	W	13	1	N	14	1	4	.4	2	.2	13	1	19	3	23	4	14	2
	E	32	3	S	5	1	3	.3	5	1	9	1	7	1	9	1	28	4
	ST	44	4		19	2	7	1	7	1	22	2	26	4	33	5	42	6
HOOSIER	W	17	.3	N	**	**	6	.1	6	.1	11	.2	50	1	25	.3	**	**
	E	17	.3	S	17	.3	22	.4	6	.1	**	**	**	**	25	.3	**	**
	ST	33	1		17	.3	28	1	11	.2	11	.2	50	1	50	1	**	**
HILLBILLY	W	19	5	N	18	5	11	3	4	1	6	2	4	1	32	12	22	8
	E	32	9	S	5	1	3	1	1	.3	1	.2	7	3	16	6	19	7
	ST	51	14		23	6	14	4	6	2	6	2	11	4	48	17	41	15

(CONTINUED) A RUSTIC

		TENNESSEE A	TENNESSEE B		GEORGIA A	GEORGIA B	ALABAMA A	ALABAMA B	MISSISSIPPI A	MISSISSIPPI B	FLORIDA A	FLORIDA B	LOUISIANA A	LOUISIANA B	ARKANSAS A	ARKANSAS B	OKLAHOMA A	OKLAHOMA B
JACKPINE SAVAGE	W	**	**	N	**	**	50	.1	**	**	**	**	**	**	**	**	**	**
	E	50	.1	S	**	**	**	**	**	**	**	**	**	**	**	**	**	**
	ST	50	.1		**	**	50	.1	**	**	**	**	**	**	**	**	**	**
MOSSBACK	W	**	**	N	**	**	25	.1	**	**	25	.1	17	.3	50	1	**	**
	E	**	**	S	50	.2	**	**	**	**	**	**	**	**	**	**	33	1
	ST	**	**		50	.2	25	.1	**	**	25	.1	17	.3	50	1	33	1
MOUNTAINBOOMER					(NO RESPONSE)													
	E	100	1	S	**	**	**	**	**	**	**	**	**	**	**	**	**	**
	ST	100	1		**	**	**	**	**	**	**	**	**	**	**	**	**	**
PUMPKIN HUSKER	W	**	**	N	**	**	100	.1	**	**	**	**	**	**	**	**	**	**
					(NO RESPONSE)													
	ST	**	**		**	**	100	.1	**	**	**	**	**	**	**	**	**	**
RAILSPLITTER	W	**	**	N	**	**	**	**	**	**	**	**	**	**	**	**	100	1
					(NO RESPONSE)													
	ST	**	**		**	**	**	**	**	**	**	**	**	**	**	**	100	1
CRACKER	W	**	**	N	19	1	4	.3	1	.1	27	2	**	**	**	**	**	**
	E	4	.3	S	30	2	**	**	**	**	13	1	**	**	**	**	**	**
	ST	4	.3		49	3	4	.3	1	.1	40	3	**	**	**	**	**	**
REDNECK	W	27	1	N	5	.1	23	1	9	.2	9	.2	17	.3	17	.3	**	**
	E	**	**	S	**	**	9	.2	18	.4	**	**	17	.3	50	1	**	**
	ST	27	1		5	.1	32	1	27	1	9	.2	33	1	67	1	**	**
SHARECROPPER	W	31	2	N	27	2	5	.3	2	.1	4	.2	5	.3	14	1	9	1
	E	13	1	S	13	1	2	.1	**	**	4	.2	5	.3	36	3	32	3
	ST	44	2		40	2	7	.4	2	.1	7	.4	9	1	50	4	41	3
STUMP FARMER	W	**	**	N	25	.2	13	.1	**	**	**	**	50	1	50	1	**	**
	E	25	.2	S	25	.2	**	**	13	.1	**	**	**	**	**	**	**	**
	ST	25	.2		50	.4	13	.1	13	.1	**	**	50	1	50	1	**	**
SWAMP ANGEL	W	25	.1	N	25	.1	25	.1	**	**	**	**	**	**	**	**	**	**
	E	**	**	S	25	.1	**	**	**	**	**	**	**	**	100	.3	**	**
	ST	25	.1		50	.2	25	.1	**	**	**	**	**	**	100	.3	**	**
YAHOO	W	13	.1	N	25	.2	**	**	13	.1	**	**	**	**	**	**	**	**
	E	13	.1	S	**	**	25	.2	13	.1	**	**	**	**	25	.3	75	1
	ST	25	.2		25	.2	25	.2	25	.2	**	**	**	**	25	.3	75	1
YOKEL	W	16	.4	N	12	.3	8	.2	4	.1	12	.3	6	.3	29	2	24	1
	E	32	1	S	4	.1	4	.1	8	.2	**	**	**	**	6	.3	35	2
	ST	[illegible]	[illegible]		16	.4	12	.3	12	.3	12	.3	6	.3	35	2	59	4

ITEM (130) (CONTINUED) A RUSTIC

		TENNESSEE C	TENNESSEE D		GEORGIA C	GEORGIA D	ALABAMA C	ALABAMA D	MISSISSIPPI C	MISSISSIPPI D	FLORIDA C	FLORIDA D	LOUISIANA C	LOUISIANA D	ARKANSAS C	ARKANSAS D	OKLAHOMA C	OKLAHOMA D
BACKWOODSMAN	W	42	3	N	61	6	73	6	50	4	77	9	100	2	43	2	43	2
	E	58	4	S	39	4	27	2	50	4	23	3	**	**	57	3	57	3
	ST		6			10		9		8		12		2		5		5
CLODHOPPER	W	47	9	N	72	8	75	7	50	4	80	7	75	7	79	10	43	7
	E	53	10	S	28	3	25	2	50	4	20	2	25	2	21	3	57	9
	ST		19			11		9		8		9		9		12		15
COUNTRY GENTLEMAN	W	58	1	N	67	2	50	1	100	1	**	**	100	2	71	3	**	**
	E	42	1	S	33	1	50	1	**	**	**	**	**	**	29	1	**	**
	ST		2			3		2		1		**		2		5		**
COUNTRY JAKE	W	64	4	N	100	1	75	[illegible]	43	[illegible]	100	1	**	**	67	4	14	1
	E	36	2	S	**	**	25	2	57	6	**	**	100	2	33	2	86	4
	ST		6			1		6		10		1		2		6		5
COUNTRY MAN	W	50	5	N	71	9	71	9	75	13	44	4	75	7	67	5	100	1
	E	50	5	S	29	4	29	4	25	4	56	4	25	2	33	3	**	**
	ST		10			13		13		17		8		9		8		1
HAYSEED	W	64	3	N	75	3	100	3	100	1	67	2	100	2	33	2	33	4
	E	36	2	S	25	1	**	**	**	**	33	1	**	**	67	4	67	7
	ST		5			4		3		1		3		2		6		11
HICK	W	29	2	N	72	5	57	3	29	3	57	11	73	18	71	6	33	4
	E	71	6	S	28	2	43	2	71	7	43	8	27	7	29	3	67	9
	ST		9			7		6		10		19		25		9		13
HOOSIER	W	50	1	N	**	**	20	1	50	1	100	2	100	5	50	1	**	**
	E	50	1	S	100	1	80	3	50	1	**	**	**	**	50	1	**	**
	ST		1			1		4		3		2		5		1		**
HILLBILLY	W	38	11	N	77	18	78	23	80	17	88	13	36	9	67	21	54	16
	E	62	18	S	23	5	22	6	20	4	12	2	64	16	33	10	46	14
	ST		28			23		29		21		15		25		31		30

(CONTINUED) A RUSTIC

		TENNESSEE C	TENNESSEE D		GEORGIA C	GEORGIA D	ALABAMA C	ALABAMA D	MISSISSIPPI C	MISSISSIPPI D	FLORIDA C	FLORIDA D	LOUISIANA C	LOUISIANA D	ARKANSAS C	ARKANSAS D	OKLAHOMA C	OKLAHOMA D
JACKPINE	W	**	**	N	**	**	100	1	**	**	**	**	**	**	**	**	**	**
SAVAGE	E	100	.2	S	**	**	**	**	**	**	**	**	**	**	**	**	**	**
	ST		.2			**		1		**		**		**		**		**
MOSSBACK	W	**	**	N	**	**	100	1	**	**	100	1	100	2	100	2	**	**
	E	**	**	S	100	1	**	**	**	**	**	**	**	**	**	**	100	1
	ST		**			1		1		**		1		2		2		1
MOUNTAINBOOMER					(NO RESPONSE)													
	E	100	1	S	**	**	**	**	**	**	**	**	**	**	**	**	**	**
	ST		1			**		**		**		**		**		**		**
PUMPKIN	W	**	**	N	**	**	100	1	**	**	**	**	**	**	**	**	**	**
HUSKER					(NO RESPONSE)													
	ST		**			**		1		**		**		**		**		**
RAILSPLITTER	W	**	**	N	**	**	**	**	**	**	**	**	**	**	**	**	100	2
					(NO RESPONSE)													
	ST		**			**		**		**		**		**		**		2
CRACKER	W	**	**	N	39	5	100	2	100	1	67	16	**	**	**	**	**	**
	E	100	1	S	61	7	**	**	**	**	33	8	**	**	**	**	**	**
	ST		1			12		2		1		24		**		**		**
REDNECK	W	100	1	N	100	.3	71	4	33	3	100	2	50	2	25	1	**	**
	E	**	**	S	**	**	29	2	67	6	**	**	50	2	75	2	**	**
	ST		1			.3		6		8		2		5		3		**
SHARECROPPER	W	71	4	N	68	6	75	2	100	1	50	2	50	2	27	2	22	1
	E	29	1	S	32	3	25	1	**	**	50	2	50	2	73	5	78	5
	ST		5			8		3		1		4		5		7		7
STUMP FARMER	W	**	**	N	50	1	100	1	**	**	**	**	100	5	100	1	**	**
	E	100	.4	S	50	1	**	**	100	1	**	**	**	**	**	**	**	**
	ST		.4			1		1		1		**		5		1		**
SWAMP ANGEL	W	100	.2	N	50	.3	100	1	**	**	**	**	**	**	**	**	**	**
	E	**	**	S	50	.3	**	**	**	**	**	**	**	**	100	1	**	**
	ST		.2			1		1		**		**		**		1		**
YAHOO	W	50	.2	N	100	1	**	**	50	1	**	**	**	**	**	**	**	**
	E	50	.2	S	**	**	100	2	50	1	**	**	**	**	100	1	100	2
	ST		.4			1		2		3		**		**		1		2
YOKEL	W	33	1	N	75	1	67	2	33	1	100	3	100	2	83	3	40	3
	E	67	2	S	25	.3	33	1	67	3	**	**	**	**	17	1	60	4
						[illegible]		[illegible]		4		3		2		4		7

ITEM (131)
WORK SHEET (74)

CHARACTERISTICS
OBSTINATE

		TENNESSEE A	TENNESSEE B		GEORGIA A	GEORGIA B	ALABAMA A	ALABAMA B	MISSISSIPPI A	MISSISSIPPI B	FLORIDA A	FLORIDA B	LOUISIANA A	LOUISIANA B	ARKANSAS A	ARKANSAS B	OKLAHOMA A	OKLAHOMA B
BULL HEADED	W	16	5	N	19	6	6	2	4	1	8	2	9	4	23	9	22	9
	E	26	8	S	11	4	3	1	3	1	5	2	9	4	15	6	23	9
	ST	42	13		30	10	9	3	7	2	12	4	18	7	38	15	44	18
CONTRARY	W	23	5	N	15	3	8	2	5	1	8	2	12	2	26	5	16	3
	E	24	5	S	10	2	1	.3	3	1	2	.4	10	2	22	4	14	3
	ST	47	10		25	5	9	2	8	2	10	2	22	4	48	9	30	5
HEADSTRONG	W	23	3	N	20	3	7	1	4	1	4	1	9	1	33	5	14	2
	E	24	3	S	9	1	2	.3	4	1	3	.4	2	.3	16	3	26	4
	ST	47	6		28	4	9	1	8	1	7	1	12	2	49	8	40	6
ORNERY	W	13	1	N	25	3	7	1	4	.4	10	1	12	1	12	1	18	1
	E	14	1	S	12	1	4	.4	4	.4	9	1	6	.3	29	2	24	1
	ST	26	3		37	4	11	1	8	1	18	2	18	1	41	3	41	3
OTSNY	W	**	**	N	50	.3	**	**	17	.1	17	.1	**	**	**	**	**	**
	E	17	.1	S	**	**	**	**	**	**	**	**	**	**	**	**	**	**
	ST	17	.1		50	.3	**	**	17	.1	17	.1	**	**	**	**	**	**
OWLY(A)	W	**	**	N	100	.1	**	**	**	**	**	**	**	**	**	**	**	**
					(NO RESPONSE)													
	ST	**	**		100	.1	**	**	**	**	**	**	**	**	**	**	**	**
PIG HEADED	W	30	1	N	13	1	3	.1	3	.1	8	.3	13	1	7	.3	20	1
	E	35	1	S	3	.1	5	.2	3	.1	**	**	7	.3	27	1	27	1
	ST	65	3		15	1	8	.3	5	.2	8	.3	20	1	33	2	47	3
SET	W	17	.4	N	25	1	4	.1	**	**	8	.2	**	**	29	1	29	1
	E	21	1	S	8	.2	4	.1	4	.1	8	.2	29	1	**	**	14	.3
	ST	38	1		33	1	8	.2	4	.1	17	.4	29	1	29	1	43	1
SOT	W	25	1	N	25	1	5	.1	**	**	10	.2	**	**	**	**	**	**
	E	20	.4	S	15	.3	**	**	**	**	**	**	**	**	**	**	100	.3
	ST	45	1		40	1	5	.1	**	**	10	.2	**	**	**	**	100	.3
STUBBORN	W	17	7	N	17	7	9	4	4	2	8	3	4	2	28	13	16	8
	E	27	11	S	10	4	3	1	2	1	3	1	7	3	21	10	25	12
	ST	44	19		27	12	12	5	6	3	11	5	10	5	49	23	41	20

ITEM (131) (CONTINUED) OBSTINATE

ITEM (131)		TENNESSEE C	TENNESSEE D		GEORGIA C	GEORGIA D	ALABAMA C	ALABAMA D	MISSISSIPPI C	MISSISSIPPI D	FLORIDA C	FLORIDA D	LOUISIANA C	LOUISIANA D	ARKANSAS C	ARKANSAS D	OKLAHOMA C	OKLAHOMA D
BULL HEADED	W	38	9	N	63	17	71	16	52	13	62	17	50	17	60	15	49	16
	E	62	15	S	37	10	29	6	48	12	38	11	50	17	40	10	51	16
	ST		24			26		22		24		27		34		25		32
CONTRARY	W	49	9	N	60	9	84	13	65	13	81	12	55	10	54	8	53	5
	E	51	9	S	40	6	16	2	35	7	19	3	45	9	46	7	47	5
	ST		18			14		15		20		15		19		14		10
HEADSTRONG	W	48	5	N	69	7	75	7	50	6	56	4	80	7	67	8	35	4
	E	52	6	S	31	3	25	2	50	6	44	3	20	2	33	4	65	7
	ST		11			10		10		12		6		9		13		11
ORNERY	W	48	2	N	68	7	64	6	50	5	53	7	67	3	29	1	43	2
	E	52	3	S	32	3	36	3	50	5	47	6	33	2	71	3	57	3
	ST		5			11		9		9		13		5		4		5
OTSNY	W	**	**	N	100	1	**	**	100	1	100	1	**	**	**	**	**	**
	E	100	.1	S	**	**	**	**	**	**	**	**	**	**	**	**	**	**
	ST		.1			1		**		1		1		**		**		**
OWLY(A)	W	**	**	N	100	.2	**	**	**	**	**	**	**	**	**	**	**	**
					(NO RESPONSE)													
	ST		**			.2		**		**		**		**		**		**
PIG HEADED	W	46	2	N	83	1	33	1	50	1	100	2	67	3	20	1	43	2
	E	54	3	S	17	.2	67	2	50	1	**	**	33	2	80	2	57	3
	ST		5			2		2		2		2		5		3		5
SET	W	44	1	N	75	2	50	1	**	**	50	1	**	**	100	1	67	1
	E	56	1	S	25	1	50	1	100	1	50	1	100	3	**	**	33	1
	ST		2			2		2		1		3		3		1		2
SOT	W	56	1	N	63	1	100	1	**	**	100	1	**	**	**	**	**	**
	E	44	1	S	38	1	**	**	**	**	**	**	**	**	**	**	100	1
	ST		2			2		1		**		1		**		**		1
STUBBORN	W	39	13	N	63	20	76	30	65	20	73	23	36	9	57	22	40	14
	E	61	21	S	37	12	24	10	35	10	27	8	64	16	43	17	60	21
	ST		34			32		39		30		31		24		39		36

ITEM (132)
WORK SHEET (75)

CHARACTERISTICS
HE GOT AWFULLY ________

		TENNESSEE			GEORGIA		ALABAMA		MISSISSIPPI		FLORIDA		LOUISIANA		ARKANSAS		OKLAHOMA	
		A	B		A	B	A	B	A	B	A	B	A	B	A	B	A	B
ASHY	W	19	.3	N	38	1	6	.1	6	.1	6	.1	100	.3	**	**	**	**
	E	19	.3	S	6	.1	**	**	**	**	**	**	**	**	**	**	**	**
	ST	38	1		44	1	6	.1	6	.1	6	.1	100	.3	**	**	**	**
HET UP	W	20	2	N	23	2	6	1	4	.3	8	1	**	**	29	2	29	2
	E	18	2	S	8	1	**	**	5	.4	7	1	**	**	19	1	24	2
	ST	39	3		31	3	6	1	8	1	16	1	**	**	48	4	52	4
HOT	W	20	2	N	19	2	3	.3	4	.4	4	.4	16	1	20	2	16	1
	E	28	3	S	11	1	4	.4	4	.4	1	.1	4	.2	36	[illegible]	8	1
	ST	48	5		30	1	[illegible]	1	[illegible]	1	5	1	20	2	56	5	24	2
MAD	W	19	11	N	17	11	7	4	4	3	6	4	7	5	26	17	13	9
	E	26	16	S	13	8	2	1	2	1	3	2	9	6	27	18	17	11
	ST	45	27		30	18	9	6	6	4	10	6	16	10	54	35	30	19
OWLY(B)	W	100	.1	N	**	**	**	**	**	**	**	**	**	**	50	.3	**	**
	E	**	**	S	**	**	**	**	**	**	**	**	**	**	50	.3	**	**
	ST	100	.1		**	**	**	**	**	**	**	**	**	**	100	1	**	**
RILED	W	22	3	N	17	2	7	1	3	1	9	1	9	1	32	4	26	3
	E	27	4	S	8	1	2	.3	1	.2	4	1	12	1	12	1	9	1
	ST	49	7		24	4	9	1	5	1	13	2	21	3	44	5	35	4
ROILED	W	7	.1	N	40	1	13	.2	7	.1	7	.1	**	**	**	**	100	.3
	E	13	.2	S	7	.1	**	**	**	**	7	.1	**	**	**	**	**	**
	ST	20	.3		47	1	13	.2	7	.1	13	.2	**	**	**	**	100	.3
UGLY	W	27	2	N	13	1	7	.4	3	.2	12	1	5	.3	40	3	10	1
	E	13	1	S	17	1	7	.4	**	**	?	.1	5	.3	30	2	10	1
	ST	40	2		30	2	13	1	3	.2	13	1	10	1	70	5	20	1
WRATHY	W	23	.3	N	62	1	8	.1	**	**	**	**	**	**	50	1	13	.3
	E	**	**	S	**	**	**	**	8	.1	**	**	**	**	13	.3	25	1
	ST	23	.3		62	1	8	.1	8	.1	**	**	**	**	63	2	38	1

(CONTINUED) HE GOT AWFULLY ________

ITEM (132)		TENNESSEE C	TENNESSEE D		GEORGIA C	GEORGIA D	ALABAMA C	ALABAMA D	MISSISSIPPI C	MISSISSIPPI D	FLORIDA C	FLORIDA D	LOUISIANA C	LOUISIANA D	ARKANSAS C	ARKANSAS D	OKLAHOMA C	OKLAHOMA D
ASHY	W	50	1	N	86	2	100	1	100	2	100	1	100	2	**	**	**	**
	E	50	1	S	14	.3	**	**	**	**	**	**	**	**	**	**	**	**
	ST		1			2		1		2		1		2		**		**
HET UP	W	53	4	N	73	6	100	5	43	5	54	7	**	**	60	4	55	7
	E	47	3	S	27	2	**	**	57	6	46	6	**	**	40	3	45	5
	ST		7			9		5		11		13		**		6		12
HOT	W	42	4	N	64	6	43	3	50	6	80	4	80	9	36	3	67	4
	E	58	6	S	36	3	57	4	50	6	20	1	20	2	64	6	33	2
	ST		10			9		8		13		5		11		9		7
MAD	W	42	24	N	58	33	76	46	72	41	66	36	45	30	49	30	44	26
	E	58	34	S	42	24	24	14	28	16	34	18	55	36	51	31	56	33
	ST		59			58		60		57		54		66		62		59
OWLY(B)	W	100	.2	N	**	**	**	**	**	**	**	**	**	**	50	1	**	**
	E	**	**	S	**	**	**	**	**	**	**	**	**	**	50	1	**	**
	ST		.2			**		**		**		**		**		1		**
RILED	W	44	7	N	69	8	77	11	71	8	68	13	43	7	73	7	75	10
	E	56	9	S	31	4	23	3	29	3	32	6	57	9	27	3	25	3
	ST		16			11		14		11		18		16		10		13
ROILED	W	33	.2	N	86	2	100	2	100	2	50	1	**	**	**	**	100	1
	E	67	.4	S	14	.3	**	**	**	**	50	1	**	**	**	**	**	**
	ST		1			2		2		2		2		**		**		1
UGLY	W	67	4	N	44	3	50	4	100	3	88	7	50	2	57	5	50	2
	E	33	2	S	56	3	50	4	**	**	13	1	50	2	43	4	50	2
	ST		5			6		9		3		8		5		9		4
WRATHY	W	100	1	N	100	3	100	1	**	**	**	**	**	**	80	3	33	1
	E	**	**	S	**	**	**	**	100	2	**	**	**	**	20	1	67	2
	ST		1			3		1		2		**		**		3		3

CHARACTERISTICS
(NO TEXT)

ITEM (133)
WORK SHEET (75)

		TENNESSEE			GEORGIA		ALABAMA		MISSISSIPPI		FLORIDA		LOUISIANA		ARKANSAS		OKLAHOMA	
		A	B		A	B	A	B	A	B	A	B	A	B	A	B	A	B
ALL IN	W	24	3	N	14	2	9	1	4	1	6	1	2	.3	23	5	27	5
	E	22	3	S	11	1	1	.1	1	.1	8	1	7	1	14	3	27	5
	ST	46	5		25	3	10	1	5	1	14	2	9	2	38	8	54	11
BEAT OUT	W	42	1	N	17	.2	8	.1	8	.1	**	**	25	.3	**	**	25	.3
	E	8	.1	S	17	.2	**	**	**	**	**	**	**	**	25	.3	25	.3
	ST	50	1		33	.4	8	.1	8	.1	**	**	25	.3	25	.3	50	1
BUSHED	W	24	1	N	7	.3	7	.3	9	.4	13	1	8	1	16	1	28	3
	E	29	1	S	**	**	4	.2	2	.1	4	.2	8	1	20	2	20	2
	ST	53	2		7	.3	11	1	11	1	18	1	16	1	36	3	40	4
DONE OUT	W	14	1	N	14	.1	14	.1	**	**	**	**	**	**	100	.3	**	**
	E	29	.2	S	14	.1	14	.1	**	**	**	**	**	**	**	**	**	**
	ST	43	.3		29	.2	29	.2	**	**	**	**	**	**	100	.3	**	**
DONE UP	W	22	.2	N	11	.1	**	**	11	.1	11	.1	**	**	60	1	20	.3
	E	33	.3	S	11	.1	**	**	**	**	**	**	**	**	**	**	20	.3
	ST	56	1		22	.2	**	**	11	.1	11	.1	**	**	60	1	40	1
FAGGED OUT	W	23	3	N	20	3	7	1	3	.4	6	1	10	1	29	4	12	2
	E	19	3	S	12	2	2	.3	4	1	3	1	10	1	20	3	20	3
	ST	42	6		32	5	9	1	7	1	10	1	20	3	49	7	32	5
GIVE OUT	W	14	4	N	20	5	8	2	4	1	5	1	11	2	30	6	15	3
	E	29	7	S	15	4	1	.2	2	.4	3	1	2	.3	23	4	19	4
	ST	43	11		35	9	8	2	5	1	8	2	13	3	53	10	34	6
PERISHED	W	20	.1	N	**	**	20	.1	**	**	**	**	**	**	50	.3	50	.3
	E	20	.1	S	40	.2	**	**	**	**	**	**	**	**	**	**	**	**
	ST	40	.2		40	.2	20	.1	**	**	**	**	**	**	50	.3	50	.3
KILLED	W	**	**	N	100	.1	**	**	**	**	**	**	**	**	100	.3	**	**
					(NO RESPONSE)													
	ST	**	**		100	.1	**	**	**	**	**	**	**	**	100	.3	**	**
PETERED OUT	W	18	2	N	18	2	6	1	2	.2	8	1	12	1	27	3	15	2
	E	33	4	S	8	1	2	.2	2	.3	4	1	6	1	15	2	24	3
	ST	50	7		27	4	8	1	4	1	11	2	18	2	42	5	39	5

(CONTINUED) (NO TEXT)

		TENNESSEE A	TENNESSEE B		GEORGIA A	GEORGIA B	ALABAMA A	ALABAMA B	MISSISSIPPI A	MISSISSIPPI B	FLORIDA A	FLORIDA B	LOUISIANA A	LOUISIANA B	ARKANSAS A	ARKANSAS B	OKLAHOMA A	OKLAHOMA B
PLAYED OUT	W	41	3	N	11	1	6	1	5	.4	6	1	4	.3	19	2	15	1
	E	14	1	S	5	.4	5	.4	5	.4	1	.1	7	1	44	4	11	1
	ST	54	4		16	1	11	1	10	1	8	1	11	1	63	6	26	3
TUCKERED	W	24	1	N	18	1	6	.2	9	.3	12	.4	**	**	27	1	18	1
	E	12	.4	S	6	.2	**	**	3	.1	9	.3	9	.3	18	1	27	1
	ST	36	1		24	1	6	.2	12	.4	21	1	9	.3	45	2	45	2
TUCKERED OUT	W	21	3	N	14	2	6	1	7	1	9	1	6	1	33	4	27	3
	E	27	3	S	6	1	2	.3	3	.4	4	1	**	**	18	2	15	2
	ST	48	6		20	3	9	1	10	1	13	2	6	1	52	6	42	5
USED UP	W	11	.1	N	56	1	**	**	11	.1	**	**	33	.3	**	**	**	**
	E	11	.1	S	**	**	**	**	**	**	11	.1	33	.3	**	**	33	.3
	ST	22	.2		56	1	**	**	11	.1	11	.1	67	1	**	**	33	.3
WORN OUT	W	20	7	N	18	7	7	2	4	1	8	3	5	2	26	10	15	5
	E	24	9	S	12	4	2	1	2	1	3	1	7	3	25	9	22	8
	ST	44	17		30	11	9	3	6	2	11	4	12	4	52	19	36	13

ITEM (133) (CONTINUED) (NO TEXT)

		TENNESSEE C	TENNESSEE D		GEORGIA C	GEORGIA D	ALABAMA C	ALABAMA D	MISSISSIPPI C	MISSISSIPPI D	FLORIDA C	FLORIDA D	LOUISIANA C	LOUISIANA D	ARKANSAS C	ARKANSAS D	OKLAHOMA C	OKLAHOMA D
ALL IN	W	53	5	N	55	4	92	9	83	6	44	5	20	2	62	7	50	10
	E	47	4	S	45	4	8	1	17	1	56	6	80	8	38	4	50	10
	ST		9			8		10		7		11		10		11		19
BEAT OUT	W	83	1	N	50	1	100	1	100	1	**	**	100	2	**	**	50	1
	E	17	.1	S	50	1	**	**	**	**	**	**	**	**	100	1	50	1
	ST		1			1		1		1		**		2		1		1
BUSHED	W	46	2	N	100	1	60	3	80	5	75	4	50	4	44	2	58	5
	E	54	2	S	**	**	40	2	20	1	25	1	50	4	56	3	42	3
	ST		4			1		4		6		6		8		5		8
DONE OUT	W	33	.1	N	50	.2	50	1	**	**	**	**	**	**	100	1	**	**
	E	67	.3	S	50	.2	50	1	**	**	**	**	**	**	**	**	**	**
	ST		1			1		2		**		**		**		1		**
DONE UP	W	40	.3	N	50	.2	**	**	100	1	100	1	**	**	100	2	50	1
	E	60	1	S	50	.2	**	**	**	**	**	**	**	**	**	**	50	1
	ST		1			1		**		1		1		**		2		1
FAGGED OUT	W	54	6	N	63	8	77	8	40	5	64	6	50	8	60	6	38	3
	E	46	5	S	37	5	23	3	60	7	36	3	50	8	40	4	62	5
	ST		10			13		11		11		10		16		10		8
GIVE OUT	W	33	6	N	58	13	90	15	69	10	65	9	86	12	57	8	44	5
	E	67	11	S	42	10	10	2	31	5	35	5	14	2	43	6	56	6
	ST		17			23		17		15		14		14		15		12
PERISHED	W	50	.1	N	**	**	100	1	**	**	**	**	**	**	100	1	100	1
	E	50	.1	S	100	1	**	**	**	**	**	**	**	**	**	**	**	**
	ST		.3			1		1		**		**		**		1		1
KILLED	W	**	**	N	100	.2	**	**	**	**	**	**	**	**	100	1	**	**
					(NO RESPONSE)													
	ST		**			.2		**		**		**		**		1		**
PETERED OUT	W	35	4	N	69	7	80	7	40	2	67	7	67	8	64	5	38	3
	E	65	7	S	31	3	20	2	60	3	33	3	33	4	36	3	62	5
	ST		11			10		8		6		10		12		7		8

(CONTINUED) (NO TEXT)

		TENNESSEE C	TENNESSEE D		GEORGIA C	GEORGIA D	ALABAMA C	ALABAMA D	MISSISSIPPI C	MISSISSIPPI D	FLORIDA C	FLORIDA D	LOUISIANA C	LOUISIANA D	ARKANSAS C	ARKANSAS D	OKLAHOMA C	OKLAHOMA D
PLAYED OUT	W	74	5	N	69	2	56	4	50	5	83	3	33	2	29	3	57	3
	E	26	2	S	31	1	44	3	50	5	17	1	67	4	71	6	43	2
	ST		7			4		8		9		4		6		9		5
TUCKERED	W	67	1	N	75	2	100	2	75	3	57	3	**	**	60	2	40	1
	E	33	1	S	25	1	**	**	25	1	43	2	100	2	40	1	60	2
	ST		2			2		2		5		5		2		3		3
TUCKERED OUT	W	44	4	N	68	5	73	7	69	10	69	8	100	4	65	6	64	6
	E	56	6	S	32	2	27	3	31	5	31	3	**	**	35	3	36	3
	ST		10			7		9		15		11		4		9		9
USED UP	W	50	.1	N	100	1	**	**	100	1	**	**	50	2	**	**	**	**
	E	50	.1	S	**	**	**	**	**	**	100	1	50	2	**	**	100	1
	ST		.3			1		**		1		1		4		**		1
WORN OUT	W	44	12	N	61	18	75	20	67	16	71	20	42	10	51	14	41	10
	E	56	15	S	39	12	25	7	33	8	29	8	58	14	49	14	59	14
	ST		27			30		27		24		28		24		28		24

ITEM (134)
WORK SHEET (76)

ACTIONS
TO BECOME ILL

		TENNESSEE A	TENNESSEE B		GEORGIA A	GEORGIA B	ALABAMA A	ALABAMA B	MISSISSIPPI A	MISSISSIPPI B	FLORIDA A	FLORIDA B	LOUISIANA A	LOUISIANA B	ARKANSAS A	ARKANSAS B	OKLAHOMA A	OKLAHOMA B
BE TAKEN SICK	W	17	2	N	20	3	9	1	4	1	7	1	5	.3	35	3	25	2
	E	11	1	S	21	3	2	.2	3	.4	6	1	5	.3	20	1	10	1
	ST	28	4		41	5	11	1	7	1	13	2	10	1	55	4	35	3
GET SICK	W	19	11	N	18	11	7	4	4	2	6	4	6	4	29	19	14	9
	E	29	17	S	10	6	2	1	2	1	3	2	8	5	23	15	21	14
	ST	48	29		28	17	9	5	6	4	9	5	14	9	52	34	34	23
TAKE SICK	W	19	2	N	22	3	4	1	6	1	6	1	11	1	31	4	17	2
	E	24	3	S	8	1	3	.4	4	1	3	.4	17	2	19	2	6	1
	ST	43	5		29	4	8	1	10	1	9	1	28	4	50	6	22	3

		TENNESSEE C	TENNESSEE D		GEORGIA C	GEORGIA D	ALABAMA C	ALABAMA D	MISSISSIPPI C	MISSISSIPPI D	FLORIDA C	FLORIDA D	LOUISIANA C	LOUISIANA D	ARKANSAS C	ARKANSAS D	OKLAHOMA C	OKLAHOMA D
BE TAKEN SICK	W	61	6	N	48	10	86	16	56	9	53	11	50	3	64	6	71	6
	E	39	4	S	52	11	14	3	44	7	47	10	50	3	36	3	29	3
	ST		10			21		19		16		21		5		9		9
GET SICK	W	40	30	N	63	41	76	52	68	42	68	44	44	30	56	43	40	32
	E	60	46	S	37	24	24	16	32	20	32	21	56	38	44	34	60	49
	ST		77			66		68		62		65		68		77		81
TAKE SICK	W	44	6	N	74	10	56	7	58	13	64	9	40	11	61	9	75	8
	E	56	8	S	26	4	44	5	42	9	36	5	60	16	39	6	25	3
	ST		14			14		12		22		14		27		15		10

ACTIONS
TO BECOME ILL WITH A COLD

ITEM (135)
WORK SHEET (76)

		TENNESSEE			GEORGIA		ALABAMA		MISSISSIPPI		FLORIDA		LOUISIANA		ARKANSAS		OKLAHOMA	
		A	B		A	B	A	B	A	B	A	B	A	B	A	B	A	B
CATCH A COLD	W	14	4	N	15	5	7	2	5	1	9	3	11	3	19	6	19	6
	E	27	8	S	13	4	3	1	3	1	4	1	15	5	15	5	20	6
	ST	41	13		29	9	10	3	7	2	13	4	26	8	35	10	39	12
CATCH COLD	W	25	6	N	14	3	6	1	6	1	6	1	6	1	19	5	17	4
	E	25	5	S	10	2	2	1	3	1	3	1	10	3	22	6	26	7
	ST	50	11		23	5	8	2	8	2	9	2	15	4	42	11	43	11
GET A COLD	W	28	1	N	18	1	8	.3	5	.2	5	.2	**	**	26	2	16	1
	E	30	1	S	5	.2	**	**	3	.1	**	**	11	1	26	2	21	1
	ST	58	2		23	1	8	.3	8	.3	5	.2	11	1	53	4	37	3
TAKE A COLD	W	19	4	N	15	3	7	1	5	1	5	1	7	1	48	8	9	1
	E	31	7	S	13	3	2	.4	1	.2	3	1	2	.3	20	3	14	2
	ST	49	11		29	6	8	2	6	1	8	2	9	1	68	11	23	4
TAKE COLD	W	20	5	N	26	7	6	2	3	1	6	1	4	1	35	9	8	2
	E	20	5	S	11	3	1	.3	3	1	4	1	3	1	28	7	22	6
	ST	40	10		37	9	7	2	6	1	10	3	7	2	63	16	31	8

		TENNESSEE			GEORGIA		ALABAMA		MISSISSIPPI		FLORIDA		LOUISIANA		ARKANSAS		OKLAHOMA	
		C	D		C	D	C	D	C	D	C	D	C	D	C	D	C	D
CATCH A COLD	W	35	9	N	53	15	71	25	64	20	69	26	41	20	55	11	48	16
	E	65	18	S	47	13	29	10	36	12	31	12	59	30	45	9	52	17
	ST		27			29		35		32		38		50		20		32
CATCH COLD	W	50	12	N	58	10	72	15	67	17	65	13	36	9	47	10	39	12
	E	50	12	S	42	7	28	6	33	9	35	7	64	16	53	11	61	18
	ST		23			17		20		26		19		25		21		30
GET A COLD	W	48	2	N	78	2	100	3	67	3	100	2	**	**	50	3	43	3
	E	52	3	S	22	1	**	**	33	1	**	**	100	5	50	3	57	4
	ST		5			3		3		4		2		5		7		7
TAKE A COLD	W	38	9	N	54	11	78	16	83	14	65	11	75	7	70	15	40	4
	E	62	14	S	46	9	22	5	17	3	35	6	25	2	30	6	60	6
	ST		23			21		20		17		17		9		21		10
TAKE COLD	W	50	11	N	71	22	83	17	50	10	56	14	60	7	56	17	27	6
	E	50	11	S	29	9	17	3	50	10	44	11	40	5	44	14	73	16
	ST		21			31		20		20		24		11		31		21

CHARACTERISTICS
SICK

ITEM (136)
WORK SHEET (80)

		TENNESSEE A	TENNESSEE B		GEORGIA A	GEORGIA B	ALABAMA A	ALABAMA B	MISSISSIPPI A	MISSISSIPPI B	FLORIDA A	FLORIDA B	LOUISIANA A	LOUISIANA B	ARKANSAS A	ARKANSAS B	OKLAHOMA A	OKLAHOMA B
AT HIS STOMACH	W	19	14	N	19	14	7	5	4	3	5	4	7	6	28	22	17	13
	E	28	21	S	10	7	3	2	2	1	3	2	4	3	24	19	19	15
	ST	48	35		28	21	9	7	6	4	9	7	11	9	53	41	36	28
IN HIS STOMACH	W	25	1	N	20	1	7	.3	5	.2	9	.4	**	**	44	1	11	.3
	E	16	1	S	9	.4	**	**	5	.2	5	.2	11	.3	22	1	11	.3
	ST	41	2		30	1	7	.3	9	.4	14	1	11	.3	67	2	22	1
ON HIS STOMACH	W	**	**	N	10	1	4	.3	1	.1	25	2	**	**	**	**	**	**
	E	6	.4	S	40	3	3	.2	6	.4	3	.2	**	**	100	1	**	**
	ST	6	.4		51	4	7	1	7	1	28	2	**	**	100	1	[illegible]	**
TO HIS STOMACH	W	41	1	N	15	.4	4	.1	4	.1	7	.2	14	1	21	1	14	1
	E	7	.2	S	**	**	4	.1	4	.1	15	.4	21	1	14	1	14	1
	ST	48	1		15	.4	7	.2	7	.2	22	1	36	2	36	2	29	1
OF HIS STOMACH	W	29	.4	N	21	.3	7	.1	**	**	7	.1	**	**	9	.3	**	**
	E	29	.4	S	**	**	**	**	**	**	7	.1	73	3	18	1	**	**
	ST	57	1		21	.3	7	.1	**	**	14	.2	73	3	27	1	**	**

		TENNESSEE C	TENNESSEE D		GEORGIA C	GEORGIA D	ALABAMA C	ALABAMA D	MISSISSIPPI C	MISSISSIPPI D	FLORIDA C	FLORIDA D	LOUISIANA C	LOUISIANA D	ARKANSAS C	ARKANSAS D	OKLAHOMA C	OKLAHOMA D
AT HIS STOMACH	W	41	36	N	66	52	73	62	70	56	62	41	67	42	54	47	47	44
	E	59	53	S	34	27	27	23	30	24	38	25	33	21	46	40	53	49
	ST		89			79		86		80		66		63		88		93
IN HIS STOMACH	W	61	3	N	69	4	100	4	50	4	67	4	**	**	67	3	50	1
	E	39	2	S	31	2	**	**	50	4	33	2	100	3	33	2	50	1
	ST		5			5		4		7		6		3		5		2
ON HIS STOMACH	W	**	**	N	21	3	60	4	20	2	89	18	**	**	**	**	**	**
	E	100	1	S	79	11	40	3	80	7	11	2	**	**	100	2	**	**
	ST		1			13		6		9		20		**		2		**
TO HIS STOMACH	W	85	3	N	100	2	50	1	50	2	33	2	40	5	60	2	50	2
	E	15	1	S	**	**	50	1	50	2	67	4	60	8	40	2	50	2
	ST		3			2		3		4		6		13		4		5
OF HIS STOMACH	W	50	1	N	100	1	100	1	**	**	50	1	**	**	33	1	**	**
	E	50	1	S	**	**	**	**	**	**	50	1	100	21	67	2	**	**
	ST		2			1		1		**		2		21		2		**

TABLE I

ACTIONS TO

ITEM (137)
WORK SHEET (81)

		TENNESSEE			GEORGIA		ALABAMA		MISSISSIPPI		FLORIDA		LOUISIANA		ARKANSAS		OKLAHOMA	
		A	B		A	B	A	B	A	B	A	B	A	B	A	B	A	B
COURT	W	21	6	N	19	6	7	2	5	1	6	2	10	3	24	6	17	4
	E	20	6	S	16	5	1	.3	3	1	3	1	7	2	16	4	26	6
	ST	40	12		35	10	8	2	8	2	8	2	17	4	40	10	43	11
GO WITH	W	21	11	N	16	8	7	3	4	2	6	3	6	3	22	13	19	11
	E	27	14	S	10	5	3	1	1	1	3	2	8	5	24	14	22	13
	ST	48	24		27	14	10	5	5	3	10	5	14	8	46	27	41	24
KEEP COMPANY WITH	W	22	2	N	20	2	7	1	3	.2	5	.4	**	**	61	5	9	1
	E	26	2	S	8	1	3	.2	1	.1	5	.4	**	**	26	2	4	.3
	ST	49	4		28	2	9	1	4	.3	11	1	**	**	87	7	13	1
SIT UP TO	W	56	1	N	13	.2	6	.1	**	**	**	**	**	**	33	.3	**	**
	E	6	.1	S	**	**	6	.1	6	.1	6	.1	**	**	67	1	**	**
	ST	63	1		13	.2	13	.2	6	.1	6	.1	**	**	100	1	**	**
SPARK WITH	W	13	1	N	23	1	2	.1	4	.2	12	1	18	1	45	2	9	.3
	E	35	2	S	4	.2	**	**	4	.2	4	.2	**	**	9	.3	18	1
	ST	48	3		27	1	2	.1	8	.4	15	1	18	1	55	2	27	1
TALK TO	W	19	1	N	19	1	3	.1	10	.3	3	.1	11	.3	33	1	**	**
	E	32	1	S	10	.3	3	.1	**	**	**	**	44	1	**	**	11	.3
	ST	52	2		29	1	6	.2	10	.3	3	.1	56	2	33	1	11	.3
WALK OUT WITH	W	**	**	N	33	.4	**	**	8	.1	**	**	**	**	**	**	**	**
	E	33	.4	S	17	.2	**	**	8	.1	**	**	67	1	33	.3	**	**
	ST	33	.4		50	1	**	**	17	.2	**	**	67	1	33	.3	**	**
WOO	W	28	1	N	20	1	12	.3	**	**	12	.3	11	.3	33	1	11	.3
	E	12	.3	S	8	.2	4	.1	**	**	4	.1	**	**	33	1	11	.3
	ST	40	1		28	1	16	.4	**	**	16	.4	11	.3	67	2	22	1

ITEM (137) (CONTINUED) TO

		TENNESSEE C	TENNESSEE D		GEORGIA C	GEORGIA D	ALABAMA C	ALABAMA D	MISSISSIPPI C	MISSISSIPPI D	FLORIDA C	FLORIDA D	LOUISIANA C	LOUISIANA D	ARKANSAS C	ARKANSAS D	OKLAHOMA C	OKLAHOMA D
COURT	W	52	13	N	54	19	88	24	61	22	67	17	58	16	61	12	40	11
	E	48	12	S	46	16	13	3	39	14	33	9	42	11	39	8	60	17
	ST		25			34		28		37		26		27		20		29
GO WITH	W	43	22	N	61	28	70	38	74	32	65	33	41	20	47	25	45	29
	E	57	30	S	39	18	30	16	26	11	35	18	59	30	53	28	55	34
	ST		52			45		54		43		51		50		52		63
KEEP COMPANY WITH	W	46	4	N	71	5	71	6	67	3	50	4	**	**	70	10	67	2
	E	54	4	S	29	2	29	2	33	2	50	4	**	**	30	4	33	1
	ST		8			7		8		5		9		**		14		3
SIT UP TO	W	90	2	N	100	1	50	1	**	**	**	**	**	**	33	1	**	**
	E	10	.2	S	**	**	50	1	100	2	100	1	**	**	67	1	**	**
	ST		2			1		2		2		1		**		2		**
SPARK WITH	W	28	2	N	86	4	100	1	50	3	75	6	100	5	83	4	33	1
	E	72	4	S	14	1	**	**	50	3	25	2	**	**	17	1	67	2
	ST		5			5		1		6		9		5		4		3
TALK TO	W	38	1	N	67	2	50	1	100	5	100	1	20	2	100	2	**	**
	E	63	2	S	33	1	50	1	**	**	**	**	80	9	**	**	100	1
	ST		4			3		2		5		1		11		2		1
WALK OUT WITH	W	**	**	N	67	1	**	**	50	2	**	**	**	**	**	**	**	**
	E	100	1	S	33	1	**	**	50	2	**	**	100	5	100	1	**	**
	ST		1			2		**		3		**		5		1		**
WOO	W	70	2	N	71	2	75	3	**	**	75	3	100	2	50	2	50	1
	E	30	1	S	29	1	25	1	**	**	25	1	**	**	50	2	50	1
	ST		2			2		5		**		4		2		4		2

ACTIONS
TO REJECT A SUITOR

ITEM (138)
WORK SHEET (82)

		TENNESSEE			GEORGIA		ALABAMA		MISSISSIPPI		FLORIDA		LOUISIANA		ARKANSAS		OKLAHOMA	
		A	B		A	B	A	B	A	B	A	B	A	B	A	B	A	B
GIVE HIM THE AIR	W	19	1	N	13	1	4	.3	6	.4	7	1	9	1	23	3	17	2
	E	24	2	S	10	1	4	.3	3	.2	7	1	11	1	17	2	23	3
	ST	43	3		24	2	9	1	9	1	15	1	20	3	40	5	40	5
GIVE HIM THE BOUNCE	W	45	1	N	9	.1	**	**	**	**	**	**	**	**	40	1	**	**
	E	27	.3	S	9	.1	**	**	9	.1	**	**	40	1	**	**	20	.3
	ST	73	1		18	.2	**	**	9	.1	**	**	40	1	40	1	20	.3
GIVE A COLD SHOULDER	W	17	4	N	18	4	5	1	4	1	7	1	11	2	30	5	11	2
	E	33	7	S	11	2	3	1	3	1	1	.2	15	3	11	2	22	4
	ST	50	10		29	6	8	2	7	1	8	2	26	4	41	7	33	5
GIVE HIM THE MITTEN	W	71	1	N	**	**	**	**	**	**	14	.1	**	**	60	1	20	.3
	E	**	**	S	**	**	**	**	**	**	14	.1	**	**	**	**	20	.3
	ST	71	1		**	**	**	**	**	**	29	.2	**	**	60	1	40	1
JILT HIM	W	23	5	N	20	4	8	2	2	1	8	2	5	1	27	6	15	3
	E	19	4	S	9	2	2	1	6	1	2	.4	13	3	24	5	16	4
	ST	42	9		29	6	10	2	8	2	10	2	18	4	52	12	31	7
KICK HIM	W	6	.2	N	26	1	3	.1	**	**	17	1	**	**	**	**	**	**
	E	11	.4	S	34	1	**	**	**	**	3	.1	**	**	100	.3	**	**
	ST	17	1		60	2	3	.1	**	**	20	1	**	**	100	.3	**	**
THROW HIM OVER	W	19	1	N	4	.1	8	.2	4	.1	4	.1	**	**	17	.3	50	1
	E	27	1	S	15	.4	**	**	8	.2	12	.3	**	**	**	**	33	1
	ST	46	1		19	1	8	.2	12	.3	15	.4	**	**	17	.3	83	2
TURN HIM DOWN	W	20	8	N	21	8	7	3	5	2	7	3	4	2	31	14	17	8
	E	22	9	S	10	4	2	1	1	.4	4	2	2	1	25	12	20	9
	ST	43	17		31	12	9	4	6	2	11	4	6	3	57	26	37	17

ITEM (138) (CONTINUED) TO REJECT A SUITOR

		TENNESSEE C	TENNESSEE D		GEORGIA C	GEORGIA D	ALABAMA C	ALABAMA D	MISSISSIPPI C	MISSISSIPPI D	FLORIDA C	FLORIDA D	LOUISIANA C	LOUISIANA D	ARKANSAS C	ARKANSAS D	OKLAHOMA C	OKLAHOMA D
GIVE HIM THE	W	45	3	N	56	3	50	4	67	6	50	5	43	8	57	6	43	6
AIR	E	55	4	S	44	3	50	4	33	3	50	5	57	10	43	4	57	8
	ST		7			6		7		10		10		18		10		14
GIVE HIM THE	W	63	1	N	50	.3	**	**	**	**	**	**	**	**	100	1	**	**
BOUNCE	E	38	1	S	50	.3	**	**	100	2	**	**	100	5	**	**	100	1
	ST		2			1		**		2		**		5		1		1
GIVE A COLD	W	34	8	N	62	13	60	11	62	13	87	13	42	13	74	10	33	5
SHOULDER	E	66	16	S	38	8	40	7	38	8	13	2	58	18	26	3	67	10
	ST		24			21		19		21		15		30		13		15
GIVE HIM THE	W	100	1	N	**	**	**	**	**	**	50	1	**	**	100	2	50	1
MITTEN	E	**	**	S	**	**	**	**	**	**	50	1	**	**	**	**	50	1
	ST		1			**		**		**		2		**		2		2
JILT HIM	W	55	12	N	70	15	76	20	29	8	80	16	27	8	53	12	47	9
	E	45	10	S	30	6	24	6	71	19	20	4	73	20	47	10	53	10
	ST		21			21		26		27		20		28		22		18
KICK HIM	W	33	.4	N	43	3	100	1	**	**	86	6	**	**	**	**	**	**
	E	67	1	S	57	4	**	**	**	**	14	1	**	**	100	1	**	**
	ST		1			8		1		**		7		**		1		**
THROW HIM	W	42	1	N	20	.3	100	2	33	2	25	1	**	**	100	1	60	3
OVER	E	58	2	S	80	1	**	**	67	3	75	3	**	**	**	**	40	2
	ST		3			2		2		5		4		**		1		5
TURN HIM	W	48	19	N	67	28	78	35	82	29	65	28	63	13	56	28	47	21
DOWN	E	52	21	S	33	14	22	10	18	6	35	15	38	8	44	22	53	24
	ST		40			42		44		35		43		20		50		46

SOCIAL LIFE
A NOISY PRANKISH CELEBRATION AFTER A WEDDING

ITEM (139)
WORK SHEET (82)

		TENNESSEE			GEORGIA		ALABAMA		MISSISSIPPI		FLORIDA		LOUISIANA		ARKANSAS		OKLAHOMA	
		A	B		A	B	A	B	A	B	A	B	A	B	A	B	A	B
BELLING	W	27	.3	N	9	.1	9	.1	9	.1	**	**	**	**	100	.3	**	**
	E	27	.3	S	18	.2	**	**	**	**	**	**	**	**	**	**	**	**
	ST	55	1		27	.3	9	.1	9	.1	**	**	**	**	100	.3	**	**
BELLING BEE					(NO RESPONSE)													
	E	100	.1	S	**	**	**	**	**	**	**	**	**	**	**	**	**	**
	ST	100	.1		**	**	**	**	**	**	**	**	**	**	**	**	**	**
BULL BAND(ING)	W	60	.3	N	20	.1	**	**	20	.1	**	**	**	**	**	**	**	**
					(NO RESPONSE)													
	ST	60	.3		20	.1	**	**	20	.1	**	**	**	**	**	**	**	**
CALATHUMP	W	67	.2	N	33	.1	**	**	**	**	**	**	**	**	**	**	**	**
					(NO RESPONSE)													
	ST	67	.2		33	.1	**	**	**	**	**	**	**	**	**	**	**	**
HORNING	W	**	**	N	**	**	13	.1	13	.1	**	**	**	**	**	**	**	**
	E	25	.2	S	25	.2	13	.1	13	.1	**	**	50	.3	**	**	50	.3
	ST	25	.2		25	.2	25	.2	25	.2	**	**	50	.3	**	**	50	.3
HORNING BEE	W	25	.1	N	**	**	**	**	**	**	**	**	**	**	**	**	**	**
	E	50	.2	S	25	.1	**	**	**	**	**	**	**	**	**	**	**	**
	ST	75	.3		25	.1	**	**	**	**	**	**	**	**	**	**	**	**
SERENADE	W	12	5	N	24	11	5	2	2	1	8	4	15	1	30	3	4	.3
	E	29	13	S	15	7	.4	.2	2	1	2	1	4	.3	37	4	11	1
	ST	41	19		39	18	6	3	3	2	11	5	19	2	67	6	15	1
SHIVAREE	W	36	7	N	4	1	4	1	4	1	9	2	5	3	35	23	19	13
	E	28	6	S	2	.3	4	1	2	.3	8	2	6	4	18	12	17	11
	ST	65	13		5	1	8	2	5	1	17	3	10	7	53	35	36	24
SKIMMELTON					(NO RESPONSE)													
	E	**	**	S	100	.1	**	**	**	**	**	**	**	**	**	**	**	**
	ST	**	**		100	.1	**	**	**	**	**	**	**	**	**	**	**	**
TIN PANNING	W	30	1	N	20	1	13	.4	3	.1	3	.1	17	.3	17	.3	17	.3
	E	10	.3	S	7	.2	**	**	3	.1	10	.3	**	**	33	1	17	.3
	ST	40	1		27	1	13	.4	7	.2	13	.4	17	.3	50	1	33	1

ITEM (139)

(CONTINUED) A NOISY PRANKISH CELEBRATION AFTER A WEDDING

		TENNESSEE			GEORGIA		ALABAMA		MISSISSIPPI		FLORIDA		LOUISIANA		ARKANSAS		OKLAHOMA	
		C	D		C	D	C	D	C	D	C	D	C	D	C	D	C	D
BELLING	W	50	1	N	33	1	100	2	100	3	**	**	**	**	100	1	**	**
	E	50	1	S	67	1	**	**	**	**	**	**	**	**	**	**	**	**
	ST		2			2		2		3		**		**		1		**
BELLING BEE					(NO RESPONSE)													
	E	100	.2	S	**	**	**	**	**	**	**	**	**	**	**	**	**	**
	ST		.2			**		**		**		**		**		**		**
BULL BAND(ING)	W	100	1	N	100	1	**	**	100	3	**	**	**	**	**	**	**	**
					(NO RESPONSE)													
	ST		1			1		**		3		**		**		**		**
CALATHUMP	W	100	1	N	100	1	**	**	**	**	**	**	**	**	**	**	**	**
					(NO RESPONSE)													
	ST		1			1		**		**		**		**		**		**
HORNING	W	**	**	N	**	**	50	2	50	3	**	**	**	**	**	**	**	**
	E	100	1	S	100	1	50	2	50	3	**	**	100	4	**	**	100	1
	ST		1			1		4		6		**		4		**		1
HORNING BEE	W	33	.2	N	**	**	**	**	**	**	**	**	**	**	**	**	**	**
	E	67	1	S	100	1	**	**	**	**	**	**	**	**	**	**	**	**
	ST		1			1		**		**		**		**		**		**
SERENADE	W	29	16	N	61	53	92	49	53	26	79	44	80	15	44	7	25	1
	E	71	38	S	39	34	8	4	47	23	21	12	20	4	56	8	75	4
	ST		54			87		53		48		56		19		15		5
SHIVAREE	W	56	21	N	70	4	47	15	70	23	55	21	47	35	66	53	53	48
	E	44	16	S	30	2	53	17	30	10	45	18	53	38	34	28	47	42
	ST		37			5		32		32		39		73		81		90
SKIMMELTON					(NO RESPONSE)													
	E	**	**	S	100	1	**	**	**	**	**	**	**	**	**	**	**	**
	ST		**			1		**		**		**		**		**		**
TIN PANNING	W	75	3	N	75	3	100	9	50	3	25	1	100	4	33	1	50	1
	E	25	1	S	25	1	**	**	50	3	75	4	**	**	67	2	50	1
	ST		4			4		9		6		5		4		3		3

ACTIONS
TO ABSENT ONESELF FROM SCHOOL

ITEM (140)
WORK SHEET (83)

		TENNESSEE A	TENNESSEE B		GEORGIA A	GEORGIA B	ALABAMA A	ALABAMA B	MISSISSIPPI A	MISSISSIPPI B	FLORIDA A	FLORIDA B	LOUISIANA A	LOUISIANA B	ARKANSAS A	ARKANSAS B	OKLAHOMA A	OKLAHOMA B
BAG SCHOOL	W	50	.1	N	50	.1	**	**	**	**	**	**	**	**	**	**	**	**
					(NO RESPONSE)													
	ST	50	.1		50	.1	**	**	**	**	**	**	**	**	**	**	**	**
BOLT	W	**	**	N	**	**	**	**	100	.1	**	**	**	**	**	**	**	**
					(NO RESPONSE)													
	ST	**	**		**	**	**	**	100	.1	**	**	**	**	**	**	**	**
COOK JACK					(NO RESPONSE)													
					(NO RESPONSE)													
					(NO RESPONSE)													
LAY OUT	W	11	2	N	21	4	4	1	2	.3	1	.2	**	**	25	.3	**	**
	E	58	12	S	3	1	**	**	1	.1	**	**	**	**	25	.3	50	1
	ST	69	14		24	5	4	1	2	.4	1	.2	**	**	50	1	50	1
LIE OUT	W	**	**	N	36	.4	**	**	9	.1	9	.1	**	**	**	**	**	**
	E	36	.4	S	9	.1	**	**	**	**	**	**	**	**	**	**	**	**
	ST	36	.4		45	1	**	**	9	.1	9	.1	**	**	**	**	**	**
PLAY TRUANT	W	28	2	N	17	1	19	1	**	**	9	1	**	**	27	1	13	1
	E	17	1	S	4	.2	**	**	2	.1	6	.3	**	**	40	2	20	1
	ST	44	2		20	1	19	1	2	.1	15	1	**	**	67	4	33	2
RUN OUT OF SCHOOL	W	25	.1	N	**	**	**	**	25	.1	**	**	**	**	**	**	**	**
	E	25	.1	S	**	**	**	**	25	.1	**	**	**	**	**	**	**	**
	ST	50	.2		**	**	**	**	50	.2	**	**	**	**	**	**	**	**
SKIP CLASS	W	24	2	N	12	1	10	1	4	.4	4	.4	7	1	15	3	24	5
	E	26	2	S	9	1	4	.4	1	.1	5	1	7	1	9	2	37	7
	ST	50	5		21	2	14	1	5	1	10	1	15	3	24	5	61	12
PLAY HOOKEY	W	21	12	N	18	10	7	4	6	3	9	5	6	4	35	24	13	9
	E	16	9	S	14	8	3	2	3	2	4	2	8	5	22	15	15	10
	ST	37	21		31	18	10	6	8	5	13	7	14	10	57	39	28	19
SKIP SCHOOL	W	17	2	N	13	1	7	1	2	.2	14	2	4	1	19	3	13	2
	E	22	2	S	13	1	5	1	1	.1	7	1	6	1	21	4	38	6
	ST	39	4		25	3	13	1	3	.3	21	2	10	2	40	7	50	9
SLIP OFF FROM SCHOOL	W	27	2	N	25	1	2	.1	2	.1	2	.1	9	.3	36	1	**	**
	E	34	2	S	7	.4	**	**	2	.1	**	**	**	**	9	.3	45	2
	ST	61	4		32	2	2	.1	4	.2	2	.1	9	.3	45	2	45	2

ITEM (140) (CONTINUED) TO ABSENT ONESELF FROM SCHOOL

		TENNESSEE			GEORGIA		ALABAMA		MISSISSIPPI		FLORIDA		LOUISIANA		ARKANSAS		OKLAHOMA	
		C	D		C	D	C	D	C	D	C	D	C	D	C	D	C	D
BAG SCHOOL	W	100	.2	N	100	.3	**	**	**	**	**	**	**	**	**	**	**	**
					(NO RESPONSE)													
	ST		.2			.3		**		**		**		**		**		**
BOLT	W	**	**	N	**	**	**	**	100	2	**	**	**	**	**	**	**	**
					(NO RESPONSE)													
	ST		**			**		**		2		**		**		**		**
COOK JACK					(NO RESPONSE)													
					(NO RESPONSE)													
	ST		**			**		**		**		**		**		**		**
LAY OUT	W	16	4	N	89	14	100	8	75	5	100	3	11	**	50	1	**	**
	E	84	23	S	11	2	**	**	25	2	**	**	**	**	50	1	100	2
	ST		27			16		8		6		2		**		1		2
LIE OUT	W	**	**	N	80	1	**	**	100	2	100	1	**	**	**	**	**	**
	E	100	1	S	20	.3	**	**	**	**	**	**	**	**	**	**	**	**
	ST		1			2		**		2		1		**		**		**
PLAY TRUANT	W	63	3	N	82	3	100	10	**	**	63	4	**	**	40	3	40	2
	E	38	2	S	18	1	**	**	100	2	38	3	**	**	60	4	60	2
	ST		5			4		10		2		7		**		6		4
RUN OUT OF SCHOOL	W	50	.2	N	**	**	**	**	50	2	**	**	**	**	**	**	**	**
	E	50	.2	S	**	**	**	**	50	2	**	**	**	**	**	**	**	**
	ST		.4			**		**		3		**		**		**		**
SKIP CLASS	W	48	4	N	58	4	69	9	80	6	44	4	50	10	62	5	39	11
	E	52	5	S	42	3	31	4	20	2	56	4	50	10	38	3	61	16
	ST		9			6		13		8		8		20		8		27
PLAY HOOKEY	W	56	23	N	56	32	71	39	67	48	69	42	44	29	61	42	47	20
	E	44	18	S	44	25	29	16	33	23	31	19	56	37	39	27	53	23
	ST		41			57		55		71		61		66		69		43
SKIP SCHOOL	W	44	4	N	50	5	57	8	67	3	65	13	40	5	47	6	25	5
	E	56	5	S	50	5	43	6	33	2	35	7	60	7	53	6	75	15
	ST		9			9		14		5		20		12		12		20
SLIP OFF FROM SCHOOL	W	44	3	N	78	5	100	1	50	2	100	1	100	2	80	3	**	**
	E	56	4	S	22	1	**	**	50	2	**	**	**	**	20	1	100	4
	ST		7			6		1		3		1		2		3		4

THE HOUSE AND ITS ENVIRONS
A PLACE WHERE FIRE ENGINES ARE KEPT

ITEM (141)
WORK SHEET (84)

		TENNESSEE			GEORGIA		ALABAMA		MISSISSIPPI		FLORIDA		LOUISIANA		ARKANSAS		OKLAHOMA	
		A	B		A	B	A	B	A	B	A	B	A	B	A	B	A	B
FIRE HALL	W	23	7	N	14	4	6	2	1	.2	.3	.1	**	**	**	**	**	**
	E	54	15	S	1	.3	.3	.1	.3	.1	**	**	100	.3	**	**	**	**
	ST	78	22		15	4	6	2	1	.3	.3	.1	100	.3	**	**	**	**
FIRE HOUSE	W	17	2	N	22	2	10	1	3	.3	3	.3	10	1	33	3	5	.3
	E	20	2	S	11	1	3	.3	3	.3	8	1	29	2	10	1	14	1
	ST	37	4		33	3	13	1	7	1	11	1	38	3	43	3	19	1
FIRE STATION	W	17	9	N	21	11	7	4	6	3	12	6	7	6	28	22	17	14
	E	9	5	S	16	8	4	2	3	2	5	3	6	5	24	19	19	15
	ST	26	14		37	20	11	6	9	5	17	9	13	10	52	42	36	29

		TENNESSEE			GEORGIA		ALABAMA		MISSISSIPPI		FLORIDA		LOUISIANA		ARKANSAS		OKLAHOMA	
		C	D		C	D	C	D	C	D	C	D	C	D	C	D	C	D
FIRE HALL	W	30	17	N	93	14	94	18	67	4	100	1	**	**	**	**	**	**
	E	70	39	S	8	1	6	1	33	2	**	**	100	3	**	**	**	**
	ST		56			15		19		5		1		3		**		**
FIRE HOUSE	W	47	4	N	67	8	75	11	50	5	30	3	25	5	78	6	25	1
	E	53	5	S	33	4	25	4	50	5	70	7	75	16	22	2	75	4
	ST		9			11		14		11		10		21		7		5
FIRE STATION	W	65	23	N	57	42	66	44	66	55	69	61	55	42	53	50	48	45
	E	35	12	S	43	31	34	23	34	29	31	28	45	34	47	43	53	50
	ST		35			73		67		84		89		76		93		95

CHARACTERISTICS
A HOBGOBLIN TO THREATEN CHILDREN WITH

ITEM (142)
WORK SHEET (90)

		TENNESSEE			GEORGIA		ALABAMA		MISSISSIPPI		FLORIDA		LOUISIANA		ARKANSAS		OKLAHOMA	
		A	B		A	B	A	B	A	B	A	B	A	B	A	B	A	B
BAD MAN	W	26	3	N	16	2	9	1	3	.3	8	1	**	**	43	5	3	.3
	E	24	3	S	6	1	6	1	1	.1	2	.2	3	.3	23	3	27	3
	ST	50	5		21	2	15	2	4	.4	10	1	3	.3	67	7	30	3
BLACK MAN	W	30	.3	N	30	.3	**	**	**	**	**	**	**	**	100	.3	**	**
	E	20	.2	S	10	.1	**	**	10	.1	**	**	**	**	**	**	**	**
	ST	50	1		40	.4	**	**	10	.1	**	**	**	**	100	.3	**	**
BOOGER MAN	W	16	9	N	19	10	6	3	4	2	7	4	6	3	34	16	12	6
	E	27	14	S	14	8	2	1	2	1	3	1	8	4	19	9	21	10
	ST	43	[illegible]		11	18	8	4	6	3	10	5	14	7	53	26	33	16
BOOGEY MAN	W	23	4	N	13	2	8	2	7	1	9	2	13	3	16	4	33	8
	E	19	4	S	5	1	4	1	4	1	6	1	14	3	10	2	14	3
	ST	43	8		19	4	13	2	11	2	15	3	27	6	25	6	48	11
OLD HARRY	W	75	.3	N	25	.1	**	**	**	**	**	**	**	**	50	.3	**	**
	E	**	**	S	**	**	**	**	**	**	**	**	**	**	**	**	50	.3
	ST	75	.3		25	.1	**	**	**	**	**	**	**	**	50	.3	50	.3
OLD NICK	W	26	1	N	22	1	13	.3	**	**	4	.1	**	**	67	1	**	**
	E	17	.4	S	9	.2	4	.1	4	.1	**	**	**	**	**	**	33	.3
	ST	43	1		30	1	17	.4	4	.1	4	.1	**	**	67	1	33	.3
OLD SCRATCH	W	30	2	N	19	1	8	.4	**	**	4	.2	33	.3	33	.3	**	**
	E	25	1	S	8	.4	2	.1	4	.2	2	.1	**	**	33	.3	**	**
	ST	55	3		26	1	9	1	4	.2	6	.3	33	.3	67	1	**	**
RAWHEAD AND BLOODYBONES	W	21	2	N	19	1	3	.2	3	.2	7	1	14	.3	14	.3	**	**
	E	26	2	S	21	2	1	.1	**	**	**	**	14	.3	43	1	14	.3
	ST	47	4		40	3	4	.3	3	.2	7	1	29	1	57	1	14	.3
PLAT EYE					(NO RESPONSE)													
	E	100	.1	S	**	**	**	**	**	**	**	**	**	**	**	**	**	**
	ST	100	.1		**	**	**	**	**	**	**	**	**	**	**	**	**	**

(CONTINUED) A HOBGOBLIN TO THREATEN CHILDREN WITH

ITEM (142)		TENNESSEE C	TENNESSEE D		GEORGIA C	GEORGIA D	ALABAMA C	ALABAMA D	MISSISSIPPI C	MISSISSIPPI D	FLORIDA C	FLORIDA D	LOUISIANA C	LOUISIANA D	ARKANSAS C	ARKANSAS D	OKLAHOMA C	OKLAHOMA D
BAD MAN	W	52	6	N	73	6	60	10	75	5	80	8	**	**	65	11	11	1
	E	48	6	S	27	2	40	7	25	2	20	2	100	3	35	6	89	9
	ST		12			8		16		7		10		3		17		10
BLACK MAN	W	60	1	N	75	1	**	**	**	**	**	**	**	**	100	1	**	**
	E	40	.4	S	25	.3	**	**	100	2	**	**	**	**	**	**	**	**
	ST		1			1		**		2		**		**		1		**
BOOGER MAN	W	38	20	N	58	35	76	34	65	33	74	39	42	20	63	38	36	19
	E	62	32	S	42	26	24	11	35	18	26	14	58	28	37	22	64	33
	ST		52			61		45		51		53		48		61		51
BOOGEY MAN	W	55	10	N	71	8	65	16	65	21	61	17	47	20	63	9	70	24
	E	45	8	S	29	3	35	9	35	11	39	11	53	23	38	5	30	10
	ST		18			12		25		33		28		43		14		35
OLD HARRY	W	100	1	N	100	.3	**	**	**	**	**	**	**	**	100	1	**	**
	E	**	**	S	**	**	**	**	**	**	**	**	**	**	**	**	100	1
	ST		1			.3		**		**		**		**		1		1
OLD NICK	W	60	1	N	71	2	75	3	**	**	100	1	**	**	100	2	**	**
	E	40	1	S	29	1	25	1	100	2	**	**	**	**	**	**	100	1
	ST		2			2		4		2		1		**		2		1
OLD SCRATCH	W	55	4	N	71	3	80	4	**	**	67	2	100	3	50	1	**	**
	E	45	3	S	29	1	20	1	100	3	33	1	**	**	50	1	**	**
	ST		7			5		5		3		3		3		2		**
RAWHEAD AND BLOODYBONES	W	44	3	N	48	5	67	2	100	3	100	5	50	3	25	1	**	**
	E	56	4	S	52	5	33	1	**	**	**	**	50	3	75	3	100	1
	ST		8			10		3		3		5		5		3		1
PLAT EYE					(NO RESPONSE)													
	E	100	.2	S	**	**	**	**	**	**	**	**	**	**	**	**	**	**
	ST		.2			**		**		**		**		**		**		**

ITEM (143)
WORK SHEET (93)

ACTIONS
A GREETING AT CHRISTMAS TIME

		TENNESSEE A	TENNESSEE B		GEORGIA A	GEORGIA B	ALABAMA A	ALABAMA B	MISSISSIPPI A	MISSISSIPPI B	FLORIDA A	FLORIDA B	LOUISIANA A	LOUISIANA B	ARKANSAS A	ARKANSAS B	OKLAHOMA A	OKLAHOMA B
CHRISTMAS BOX	W	17	.1	N	50	.3	**	**	**	**	**	**	**	**	**	**	**	**
	E	17	.1	S	17	.1	**	**	**	**	**	**	**	**	**	**	**	**
	ST	33	.2		67	.4	**	**	**	**	**	**	**	**	**	**	**	**
CHRISTMAS GIFT	W	18	5	N	22	7	4	1	4	1	2	1	3	1	39	9	13	3
	E	31	9	S	10	3	2	1	3	1	2	1	5	1	21	5	19	4
	ST	50	15		32	10	6	2	7	2	5	1	8	2	60	13	32	7
MERRY CHRISTMAS	W	20	14	N	18	12	7	5	4	3	9	6	7	5	24	18	15	12
	E	23	16	S	11	7	3	2	2	2	4	3	8	6	23	17	22	16
	ST	42	29		28	20	10	7	7	5	13	9	15	12	47	35	37	28

		TENNESSEE C	TENNESSEE D		GEORGIA C	GEORGIA D	ALABAMA C	ALABAMA D	MISSISSIPPI C	MISSISSIPPI D	FLORIDA C	FLORIDA D	LOUISIANA C	LOUISIANA D	ARKANSAS C	ARKANSAS D	OKLAHOMA C	OKLAHOMA D
CHRISTMAS BOX	W	50	.2	N	75	1	**	**	**	**	**	**	**	**	**	**	**	**
	E	50	.2	S	25	.3	**	**	**	**	**	**	**	**	**	**	**	**
	ST		.4			1		**		**		**		**		**		**
CHRISTMAS GIFT	W	37	12	N	69	22	72	15	52	17	50	7	40	5	65	18	40	8
	E	63	21	S	31	10	28	6	48	15	50	7	60	8	35	10	60	12
	ST		33			33		21		32		14		14		27		21
MERRY CHRISTMAS	W	46	31	N	62	41	74	58	66	45	70	60	47	41	51	37	42	33
	E	54	35	S	38	25	26	21	34	23	30	26	53	46	49	36	58	46
	ST		66			66		79		68		86		86		73		79

ACTIONS
TO COAST LYING DOWN FLAT

ITEM (144)
WORK SHEET (95)

		TENNESSEE A	TENNESSEE B		GEORGIA A	GEORGIA B	ALABAMA A	ALABAMA B	MISSISSIPPI A	MISSISSIPPI B	FLORIDA A	FLORIDA B	LOUISIANA A	LOUISIANA B	ARKANSAS A	ARKANSAS B	OKLAHOMA A	OKLAHOMA B
BELLY BOOSTER	W	20	1	N	20	1	**	**	3	.1	20	1	7	.3	64	3	7	.3
	E	20	1	S	13	1	5	.2	**	**	**	**	**	**	7	.3	14	1
	ST	40	2		33	1	5	.2	3	.1	20	1	7	.3	71	4	21	1
BELLY BUMP	W	38	1	N	6	.1	6	.1	6	.1	**	**	**	**	75	1	**	**
	E	25	.4	S	19	.3	**	**	**	**	**	**	**	**	25	.3	**	**
	ST	63	1		25	.4	6	.1	6	.1	**	**	**	**	100	1	**	**
BELLY BUMPER	W	10	1	N	34	2	2	.1	4	.2	10	1	**	**	50	1	13	.3
	E	20	1	S	14	1	2	.1	2	.1	2	.1	**	**	25	1	13	.3
	ST	30	2		48	2	4	.2	6	.3	12	1	**	**	75	2	25	1
BELLY BUNKER	W	75	.3	N	**	**	**	**	25	.1	**	**	**	**	50	.3	**	**
	E	**	**	S	**	**	**	**	**	**	**	**	50	.3	**	**	**	**
	ST	75	.3		**	**	**	**	25	.1	**	**	50	.3	50	.3	**	**
BELLY BUNT	W	33	.1	N	33	.1	**	**	**	**	**	**	**	**	**	**	**	**
	E	**	**	S	33	.1	**	**	**	**	**	**	**	**	**	**	**	**
	ST	33	.1		67	.2	**	**	**	**	**	**	**	**	**	**	**	**
BELLY BUST(A)	W	19	1	N	22	1	7	.2	7	.2	7	.2	28	2	11	1	**	**
	E	30	1	S	4	.1	**	**	**	**	4	.1	22	1	33	2	6	.3
	ST	48	1		26	1	7	.2	7	.2	11	.3	50	3	44	3	6	.3
BELLY BUSTER(A)	W	18	3	N	17	3	12	2	3	.4	6	1	**	**	43	8	13	3
	E	25	4	S	10	1	1	.2	2	.3	5	1	4	1	19	4	21	4
	ST	43	6		27	4	13	2	5	1	11	2	4	1	62	12	34	6
BELLY DOWN	W	29	1	N	13	.3	**	**	4	.1	4	.1	**	**	**	**	**	**
	E	21	1	S	25	1	4	.1	**	**	**	**	**	**	75	1	25	.3
	ST	50	1		38	1	4	.1	4	.1	4	.1	**	**	75	1	25	.3
BELLY FLOP(A)	W	**	**	N	17	.1	**	**	17	.1	17	.1	**	**	50	.3	**	**
	E	17	.1	S	**	**	17	.1	**	**	17	.1	**	**	50	.3	**	**
	ST	17	.1		17	.1	17	.1	17	.1	33	.2	**	**	100	1	**	**
BELLY FLOPPER(A)	W	40	.4	N	20	.2	10	.1	**	**	**	**	**	**	**	**	**	**
	E	**	**	S	10	.1	10	.1	10	.1	**	**	**	**	**	**	**	**
	ST	40	.4		30	.3	20	.2	10	.1	**	**	**	**	**	**	**	**

(CONTINUED) TO COAST LYING DOWN FLAT

		TENNESSEE			GEORGIA		ALABAMA		MISSISSIPPI		FLORIDA		LOUISIANA		ARKANSAS		OKLAHOMA	
		A	B		A	B	A	B	A	B	A	B	A	B	A	B	A	B
BELLY GRINDER	W	25	.1	N	**	**	**	**	25	.1	**	**	**	**	50	.3	**	**
	E	**	**	S	25	.1	25	.1	**	**	**	**	**	**	50	.3	**	**
	ST	25	.1		25	.1	25	.1	25	.1	**	**	**	**	100	1	**	**
BELLY GUT	W	**	**	N	**	**	**	**	**	**	50	.1	**	**	**	**	**	**
	E	50	.1	S	**	**	**	**	**	**	**	**	**	**	**	**	**	**
	ST	50	.1		**	**	**	**	**	**	50	.1	**	**	**	**	**	**
BELLY GUTTER	W	100	.1	N	**	**	**	**	**	**	**	**	**	**	**	**	**	**
					(NO RESPONSE)													
	ST	100	.1		**	**	**	**	**	**	**	**	**	**	**	**	**	**
BELLY KACHUG	W	**	**	N	**	**	**	**	**	**	33	.1	**	**	**	**	**	**
	E	33	.1	S	**	**	33	.1	**	**	**	**	**	**	**	**	**	**
	ST	33	.1		**	**	33	.1	**	**	33	.1	**	**	**	**	**	**
BELLY KACHUNK	W	33	.1	N	**	**	**	**	**	**	**	**	**	**	**	**	**	**
	F	**	**	S	67	.2	**	**	**	**	**	**	**	**	**	**	**	**
	ST	33	.1		67	.2	**	**	**	**	**	**	**	**	**	**	**	**
BELLY WHACK	W	**	**	N	100	.1	**	**	**	**	**	**	**	**	**	**	**	**
					(NO RESPONSE)													
	ST	**	**		100	.1	**	**	**	**	**	**	**	**	**	**	**	**
BELLY WOP	W	**	**	N	33	.2	**	**	**	**	**	**	**	**	100	.3	**	**
	E	33	.2	S	17	.1	17	.1	**	**	**	**	**	**	**	**	**	**
	ST	33	.2		50	.3	17	.1	**	**	**	**	**	**	100	.3	**	**
BELLY WOPPER	W	13	.3	N	42	1	4	.1	**	**	4	.1	**	**	40	1	**	**
	E	25	1	S	8	.2	4	.1	**	**	**	**	20	.3	**	**	40	1
	ST	38	1		50	1	8	.2	**	**	4	.1	20	.3	40	1	40	1
BELLY SLAM	W	14	.1	N	57	.4	29	.2	**	**	**	**	**	**	**	**	**	**
	E	**	**	S	**	**	**	**	**	**	**	**	50	.3	50	.3	**	**
	ST	14	.1		57	.4	29	.2	**	**	**	**	50	.3	50	.3	**	**

(CONTINUED) TO COAST LYING DOWN FLAT

ITEM (144)		TENNESSEE C	TENNESSEE D		GEORGIA C	GEORGIA D	ALABAMA C	ALABAMA D	MISSISSIPPI C	MISSISSIPPI D	FLORIDA C	FLORIDA D	LOUISIANA C	LOUISIANA D	ARKANSAS C	ARKANSAS D	OKLAHOMA C	OKLAHOMA D
BELLY BOOSTER	W	50	5	N	62	6	**	**	100	5	100	21	100	7	90	12	33	4
	E	50	5	S	38	4	100	5	**	**	**	**	**	**	10	1	67	7
	ST		10			10		5		5		21		7		14		11
BELLY BUMP	W	60	4	N	25	1	100	3	100	5	**	**	**	**	75	4	**	**
	E	40	3	S	75	2	**	**	**	**	**	**	**	**	25	1	**	**
	ST		6			3		3		5		**		**		5		**
BELLY BUMPER	W	33	3	N	71	14	50	3	67	11	83	13	**	**	67	5	50	4
	E	67	6	S	29	6	50	3	33	5	17	3	**	**	33	3	50	4
	ST		10			19		5		16		15		**		8		7
BELLY BUNKER	W	100	2	N	**	**	**	**	100	5	**	**	**	**	100	1	**	**
	E	**	**	S	**	**	**	**	**	**	**	**	100	7	**	**	**	**
	ST		2			**		**		5		**		7		1		**
BELLY BUNT	W	100	1	N	50	1	**	**	**	**	**	**	**	**	**	**	**	**
	E	**	**	S	50	1	**	**	**	**	**	**	**	**	**	**	**	**
	ST		1			2		**		**		**		**		**		**
BELLY BUST(A)	W	38	3	N	86	5	100	5	100	11	67	5	56	33	25	3	**	**
	E	62	5	S	14	1	**	**	**	**	33	3	44	27	75	8	100	4
	ST		8			6		5		11		8		60		11		4
BELLY BUSTER(A)	W	42	17	N	64	20	89	46	57	21	56	23	**	**	70	32	39	26
	E	58	23	S	36	11	11	5	43	16	44	18	100	13	30	14	61	41
	ST		40			31		51		37		41		13		45		67
BELLY DOWN	W	58	5	N	33	2	**	**	100	5	100	3	**	**	**	**	**	**
	E	42	3	S	67	5	100	3	**	**	**	**	**	**	100	4	100	4
	ST		8			7		3		5		3		**		4		4
BELLY FLOP(A)	W	**	**	N	100	1	**	**	100	5	50	3	**	**	50	1	**	**
	E	100	1	S	**	**	100	3	**	**	50	3	**	**	50	1	**	**
	ST		1			1		3		5		5		**		3		**
BELLY FLOPPER(A)	W	100	3	N	67	2	50	3	**	**	**	**	**	**	**	**	**	**
	E	**	**	S	33	1	50	3	100	5	**	**	**	**	**	**	**	**
	ST		3			2		5		5		**		**		**		**

(CONTINUED) TO COAST LYING DOWN FLAT

		TENNESSEE C	TENNESSEE D		GEORGIA C	GEORGIA D	ALABAMA C	ALABAMA D	MISSISSIPPI C	MISSISSIPPI D	FLORIDA C	FLORIDA D	LOUISIANA C	LOUISIANA D	ARKANSAS C	ARKANSAS D	OKLAHOMA C	OKLAHOMA D
BELLY GRINDER	W	100	1	N	**	**	**	**	100	5	**	**	**	**	50	1	**	**
	E	**	**	S	100	1	100	3	**	**	**	**	**	**	50	1	**	**
	ST		1			1		3		5		**		**		3		**
BELLY GUT	W	**	**	N	**	**	**	**	**	**	100	3	**	**	**	**	**	**
	E	100	1	S	**	**	**	**	**	**	**	**	**	**	**	**	**	**
	ST		1			**		**		**		3		**		**		**
BELLY GUTTER	W	100	1	N	**	**	**	**	**	**	**	**	**	**	**	**	**	**
					(NO RESPONSE)													
	ST		1			**		**		**		**		**		**		**
BELLY KACHUG	W	**	**	N	**	**	**	**	**	**	100	[illegible]	**	**	**	**	**	**
	E	100	1	S	**	**	100	3	**	**	**	**	**	**	**	**	**	**
	ST		1			**		3		**		3		**		**		**
BELLY KACHUNK	W	100	1	N	**	**	**	**	**	**	**	**	**	**	**	**	**	**
	E	**	**	S	100	2	**	**	**	**	**	**	**	**	**	**	**	**
	ST		1			2		**		**		**		**		**		**
BELLY WHACK	W	**	**	N	100	1	**	**	**	**	**	**	**	**	**	**	**	**
					(NO RESPONSE)													
	ST		**			1		**		**		**		**		**		**
BELLY WOP	W	**	**	N	67	2	**	**	**	**	**	**	**	**	100	1	**	**
	E	100	1	S	33	1	100	3	**	**	**	**	**	**	**	**	**	**
	ST		1			2		3		**		**		**		1		**
BELLY WOPPER	W	33	2	N	83	8	50	3	**	**	100	3	**	**	100	3	**	**
	E	67	4	S	17	2	50	3	**	**	**	**	100	7	**	**	100	7
	ST		6			10		5		**		3		7		3		7
BELLY SLAM	W	100	1	N	100	3	100	5	**	**	**	**	**	**	**	**	**	**
	E	**	**	S	**	**	**	**	**	**	**	**	100	7	100	1	**	**
	ST		1			3		5		**		**		7		1		**

TABLE I

ACTIONS
TO HIT THE WATER FLAT WHEN DIVING

ITEM (145)
WORK SHEET (95)

		TENNESSEE			GEORGIA		ALABAMA		MISSISSIPPI		FLORIDA		LOUISIANA		ARKANSAS		OKLAHOMA	
		A	B		A	B	A	B	A	B	A	B	A	B	A	B	A	B
BELLY FLOP(B)	W	6	.2	N	24	1	3	.1	9	.3	12	.4	8	.3	17	1	25	1
	E	15	1	S	12	.4	3	.1	3	.1	15	1	**	**	17	1	33	1
	ST	21	1		35	1	6	.2	12	.4	26	1	8	.3	33	1	58	3
BELLY FLOPPER(B)	W	38	.3	N	**	**	**	**	13	.1	**	**	**	**	50	.3	50	.3
	E	**	**	S	25	.2	**	**	13	.1	13	.1	**	**	**	**	**	**
	ST	38	.3		25	.2	**	**	25	.2	13	.1	**	**	50	.3	50	.3
BELLY BUST(B)	W	16	1	N	20	2	5	.4	6	1	9	1	6	1	19	3	8	1
	E	16	1	S	15	1	5	.4	1	.1	6	1	33	4	8	1	25	3
	ST	33	3		35	3	10	1	8	1	15	1	39	5	28	4	33	4
BELLY BUSTER(B)	W	17	11	N	20	13	8	5	5	3	8	5	8	5	31	20	16	10
	E	23	15	S	13	8	2	1	2	1	3	2	3	2	21	14	19	12
	ST	40	25		33	21	10	7	6	4	11	7	12	8	53	34	36	23

		TENNESSEE			GEORGIA		ALABAMA		MISSISSIPPI		FLORIDA		LOUISIANA		ARKANSAS		OKLAHOMA	
		C	D		C	D	C	D	C	D	C	D	C	D	C	D	C	D
BELLY FLOP(B)	W	29	1	N	67	3	50	1	75	6	44	5	100	3	50	2	43	4
	E	71	2	S	33	2	50	1	25	2	56	6	**	**	50	2	57	5
	ST		2			5		3		8		10		3		4		8
BELLY FLOPPER(B)	W	100	1	N	**	**	**	**	50	2	**	**	**	**	100	1	100	1
	E	**	**	S	100	1	**	**	50	2	100	1	**	**	**	**	**	**
	ST		1			1		**		4		1		**		1		1
BELLY BUST(B)	W	50	5	N	57	7	50	5	83	10	58	8	14	6	70	6	25	4
	E	50	5	S	43	5	50	5	17	2	42	6	86	33	30	3	75	11
	ST		9			11		11		12		14		39		9		14
BELLY BUSTER(B)	W	42	37	N	61	50	78	68	70	54	74	56	71	42	59	51	46	35
	E	58	51	S	39	33	22	19	30	23	26	19	29	17	41	35	54	41
	ST		87			83		86		77		75		58		86		76

ITEM (146)
WORK SHEET (96)

ACTIONS
THE BABY MOVES ON ALL FOURS ACROSS THE FLOOR

		TENNESSEE A	TENNESSEE B		GEORGIA A	GEORGIA B	ALABAMA A	ALABAMA B	MISSISSIPPI A	MISSISSIPPI B	FLORIDA A	FLORIDA B	LOUISIANA A	LOUISIANA B	ARKANSAS A	ARKANSAS B	OKLAHOMA A	OKLAHOMA B
CRAWLS	W	18	15	N	19	16	7	6	4	4	8	7	7	6	30	28	15	13
	E	23	19	S	12	10	2	2	2	2	4	3	8	7	23	21	18	16
	ST	41	34		31	25	10	8	7	5	12	9	15	13	53	48	32	30
CREEPS	W	13	.3	N	21	1	**	**	8	.2	**	**	**	**	80	4	7	.3
	E	17	.4	S	13	.3	4	.1	4	.1	21	1	**	**	7	.3	7	.3
	ST	29	1		33	1	4	.1	13	.3	21	1	**	**	87	5	13	1

		TENNESSEE C	TENNESSEE D		GEORGIA C	GEORGIA D	ALABAMA C	ALABAMA D	MISSISSIPPI C	MISSISSIPPI D	FLORIDA C	FLORIDA D	LOUISIANA C	LOUISIANA D	ARKANSAS C	ARKANSAS D	OKLAHOMA C	OKLAHOMA D
CRAWLS	W	44	43	N	62	60	75	74	64	61	70	66	46	46	57	52	45	44
	E	56	55	S	38	37	25	24	36	34	30	29	54	54	43	39	55	54
	ST		98			97		99		95		95		100		91		98
CREEPS	W	43	1	N	63	2	**	**	67	4	**	**	**	**	92	8	50	1
	E	57	1	S	38	1	100	1	33	2	100	5	**	**	8	1	50	1
	ST		2			3		1		5		5		**		9		2

ITEM (147)
WORK SHEET (98)

ACTIONS
TO CARRY A HEAVY SUITCASE

		TENNESSEE A	TENNESSEE B		GEORGIA A	GEORGIA B	ALABAMA A	ALABAMA B	MISSISSIPPI A	MISSISSIPPI B	FLORIDA A	FLORIDA B	LOUISIANA A	LOUISIANA B	ARKANSAS A	ARKANSAS B	OKLAHOMA A	OKLAHOMA B
CARRY	W	18	11	N	16	9	8	5	5	3	8	5	5	4	28	21	16	12
	E	27	16	S	9	6	2	1	2	1	4	2	8	6	22	17	21	16
	ST	45	27		25	15	10	6	8	5	12	7	13	10	50	37	37	28
FREIGHT					(NO RESPONSE)													
					(NO RESPONSE)													
					(NO RESPONSE)													
HIKE	W	67	.2	N	33	.1	**	**	**	**	**	**	**	**	**	**	100	.3
					(NO RESPONSE)													
	ST	67	.2		33	.1	**	**	**	**	**	**	**	**	**	**	100	.3
LUG	W	16	2	N	24	3	9	1	1	.2	5	1	14	2	27	4	16	3
	E	23	3	S	14	2	2	.3	2	.3	3	.4	16	3	14	2	14	2
	ST	39	6		38	5	11	2	4	1	8	1	30	5	41	6	30	5
PACK	W	45	1	N	7	.2	7	.2	3	.1	3	.1	**	**	45	2	9	.3
	E	24	1	S	**	**	**	**	7	.2	3	.1	**	**	27	1	18	1
	ST	69	2		7	.2	7	.2	10	.3	7	.2	**	**	73	3	27	1
TOTE	W	17	4	N	29	7	5	1	4	1	9	2	23	2	32	3	5	.3
	E	9	2	S	18	4	1	.3	3	1	4	1	9	1	23	2	9	1
	ST	26	6		47	11	6	2	8	2	13	3	32	3	55	4	14	1

		TENNESSEE C	TENNESSEE D		GEORGIA C	GEORGIA D	ALABAMA C	ALABAMA D	MISSISSIPPI C	MISSISSIPPI D	FLORIDA C	FLORIDA D	LOUISIANA C	LOUISIANA D	ARKANSAS C	ARKANSAS D	OKLAHOMA C	OKLAHOMA D
CARRY	W	40	26	N	63	29	77	49	70	44	68	41	37	21	55	40	44	35
	E	60	39	S	38	17	23	15	30	19	32	20	63	36	45	33	56	44
	ST		65			46		65		63		61		57		73		79
FREIGHT					(NO RESPONSE)													
					(NO RESPONSE)													
	ST		**			**		**		**		**		**		**		**
HIKE	W	100	1	N	100	.3	**	**	**	**	**	**	**	**	**	**	100	1
					(NO RESPONSE)													
	ST		1			.3		**		**		**		**		**		1
LUG	W	42	6	N	62	11	81	14	40	3	64	6	46	13	67	9	54	7
	E	58	8	S	38	6	19	3	60	4	36	4	54	15	33	4	46	6
	ST		14			17		17		7		10		28		13		13
PACK	W	65	3	N	100	1	100	2	33	1	50	1	**	**	63	4	33	1
	E	35	2	S	**	**	**	**	67	3	50	1	**	**	38	2	67	2
	ST		5			1		2		4		2		**		6		3
TOTE	W	66	10	N	62	22	80	13	56	14	67	18	71	11	58	5	33	1
	E	34	5	S	38	14	20	3	44	11	33	9	29	4	42	4	67	2
	[illegible]		[illegible]			36		16		26		27		15		9		3

Table II

Totals of Words Used

This table contains all words in the questionnaire arranged in ascending order of frequency of reporting. The first entries are at zero; the last at over one thousand. In the lower ranges, four responses or more are considered positive evidence of actual choice especially if the responses form a geographic cluster when mapped. Below this number, the responses are best viewed as a record of total lack of use in the sense indicated; that is, silence is interpreted as a statement by one thousand persons that the questionnaire word is not a part of the local vocabulary in that meaning.

EACEWORM
BABY COACH
CUBBIE
LATTERMATH
CREEPER
CHANCE
GOOSE DROWNDER
TEMPEST
OVERDEN
DUTCH CAP
HAY DOODLES
LOPPERED MILK
COOK JACK
FREIGHT
1 DOMINIE
1 PUMPKIN HUSKER
1 CO-DICK
1 CRULL(B)
1 TEAMING
1 HOG BOIST
1 FLAW

1 SHELF
1 DOODLES
1 CLOCK SHELF
1 CLOTHES PRESS(A)
1 COCK LOFT
1 RIDD UP
1 DANDLE
1 INTERVALE(A)
1 COULEE(B)
1 TARVIA
1 BONNY CLAPPER
1 SKIMMELTON
1 BOLT
1 OWLY(A)
1 PLAT EYE
1 BELLY GUTTER
1 BELLY WHACK
1 BELLING BEE
2 ANGLEDOG
2 EAR SEWER
2 YARD-AX

2 JACKPINE SAVAGE
2 MOTTE
2 BEE
2 KIP, KIP
2 CO-DAY
2 CRULL(A)
2 CUSSIE
2 JUTE BAG
2 SPOUTING
2 HAND IRONS
2 SCAFFOLD
2 DAGO
2 HAP
2 TARVIA ROAD
2 DONNICK
2 BLART
2 POT CHEESE
2 BAG SCHOOL
2 KILLED
2 BELLY GUT
3 WARTY TOAD

3 CHAIR BACKER
3 RAINWORM
3 RAILSPLITTER
3 HISTE
3 ROWEN
3 AWENDAW
3 CO-DACK
3 KIT, KIT
3 BREATH HARP
3 FILLS
3 COW POUND
3 JUTE SACK
3 PRESS(A)
3 PITCH PINE
3 BEST ROOM
3 INTERVALE(B)
3 BORROW DITCH
3 LODGE
3 SHAKEDOWN
3 CLEAVESTONE
3 OPEN SEED PEACH

3 RARE RIPES
3 CAP
3 OWLY(B)
3 BELLY KACHUG
3 BELLY KACHUNK
3 BELLY BUNT
3 CALATHUMP
4 BABY CAB
4 MUDWORM
4 CADE
4 LAUGH
4 COSSIE
4 HOG CRAWL
4 TOOT
4 COFFEE SACK
4 HAY CAP
4 BARRACK
4 ANCHOR ICE
4 SKY PARLOR
4 HAY TUMBLES
4 HICKY HORSE
4 BLARE

4 COMFORTABLE
4 FLITCH
4 MUTTON CORN
4 GRINNIE
4 HORNING BEE
4 RUN OUT OF SCHOOL
4 HIKE
5 SUGAR LOT
5 BIBLE BANGER
5 GREY FROG
5 WART FROG
5 WIDDIE
5 AFTERMATH
5 RIZ BREAD
5 FAT CAKE(B)
5 CUPPIN
5 COW BRAKE
5 TUMBLES
5 SHALE
5 COCK HORSE
5 BARROW DITCH

5 LIVE FOREVERS
5 THICK MILK
5 BONNY CLABBER
5 OPEN SEED
5 SUGAR CORN
5 DUTCH CHEESE
5 SWAMP ANGEL
5 BULL BAND(ING)
6 DRY-LAND FROG
6 SUGAR PLACE
6 CO-CHEE
6 CHOOK, CHOOK
6 WHINNER
6 LUCKY BONE
6 STOPPLE(A)
6 ZIGZAG FENCE
6 NEB
6 MOW
6 OVERHEAD
6 BIG HOUSE
6 REDD UP

6 BARN CHAMBER
6 SWALE(A)
6 DORNICK
6 DOPE
6 SEWEE BEANS
6 BELLY BUNKER
6 OLD HARRY
6 BELLY GRINDER
6 OTSNY
6 CHRISTMAS BOX
7 MOUNTAINBOOMER
7 CRAWS
7 SAP BUSH
7 FAT CAKE(A)
7 COME BOSS(IE)
7 BOSS(IE)(A)
7 TAP(C)
7 STOOP(A)
7 SPEAR
7 ARMOR
7 WHET SEED

7 SEEP(A)

7 BERM

7 MEW(A)

7 FREE PEACH

7 GARDEN CORN

7 WHEAT CAKES

7 SALLET BEANS

7 LOBBERED MILK

7 PERISHED

7 BELLY WOP

8 CHUCK, CHUCK

8 SO-WENCH

8 NEAR-SIDE HORSE

8 SEOK

8 THILLS

8 NEAP

8 SWILL PAIL

8 SIVVY BEANS

8 GROUND NUTS

8 CRUDDLED MILK

8 BELLY FLOP(A)

8 DONE OUT

9 SEWING NEEDLE

9 ROCK MAPLE

9 NAN(NIE)

9 PAVE

9 DOUBLE EVENER

9 PALE GARDEN

9 WHIFFLETREE

9 OPEN PEACH

9 BELLY SLAM

10 TOWN WORM

10 NIGHT WALKER

10 MOSSBACK

10 BOSS(IE)(B)

10 FARM LOT

10 SEAGRASS SACK

10 BREATH HARP(B)

10 CORK STOPPLE

10 DO UP

10 PRESS(B)

10 SQUALL

10 WHETTER

10 CRY

10 WHET

10 FLANNEL CAKES

10 BELLY FLOPPER(B)

10 HORNING

10 BELLY FLOPPER(A)

11 DARNING NEEDLE

11 DUST WEB

11 KUT, KUT

11 POO-WEE

11 WHEAT BREAD

11 SHIPPLETREE

11 SNAKE FENCE

11 EVENER

11 SPREADER

11 SWIVELTREE

11 FRY PAN

11 EAVES SPOUTS

11 MOWS

11 ELECTRIC(AL) SHOWER

11 GREEN CORN

11 POTATO ONIONS

11 LIE OUT

11 BLACK MAN

12 MY RELATIONS(A)

12 STUMP FARMER

12 COME

12 SHAFE

12 NIGH HORSE

12 PORTICO(A)

12 STOOK

12 FAT PINE

12 ARMOIRE

12 BARROW PIT

12 SWALE(C)

12 BORROW PIT

12 GIVE HIM THE MITTEN

12 BELLING

12 YAHOO

12 USED UP
13 NUT CAKE
13 CLOTHES PRESS(B)
13 DOGS
13 SPOUTS
13 FLYING MARE
13 SHUCK(A)
13 HEART(B)
14 HARD MAPLE
14 GUNNY BAG
14 FATWOOD
14 LIGHTWOOD KNOT FLOATER
14 SHALE ICE
14 WOOD BUCK
14 SAW JACK(A)
14 TRESTLE(B)
14 OPEN STONE PEACH
14 DONE UP
15 COME UP
15 CO-NIN(NIE)
15 WORM FENCE
15 SHOOK
15 BUCK
15 WALK OUT WITH
16 MY RELATION
16 JOHNNY CAKE
16 FRYER
16 HAY MOW
16 SCUM
16 CARBON OIL
16 TO SHUCK(C)
16 GIVE HIM THE BOUNCE
16 ROILED
16 BEAT OUT
17 SUGAR BUSH
17 JUNE BUG
17 DRAWING
17 BACK CHUNK
17 TO POD
17 PONHAWS
17 PONHOSS
17 ASHY
18 FRIED CAKE(B)
18 PULLING BONE
18 JACK(A)
18 SITTING ROOM
18 GARRET
18 A PIECE
19 A WAYS
19 FRIED CAKE(A)
19 COO-CHICK
19 SURFACE TREATED ROAD
19 SWALE(B)
19 PIECE MEAL
19 SIT UP TO
20 FIRE BUG
20 STY
20 SAWBUCK(A)
20 QUARTER BEFORE ELEVEN
20 COAL PAIL
20 JACK(B)
20 HEART(A)
20 JERKY
20 KITCHEN GARDEN
20 BELLY BUMP
21 SAP ORCHARD
21 FEATURES
21 HERE
21 COME BOSS(IE)
21 SOO(D)
21 RAISED DOUGHNUT(A)
21 PIAZZA
21 JERKED BEEF
21 SLAPJACKS
21 SOT
21 WRATHY
22 HOOSIER
22 CARTING
22 COCKS
22 WOOD HOUSE(B)
22 BLAT
22 BELLER(C)
23 DEVILS DARNING NEEDLE

23 BREAKBONE
23 CRULLER(A)
23 CRULLER(B)
23 RICK(A)
23 SHELL OATS
24 MOMMER
24 SHEEP
24 SLOP PAIL
24 TAP(A)
24 COW YARD
24 MANTEL SHELF
24 HAYCOCKS
24 HEINZ
24 SNAPS
25 DEW WEB
25 YEAST BREAD
25 WHINKER
25 PALE FENCE
25 BREAKING AWAY
25 DRAW(A)
25 CRIPPLE
25 OF HIS STOMACH
26 DEW WORM
26 ROLLER SHADES
26 HUM
26 OLD NICK
27 WEB(A)
28 REDNECK
28 COULEE
28 FICE
28 SWILL BUCKET
28 SMEARCASE
28 BELLY DOWN
29 SUGAR CAMP
29 EEL WORM
29 HERE BOSS(IE)
29 MEW(B)
29 TOTING
29 POLE
29 TRASH MOVER
29 LOG IRONS
29 HARD PEACH
29 BELLY WOPPER
30 PULL BONE
30 SLAB
30 SLAT FENCE
30 OPEN STONE
31 THE REVEREND
31 SUGAR ORCHARD
31 CO-JACK
31 PIKE
31 FLYING JENNY
31 FLYING DUTCHMAN
31 PIG STY
31 SHUCK(B)
31 SET
32 GRANNY DOCTOR
32 COUNTRY GENTLEMAN
32 COME NAN(NIE)
32 TIDY UP
32 BELLOW(C)
32 TEETER
32 GRIDDLE CAKES
32 THROW HIM OVER
33 WHIRLYJIG
34 BOG
34 GUANO SACK
34 WOO
35 GIDDY-AP
35 DOUBLE SWINGLETREE
35 HAY RICK
35 FIRE IRONS
35 SAW JACK(B)
35 CURDLED MILK
36 LOO(A)
36 KICK HIM
36 TIN PANNING
37 GODMOTHER
37 SPIDER NEST
37 GEE-UP
37 COAL HOD
37 GROUND PEAS
38 WEB(B)
38 COME CALF(IE)
38 NEAR HORSE

38 STEP
38 CROCUS SACK
38 MOUTH HARP(A)
38 MANTEL BOARD
38 RICKS(B)
38 BAYOU(B)
38 CURD(S)
39 PAPPY
39 POP
39 BAIT WORM
39 POISON IVORY
39 BIDDIE
39 COVERLET
39 MACADAM ROAD
39 CREEPS
40 SUGAR GROVE
40 MY KIN
40 RACK(A)
40 HAND STACKS
40 COVERLID
40 TALK TO
40 PACK
41 MY RELATIONS(B)
41 TOOL HOUSE(B)
41 GALLERY
41 TEETER BOARD
41 FRITTERS
41 TO HIS STOMACH
42 MOMMY
42 SPIDER
42 BEANS
42 YOKEL
43 CO-CALF(IE)
43 WOO-EE
43 MOUTH HARP(B)
43 HEAPS
43 PINE
43 RINN
44 TOAD STRANGLER
44 KERNEL(A)
44 CURD CHEESE
44 TUCKERED
45 LINE HORSE
45 SADDLE HORSE
45 LOO(B)
45 BELLY BUST(A)
46 RAIN TROUGHS
46 BELLY FLOP(B)
47 FIREBOARD
47 PARKING
48 CO-WENCH
48 SCRUB
48 TREE LAWN
48 STOPPLE(B)
48 FROGSTOOL
49 MY PEOPLE(B)
49 OILED ROAD
49 SPIGOT(A)
50 HOP TOAD
50 EAVES TROUGHS
50 SCALLION(S)
50 LUNCH
51 PAW
51 PORTICO(B)
51 SIDE PORK
52 MAMMY
52 BIND
52 CAKE DOUGHNUT
52 RIDY HORSE(B)
53 CO-SHEEP
53 WARDROBE(A)
53 IN HIS STOMACH
54 TRESTLE(A)
54 BAR DITCH
54 HARD ROAD
54 SPIGOT(C)
54 BELLY BOOSTER
55 PARSON
55 SOO(A)
55 PLATFORM
55 PARLOR
55 PIG HEADED
56 MAW
56 A PIECE
56 OLD SCRATCH
57 FEED LOT
57 CURTAINS
57 BUNK

58 CO-BOSS(IE)
58 JUICE HARP(A)
58 FAIRING UP
58 TIED QUILT
58 BELLY BUMPER
59 GLOW WORM
59 WHIRLYGIG
59 GET A COLD
60 ANGLEWORM
60 PONE BREAD
60 MUSH ICE
60 CEMENT ROAD
60 FISTE
60 PINDERS
61 STEPS
63 SOOK BOSS(IE)
63 SPARK WITH
64 MY PEOPLE(A)
64 COUNTRY JAKE
64 STONE FENCE
64 VERANDA(B)
64 WINDOW BLINDS

64 PARKING STRIP
65 CO-EE
66 BOULEVARD
66 BAR PIT
66 HYDRANT(A)
66 FRENCH HARP(B)
67 CRACKER
67 SOONER
67 POKE
67 JEWS HARP(A)
67 SLIP OFF FROM SCHOOL
68 WATER GUTTER
69 MAPLE ORCHARD
69 RIDY HORSE(A)
69 VERANDA(A)
69 DRESSING GRAVY
69 CLABBER CHEESE
69 FAMILY GARDEN
69 ON HIS STOMACH
69 PLAY TRUANT

70 HAYSEED
70 SUGAR TREE GROVE
70 HOG HOUSE
70 BUSHED
72 LEADER
72 BREAD DOUGHNUT
73 HUSK(A)
74 SO
74 BAWL(C)
74 SWINGLETREE
75 TOOL SHED(B)
76 CLEARSTONE
76 CORN DODGER(S)
77 SHARECROPPER
77 LAG LINE
77 COMMON DOG
77 YOUNG ONIONS
78 CARRYING
78 SWEET CORN
79 HARD SURFACE ROAD(A)
80 GRADER DITCH

80 LAMP OIL
80 PIT(B)
80 UGLY
80 RAWHEAD AND BLOODYBONES
81 PALINGS
81 GARDEN PATCH
82 SOFT PEACH
82 FLITTERS
82 CORN PONE
83 WHEEL HORSE
83 HOO-EE
83 BELLER(A)
83 KERNEL(B)
84 SOOK
84 WOOD HOUSE(A)
84 LAGGING LINE
86 BOULEVARD STRIP
86 MULTIPLIERS
87 HORSE(B)
87 BURLAP SACK
88 CRABS

89 FISHWORM
89 SO-BOSS(IE)
90 MY FOLKS(B)
91 WHITE BREAD
91 BELLOW(A)
92 MY RELATIVES(A)
93 BLUFF
93 SAWBUCK(B)
93 DIP
94 STARTING LINE
94 LOAD
94 MOUTH ORGAN
95 CRAYFISH
95 SOO-WEE
96 COW LOT(B)
98 CLEARSEED PEACH
98 SOWBELLY
99 WHICKER
99 SHEEPIE
99 SPICKET(A)
99 KEEP COMPANY WITH
100 FIRE DOGS
100 STONE
102 HUSK(C)
102 GIVE HIM THE AIR
103 PAIL(A)
103 STORM
103 STONE(A)
104 BACKWOODSMAN
104 BAYOU(A)
104 SALAD
104 HET UP
106 MA
106 SUGAR MAPLE GROVE
106 LIGHTWOOD
106 PLAYED OUT
107 HUSK(B)
107 SAW BOSS(IE)
108 HARP
108 BLINDS
108 HARD SURFACE ROAD(B)
109 GRANNY
109 LOFT(B)
110 GRANNY WOMAN
110 PAVEMENT(B)
110 GUNNY SACK
111 MY FAMILY(B)
112 PA
112 SOOKIE, SUUKIE
113 POISON VINE
113 PRESS PEACH
113 FIRE HOUSE
115 TO HULL(C)
116 CHORE TIME
116 BELLY BUST(B)
118 HOT
119 THUNDER SHOWER
119 HEAD CHEESE
120 CLAPBOARDS
120 ORNERY
121 FATHER
121 MOM
122 PRAIRIE
122 TURN
123 QUARTER TO ELEVEN
124 FEED TIME
125 MAPLE GROVE
127 FRONT ROOM
127 BELLER(B)
128 FIREFLY
128 WOOD SHED(B)
129 FATBACK
129 ASH BREAD
133 SOOK(IE)
133 TAP(B)
133 FAIRING OFF
133 CLINGSTONE PEACH
133 BAD MAN
135 GIDDY-UP
135 BLEAT
136 MIDDLIN MEAT
138 HICK
138 TOOL HOUSE(A)

140 COUNTRY MAN
140 A BITE
140 HOE CAKE(S)
142 SPIDERS WEB(A)
142 SPICKET(C)
142 BURLAP BAG
142 SPICKET(B)
142 QUARTER OF ELEVEN
145 BATTER BREAD
146 SKIP CLASS
148 CUR DOG
148 BE TAKEN SICK
149 GUTTER(B)
150 VOLUNTEER (CROP)
151 GOOBERS
152 MOO(A)
152 PARKWAY
152 TAKE SICK
156 ASH PONE
156 DRAG
157 TUCKERED OUT
159 PRESSED MEAT
159 SKIP SCHOOL
160 STONE(B)
161 MARSH
162 PIGOO-WEE
164 WOOD SHED(A)
164 COUNTERPIN
164 SALLET
164 PETERED OUT
168 COUNTERPANE
169 SUGAR TREE
169 FISH BAIT
169 GIDDAP
169 BELLOW(B)
170 HEADSTRONG
172 SHELL(B)
172 COOKIE
172 ALL IN
173 BLATE
173 FLAPJACKS
174 NO-COUNT
176 MY PARENTS
178 TOOL SHED(A)
178 RILED
179 CRAWDAD(DIE)S
183 BREAD
184 ELECTRIC(AL) STORM
184 SIDEWALK PLOT
184 LUG
185 HOG(S) HEAD CHEESE
185 FAGGED OUT
186 LEAN-TO SHED
187 SNAKE FEEDER
191 ROCK FENCE
192 SHALLOTS
192 SHEAF
193 DOUBLE SINGLETREE
193 STRAIGHTEN UP
195 CLODHOPPER
196 BELLY BUSTER(A)
197 CLING
199 PAIL(B)
200 CROKER SACK
200 HOME MADE CHEESE
200 LAY OUT
201 PLUM PEACH
204 SPIGOT(B)
204 DOG IRONS
206 GLASS CORK
206 CLING PEACH
209 CORK STOPPER(B)
212 RACK(B)
213 SLOUGH
215 LOCAL PREACHER
215 KOPE
215 FAUCET(C)
215 MIDDLIN(S)
216 COMFORTER
217 CLEARING OFF
222 SOO-PIG
223 PILES

224 FREESTONE PEACH
225 LOW(A)
228 CORK STOPPER(A)
231 BROTHER SO-AND-SO
236 SPIDERS WEB(B)
236 LOW(B)
239 TEN FORTY FIVE
240 SHED
241 EAVES
241 GULLY WASHER
242 COBWEB(B)
242 CLABBER MILK
243 CLABBERED MILK
243 SALT PORK
244 SEEP(B)
245 FISHING WORM
246 BOOGEY MAN
246 GIVE A COLD SHOULDER
247 DAD
247 RAISED DOUGHNUT(B)
247 NEIGH
249 KETTLE
252 MANTELPIECE
253 BACON
253 LOAF BREAD
254 BACK STICK
255 CLOTHES CLOSET
255 CONTRARY
256 COO-SHEEP
257 TAKE A COLD
257 TOTE
258 TAKES AFTER
258 SAH
259 DRAW(B)
260 WEATHERBOARDS
262 FAUCET(B)
266 ASH CAKE
267 CHIPPED BEEF
267 C A L L B Y N A M E
267 JILT HIM
270 TOAD
271 FIRE HALL
272 SIDING
273 MONGREL
275 (GEORGIA) WIGGLER
275 TIME TO FEED
275 CORK
275 SKIM
278 HOG LOT
279 C L U C K
279 PALING FENCE
280 HOT CAKES
281 PORCH(B)
283 NIGHT CRAWLER
284 STOREROOM(A)
285 CATCH COLD
286 MOSQUITO HAWK
288 CLEAR SEED
291 GIVE OUT
292 A LITTLE WAYS
295 FAVORS
295 PAPA
295 SIDE MEAT
296 BATTER CAKES
302 RESEMBLES
304 STOOP(B)
307 CLOUDBURST
308 WHINNY
308 TAW LINE
309 LOFT
310 HAY SHOCKS
311 FRENCH HARP(A)
311 SPRING ONIONS
314 SUNSET
315 PAVEMENT(A)
318 TAKE COLD
323 DRAGON FLY
324 JACKLEG PREACHER
325 HORSE(A)
327 STOPPER
333 SHOCKS(A)

334 TOW SACK
339 MY FOLKS(A)
342 CLINGSTONE
343 CHIPMUNK
349 PIT(A)
352 CHRISTMAS GIFT
353 EARTHWORM
356 SHAVS
357 COURT
359 FRYING PAN
362 SECOND CUTTING
363 DOWNPOUR
367 HARMONICA
368 HILLBILLY
368 HULL(A)
369 FREESTONE
370 DOUGHNUT(B)
372 WHET STONE
374 QUARTER TILL ELEVEN
374 SHIVAREE
375 AFTERNOON
375 TAW
378 EVENING
379 JUICE HARP(B)
382 BARN LOT
382 SCRAPPLE
383 CONCRETE ROAD
385 CATCH A COLD
392 SUNUP
395 RED WORM
397 SHADES
398 SUNRISE
399 SACK
402 SAW
404 VEGETABLE GARDEN
405 CLUMP
405 ANDIRONS
405 SAW HORSE(B)
407 BOTTOMS
410 SMOKEHOUSE
415 CLEARING UP
417 CUR
423 PIG PEN
423 SNAP BEANS
424 BULL HEADED
425 PIGGY, PIGGY
426 CHICKIE, CHICKIE
426 WISHBONE
427 BARN LOFT
427 PAVED ROAD
429 A LITTLE WAY
433 LEAD HORSE
439 LIMA BEANS
440 HYDRANT(B)
446 SKIN
447 SNAKE DOCTOR
451 SLIPPERY
454 BAG
455 A LITTLE PIECE
466 NICKER
466 WORN OUT
467 SERENADE
469 W H I S T L E
470 SUNDOWN
472 BAWL(B)
474 STONE WALL
476 BABY CARRIAGE
480 MY RELATIVES(B)
480 SECOND CROP
483 ROCK WALL
491 SPIDER WEB(A)
493 THUNDER STORM
493 ROASTING EARS
497 COW PEN
500 STOREROOM(B)
502 ARMLOAD
503 GREEN BEANS
505 MANTEL
509 TURN HIM DOWN
511 JEWS HARP(B)
512 SOOK COW
522 POT
531 COAL BUCKET
532 COAL OIL

533 DRIED BEFF
537 SHAFTS
538 LOOKS LIKE
538 WEATHERBOARDING
539 MOTHER
540 STRING BEANS
542 HAY LOFT
543 COAL SCUTTLE
543 SKILLET
544 ARMFUL
550 STUBBORN
553 MAMA
566 CLOSET
567 MY KINFOLKS
571 SPOON BREAD
592 MY FAMILY(A)
593 COW LOT(A)
594 DADDY
597 GROVE
598 BUCKET(B)
600 POISON OAK
600 GET UP

605 MOO(B)
607 KINDLING WOOD
609 BAWL(A)
610 SOOK CALF(IE)
611 POLECAT
617 CHICK, CHICK
619 WARDROBE(B)
620 SPIDER WEB(B)
623 GREEN ONIONS
626 GARDEN
627 SHELL(A)
636 FEEDING TIME
643 FAUCET(A)
649 BUNDLE
650 BARN YARD
652 HOG PEN
653 CLABBER
653 GO WITH
657 WINDOW SHADES
660 BOOGER MAN
663 COBWEB(A)

663 RIND
667 PANCAKES
669 LIVING ROOM
671 POISON IVY
673 GROUND SQUIRREL
681 CLEAN UP
682 SLICK
682 SEED(A)
683 KEROSCNE
683 PORCH(A)
683 COTTAGE CHEESE
684 SUGAR MAPLE
689 SLOP BUCKET
689 ATTIC
700 SWAMP
704 DOUBLETREE
707 BUCKET(A)
712 SAW HORSE(A)
720 BOTTOM LAND
725 HULL(B)
729 SOUSE

736 BABY BUGGY
736 DITCH
736 PLAY HOOKEY
740 FIRE STATION
740 SKUNK
745 LIGHT-BREAD
746 COMFORT
757 MEADOW
764 BACKLOG
764 GET SICK
764 MAD
771 CORN ON THE COB
772 PICKET FENCE
774 WHET ROCK
780 CARRY
798 BELLY BUSTER(B'
811 CRAWFISH
811 BUTTER BEANS
820 GUTTERS
839 BLACKTOP
844 SAUCE

861 MIDWIFE

864 SEED(B)

876 MERRY CHRISTMAS

878 PULLY BONE

879 SHOCK(B)

887 TOAD FROG

889 BEDSPREAD

908 PEANUTS

914 SINGLETREE

920 GREENS

933 AT HIS STOMACH

947 A SNACK

972 TOADSTOOL

984 HARROW

989 HAULING

993 TO SHELL(C)

998 DOUGHNUT(A)

1017 ROCK

1022 SHUCK(D)

1027 TONGUE

1044 SEESAW

1049 CORN BREAD

1049 CRAWLS

1060 RAIL FENCE

1065 PALLET

1068 LIGHTNING BUG

1094 HAYSTACK

Table III

Volunteered Word List

This list contains all the words recovered from computer memory which informants volunteered in the course of answering the questionnaire. It is in an alphabetical order determined by a computer's view of that order.

The numbers in parentheses specify the Item number under which the word was identified. The two letter abbreviations to the right of these numbers signify the states from which the word was volunteered; AL, Alabama; AR, Arkansas; FL, Florida; GA, Georgia; LA, Louisiana; MI, Mississippi; OK, Oklahoma; TE, Tennessee. An abundance of these abbreviations after an entry indicates the relative prevalence of that word; a small number of them, however, is not sufficient evidence to persuade investigators that additional search for that word is pointless.

Aside from adding to the list of local words, the volunteered entries indicate semantic change as in *pioneer,* apparently in a derogatory sense, and lexical blending as in *fat lighter* and *fat splinters* out of the *fat pine, fatwood, lightwood, liteard* background.

ALL WEATHER ROAD	(61)	TE
ASPHALT ROAD	(61)	AR FL GA OK TE
BAKER BREAD	(84)	TE
BACK PORCH	(25)	MI
BACKROOM	(17)	AR
BACKWOOD(S) CRACKER	(130)	FL
BACKWOOD(S) HOOSIER	(130)	GA
BALE(S)	(89)	LA TE
BAIT(S)	(113)	AL AR FL GA LA MI TE
BEAT	(133)	FL GA TE
BELLY SLIDE	(144)	GA OK TE
BETWEEN MEALS	(95)	AR GA LA MI TE
BEET GREENS	(104)	TE
BISCUIT EATER	(65)	AR
BIG WORM	(113)	AL
BLACKLAND WORM	(113)	MI
BLOODY BONES	(142)	TE
BLOWING HARP	(40)	GA
BOTTOM LAND PASTURE	(58)	FL
BOTTOM PASTURE	(58)	MI
BOXING	(15)	AL AR GA MI TE
BOILER	(35)	AL LA
BOILING POT	(35)	TE
BRANCH BOTTOM	(58)	TE
BRUSH OFF	(138)	GA
BREAK UP	(138)	FL LA TE
BREAKING UP	(5)	AL AR LA
BREAKING OFF	(5)	AR FL GA TE
BREAST BONE	(69)	FL GA TE
BRICK BAT	(64)	TE
BULL FROG	(112)	MI
BULLFROG STRANGLER	(6)	FL OK
BUTT HEADED	(131)	TE
BUTTERMILK	(93)	AL AR FL GA LA MI OK TE
BUNCH (OF TREES)	(120)	AL GA LA TE
BUNDLES	(89)	AL
BUNG	(36)	GA
BUG OUT	(140)	OK
CATALPA WORM	(113)	AL
CANE PATCH	(119)	FL
CEDAR CHEST	(22)	GA
CEDAR ROBE	(22)	LA
CHUNK	(64)	OK
CHIFFEROBE	(22)	LA MI TE
CHIFFONIER	(22)	AL AR FL GA LA MI OK TE
CHITTLING BREAD	(90)	MI
CITY HALL	(141)	TE
CIGALLE	(115)	LA
CLEARING	(5)	AL MI
CLOD KNOCKER	(130)	GA
CLOTHES CABINET	(22)	FL
CLOTHES RACKS	(22)	AR GA OK TE
CLOUD BREAK	(6)	FL
COTTON HOUSE	(17)	FL
COMMON CUR	(65)	OK
COUNTERSPREAD	(54)	GA
COUNTRY CRACKER	(130)	GA
COUNTRY HOOSIER	(130)	MI TE
CONCAVE	(59)	TE
COVER CROP	(87)	MI
COW BARN	(26)	GA
COW CORRAL	(26)	AR
COW FIELD	(26)	AL AR FL GA LA MI TE
COW HOUSE	(26)	AL AR GA MI TE
COW PASTURE	(26)	AL AR FL GA LA MI OK TE
COW SHED	(26)	AL AR FL GA LA MI OK TE
COW STALL	(26)	GA
COW WOODS	(26)	AL AR GA MI TE
COWBOY BRITCHES	(69)	MI
CORN CAKE	(84)	AR
CORN MEAL MUSH	(84)	OK TE
CORN MUSH	(84)	AL AR FL GA TE
CORN PONE MUSH	(84)	AR
CORN SACK	(38)	FL
CORN (MEAL) DUMPLINGS	(90)	AL AR FL GA LA MI OK TE
CORRAL	(26)	GA OK
CRACKLING BREAD	(90)	AL FL LA MI OK TE
CRAWDABS	(116)	TE
CRAWJACKS	(116)	AL
CRUMBING WORM	(113)	MI
CREEK BOTTOM	(58)	LA MI TE
CUT CLASSES	(140)	AL AR FL GA LA MI OK TE
CURB	(62)	AR
DATE	(137)	AL AR GA MI OK TE
DEADLINE	(50)	GA
DELTA	(57)	LA
DELUGE	(6)	AR
DEN	(8)	MI

DEVIL CHASER	(12	FL
DEVIL'S HORSE	(115	TE
DEVIL'S SNUFFBOX	(10	TE
DISC	(45	AR FL
DITCH HIM	(138	TE
DITCHLINE	(63)	GA
DOUBLE ARMFUL	(46)	AL
DOUBLE HITCH	(43)	GA
DRAG HARROW	(45)	GA TE
DRAG TOOTH HARROW	(45)	FL
DRAIN	(58)	FL
DRAIN PIPES	(16)	OK
DRAIN(AGE) DITCH	(63)	AL AR GA TE
DRAW HORSE	(47)	AL AR FL GA LA MI OK TE
DRAWING ROOM	(8)	MI TE
DREAN	(63)	GA
DRESSING	(90)	AR GA MI
DROP HIM	(138	AR TE
DROP SIDING	(15)	LA TE
DRY HOLLOW	(58)	GA
DUKE'S MIXTURE	(65)	AR
DUSKY DARK	(3)	TE
DUSK(Y) DARK	(3)	GA
EGG BREAD	(84)	GA
ENGINE HOUSE	(141)	LA MI
EXHORTER	(129)	TE
FAT LIGHTER	(12)	AL
FAT SPLINTERS	(12)	AL AR FL GA LA MI TE
FATBACK BACON	(87)	TE
FATTY BREAD	(90)	FL
FARMER	(130)	MI OK
FETCH	(147)	GA
FIDDLE WORM	(113)	AL
FIRE DEPARTMENT	(141)	GA TE
FIREPLACE ROOM	(8)	AL GA TE
FIREWOOD	(12)	OK
FLAT (A)	(57)	AL AR GA MI OK TE
FLAT (B)	(58)	GA
FLEET FOOTED PREACHER	(129)	FL
FLOOD	(6)	AL AR FL
FLORIDA ROOM	(8)	AL AR GA MI OK TE
FLYING HORSE	(49)	MI
FRESH ONIONS	(101)	OK
FROG	(112)	AL AR FL GA LA MI OK TE
FROG STRANGLER	(6)	FL OK
GALLOPING FENCE	(29)	GA
GARDEN PLOT	(96)	TE
GEE HORSE	(79)	MI
GEORGIA CHICKEN	(87)	FL
GIVE A MAROON HARPOON	(138)	TE
GIVE HIM A DEAR JOHN	(138)	TE
GIVE HIM THE GATE	(138)	FL OK TE
GIVE HIS WALKING PAPERS	(138)	AL GA
GLASS STOPPER	(39)	AL AR FL GA LA MI OK TE
GO CART	(125)	LA
GO STEADY	(137)	TE
GO TO SEE	(137)	GA
GRADER FURROW	(63)	TE
GRASS PLOT	(62)	AL AR FL GA MI TE
GRASS STRIP	(62)	AL AR FL GA LA MI OK TE
GRAVEL ROAD	(61)	AR
GRAVY	(92)	FL
GRUB WORM	(113)	AL AR GA MI OK TE
GREEN STRIP	(62)	TE
GROUND GLASS STOPPER	(39)	GA
GROUND MOLE	(110)	AL AR GA MI TE
GRIND ROCK	(52)	LA MI
GRIND STONE	(52)	AL AR FL GA LA MI OK TE
GRINDING STONE	(52)	LA
GULLY	(63)	GA TE
GUT RIPPER	(144)	TE
GUTTER PIPE	(16)	AL LA MI
HAS HAD IT	(133)	AL
HALF BREED	(65)	TE
HAW HORSE	(79)	TE
HAY COTS	(20)	GA
HAY DUMP	(20)	GA
HAY MOUNDS	(20)	FL OK
HAY RACKS	(19)	GA TE
HAY SHOCK	(20)	FL
HAR	(45)	AR
HARD SHOWER	(6)	AR GA
HARD TOP	(61)	AL AR
HARR	(45)	AR
HEAD MEAT	(91)	AL AR GA OK TE
HEAD TAW	(50)	AL AR GA
HEATED UP	(132)	TE
HEAVY PAN	(35)	OK

HITCH	(43)	OK
HIGHWAY	(59)	GA
HOLLER FIELD	(58)	TE
HOLLERING DISTANCE	(80)	TE
HOLY ROLLER	(129)	FL
HOT AND BOTHERED	(132)	MI
HOT HEADED	(132)	TE
HOT UNDER THE COLLAR	(132)	GA TE
HOUND	(65)	AR TE
HOUND DOG	(65)	AL FL TE
HOPPIE TOAD	(112)	FL OK TE
HUSH PUPPIES	(84)	FL
HULL	(88)	TE
ICE SHELL	(9)	FL
IRON POT	(35)	GA
IRON SKILLET	(34)	GA
JACK HORSE	(47)	GA
JAWS HARP	(40)	GA
JOWLS	(91)	TE
JUNK HOUSE	(17)	GA
KUSH KUSH	(84)	FL GA LA TE
LANDING	(25)	LA
LAP LUNCH	(95)	GA
LAY PREACHER (PARTTIME)	(129)	AL AR FL GA LA OK TE
LAY READER	(129)	AL GA TE
LEADING HORSE	(79)	MI
LEAN-TO (SHED)	(17)	AL AR FL GA LA MI OK TE
LEAVE HIM	(138)	OK
LEFT HORSE	(79)	AL AR FL LA
LITEARD	(12)	FL
LITTLE HOUSE	(17)	TE
LIGHT PONE	(83)	AL AR FL GA LA MI OK TE
LIGHTERED WOOD	(12)	FL
LOAFERING DOG	(65)	GA
LOCAL YOKEL	(130)	OK
LOCKER	(22)	LA
LOW GROUND	(57)	AR FL
LOWLAND	(58)	AL GA MI OK TE
LOG HEADED	(131)	AL AR FL GA MI OK TE
LOG REST	(11)	GA
LUMBER ROOM	(17)	MI
MAUL STICK PREACHER	(129)	TE
MAPLE TREE	(118)	AL AR FL GA LA MI
MEAT SKINS	(88)	FL TE
MERRY-GO-ROUND	(49)	AL AR FL GA LA MI OK TE
MILK BUCKET	(32)	OK
MILK TIME	(70)	LA
MOLASSES CAKE	(85)	TE
MOUNTAIN HOOSIER	(130)	GA TE
MUSH	(84)	AR TE
MUSH BREAD	(84)	AL AR FL GA LA MI OK TE
MUSHROOM	(109)	GA MI TE
MUTT	(65)	AR GA TE
NAUSEATED	(136)	AL
NEST ONIONS	(101)	AL AR FL GA MI OK TE
NEUTRAL GROUND	(62)	LA MI
NICK NACKS	(95)	TE
OFF HORSE	(79)	AL AR MI
OIL STONE	(52)	AR
OLD WOOLY BLACK	(142)	AL FL GA LA MI TE
ONE HORSE PREACHER	(129)	GA
OPEN HEART	(99)	TE
OUTHOUSE	(17)	AR MI
OUR TRIBE	(124)	TE
PASTURE	(26)	AL AR FL GA LA MI OK TE
PASTURE	(58)	OK
PATCH (OF WOODS)	(120)	AR TE
PATIO	(25)	AL AR FL GA LA MI OK TE
PAPER BAG	(37)	AL AR
PAPER SACK	(37)	AR GA LA
PEAT SACK	(38)	LA
PICK UP	(24)	OK
PILES (OF WHEAT)	(21)	AL AR LA MI
PINE KNOT	(12)	LA MI
PIONEER	(130)	TE
PIGGEN	(32)	TE
PLAIN DOG	(65)	OK
PLANK FENCE	(29)	AL AR FL GA LA MI OK TE
PLUNDER HOUSE	(17)	AL AR FL GA LA MI OK TE
POKE SACK	(37)	TE
POOPED OUT	(133)	AL AR FL GA LA OK TE
POOR DO	(84)	TE
POOR WHITE	(130)	GA
POP THE WHIP	(49)	AR
POISON SUMAC	(121)	AR
PRESS MEAT	(91)	GA
PULLIT BONE	(69)	TE
PUT HIM DOWN	(138)	AR LA TE

PUMP HOUSE	(17)	TE
QUILT	(55)	FL
QUIT HIM	(138)	AL GA LA MI TE
RAN OUT OF SCHOOL	(140)	MI
RAVINE	(58)	AR GA
RAILS	(29)	AL AR FL GA LA MI OK TE
RAIL(ING) FENCE	(29)	AL AR FL GA LA MI OK TE
RAIN EAVESTROUGHS	(15)	FL
REJECT	(133)	AL
RECEPTION	(139)	AL LA MI
RED RIVER BUMPKIN	(130)	AR
RILED UP	(132)	AL AR FL GA MI OK TE
RIDGE RUNNER	(130)	GA TE
RIVER RATS	(130)	TE
ROAD DITCH	(63)	AR FL GA LA
ROAST EARS	(108)	LA OK
ROASTED PONE	(84)	LA
SALAD (SALLET) GREENS	(104)	GA MI TE
SALT BACON	(87)	TE
SALT MEAT	(87)	AL AR FL GA LA MI OK TE
SAFETY ZONE	(62)	TE
SAW BENCH	(47)	GA
SAW LOG	(47)	GA
SAW RACK	(47)	AL AR FL GA LA MI OK TE
SCULLIONS	(10.)	GA
SCYTHE STONE	(52)	AR
SCRATCHER	(45)	AR
SEASONING MEAT	(87)	TE
SECOND GROWTH	(81)	GA TE
SHAFT HIM	(138)	AL AR FL GA LA TE
SHAFTED	(138)	TE
SHARPENING STONE	(52)	LA
SHED ROOM	(17)	GA
SHELL BEANS	(103)	AL AR GA MI TE
SHELLIES	(103)	AL AR FL GA MI TE
SHOOK UP	(133)	AL
SHOOT OUT OF THE SADDLE	(138)	AL TE
SHOOTING LINE	(50)	TE
SHOT	(133)	AL
SHOWER	(6)	AL TE
SHINNERY	(120)	OK
SHIPLAP	(15)	AL AR FL GA LA MI OK TE
SIDE DITCH	(63)	MI TE
SIDE ROOM	(17)	AR TE
SIDEWALK STRIP	(62)	AL AR FL GA LA MI OK TE
SIDEWALK PREACHER	(129)	OK
SINKER	(85)	GA
SKEETER HAWK	(115)	GA
SKIF ICE	(9)	AR
SLUSH ICE	(9)	AL AR GA MI TE
SLIGHT HIM	(138)	GA
SOT (IN HIS WAYS)	(131)	AR
SOUP HOUND	(65)	LA
SOUSE MEAT	(91)	MI TE
SPARK	(137)	TE
SPLINTERS	(12)	FL GA LA MI TE
SPLIT RAIL FENCE	(29)	GA
SPOUT	(36)	AR GA MI
SPREAD	(54)	MI
SPRING FROG	(112)	FL
STACKS	(20)	GA
STEW KETTLE	(35)	AR
STEWER	(35)	AR
STORE HOUSE	(17)	GA
STOVE WOOD	(12)	OK
STREAK O LEAN	(87)	AL MI
STREAKED MEAT	(87)	AL AR FL GA LA MI OK TE
STRIP	(62)	AL GA TE
STROLLER	(125)	AL
SUN PORCH	(25)	GA TE
SUGAR MAPLE ORCHARD	(119)	AR
SUGAR TREE ORCHARD	(119)	TE
SWAG	(58)	AR LA MI TE
SWAGERS (SWAYERS)	(113)	AL AR FL GA MI OK TE
SWALLOPING	(92)	TE
SWEET CAKE	(85)	AL
TACKED QUILT	(55)	LA MI TE
TAW HEAD	(50)	AR
TAR ROAD	(61)	TE
TEA CAKE	(85)	AL LA
TEA PARTY	(139)	GA
TEETER TOTTER	(48)	AR FL LA OK TE
TERRACE	(25)	AR GA
THE BOY	(69)	TE
THE FOLKS	(124)	OK
THICKET	(120)	TE
THIN ICE	(9)	AL AR FL GA OK TE
THROW LINE	(50)	AL

TIME TO FEED UP	(70)	FL GA
TIN BUCKET	(32)	AL AR FL GA LA MI OK TE
TIRED OUT	(133)	AR LA
TO SNAP	(102)	FL OK
TOBACCO WORM	(113)	FL
TOP LINE	(50)	GA
TOP LOFT	(23)	GA
TOY LINE	(50)	TE
TRASH TOTER	(6)	GA
TRUNDLE BED	(56)	MI
TURNIP GREENS	(104)	AL FA OK TE
TURNIP SALAD	(104)	GA OK
TURTLE MAN	(142)	LA
TWILIGHT	(1)	GA
TWIN BROTHERS	(34)	MI
UNSMOKED MEAT	(87)	AL AR GA MI TE
UPSET	(132)	GA OK
UTILITY ROOM	(17)	FL GA MI OK TE
VALLEY	(56)	MI
VALLEY LAND	(57)	FL
VENETIAN BLINDS	(14)	AL TE
VEGETABLE PATCH	(96)	LA
WASH HOUSE	(17)	FL
WASHOUT	(6)	GA
WATER DITCH	(63)	TE
WATER HYDRANT	(36)	TE
WATER SPOUTS	(15)	AL AR FL GA MI TE
WATER TROUGH	(16)	AL FL GA LA MI TE
WAGON TONGUE	(41)	AL GA TE
WAX BEANS	(104)	FL
WARDROBE CLOSET	(22)	TE
WET WEATHER SPRING	(58)	TE
WHIRLING JENNY	(49)	MI
WHITE EYED	(133)	GA TE
WHITE MEAT	(87)	AL FL GA
WHITE SIDE	(87)	FL GA
WILD ONION PATCH	(58)	GA
WINDOW CURTAINS	(14)	FL
WINDROWS	(20)	AL LA TE
WINTER ONIONS	(101)	AR OK
WIGGLE WORM	(113)	AL TE
WOOD FENCE	(29)	MI
WOOD HORSE	(47)	AR MI
WOOD RACK	(47)	AL AR FL GA LA MI OK TE
WOOD SPLINTERS	(12)	GA
WOODEN (WATER) BUCKET	(32)	GA OK
WOODS	(120)	FL GA TE
WORKED UP	(132)	OK
WORM(S)	(113)	LA MI TE
YARD FAUCET	(36)	AL
(HORSE) MULE) LOT	(28)	AL AR FL GA MI LA TE

Word Maps

All word maps in this study derive from responses of individual informants whose counties or parishes of residence are shown in Map 3. Each response from that county or parish is plotted at the same point, the county seat. No attempt has been made to show the number of responses or the ages of respondents by varying the size of the map symbols.

Maps 4–75 present the specific geographic distribution of a range of local words. Some maps show a single word, others two word groups for the same thing or of the same general lexical form as in *coverlet, coverlid.* Maps 76–83 are composites which serve to identify main and subordinate dialect areas within *Southern* as redefined. Discussion of these maps is in Chapters 3–5; reference to them regularly occurs in the separate items in Chapter 6.

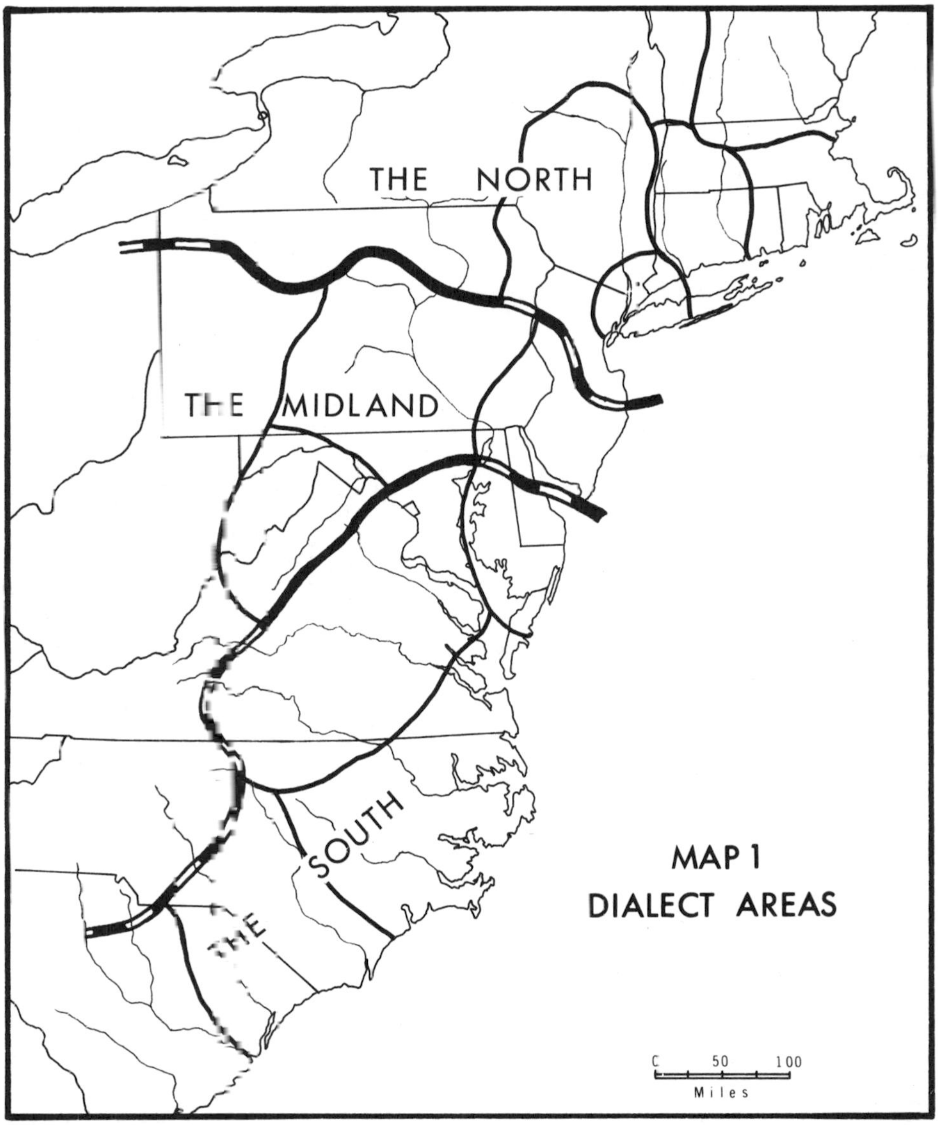
THE NORTH
THE MIDLAND
SOUTH
MAP 1
DIALECT AREAS
0 50 100
Miles

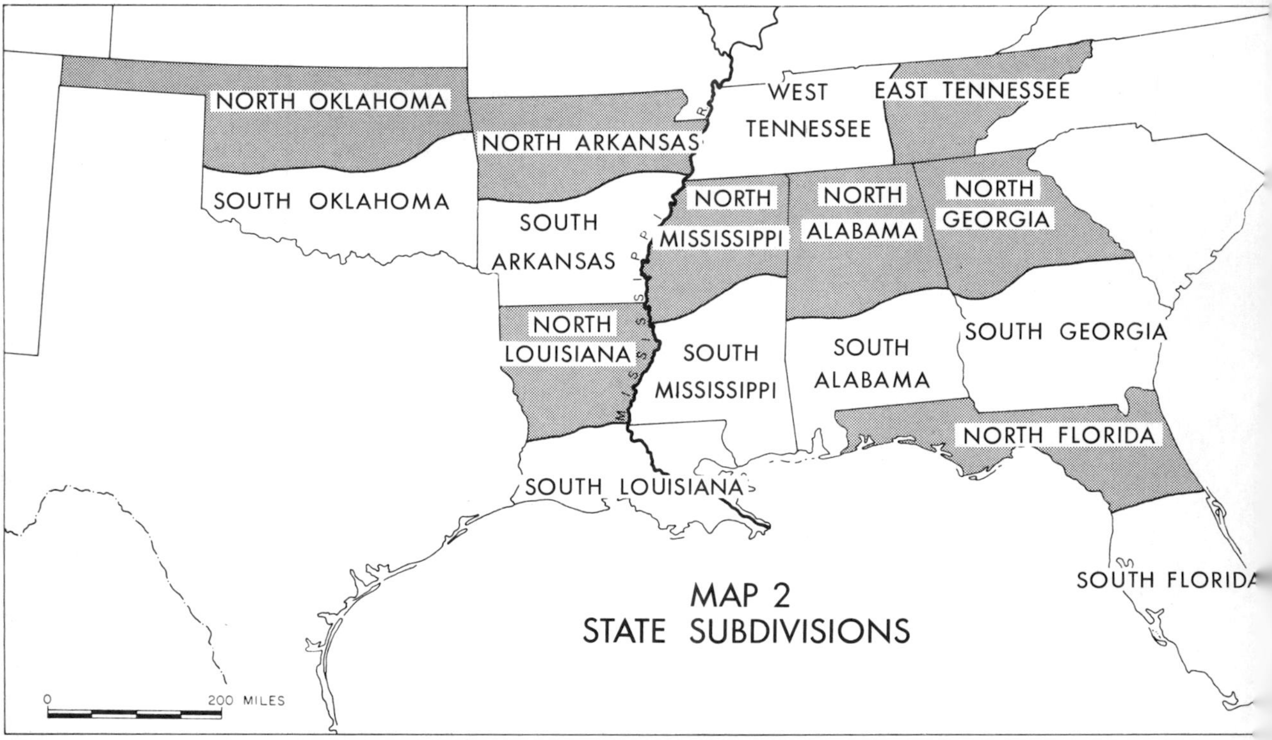
NORTH OKLAHOMA
SOUTH OKLAHOMA
NORTH ARKANSAS
SOUTH ARKANSAS
WEST TENNESSEE
EAST TENNESSEE
NORTH MISSISSIPPI
SOUTH MISSISSIPPI
NORTH ALABAMA
SOUTH ALABAMA
NORTH GEORGIA
SOUTH GEORGIA
NORTH LOUISIANA
SOUTH LOUISIANA
NORTH FLORIDA
SOUTH FLORIDA
MISSISSIPPI R.
0 200 MILES

MAP 2
STATE SUBDIVISIONS

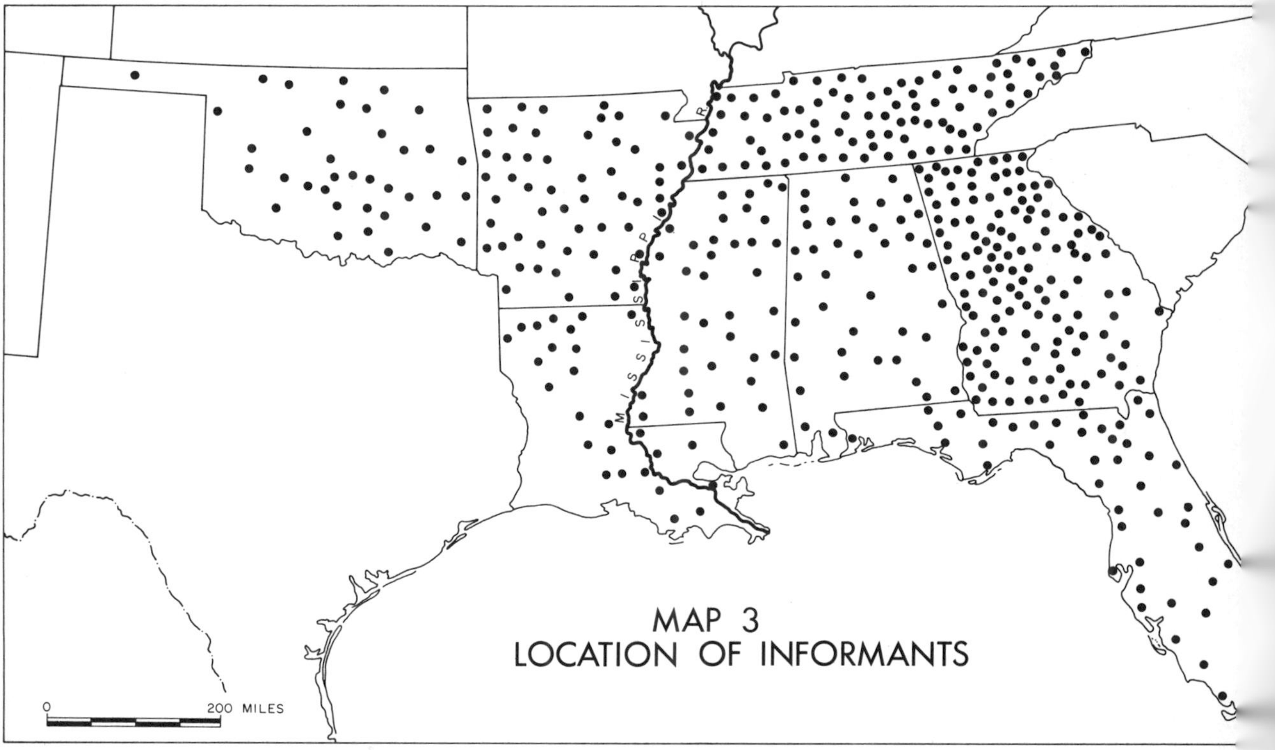
MISSISSIPPI R.
0 200 MILES

MAP 3
LOCATION OF INFORMANTS

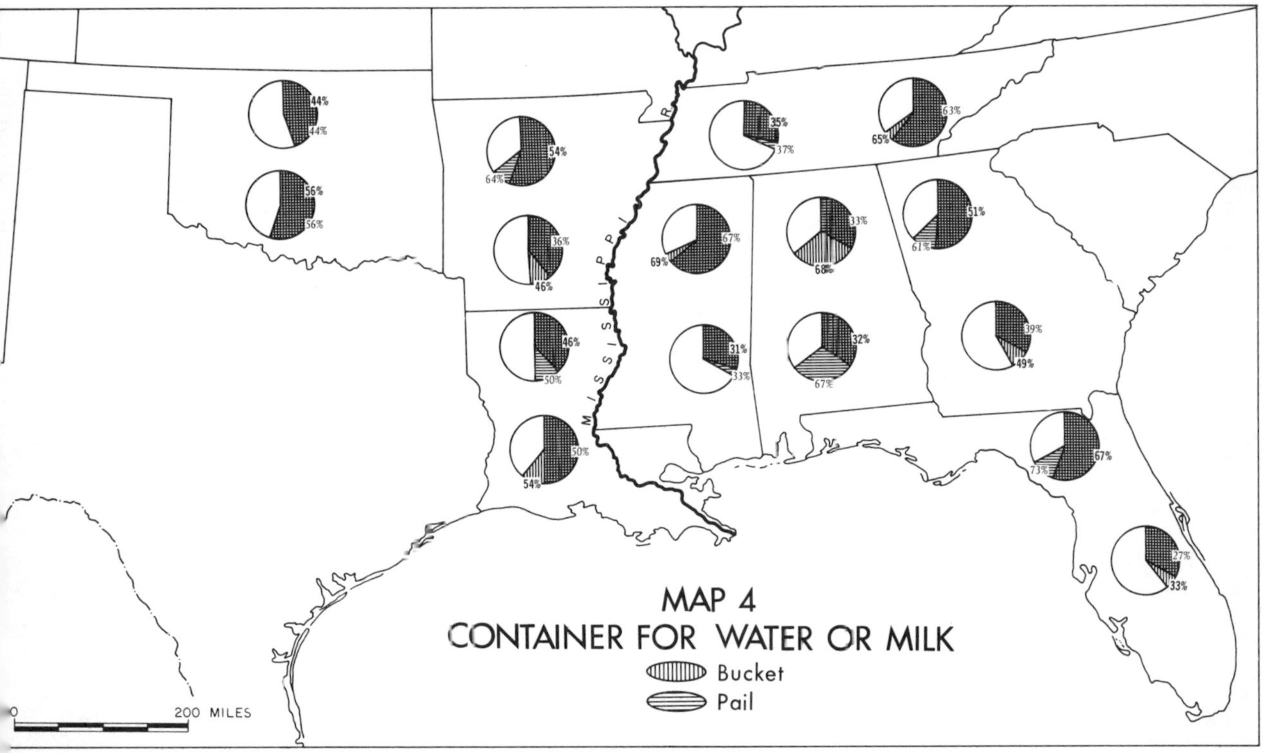
MISSISSIPPI R.
MAP 4
CONTAINER FOR WATER OR MILK
Bucket
Pail
0
200 MILES

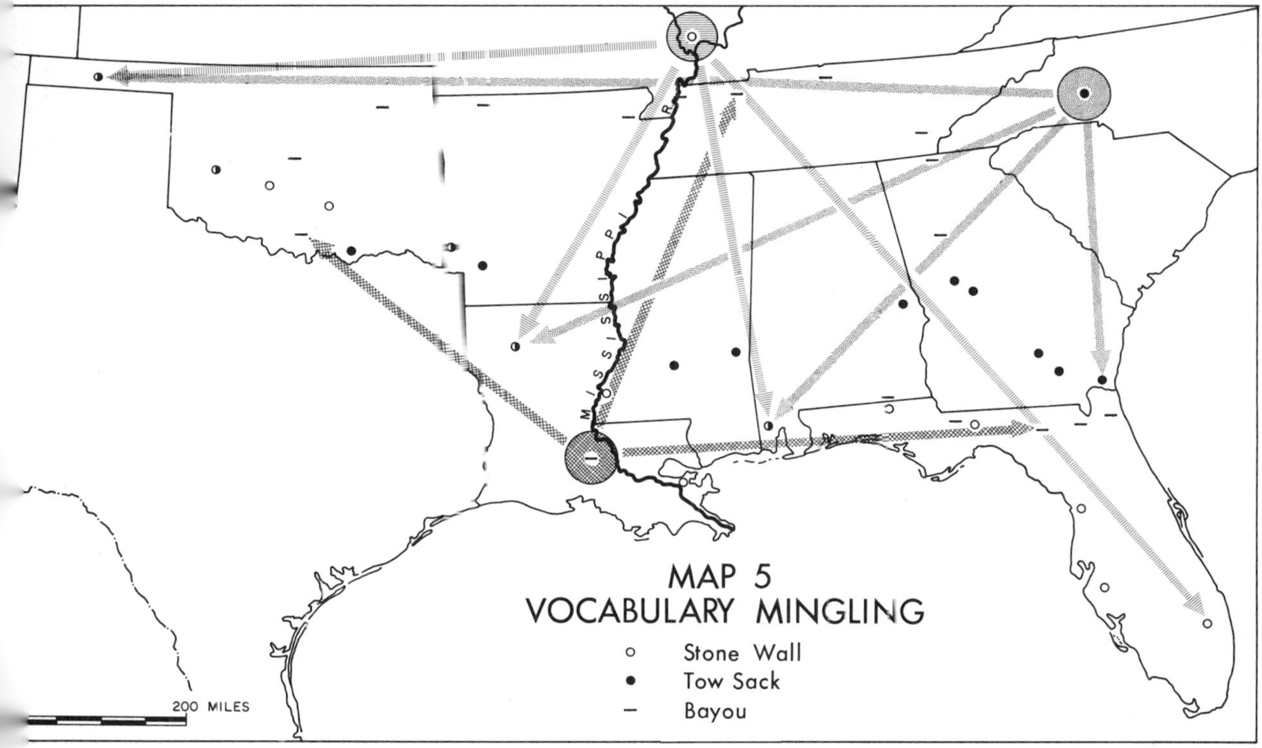
MISSISSIPPI R.
MAP 5
VOCABULARY MINGLING
Stone Wall
Tow Sack
Bayou
200 MILES

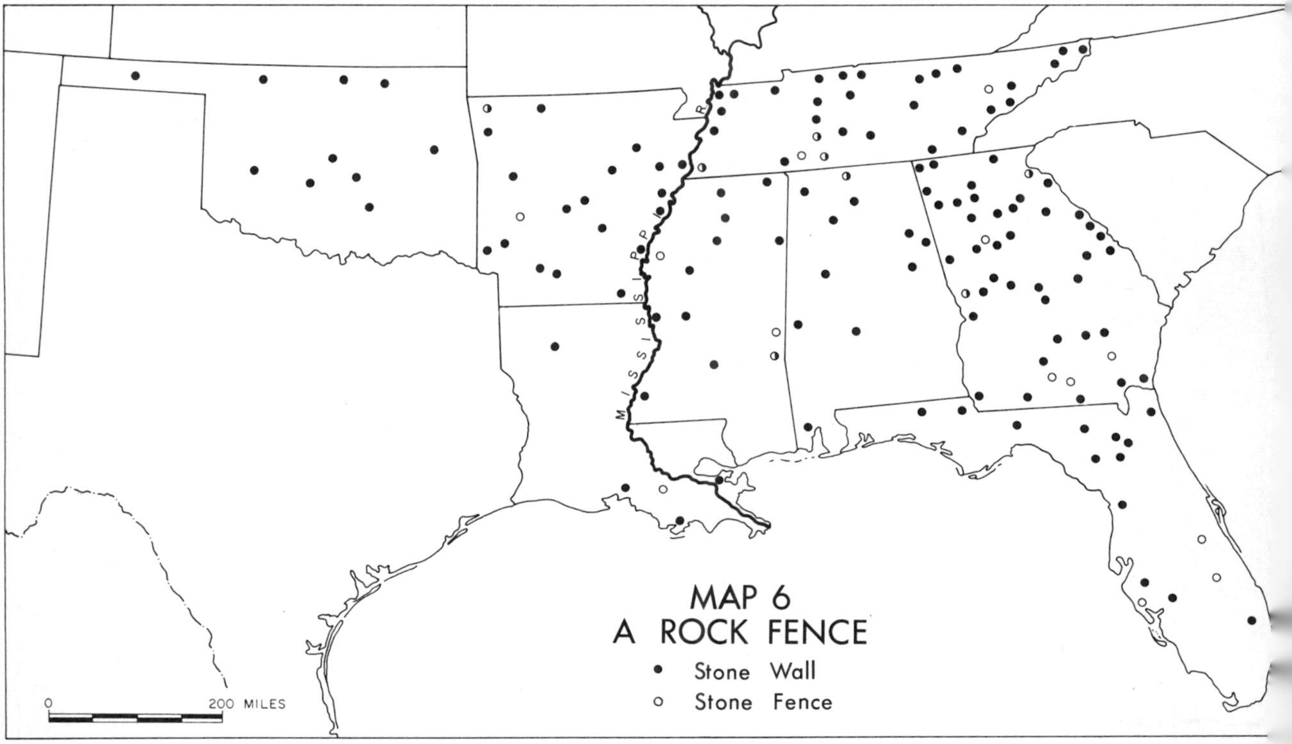
MISSISSIPPI R.
MAP 6
A ROCK FENCE
• Stone Wall
○ Stone Fence
0 200 MILES

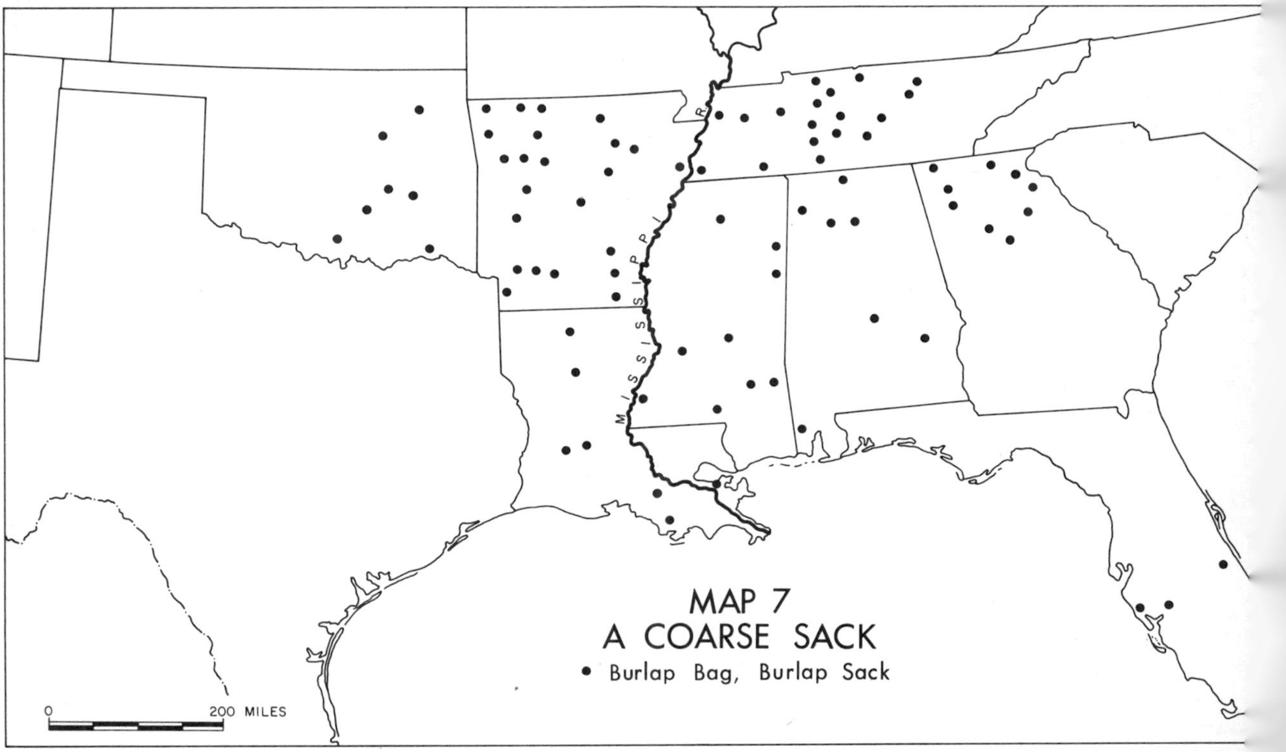
MISSISSIPPI R.
MAP 7
A COARSE SACK
• Burlap Bag, Burlap Sack
0 200 MILES

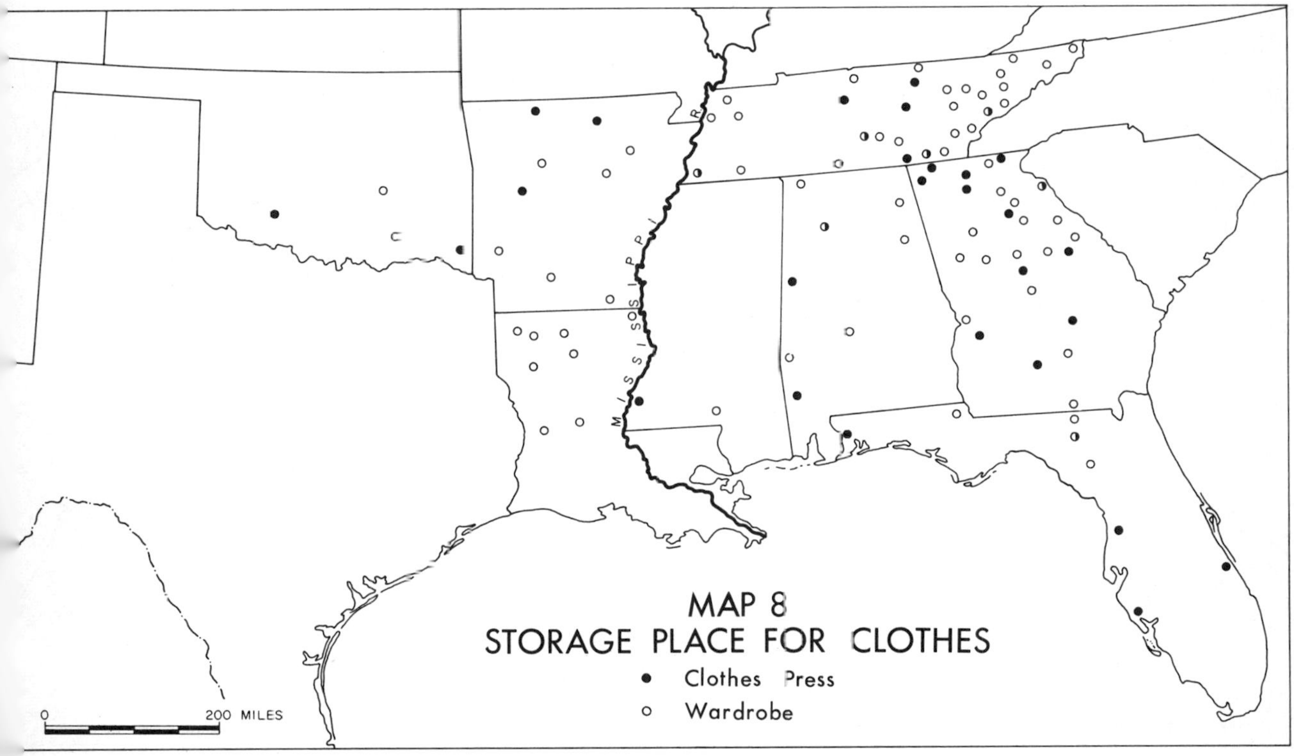
MAP 8
STORAGE PLACE FOR CLOTHES
• Clothes Press
○ Wardrobe
0
200 MILES

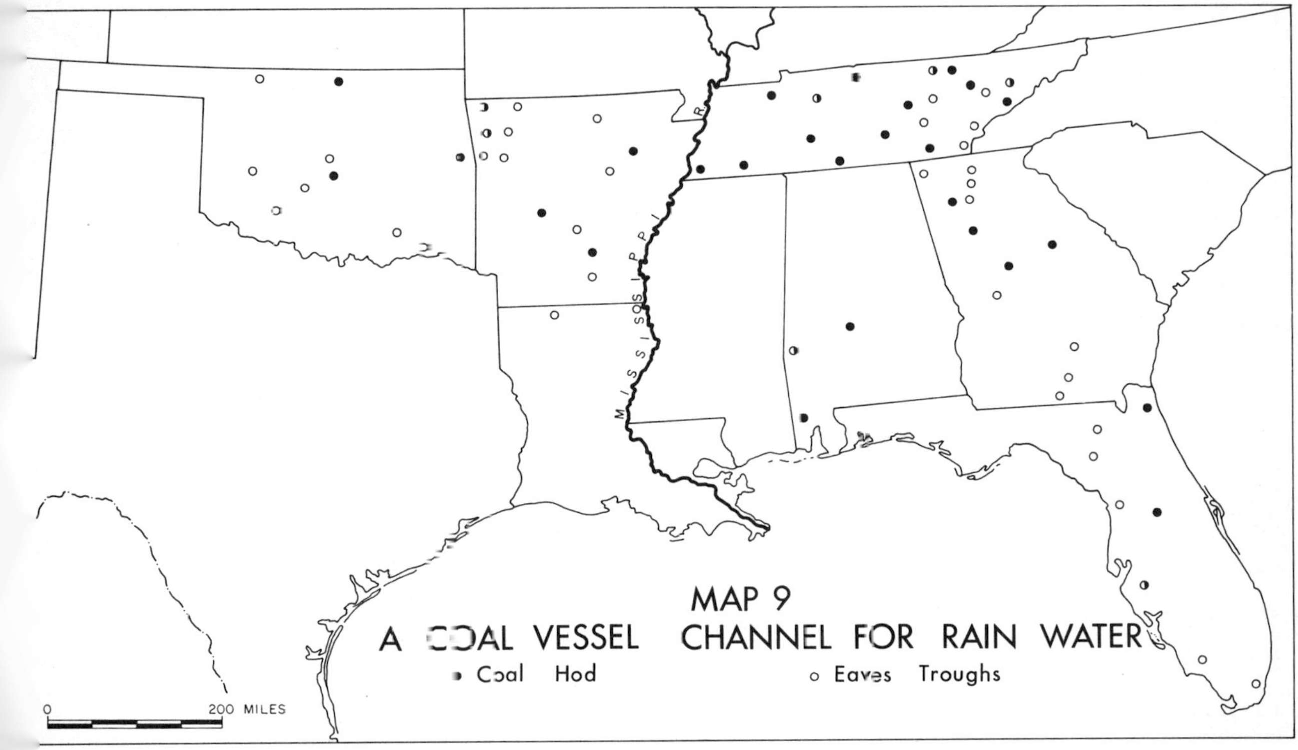
MAP 9
A COAL VESSEL CHANNEL FOR RAIN WATER
• Coal Hod
○ Eaves Troughs
0
200 MILES

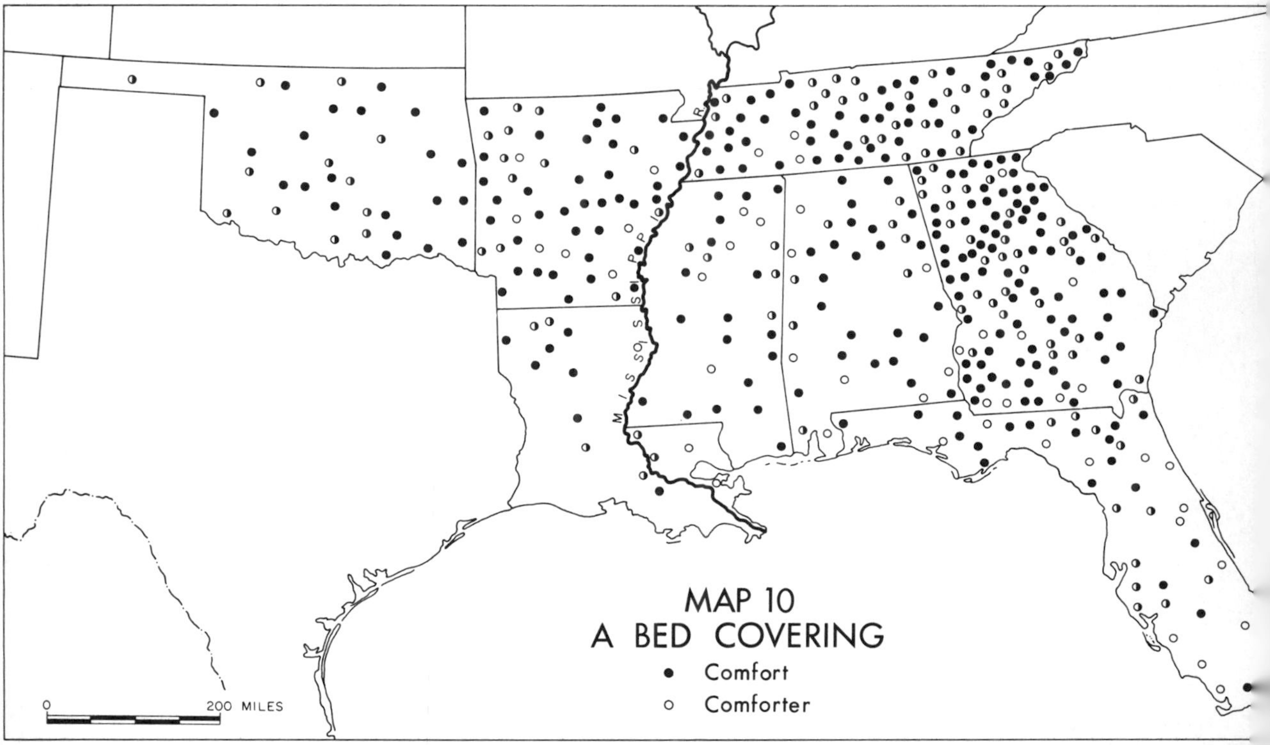
MISSISSIPPI R.
0
200 MILES
MAP 10
A BED COVERING
● Comfort
○ Comforter

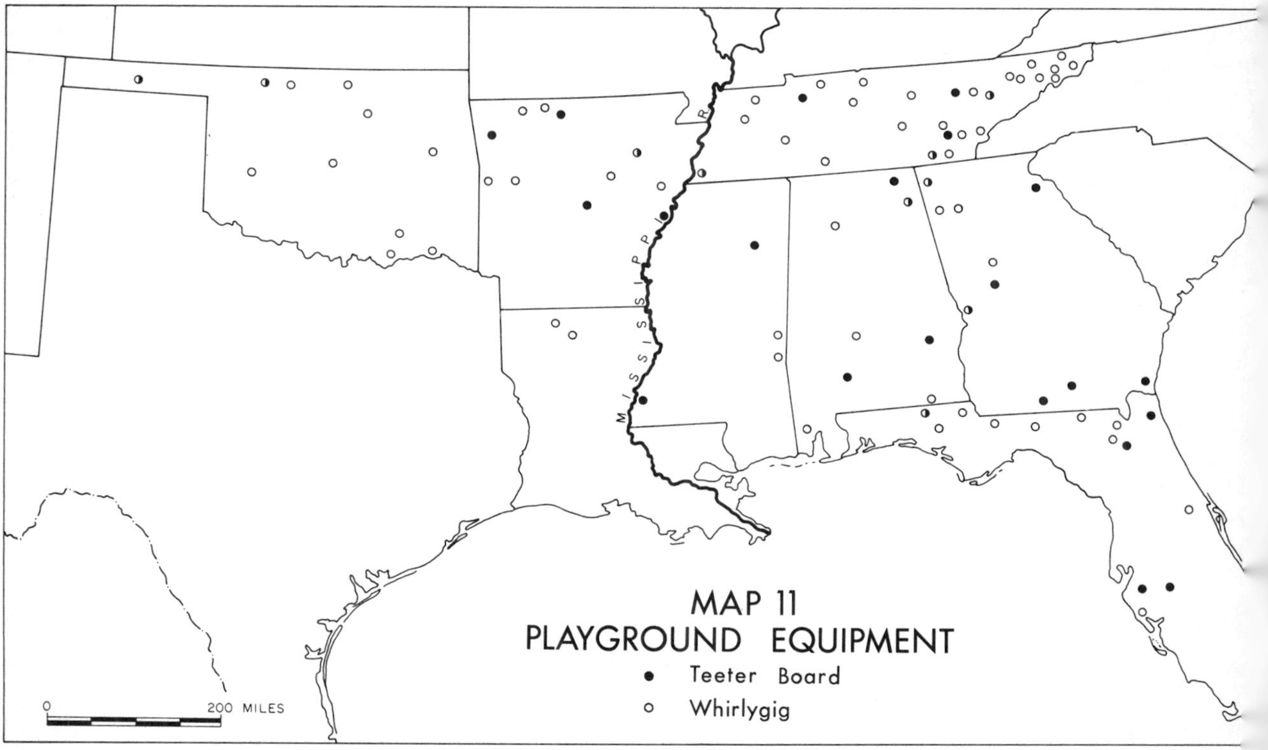
MISSISSIPPI R.
0
200 MILES
MAP 11
PLAYGROUND EQUIPMENT
● Teeter Board
○ Whirlygig

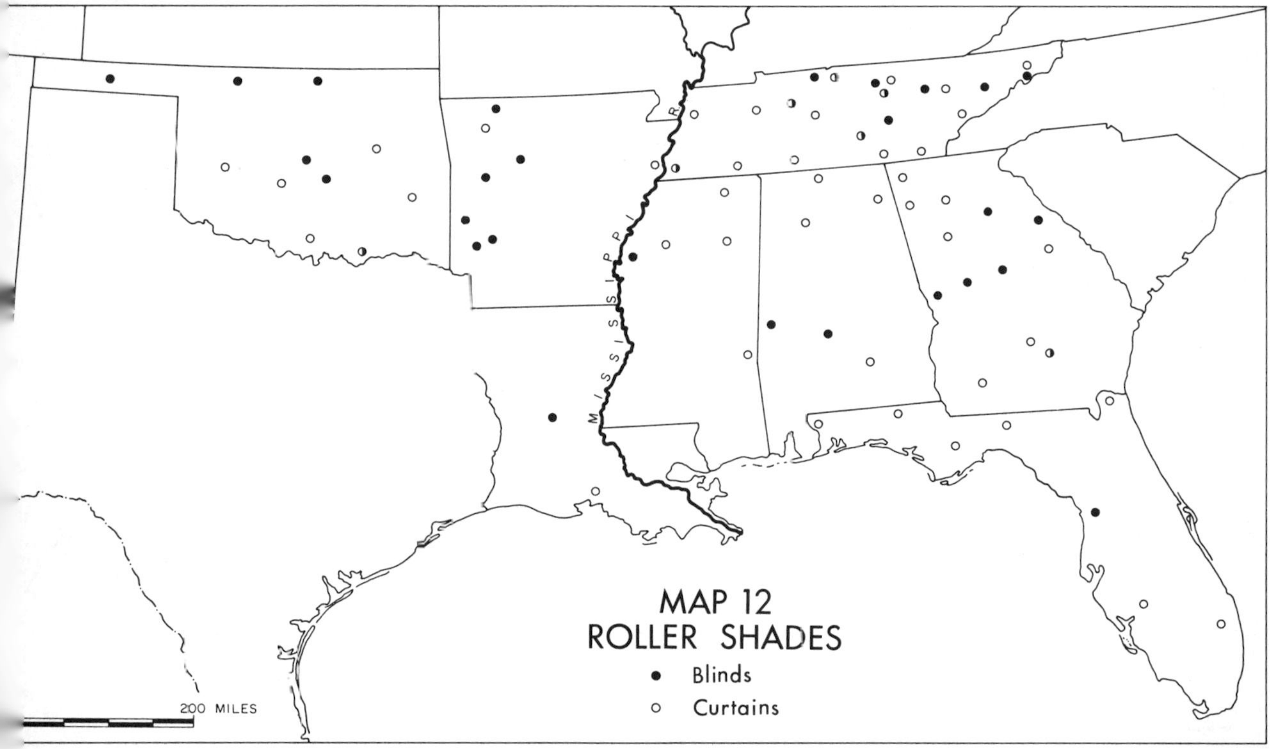
MISSISSIPPI R.
200 MILES
MAP 12
ROLLER SHADES
Blinds
Curtains

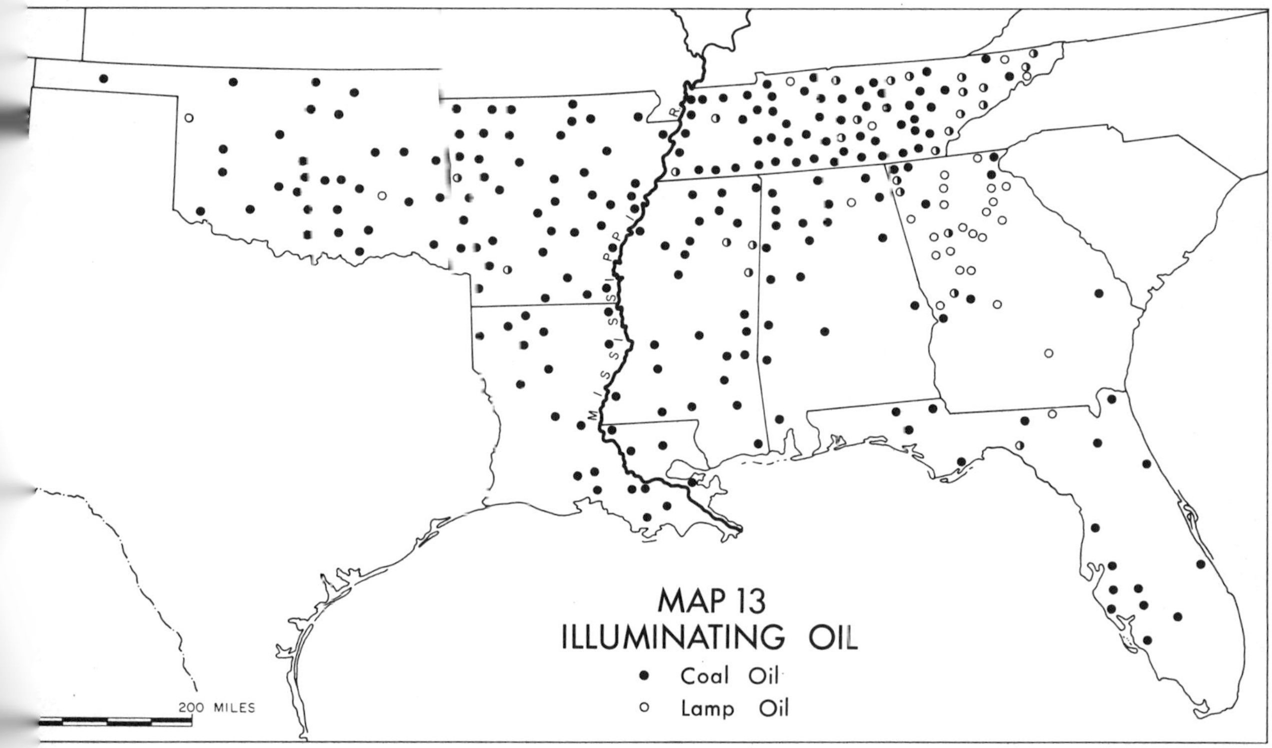
MISSISSIPPI R.
200 MILES
MAP 13
ILLUMINATING OIL
Coal Oil
Lamp Oil

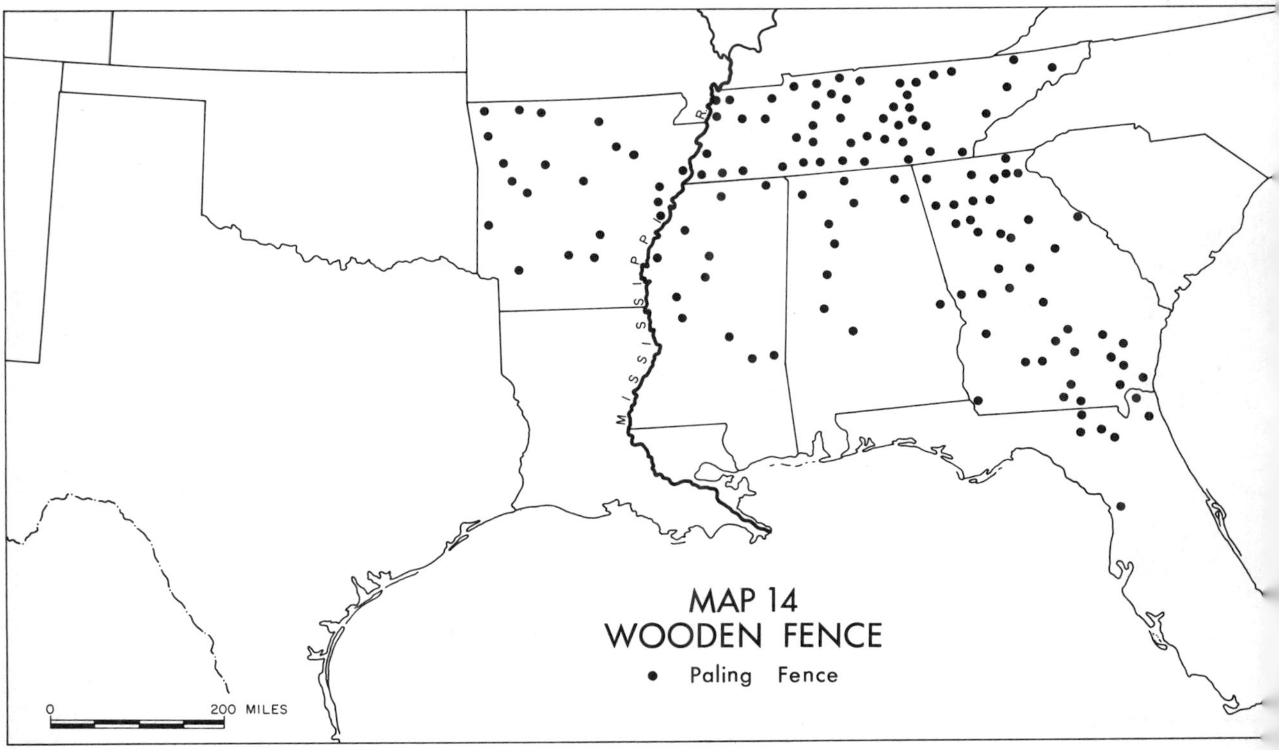
MISSISSIPPI R.
MAP 14
WOODEN FENCE
Paling Fence
0
200 MILES

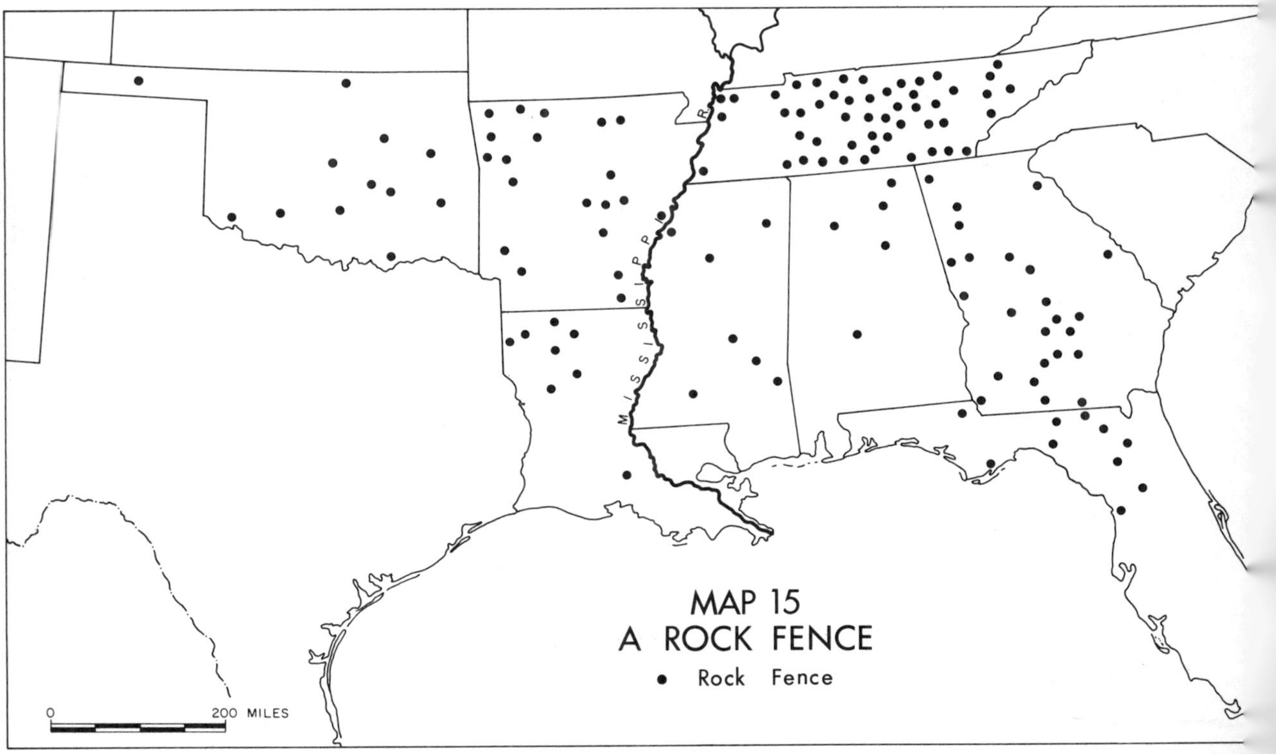
MISSISSIPPI R.
MAP 15
A ROCK FENCE
Rock Fence
0
200 MILES

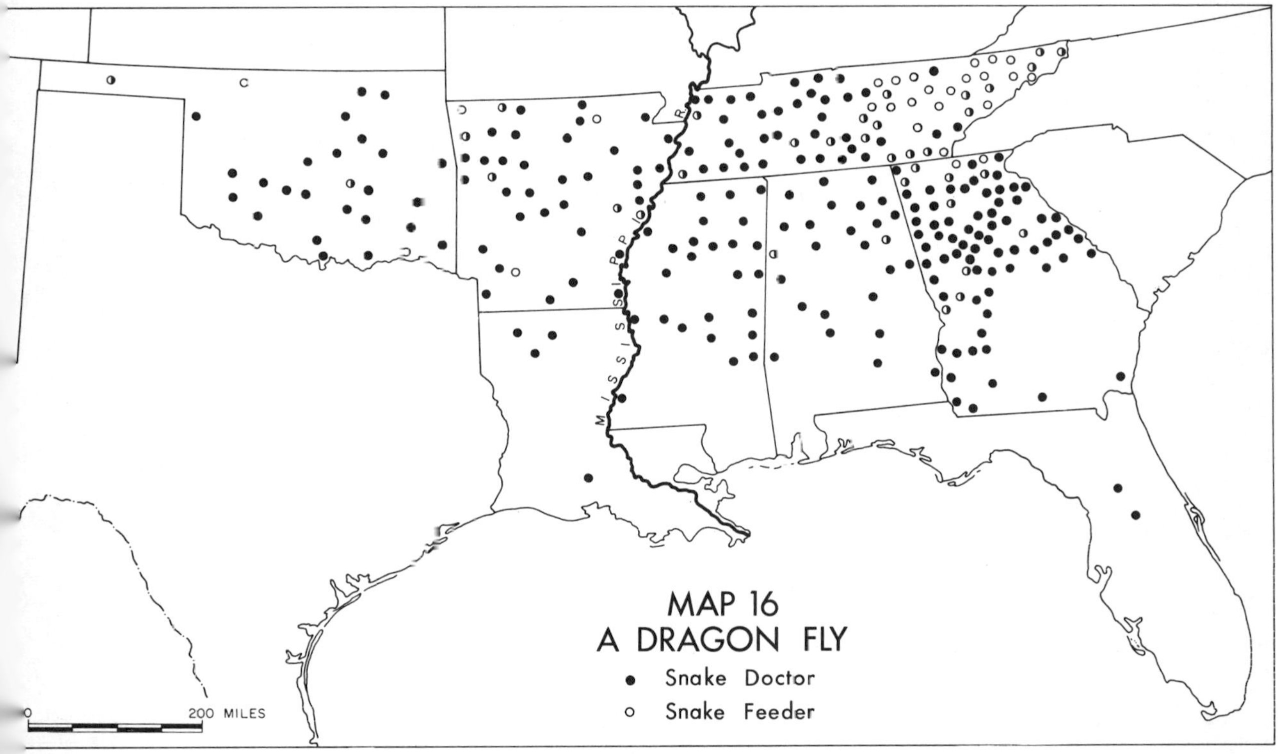
MISSISSIPPI R
0
200 MILES

MAP 16
A DRAGON FLY
• Snake Doctor
○ Snake Feeder

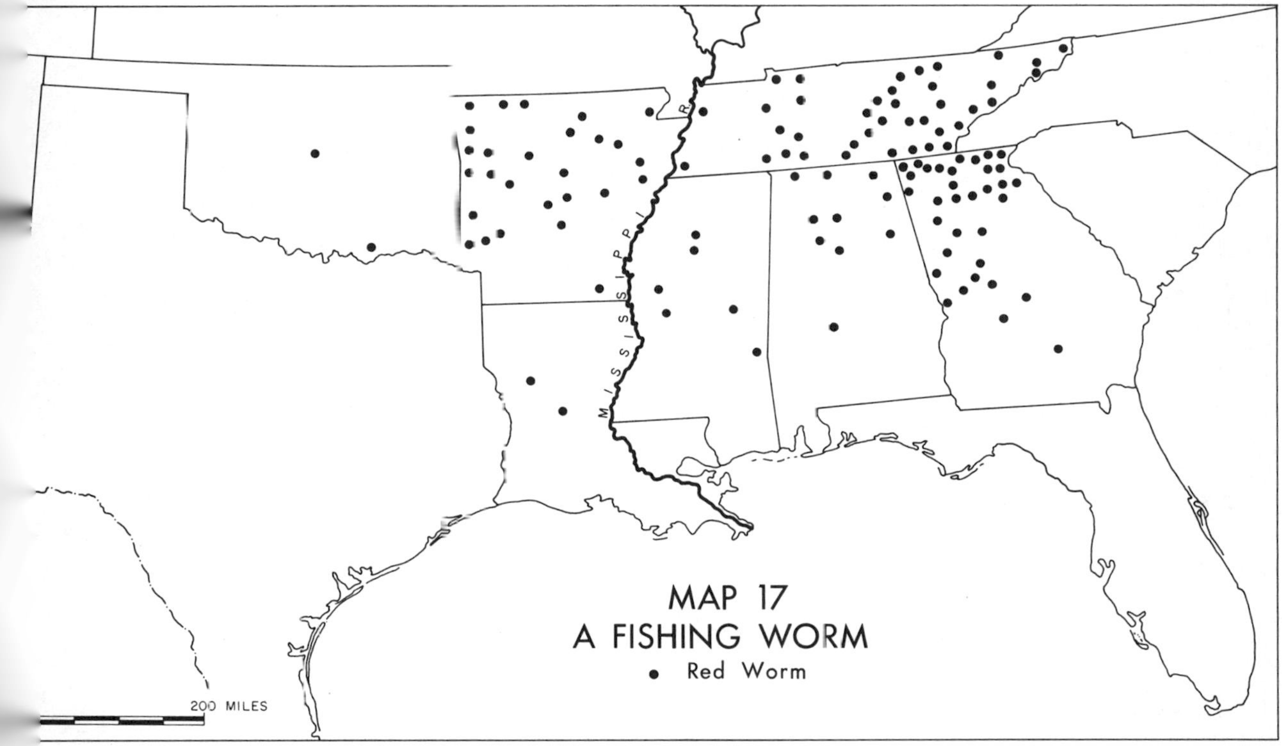
MISSISSIPPI R
200 MILES

MAP 17
A FISHING WORM
• Red Worm

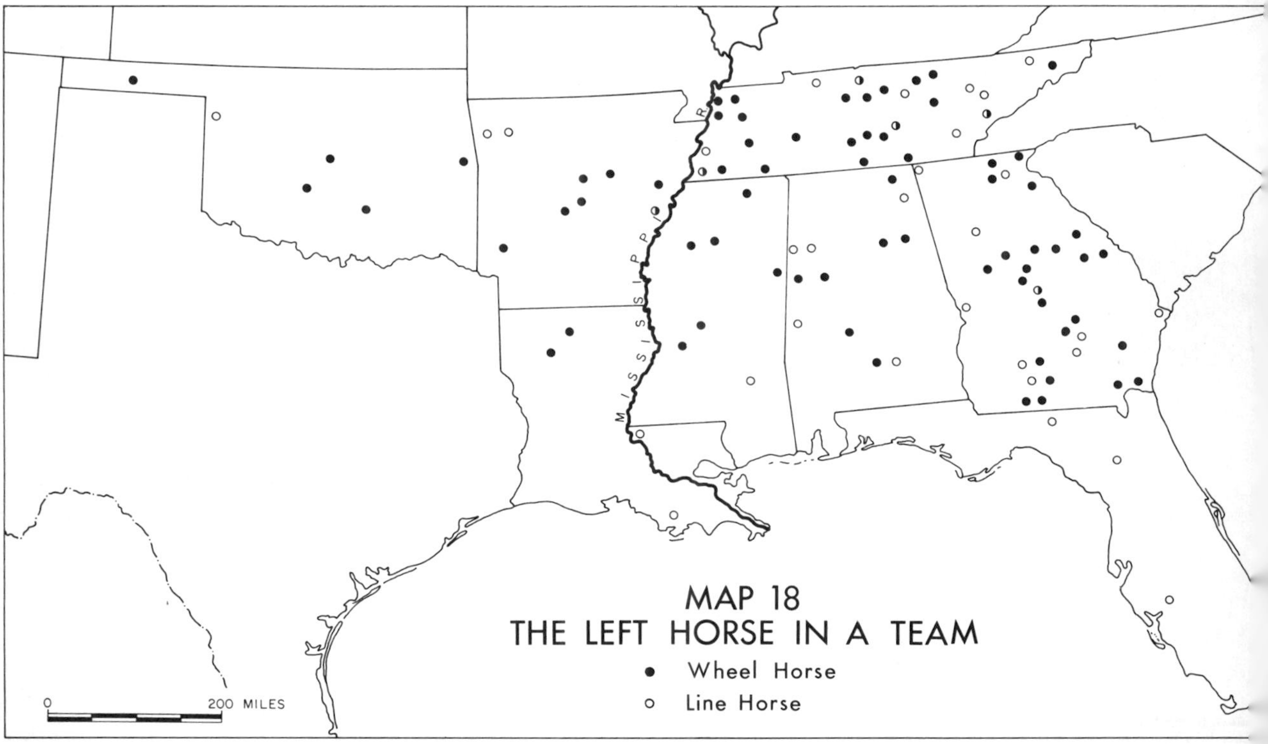
MISSISSIPPI R.
0
200 MILES

MAP 18
THE LEFT HORSE IN A TEAM
● Wheel Horse
○ Line Horse

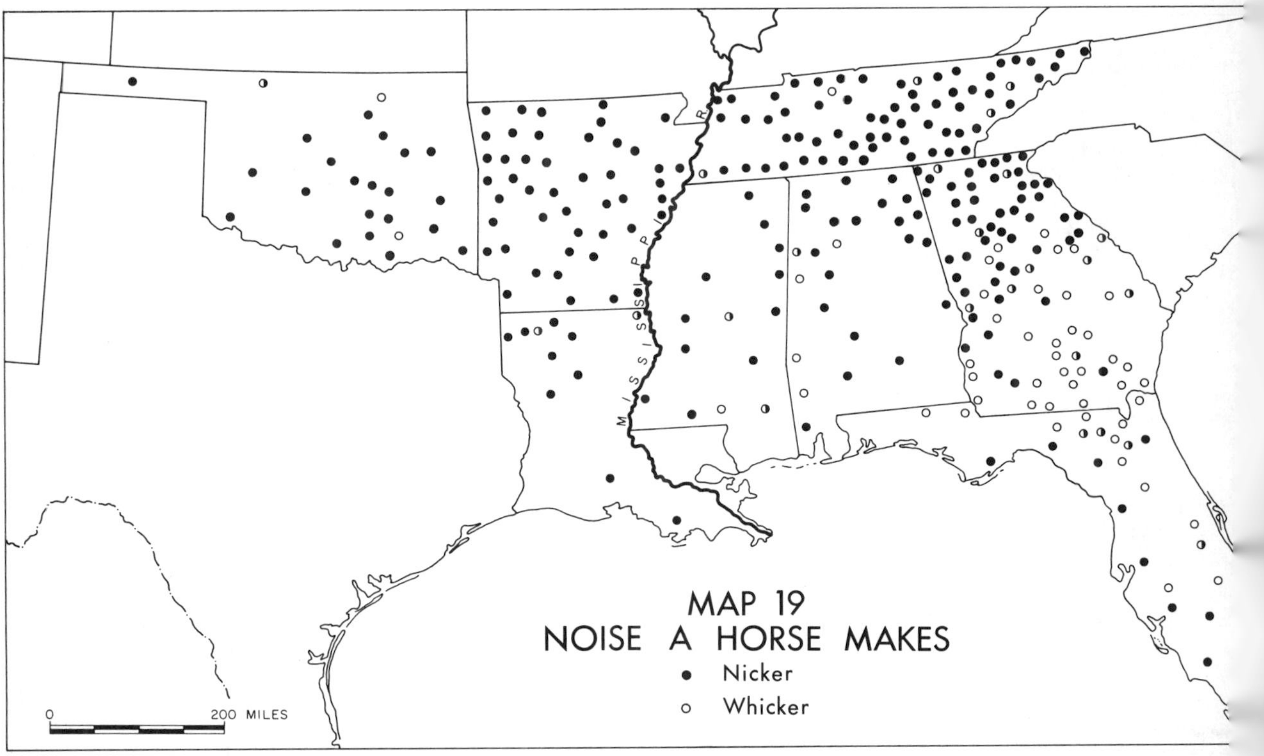
MISSISSIPPI R.
0
200 MILES

MAP 19
NOISE A HORSE MAKES
● Nicker
○ Whicker

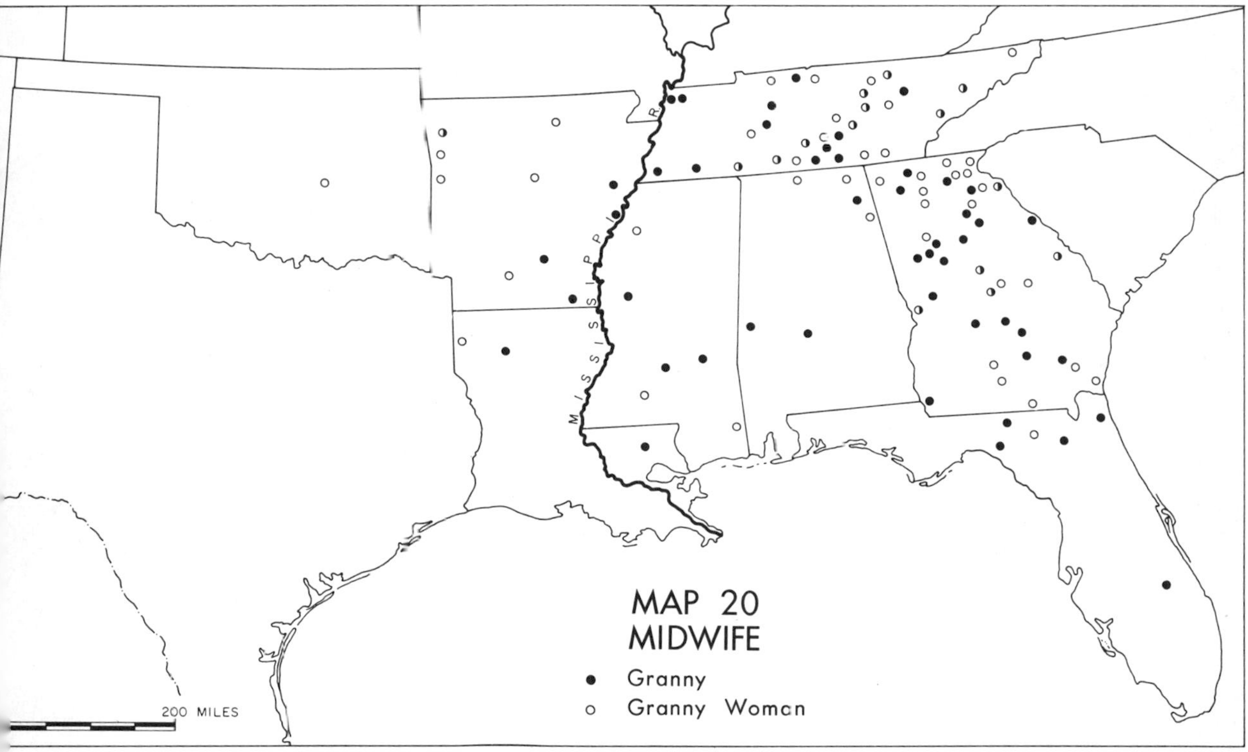
MISSISSIPPI R.
MAP 20
MIDWIFE
● Granny
○ Granny Woman
200 MILES

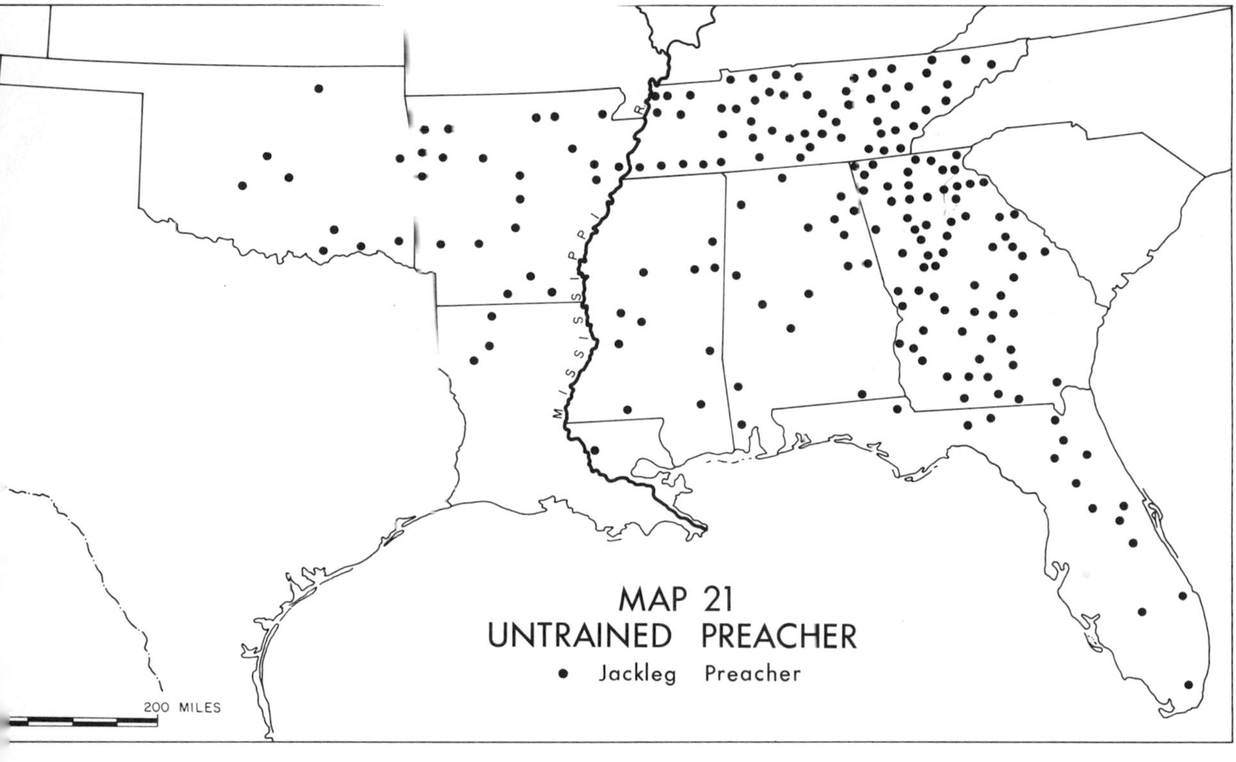
MISSISSIPPI R.
MAP 21
UNTRAINED PREACHER
● Jackleg Preacher
200 MILES

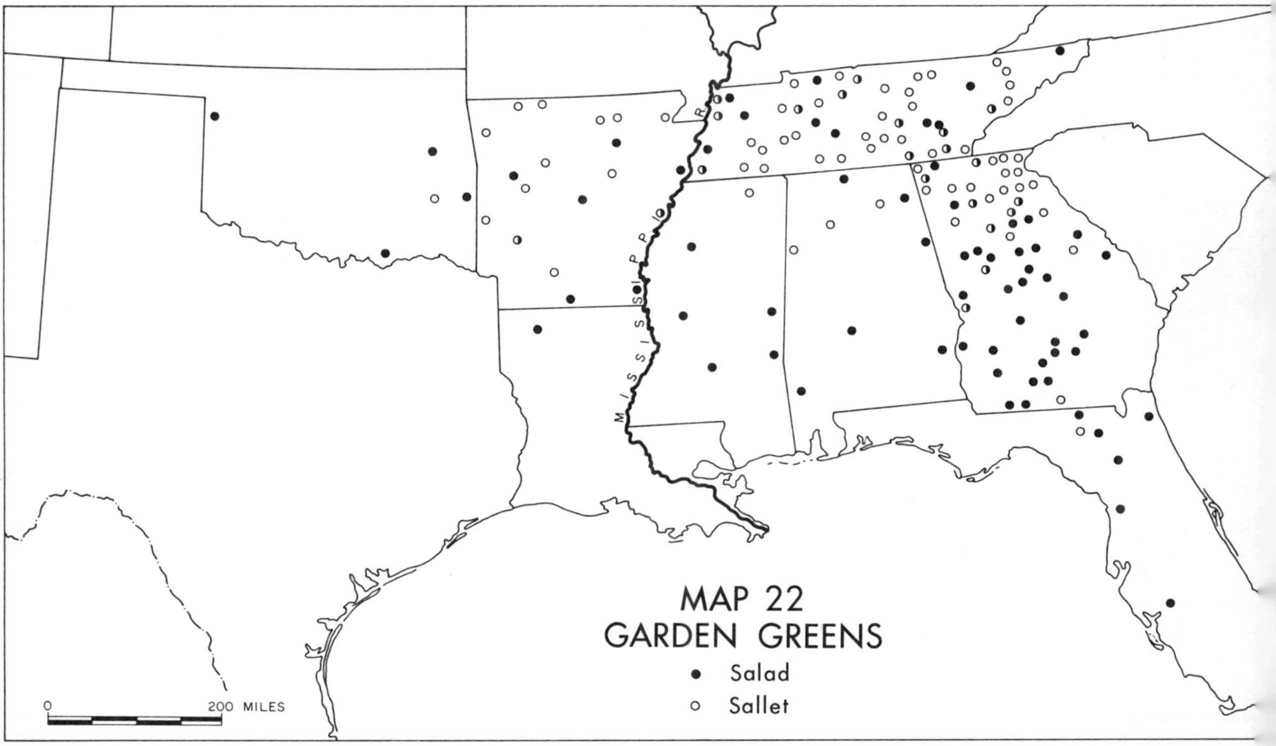
MISSISSIPPI R.
MAP 22
GARDEN GREENS
• Salad
○ Sallet
0 200 MILES

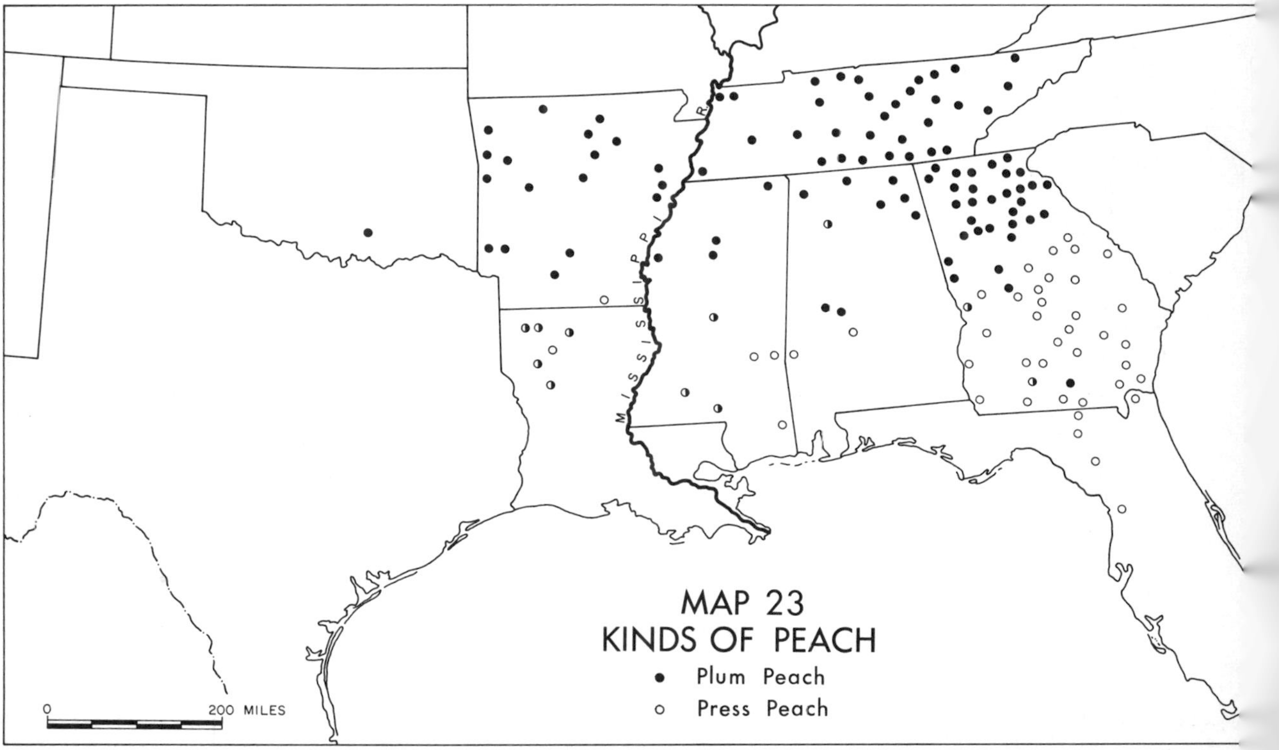
MISSISSIPPI R.
MAP 23
KINDS OF PEACH
• Plum Peach
○ Press Peach
0 200 MILES

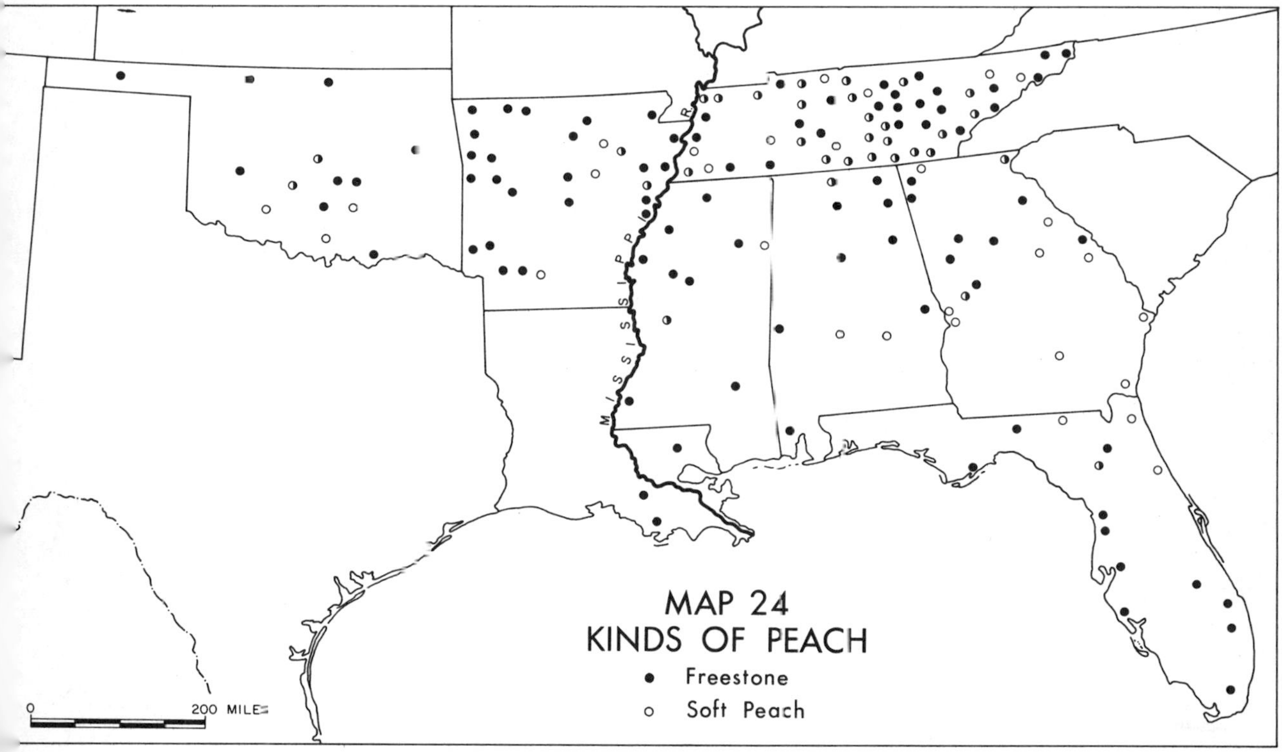
MISSISSIPPI R
MAP 24
KINDS OF PEACH
• Freestone
○ Soft Peach
0 200 MILES

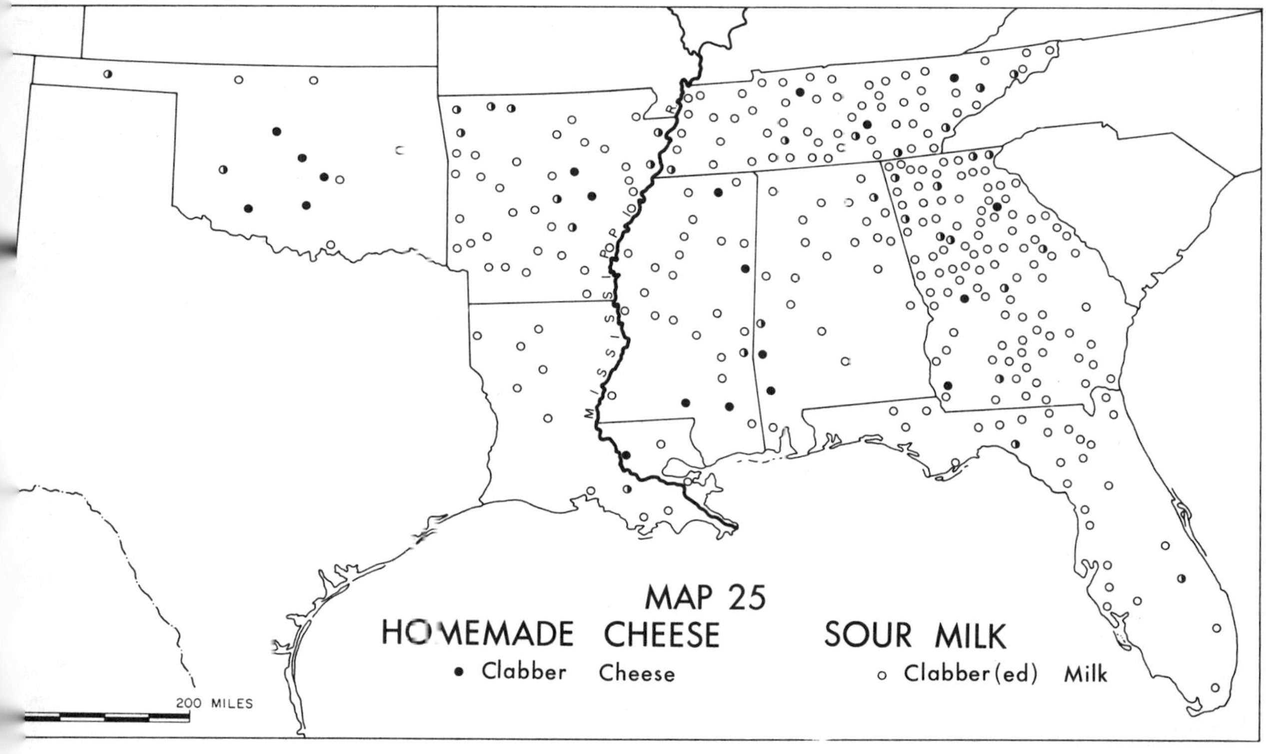
MISSISSIPPI R
MAP 25
HOMEMADE CHEESE SOUR MILK
• Clabber Cheese
○ Clabber(ed) Milk
200 MILES

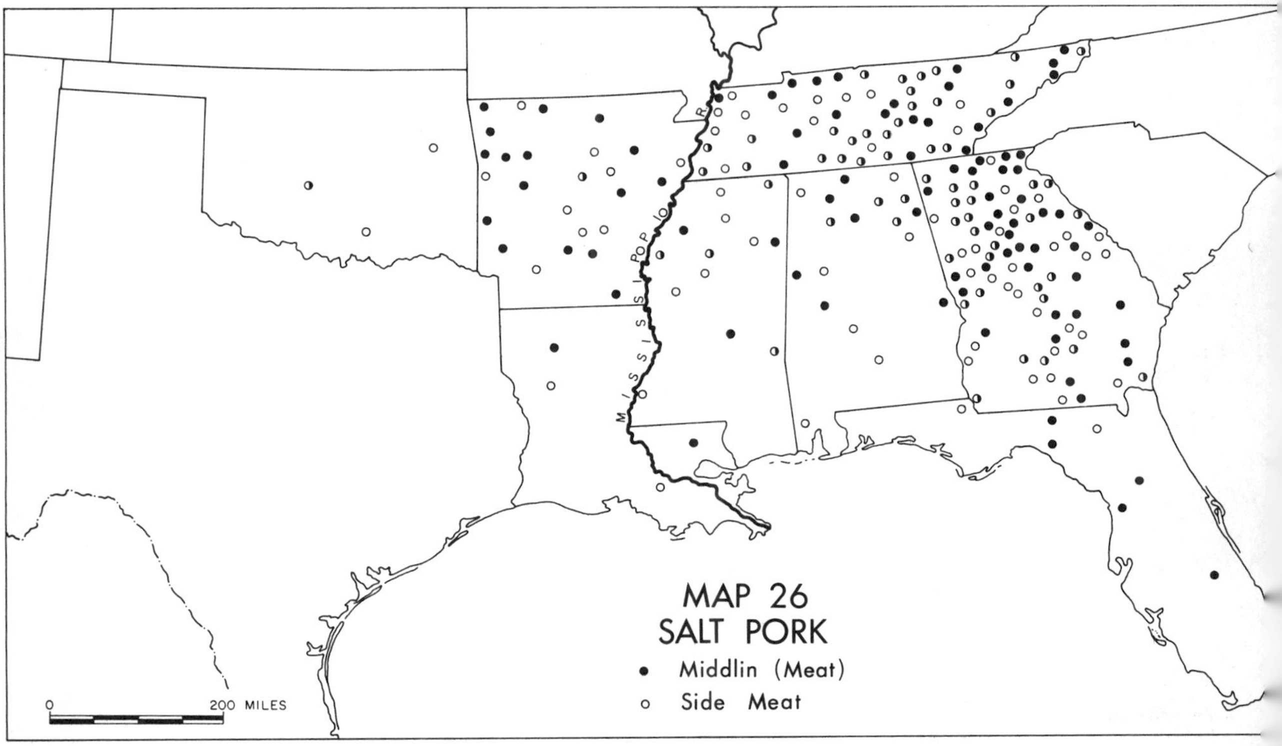
MISSISSIPPI R.
MAP 26
SALT PORK
• Middlin (Meat)
○ Side Meat
0
200 MILES

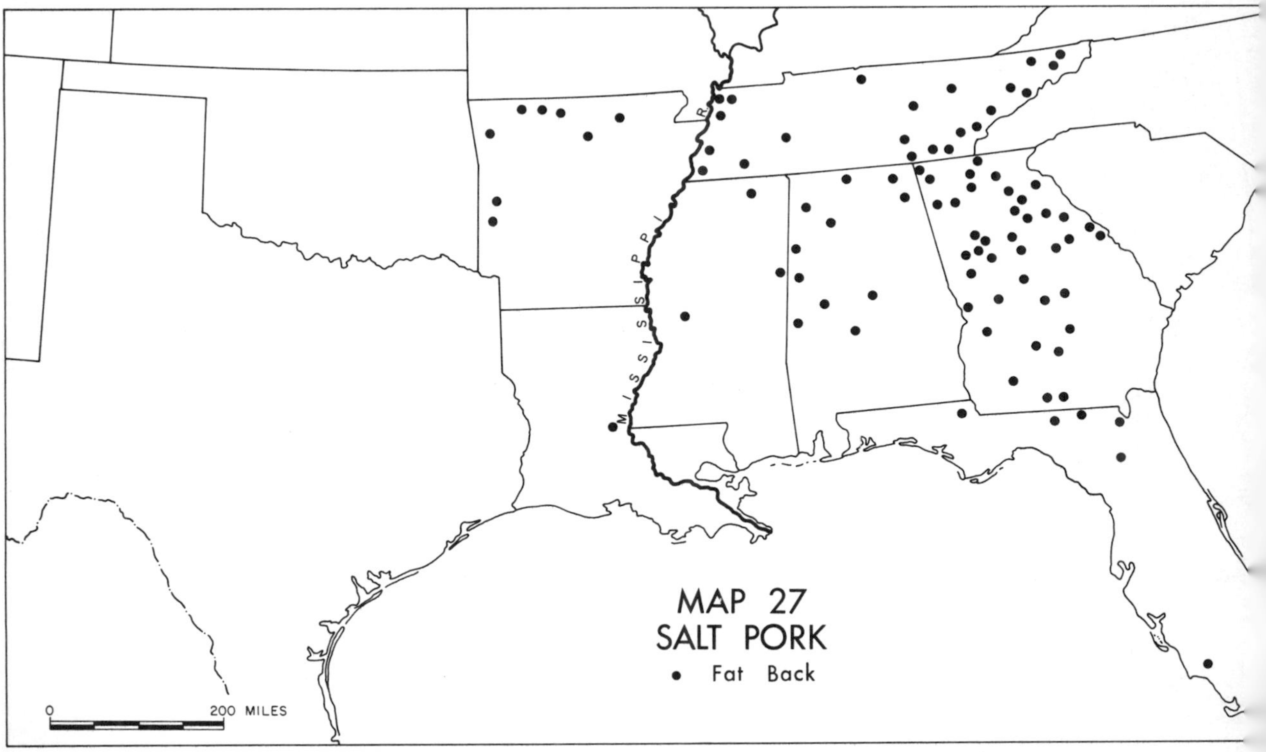
MISSISSIPPI R.
MAP 27
SALT PORK
• Fat Back
0
200 MILES

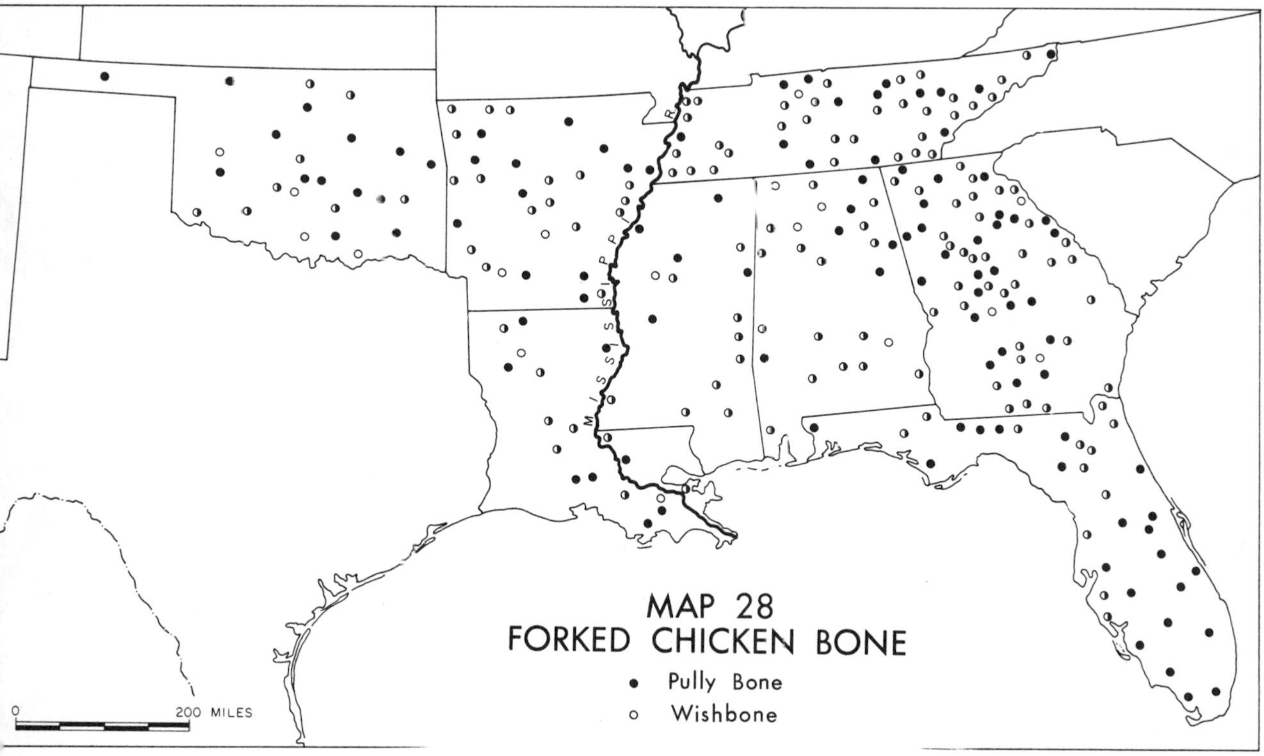
MISSISSIPPI R
0
200 MILES
MAP 28
FORKED CHICKEN BONE
• Pully Bone
○ Wishbone

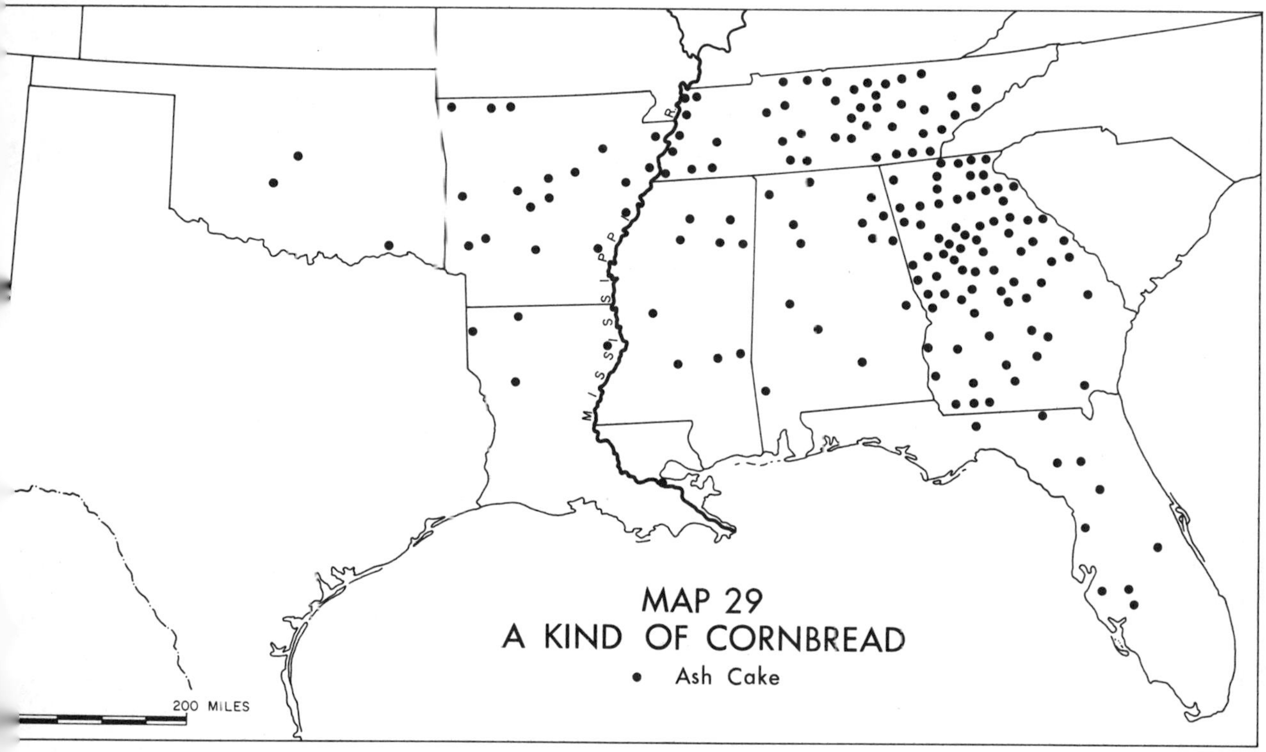
MISSISSIPPI R
200 MILES
MAP 29
A KIND OF CORNBREAD
• Ash Cake

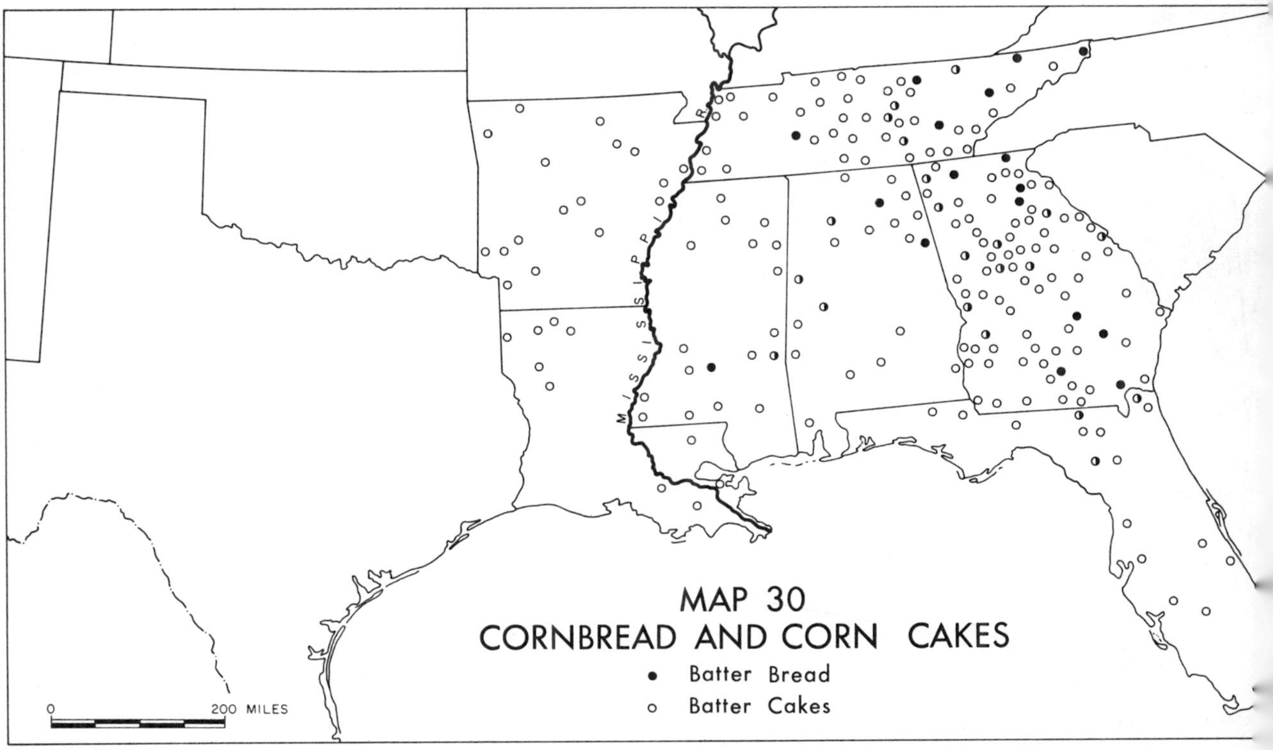
MISSISSIPPI R
MAP 30
CORNBREAD AND CORN CAKES
Batter Bread
Batter Cakes
0
200 MILES

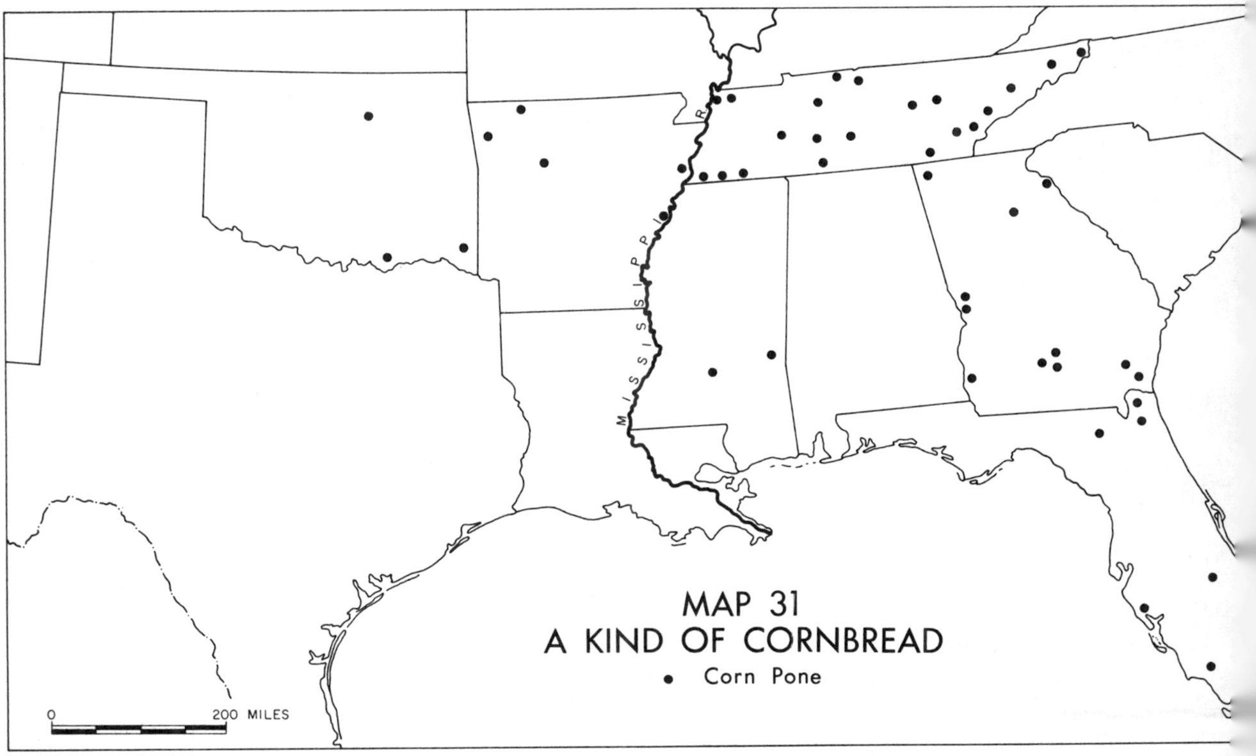
MISSISSIPPI R
MAP 31
A KIND OF CORNBREAD
Corn Pone
0
200 MILES

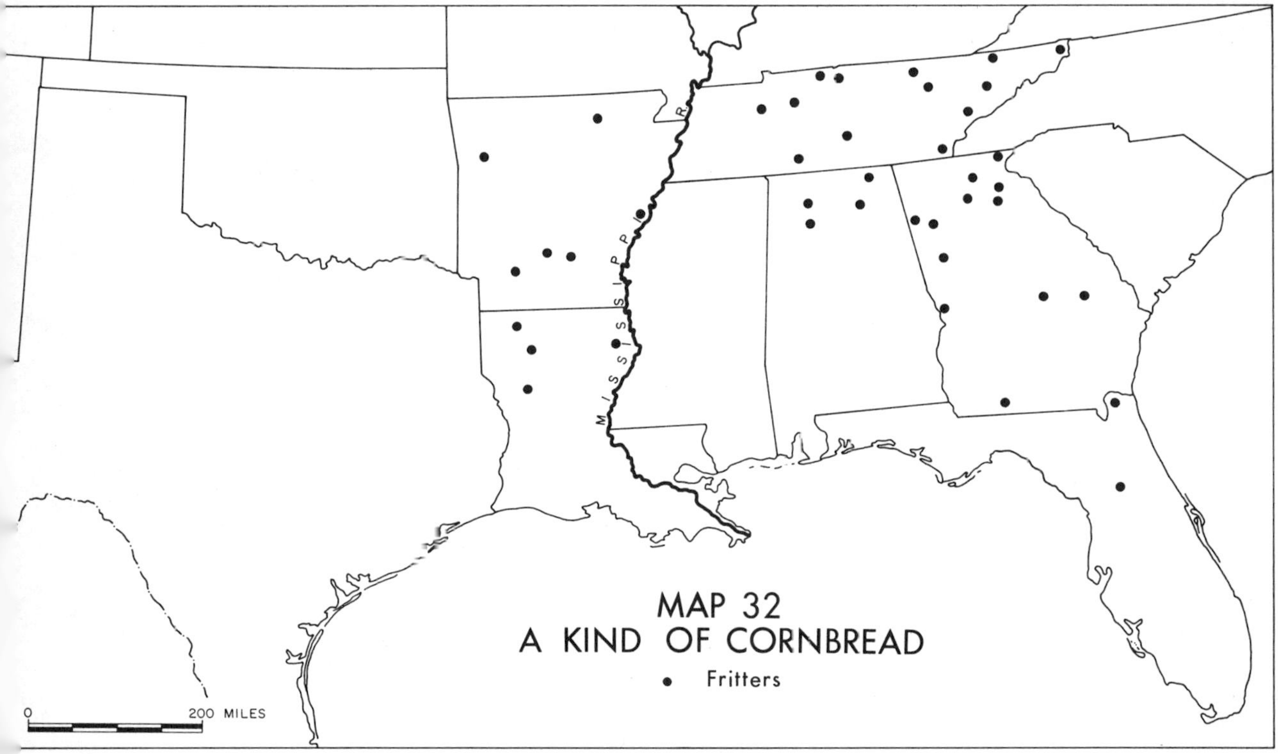
MAP 32
A KIND OF CORNBREAD
Fritters
0
200 MILES
R.
MISSISSIPPI

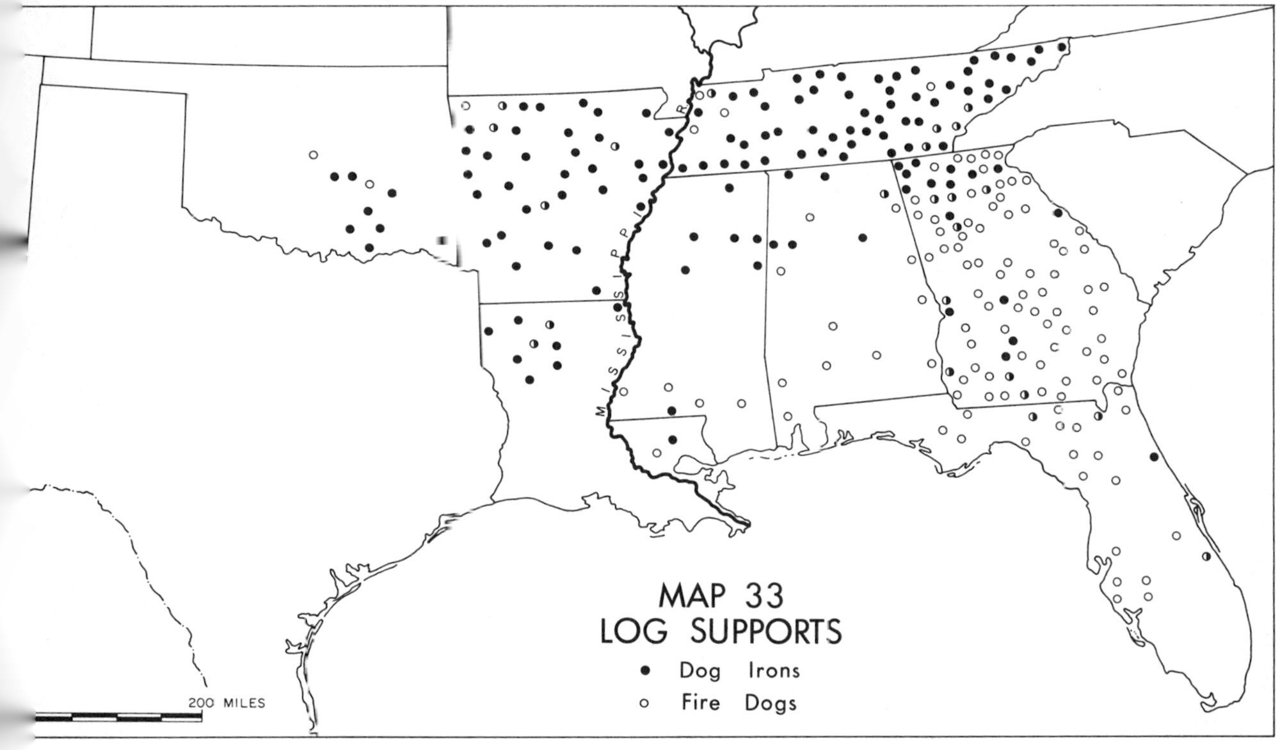
MAP 33
LOG SUPPORTS
Dog Irons
Fire Dogs
200 MILES
R.
MISSISSIPPI

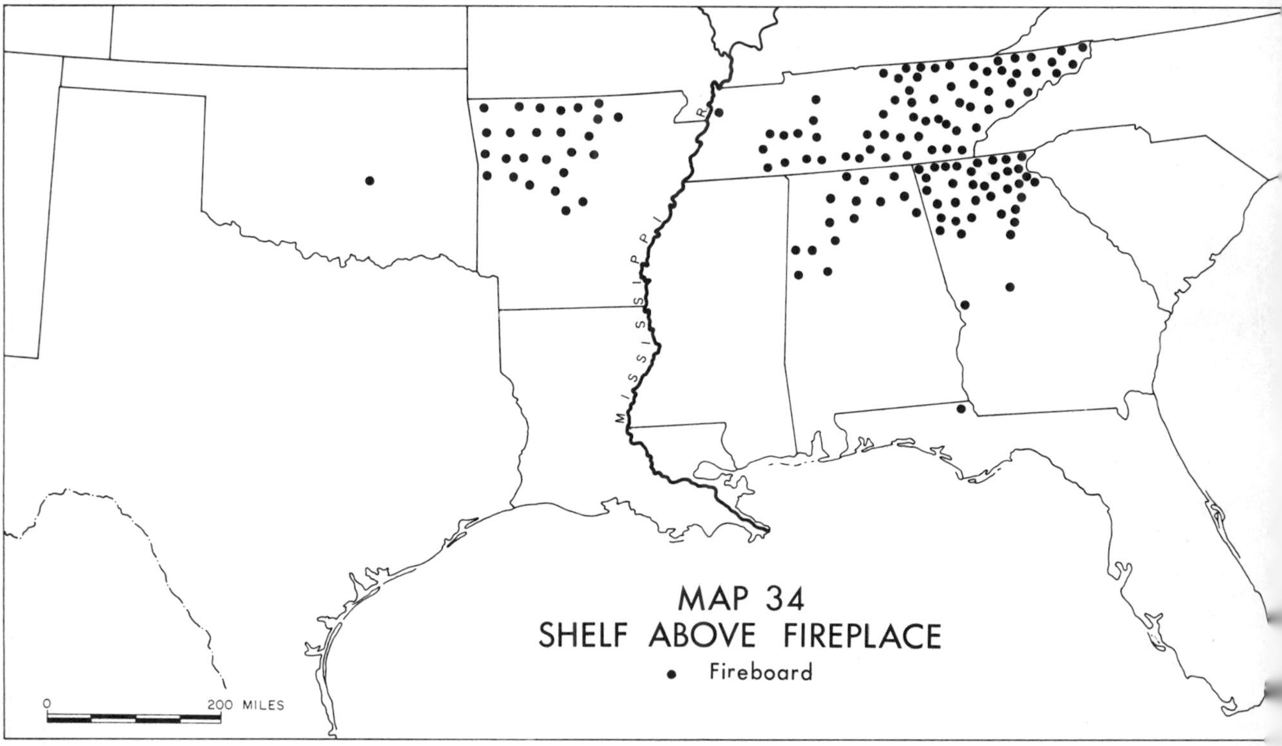
MISSISSIPPI R.
0
200 MILES

MAP 34
SHELF ABOVE FIREPLACE
• Fireboard

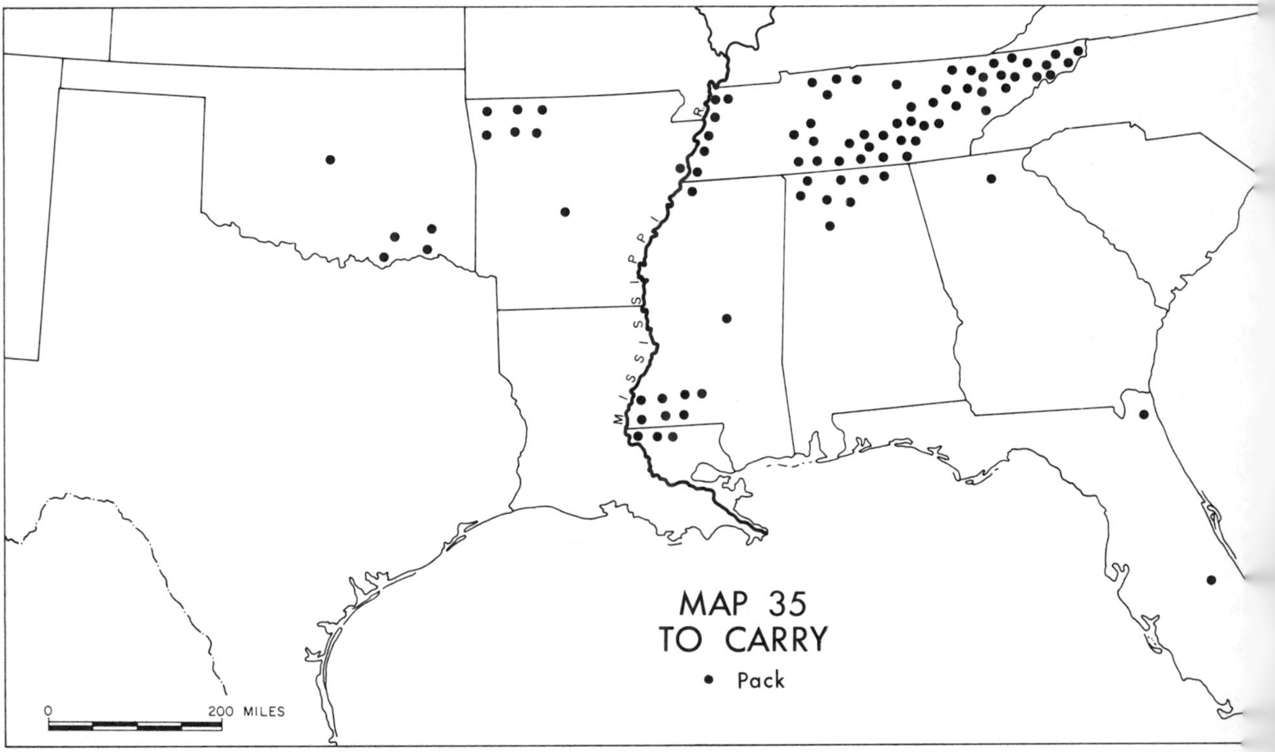
MISSISSIPPI R.
0
200 MILES

MAP 35
TO CARRY
• Pack

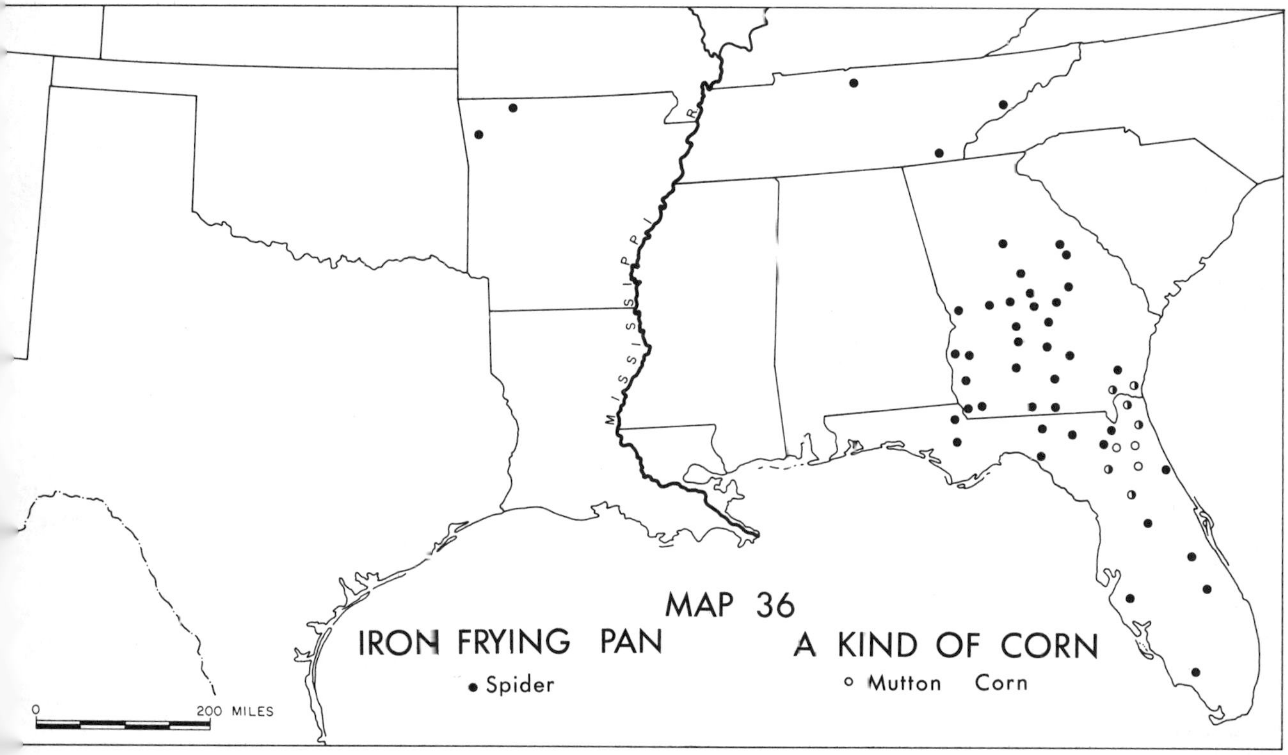
MISSISSIPPI R.
MAP 36
IRON FRYING PAN
• Spider
A KIND OF CORN
○ Mutton Corn
0
200 MILES

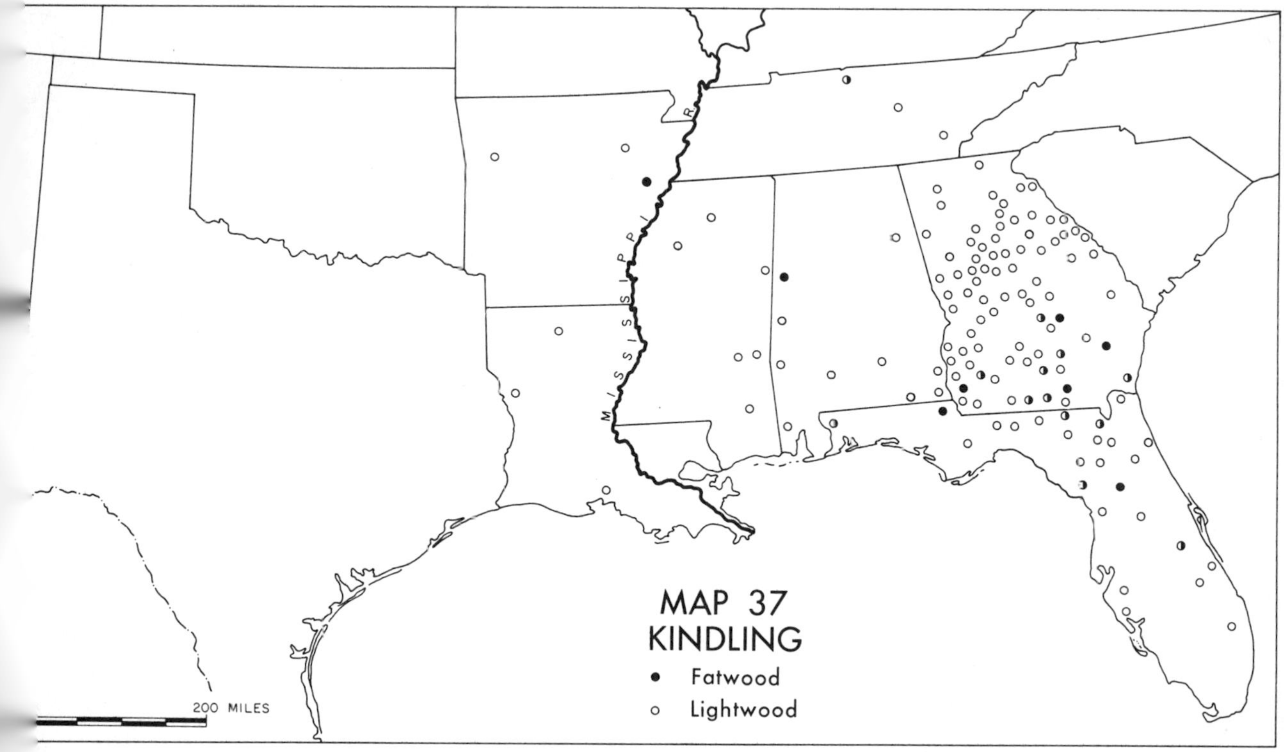
MISSISSIPPI R.
MAP 37
KINDLING
• Fatwood
○ Lightwood
200 MILES

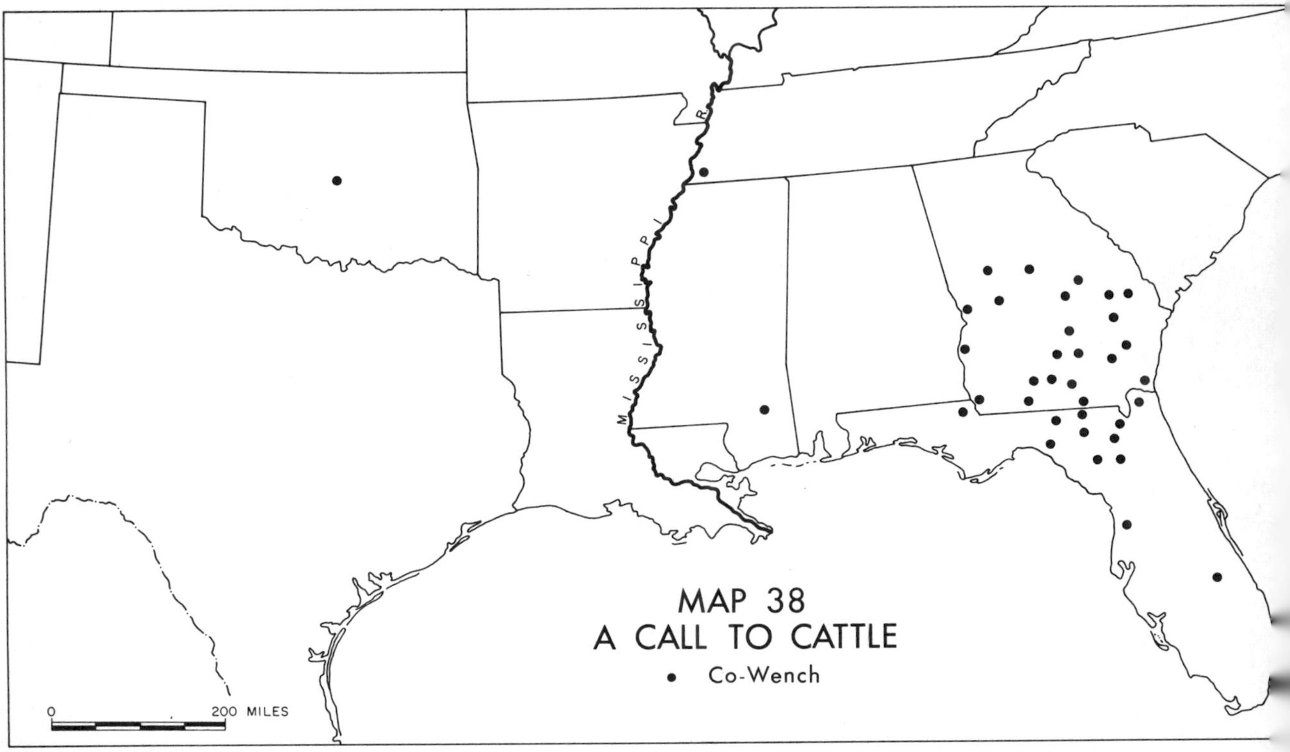
MISSISSIPPI R.
0 200 MILES

MAP 38
A CALL TO CATTLE
• Co-Wench

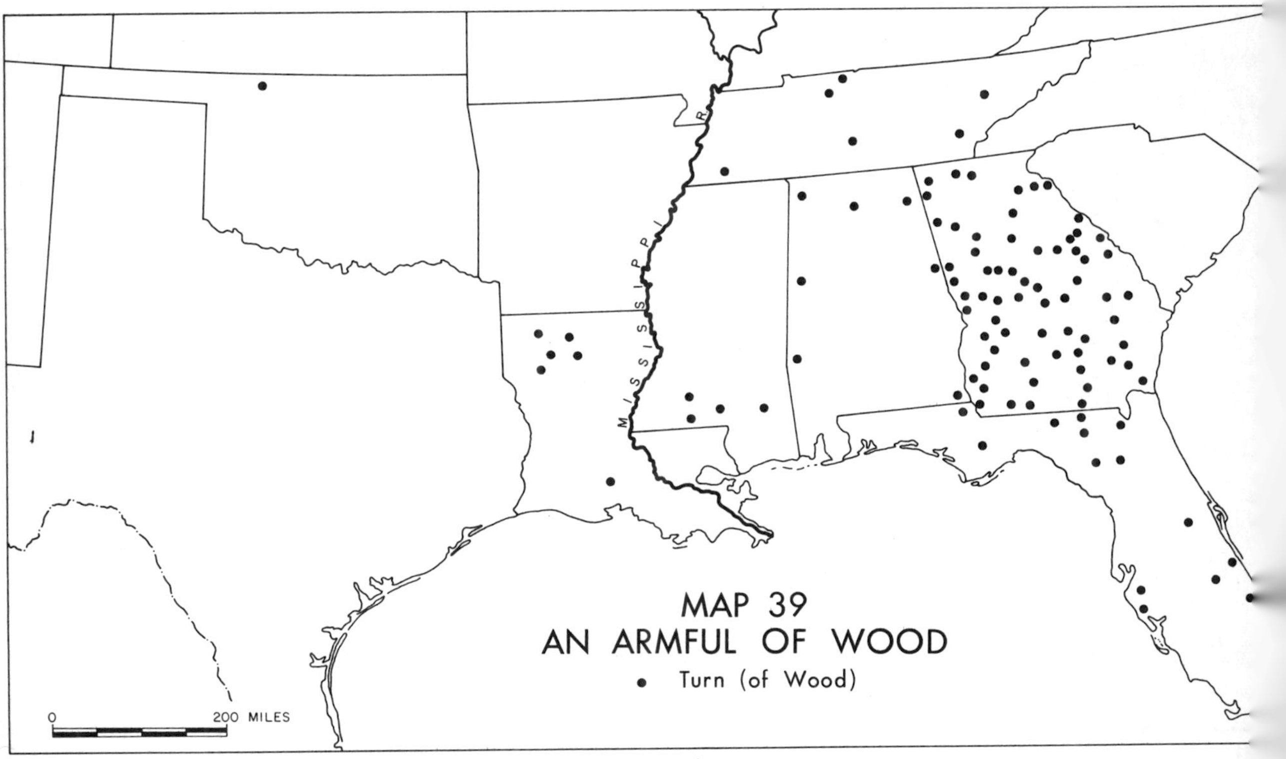
MISSISSIPPI R.
0 200 MILES

MAP 39
AN ARMFUL OF WOOD
• Turn (of Wood)

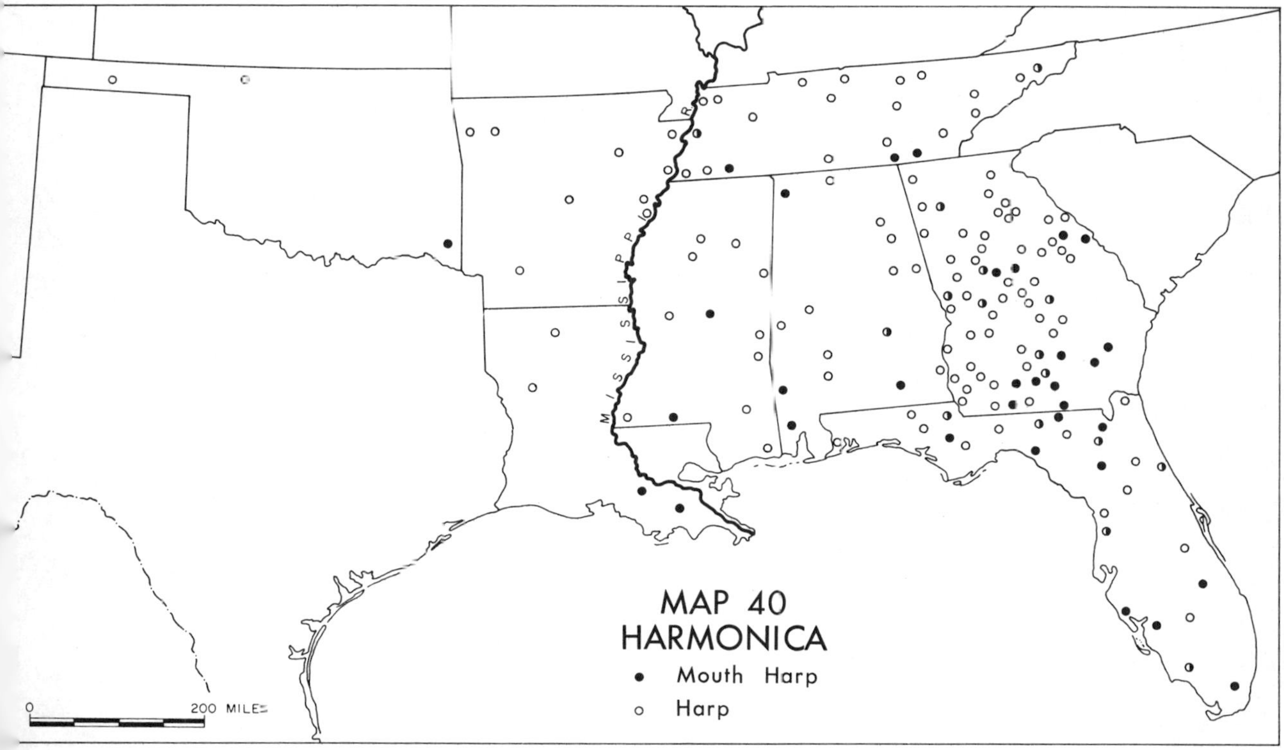
MISSISSIPPI R
MAP 40
HARMONICA
Mouth Harp
Harp
0
200 MILES

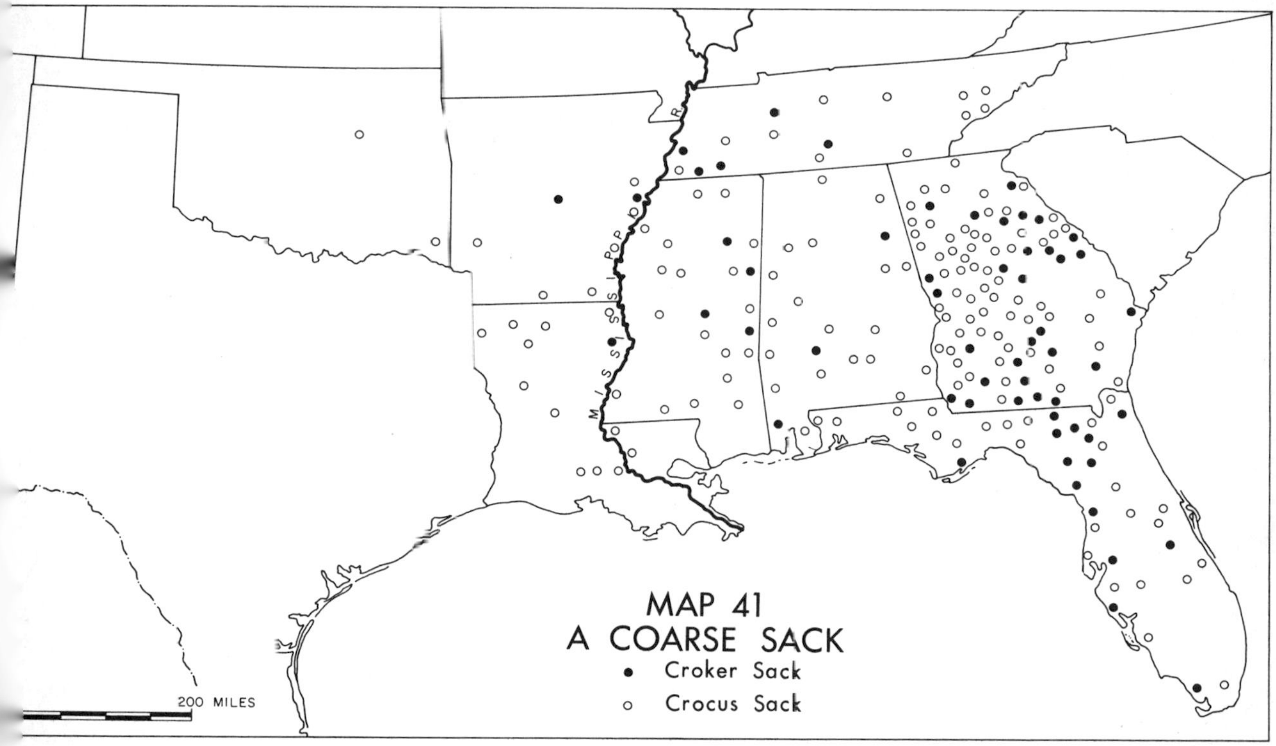
MISSISSIPPI R
MAP 41
A COARSE SACK
Croker Sack
Crocus Sack
200 MILES

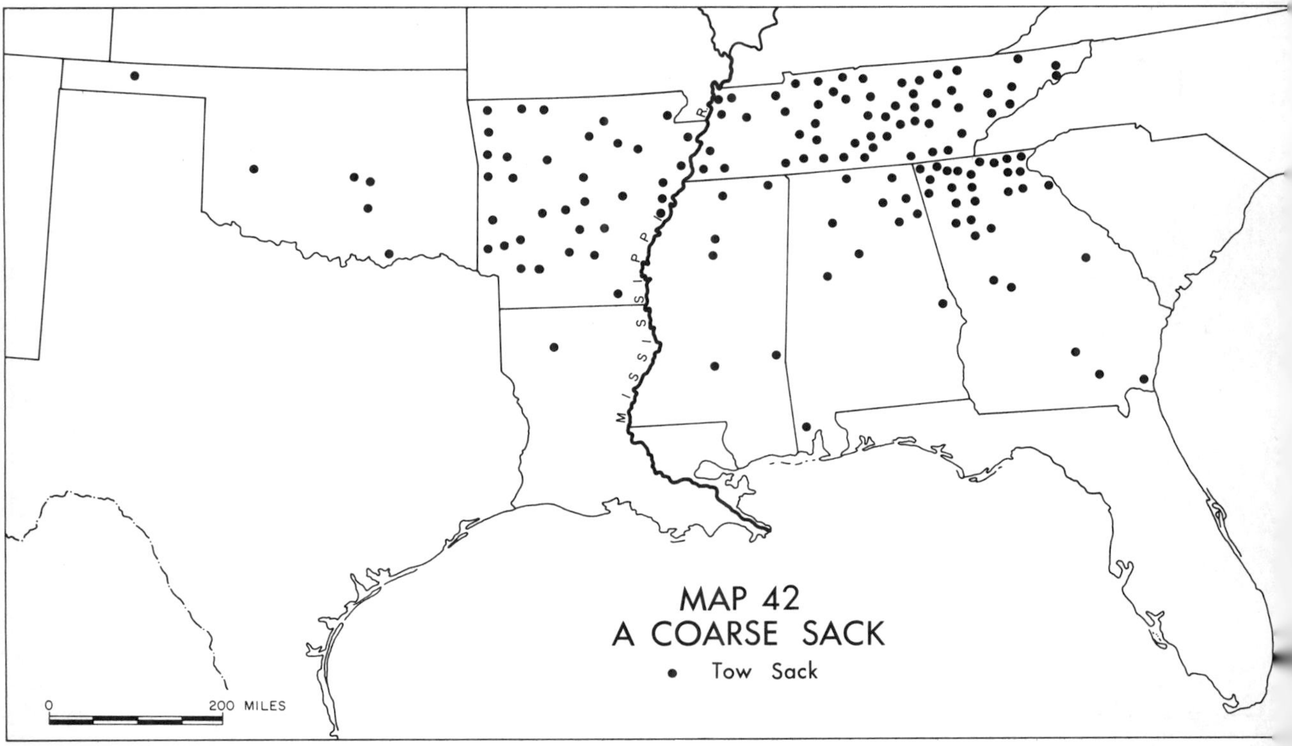
MISSISSIPPI R.
MAP 42
A COARSE SACK
Tow Sack
0 200 MILES

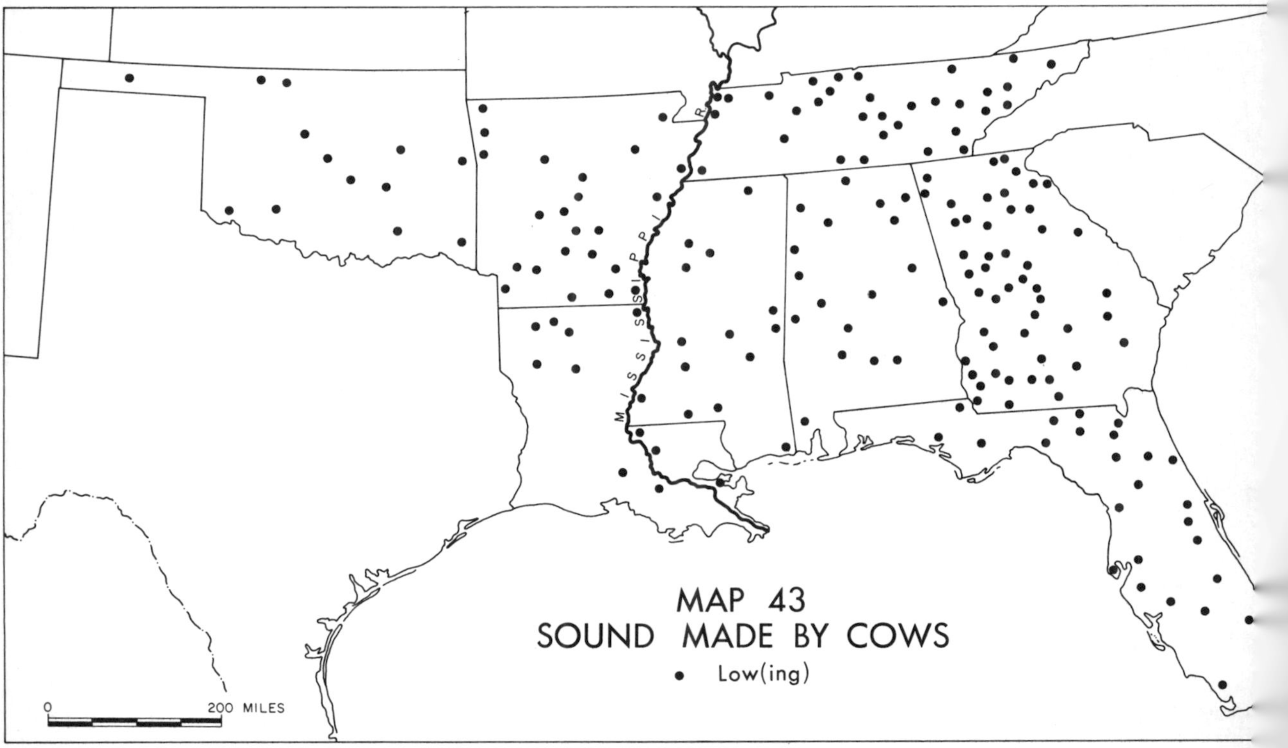
MISSISSIPPI R.
MAP 43
SOUND MADE BY COWS
Low(ing)
0 200 MILES

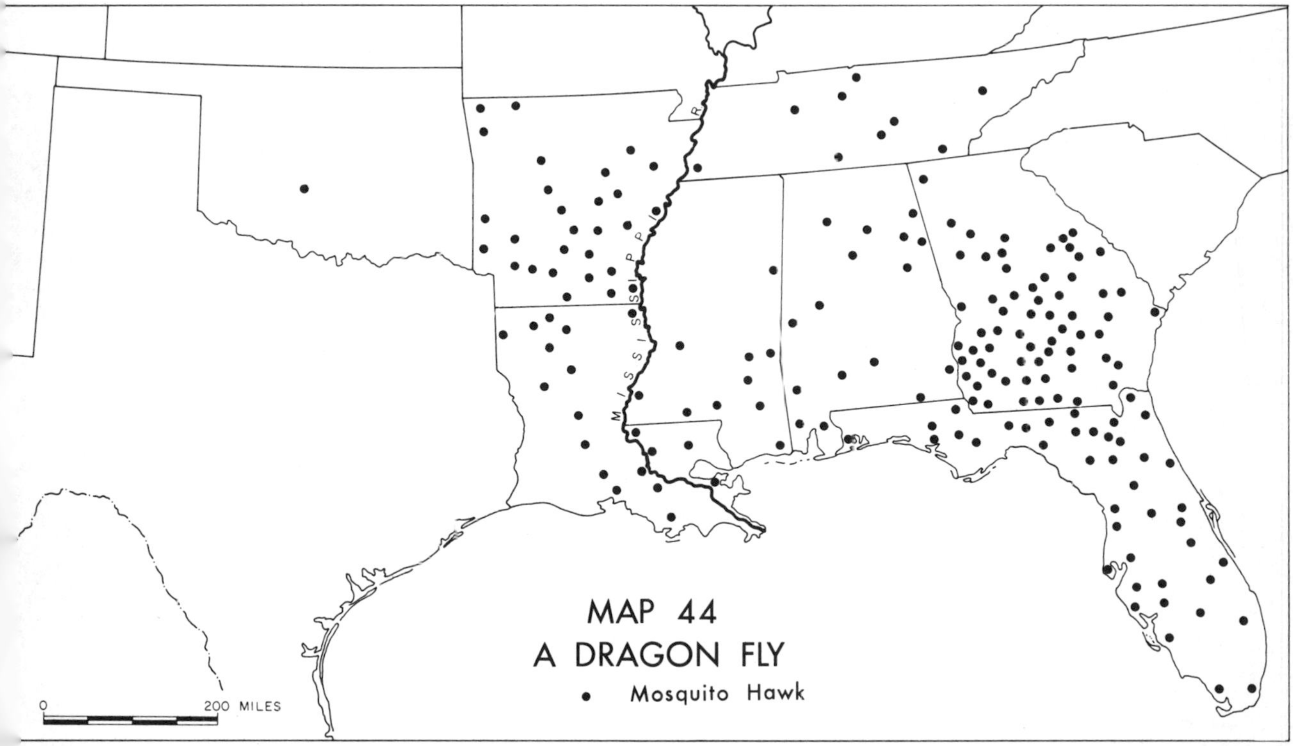
MISSISSIPPI R.
0
200 MILES

MAP 44
A DRAGON FLY
• Mosquito Hawk

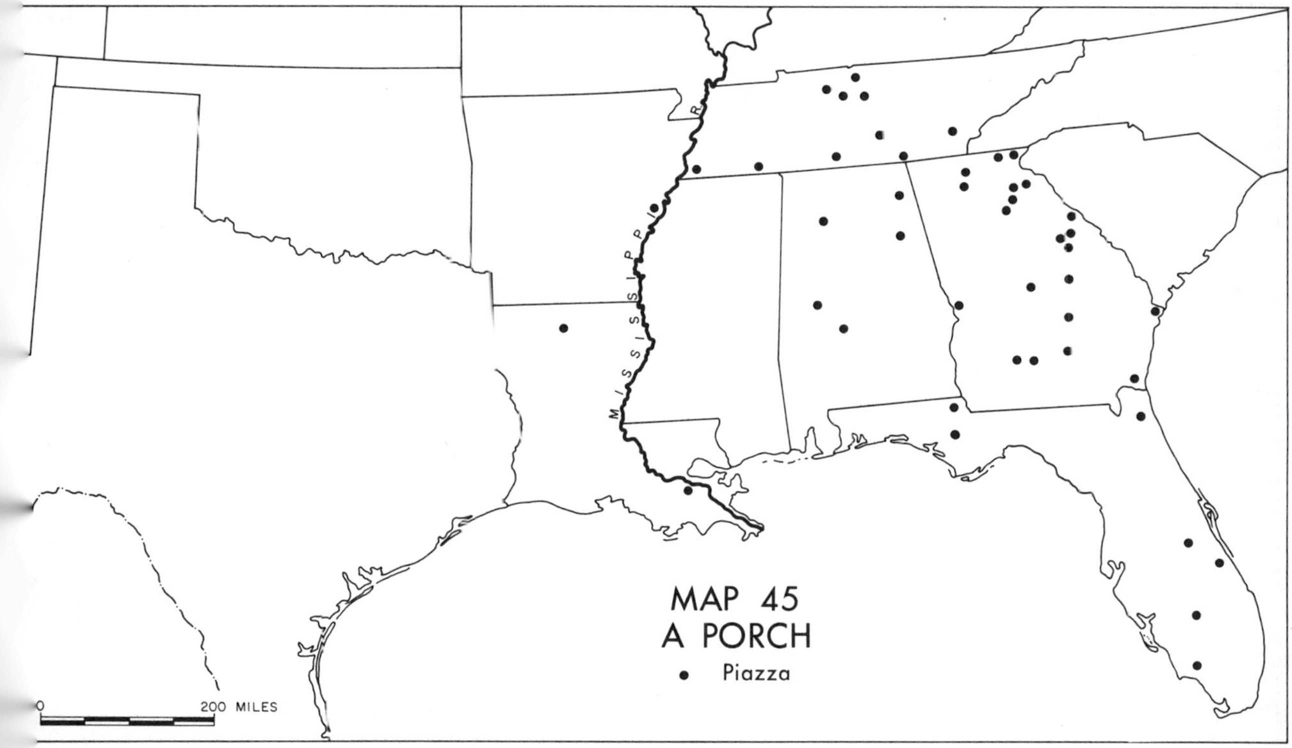
MISSISSIPPI R.
0
200 MILES

MAP 45
A PORCH
• Piazza

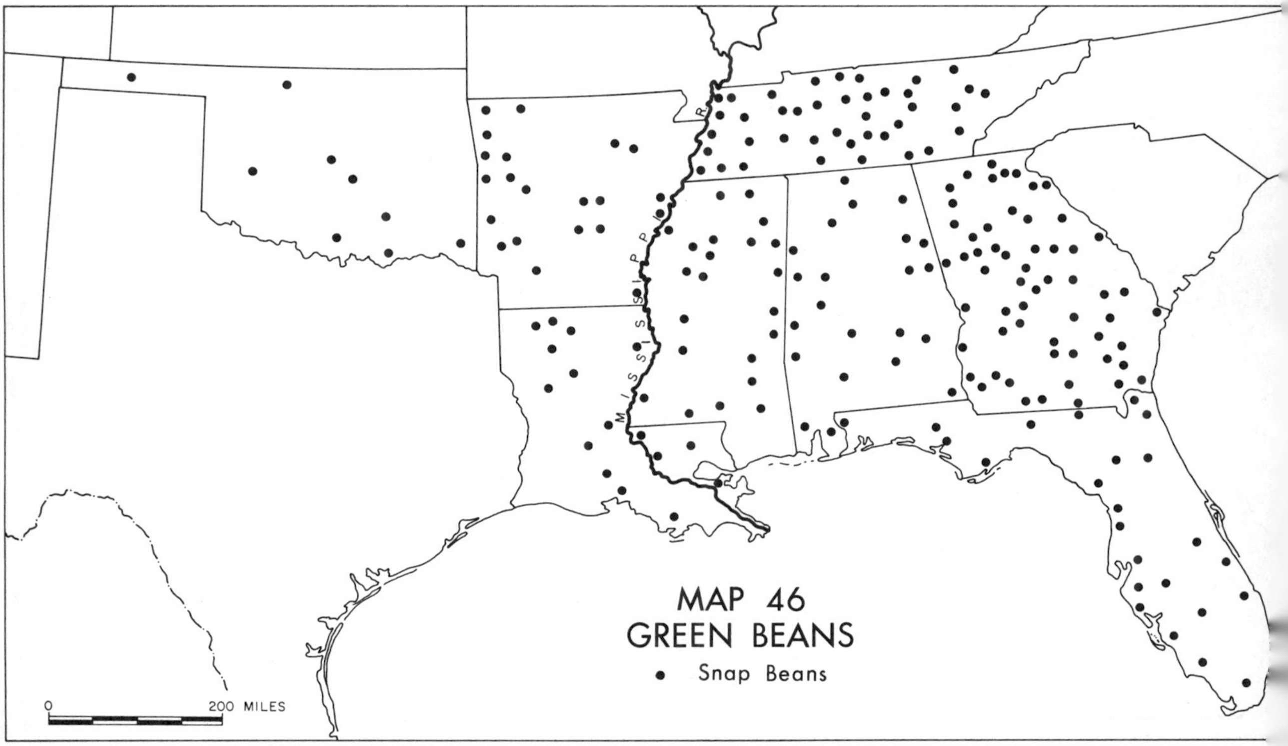
MISSISSIPPI R.
MAP 46
GREEN BEANS
Snap Beans
0
200 MILES

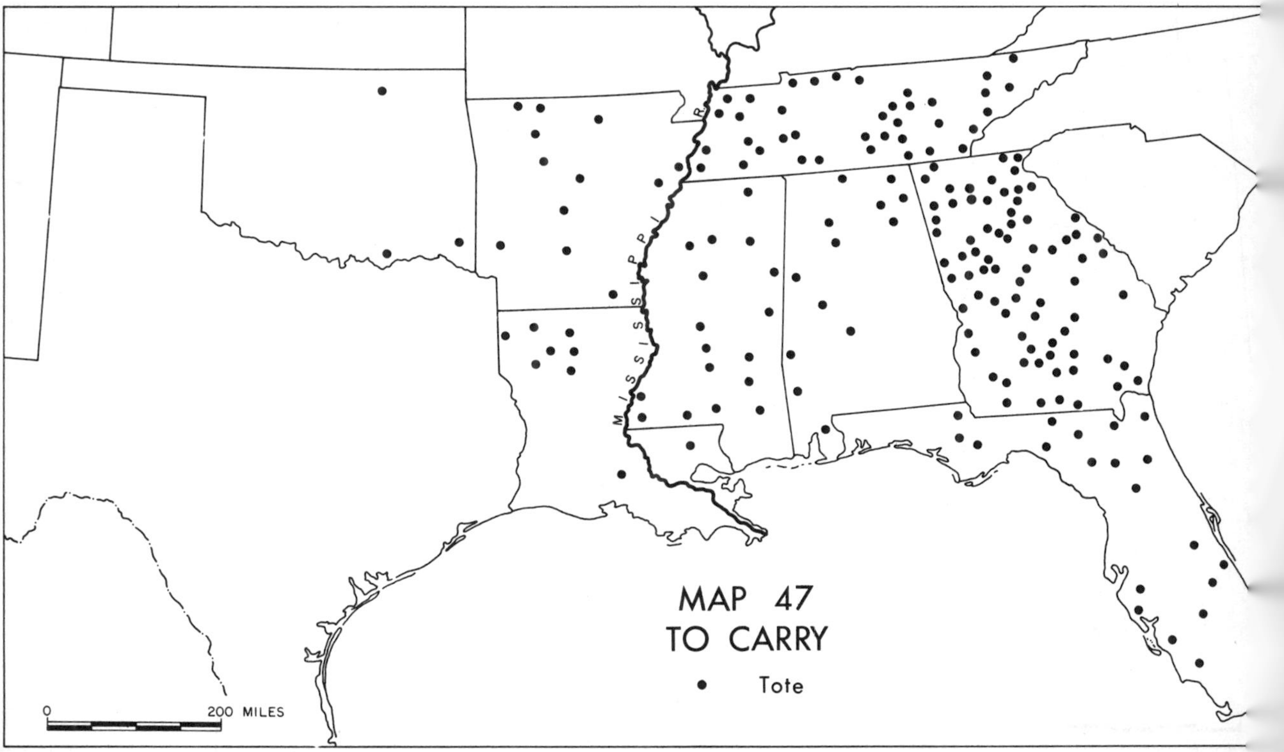
MISSISSIPPI R.
MAP 47
TO CARRY
Tote
0
200 MILES

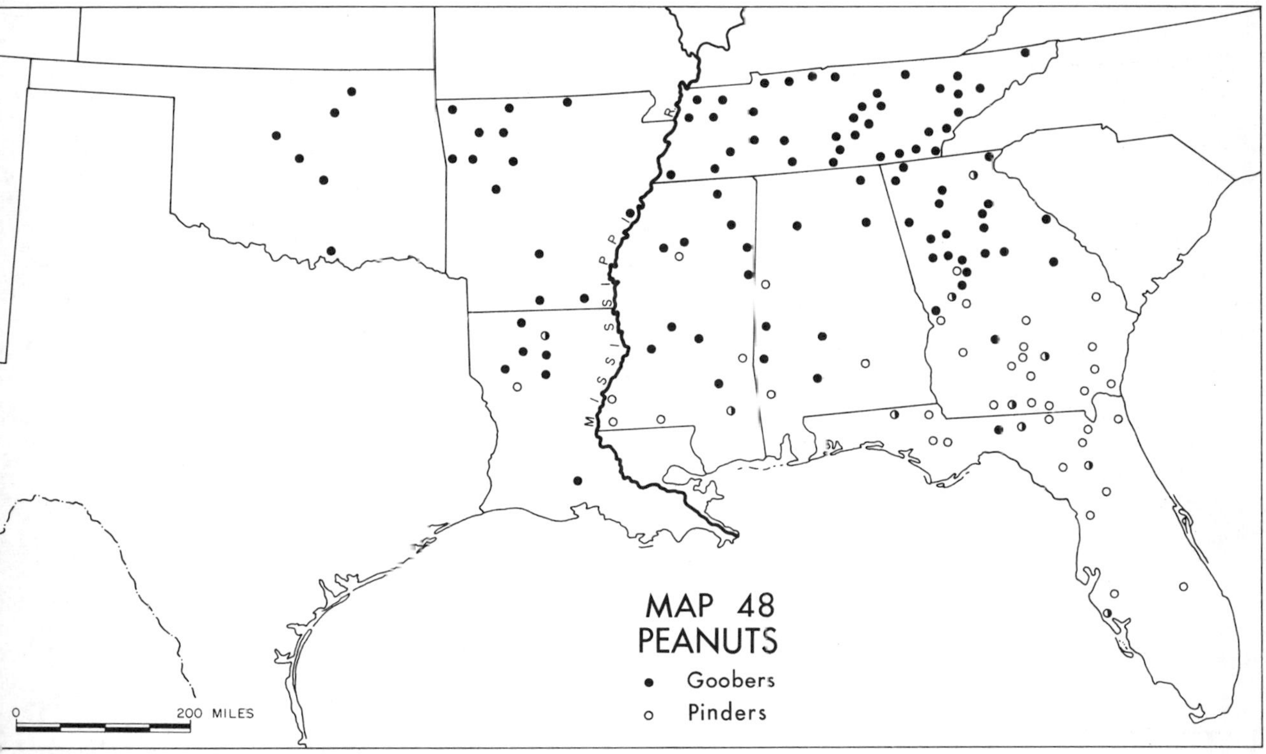
R.
MISSISSIPPI
MAP 48
PEANUTS
Goobers
Pinders
0
200 MILES

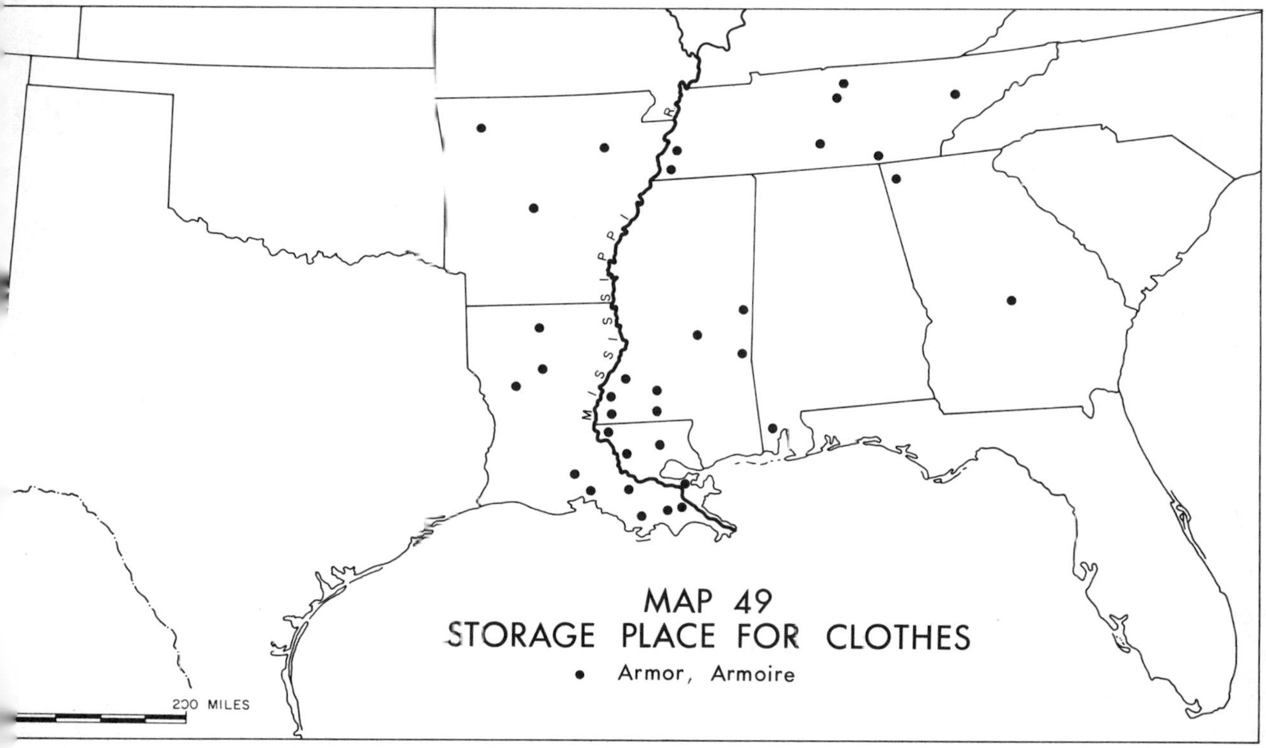
R.
MISSISSIPPI
MAP 49
STORAGE PLACE FOR CLOTHES
Armor, Armoire
200 MILES

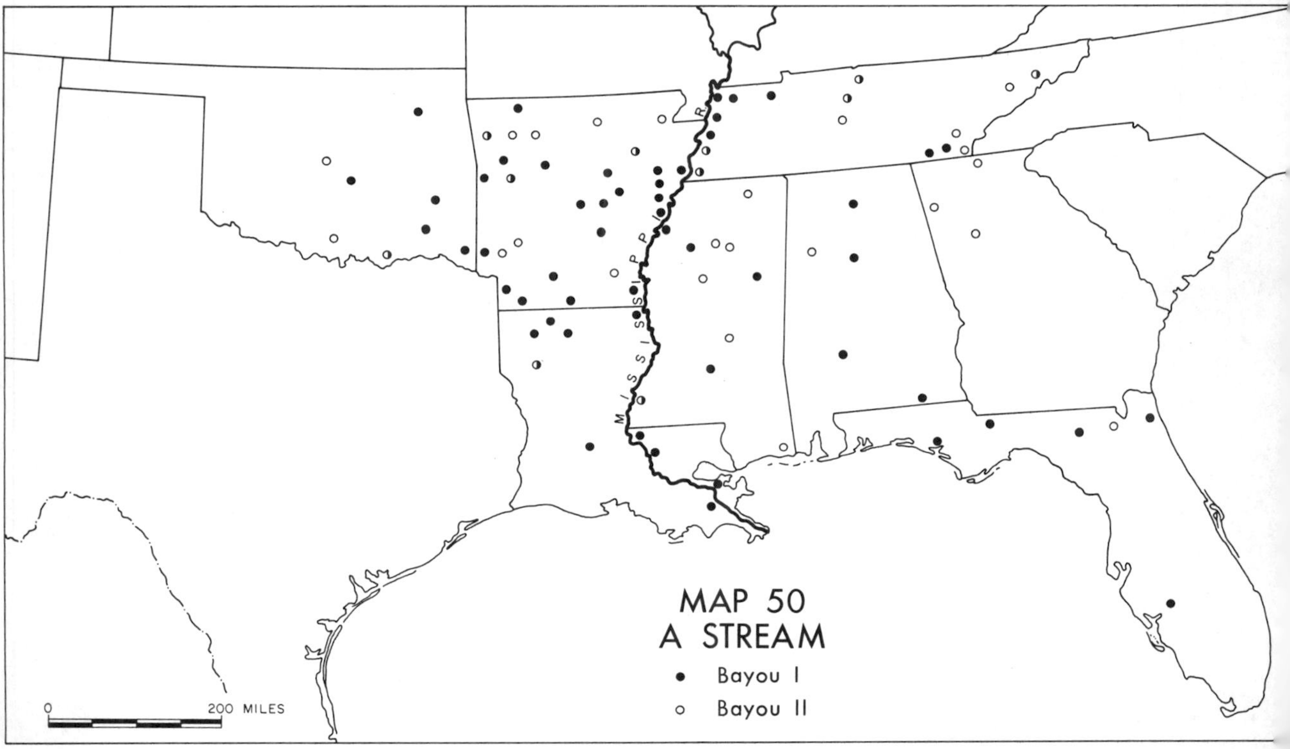
MISSISSIPPI R.
MAP 50
A STREAM
• Bayou I
○ Bayou II
0 200 MILES

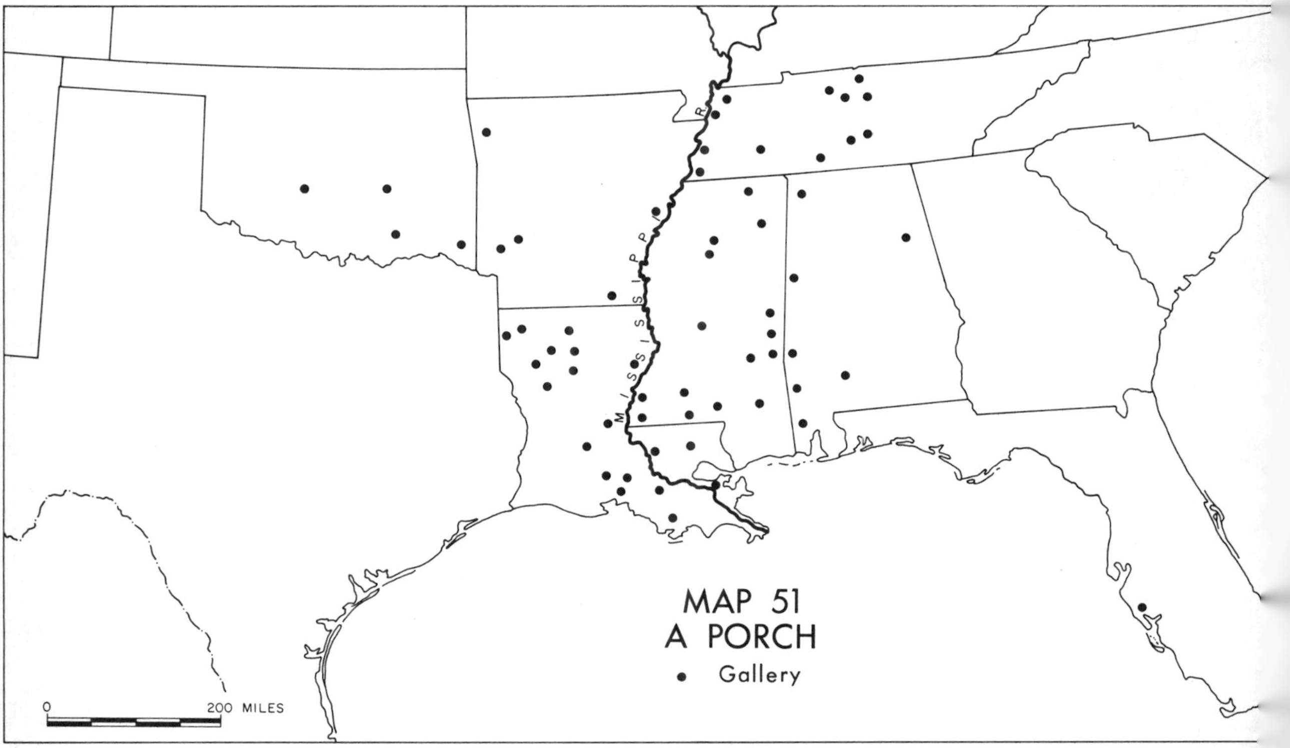
MISSISSIPPI R.
MAP 51
A PORCH
• Gallery
0 200 MILES

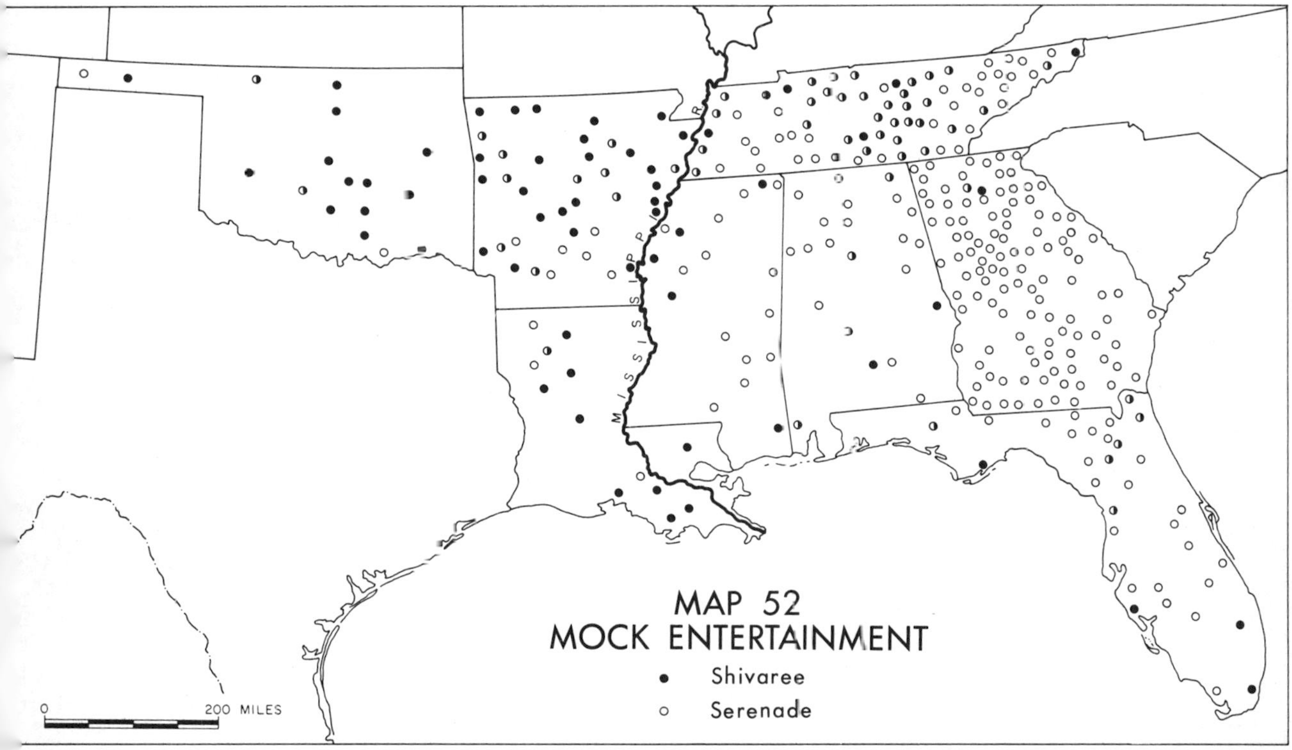
MISSISSIPPI R.
0
200 MILES
Shivaree
Serenade

MAP 52
MOCK ENTERTAINMENT

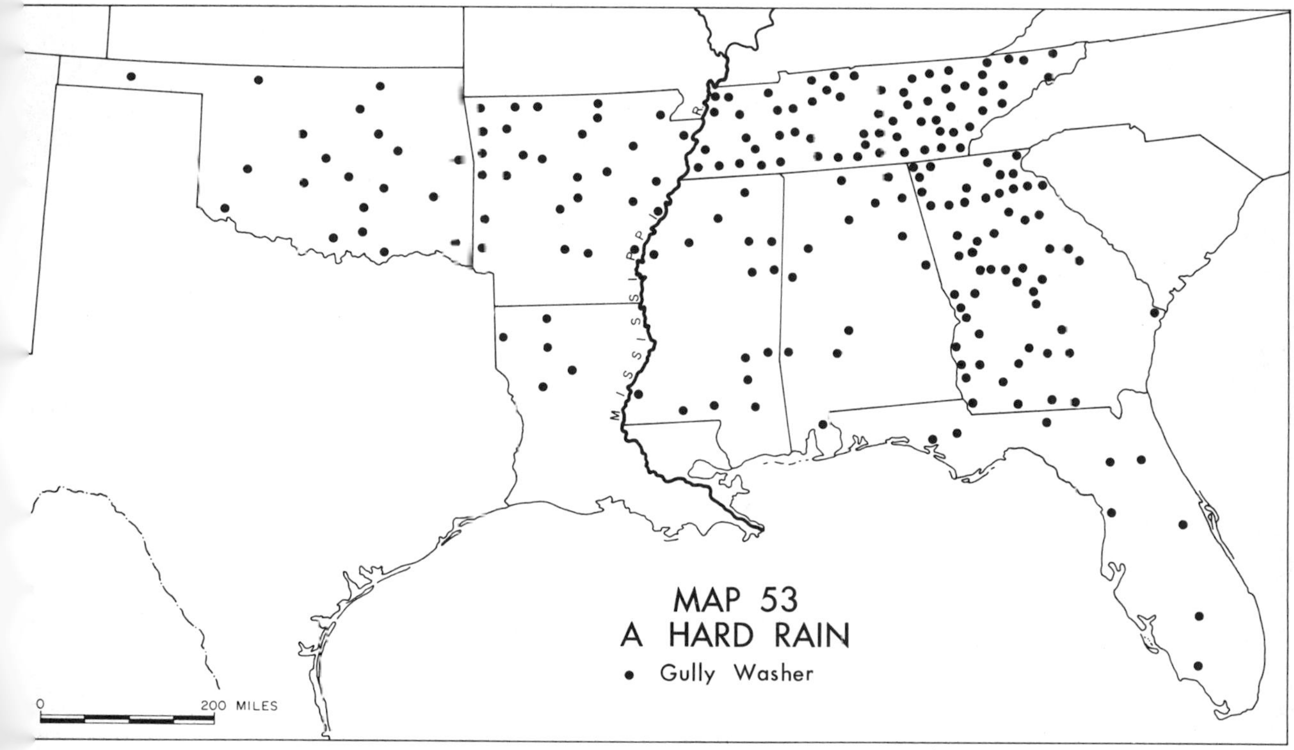
MISSISSIPPI R.
0
200 MILES
Gully Washer

MAP 53
A HARD RAIN

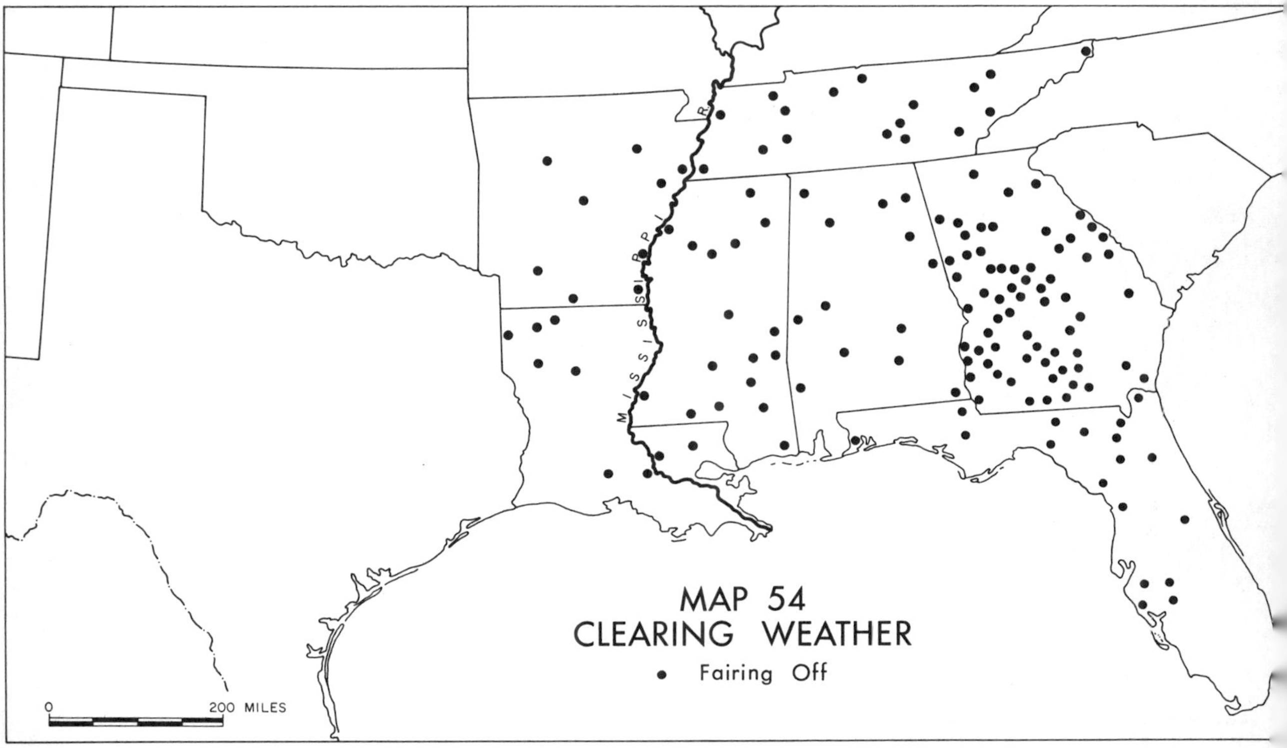
MISSISSIPPI R.
0
200 MILES

MAP 54
CLEARING WEATHER
• Fairing Off

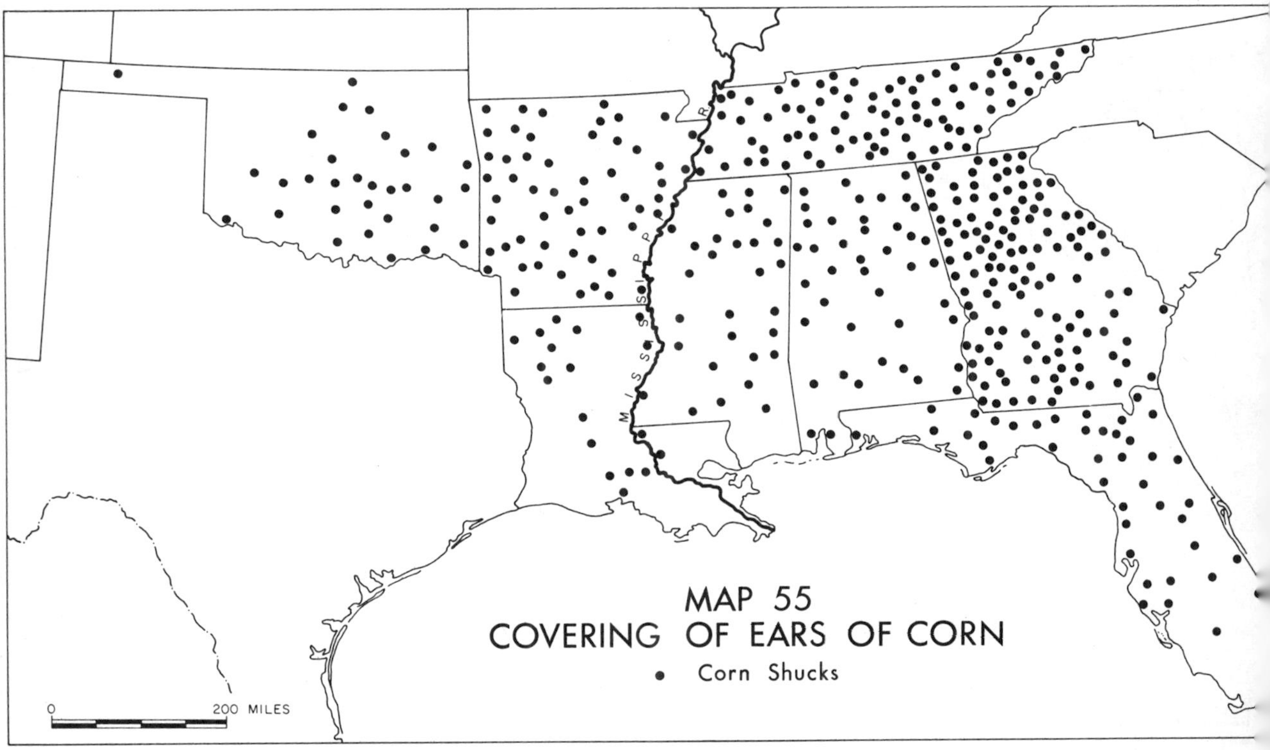
MISSISSIPPI R.
0
200 MILES

MAP 55
COVERING OF EARS OF CORN
• Corn Shucks

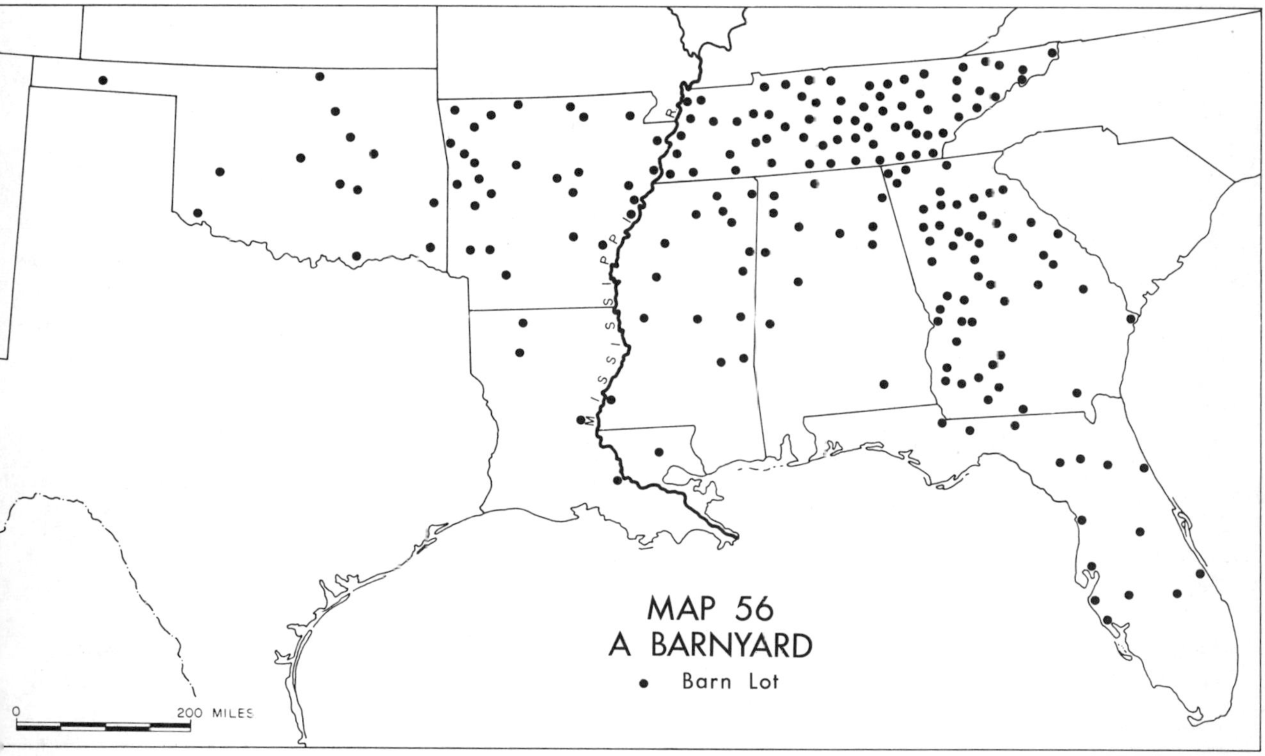
MISSISSIPPI R
0
200 MILES

MAP 56
A BARNYARD
• Barn Lot

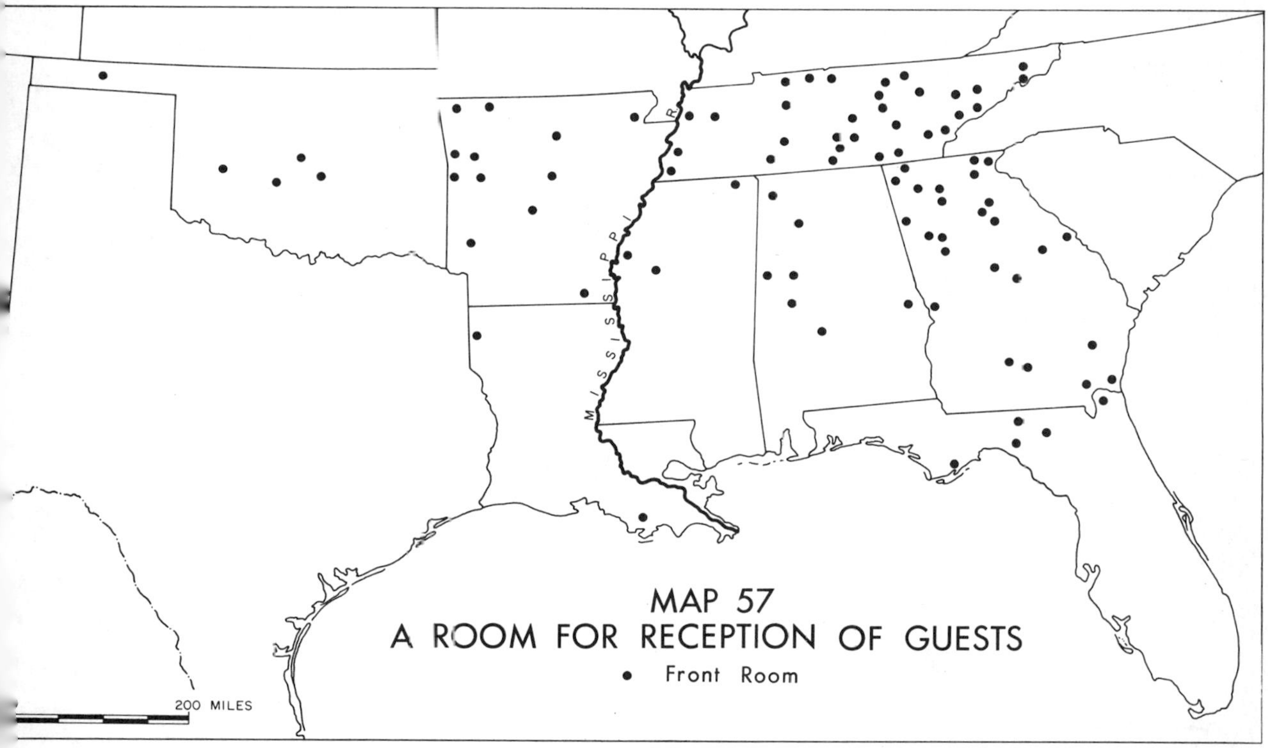
MISSISSIPPI R
200 MILES

MAP 57
A ROOM FOR RECEPTION OF GUESTS
• Front Room

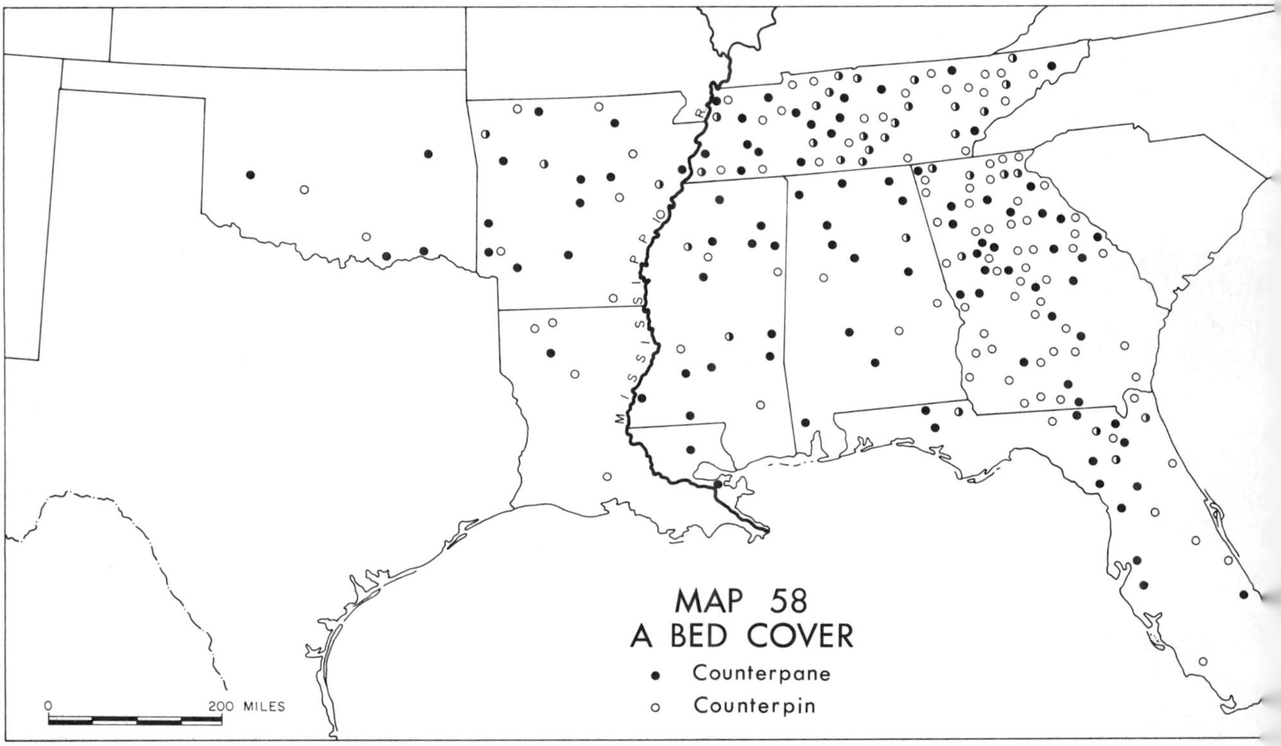
MISSISSIPPI R.
MAP 58
A BED COVER
Counterpane
Counterpin
0
200 MILES

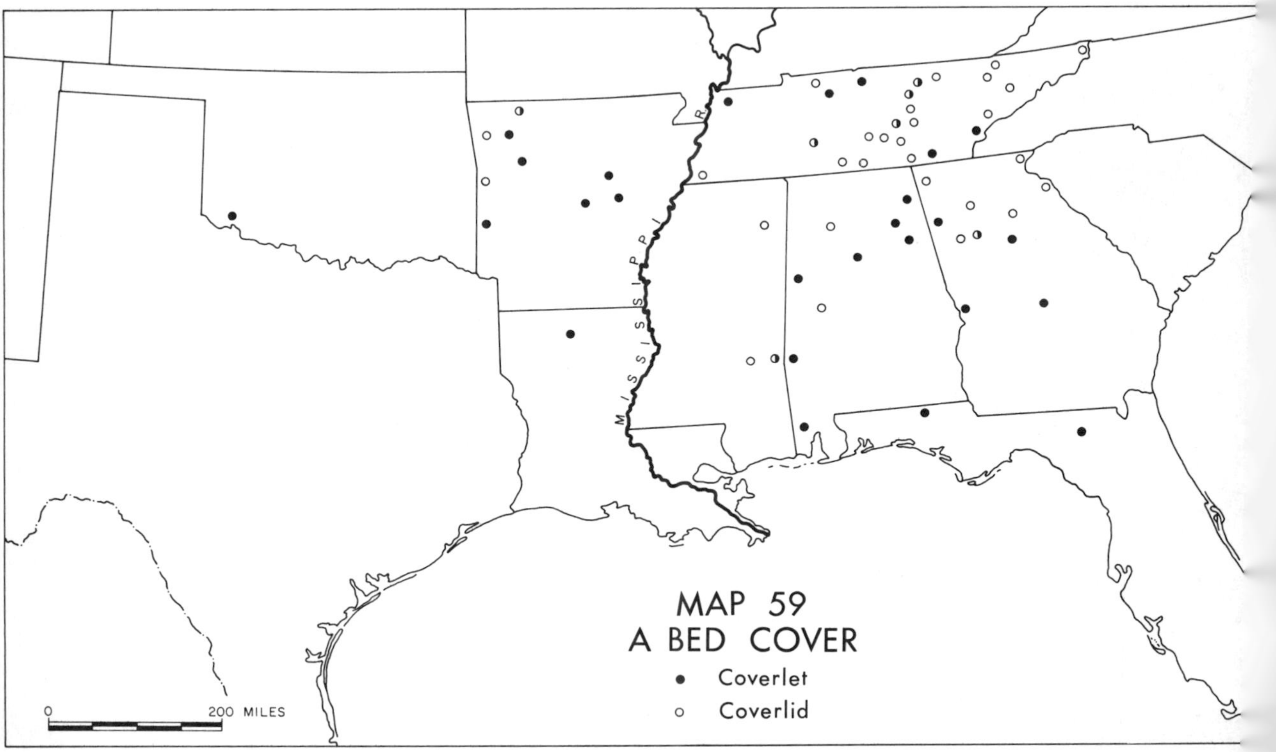
MISSISSIPPI R.
MAP 59
A BED COVER
Coverlet
Coverlid
0
200 MILES

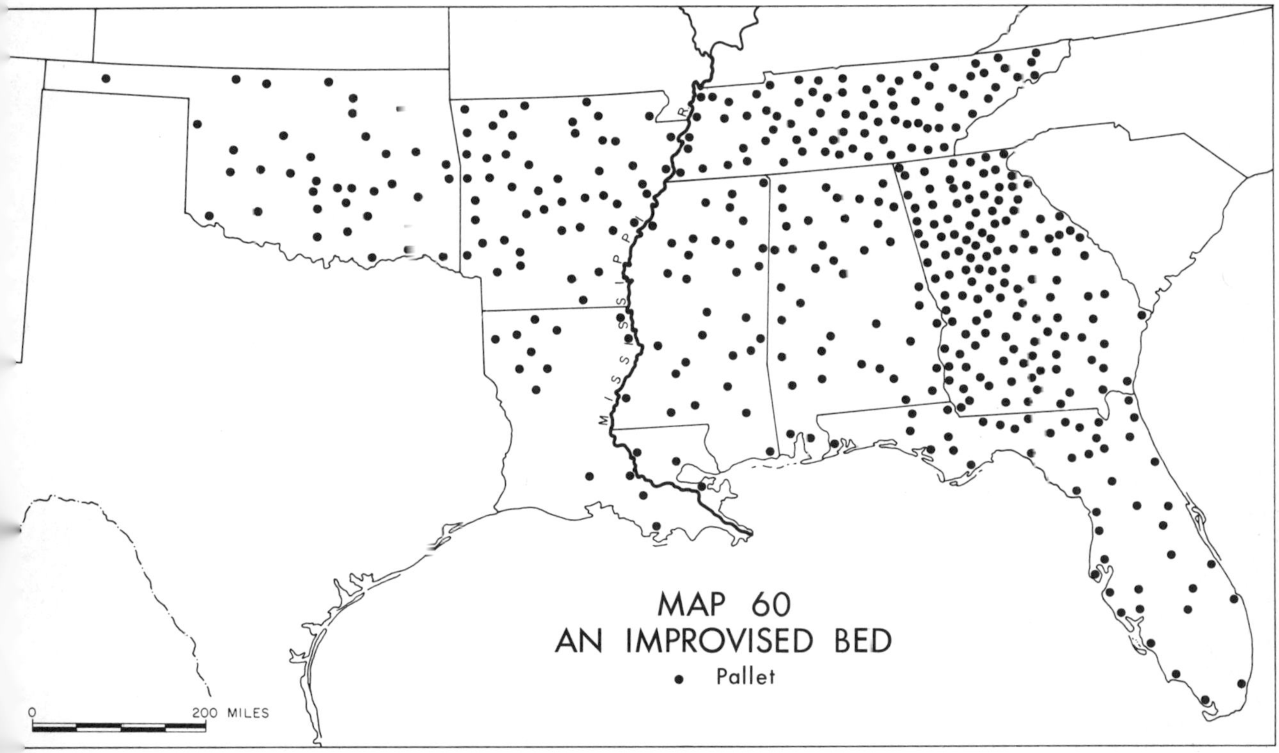
MISSISSIPPI R.
MAP 60
AN IMPROVISED BED
• Pallet
0 200 MILES

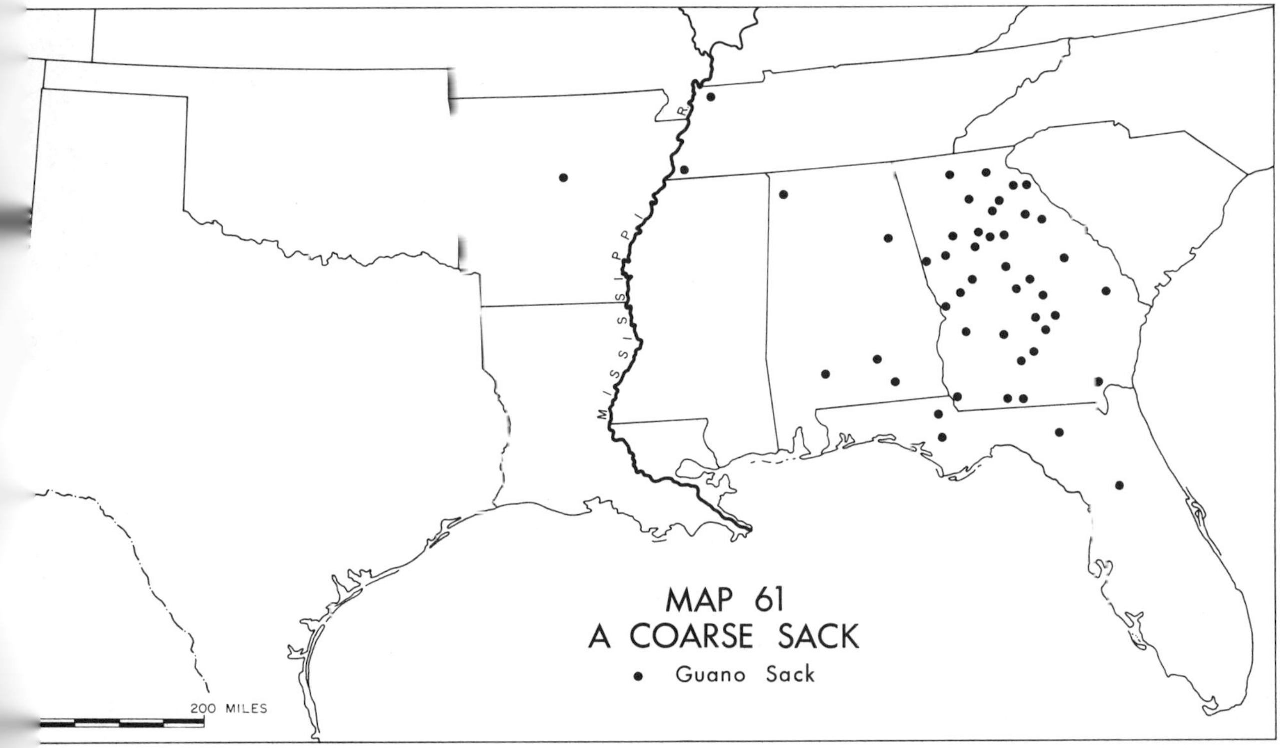
MISSISSIPPI R.
MAP 61
A COARSE SACK
• Guano Sack
200 MILES

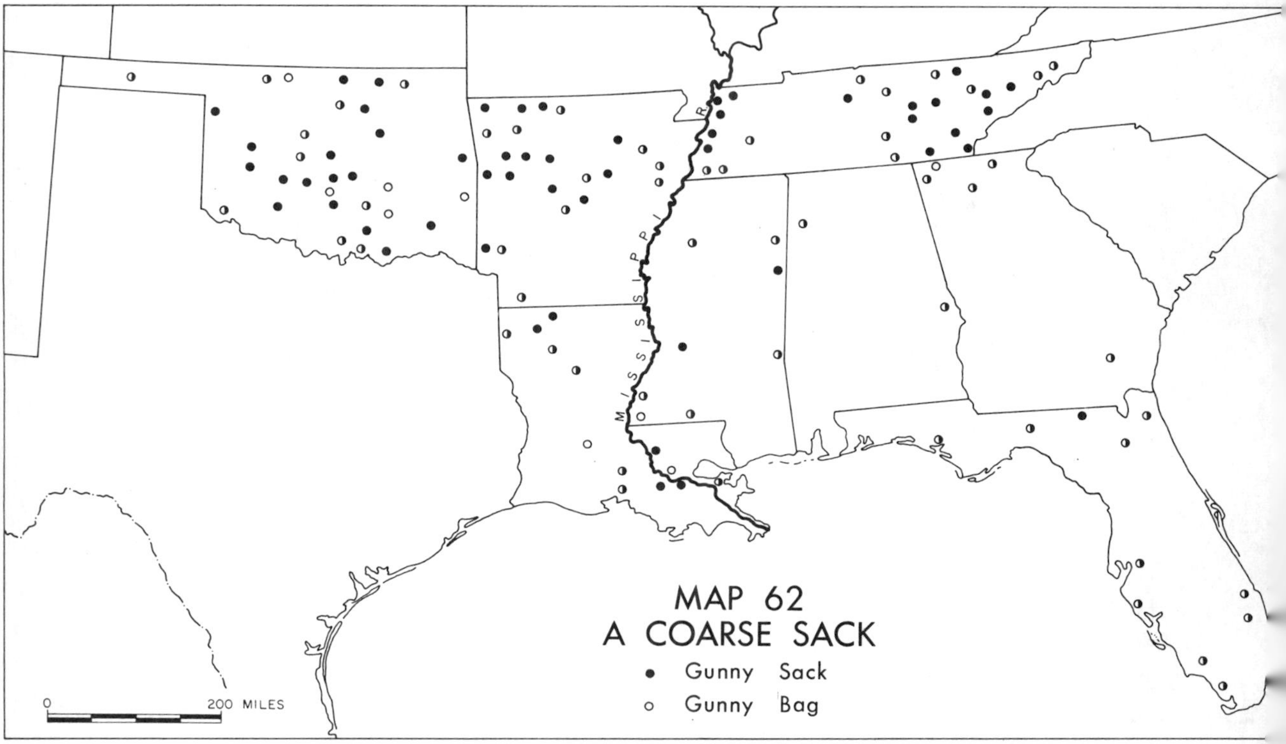
MISSISSIPPI R.
MAP 62
A COARSE SACK
• Gunny Sack
○ Gunny Bag
0
200 MILES

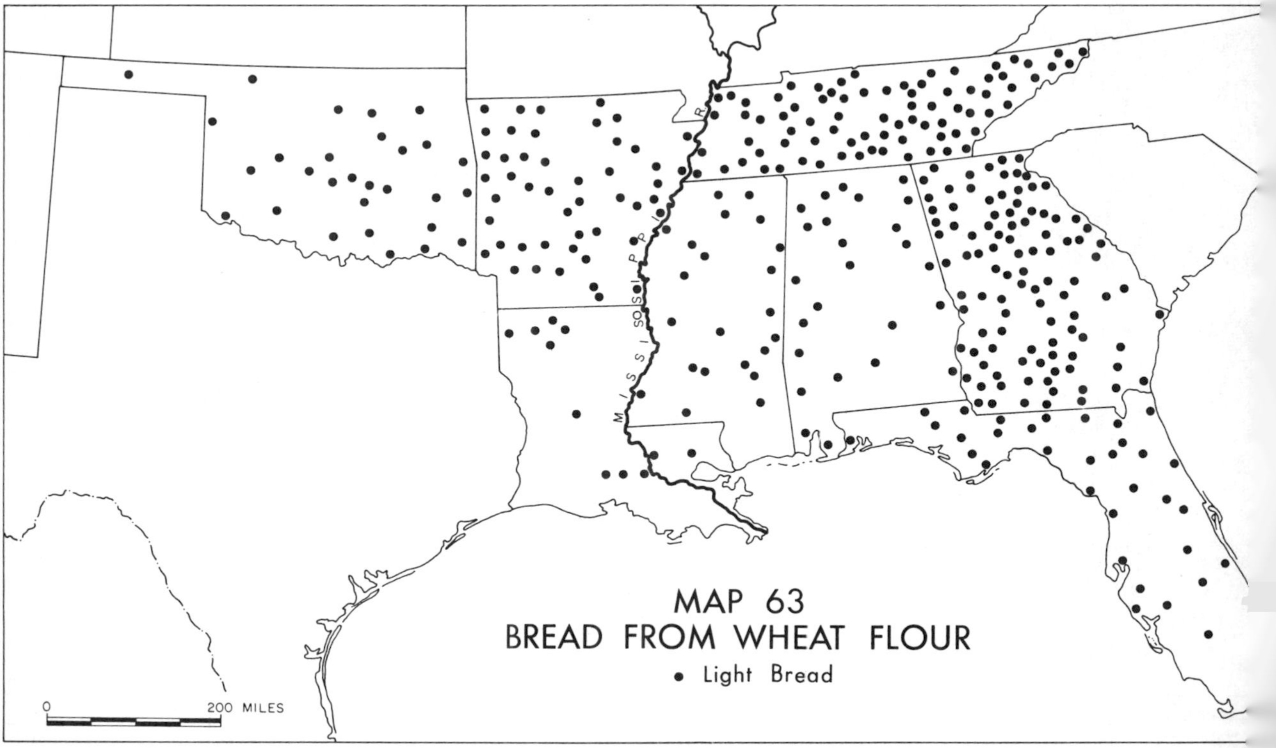
MISSISSIPPI R.
MAP 63
BREAD FROM WHEAT FLOUR
• Light Bread
0
200 MILES

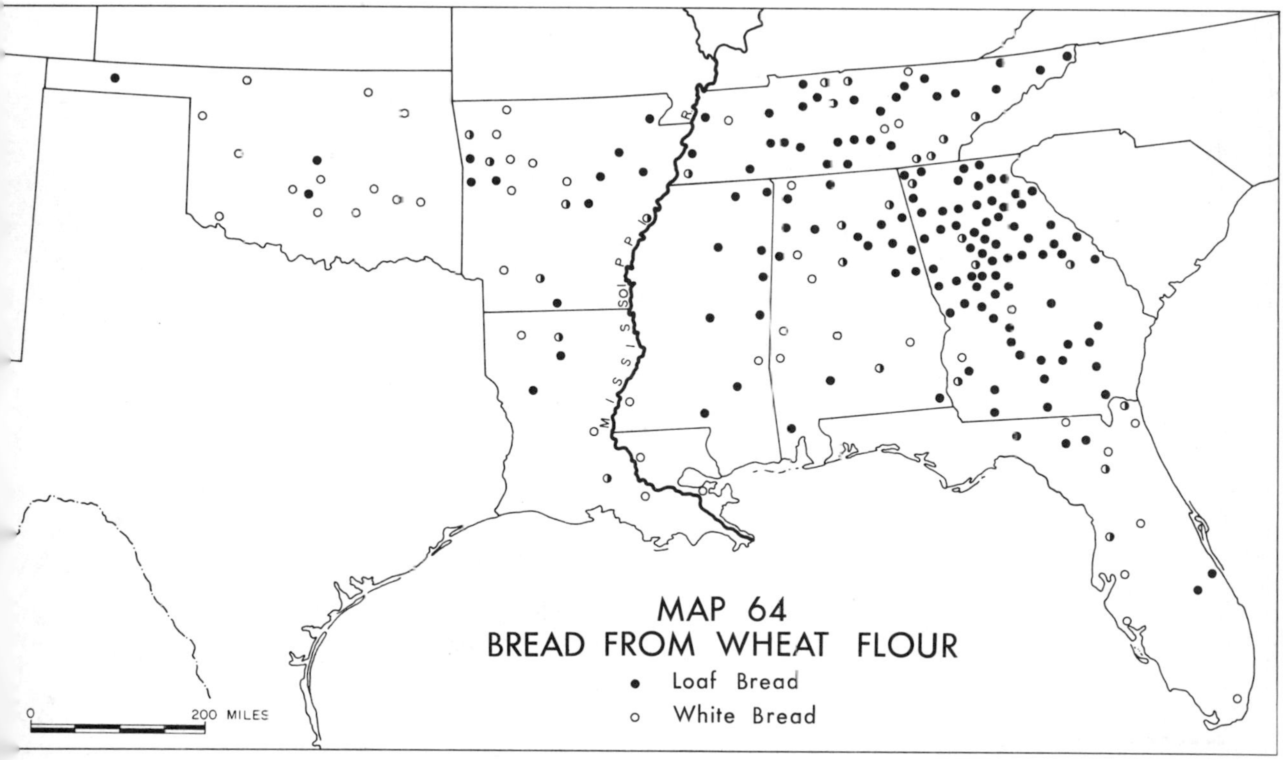
MISSISSIPPI R.
0
200 MILES

MAP 64
BREAD FROM WHEAT FLOUR
• Loaf Bread
○ White Bread

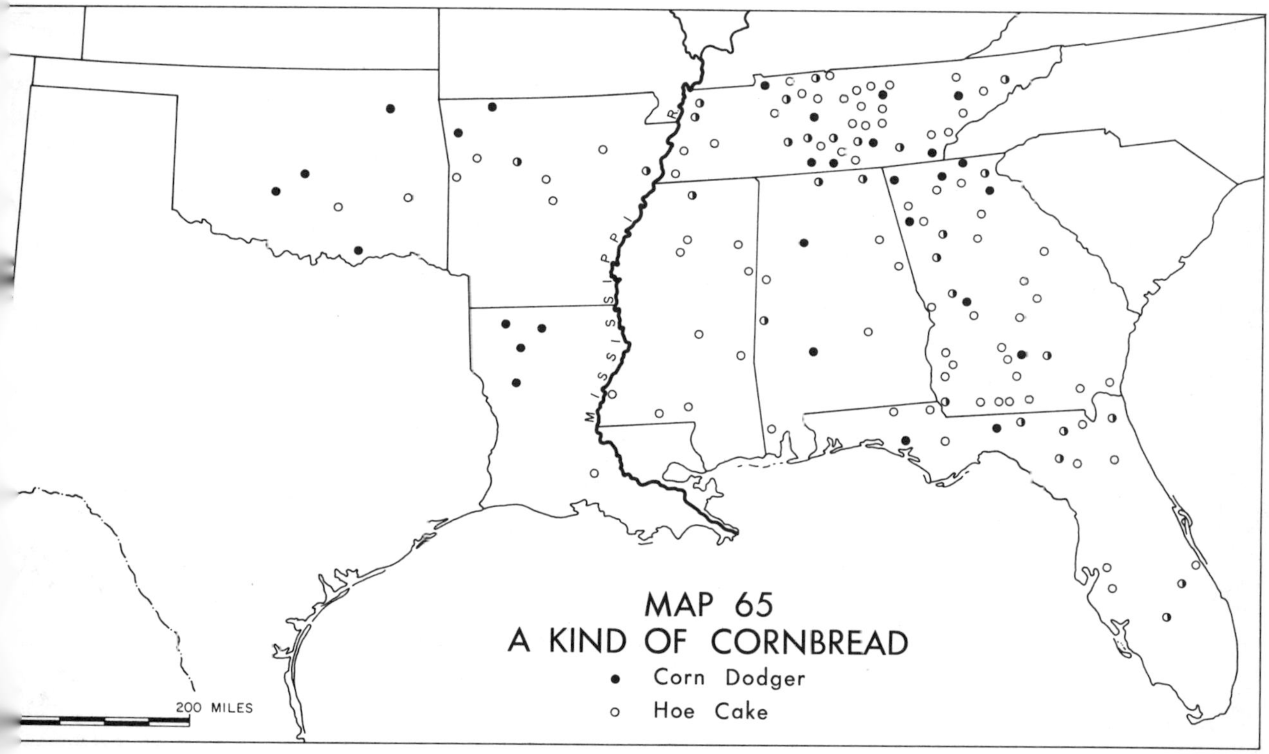
MISSISSIPPI R.
200 MILES

MAP 65
A KIND OF CORNBREAD
• Corn Dodger
○ Hoe Cake

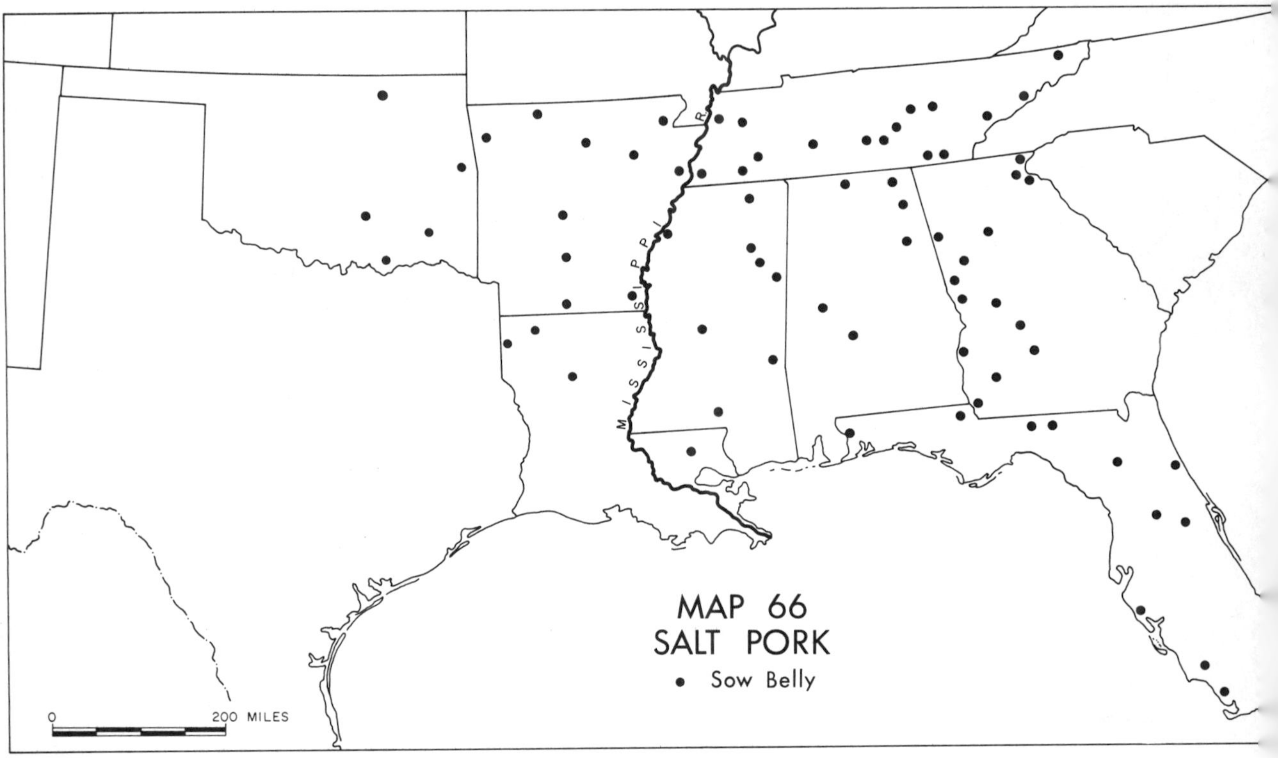
R
MISSISSIPPI
MAP 66
SALT PORK
• Sow Belly
0
200 MILES

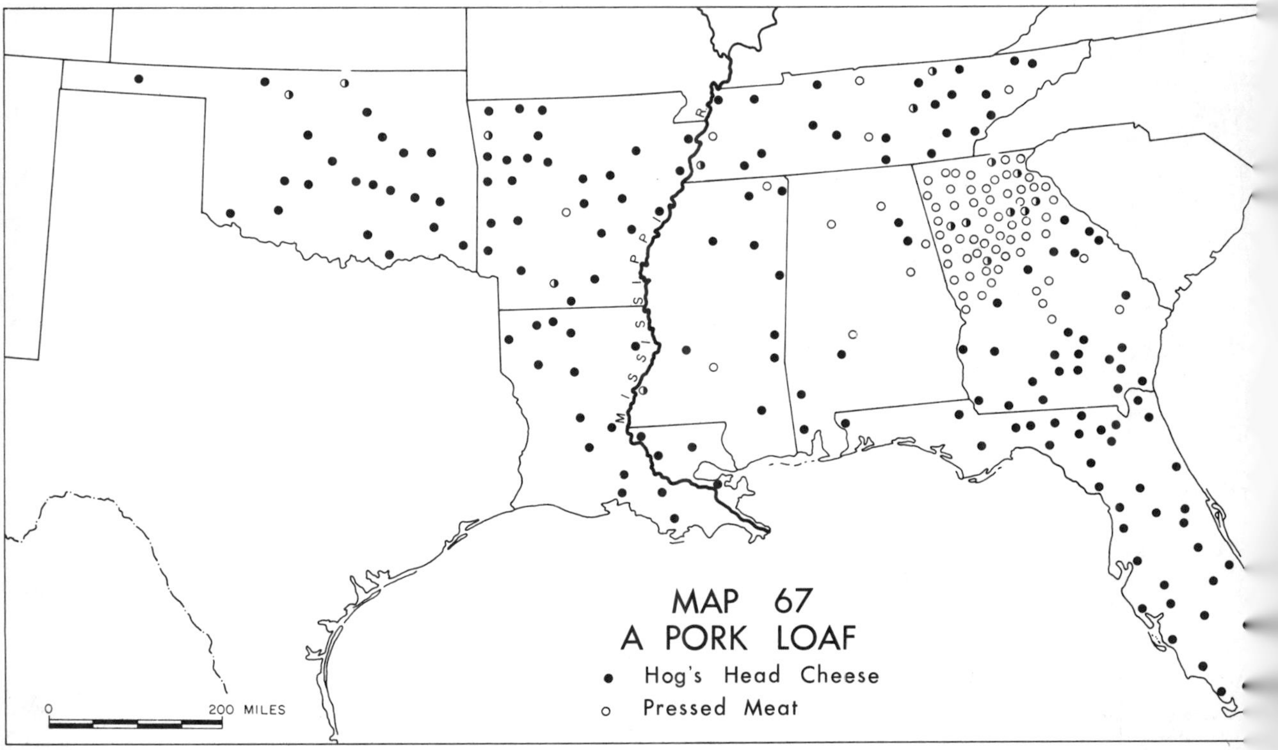
R
MISSISSIPPI
MAP 67
A PORK LOAF
• Hog's Head Cheese
○ Pressed Meat
0
200 MILES

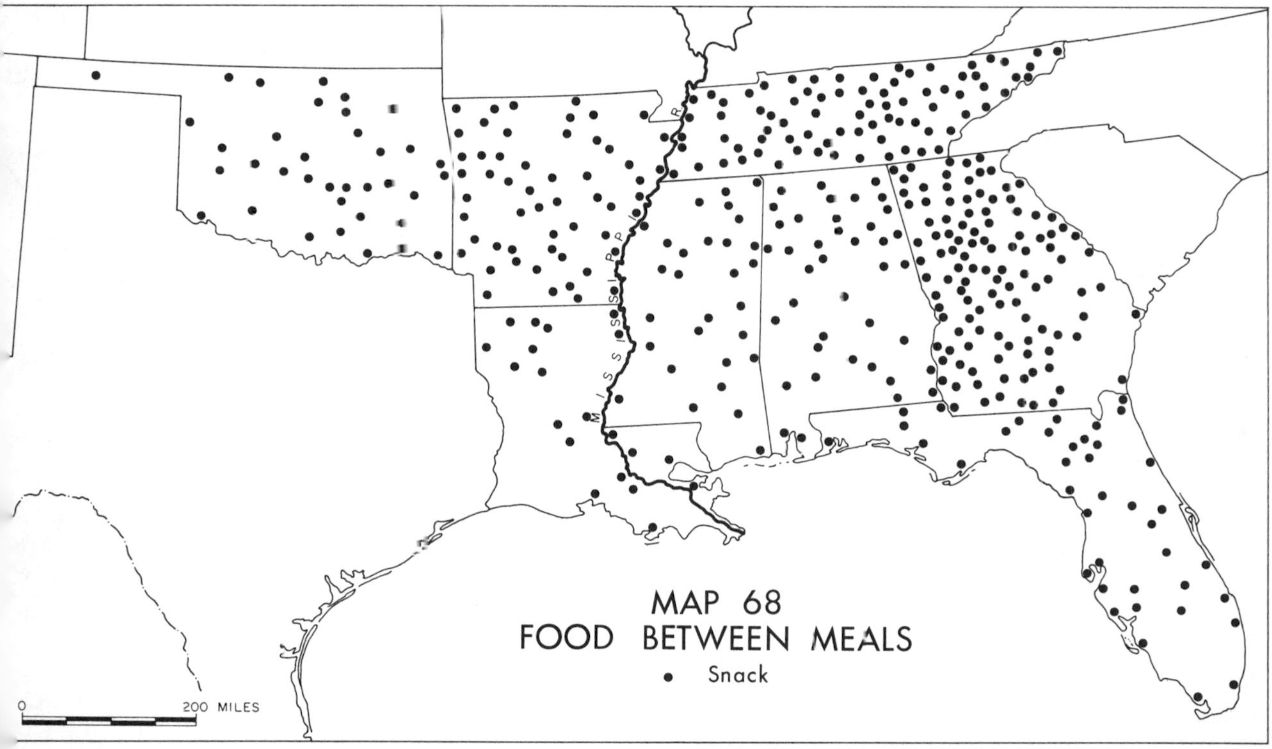
MISSISSIPPI R.
0
200 MILES
MAP 68
FOOD BETWEEN MEALS
• Snack

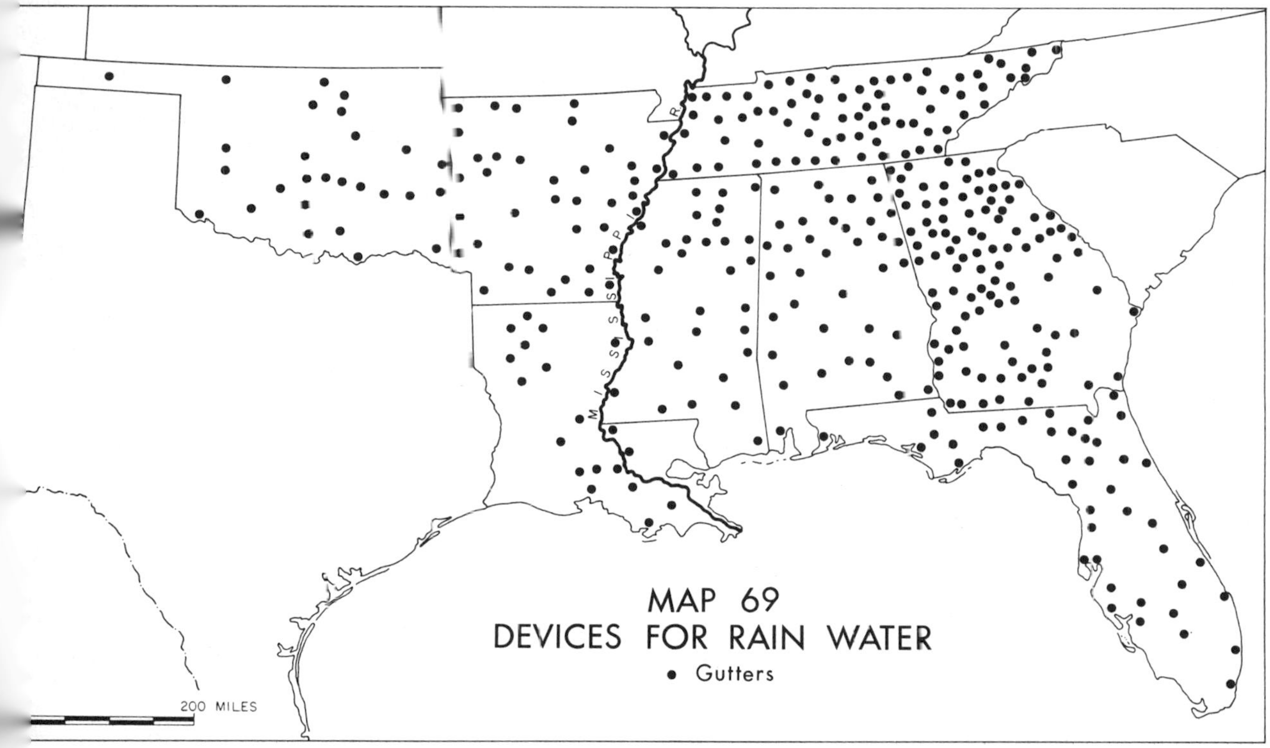
MISSISSIPPI R.
200 MILES
MAP 69
DEVICES FOR RAIN WATER
• Gutters

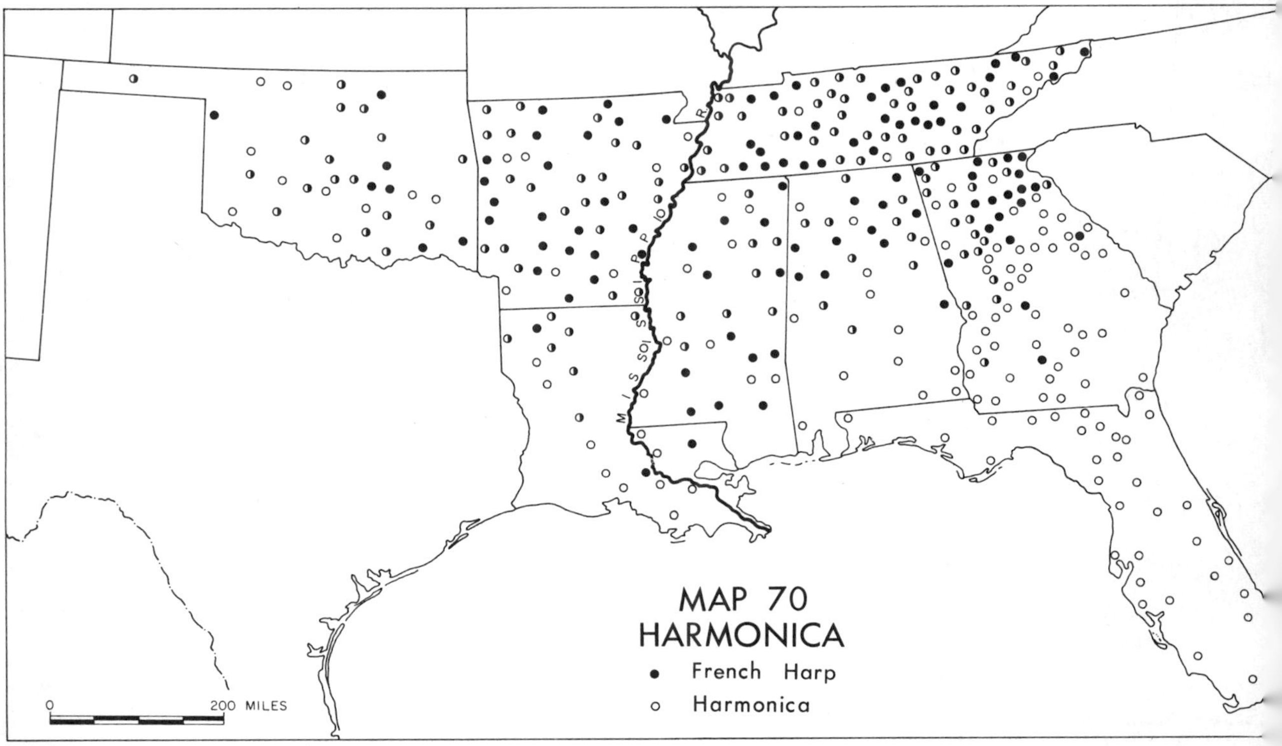
MISSISSIPPI R.
MAP 70
HARMONICA
French Harp
Harmonica
0
200 MILES

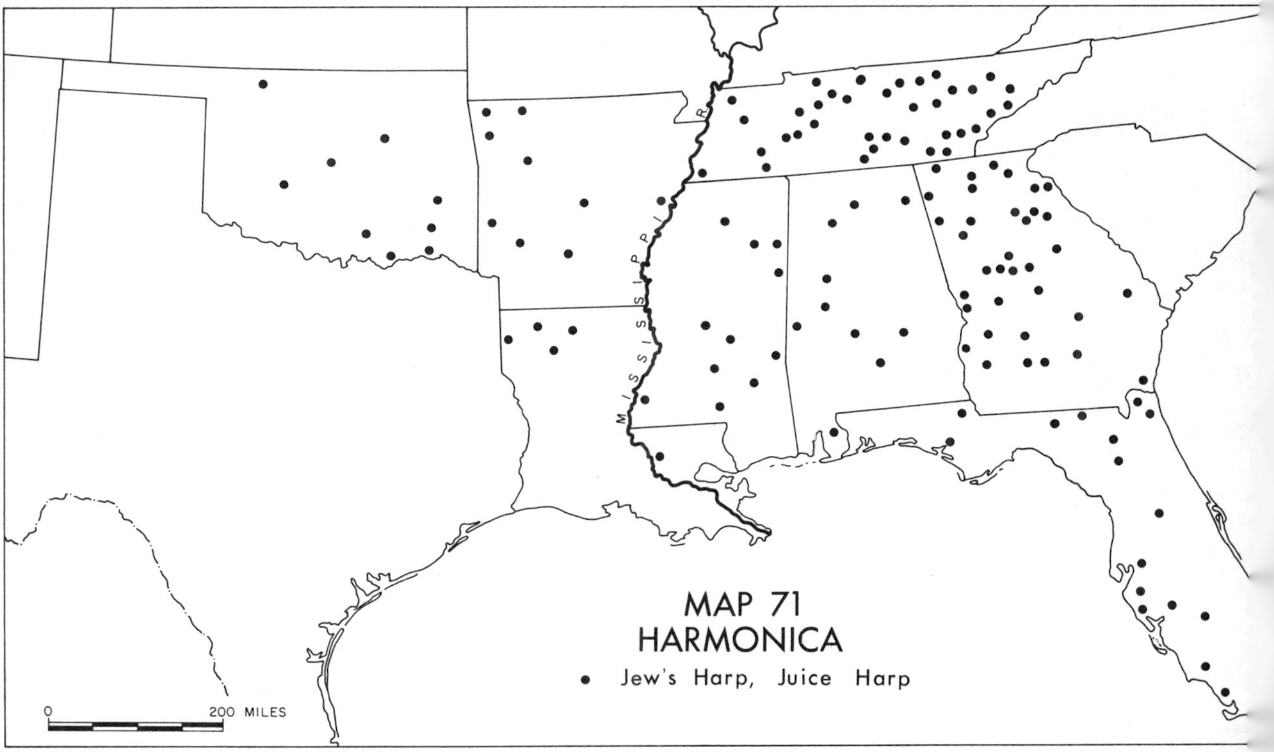
MISSISSIPPI R.
MAP 71
HARMONICA
Jew's Harp, Juice Harp
0
200 MILES

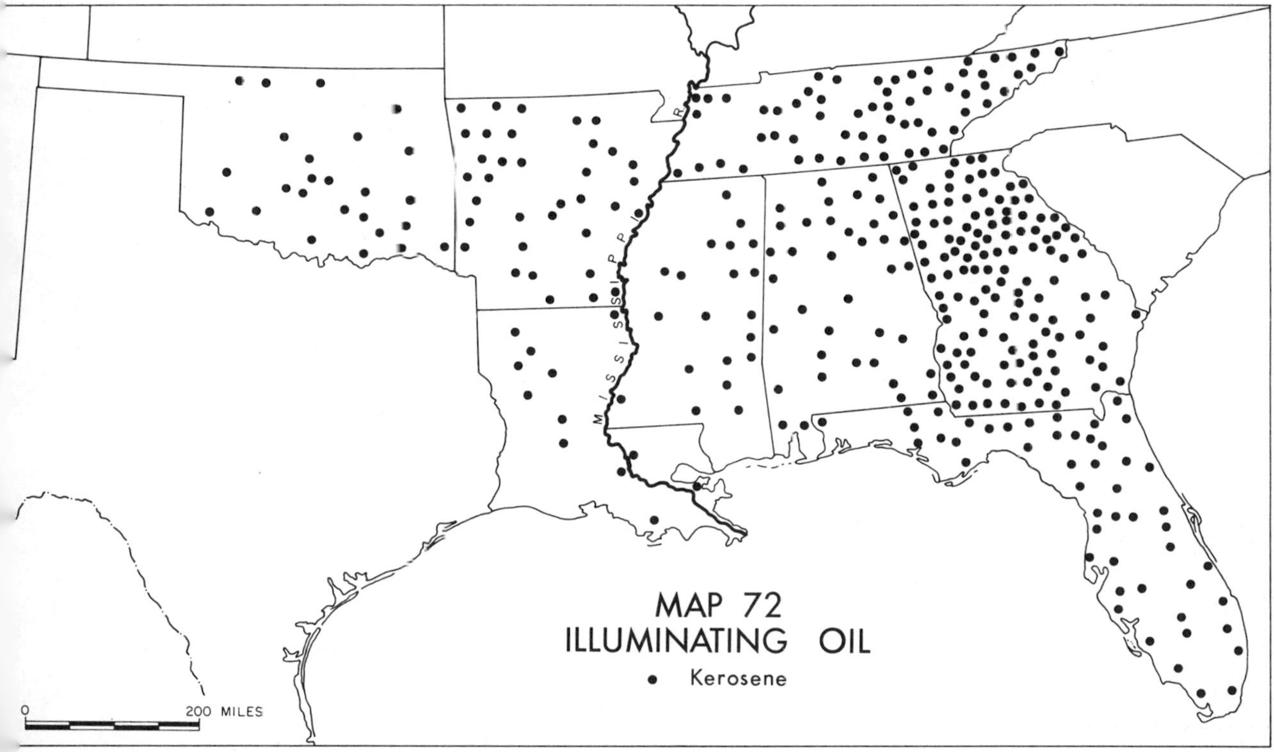
MAP 72
ILLUMINATING OIL
Kerosene
MISSISSIPPI R.
0
200 MILES

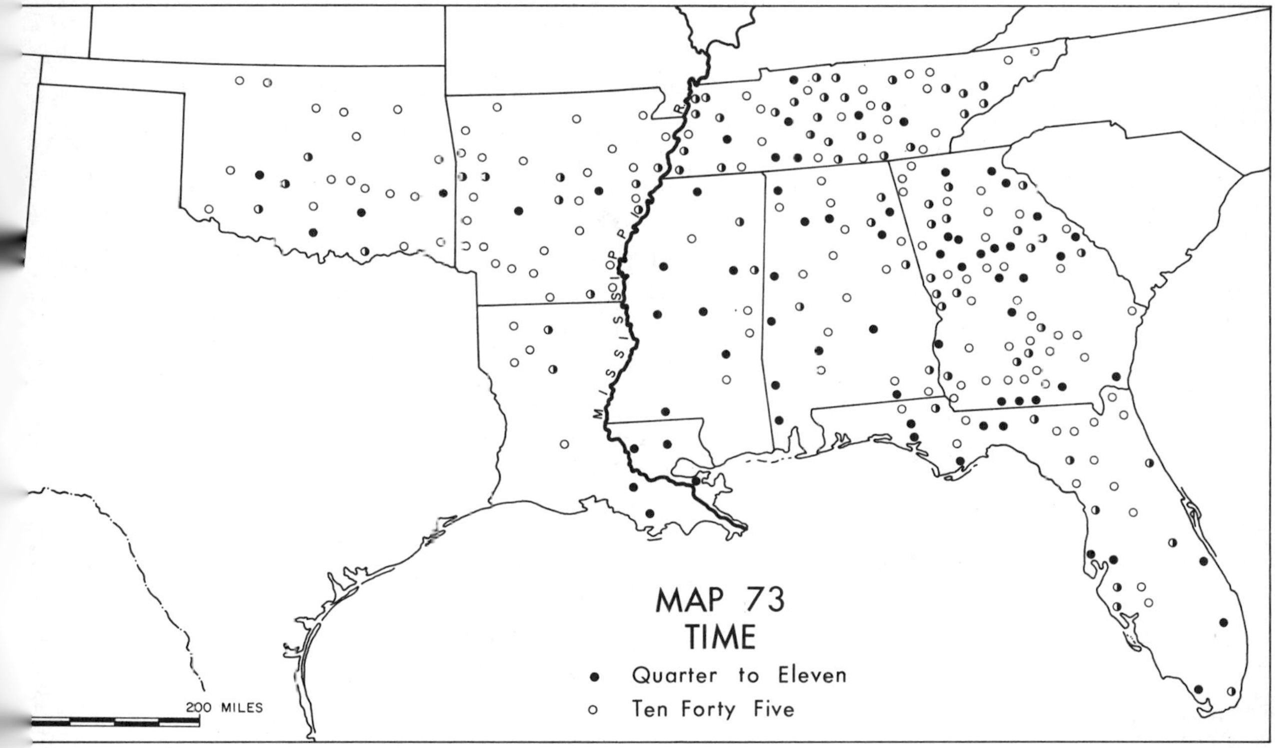
MAP 73
TIME
Quarter to Eleven
Ten Forty Five
MISSISSIPPI R.
200 MILES

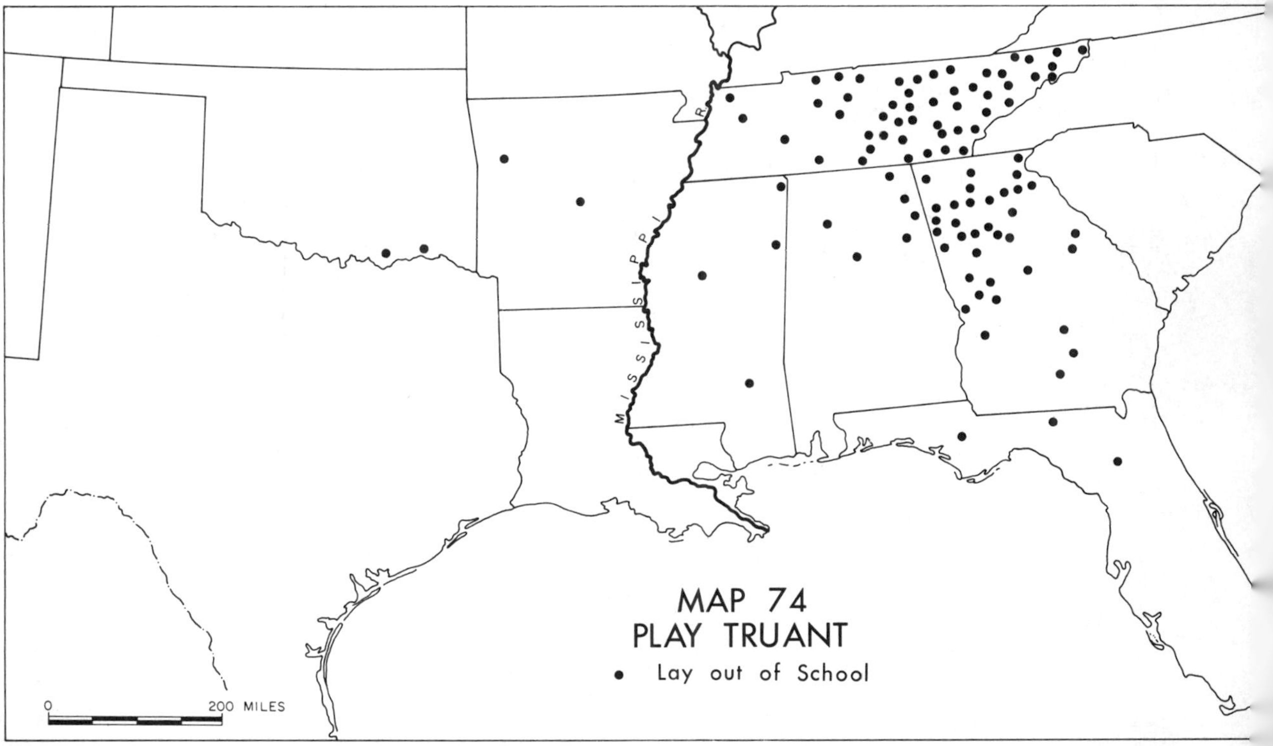
MISSISSIPPI R.
0 200 MILES

MAP 74
PLAY TRUANT
• Lay out of School

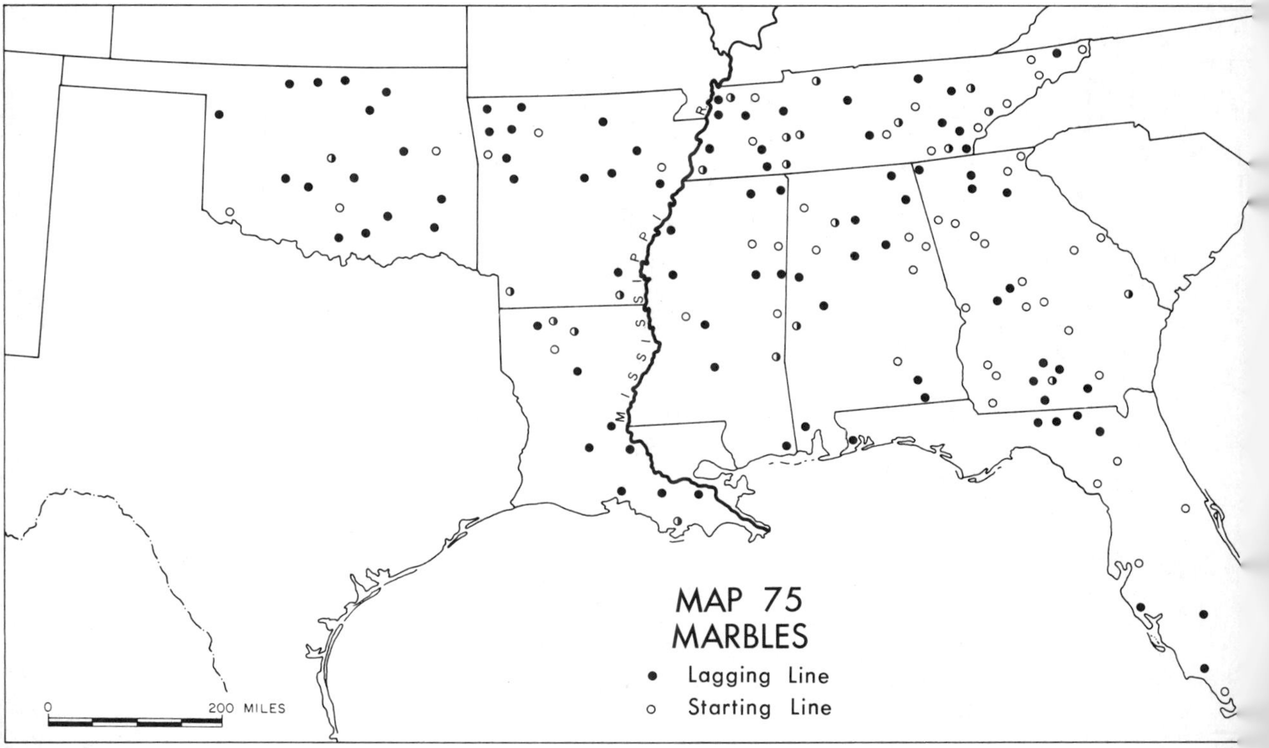
MISSISSIPPI R.
0 200 MILES

MAP 75
MARBLES
• Lagging Line
○ Starting Line

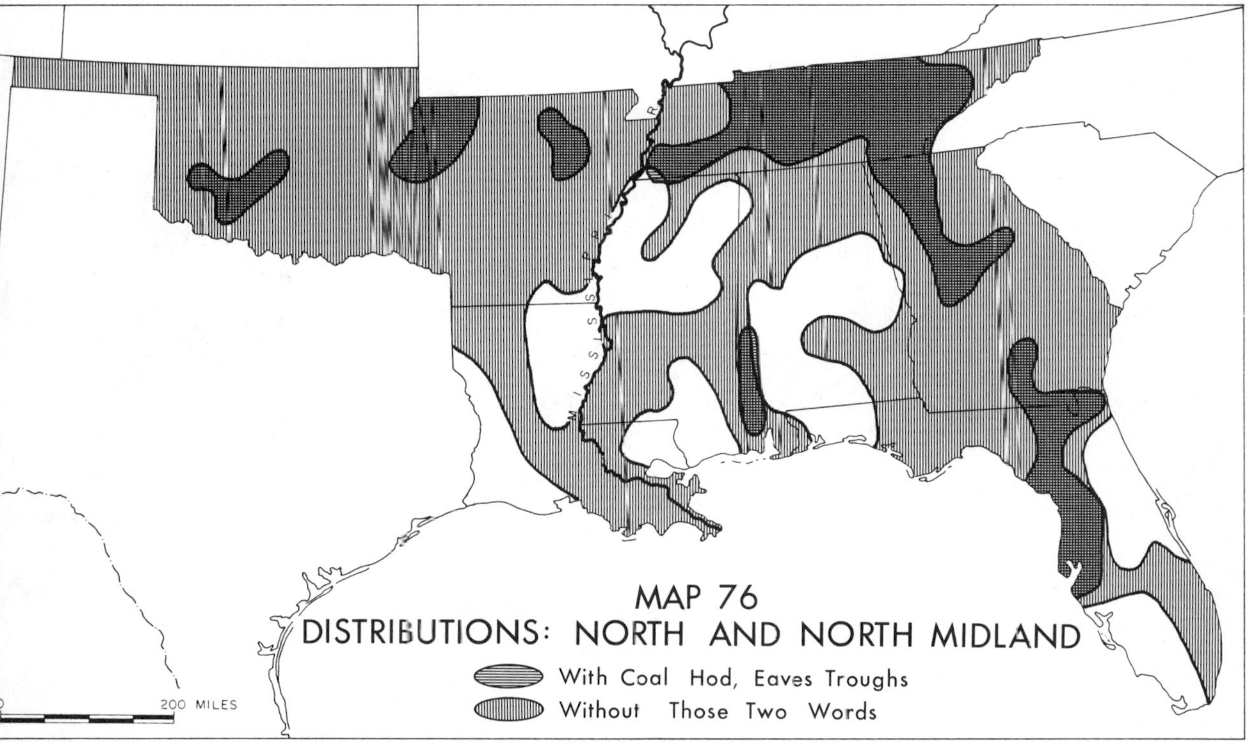
MAP 76
DISTRIBUTIONS: NORTH AND NORTH MIDLAND
With Coal Hod, Eaves Troughs
Without Those Two Words
200 MILES
MISSISSIPPI R.

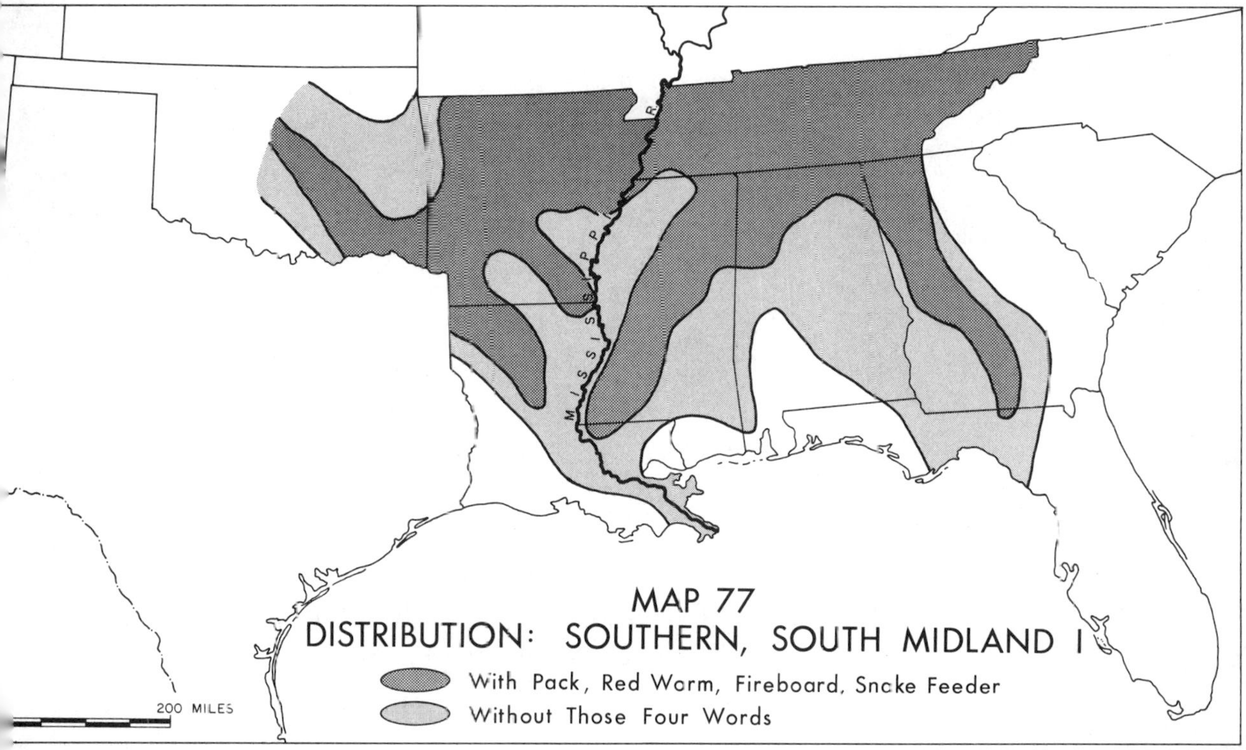
MAP 77
DISTRIBUTION: SOUTHERN, SOUTH MIDLAND I
With Pack, Red Worm, Fireboard, Snake Feeder
Without Those Four Words
200 MILES
MISSISSIPPI R.

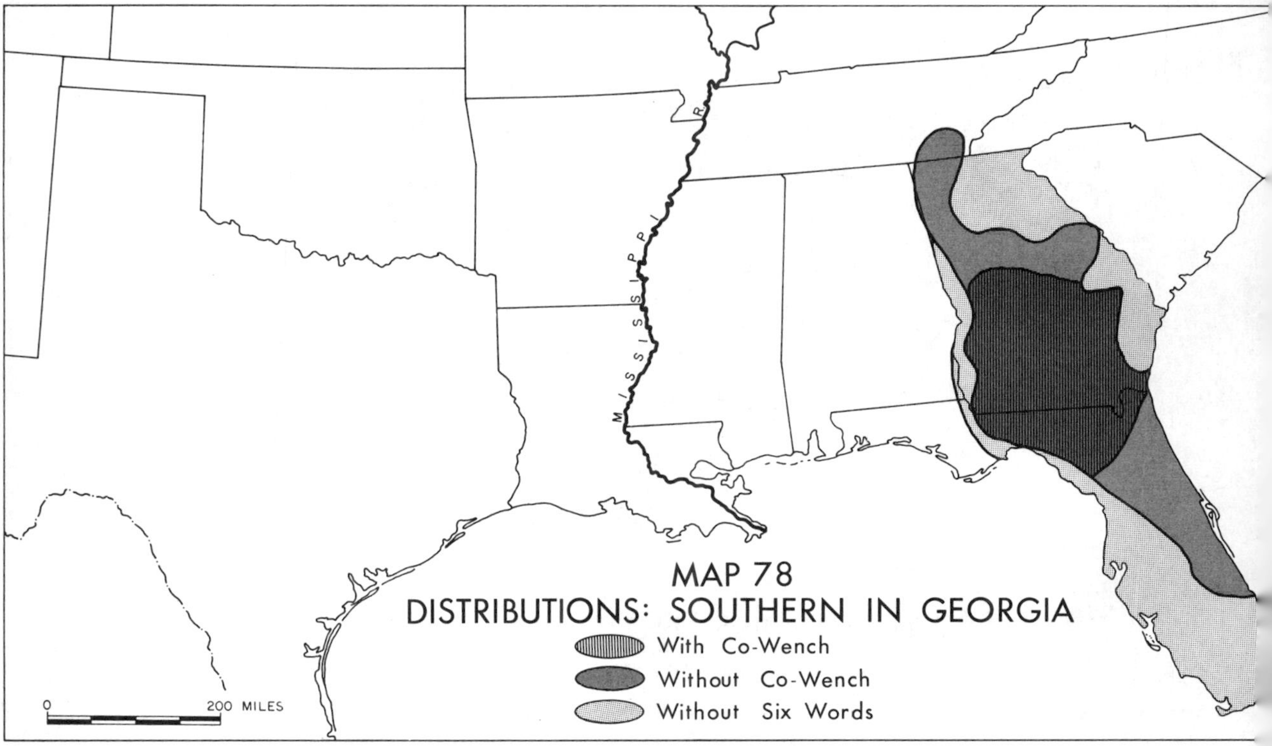
MISSISSIPPI R.
With Co-Wench
Without Co-Wench
Without Six Words
0
200 MILES

MAP 78
DISTRIBUTIONS: SOUTHERN IN GEORGIA

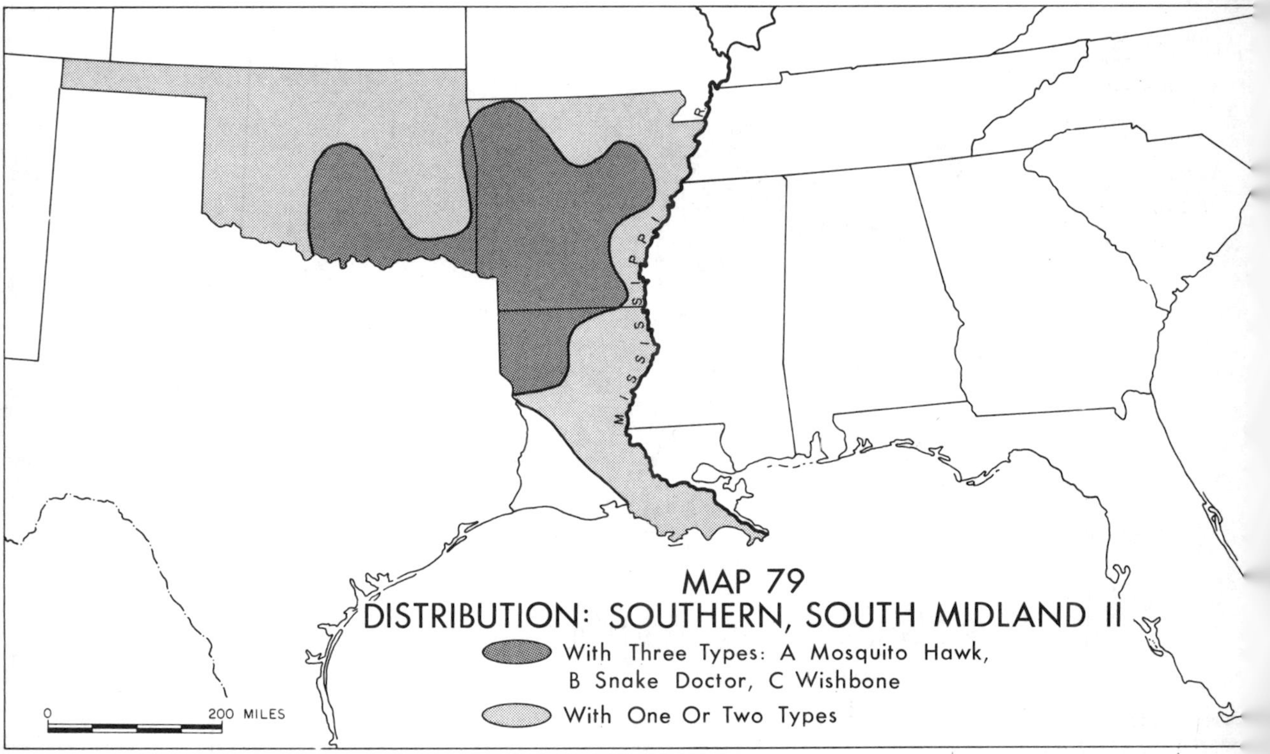
MISSISSIPPI R.
With Three Types: A Mosquito Hawk, B Snake Doctor, C Wishbone
With One Or Two Types
0
200 MILES

MAP 79
DISTRIBUTION: SOUTHERN, SOUTH MIDLAND II

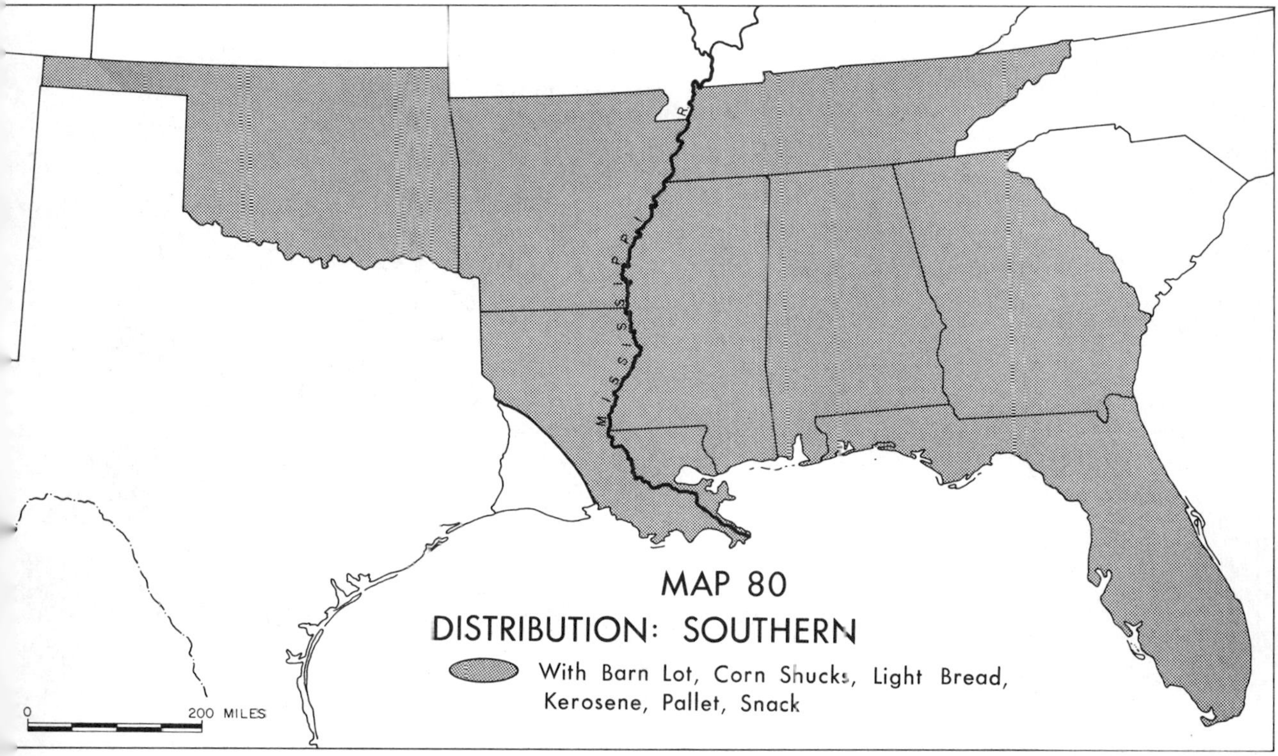
MISSISSIPPI R
0 200 MILES

MAP 80
DISTRIBUTION: SOUTHERN

With Barn Lot, Corn Shucks, Light Bread, Kerosene, Pallet, Snack

MAP 81
REPRESESENTATIVE WORD BOUNDARIES

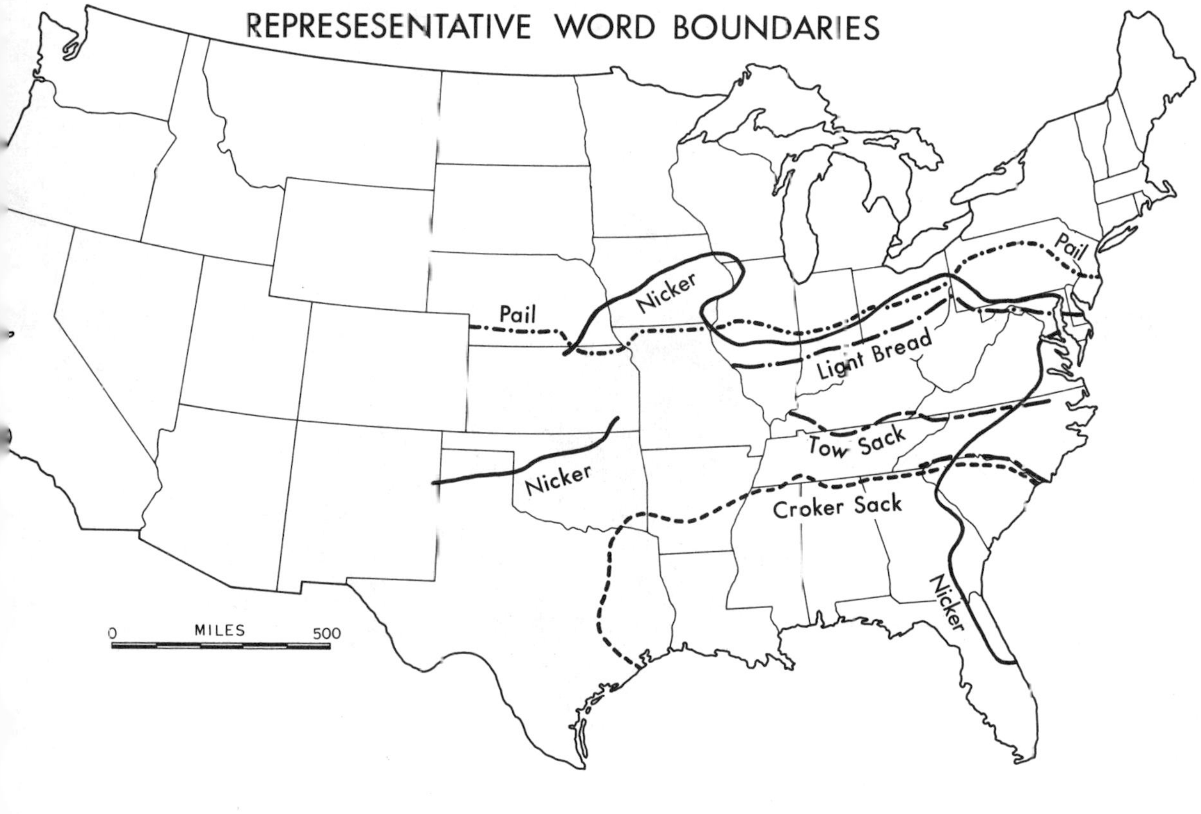
Pail
Nicker
Pail
Light Bread
Tow Sack
Nicker
Croker Sack
Nicker
0 MILES 500

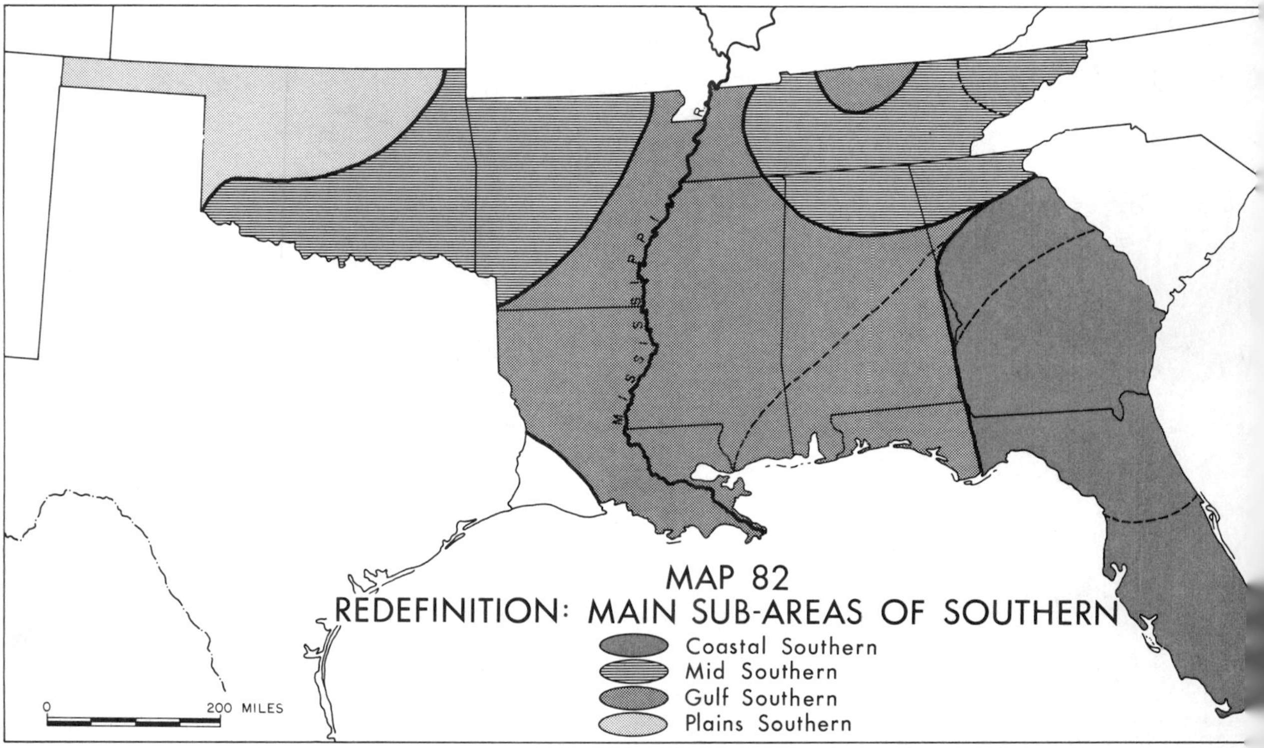
MISSISSIPPI R
Coastal Southern
Mid Southern
Gulf Southern
Plains Southern
0
200 MILES

MAP 82
REDEFINITION: MAIN SUB-AREAS OF SOUTHERN

MAP 83
REDEFINITION: SOUTHERN

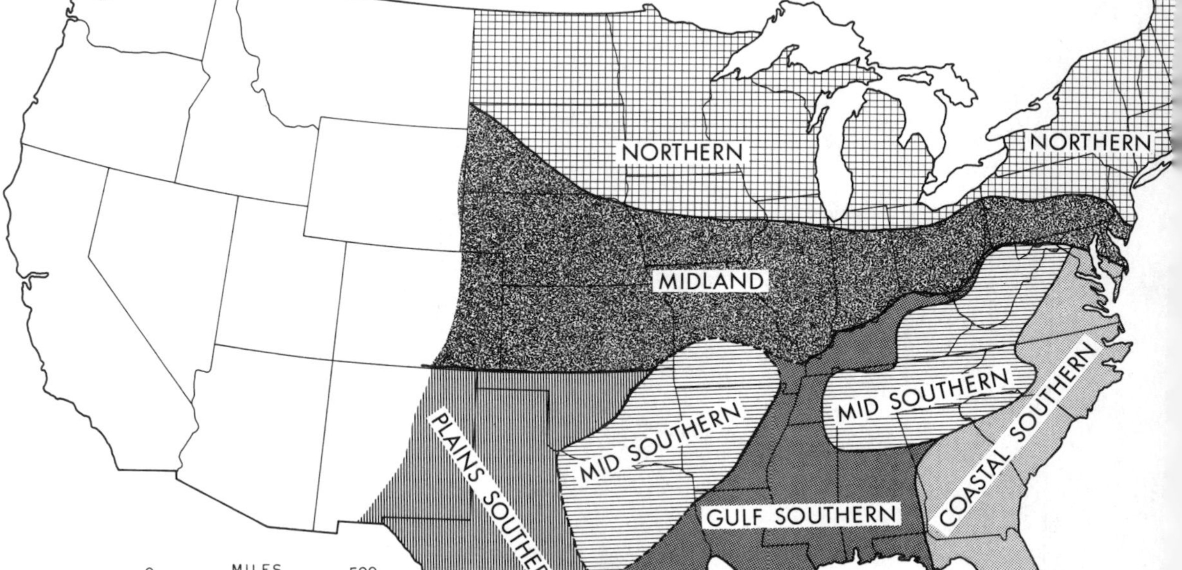
NORTHERN
NORTHERN
MIDLAND
MID SOUTHERN
MID SOUTHERN
PLAINS SOUTHERN
GULF SOUTHERN
COASTAL SOUTHERN
0
MILES
500

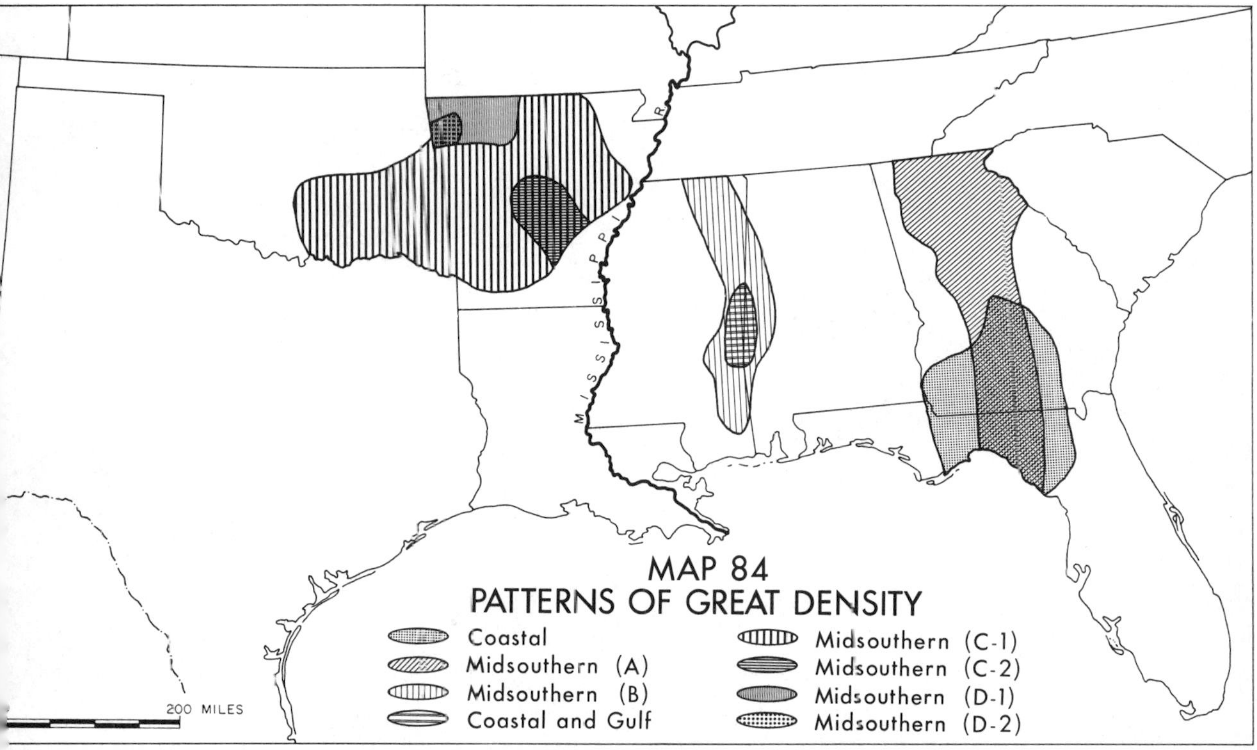
MISSISSIPPI R.
MAP 84
PATTERNS OF GREAT DENSITY
Coastal
Midsouthern (A)
Midsouthern (B)
Coastal and Gulf
Midsouthern (C-1)
Midsouthern (C-2)
Midsouthern (D-1)
Midsouthern (D-2)
200 MILES

Notes

Selected Bibliography

Word Index

Topical Index

Notes

1 The Setting for Uniformity or Variation

1. Harry R. Warfel, ed. "Introduction," *Letters of Noah Webster* (New York, 1953), p. xxxv.
2. *Dissertations on the English Language: with Notes, Historical and Critical* (Boston, 1789), p. 36. Webster's topic here is speech; three paragraphs later (pp. 37–38) it is print: "To learn the English language in its purity, it is necessary to examin [*sic*] the best authors from Chaucer to the present time." The developed uniformity would be all inclusive.
3. *Ibid.*, p. 19.
4. From William Wirt, *The Life and Character of Patrick Henry* as reprinted in Robert M. Estrich and Hans Sperber, *Three Keys to Language* (New York, 1952), p. 328. Wirt's comment on the quotation is "the accuracy of Mr. Page's memory is questioned in this particular, by the acquaintances of Mr. Henry, who say, that he was too good a grammarian to have uttered such a sentence, although they admit the inaccuracy of his pronunciation, in some of the words imputed to him." The reflected attitude toward books, however, is important as a counter to the idea that books are essential in language transmission.
5. Cover terms such as Old Southwest, Gulf South, or South Central States could serve. *Interior South,* however, emphasizes an important aspect of this study, the dissemination of a vocabulary from the Atlantic states to parts of the interior. In this context, Georgia is both a point of origin and an area for dissemination. Florida is included because of its associated linguistic history. Three states of the interior, Kentucky, Texas, and Missouri, are not represented either because other scholars were surveying the regional English there or because an opportunity to conduct a survey did not develop.
6. For this portion of Boone's life on the frontier, see John Bakeless, *Daniel Boone, Master of the Wilderness* (New York, 1939), pp. 17–123. A survey of conditions on the seaboard and in the backwoods before 1776 is Carl Bridenbaugh, *Myths and Realities, Societies of the Colonial South* (Baton Rouge, La., 1952). An introduction to the expanding agricultural frontier for the nation in general is Paul W. Gates, *The Farmer's Age: Agriculture, 1815–1860,* in *The Economic History of the United States,* ed. Henry David et. al. (New York, 1960), III. William O. Lynch, "The Westward Flow of Southern Colonists before 1861," *Journal of Southern History,* IX (1943), 303–27, assembles and interprets the census data which I have followed here. For instances of misreading the evidence of soil and vegetation, see Archer B. Hulbert, *Soil, Its Influences on the History of the United States* (New Haven, Conn., 1930), pp. 77 ff.
7. The great diversity of social groups in the Interior South is shown in Gates, *The Farmer's Age,* pp. 5–21 and 134–155. Recognition is given there to independent farmers, to the small slave owners, and to groups other than the big planters.
8. From William C. Bagley, Jr., *Soil Exhaustion and the Civil War* (Washington, D.C., 1942), p. 22; this doctoral essay provides readers with a collection of remarks on poor soil management (pp. 10–33) from colonial days to 1860. Only a few Virginia or Carolina planters can be named who actually moved their plantations or established new ones in this dramatic fashion. In *The Mind of the South* (Anchor Book, 1954), pp. 27–28, W. J. Cash guesses that there were "less than five hundred" of the Virginia aristocrats. He traces the new cotton aristocracy to "the pushing, the ambitious, among the old coon-hunting population of the backcountry."
9. Population movements described here are those of free white persons; exact numbers for given censuses in each state are in Lynch, "Westward Flow," beginning with p. 304n6. The different pattern of movement for the slave population begins in his study, p. 311.
10. For brief summaries, see Samuel E. Morrison, *The Oxford History of the American People* (New York, 1965), pp. 402–3, 472–79, 888–91.

2 Procedures and Assumptions

1. For Linguistic Atlas procedures see Hans Kurath et. al., *Handbook of the Linguistic Geography of New England* (Washington, D.C., 1939), pp. 39–54. Other procedures for obtaining spoken responses are in Eugen Dieth and Harold Orton, "A Questionnaire for a Linguistic Atlas of England," *Survey of English Dialects* (Leeds, England, 1962); Stanley M. Sapon, *A Pictorial Linguistic Interview Manual,* offset (Columbus, Ohio, 1957); and Lyle V. Jones and Joseph M. Wepman, *A spoken word count* [*sic*] (Chicago, 1966). A technique which uses a standard text as a control for obtaining pronunciation alone is in Charles K. Thomas, *An Introduction to the Phonetics of American English,* 2nd ed. (New York, 1958).

2. (Ann Arbor, Mich., 1949).
3. For additional details about the questionnaire see Appendix B. *Word* as used in discussing the synonyms refers to any lexical entry treated as a self-contained unit.
4. See Tables of Percentages of Use, pp. 65ff.
5. The private worlds concept is advanced by W. V. O. Quine, *Word and Object* (Cambridge, Mass., 1960), particularly pp. 26–27. Some difficulties which arise when a researcher undertakes to measure the connections between word and meaning are in *Readings in the Psychology of Language,* ed. Leon A. Jakobovits and Murray S. Miron (Englewood Cliffs, N.J., 1967), especially pp. 355 ff.
6. See *The American College Dictionary* (1967). Not entirely so its contemporaries: *Webster's Seventh New Collegiate Dictionary* (1963) tentatively connects *lunch* with *nuncheon,* "a light snack." The college edition of *Webster's New World Dictionary* (1960) traces it to Spanish *lonja,* "a slice of ham."
7. Each word in the synonym lists was examined for its special American senses in *A Dictionary of American English on Historical Principles,* ed. Sir William Craigie et. al., 4 vols. (Chicago, 1936); *A Dictionary of Americanisms on Historical Principles,* ed. Mitford M. Mathews, 2 vols. (Chicago, 1951); and, for its classification as dialectal or nondialectal, in *American Dialect Dictionary,* ed. Harold Wentworth (New York, 1944). With reference to the last source one can only regret that Professor Cassidy's projected "Dictionary of American Regional English" has not reached publication.

8. Negro and American Indian informants were sought. No records were obtained from the latter, and only five from the former. Those five are not a part of the present tabulations simply because five do not form a useful statistical group for comparison with one thousand other informants. For an introduction to difficulties in analyses of Negro usage, see J. L. Dillard, "Non-Standard Negro Dialects—Convergence or Divergence?" *The Florida FL Reporter,* LXV (1968), 1–3. In my selected records are the responses of 589 women, 50 persons educated beyond the twelfth grade, and over 400 beyond the sixth. Some informants are between the ages of 18 and 40, just less than 400 between 40 and 69, and over 330 between 70 and 90. It is hoped that the exact figures will be made available in the form of computer tapes. The parental birthplaces in part are indicated in the table below. For full details on the birthplace of parents and grandparents, turn to Appendix A.

FROM	TO							
	ALA.	ARK.	FLA.	GA.	LA.	MISS.	OKLA.	TENN.
Alabama	132	7	7	14	3	11	8	12
Arkansas		121			3		10	
Florida			103	6				
Georgia	13	8	33	440		1	1	13
Louisiana	1	7			47	2		1
Mississippi	3	17			3	72	2	5
Oklahoma		1				1	43	
Tennessee	4	33	3	17		3	5	330

9. Additional details of computer processing are given in Appendix C. Discussion of problems related to preparing field records for computer processing are in E. Bagby Atwood, *The Regional Vocabulary of Texas* (Austin, Tex., 1962), pp. 256 ff. One should augment this general description with Roger W. Shuy, "An Automated Retrieval Program for the Linguistic Atlas of the United States and Canada," *Computation in Linguistics,* ed. Paul L. Garvin and Bernard Spolsky (Bloomington, Ind., 1966), pp. 60–75. Gordon R. Wood, *Sub-Regional Speech Variations in Vocabulary, Grammar, and Pronunciation* (Cooperative Research Project No. 3046, United States Office of Education, final report. Edwardsville, Ill., 1967) comments on computer analysis of transcriptions from tape records of American English.
10. Atwood, *Regional Vocabulary,* reached similar conclusions after examining field records.
11. The county record is a part of the total computer tape.
12. If the researcher is interested in securing responses that will reflect the language at the precise moment, a printed questionnaire is an effective instrument to use. Spoken interviews produce variables of time between the separate records. Field work for the *Linguistic Atlas of New England* began in 1931; interviewing was completed in 1933; the atlas itself was published

from 1939 to 1943. Continuity or change can be studied in the reinvestigation reported in Audrey H. Duckert, "The *Linguistic Atlas of New England* Revisited," *Publication of the American Dialect Society,* XXXIX (1963), 8–15. In contrast, the questionnaires used here were prepared, distributed, and returned within a two-year period.

In addition to Atwood and Kurath, already cited, these are immediately pertinent: Raven I. McDavid, Jr. "The Dialects of American English," and supporting maps in W. Nelson Francis, *The Structure of American English* (New York, 1958), pp. 480–543 and 579–85; Harold B. Allen, "Minor Dialect Areas of the Upper Midwest," *Publication of the American Dialect Society,* XXX (1958), 3–16; Albert H. Marckwardt, "Principal and Subsidiary Dialect Areas in the North Central States," *Publication of the American Dialect Society,* XXVII (1957), 3–15; the reprinting of Allen and Marckwardt with a modification of maps in *Readings in Applied Linguistics,* ed. Harold B. Allen (New York, 1964), pp. 220–41; Clyde T. Hankey, "A Colorado Word Geography," *Publication of the American Dialect Society,* XXXIV (1960), 1–76; and, for details not in those sources, Carroll E. Reed, *Dialects of American English* (Cleveland and New York, 1967). Recent selective bibliographies are *Linguistics and English Linguistics,* comp. Harold B. Allen (New York, 1966), particularly pp. 57–60 and 81–82; *An Annotated Bibliography of Southern Speech,* comp. by Lee Pederson (Atlanta, Ga., 1968).

13. For a comparison of modified phonemic respellings with conventional spellings see Wood, *Sub-Regional Speech Variations.* Theoretical support for procedures for moving from phonetic to lexical to semantic levels is being developed by Sydney M. Lamb. A brief but clear illustration of the general workings of that procedure is David C. Bennet, "English Prepositions: A Stratificational Approach," *Journal of Linguistics,* IV (1968), 153–72. An adverse review of Lamb's *Outline of Stratificational Grammar* (1966) is in the same journal, pp. 287–95.

3 Gradations in Uniformity

1. The larger linguistic setting for such concepts as gradation is examined in Dwight L. Bolinger, *Generality, Gradience, and the All-or-None,* in Janua Linguarum, XIV (The Hague, The Netherlands, 1961).
2. The use of legal papers, commercial accounts, plantation books, church records, letters, children's writings, student compositions, and diaries and journals to document historical elements in the development of American English is well illustrated in Norman E. Eliason, *Tarheel Talk: An Historical Study of the English Language in North Carolina to 1860* (Chapel Hill, N.C., 1956). Though badly needed, nothing like it has appeared for the states of the Interior South.
3. Harold B. Allen called this to my attention in 1963 in private correspondence. Among other places, he mentioned upstate New York as an area from which instances had been reported. His forthcoming Atlas study of the Upper Midwest will report the instances he and his co-workers found there. Until we have a printed record of its distributions in the states that lie east of his area of investigation, we will be at something of a loss to account for its dissemination. Of course, with the present report and the Allen Atlas, a researcher could consult the Atlas files if he wishes to fill in the gap. Meanwhile as a matter of convenience, I have taken an oversimplified explanation as workable: *mosquito hawk* came into the Interior South only from the South Atlantic states.
4. See Gordon R. Wood, "Word Distribution in the Interior South," *Publication of the American Dialect Society,* XXXV (1961), 2–3.
5. Hans Kurath, *A Word Geography of the Eastern United States* (Ann Arbor, Mich., 1949), p. 35.
6. *Ibid.,* p. 46. He conjectures that the Maryland word *guano sack* spread to the Shenandoah Valley, "presumably as a Baltimore trade word." Ships bearing cargo from Peru could dock at Savannah before going to Baltimore, or docking at Baltimore could come south to Savannah. In either case, it is the Savannah-Augusta trade areas that distribute products in Georgia and thus send the product name along with it. West of Georgia other ports contribute to the diffusion, e.g. Mobile, Alabama.
7. Kendall Beaton, "Founders' Incentives: The Pre-Drake Refining Industry," *Oil's First Century; Papers Given at the Centennial Seminar on the History of the Petroleum Industry,* Harvard Business School, Nov. 13–14, 1959, compiled and edited by the staff of *The Business History Review* (Cambridge, Mass., 1960), pp. 7–19.
8. E. Bagby Atwood, *The Regional Vocabulary of Texas* (Austin, Tex., 1962), pp. 104–19, links some of the Texas vocabulary with Sears, Roebuck and Co. catalog entries as well as with other commercial sources. See also Arthur G. Kimball, "Sears-Roebuck and Regional Terms," *American Speech,* XXXVIII (1963), pp. 209–13.
9. One is reasonably certain that a word volunteered in seven of the eight states will be found

frequently in the course of interviews. On the other hand, there is a chance that some infrequently volunteered words occur more often and over a larger part of the area than this record indicates.

10. If the record shows one hundred percent for one of the states, obviously that state is the only one in which the given word occurs; the other states on that side of the Mississippi have zero percent.
11. The choice of words derives mainly from lists in Kurath, *Word Geography,* Tables I, II, III, IV, and V, pp. 12–48.
12. In the scattergrams no attempt has been made to show the number of words which occur at zero percent in one or more of the eight states. The record can be obtained from the item entries individually in Table I.
13. A different dimension would emerge if the relative values for the number of informants in each state were weighted so that computer percentages would have an identical base from state to state. As it is, the larger number of counties and thus the larger number of informants in Tennessee or Georgia distorts relationships when we compare numbers of responses from state to state. The computation involved, however, took more time than was justified. Readers can mentally stretch the smaller triangles until the right edges match; then the altitude of the triangles, i.e., the position on the state-wide scale of relative importance, can be compared.
14. Kurath, *Word Geography,* p. 50.
15. Atwood, *Regional Vocabulary,* pp. 109–23.
16. A blank in the right-hand column does not indicate the absence of a synonym; obviously synonyms are at hand. Rather it is an indication that the Texas vocabulary did not include one of the questionnaire synonyms in the pertinent segment of discussion. Readers will consult the entries in Tables I and II for possible words and for the ranges of obsolescence or innovation that they indicate.
17. *Regional Vocabulary,* p. 122.

4 The Geography of Some Words

1. Column C of Table I is the source of mapping under discussion. The state total for each word by itself is one hundred percent; the subdivisional total is printed as a percent of that. Smaller subdivisions such as East, Middle, and West Tennessee, justified by custom, could have been shown in the computer printout; the calculations would have been appreciably increased and the resulting tables would have been very difficult to read. Computer tapes are in my opinion the better place to store these records.
2. This choice of number, shape, and size of symbols is largely in response to problems of reducing draft maps to their present printed dimensions. E. Bagby Atwood, dealing with maps of a smaller part of this whole region, attempted to show "all occurrences on maps" in selected instances (*The Regional Vocabulary of Texas* [Austin, Tex., 1962], p. 130). His remarks continue, "although the incidence of a word in a given community is never suppressed, the actual number of occurrences should not necessarily be regarded as exact."
3. The eastern edge of *gallery* and the western edge of *piazza* overlap; this overlapping may serve to mark a boundary for Louisiana influences on local word choice. As is shown by Atwood's isoglosses, *Ibid.,* Figure 16, p. 97, the Louisiana patterns of word distribution among parishes are intricate. My evidence from the questionnaire is insufficient to support anything but the most tentative guess as to the nature of this influence beyond Louisiana. Historical studies suggest that the influence dates from early times and extends up to the turn of the century if not beyond it. See, for instance, the relationship between New Orleans agents and the upriver planters, farmers, and merchants in Thomas P. Abernethy, "The Early Development of Commerce and Banking in Tennessee," *Mississippi Valley Historical Review,* XIV (1927), 316–17. The civilizing presence of urban life along the Mississippi River at the earliest stages of our national expansion is the central topic of *The Frontier Re-examined,* ed. John F. McDermott (Urbana, Ill., 1966).
4. The dialect areas are those operationally defined in Hans Kurath, *A Word Geography of the Eastern United States* (Ann Arbor, Mich., 1949), and shown here in Map 1. Reasons for putting quotation marks around identifying labels are given in Chap. 5.
5. *Curtains* should possibly have been excluded since its Atlantic setting is in two separate dialect areas in Kurath (*Ibid.,* Table VI, p. 49). It and maps of *piazza, gutters, spider,* and *low,* all of which are in the same list, are here placed in sequences that permit one to examine them in a related context of parallel diffusions. At this point in the analysis, since each map is a statement of unique distributions within the Interior South, the order is immaterial. Later in this chapter maps drawn from these sequences are combined, and for that kind of map making sequence and selection are obviously important.
6. Commenting on the presence of "Southern" words in Texas, Atwood said that "the planter class enjoyed an inordinate prestige in early Texas, and exercised an influence far out of proportion to their numbers." *Regional Vocabulary,* p. 88.
7. For early influences of French culture on Eng-

lish-speaking settlers along the Mississippi, see McDermott, *Frontier.*

8. The word maps are those of *pack, dog irons, fireboard, snake feeder, red worm, French harp, mouth harp, rock fence, ash cake, tow sack, clabber(ed) milk, wheel horse, line horse, batter bread.*
9. See Chap. 5.
10. The word maps are those of *co-wench, fatwood, press peach, spider, turn of wood, mosquito hawk, fire dogs, lightwood, whicker, pinders,* and *piazza.*
11. The maps here are considered in three groups; the absence of one or more members of a given group simplifies the problems of display since the researcher has to keep track only of group presence rather than of specific word presence. The maps by group are those of (A) *earthworm, mosquito hawk, plum peach, sallet, dog irons*; (B) *wheel horse, line horse, fireboard, snake doctor, snap beans*; (C) *red worm, rock fence, jackleg preacher, tow sack, wishbone, blinds, clabber(ed) milk.*
12. For a supplementary range of gradations at the edge of these areas see the discussion in which this analysis was first proposed: Gordon R. Wood, "Dialect Contours in the Southern States," *American Speech,* XXXVIII (1963), pp. 243–56. From east to west the pertinent maps are for Georgia those of *jew's harp, juice harp, comforter, fat back, dog irons, middling(s), ash cake, (hay) cock* or *rick,* and *stack,* along with *mosquito hawk, press peach, fatwood, spider, whicker, co-wench;* for Mississippi and Alabama those of *clabber cheese, coverlet, coverlid, jew's harp, juice harp, comforter, fatback, middling(s), jackleg preacher, ash cake, red worm, plum peach, water gutter, whet stone,* along with *mosquito hawk, press peach, whicker, gallery, pull bone;* for Arkansas and Oklahoma those of *dog irons, snake doctor, flying jenny, red worm, tow sack, fairing off, side meat, wheel horse,* and *line horse;* and for northwest Arkansas *mosquito hawk, tin panning, jerked beef, snake feeder, ridy horse, fatback, salad, sallet, (hay) cock* or *rick, hand stack, spider, blinds, coal hod, tied quilt, breaking off, (hog's) head cheese, corn dodger, big house, worm fence, pressed meat, coverlet, coverlid, sow belly, smearcase.* Seeming differences in count arise from the researcher's decision to treat as a single word all phonological variants such as *coverlet, coverlid.*

5 The *Southern* Dialect Area Redefined

1. Hans Kurath, *A Word Geography of the Eastern United States* (Ann Arbor, Mich., 1949), pp. 11–49. For variations on boundaries and labels compare Charles K. Thomas, *The Phonetics of American English,* 2nd ed. (New York, 1958); Virginia McDavid's work in W. Nelson Francis, *The Structure of American English* (New York, 1958), pp. 580–85 or its somewhat more available modification in Raven I. McDavid, Jr. and John T. Muri, "Americans Speaking" (*National Council of Teachers of English Pamphlet,* Champaign, Ill., 1967); John Nist, *A Structural History of English* (New York, 1966); Margaret Schlauch, *The English Language in Modern Times* (Warsaw and London, 1959). Changing views are reflected by the difference in maps in the first and second editions of Albert C. Baugh, *A History of the English Language* (New York, 1935 and 1957).
2. E. Bagby Atwood, *The Regional Vocabulary of Texas* (Austin, Tex., 1962), pp. 85–87.
3. Gordon R. Wood, "Word Distribution in the Interior South," *Publication of the American Dialect Society,* XXXV (1961), 10–11; "Dialect Contours in the Southern States," *American Speech,* XXXVIII (1963), 245–46.
4. Kurath's Table III, (*Word Geography,* p. 38), The Southern Area has as subdivision labels, The South and the South Midland, The South, Virginia and the South Midland, The Carolinas and the South Midland, and The Southern Coast. One of Atwood's tables (*Regional Vocabulary,* p. 84), has these among its other regional labels: South Midland, Coastal Southern, General Southern, and All Southern.
5. Wood, first mapped in "Word Distribution" and "Dialect Contours."
6. Atwood, *Regional Vocabulary,* p. 87, "We may . . . classify the Trans-Pecos as a transitional area, since the drop in Southern words is very consistent, although not so great as to justify the conception of a dialect boundary."
7. The Ohio lies below some Southern features. If one examines the Atlas records for *light bread,* for example, its northern boundary will be seen to cross central Ohio, Indiana, and Illinois. That line has been suggested in Map 83; actual placing, of course, awaits the publication of this Midwest portion of the Linguistic Atlas.

   The first suggestion that I know of which comments on placing the "South Midland" element in this new relationship to the major dialects which surround it is Norman Eliason's. In *Tarheel Talk: An Historical Study of the English Language in North Carolina to 1860* (Chapel Hill, N.C., 1956), p. 16, n. 12, he writes: "I am inclined to think that when all of the *Atlas* data are weighed, especially pronunciation, this area will be assigned to Southern."
8. When the North Central Atlas appears, some

data presented here can and will be reinterpreted in the light of facts given there. Similarly Atlases now in press—Harold Allen's of the Upper Midwest and William R. Van Riper's of Oklahoma—will permit one to affirm or modify interpretations offered here. For the Interior South, the pronunciation isoglosses may fall in quite different patterns from those based on vocabulary. An attempt at comparing the presence or absence of common features in vocabulary, pronunciation and grammar is in Gordon R. Wood, *Sub-Regional Speech Variations in Vocabulary, Grammar, and Pronunciation* (Cooperative Research Project No. 3046, United States Office of Education, final report. Edwardsville, Ill., 1967); a few distinctive features were found to correspond in their geographic distribution, but the inquiry needs to cover a larger area.

9. A recent review of performance is by Raven I. McDavid, Jr., "Dialect Labels in the Merriam Third," *Publication of the American Dialect Society,* XLVII (1967), 1–22.

6 The Choice of Synonyms

1. These topical entries have the following format: heading, text, discussion, and notes. The heading is a broad classificational label which identifies the topic or one of its subparts. Next is Item followed by one or more numbers, a reference to the number preceding ITEM in Table I; an entry, "Items 6, 7" for example, directs the reader to ITEM 6 and then to ITEM 7. The final, optional entry is to the Word Geography and to one or more maps there as in "Map 34."

   The notes list volunteered words, sending the reader to the table of Volunteered Words for information about the state or states from which they were volunteered; the occasional presence of a word in a note and its absence from the table proper indicates that computer retrieval did not recover this word from storage. Following the volunteered words, if any, are references to questionnaire words which are listed in *ADD (American Dialect Dictionary), DA (Dictionary of Americanisms),* and *DAE (Dictionary of American English)*; the notation *DA, DAE* means that the listed words appear in either dictionary or both. These entries are intended as a note on the current view of standard reference works as to the meaning, social standing, and first printed record of the entry reported. The final notation is to the presence of maps in other word geographies, e.g. Atwood, Map 90, Kurath, Figure 63, referring to E. Bagby Atwood, *The Regional Vocabulary of Texas* (Austin, Tex., 1962); and Hans Kurath, *A Word Geography of the Eastern United States* (Ann Arbor, Mich., 1949).

   The format for Table I is described in the explanatory pages which go before it; similar explanatory pages go before the other tables. Calculations in Table I supersede those in Gordon R. Wood, "Word Distribution in the Interior South," *Publication of the American Dialect Society,* XXXV (1961), 5–13.

2. *ADD: gully washer, goose drownder,* and *toad strangler. DA: electrical storm, cloudburst,* 19 c.; *goose drownder, gully washer, toad strangler* 20 c. Atwood (*Regional Vocabulary*), Maps 89, 119.
3. *ADD: fair off, fair up. DA, DAE: breaking away* 18 c.; *clearing off, fairing off, fairing up* 19 c. Atwood (*Regional Vocabulary*), Maps 90, 123.
4. Other volunteered words *ice shell, skim (of) ice, slush ice, thin ice, thin sheet ice. ADD: skim. DA, DAE: anchor ice* in another sense, and *skim, mush ice* 19 c.
5. Other volunteered words: *low ground, river bottom, valley land. DA, DAE: bottoms* 17 c., *bottom land* 18 c. Kurath (*Word Geography*), Figures 90, 91.
6. In addition to the words also volunteered for the preceding entry (*n.* 5) are these: *bottom pasture, branch bottom, creek bottom, drain, dry hollow, holler field, pasture, wild onion patch, wet weather spring. DA, DAE: slough* and *swale* 17 c., *bayou, prairie, swale* 18 c. (though the present sense of *prairie* is not reported until 20 c.), and *coulee, draw* 19 c. in senses close to that of the questionnaire. *DAE: bog, meadow, swamp* in 17 c., and *seep* in 19 c., and discusses the possibilities of local use in England of various of these words. Atwood, Map 53. Kurath, Figure 91.
7. Additional volunteered words: *bunch (of), patch (of) trees, woods. ADD: shinnery, DAE* dates *bluff* in the sense of a steep bank from 17 c. Harold B. Allen, "Minor Dialect Areas of the Upper Midwest," *Publication of the American Dialect Society,* XXX (1958), 9, discusses the change of *thicket* from the meaning of "shrubbery" to that of a "small grove of trees." He also notes how the American sense of *bluff* might have developed from the sense of an "eroded bank" to that of a "clump of trees." In the Midwest *bluff* is a Canadian immigrant. Obviously this word needs further search. *Ibid.,* Maps 3, 4.
8. Volunteered: *maple tree. ADD: sugar tree. DA, DAE: sugar maple, sugar tree, hard maple, rock maple* 18 c. Kurath, Figures 17, 143.
9. Additional volunteered words: *sugar maple orchard, sugar tree orchard. DA, DAE: sugar*

camp, sugar grove 18 c.; *maple orchard, sap orchard, sugar bush, sugar orchard* 19 c. Kurath, Figures 144, 145.

For sugar production from cane, see Paul W. Gates, *The Farmer's Age: Agriculture, 1815–1860,* in *The Economic History of the United States,* ed. Henry David et. al. (New York, 1960), pp. 122–27, 435.

10. *ADD:* the *ivory* element in *poison ivory. DA, DAE: poison ivy, poison oak,* and *poison vine* 18 c. Atwood, Map 91.
11. *DA: devil's snuffbox* in this sense 20 c.
12. *ADD: polecat. DA, DAE: polecat, skunk* 17 c. Kurath, Figures 42, 137.
13. Volunteered: *ground mole. ADD: grinnie. DAE: ground squirrel* 18 c., *chipmunk* 19 c. Kurath, Figure 138.
14. Volunteered: *bull frog, frog, hoppie toad, spring frog. ADD: hoppie toad, toad frog. DAE: hop toad* 19 c. Atwood, Map 113.
15. *ADD: lightning bug, firefly. DA, DAE: firefly, fire bug, glow worm, lightning bug* 18 c.; *DAE: June bug* 19 c., but in a sense different from the one here.
16. Additional volunteered words: *devil's horse, water bug. ADD: snake doctor. DA: mosquito hawk* 18 c., *snake doctor* 19 c.; *DAE: dragon fly* 17 c.; *devil's darning needle* 19 c.; *DA, DAE: snake feeder* 19 c. Atwood, Maps 66, 120. Kurath, Figures 15, 34, 141.
17. Volunteered: *crawdabs, crawjacks. ADD: crawdad, crawdab. DA, DAE: crawfish* 17 c.; *crayfish, crabs* (not clear about the sense) 19 c., *crawdad* 20 c.
18. Additional volunteered words: *bait(s), big worm, black land worm, catalpa worm, crumbing worm,* and the generic *worm(s). ADD: angleworm, eaceworm, eel worm, dew worm, fishing worm, mudworm,* and *red worm. DAE: earthworm* 18 c., *angle worm* 19 c. Atwood, Map 68. Kurath, Figures 28, 139, 140.
19. Volunteered: *dust(y) dark, dusky dark. ADD: afternoon, evening, sunrise, sunup, sunset, duskdark. DAE: sunup, sundown* 18 c. Atwood, Maps 92, 123.
20. Volunteered: *milk time, time to feed up. DAE: chore* by itself 18 c. Atwood, Map 80. Kurath, Figure 44.
21. Volunteered: *hollering distance. DAE: a piece* 18 c. Atwood, Map 77. Kurath, Figure 111.
22. Volunteered: *double armful.* Atwood, Map 58. Kurath, Figure 73.
23. *ADD: pa, pap,* and variants; *ma, maw,* and variants.
24. Volunteered: (for first sense) *the folks*; (for second sense) *our tribe. ADD: folks, kin, kinfolks.*
25. *ADD: favors, features. DAE: favors* 18 c.
26. *ADD: granny, granny doctor, granny woman. DA, DAE: granny* 18 c. Kurath, Figure 149.
27. Volunteered: *devil chaser, exhorter, fleet footed preacher, holy roller, maul stick preacher, one horse preacher, sidewalk preacher. DA: preacher* 17 c., *jackleg* in *jackleg lawyer* 18 c.
28. Volunteered: (with adverse sense) *backwood cracker, backwood hoosier, clod knocker, country cracker, country hoosier, local yokel, mountain hoosier, ridge runner, Red River bumpkin, river rats, poor white* (neutral under some circumstances), *farmer, pioneer. ADD: country jake, cracker, hayseed, hick, hillbilly, hoosier, mountain boomer, red neck, sharecropper, yahoo,* and (?) *yokel. DA, DAE: backwoods man, cracker* 18 c., *country jake, hayseed, hoosier, jackpine* (but not *jackpine savage*), *mossback, mountain boomer, rail splitter* 19 c., and *hillbilly, sharecropper* 20 c.
29. Volunteered: *ADD: booger, boogerman, bloody bones, turtle man. DAE,* citing testimony from the New England witchcraft trials: *blackman* 17 c.
30. Other volunteered words: *go steady, go to see, spark. ADD: sit up to, spark, talk to. DA, DAE: spark with* 18 c.; *go with* and the *-ing* form of *court* 19 c. Atwood, Map 111.
31. Volunteered: *brush off, break up, ditched him, drop him, give him the gate, a dear John, the shaft, his walking papers, a maroon harpoon, leave him, put him down, quit him, reject him, shafted him, shoot him out of the saddle, slight him. ADD: kick. DAE: turn down, give the bounce, give the mitten, kick him* 19 c. Note that in the computer text *give him a cold shoulder* is printed as *give a cold shoulder,* a requirement imposed by the amount of space reserved for text words in the computer programming.
32. *ADD: belling, bull banding, horning, serenade, shivaree, skimmelton. DA, DAE: belling, shivaree, tin panning, horning* 19 c. Atwood, Map 46. Kurath, Figure 154. McDavid (in Francis, *Structure*), Map 6.
33. Additional volunteered words: *bug out, ran out of school. ADD: lay out. DA, DAE: play hookey* 19 c. Kurath, Figures 157, 158.
34. Volunteered: (first sense) *teeter totter,* (second sense) *flying horses, merry-go-round, pop the whip, whirling jenny. ADD: ridy horse, seesaw, teeter, flying jinny. DA, DAE: teeter board* 19 c. Atwood, Map 112. Kurath, Figures 5b, 13, 79.
35. Additional volunteered words: *deadline, shooting line, taw head, toe line, toy line, throw line.*
36. Volunteered: *blowing harp, jaws harp. ADD: French harp, harp, mouth harp. DA, DAE: jew's harp* 17 c.; *harmonica, French harp, mouth organ* 19 c.; *mouth harp* 20 c. Atwood, Map 59.
37. Volunteered: *belly slide, gut ripper. ADD: belly buster,* etc. *DA: belly bumper, belly gutter* 19 c.

38. *ADD: Christmas gift. DAE: Christmas gift* 19 c. Atwood, Maps 71, 122. Kurath, Figures 42, 161.
39. Volunteered: *nauseated. ADD: sick at,* etc., *take sick.* Kurath, Figure 152.
40. Additional volunteered words: *beat, has had it, shot, tired out, white eyed. ADD: do out, perished, tuckered out. DA, DAE: worn out* 18 c.; *bushed, done out, fagged out, petered out, played out, tuckered out, used up* 19 c.; *done up* 20 c.
41. Additional volunteered words: *heated up, hot and bothered, hot headed, riled up, shook up, upset, worked up. ADD: ashy, het, mad* (as noun), *rile, ugly* (?), *wrathy. DA, DAE: ashy, het, mad, riled, ugly, wrathy* 19 c. *DAE* cites *OED* label for *mad,* "dialectal and U.S. slang," and *riled,* "chiefly U.S. and colloquial."
42. Volunteered: *butt headed, log headed, sot in his ways. ADD: ornery, set, sot. DA, DAE: ornery, bullheaded, set* 19 c.
43. Volunteered words: *fetch, pick up. ADD: lug, pack, tote, drawing. DA, DAE: tote, carting* 17 c.; *pack, drawing, do up* 19 c. Atwood, Maps 62, 65. Kurath, Figure 76.
44. Volunteered: *garden plot, vegetable patch. ADD: patch. DAE* dates *garden, kitchen garden* 17 c.; *garden patch, vegetable garden* 19 c.
45. Additional volunteered words: *wax beans. ADD: butter beans, lima beans, shelly beans, shellies, sivvy beans, snap beans, snaps, string beans. DA, DAE: sewee beans, snap beans* 18 c.; *butter beans, lima beans* 19 c. *DAE* to *shell* 17 c., to *shuck* (with reference to corn) 19 c. Atwood, Map 63. Kurath, Figures 40, 132, 133.
46. *ADD: shell.*
47. *ADD: mutton corn, roasting ears. DAE: green corn* 17 c., *roasting ears* 18 c. Kurath, Figure 41.
48. *ADD: goobers, ground peas, pinders. DAE: ground nuts, ground peas* 18 c., *peanuts, goobers, pinders* 19 c. McDavid (in Francis), Map 6.
49. Volunteered: *beet greens, salad* or *sallet greens, turnip greens, turnip salad. ADD: greens, sallet. DAE: salad* 17 c., *greens* 18 c. Kurath, Figure 131.
50. Volunteered: *fresh onions, nest onions, scullions, winter onions. ADD: scallions, shell oats. DAE: potato onions* 19 c.
51. Volunteered: *open heart. DAE: clingstone* 18 c., *cling, freestone* 19 c. Atwood, Map 107. Kurath, Figures 35, 128, 129, 130.
52. *DAE: pit* 19 c.
53. Volunteered: *bales, hay cots, hay dump, hay mounds, stacks, windrows, hay racks, hay shock, bundles, piles. ADD: bind, shock(s), shook, stook. DA: shock* 19 c., *DAE: bundle* 18 c.; transfer of sense of *shocks* to corn stalks, *shook* in the sense of "a bundle of staves" 19 c. Kurath, Figures 58, 59, 60.
54. For the growth of the food distributing industry see Gates, *Farmer's Age,* pp. 94–98, 156–78, 216, 241, 257–62, 270. The increase of fresh and processed foods in the twentieth century is shown in the tables of *Consumption of Food in United States, 1909–48* (U.S. Department of Agriculture Miscellaneous Publication No. 691. Washington, D.C., 1949). One must deduce the particulars from these general records since accurate local reports before 1900 are lacking.
55. *ADD: chipped beef, dried beef. DA, DAE: dried beef, jerked beef* 18 c.; *chipped beef, jerky* 19 c.
56. Additional volunteered words: *fatback bacon, Georgia chicken, salt meat, seasoning meat, streaked meat, unsmoked meat, white side; jowls, souse meat, hull. ADD: fat back, side meat, sow belly, souse. DA, DAE: middlins* 18 c.; *side meat, sow belly, head cheese, hog's head cheese, souse* 19 c.; *fat back* 20 c. Atwood, Maps 47, 54, 75. Kurath, Figures 122, 129.
57. *ADD: clabber, bonny clabber, lobbered milk; cottage cheese, clabber cheese, Dutch cheese, smearcase. DAE: curds* (perhaps in another sense) 17 c., *bonny clabber* 18 c.; *clabber, cottage cheese, smearcase* 19 c. Atwood, Maps 41, 52. Kurath, Figures 2, 10, 23, 124.
58. Additional volunteered words: *baker bread, light pone, chittling bread, egg bread, crackling bread, dressing, hush puppies, fatty bread, mush bread, poor do, roasted pone, twin brothers. ADD: corn bread, corn dodger, corn pone, hoe cake, Johnny cake, pone bread, ash cake, batter bread. DA, DAE: corn bread, hoe cake, Johnny cake, pone bread* 18 c.; *corn dodger, corn pone, ash cake, ash pone, batter bread* 19 c.; *spoon bread* 20 c. Atwood, Maps 45, 84; Kurath, Figures 30, 116, 119.
59. *ADD: ponhaws, ponhoss, scrapple. DA: ponhaws, scrapple* 19 c. Kurath, Figure 23.
60. Additional volunteered words: *molasses cake, sinker, sweet cake. ADD: doughnut, cruller, fried cake, flannel cakes, flapjacks, griddle cakes, hot cakes, pancakes, slap jacks. DA, DAE: fritters, pancakes, hot cakes* 17 c.; *cookie* 18 c.; *cruller, doughnut, fried cake, nut cake, batter cakes, flannel cakes, flapjacks, griddle cakes, slap jacks* 19 c. Atwood, Map 103. Kurath, Figures 14, 120.
61. Additional volunteered words: *gravy; breast bone, the boy, cowboy britches, pullit bone; lap lunch, in between meals. ADD: dip, pulling bone, wishbone, lucky bone, pully bone. DAE: dip, pulling bone, wishbone, lunch* 19 c. Atwood, Maps 42, 72, 124. Kurath, Figures 98, 127.
62. Volunteered: *biscuit eater, common cur, duke's mixture, half breed, hound, hound dog, loafering dog, mutt, plain dog, soup hound. ADD: fiste, no-count, sooner* as element of *sooner*

dog. DA, DAE: cur dog, fiste 18 c.; *scrub, sooner, no-count* 19 c. in other contexts.

63. Volunteered: *gee horse, haw horse, leading horse, left horse, off horse. ADD: whinny, nicker, whicker, whinner, come up, gee-up, gidd-ap. DAE: saddle horse* (in another sense), *wheel horse,* 18 c., *get up* 19 c. Atwood, Map 67. Kurath, Figures 10, 33, 34, 40, 97, 107, 108, 109, 110.
64. *ADD: suke, blat, blate, bleat, beller, low. DA, DAE: blat; bossie* and *sookie* (the latter as applied to pigs) 19 c. Atwood, Map 61. Kurath, Figures 4, 15, 16, 29, 96, 99.
65. *ADD: pig, suke.* Kurath, Figure 104.
66. *ADD: biddy* as a noun. Kurath, Figure 106.
67. Volunteered: *plank fence, railing fence, galloping fence, split rail fence; chunk. ADD: chunk; stone* and *rock wall* and *fence; dornick* (one citation notes its prevalence in Arkansas). *DA, DAE: stone fence, stone wall, rail fence, worm fence, pale fence* 17 c.; *dornick, snake fence, zig zag fence, picket fence, paling fence, palings* 19 c. Thomas Pyles, *Words and Ways of American English* (New York, 1952) suggests (p. 10) that "Perhaps American verbal prudery was partially responsible for the original avoidance of *stone* in most sections of the country" and the substitution of *rock* for it in its American sense. Atwood, Maps 74, 81, 120. Kurath, Figures 18, 39, 41, 63, 64, 65.
68. Volunteered: *cow corral, cow field, cow pasture, cow woods, cow barn, cow shed, cow house, cow stall. ADD: barn lot, cuppin. DA, DAE: barn yard, cow lot, cow pen, cow yard, hog pen, hog house* 17 c.; *barn lot* 18 c.; *cuppin, pig pen, pig sty* 19 c. Atwood, Map 19. Kurath, Figures 61, 62.
69. Additional volunteered words: *backroom, junk house, lean to, little house, lumber room, outhouse, plunder house, pump house, side room, shed room, store house. DAE: lean-to* and *tool* by themselves 17 c.; *shed, wood house* 17 c.; *wood shed* 19 c. Atwood, Map 39.
70. A link between the spread of patterns of domestic architecture and the distribution of regional words occurs in F. Kniffen, "Folk Housing: Key to Diffusion," *Annals,* Association of American Geographers, LV (1965), 549–77. In that study the authority cited for word distribution is not the most renowned of the present dialect researchers. The usefulness of this architectural study for the present investigation is that it illustrates a local range of objects which can be meant by one name. *Gallery,* for example, is not necessarily limited to Greek revival mansions with lofty, fluted pillars in front.
71. Additional volunteered words: *drop siding; drains, drain pipes, gutter pipe, rain-eaves troughs; back porch, landing, sun porch, terrace. ADD: porch, gallery, piazza, stoop, veranda. DA, DAE: clapboards, weatherboards, gutters, piazza* 17 c.; *gallery, stoop* 18 c.; *siding, eaves spouts, eaves troughs, porch, veranda* 19 c. *Gallery* in *DAE* is supported by evidence from George Washington; its westward dissemination may reflect additional sources beyond Louisiana French. Atwood, Map 57. Kurath, Figures 35, 43, 53, 54.
72. Additional volunteered words: *den, drawing room, top loft. ADD: big house, front room, fireboard; loft, sky parlor. DA, DAE: parlor, garret* 17 c.; *best room, sitting room, mantelpiece, loft* 18 c.; *living room, front room, mantel, mantel shelf, attic* 19 c. Atwood, Map 73, 110. Kurath, Figures 27, 28, 46, 47.
73. Additional volunteered words: *clothes cabinet, cedar chest, cedar robe, chifferobe, clothes racks,* and *locker.* The last two present difficult semantic problems which require search to reveal the local range of meanings. *ADD: armor, clothes press. DA, DAE: armoire, clothes closet, wardrobe* 19 c. Atwood, Map 50. Kurath, Figures 50, 52.
74. Volunteered: *trundle bed, counterspread, spread, quilt, tacked quilt. ADD: pallet, bedspread, counterpin, coverlid, comfort, comforter, hap. DA, DAE: counterpane, coverlet, coverlid* 17 c.; *bedspread, comfort, comforter* 19 c. Atwood, Map 51. Kurath, Figures 88, 89.
75. Additional volunteered word: *window curtains. ADD: blinds, curtains, shades. DAE* cites *curtains* in a passage from 1640 but in a different sense there; *DA, DAE: blinds, shades, window shades* 19 c. in the sense used in the questionnaire. Kurath, Figures 16, 49.
76. Volunteered: *log rest; draw horse, jack horse, saw bench, saw log, saw rack, trestle bench, wood horse, wood rack. DAE: andirons, dogs, fire irons* 17 c.; *dog irons, firedogs,* 18 c.; *saw horse, buck, saw buck* 19 c. Atwood, Maps 102, 108. Kurath, Figures 48, 81.
77. Additional volunteered words: *milk bucket, tin bucket, wooden water bucket. ADD: bucket, pail, coal hod. DAE: bucket* 17 c.; *swill pail* 18 c.; *coal hod, coal scuttle* 19 c. Atwood, Map 106. Kurath, Figures 50, 66, 82.
78. Volunteered: *boiler, boiling pot, heavy pan, iron pot, stew kettle, stewer, iron skillet. ADD: creeper, frying pan, fry pan, skillet, spider. DA, DAE: frying pan, kettle, skillet, pot* 17 c.; *spider* 18 c.; *fry pan, creeper* 19 c. Kurath, Figures 6, 43, 68.
79. Volunteered: *glass stopper.*
80. Volunteered: *bung, spout, water hydrant, yard faucet. ADD: hydrant, spicket. DA, DAE: faucet, hydrant* 19 c. *DAE* cites a 17 c. passage with *faucet* as the name of a spigot by which liquids

may be drawn from a cask. Atwood, Map 87. Kurath, Figures 42, 69.

81. Additional volunteered words: *drag harrow, drag tooth harrow, harr, scratcher; hitch, double hitch, wagon tongue.* ADD: *thills, swiveltree.* DA, DAE: *drag, harrow* 17 c.; *fills, swingletree* 18 c., *neap, singletree, double tree, whiffletree* 19 c. Kurath, Figures 4, 9, 41, 74, 75, 77.
82. Volunteered: *paper bag, paper sack, poke sack, corn sack, peat sack.* ADD: *poke, sack, crocus sack, croker sack, gunny sack, tow sack.* DA, DAE: *crocus* (as a cloth) and *sack* 17 c.; *guano sack, gunny sack,* and *jute* (as a cloth) 19 c. Atwood, Maps 39, 69, 94, 123, 125. Kurath, Figures 17, 32, 71.
83. Volunteered: *stroller, go-cart.* DAE: *baby carriage* 19 c. Kurath, Figure 147.
84. Additional volunteered words: *grind rock, oil stone, sharpening stone, scythe stone.* ADD: *whet, whet rock.* DAE: *whet stone* 17 c. Atwood Maps 88, 123. Kurath, Figures 38, 83.
85. Additional volunteered words: *fat splinters, firewood, pine knot, splinters, stove wood.* ADD: *fat pine, fatwood, lightwood; kerosene, coal oil, lamp oil.* DA, DAE: *fat pine, pitch pine, back log* 17 c.; *lightwood, pine* 18 c.; *back stick, kerosene, coal oil* 19 c. Atwood, Map 109. Kurath, Figures 4, 29, 84.
86. Volunteered words: *city hall, engine house, fire department.* DA: *fire hall, fire house* 20 c.
87. Volunteered: *asphalt road, all weather road, gravel road, hard top, tar road, highway.* ADD: *pike, slab.* DA, DAE: *pavement* 17 c.; *macadam road* (not in this sense), *pike* 19 c.; *blacktop* 20 c.
88. Volunteered: *curb, grass plot, grass strip, green strip, neutral ground, safety zone, sidewalk strip, strip; ditchline, drainage ditch, drean* (pronunciation), *grader furrow, gully, road ditch, side ditch, water ditch.* ADD: *berm.* DA, DAE: *gutter* 17 c.; *sidewalk* (but not *sidewalk plot*), 18 c.; *grade* (for road construction), *berm* and *boulevard* (not in this sense), *parking* 19 c. For occurrences of *bar pit, borrow pit* see Allen, "Minor Dialect Areas," Map 4.

Selected Bibliography

Abbreviations

ADD	*American Dialect Dictionary*
AS	*American Speech*
DA	*A Dictionary of Americanisms on Historical Principles*
DAE	*A Dictionary of American English on Historical Principles*
JL	*Journal of Linguistics*
PADS	*Publication of the American Dialect Society*

Allen, Harold B. "Minor Dialect Areas of the Upper Midwest," *PADS,* XXX (1958), 3–16.

American Dialect Dictionary, ed. Harold Wentworth. New York: Crowell, 1944.

An Annotated Bibliography of Southern Speech, comp. Lee Pederson. Southeastern Educational Laboratory Monograph No. 1. Atlanta, Ga., 1968.

Atwood, E. Bagby. *The Regional Vocabulary of Texas.* Austin: University of Texas Press, 1962.

Baugh, Albert C. *A History of the English Language,* 1st and 2nd eds. New York: Appleton-Century-Crofts, 1935, 1957.

Bennett, David C. "English Prepositions: A Stratificational Approach," *JL,* IV (1968), 153–72.

Bolinger, Dwight L. *Generality, Gradience, and the All-or-None.* Janua Linguarum, XIV. The Hague: Mouton, 1961.

A Compilation of the Work Sheets of the Linguistic Atlas of the United States and Canada and Associated Projects, comp. Raven I. McDavid, Jr. and Virginia McDavid. Mimeographed. Ann Arbor: University of Michigan, 1951.

A Dictionary of American English on Historical Principles, ed. Sir William Craigie, J. R. Hulbert, *et. al.* 4 vols. Chicago: University of Chicago Press, 1936.

A Dictionary of Americanisms on Historical Principles, ed. Mitford M. Mathews. 2 vols. Chicago: University of Chicago Press, 1951.

Dillard, J. L. "Non-Standard Negro Dialects—Convergence or Divergence?" *The Florida FL Reporter,* LXV (1968), 1–3.

Duckert, Audrey H. *"The Linguistic Atlas of New England* Revisited," *PADS,* XXXIX (1963), 8–15.

Eliason, Norman E. *Tarheel Talk: An Historical Study of the English Language in North Carolina to 1860.* Chapel Hill: The University of North Carolina Press, 1956.

Estrich, Robert M. and Hans Sperber. *Three Keys to Language.* New York: Rinehart, 1952.

Francis, W. Nelson. *The Structure of American English.* New York: Ronald, 1958.

Hankey, Clyde T. "A Colorado World Geography," *PADS,* XXXIV (1960), 1–76.

Jones, Lyle V. and Joseph M. Wepman. *A spoken word count* [sic]. Chicago: Language Research Associates, 1966.

Kimball, Arthur G. "Sears-Roebuck and Regional Terms," *AS,* XXXVIII (1963), 209–13.

Kurath, Hans, *et. al. Handbook of the Linguistic Geography of New England.* Washington, D.C.: American Council of Learned Societies, 1939.

Kurath, Hans. *A Word Geography of the Eastern United States.* Ann Arbor: University of Michigan Press, 1949.

Marckwardt, Albert H. "Principal and Subsidiary Dialect Areas in the North Central States," *PADS,* XXVII (1957), 3–15.

McDavid, Raven I. Jr., "Dialect Labels in the Merriam *Third," PADS,* XLVII (1967), 1–22.

McDavid, Raven I. Jr. and John T. Muri. *Americans Speaking: A Pamphlet to Accompany the NCTE Recording.* Champaign: National Council of Teachers of English, 1967.

McDavid, Raven I. Jr. and Virginia McDavid. "The Dialects of American English" and "Appendix [Maps]," chapters in Francis, *Structure* (above), pp. 480–543, 580–85.

Nist, John. *A Structural History of English.* New York: St. Martin's, 1966.

Orton, Harold and Eugen Dieth. *Survey of English Dialects: Introduction.* Leeds: Arnold for the University of Leeds, 1962.

Quine, William V. O. *Word and Object.* Cambridge, Mass.: M.I.T. Press, and New York: Wiley, 1964.

Readings in the Psychology of Language, ed. Leon A. Jakobovits and Murray S. Miron. Englewood Cliffs: Prentice-Hall, 1967.

Reed, Carroll E. *Dialects of American English.* Cleveland: World, 1967.

Sapon, Stanley M. *A Pictorial Linguistic Interview Manual.* Photo offset. Columbus, Ohio: Ohio State University, 1957.

Schlauch, Margaret. *The English Language in Modern Times (since 1400).* Warsaw: Pánstwowe Wydawnictwo Naukowe, and London: Oxford University Press, 1959.

Shuy, Roger W. "An Automated Retrieval Program for the Linguistic Atlas of the United States and Canada," *Computation in Linguistics,* ed. Paul L. Garvin and Bernard Spolsky. Bloomington: Indiana University Press, 1966.

Thomas, Charles K. *An Introduction to the Phonetics of American English,* 2nd ed. New York: Ronald, 1958.

Warfel, Harry R., ed. *Letters of Noah Webster*. New York: Library, 1953.

Webster, Noah. *Dissertations on the English Language with Notes Historical and Critical*. Scholars' Facsimiles and Reprints. Gainesville, Fla., 1951.

Wood, Gordon R. "Dialect Contours in the Southern States," *AS*, XXXVIII (1963), 243–56.

Wood, Gordon R. *Sub-Regional Speech Variations in Vocabulary, Grammar, and Pronunciation*. Final Report. Photo offset. Edwardsville, Ill.: Southern Illinois University, 1967.

Wood, Gordon R. "Word Distribution in the Interior South," *PADS*, XXXV (1961), 1–16.

Word Index

Words in this list appear in the questionnaire proper or were volunteered in answering it. The first class is unmarked: *aftermath*; the second is followed by an asterisk: *asphalt road**. Each has an identifying number, the item number in the questionnaire; *aftermath* #81 and *asphalt road** #61 illustrate the convention. For the record of state occurrences of volunteered words, readers will consult pp. 312–15.

Definitions by necessity are approximate and sometimes redundant.

aftermath #81: a second growth, 188, 299
afternoon #1: latter part of the day, 36, 65, 308, 368*n*
all in #133: exhausted, 40, 271, 273, 306
all-weather road #61: tar road, 371*n*
anchor ice #9: thin layer of ice, 33, 73, 299, 367*n*
andirons #11: log supports, 49, 76, 77, 308, 370*n*
angledog #113: worm used for bait, 36, 237, 238, 298
angleworm #113: worm used for bait, figure 5, *14–15*; 237, 238, 304, 368*n*
armful #46: an amount of wood, 37, 128, 309
arm load #46: an amount of wood, 13; figure 5, *14–15*; 37, 128, 308
armor #22: movable storage place, 49, 94, 299; map 49, *341*; 370*n*
armoire #22: movable storage place, 21, 25, 49, 94, 300; map 49, *341*; 370*n*
ash bread #84: corn bread cooked in ashes, 44, 193, 305
ash cake #84: corn bread cooked in ashes, 17; figure 9, *18–19*; 25, 44, 193, 307; map 29, *331*; 369*n*
ash pone #84: corn bread cooked in ashes, 44, 193, 306, 369*n*
ashy #132: enraged, 40, 269, 279, 301, 369*n*
*asphalt road** #61: tar road, 371*n*
attic #23: unfinished room beneath the roof, 22, 49, 95, 309, 370*n*
awendaw bread #84: soft corn bread, 44, 194, 298

baby buggy #125: a vehicle, 16; figure 5, *14–15*; 51, 258, 309
baby cab #125: a vehicle, 51, 258, 299
baby carriage #125: a vehicle, 51, 258, 308, 371*n*
baby coach #125: a vehicle, 51, 258, 298
back chunk #13: log at back of a fire, 32, 52, 79, 301
backlog #13: log at back of a fire, 32, 52, 79, 309, 371*n*
*back porch** #25: small porch, 370*n*
*back room** #17: room joined to a house, 370*n*
back stick #13: log at back of a fire, 32, 52, 79, 307, 371*n*
*backwoods cracker** #130: a rustic, 368*n*
*backwoods hoosier** #130: a rustic, 38, 368*n*
backwoodsman #130: a rustic, 38, 263, 265, 305, 368*n*
bacon #87: salted hog meat, 43, 44, 201, 202, 307
bad man #142: hobgoblin, 22, 38, 287, 288, 305
bag #37: a paper container, 51, 114, 308
bag school #140: to absent oneself from school, 39, 284, 285, 298
*bait(s)** #113: worm used for bait, 368*n*
bait worm #113: worm used for bait, 36, 237, 238, 303
*baker bread** #83: loaf of white bread, 13, 369*n*
*bale(s)** #89: bundles of wheat stalks, 369*n*
bar ditch #63: ditch beside a graded road, 53, 156, 157, 303
barn chamber #18: upper storage room in a barn, 47, 87, 88, 299
barn loft #18: upper storage room in a barn, 47, 87, 88, 308
barn lot #28: yard adjoining the barn, 28, 47, 103, 308; map 56, *345*; map 80, *357*; 370*n*
barn yard #28: yard adjoining the barn, 47, 103, 309, 370*n*
bar pit #63: ditch beside a graded road, 53, 156, 157, 304, 371*n*
barrack #19: large pile of hay, 43, 89
barrow ditch #63: ditch beside a graded road, 156, 157, 299
barrow pit #63: ditch beside a graded road, 53, 156, 157, 300
batter bread #84: soft corn bread, 17; figure 9, *18–19*; 25, 44, 194, 306; map 30, *332*; 366*n*, 369*n*
batter cakes #86: flat cakes made with flour, 22, 25, 29, 45, 199, 200, 299, 307; map 30, *332*; 369*n*
bawl (A) #66: sound from a weaned calf, 13, 46, 162, 309
bawl (B) #67: gentle sound from a cow, 13; figure 5, *14–15*; 46, 163, 164, 308
bawl (C) #67: loud sound from a cow, 13; figure 5, *14–15*; 46, 165, 166, 304
bayou (A) #58: swamp, 24, 25, 33, 34, 144, 145, 305; map 5, *319*; map 50, *342*; 367*n*
bayou (B) #58: low grassland, 24, 25, 33, 34, 147, 148, 303; map 5, *319*; map 50, *342*; 367*n*
*beans** #103: beans eaten in pods, 41, 225, 303
*beat** #133: exhausted, 369*n*
beat out #133: exhausted, 40, 271, 273, 301
bedspread #54: fancy bed cover, 22, 49, 140, 310, 370*n*
bee #78: a call to chickens, 183, 184, 298
*beet greens** #104: edible tops of turnips, 42, 369*n*
beller (A) #66: sound from a weaned calf, 161, 162, 304, 370*n*
beller (B) #67: gentle sound from a cow, 46, 163, 164, 305. 370*n*
beller (C) #67: loud sound from a cow, 46, 165, 166, 301, 370*n*
belling #139: noisy celebration after a wedding, 39, 282, 283, 300, 368*n*
belling bee #139: noisy celebration after a wedding, 39, 282, 283, 298
bellow (A) #66: sound from a weaned calf, 161, 162, 305

Topical Index